ninth edition

STRATEGIC MANAGEMENT and BUSINESS POLICY

Concepts

Thomas L. Wheelen
University of South Florida

J. David Hunger
Iowa State University

PEARSON

Prentice
Hall

Upper Saddle River, New Jersey 07458

WX 200
Organisation & administratn

Library of Congress Cataloging-in-Publication Data

Wheelen, Thomas L.
   Strategic management and business policy / Thomas L. Wheelen, J. David Hunger.--9th ed.
     p. cm.
   Rev. ed. of: Strategic management and business policy. Concepts / Thomas L. Wheelen,
J. David Hunger. 8th ed. c2002.
   Various multi-media instructional aids, including a Web site, are available to supplement the text.
   Includes bibliographical references and index.
   ISBN 0-13-142405-X
    1. Strategic planning. I. Hunger, J. David. Wheelen, Thomas L. Strategic
management and business policy. Concepts. III. Title.

HD30.28.W43 2004c
658.4'012--dc21

Senior Managing Editor (Editorial): Jennifer Glennon
Editor-in-Chief: Jeff Shelstad
Assistant Editor: Melanie Olsen
Editorial Assistant: Kelly Wendrychowicz
Media Project Manager: Jessica Sabloff
Executive Marketing Manager: Shannon Moore
Marketing Assistant: Patrick Danzuso
Senior Managing Editor (Production): Judy Leale
Production Editor: Cindy Spreder
Permissions Supervisor: Suzanne Grappi
Associate Director, Manufacturing: Vincent Scelta
Production Manager: Arnold Vila
Buyer: Diane Peirano
Design Manager: Maria Lange
Designer: Steve Frim
Interior Design: Lee Goldstein
Cover Design: Steve Frim
Cover Illustration/Photo: Hermann/Starke—CORBIS
Illustrator (Interior): UG / GGS Information Services, Inc.
Manager, Print Production: Christy Mahon
Print Production Liaison: Ashley Scattergood
Composition: UG / GGS Information Services, Inc.
Full-Service Project Management: UG / GGS Information Services, Inc.
Printer/Binder: Courier-Kendallville

Credits and acknowledgments borrowed from other sources and reproduced, with permission, in this textbook appear on appropriate page within text.

Pearson Prentice Hall™ is a trademark of Pearson Education, Inc.
Pearson® is a registered trademark of Pearson plc.
Prentice Hall® is a trademark of Pearson Education, Inc.

Pearson Education LTD   Pearson Education Australia PTY, Limited
Pearson Education Singapore, Pte. Ltd   Pearson Education North Asia Ltd
Pearson Education, Canada, Ltd   Pearson Educación de Mexico, S.A. de C.V.
Pearson Education–Japan   Pearson Education Malaysia, Pte. Ltd

10 9 8 7 6 5 4
ISBN 013-142405-X

ninth edition

STRATEGIC MANAGEMENT and BUSINESS POLICY

Concepts

Dedicated to

Kathy
Richard
Tom

Betty
Kari, Jeff, Maddie, and Megan
Suzi, Nick, and Summer
Lori
Merry
Smokey

And to the Prentice Hall sales representatives who work so hard to promote this book, we thank you!

Tara Algeo	Kate Derrick	Dave Hill
Peter Ancona	George Devenny	Kristen Hodge
Geralyn Applegate	Sue Dikun	Brett Holmes
Larry Armstrong	Dana Duncan	Carole Horton
Tracy Augustine	Beverly Dunn	David Hough
Jonathan Axelrod	Scott Dustan	Jody Ipsen
Hal Balmer	Susan Fackert	David Jackson
Cordelia Barrera	Trey Feigle	Susan Jackson
Kelly Bell	Marissa Feliberty	Connie James
William Beville	Dennis Fernandes	Vince Jansen
Jennifer Blackburn	Mary Fernandez	Leah Johnson
Joan Blasco-Paul	John Fishback	Susan Joseph
Melissa Blum	Sean Fisher	Curtis Ketterman
Sara Bredbenner	Jonathan Fitting	Stacy Keyser
Jeanne Bronson	Steve Foster	Romayne Kilde
Julie Burgmeier	Mary Gallagher	Sally Kissel
Shauna Burgmeier	Cheryle Gehrlich	Tammy Knight
Ruth Cardiff	Sybil Geraud	Susan Koller
Darrin Carr	Carolyn Chazi-Tehrani	Eric Krassow
Michael Carrigg	David Gillespie	Daniel Krauss
Andrea Catullo	Chip Gillikin	Steven Ladd
Meredith Chandler	Eric Gilmore	Kelly Lambing
Natalie Cherry	Evan Girard	Sharon Lavoy
Krista Christenson	Kevin Glynn	Kristen Lindley
Matt Christopherson	Keri Goldberg-Leonard	Stacie Lipten
Catherine Colucci	Katherine Grassi	Tricia Liscio
Thayne Conrad	Lisa Greer	Tracy Long
Cyndi Crimmins	Doug Greive	David Lopez
Meilynn D'Alessandro	Edith Hall	Jennifer Lucking
Sarah Davis	Melissa Hallett	Kimberly Manzi
Matthew DeGroat	Alison Harvey	Meredith Margraf
Matt Denham	Julie Hildebrand	Patrick Mast

Jennifer Matty

Joshua McClary

Eileen McClay

Regina McCray

Brian McGarry

Milton McGowen

Irene McGuinness

Lou McGuire

Ryan McHenry

Jeff McIlroy

Sally McPherson

Mary Meyer

Laura Middleton

Sue Miller

Ashley Millinor

Paul Misselwitz

Becky Mitchell

Kate Moore

Karen Moreau

Julie Morel

Katie Morgan

Joseph Murray

Pete Nasta

Celeste Nossiter

Meghan O'Donnell

Kevin O'Sullivan

Tori Olson Alves

Nancy Palmer

Deborah Patterson

Emilia Pawlowski

Antoinette Payne

Mick Pfaff

Carol Pharo

Andrew Pollard

David Ramsey

Allison Rauch

Karen Reifsteck

Leann Reisinger

Julie Resler

Mary Rhodes

Anne Riddick

Molly Riggs

Dan Rinn

Dorothy Rosene

Richard Rowe

Brad Sallmen

Corrina Schultz

Terra Schultz

Steven Shapiro

Brent Sheppard

Mark Sibla

Wayne Siegert

Phyllis Simon

Donald Smith

Ann Sorenson

Beth Spencer

Richard Spencer

Joe Sturino

Cindy Sullivan

Dan Sullivan

Chuck Synovec

Moira Tarpy

Mark Templeman

Devorah Tharp

David Theisen

Derek Thibodeau

Frank Timoney

Catherine Traywick

Nugent Tyra

Karen Villagomez

David Visser

Jennifer Walters

Michael Ward

Mary Weatherly

LeDawn Webb

Ann Weiss

Eric Weiss

Jim West

Hannah Whitlock

Read Wickham

Alissa Wilmoth

Jennifer Woodle

Sharon Young

Brief Contents

PART ONE   Introduction to Strategic Management and Business Policy   1

   Chapter 1   **Basic Concepts of Strategic Management**   1

   Chapter 2   **Corporate Governance and Social Responsibility**   25

PART TWO   Scanning the Environment   51

   Chapter 3   **Environmental Scanning and Industry Analysis**   51

   Chapter 4   **Internal Scanning: Organizational Analysis**   80

PART THREE   Strategy Formulation   108

   Chapter 5   **Strategy Formulation: Situation Analysis and Business Strategy**   108

   Chapter 6   **Strategy Formulation: Corporate Strategy**   136

   Chapter 7   **Strategy Formulation: Functional Strategy and Strategic Choice**   164

PART FOUR   Strategy Implementation and Control   191

   Chapter 8   **Strategy Implementation: Organizing for Action**   191

   Chapter 9   **Strategy Implementation: Staffing and Directing**   217

   Chapter 10   **Evaluation and Control**   241

PART FIVE   Other Strategic Issues   277

   Chapter 11   **Strategic Issues in Managing Technology and Innovation**   277

   Chapter 12   **Strategic Issues in Entrepreneurial Ventures and Small Businesses**   301

   Chapter 13   **Strategic Issues in Not-For-Profit Organizations**   324

PART SIX   Introduction to Case Analysis   341

   Chapter 14   **Suggestions for Case Analysis**   341

Contents

Preface xxi

PART ONE Introduction to Strategic Management and Business Policy 1

Chapter 1 Basic Concepts of Strategic Management 1

  1.1 The Study of Strategic Management 2

     Phases of Strategic Management 3

     Benefits of Strategic Management 4

  1.2 Globalization and Electronic Commerce: Challenges to Strategic Management 5

     Impact of Globalization 5

     Impact of Electronic Commerce 5

     GLOBAL ISSUE: Regional Trade Associations Replace National Trade Barriers 6

  1.3 Theories of Organizational Adaptation 7

  1.4 Creating a Learning Organization 8

  1.5 Basic Model of Strategic Management 9

     Environmental Scanning 9

     Strategy Formulation 10

     Strategy Implementation 15

     Evaluation and Control 16

     Feedback/Learning Process 16

  1.6 Initiation of Strategy: Triggering Events 16

     INTERNET ISSUE: Triggering Event at Sun Microsystems 17

  1.7 Strategic Decision Making 18

     What Makes a Decision Strategic 18

     Mintzberg's Modes of Strategic Decision Making 18

     Strategic Decision-Making Process: Aid to Better Decisions 19

  1.8 **Impact of the Internet on Strategic Management 22**

Chapter 2 Corporate Governance and Social Responsibility 25

  2.1 Corporate Governance: Role of the Board of Directors 26

     Responsibilities of the Board 27

     Members of a Board of Directors 29

THEORY AS IT APPLIES: Agency Theory Versus Stewardship Theory in Corporate Governance 30

Nomination and Election of Board Members 32

Organization of the Board 33

Trends in Corporate Governance 34

2.2 Corporate Governance: The Role of Top Management 35

Responsibilities of Top Management 35

2.3 Social Responsibilities of Strategic Decision Makers 37

Responsibilities of a Business Firm 37

Corporate Stakeholders 39

2.4 Ethical Decision Making 40

GLOBAL ISSUE: Unethical Practices at Enron and WorldCom Exposed by "Whistleblowers" 40

Some Reasons for Unethical Behavior 41

Encouraging Ethical Behavior 42

2.5 **Impact of the Internet on Corporate Governance and Social Responsibility 44**

INTERNET ISSUE: Governments Act to Protect Society by Regulating the Internet 45

PART ENDING VIDEO CASE: Newbury Comics, Inc. 50

PART TWO   Scanning the Environment 51

Chapter 3   **Environmental Scanning and Industry Analysis 51**

3.1 Environmental Scanning 52

Identifying External Environmental Variables 52

GLOBAL ISSUE: Identifying Potential Markets in Developing Nations 58

Identifying External Strategic Factors 59

3.2 Industry Analysis: Analyzing the Task Environment 60

Porter's Approach to Industry Analysis 60

Industry Evolution 64

Categorizing International Industries 64

International Risk Assessment 65

Strategic Groups 66

Strategic Types 66

Hypercompetition 67

Using Key Success Factors to Create an Industry Matrix 69

3.3 Competitive Intelligence 70

3.4 Forecasting 71

Danger of Assumptions 71

Useful Forecasting Techniques 72

3.5 Synthesis of External Factors—EFAS 73

3.6 **Impact of the Internet on Environmental Scanning and Industry Analysis 74**

INTERNET ISSUE: Competitor Information Available on the Internet 76

Chapter 4   Internal Scanning: Organizational Analysis 80

4.1 A Resource-Based Approach to Organizational Analysis 81

Using Resources to Gain Competitive Advantage 82

Determining the Sustainability of an Advantage 82

4.2 Value Chain Analysis 84

Industry Value Chain Analysis 84

Corporate Value Chain Analysis 85

4.3 Scanning Functional Resources 87

Basic Organizational Structures 87

Corporate Culture: The Company Way 88

Strategic Marketing Issues 89

GLOBAL ISSUE: ABB Uses Corporate Culture as a Competitive Advantage 90

Strategic Financial Issues 91

Strategic Research and Development (R&D) Issues 92

Strategic Operations Issues 95

Strategic Human Resource Management (HRM) Issues 97

Strategic Information Systems/Technology Issues 99

INTERNET ISSUE: The Growing Global Internet Economy 99

4.4 The Strategic Audit: A Checklist for Organizational Analysis 100

4.5 Synthesis of Internal Factors: IFAS 101

4.6 **Impact of the Internet on Internal Scanning and Organizational Analysis 102**

PART ENDING VIDEO CASE: Newbury Comics, Inc. 106

PART THREE   Strategy Formulation 108

Chapter 5   Strategy Formulation: Situation Analysis and Business Strategy 108

5.1 Situational Analysis: SWOT Analysis 109

Generating a Strategic Factors Analysis Summary (SFAS) Matrix 110

Finding a Propitious Niche   112

⊞ GLOBAL ISSUE: SAB Defends Its Propitious Niche   113

5.2 Review of Mission and Objectives   114

5.3 Generating Alternative Strategies Using a TOWS Matrix   114

5.4 Business Strategies   115

Porter's Competitive Strategies   117

Cooperative Strategies   126

⊞ INTERNET ISSUE: Business to Business at Cisco Systems   130

5.5 **Impact of the Internet on Business Strategy   131**

Chapter 6   Strategy Formulation: Corporate Strategy   136

6.1 Corporate Strategy   137

6.2 Directional Strategy   138

Growth Strategies   138

THEORY AS IT APPLIES: Transaction Cost Economics Analyzes Vertical Growth Strategy   141

International Entry Options   143

⊞ GLOBAL ISSUE: Wal-Mart Enters International Markets   144

Controversies in Directional Growth Strategies   146

Stability Strategies   146

Retrenchment Strategies   148

6.3 Portfolio Analysis   151

BCG Growth-Share Matrix   151

GE Business Screen   153

International Portfolio Analysis   154

Advantages and Limitations of Portfolio Analysis   155

6.4 Corporate Parenting   156

Developing a Corporate Parenting Strategy   156

Parenting-Fit Matrix   157

Horizontal Strategy and Multipoint Competition   159

6.5 **Impact of the Internet on Corporate Strategy   159**

⊞ INTERNET ISSUE: Global Online Population   160

Chapter 7   Strategy Formulation: Functional Strategy and Strategic Choice   164

7.1 Functional Strategy   165

Core Competencies   165

The Sourcing Decision: Where Should Functions Be Housed? 166

Marketing Strategy 168

Financial Strategy 169

Research and Development (R&D) Strategy 170

Operations Strategy 171

    GLOBAL ISSUE: International Differences Alter Whirlpool's
Operations Strategy 172

Purchasing Strategy 173

Logistics Strategy 174

    INTERNET ISSUE: Staples Uses Internet to Replenish Inventory from 3M 175

Human Resources Management (HRM) Strategy 175

Information Systems Strategy 176

7.2 Strategies to Avoid 177

7.3 Strategic Choice: Selection of the Best Strategy 177

Constructing Corporate Scenarios 178

Process of Strategic Choice 183

7.4 Development of Policies 184

7.5 **Impact of the Internet on Functional Strategy 185**

PART ENDING VIDEO CASE: Newbury Comics, Inc. 190

PART FOUR   Strategy Implementation and Control 191

Chapter 8   **Strategy Implementation: Organizing for Action 191**

8.1 Strategy Implementation 192

8.2 Who Implements Strategy? 193

8.3 What Must Be Done? 194

Developing Programs, Budgets, and Procedures 194

Achieving Synergy 196

8.4 How Is Strategy to Be Implemented? Organizing for Action 197

Structure Follows Strategy 197

Stages of Corporate Development 198

Organizational Life Cycle 201

    INTERNET ISSUE: The Founder of the Modem Blocks Transition to Stage II 202

Advanced Types of Organizational Structures 204

Reengineering and Strategy Implementation 207

Designing Jobs to Implement Strategy 208

THEORY AS IT APPLIES: Designing Jobs with the Job Characteristics Model 209

8.5 International Issues in Strategy Implementation 209

Stages of International Development 210

Centralization Versus Decentralization 210

🌐 GLOBAL ISSUE: FedEx Provides the Infrastructure for Companies to Become Global 211

8.6 Impact of the Internet on Organizational Design and Structure 212

Chapter 9 Strategy Implementation: Staffing and Directing 217

9.1 Staffing 218

Staffing Follows Strategy 219

Selection and Management Development 221

Problems in Retrenchment 222

International Issues in Staffing 224

9.2 Leading 225

Managing Corporate Culture 225

Action Planning 229

Management By Objectives 231

Total Quality Management 232

International Considerations in Leading 232

🌐 GLOBAL ISSUE: Cultural Differences Create Implementation Problems in Merger 234

9.3 Impact of the Internet on Staffing and Leading in Organizations 235

Static Intranet Applications 235

Dynamic Intranet Applications 236

📡 INTERNET ISSUE: Virtual Teams Use the Net to Operate at Long Distance 236

Advantages and Disadvantages of Intranets 237

Chapter 10 Evaluation and Control 241

10.1 Evaluation and Control in Strategic Management 243

10.2 Measuring Performance 243

Appropriate Measures 243

Types of Controls 243

Activity-Based Costing 245

Primary Measures of Corporate Performance 246

📡 INTERNET ISSUE: "Eyeballs" and "MUUs": Questionable Performance Measures 248

Primary Measures of Divisional and Functional Performance 252

International Measurement Issues 254

🌐 GLOBAL ISSUE: The Impact of Piracy on International Trade 255

10.3 Strategic Information Systems 256

Enterprise Resource Planning (ERP) 256

Divisional and Functional IS Support 257

10.4 Problems in Measuring Performance 257

Short-Term Orientation 258

Goal Displacement 258

10.5 Guidelines for Proper Control 259

10.6 Strategic Incentive Management 260

10.7 Using the Strategic Audit to Evaluate Corporate Performance 262

10.8 **Impact of the Internet on Evaluation and Control 262**

Appendix 10.A Strategic Audit of a Corporation 265

PART ENDING VIDEO CASE: Newbury Comics, Inc. 274

PART FIVE Other Strategic Issues 277

Chapter 11 **Strategic Issues in Managing Technology and Innovation 277**

11.1 Role of Management 278

11.2 Environmental Scanning 280

External Scanning 280

Internal Scanning 283

Resource Allocation Issues 283

11.3 Strategy Formulation 284

GLOBAL ISSUE: Impact of R&D on Competitive Advantage in China 285

Product Versus Process R&D 285

Technology Sourcing 286

Importance of Technological Competence 288

Product Portfolio 289

11.4 Strategy Implementation 290

Developing an Innovative Entrepreneurial Culture 290

Organizing for Innovation: Corporate Entrepreneurship 291

11.5 Evaluation and Control 294

INTERNET ISSUE: Software Company Challenges Hackers to Attack Its Product 295

11.6 **Impact of the Internet on Managing Technology and Innovation 296**

Chapter 12 **Strategic Issues in Entrepreneurial Ventures and Small Businesses 301**

12.1 Importance of Small Business and Entrepreneurial Ventures 301

GLOBAL ISSUE: Entrepreneurship: Some Countries Are More Supportive
Than Others 302

Definition of Small-Business Firms and Entrepreneurial Ventures   303

The Entrepreneur as a Strategist   303

12.2   Use of Strategic Planning and Strategic Management   304

Degree of Formality   304

Usefulness of Strategic Management Model   305

Usefulness of Strategic Decision-Making Process   305

12.3   Issues in Corporate Governance   308

12.4   Issues in Environmental Scanning and Strategy Formulation   309

Sources of Innovation   309

Factors Affecting a New Venture's Success   311

INTERNET ISSUE: Web Site Provides Local Business a Global Presence   312

12.5   Issues in Strategy Implementation   313

Substages of Small Business Development   313

Transfer of Power and Wealth in Family Businesses   315

12.6   Issues in Evaluation and Control   316

12.7   **Impact of the Internet on Entrepreneurial Ventures and Small Businesses   318**

Chapter 13   Strategic Issues in Not-For-Profit Organizations   324

13.1   Why Not-For-Profit?   325

GLOBAL ISSUE: Which Is Best for Society: Business or Not-For-Profit?   326

13.2   Importance of Revenue Source   326

Sources of Not-For-Profit Revenue   327

Patterns of Influence on Strategic Decision Making   327

Usefulness of Strategic Management Concepts and Techniques   329

13.3   Impact of Constraints on Strategic Management   329

Impact on Strategy Formulation   330

Impact on Strategy Implementation   331

Impact on Evaluation and Control   332

13.4   Popular Not-For-Profit Strategies   332

Strategic Piggybacking   332

Mergers   333

Strategic Alliances   333

13.5   **Impact of the Internet on Not-For-Profit Organizations   335**

Taxation   335

Improvement of Government Services   335

Impact on Other Not-For-Profit Organizations   336

INTERNET ISSUE: The Not-For-Profit Organizations That Rule the Internet   336

PART SIX Introduction to Case Analysis 341

Chapter 14 **Suggestions for Case Analysis 341**

    14.1 The Case Method 342

    14.2 Researching the Case Situation 342

    14.3 Financial Analysis: A Place to Begin 342

        Analyzing Financial Statements 343

        Common-Size Statements 346

        Z-Value, Index of Sustainable Growth, and Free Cash Flow 346

        Useful Economic Measures 347

        GLOBAL ISSUE: Why Consider Inflation in Case Analysis? 348

    14.4 Format for Case Analysis: The Strategic Audit 348

    14.5 **Impact of the Internet on Case Analysis 351**

        Finding a Company's Web Site 351

        INTERNET ISSUE: Top 10 Internet Scams 352

        Using a Search Engine 352

        Finding More Information 352

Appendix 14.A Resources for Case Research 355

Appendix 14.B Suggested Case Analysis Methodology Using the Strategic Audit 357

Appendix 14.C Example of Student-Written Strategic Audit 361

    Glossary G-1

    Name Index I-1

    Subject Index I-13

Preface

We wrote *Concepts in Strategic Management and Business Policy* to introduce you to strategic management—a field of inquiry that focuses on the organization as a whole and its interactions with its environment. The corporate world is in the process of transformation driven by information technology (in particular the Internet) and globalization. Strategic management takes a panoramic view of this changing corporate terrain and attempts to show how large and small firms can be more effective and efficient not only in today's world, but in tomorrow's as well.

The text has been class-tested in strategy courses and revised based on feedback from students and instructors. For the most part, the text is unchanged from the eighth edition. The only changes are the additions of Enron, Tyco, and Worldcom examples in Chapter 2 and the inclusion of a glossary of key terms at the back of the book. The first 10 chapters are organized around a strategic management model that prefaces each chapter and provides a structure for both content and case analysis. We emphasize those concepts that have proven to be most useful in understanding strategic decision-making and in conducting case analysis. Our goal was to make the text as comprehensive as possible without getting bogged down in any one area. Endnote references are provided for those who wish to learn more about any particular topic. The primary changes from the eighth edition are the selection of cases. We included new versions of eight popular full-length cases and five entirely new cases. We also added a special category of ten experiential cases called Internet Research Mini-Cases. All of the cases are about actual organizations. The firms range in size from large, established multinationals to small, entrepreneurial ventures, and cover a broad variety of issues. As an aid to case analysis, we propose the strategic audit as an analytical technique.

Objectives

This book focuses on the following objectives, typically found in most strategic management and business policy courses:

- To develop an understanding of strategic management concepts, research, and theories.
- To develop a framework of analysis to enable a student to identify central issues and problems in complex, comprehensive cases; to suggest alternative courses of action; and to present well-supported recommendations for future action.
- To develop conceptual skills so that a student is able to integrate previously learned aspects of corporations.
- To develop an understanding of the global economy and the Internet and their current and potential impact on business activities in any location.
- To develop an understanding of the role of corporate governance in strategic management.
- To develop the ability to analyze and evaluate, both quantitatively and qualitatively, the performance of the people responsible for strategic decisions.
- To bridge the gap between theory and practice by developing an understanding of when and how to apply concepts and techniques learned in earlier courses on marketing, accounting, finance, management, operations, and information systems.

- To improve research capabilities necessary to gather and interpret key environmental data.
- To develop a better understanding of the present and future environments in which corporations must function.
- To develop analytical and decision-making skills for dealing with complex conceptual problems in an ethical manner.

This book achieves these objectives by presenting and explaining concepts and theories useful in understanding the strategic management process. It critically analyzes studies in the field of strategy to acquaint the student with the literature of this area and to help develop the student's research capabilities. It also suggests a model of strategic management. It recommends the strategic audit as one approach to the systematic analysis of complex organization-wide issues. Through a series of special issue and comprehensive cases (available in the combined text and the cases text), it provides the student with an opportunity to apply concepts, skills, and techniques to real-world corporate problems. The book focuses on the business corporation because of its crucial position in the economic system of the world and in the material development of any society.

Time-Tested Features

This edition contains many of the same features and content that helped make previous editions successful. Some of the features are the following:

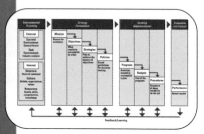

- A **strategic management model** runs throughout the first 10 chapters as a unifying concept. (Explained in Chapter 1)

chapter 2

Corporate Governance and Social Responsibility

- **Corporate governance** is examined in terms of the roles, responsibilities, and interactions of top management and the board of directors. (Chapter 2) Most of the cases contain information about the company's board of directors and top management.

2.3 Social Responsibilities of Strategic Decision Makers

Should strategic decision makers be responsible only to shareholders, or do they have broader responsibilities? The concept of **social responsibility** proposes that a private corporation has responsibilities to society that extend beyond making a profit. Strategic decisions often affect more than just the corporation. A decision to retrench by closing some plants and discontinuing product lines, for example, affects not only the firm's workforce, but also the communities where the plants are located and the customers that have no other source for the discontinued product. Such situations raise questions of the appropriateness of certain missions, objectives, and strategies of business corporations. Managers must be able to deal with these conflicting interests in an ethical manner to formulate a viable strategic plan.

RESPONSIBILITIES OF A BUSINESS FIRM

What are the responsibilities of a business firm, and how many of them must be fulfilled? Milton Friedman and Archie Carroll offer two contrasting views of the responsibilities of business firms to society.

- **Social responsibility and managerial ethics** are examined in detail in terms of how they affect strategic decision making. (Chapter 2)

- Equal emphasis is placed on **environmental scanning** of the societal environment as well as on the task environment. Topics include forecasting and Miles and Snow's typology in addition to Porter's industry analysis. (Chapter 3) ▶

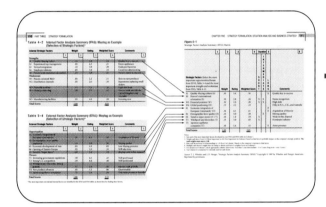

- **Core and distinctive competencies** are examined within the framework of the resource-based view of the firm. (Chapter 4)

- Internal and external strategic factors are emphasized through the use of specially-designed **EFAS, IFAS,** and **SFAS tables**. (Chapters 3, 4, and 5) ◀

- Two chapters deal with issues in **strategy implementation**, such as organizational and job design plus strategy-manager fit, action planning, and corporate culture. (Chapters 8 and 9)

- A separate chapter on **evaluation and control** explains the importance of measurement and incentives to organizational performance. (Chapter 10)

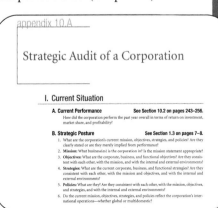

- The **strategic audit**, a way to operationalize the strategic decision-making process, provides a tested methodology in case analysis. (Chapter 10) ▶

- Special chapters deal with strategic issues in **managing technology and innovation, entrepreneurial ventures and small businesses,** and **not-for-profit organizations.** (Chapters 11, 12, and 13, respectively) These issues are often ignored by other strategy textbooks.

chapter 14
PART SIX
Introduction to Case Analysis

Suggestions
for Case Analysis

A few years ago, AlliedSignal's free cash flow measure turned negative. Although the company reported a 16% gain in net income for the second quarter, the free cash flow was a negative $90 million. Top management dismissed the cash flow situation as only temporary, arguing that capital spending and increasing inventory during the first part of the year was needed to fuel the company's sales growth expected later in the year. A company spokesman predicted that the free cash flow for the year should hit $300 million and concluded, "There's no problem with cash flow here."

"Not so!" responded Jeffrey Fotta, President of Boston's Ernst Institutional Research. Fotta contended that Allied's growing sales and earnings masked a serious problem in the company. Over the past year, Allied's push to boost sales had caused it difficulty in meeting its cash needs from operations. "They're growing too fast and not getting the returns from capital investments they need to get. Allied peaked in mid 1995, and returns have been deteriorating since." Fotta predicted that without major changes, AlliedSignal would have increasing difficulty continuing its double-digit sales growth."

This is an example of how one analyst used a performance measure to assess the overall health of a company. You can do the same type of in-depth analysis on a comprehensive strategic management case. This chapter provides you with various analytical techniques and suggestions for conducting this kind of case analysis.

341

- **Suggestions for in-depth case analysis** provide a complete listing of financial ratios, recommendations for oral and written analysis, and ideas for further research. (Chapter 14)

- The **Strategic Audit Worksheet** is based on the time-tested strategic audit and is designed to help students organize and structure daily case preparation in a brief period of time. The worksheet works exceedingly well for checking the level of daily student case preparation—especially for open class discussions of cases. (Chapter 14)

- **Key Theory As It Applies Capsules** in various chapters explain key theories underlying strategic management. This feature adds emphasis to the theories, but does not interrupt the flow of the text material.

Projections for the 21st Century

- From 1994 to 2010, the world population will grow from 5.607 billion to 7.32 billion.
- From 1994 to 2010, the number of nations will increase from 192 to 202.[67]

- **Projections for the 21st Century** end each chapter by forecasting what the world will be like in 2010.

- An **experiential exercise** focusing on the material covered in each chapter helps the reader to apply strategic concepts to an actual situation.

Strategic Practice Exercise

How far should people in a business firm go in gathering competitive intelligence? Where do you draw the line?

Evaluate each of the following approaches that a business firm could use to gather information about competition. For each approach, mark your feeling about its appropriateness: 1 (definitely not appropriate), 2 (probably not appropriate), 3 (undecided), 4 (probably appropriate), or 5 (definitely appropriate).

The business firm should try to get useful information about competitors by:

____ Carefully studying trade journals.
____ Wiretapping the telephones of competitors.
____ Posing as a potential customer to competitors.
____ Getting loyal customers to put out a phony "request for proposal" to solicit competitors' bids.
____ Buying competitors' products and taking them apart.
____ Hiring management consultants who have worked for competitors.
____ Rewarding competitors' employees for useful "tips."
____ Questioning competitors' customers and/or suppliers.
____ Buying and analyzing competitors' garbage.
____ Advertising and interviewing for nonexistent jobs.

____ Taking public tours of competitors' facilities.
____ Releasing false information about the company in order to confuse competitors.
____ Questioning competitors' technical people at trade shows and conferences.
____ Hiring key people away from competitors.
____ Analyzing competitors' labor union contracts.
____ Having employees date persons who work for competitors.
____ Studying aerial photographs of competitors' facilities.

After you mark each of the preceding approaches, compare your responses to those of other people in your class. For each approach, the people marking 4 or 5 should say why they thought this particular act would be appropriate. Those who marked 1 or 2 should then state why they thought this act would be inappropriate.

What does this tell you about ethics and socially responsible behavior?

Source: Developed from W. A. Jones, Jr. and N. B. Bryan, Jr., "Business Ethics and Business Intelligence: An Empirical Study of Information-Gathering Alternatives," International Journal of Management (June 1995), pp. 204–208. For actual examples of some of these activities, see J. Kerstetter, P. Burrows, J. Greene, G. Smith, and M. Conlin, "The Dark Side of the Valley," Business Week (July 17, 2000), pp. 42–43.

- A list of **key terms** and the pages in which they are discussed enable the reader to keep track of important concepts as they are introduced in each chapter.

- **Timely, well-researched, and class-tested cases** deal with interesting companies and industries. Many of the cases are about well-known, publicly held corporations—ideal subjects for further research by students wishing to "update" the cases.

- An **Industry Note for use in industry analysis** of the major home appliance industry is included for use by itself or with the Maytag case.

Features New to This 9th Edition

TEXT

We have incorporated information from some of the recent scandals in corporate governance and business ethics in Chapter 2, Corporate Governance and Social Responsibility. The opening vignette to the chapter now deals with governance issues at Tyco International. A special boxed feature highlights the "whistle blowers" who brought to light the unethical and even criminal practices at Enron and Worldcom.

NEW! We have added a Glossary to the back of the book listing the many key terms and their definitions used within the chapters. Rather than paging through the book to find a particular term, the reader can go to one spot to find the definition and the page location of any important concept and technique.

IN THE FULL-VOLUME AND CASES TEXTS—NEW CASES

We have added five new cases dealing with contemporary issues and industries.

- A new case on corporate governance: McKesson Makes a Deal
- Two new technology cases: Palm Computing and Handspring
- A new entrepreneurial venture: Adrenaline Air Sports
- A new airline case: American Airlines

NEW VERSIONS OF POPULAR CASES

We have updated eight of our most popular cases to make them even more relevant in the classroom.

- Harley-Davidson
- Carnival Cruise Lines
- Reebok
- U. S. Major Home Appliance Industry
- Maytag Corporation
- Kmart
- Wal-Mart
- Arm & Hammer

We have added the address, phone numbers, Web site and stock market symbol for each case of a publicly-held company. This table appears on pages xxxi and xxxii of this book.

NEW! INTERNET RESEARCH MINI-CASES

We have added a new exciting section of Internet Research Mini-Cases to be used as exercises for researching and analyzing companies for class discussion and presentation. These are mini-cases that introduce a particular company, but leave it to the reader to research the company on the Internet to obtain further information. It is then up to the student to analyze the company on the basis of information that has been found. These exercises are very useful to those instructors who like to assign cases for students to update and analyze. All of these cases are new and up-to-date as of 2002.

Five mini-cases are included in the book.

- eBay
- Hershey Foods
- AirTran
- Tyson Foods
- Eli Lilly

Five more mini-cases are on Prentice Hall's Website at www.prenhall.com/wheelen.

- Southwest Airlines
- Stryker
- Heinz
- Williams-Sonoma
- Pfizer

CUSTOMIZE!

Want to customize your Wheelen/Hunger cases?
This program is intended for professors who wish to build a custom casebook or custom course pack. You can either use a portion of a Prentice Hall business casebook or you can mix and match materials from several Prentice Hall books. In addition, you can add your own materials or outside cases; up to 20 percent of the text can come from outside Prentice Hall Custom Business Resources. This material can range from professor-produced material such as a syllabus and class notes to articles from business periodicals such as *The Economist, Business Week,* and many more. ***It's just a click away. Visit www.prenhall.com/custombusiness.***

Supplements

Supplemental materials are available to the instructor from the publisher. These include both Text and Case Instructor Manuals, an Instructor's Resource CD-ROM containing testing software and PowerPoints, videos, a book specific Web site, and transparency acetates in color.

INSTRUCTOR'S MANUALS

Two comprehensive Instructor's Manuals have been carefully constructed to accompany this book. The first one accompanies the text chapters; the second one accompanies the cases.

Text Instructor's Manual

To aid in discussing the 14 chapters dealing with strategic management concepts, the Text Instructor's Manual includes:

(1) ***Suggestions for Teaching Strategic Management***—discusses various teaching methods and includes suggested course syllabi.

(2) ***Chapter Notes***—includes summaries of each chapter, suggested answers to discussion questions, suggestions for using end of chapter cases exercises, plus additional discussion questions (with answers) and lecture modules.

(3) ***Multiple-Choice Test Questions***—contains approximately 100 questions for each of the 14 chapters for a total of over 1,400 questions!

(4) ***Video Guide***—includes teaching notes for the Newbury Comics video.

Case Instructor's Manual

The Case Instructor's Manual has been fully updated for this edition. To aid in case method teaching, the Case Instructor's Manual includes detailed suggestions for use, teaching objectives, and examples of student analyses for each of the 34 complete cases, plus information about using the ten Internet Research Mini-Cases. This is the most comprehensive instructor's manual available in strategic management. A standardized format is provided for each case:

(1) Case Abstract

(2) Case Issues and Subjects

(3) Steps Covered in the Strategic Decision-Making Process

(4) Case Objectives

(5) Suggested Classroom Approaches

(6) Discussion Questions

(7) Case Author's Teaching Note

(8) Student-Written Strategic Audit or Paper

(9) EFAS, IFAS, SFAS Exhibits

(10) Financial Analysis—ratios and common-size income statements

INSTRUCTOR'S RESOURCE CD-ROM

The Instructor's Resource CD-ROM contains tools to facilitate the instructor's lectures and examinations. These include PowerPoint Electronic Transparency Masters, a collection of about 150 figures and tables from the text. PowerPoints for the cases in the text are also available. The instructor may customize these presentations and can present individual slides for student handouts. The CD also contains a computerized test bank of all the multiple-choice questions (over 1,400) listed in the Text Instructor's Manual. The Instructor's Manuals have also been added to the Instructor's Resource CD-ROM, as well as the video case notes for Newbury Comics.

VIDEO: NEWBURY COMICS

This videotape features part-ending segments shot at Newbury Comics, an exciting and current popular culture retail chain. Beginning life as a store buying and selling used CDs, Newbury Comics has been expanding its product line and locations. Segments address key issues such as the company's basic model, mission and vision, and decision-making models. Accompanying case information can be found at the end of the parts in the concepts and full-volume text, and a video guide is included in the Text Instructor's Manual.

POWERPOINTS

The PowerPoint transparencies, a comprehensive package of text outlines and figures corresponding to the text and cases, are designed to aid the educator and supplement in-class lectures. The PPTs can be found on the Instructor's CD, as well as on the text Web site, located at **www.prenhall.com/wheelen.**

MY COMPANION WEBSITE

The new MyCompanion Website provides professors with a customized course Website including new communication tools, one-click navigation of chapter content, and In the News articles provided by XanEdu. It also features an online Study Guide for students and download files of both Instructor's Manuals and the PowerPoints for Instructors. **www.prenhall.com/wheelen**

ONLINE COURSES

Courses are available in *Blackboard, Course Compass,* and *WebCT*. These courses feature Companion Website and Test Item File Content in an easy-to-use system. Developed by educators for educators and their students, this online content and tools feature the most advanced educational technology and instructional design available today. The rich set of materials, communication tools, and course management resources can be easily customized to either enhance a traditional course or create the entire course online.

MASTERING STRATEGY

Mastering Strategy is the first product in the *Mastering Business* series. It offers students an interactive, multimedia experience as they follow the people and issues of CanGo, Inc., a small Internet startup. The text, video, and interactive exercises provide students an opportunity to simulate the strategic planning experience and chart the future activities for CanGo.

FINANCIAL TIMES STUDENT SUBSCRIPTION

Participating students qualify for a $10.00, 15-week subscription to the *Financial Times*. **How It Works:** Wheelen/Hunger text + subscription package will contain a 16-page full-color *Financial Times* student guide shrink-wrapped to the text. Bound inside the student guide will be a postcard which entitles the student to claim a pre-paid 15-week subscription to the *Financial Times*. Free subscription for professors who choose to use this package! Contact your local Prentice Hall representative for more information.

ACKNOWLEDGMENTS

We thank the many people at Prentice Hall who helped to make this edition possible. We are especially grateful to Jennifer Glennon, Cindy Spreder, Jessica Sabloff, Melanie Olsen, and Sandra Krausman, who took the book through the production process.

We are also very grateful to Kathy Wheelen for her first-rate administrative support and to Betty Hunger for her preparation of the subject and name indexes and the glossary. We are especially thankful to the many students who tried out the cases we chose to include in the combined book and the case book. Their comments helped us find any flaws in the cases before the book went to the printer.

In addition, we express our appreciation to Dr. Labh Hira, Dean, and Dr. Russ Laczniac, Management Department Chair, of Iowa State University's College of Business, for their support and provision of the resources so necessary to produce a textbook. We also recognize Dr. Robert L. Anderson, Dean, and Dr. Alan Balfour, Management Department Chair of the College of Business of the University of South Florida. Both of us acknowledge our debt to Dr. William Shenkir and Dr. Frank S. Kaulback, former Deans of the McIntire School of Commerce of the University of Virginia for the provision of a work climate most supportive to the original development of this book.

Lastly, to the many strategy/policy instructors and students who have expressed their problems with the strategy/policy course: we have tried to respond to your concerns as best we could by providing a comprehensive yet usable text coupled with recent and complex cases. To you, the people who work hard in the strategy/policy trenches, we acknowledge our debt. This book is yours.

T. L. W.
Tampa, Florida

J. D. H.
Ames, Iowa

STRATEGIC MANAGEMENT and BUSINESS POLICY

Concepts

chapter 1

Basic Concepts of Strategic Management

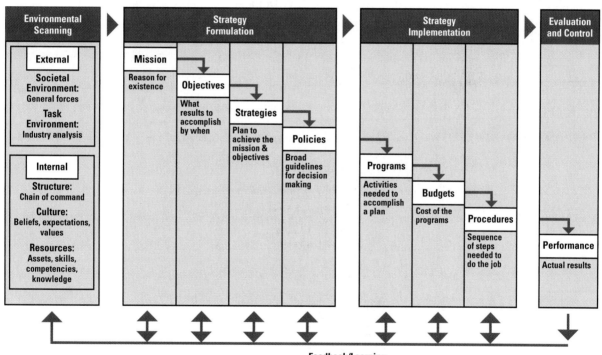

Feedback/Learning

How does a company become successful and stay successful? Certainly not by playing it safe and following the traditional ways of doing business! Even a company like General Electric, an established, old-line *Fortune* 500 company with operations throughout the world, must constantly renew itself or else be outmaneuvered by aggressive newcomers. Realizing the potential impact of the Internet on all industries, Jack Welch, Chairman of the Board, issued a challenge at a March 1999 meeting to managers of the firm's business units to, in effect, replace their own product lines before competitors could do so. They also needed to learn how to conduct their business on the Internet. Welch had witnessed his own family and colleagues complete most or all of their Christmas shopping online and decided that the company had to enter the Internet age with a vengeance. Welch directed the top 600 managers to find an internal "Internet mentor" who would tutor them in the World Wide Web. According to Welch, "There's no such thing as an 'old economy.' Commerce is the same as it was 500 years ago. People sell and people buy—whether it's from a wagon or the Internet."[1]

In early February 2000, General Electric quietly launched the General Electric Financial Network ⟨gefn.com⟩, its first financial Web site for consumers. After having already invested over $10 million in developing the new business, GE heavily advertised its Web site in the televised summer Olympics. Gefn.com was marketed as the Web site where consumers could go to simplify their investment lives and find everything from a bank account to life insurance and GE mutual funds. According to Michael Frazier, head of the GE Capital consumer unit in charge of creating gefn.com, "Make no mistake, we want to be as well known to consumers for financial security as we are for light bulbs and appliances."[2] Knowing that many of the 50+ "baby boomers" were in the market for financial services as a way to save for their retirement, gefn.com entered a market already crowded with strong competitors.

Acknowledging GE's thrust as a bold strategic move, a number of industry analysts questioned if gefn.com had what was needed to be a major competitor in this business. For example, even though the Web site allowed customers to do online banking and obtain GE insurance and loans, it did not provide the ability to trade stocks or buy non-GE mutual funds. They also wondered if gefn.com could achieve its objectives with only an Internet presence and no "bricks and mortar" branch offices in which customers and loan officers could interact. E*Trade, in contrast, had realized the limited growth potential of its online brokerage and banking businesses and had begun opening E*Trade Zone retail offices and automated teller machines.[3]

Realizing these to be important issues, GE executives claimed, nevertheless, that gefn.com would be an important new distribution channel for GE's existing financial services units. One of the fastest growing units was GE Financial Assurance (GEFA), a provider of insurance, mutual funds, and 401(k) retirement plans in 17 countries. GE planned to put links to gefn.com on the intranets of those companies that already had a relationship with GE through their insurance or retirement plans. GE executives were seriously examining the alternative of a "carefully crafted alliance" over an acquisition to enter the electronic brokerage business. Referring to GE's well-known companywide policy that a business unit must be either number one or two in market share or have the potential to achieve it, Michael Frazier argued that "being number one or number two is not as important as being big enough to control your own destiny." General Electric, as a late entrant, clearly had the resources to make an impact on this competitive and fragmented market, but did it have what was needed to become a major player in the financial services industry?

1.1 The Study of Strategic Management

Strategic management is that set of managerial decisions and actions that determines the long-run performance of a corporation. It includes environmental scanning (both external and internal), strategy formulation (strategic or long-range planning), strategy implementation, and evaluation and control. The study of strategic management, therefore, emphasizes the monitoring and evaluating of external opportunities and threats in light of a corporation's strengths and weaknesses. Originally called business policy, strategic management incorporates such topics as long-range planning and strategy. **Business policy**, in contrast, has a general management orientation and tends primarily to look inward with its concern for properly integrating the corporation's many functional activities. Strategic management, as a field of study, incorporates the integrative concerns of business policy with a heavier environmental and strategic emphasis. Therefore, strategic management has tended to replace business policy as the preferred name of the field.[4]

PHASES OF STRATEGIC MANAGEMENT

Many of the concepts and techniques dealing with strategic management have been developed and used successfully by business corporations such as General Electric and the Boston Consulting Group. Over time, business practitioners and academic researchers have expanded and refined these concepts. Initially strategic management was of most use to large corporations operating in multiple industries. Increasing risks of error, costly mistakes, and even economic ruin are causing today's professional managers in all organizations to take strategic management seriously in order to keep their company competitive in an increasingly volatile environment.

As managers attempt to better deal with their changing world, a firm generally evolves through the following four **phases of strategic management**:[5]

Phase 1. *Basic financial planning:* Managers initiate serious planning when they are requested to propose next year's budget. Projects are proposed on the basis of very little analysis, with most information coming from within the firm. The sales force usually provides the small amount of environmental information. Such simplistic operational planning only pretends to be strategic management, yet it is quite time consuming. Normal company activities are often suspended for weeks while managers try to cram ideas into the proposed budget. The time horizon is usually one year.

Phase 2. *Forecast-based planning:* As annual budgets become less useful at stimulating long-term planning, managers attempt to propose five-year plans. They now consider projects that may take more than one year. In addition to internal information, managers gather any available environmental data—usually on an ad hoc basis—and extrapolate current trends five years into the future. This phase is also time consuming, often involving a full month of managerial activity to make sure all the proposed budgets fit together. The process gets very political as managers compete for larger shares of funds. Endless meetings take place to evaluate proposals and justify assumptions. The time horizon is usually three to five years.

Phase 3. *Externally oriented planning (strategic planning):* Frustrated with highly political, yet ineffectual five-year plans, top management takes control of the planning process by initiating strategic planning. The company seeks to increase its responsiveness to changing markets and competition by thinking strategically. Planning is taken out of the hands of lower level managers and concentrated in a planning staff whose task is to develop strategic plans for the corporation. Consultants often provide the sophisticated and innovative techniques that the planning staff uses to gather information and forecast future trends. Ex-military experts develop competitive intelligence units. Upper level managers meet once a year at a resort "retreat" led by key members of the planning staff to evaluate and update the current strategic plan. Such top-down planning emphasizes formal strategy formulation and leaves the implementation issues to lower management levels. Top management typically develops five-year plans with help from consultants but minimal input from lower levels.

Phase 4. *Strategic management:* Realizing that even the best strategic plans are worthless without the input and commitment of lower level managers, top management forms planning groups of managers and key employees at many levels from various departments and work groups. They develop and integrate a series of strategic plans aimed at achieving the company's primary objectives. Strategic plans now detail the implementation, evaluation, and control issues. Rather than attempting to perfectly forecast the future, the plans emphasize probable scenarios and contingency strategies. The sophisticated annual five-year strategic plan is replaced with strategic thinking at all levels of the organization throughout the year. Strategic information, previously available only centrally to top management, is available via local area networks and intranets to people throughout the organization. Instead of a large centralized planning staff, internal and external planning consultants are available to help guide group strategy discussions. Although top management may still initiate the strategic planning process, the resulting strategies may come from anywhere in the organization. Planning is typically interactive across levels and is no longer top down. People at all levels are now involved.

General Electric, one of the pioneers of strategic planning, led the transition from strategic planning to strategic management during the 1980s.[6] By the 1990s, most corporations around the world had also begun the conversion to strategic management.

Until 1978, Maytag Corporation, the major home appliance manufacturer, could be characterized as being in Phase one of strategic management. Maytag's CEO, Daniel Krum, formed a strategic planning task force to answer the question: "If we keep doing what we're doing now, what will the Maytag Corporation look like in five years?" The answer to this question served as the impetus for the firm's subsequent expansion into a full line of major home appliances and its entry into the world market through the purchase of Hoover.

BENEFITS OF STRATEGIC MANAGEMENT

Research has revealed that organizations that engage in strategic management generally outperform those that do not.[7] The attainment of an appropriate match or "fit" between an organization's environment and its strategy, structure, and processes has positive effects on the organization's performance.[8] For example, a study of the impact of deregulation on U.S. railroads found that those railroads that changed their strategy as their environment changed outperformed those railroads that did not change their strategy.[9]

A survey of nearly 50 corporations in a variety of countries and industries found the three most highly rated benefits of strategic management to be:

- Clearer sense of strategic vision for the firm
- Sharper focus on what is strategically important
- Improved understanding of a rapidly changing environment[10]

To be effective, however, strategic management need not always be a formal process. As occurred at Maytag, it can begin with a few simple questions:

1. **Where is the organization now? (Not where do we hope it is!)**
2. **If no changes are made, where will the organization be in 1 year? 2 years? 5 years? 10 years? Are the answers acceptable?**
3. **If the answers are not acceptable, what specific actions should management undertake? What are the risks and payoffs involved?**

A survey by Bain & Company revealed the most popular management tools to be strategic planning and developing mission and vision statements—essential parts of strategic management.[11] Studies of the planning practices of actual organizations suggest that the real value of strategic planning may be more in the future orientation of the planning process itself than in any written strategic plan. Small companies, in particular, may plan informally and irregularly. Nevertheless, studies of small businesses reveal that even though the degree of formality in strategic planning may have only a small to moderate impact on a firm's profitability, formal planners have significantly greater growth in sales than do informal planners.[12]

Planning the strategy of large, multidivisional corporations can become complex and time consuming. It often takes slightly more than a year for a large company to move from situation assessment to a final decision agreement. Because of the relatively large number of people affected by a strategic decision in such a firm, a formalized, more sophisticated system is needed to ensure that strategic planning leads to successful performance. Otherwise, top management becomes isolated from developments in the business units, and lower level managers lose sight of the corporate mission and objectives.

1.2 Globalization and Electronic Commerce: Challenges to Strategic Management

Not too long ago, a business corporation could be successful by focusing only on making and selling goods and services within its national boundaries. International considerations were minimal. Profits earned from exporting products to foreign lands were considered frosting on the cake but not really essential to corporate success. During the 1960s, for example, most U.S. companies organized themselves around a number of product divisions that made and sold goods only in the United States. All manufacturing and sales outside the United States were typically managed through one international division. An international assignment was usually considered a message that the person was no longer promotable and should be looking for another job.

Similarly, until the mid-1990s, a business firm could be very successful without using the Internet for anything more than a public relations Web site. Most business was done through a sales force and a network of distributors with the eventual sale to the consumer being made through retail outlets. Few executives used a personal computer, let alone "surfed" the World Wide Web. The Internet may have been useful for research, but until recently it was not seriously viewed as a means to actually conduct normal business transactions.

IMPACT OF GLOBALIZATION

Today, everything has changed. **Globalization**, the internationalization of markets and corporations, has changed the way modern corporations do business. To reach the economies of scale necessary to achieve the low costs, and thus the low prices, needed to be competitive, companies are now thinking of a global (worldwide) market instead of a national market. Nike and Reebok, for example, manufacture their athletic shoes in various countries throughout Asia for sale on every continent. Instead of using one international division to manage everything outside the home country, large corporations are now using matrix structures in which product units are interwoven with country or regional units. International assignments are now considered key for anyone interested in reaching top management.

As more industries become global, strategic management is becoming an increasingly important way to keep track of international developments and position the company for long-term competitive advantage. For example, Maytag Corporation purchased Hoover not so much for its vacuum cleaner business, but for its European laundry, cooking, and refrigeration business. Maytag's management realized that a company without a manufacturing presence in the European Union (EU) would be at a competitive disadvantage in the changing major home appliance industry. See the 🌐 **Global Issue** feature to learn how regional trade associations are changing how international business is conducted. Similar international considerations have led to the strategic alliance between British Airways and American Airlines and to the merger between Daimler-Benz and Chrysler Corporation.

IMPACT OF ELECTRONIC COMMERCE

Electronic commerce refers to the use of the Internet to conduct business transactions. A 1999 survey conducted by Booz-Allen & Hamilton and the Economist Intelligence Unit of more than 525 top executives from a wide range of industries revealed that the Internet is reshaping the global marketplace and that it will continue to do so for many years. More than 90% of the executives believed that the Internet would transform or have a major impact on their corporate strategy within two years. According to Matthew Barrett, Chairman and CEO of the Bank of Montreal, "We are only standing at the threshold of a New World. It is as if we had just invented printing or the steam engine."[13] Not only is the Internet changing the way customers, suppliers, and companies interact, it is changing the way companies work internally.

Global Issue

Regional Trade Associations Replace National Trade Barriers

Previously known as the Common Market and the European Community, the **European Union (EU)** is the most significant trade association in the world. The goal of the EU is the complete economic integration of its 15 member countries—Austria, Belgium, Denmark, Finland, France, Germany, Greece, Ireland, Italy, Luxembourg, the Netherlands, Portugal, Spain, Sweden, and the United Kingdom—so that goods made in one part of Western Europe can move freely without ever stopping for a customs inspection. One currency, the euro, is being used throughout the region as members integrate their monetary systems. The steady elimination of barriers to free trade is providing the impetus for a series of mergers, acquisitions, and joint ventures among business corporations. The requirement of at least 60% local content to avoid tariffs has forced many American and Asian companies to abandon exporting in favor of a strong local presence in Europe. The EU has agreed to expand its membership to include the Czech Republic, Hungary, Estonia, Poland, Malta, Cyprus, and Slovenia by 2004; Latvia, Lithuania, and Slovakia by 2006; and Bulgaria and Romania by 2010. Turkey is being considered for admission in 2011.

Canada, the United States, and Mexico are affiliated economically under the **North American Free Trade Agreement (NAFTA)**. The goal of NAFTA is improved trade among the three member countries rather than complete economic integration. Launched in 1994, the agreement requires all three members to remove all tariffs among themselves over 15 years, but they are allowed to have their own tariff arrangements with nonmember countries. Cars and trucks must have 62.5% North American content to qualify for duty-free status.

Transportation restrictions and other regulations are being significantly reduced. Some Asian and European corporations are locating operations in one of the countries to obtain access to the entire North American region. Vicente Fox, President of Mexico, is proposing that NAFTA become more like the European Union in that both people and goods would have unlimited access across borders from Mexico to Canada. In addition, there have been some discussions of extending NAFTA southward to include Chile, but thus far nothing formal has been proposed.

South American countries are also working to harmonize their trading relationships with each other and to form trade associations. The establishment of the **Mercosur (Mercosul** in Portuguese) free-trade area among Argentina, Brazil, Uruguay, and Paraguay means that a manufacturing presence within these countries is becoming essential to avoid tariffs for nonmember countries. Claiming to be NAFTA's southern counterpart, Mercosur has extended free-trade agreements to Bolivia and Venezuela. With Chile and Argentina cooperating to build a tunnel through the Andes to connect both countries, it is likely that Chile may soon form some economic relationship with Mercosur.

Asia has yet no comparable regional trade association to match the potential economic power of either NAFTA or the EU. Japan, South Korea, China, and India generally operate as independent economic powers. Nevertheless, the **Association of South East Asian Nations (ASEAN)**—composed of Brunei, Indonesia, Malaysia, the Philippines, Singapore, Thailand, and Vietnam—is attempting to link its members into a borderless economic zone. Increasingly referred to as ASEAN+3, it is already including China, Japan, and South Korea in its annual summit meetings. The ASEAN nations are negotiating the linkage of the ASEAN Free-Trade Area (AFTA) with the existing FTA of Australia and New Zealand. With the EU extending eastward and NAFTA extending southward to someday connect with Mercosur, pressure is already building on the independent Asian nations to soon form an expanded version of ASEAN.

In just the few years since its introduction, it has profoundly affected the basis of competition in many industries. Instead of the traditional focus on product features and costs, the Internet is shifting the basis for competition to a more strategic level in which the traditional value chain of an industry is drastically altered. A 1999 report by AMR Research indicated that industry leaders are in the process of moving 60 to 100% of their business to business (B2B) transactions to the Internet. The net B2B marketplace includes (a) Trading Exchange Platforms like VerticalNet and i2 Technologies's TradeMatrix, which support trading communities in multiple markets; (b) Industry-Sponsored Exchanges, such as the one being built by major automakers; and (c) Net Market Makers, like e-Steel, NECX, and BuildPoint, which focus on a specific industry's value chain or business processes to mediate multiple transactions among businesses. The Garner Group predicts that the worldwide B2B market will grow from $145 billion in 1999 to $7.29 trillion in 2004, at which time it will represent 7% of the total global sales transactions.[14]

The previously mentioned survey of top executives identified the following seven trends, due at least in part, to the rise of the Internet:[15]

1. The Internet is forcing companies to transform themselves. The concept of electronically networking customers, suppliers, and partners is now a reality.

2. New channels are changing market access and branding, causing the *disintermediation* (breaking down) of traditional distribution channels. By working directly with the customers, companies are able to avoid the usual distributors, thus forming closer relationships with the end users, improving service, and reducing costs.

3. The balance of power is shifting to the consumer. Now having unlimited access to information on the Internet, customers are much more demanding than their "nonwired" predecessors.

4. Competition is changing. New technology-driven firms plus older traditional competitors are exploiting the Internet to become more innovative and efficient.

5. The pace of business is increasing drastically. Planning horizons, information needs, and customer/supplier expectations are reflecting the immediacy of the Internet. Because of this turbulent environment, time is compressed into "dog years" in which one year feels like seven years.

6. The Internet is pushing corporations out of their traditional boundaries. The traditional separation between suppliers, manufacturers, and customers is becoming blurred with the development and expansion of extranets, in which cooperating firms have access to each other's internal operating plans and processes. For example, Lockheed Martin, the aerospace company, has an extranet linking Lockheed to Boeing, a project partner, and to the U.S. Defense Department, a key customer.

7. Knowledge is becoming a key asset and a source of competitive advantage. For example, physical assets accounted for 62.8% of the total market value of U.S. manufacturing firms in 1980 but only 37.9% in 1991. The remainder of the market value is composed of intangible assets, primarily intellectual capital.[16]

1.3 Theories of Organizational Adaptation

Globalization and electronic commerce present real challenges to the strategic management of business corporations. How can any one company keep track of all the changing technological, economic, political-legal, and sociocultural trends around the world and make the necessary adjustments? This is not an easy task. Various theories have been proposed to account for how organizations obtain fit with their environment. The theory of **population ecology**, for example, proposes that once an organization is successfully established in a particular environmental niche, it is unable to adapt to changing conditions. Too much inertia prevents the organization from changing. The company is thus replaced (bought out or goes bankrupt) by other organizations more suited to the new environment. Although popular in sociology, research fails to support the arguments of population ecology.[17] **Institution theory**, in contrast, proposes that organizations can and do adapt to changing conditions by imitating other successful organizations. To its credit, many examples can be found of companies that have adapted to changing circumstances by imitating another firm's strategies. The theory does not, however, explain how or by whom successful new strategies are developed in the first place. The **strategic choice perspective** goes one step further by proposing that not only do organizations adapt to a changing environment, but that they also have the opportunity and power to reshape their environment. Because of its emphasis on managers making rational strategic decisions, the strategic choice perspective is the dominant one taken in strategic management. Its argument that adaptation is a dynamic process fits with the view of **organizational learning theory** that organizations adjust defensively to a changing environment and use knowledge offensively to improve the fit between the organization and its environment. This perspective expands the strategic choice perspective to include people at all levels becoming involved in providing input into strategic decisions.[18]

In agreement with the concepts of organizational learning theory, an increasing number of companies are realizing that they must shift from a vertically organized, top-down type of organization to a more horizontally managed, interactive organization. They are attempting to adapt more quickly to changing conditions by becoming "learning organizations."

1.4 Creating a Learning Organization

Strategic management has now evolved to the point that its primary value is in helping the organization operate successfully in a dynamic, complex environment. Inland Steel Company, for example, uses strategic planning as a tool to drive organizational change. Managers at all levels are expected to continually analyze the changing steel industry in order to create or modify strategic plans throughout the year.[19] To be competitive in dynamic environments, corporations are having to become less bureaucratic and more flexible. In stable environments such as have existed in years past, a competitive strategy simply involved defining a competitive position and then defending it. As it takes less and less time for one product or technology to replace another, companies are finding that there is no such thing as a permanent competitive advantage. Many agree with Richard D'Aveni (in his book *Hypercompetition*) that any sustainable competitive advantage lies not in doggedly following a centrally managed five-year plan, but in stringing together a series of strategic short-term thrusts (as Intel does by cutting into the sales of its own offerings with periodic introductions of new products).[20] This means that corporations must develop strategic flexibility—the ability to shift from one dominant strategy to another.[21]

Strategic flexibility demands a long-term commitment to the development and nurturing of critical resources. It also demands that the company become a **learning organization**—an organization skilled at creating, acquiring, and transferring knowledge, and at modifying its behavior to reflect new knowledge and insights. Organizational learning is a critical component of competitiveness in a dynamic environment. It is particularly important to innovation and new product development.[22] For example, Hewlett-Packard uses an extensive network of informal committees to transfer knowledge among its cross-functional teams and to help spread new sources of knowledge quickly.[23] Learning organizations are skilled at 4 main activities:

- Solving problems systematically
- Experimenting with new approaches
- Learning from their own experiences and past history as well as from the experiences of others
- Transferring knowledge quickly and efficiently throughout the organization[24]

Learning organizations avoid stability through continuous self-examination and experimentation. People at all levels, not just top management, need to be involved in strategic management—helping to scan the environment for critical information; suggesting changes to strategies and programs to take advantage of environmental shifts; and working with others to continuously improve work methods, procedures, and evaluation techniques. Motorola, for example, developed an action learning format in which people from marketing, product development, and manufacturing meet to argue and reach agreement about the needs of the market, the best new product, and the schedules of each group producing it. This action learning approach overcame the problems that arose previously when the three departments met and formally agreed on plans but continued with their work as if nothing had happened.[25]

Organizations that are willing to experiment and are able to learn from their experiences are more successful than those that do not. For example, in a study of U.S. manufacturers of diagnostic imaging equipment, the most successful firms were those that improved products sold in the United States by incorporating some of what they had learned from their manufacturing and sales experiences in other nations. The less successful firms used the foreign operations primarily as sales outlets, not as important sources of technical knowledge.[26]

1.5 Basic Model of Strategic Management

Strategic management consists of four basic elements:

- **Environmental scanning**
- **Strategy formulation**
- **Strategy implementation**
- **Evaluation and control**

Figure 1–1 shows simply how these elements interact; **Figure 1–2** expands each of these elements and serves as the model for this book.[27] The terms used in **Figure 1–2** are explained in the following pages.

ENVIRONMENTAL SCANNING

Environmental scanning is the monitoring, evaluating, and disseminating of information from the external and internal environments to key people within the corporation. Its purpose is to identify **strategic factors**—those external and internal elements that will determine the future of the corporation. The simplest way to conduct environmental scanning is through **SWOT analysis**. SWOT is an acronym used to describe those particular **S**trengths, **W**eaknesses, **O**pportunities, and **T**hreats that are strategic factors for a specific company. The **external environment** consists of variables (**O**pportunities and **T**hreats) that are outside the organization and not typically within the short-run control of top management. These

Figure 1–1
Basic Elements of the Strategic Management Process

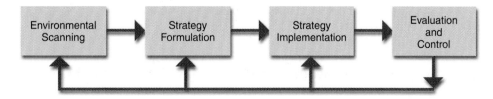

Figure 1–2
Strategic Management Model

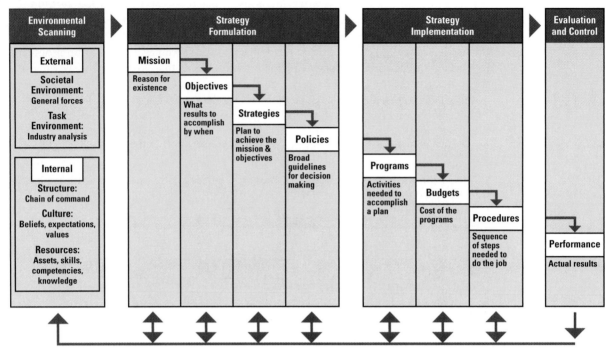

variables form the context within which the corporation exists. **Figure 1–3** depicts key environmental variables. They may be general forces and trends within the overall societal environment or specific factors that operate within an organization's specific task environment—often called its industry. (These external variables are defined and discussed in more detail in **Chapter 3**.)

The **internal environment** of a corporation consists of variables (**S**trengths and **W**eaknesses) that are within the organization itself and are not usually within the short-run control of top management. These variables form the context in which work is done. They include the corporation's structure, culture, and resources. Key strengths form a set of core competencies that the corporation can use to gain competitive advantage. (These internal variables and core competencies are defined and discussed in more detail in **Chapter 4**.)

STRATEGY FORMULATION

Strategy formulation is the development of long-range plans for the effective management of environmental opportunities and threats, in light of corporate strengths and weaknesses. It includes defining the corporate mission, specifying achievable objectives, developing strategies, and setting policy guidelines.

Mission

An organization's **mission** is the purpose or reason for the organization's existence. It tells what the company is providing to society, either a service like housecleaning or a product like automobiles. A well-conceived mission statement defines the fundamental, unique purpose

Figure 1–3
Environmental Variables

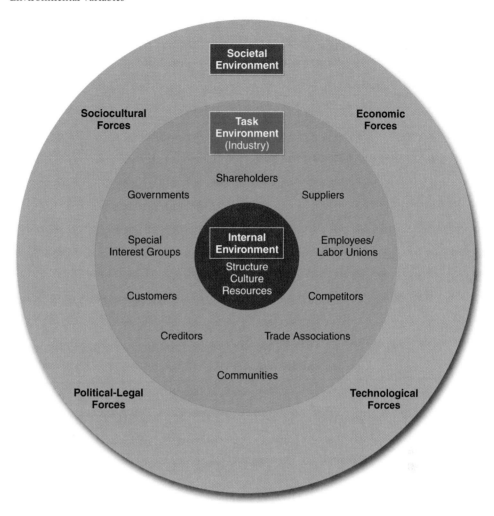

that sets a company apart from other firms of its type and identifies the scope of the company's operations in terms of products (including services) offered and markets served. It may also include the firm's philosophy about how it does business and treats its employees. It puts into words not only what the company is now, but also what it wants to become—management's strategic vision of the firm's future. (Some people like to consider vision and mission as two different concepts: A mission statement describes what the organization is now; a vision statement describes what the organization would like to become. We prefer to combine these ideas into a single mission statement.)[28] The mission statement promotes a sense of shared expectations in employees and communicates a public image to important stakeholder groups in the company's task environment. *It tells who we are and what we do as well as what we'd like to become.*

One example of a mission statement is that of Maytag Corporation:

To improve the quality of home life by designing, building, marketing, and servicing the best appliances in the world.

Another classic example is that etched in bronze at Newport News Shipbuilding, unchanged since its founding in 1886:

We shall build good ships here—at a profit if we can—at a loss if we must—but always good ships.[29]

A mission may be defined narrowly or broadly in scope. An example of a **broad** mission statement is that used by many corporations: Serve the best interests of shareowners, customers, and employees. A broadly defined mission statement such as this keeps the company from restricting itself to one field or product line, but it fails to clearly identify either what it makes or which product/markets it plans to emphasize. Because this broad statement is so general, a **narrow** mission statement, such as the preceding one by Maytag emphasizing appliances, is more useful. A narrow mission very clearly states the organization's primary business, but it may limit the scope of the firm's activities in terms of product or service offered, the technology used, and the market served. Instead of just stating it is a "railroad," a company might be better calling itself a "transportation company."

Objectives

Objectives are the end results of planned activity. They state what is to be accomplished by when and should be quantified if possible. The achievement of corporate objectives should result in the fulfillment of a corporation's mission. In effect, this is what society gives back to the corporation when the corporation does a good job of fulfilling its mission. Robert Lane, Chairman of Deere & Company, the world's largest maker of farm equipment, uses the phrase "double and double again" to express ambitious objectives for the company. "It gives us a sense that we're on the move," explained Lane. For example, one of Deere's current objectives is to double the market value (number of shares multiplied by stock price) of the company ($8 billion in 2000) to $16 billion and then to double it again to $32 billion over 10 years. Similarly, the sales objective is to have sales ($13 billion in 2000) double and double again over the next 10 years.[30]

The term "goal" is often used interchangeably with the term "objective." In this book, we prefer to differentiate the two terms. In contrast to an objective, we consider a **goal** as an open-ended statement of what one wants to accomplish with no quantification of what is to be achieved and no time criteria for completion. For example, a simple statement of "increased profitability" is thus a goal, not an objective, because it does not state how much profit the firm wants to make the next year. An objective would say something like, "increase profits 10% over last year."

Some of the areas in which a corporation might establish its goals and objectives are:

- Profitability (net profits)
- Efficiency (low costs, etc.)
- Growth (increase in total assets, sales, etc.)
- Shareholder wealth (dividends plus stock price appreciation)
- Utilization of resources (return on investment or equity)
- Reputation (being considered a "top" firm)
- Contributions to employees (employment security, wages, diversity)
- Contributions to society (taxes paid, participation in charities, providing a needed product or service)
- Market leadership (market share)
- Technological leadership (innovations, creativity)
- Survival (avoiding bankruptcy)
- Personal needs of top management (using the firm for personal purposes, such as providing jobs for relatives)

Strategies

A **strategy** of a corporation forms a comprehensive master plan stating how the corporation will achieve its mission and objectives. It maximizes competitive advantage and minimizes competitive disadvantage. For example, after Rockwell International Corporation realized that it could no longer achieve its objectives by continuing with its strategy of diversification into multiple lines of businesses, it sold its aerospace and defense units to Boeing. Rockwell instead chose to concentrate on commercial electronics, an area that management felt had greater opportunities for growth.

The typical business firm usually considers three types of strategy: corporate, business, and functional.

1. **Corporate strategy** describes a company's overall direction in terms of its general attitude toward growth and the management of its various businesses and product lines. Corporate strategies typically fit within the three main categories of stability, growth, and retrenchment. For example, Maytag Corporation followed a corporate growth strategy by acquiring other appliance companies in order to have a full line of major home appliances.

2. **Business strategy** usually occurs at the business unit or product level, and it emphasizes improvement of the competitive position of a corporation's products or services in the specific industry or market segment served by that business unit. Business strategies may fit within the two overall categories of *competitive* or *cooperative* strategies. For example, Apple Computer uses a differentiation competitive strategy that emphasizes innovative products with creative design. The distinctive design and colors of its iMac line of personal computers (when contrasted with the usual beige of the competitor's products) has successfully boosted the company's market share and profits. In contrast, British Airways followed a cooperative strategy by forming an alliance with American Airlines in order to provide global service.

3. **Functional strategy** is the approach taken by a functional area to achieve corporate and business unit objectives and strategies by maximizing resource productivity. It is concerned with developing and nurturing a *distinctive competence* (see **Chapter 4**) to provide a company or business unit with a competitive advantage. Examples of R&D functional strategies are technological followership (imitate the products of other companies) and technological leadership (pioneer an innovation). For years, Magic Chef had been a successful appliance maker by spending little on R&D but by quickly imitating the innovations of other competitors. This helped the company to keep its costs lower than its competitors and consequently to compete with lower prices. In terms of marketing functional strategies, Procter & Gamble is a master of marketing "pull"—the process of spending huge amounts on advertising in order to create customer demand. This supports P&G's competitive strategy of differentiating its products from its competitors.

Business firms use all three types of strategy simultaneously. A **hierarchy of strategy** is the grouping of strategy types by level in the organization. This hierarchy of strategy is a nesting of one strategy within another so that they complement and support one another. (See **Figure 1–4**.) Functional strategies support business strategies, which, in turn, support the corporate strategy(ies).

Just as many firms often have no formally stated objectives, many firms have unstated, incremental, or intuitive strategies that have never been articulated or analyzed. Often the only way to spot a corporation's implicit strategies is to look not at what management says, but at what it does. Implicit strategies can be derived from corporate policies, programs approved

Figure 1–4
Hierarchy of Strategy

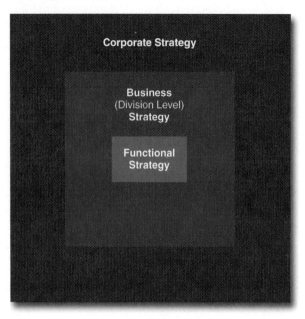

(and disapproved), and authorized budgets. Programs and divisions favored by budget increases and staffed by managers who are considered to be on the fast promotion track reveal where the corporation is putting its money and its energy.

Policies

A **policy** is a broad guideline for decision making that links the formulation of strategy with its implementation. Companies use policies to make sure that employees throughout the firm make decisions and take actions that support the corporation's mission, objectives, and strategies. For example, consider the following company policies:

- **Maytag Company:** Maytag will not approve any cost reduction proposal if it reduces product quality in any way. (This policy supports Maytag's strategy for Maytag brands to compete on quality rather than on price.)

- **3M:** Researchers should spend 15% of their time working on something other than their primary project. (This supports 3M's strong product development strategy.)

- **Intel:** Cannibalize your product line (undercut the sales of your current products) with better products before a competitor does it to you. (This supports Intel's objective of market leadership.)

- **General Electric:** GE must be number one or two wherever it competes. (This supports GE's objective to be number one in market capitalization.)

- **Nordstrom:** A "no questions asked" merchandise return policy, because the customer is always right. (This supports Nordstrom's competitive strategy of differentiation through excellent service.)

Policies like these provide clear guidance to managers throughout the organization. (Strategy formulation is discussed in greater detail in **Chapters 5**, **6**, and **7**.)

STRATEGY IMPLEMENTATION

Strategy implementation is the process by which strategies and policies are put into action through the development of programs, budgets, and procedures. This process might involve changes within the overall culture, structure, and/or management system of the entire organization. Except when such drastic corporate-wide changes are needed, however, the implementation of strategy is typically conducted by middle and lower level managers with review by top management. Sometimes referred to as operational planning, strategy implementation often involves day-to-day decisions in resource allocation.

Programs

A **program** is a statement of the activities or steps needed to accomplish a single-use plan. It makes the strategy action oriented. It may involve restructuring the corporation, changing the company's internal culture, or beginning a new research effort. For example, consider Intel Corporation, the microprocessor manufacturer. Realizing that Intel would not be able to continue its corporate growth strategy without the continuous development of new generations of microprocessors, management decided to implement a series of programs:

- They formed an alliance with Hewlett-Packard to develop the successor to the Pentium Pro chip.
- They assembled an elite team of engineers and scientists to do long-term, original research into computer chip design.

Another example is FedEx Corporation's program to install a sophisticated information system to enable its customers to track their shipments at any point in time. FedEx thus installed computer terminals at 100,000 customers and gave proprietary software to another 650,000 so shippers could label much of their own packages.[31]

Budgets

A **budget** is a statement of a corporation's programs in terms of dollars. Used in planning and control, a budget lists the detailed cost of each program. Many corporations demand a certain percentage return on investment, often called a "hurdle rate," before management will approve a new program. This ensures that the new program will significantly add to the corporation's profit performance and thus build shareholder value. The budget thus not only serves as a detailed plan of the new strategy in action, but also specifies through pro forma financial statements the expected impact on the firm's financial future.

For example, General Motors budgeted $4.3 billion during 2000 through 2004 to update and expand its Cadillac line of automobiles. With this money, the company is increasing the number of models from five to nine, and offering more powerful engines, sportier handling, and edgier styling. The company hopes to reverse its declining market share by appealing to a younger market. (The average Cadillac buyer was 67 years old in 2000.)[32]

Procedures

Procedures, sometimes termed *Standard Operating Procedures* (*SOP*), are a system of sequential steps or techniques that describe in detail how a particular task or job is to be done. They typically detail the various activities that must be carried out in order to complete the corporation's programs. For example, Delta Airlines used various procedures to cut costs. To reduce the number of employees, Delta asked technical experts in hydraulics, metal working, avionics, and other trades to design cross-functional work teams. To cut marketing expenses, Delta instituted a cap on travel agent commissions and emphasized sales to bigger accounts. Delta also changed its purchasing and food service procedures. (Strategy implementation is discussed in more detail in **Chapters 8** and **9.**)

EVALUATION AND CONTROL

Evaluation and control is the process in which corporate activities and performance results are monitored so that actual performance can be compared with desired performance. Managers at all levels use the resulting information to take corrective action and resolve problems. Although evaluation and control is the final major element of strategic management, it also can pinpoint weaknesses in previously implemented strategic plans and thus stimulate the entire process to begin again.

Performance is the end result of activities.[33] It includes the actual outcomes of the strategic management process. The practice of strategic management is justified in terms of its ability to improve an organization's performance, typically measured in terms of profits and return on investment. For evaluation and control to be effective, managers must obtain clear, prompt, and unbiased information from the people below them in the corporation's hierarchy. Using this information, managers compare what is actually happening with what was originally planned in the formulation stage. For example, the success of Delta Airline's turnaround strategy was evaluated in terms of the amount spent on each airplane seat per mile of flight. Before the "Leadership 7.5" program was instituted, the cost per seat was 9.76¢. The program needed to reach 7.5¢ to achieve the company's objective of reducing annual expenses by $2.1 billion.

The evaluation and control of performance completes the strategic management model. Based on performance results, management may need to make adjustments in its strategy formulation, in implementation, or in both. (Evaluation and control is discussed in more detail in **Chapter 10**.)

FEEDBACK/LEARNING PROCESS

Note that the strategic management model depicted in **Figure 1–2** includes a feedback/learning process. Arrows are drawn coming out of each part of the model and taking information to each of the previous parts of the model. As a firm or business unit develops strategies, programs, and the like, it often must go back to revise or correct decisions made earlier in the model. For example, poor performance (as measured in evaluation and control) usually indicates that something has gone wrong with either strategy formulation or implementation. It could also mean that a key variable, such as a new competitor, was ignored during environmental scanning and assessment.

1.6 Initiation of Strategy: Triggering Events

After much research, Henry Mintzberg discovered that strategy formulation is typically not a regular, continuous process: "It is most often an irregular, discontinuous process, proceeding in fits and starts. There are periods of stability in strategy development, but also there are periods of flux, of groping, of piecemeal change, and of global change."[34] This view of strategy formulation as an irregular process can be explained by the very human tendency to continue on a particular course of action until something goes wrong or a person is forced to question his or her actions. This period of "strategic drift" may simply result from inertia on the part of the organization or may simply reflect management's belief that the current strategy is still appropriate and needs only some "fine-tuning." Most large organizations tend to follow a particular strategic orientation for about 15 to 20 years before making a significant change in direction.[35] After this rather long period of fine-tuning an existing strategy, some sort of shock to the system is needed to motivate management to seriously reassess the corporation's situation.

A **triggering event** is something that acts as a stimulus for a change in strategy. Some possible triggering events are:

- **New CEO:** By asking a series of embarrassing questions, the new CEO cuts through the veil of complacency and forces people to question the very reason for the corporation's existence.

- **External Intervention:** The firm's bank refuses to approve a new loan or suddenly demands payment in full on an old one. A customer complains about a serious product defect.

- **Threat of a Change in Ownership:** Another firm may initiate a takeover by buying the company's common stock.

- **Performance Gap:** A performance gap exists when performance does not meet expectations. Sales and profits either are no longer increasing or may even be falling.

- **Strategic Inflection Point:** Coined by Andy Grove, Chairman of the Board of Intel Corporation, this represents what happens to a business when a major change takes place due to the introduction of new technologies, a different regulatory environment, a change in customer's values, or a change in what customers prefer.[36]

Sun Microsystems is an example of one company in which a triggering event forced its management to radically rethink what it was doing. See the **Internet Issue** feature to learn how one phone call to Sun's president stimulated a change in strategy at Sun.

Internet Issue

TRIGGERING EVENT AT SUN MICROSYSTEMS

Sun Microsystems President Edward Zander received a personal phone call in June 2000 directly from Margaret Whitman, CEO of eBay, Inc., the Internet auction firm. After a string of small computer crashes, eBay had just suffered a 22-hour outage of its Web site. Whitman called Zander to report that there was a bug in Sun's top-of-the-line server and that Sun had better fix it immediately or else lose eBay's business. A series of around-the-clock meetings at Sun revealed that the problem was that Sun's customers had no idea of how to maintain a $1 million+ computer. eBay had failed to provide sufficient air conditioning to keep the machine cool. Even though Sun had issued a software patch to fix a problem many months earlier, eBay had neglected to install it. The list went on and on. Sun soon realized that the problem was bigger than just eBay. Over 40% of the servers that manage most Web sites were made by Sun.

As more firms were expanding their business to include the Internet, this market for Sun's servers was expected to boom. Nevertheless, many of these firms were too new and small to have the proper technology infrastructure. "It suddenly hit me," said Zander. "How many future eBays are buying their first computer from us this very minute?" According to Scott McNealy, CEO of Sun, "That's when we realized that it wasn't eBay's fault. It was our fault."

Since that realization, Sun's management team has been rebuilding the company to make its servers as reliable as the telephone system. In a drastic strategic change, management decided to expand beyond simply selling servers to providing many of the technologies required to make Web servers completely reliable. It now provides storage products, e-business software, and consultants who not only supply the hardware, but also work directly with the customers to ensure that the servers are operated properly. Just as high-tech mainframe managers used to say that "No one gets fired for choosing IBM," Zander aims to have the same said of Sun Microsystems. "I want to be the sage bet for companies that need the most innovative technology," added Sun's president.

Source: P. Burrows, "Sun's Bid to Rule the Web," *Business Week E.Biz* (July 24, 2000), pp. EB 31–42.

1.7 Strategic Decision Making

The distinguishing characteristic of strategic management is its emphasis on strategic decision making. As organizations grow larger and more complex with more uncertain environments, decisions become increasingly complicated and difficult to make. In agreement with the strategic choice perspective mentioned earlier, this book proposes a strategic decision-making framework that can help people make these decisions regardless of their level and function in the corporation.

WHAT MAKES A DECISION STRATEGIC

Unlike many other decisions, **strategic decisions** deal with the long-run future of the entire organization and have three characteristics:

1. **Rare:** Strategic decisions are unusual and typically have no precedent to follow.

2. **Consequential:** Strategic decisions commit substantial resources and demand a great deal of commitment from people at all levels.

3. **Directive:** Strategic decisions set precedents for lesser decisions and future actions throughout the organization.[37]

One example of a strategic decision was that made by Monsanto to move away from being a chemical company emphasizing fertilizers and herbicides to becoming a "life sciences" enterprise, devoted to improving human health by seeking synergies in biotech, pharmaceutical research, and food products. Management decided to sell its slow-growing chemical business and invest $4 billion into R&D and a series of acquisitions. Realizing that the planet couldn't survive an expected doubling of its population without serious environmental degradation, Monsanto decided to develop genetically engineered seeds to double crop yields using less fertilizer and poisons.[38]

MINTZBERG'S MODES OF STRATEGIC DECISION MAKING

Some strategic decisions are made in a flash by one person (often an entrepreneur or a powerful chief executive officer) who has a brilliant insight and is quickly able to convince others to adopt his or her idea. Other strategic decisions seem to develop out of a series of small incremental choices that over time push the organization more in one direction than another. According to Henry Mintzberg, the three most typical approaches, or modes, of strategic decision making are entrepreneurial, adaptive, and planning.[39] A fourth mode, logical incrementalism, was added later by Quinn.

- **Entrepreneurial Mode:** Strategy is made by one powerful individual. The focus is on opportunities; problems are secondary. Strategy is guided by the founder's own vision of direction and is exemplified by large, bold decisions. The dominant goal is growth of the corporation. America Online, founded by Steve Case, is an example of this mode of strategic decision making. The company reflects his vision of the Internet provider industry. Although AOL's clear growth strategy is certainly an advantage of the entrepreneurial mode, its tendency to market its products before the company is able to support them is a significant disadvantage.

- **Adaptive Mode:** Sometimes referred to as "muddling through," this decision-making mode is characterized by reactive solutions to existing problems, rather than a proactive search for new opportunities. Much bargaining goes on concerning priorities of objectives. Strategy is fragmented and is developed to move the corporation forward incrementally. This mode is typical of most universities, many large hospitals, a large number of governmental agencies, and a surprising number of large corporations. Encyclopaedia Britannica, Inc., operated successfully for many years in this mode. It continued to rely on the door-to-door selling of its prestigious books long after dual career couples made this marketing approach obsolete. Only after it was acquired in 1996 did the company change its marketing strategy to television advertising and Internet marketing. (See ⟨www.eb.com⟩.) It now offers an online version of the encyclopedia in addition to the printed volumes.

- **Planning Mode:** This decision-making mode involves the systematic gathering of appropriate information for situation analysis, the generation of feasible alternative strategies, and the rational selection of the most appropriate strategy. It includes both the proactive search for new opportunities and the reactive solution of existing problems. Hewlett-Packard (HP) is an example of the planning mode. After a careful study of trends in the computer and communications industries, management noted that the company needed to stop thinking of itself as a collection of stand-alone products with a primary focus on instrumentation and computer hardware. Led by its new CEO, Carly Fiorina, top management felt that the company needed to become a customer-focused and integrated provider of information appliances, highly reliable information technology infrastructure, and electronic commerce services. Consequently, products were merged into packages for electronic services solutions, such as software for building internal company portals and "e-speak," a software platform that can quickly create and combine different kinds of online services. HP also sold its venerable test and measurement unit—the business in which the company had begun. HP's research labs also received significant support and were encouraged to quit focusing on incremental improvements so that they could develop "disruptive technologies," such as molecular computing, a technology to build integrated circuits using molecules.[40]

- **Logical Incrementalism:** A fourth decision-making mode, which can be viewed as a synthesis of the planning, adaptive, and, to a lesser extent, the entrepreneurial modes, was proposed by Quinn. In this mode, top management has a reasonably clear idea of the corporation's mission and objectives, but, in its development of strategies, it chooses to use "an interactive process in which the organization probes the future, experiments and learns from a series of partial (incremental) commitments rather than through global formulations of total strategies."[41] Thus, although the mission and objectives are set, the strategy is allowed to emerge out of debate, discussion, and experimentation. This approach appears to be useful when the environment is changing rapidly and when it is important to build consensus and develop needed resources before committing the entire corporation to a specific strategy.

STRATEGIC DECISION-MAKING PROCESS: AID TO BETTER DECISIONS

Good arguments can be made for using either the entrepreneurial or adaptive modes (or logical incrementalism) in certain situations. This book proposes, however, that in most situations the planning mode, which includes the basic elements of the strategic management process, is a more rational and thus better way of making strategic decisions. Research indicates that the planning mode is not only more analytical and less political than are the other modes, but it is also more appropriate for dealing with complex, changing environments.[42]

Figure 1–5
Strategic Decision-Making Process

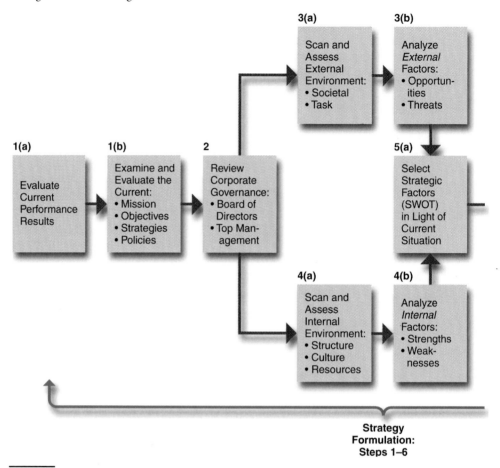

Source: T. L. Wheelen and J. D. Hunger, "Strategic Decision-Making Process," Copyright © 1994 and 1997 by Wheelen and Hunger Associates. Reprinted by permission.

We therefore propose the following eight-step **strategic decision-making process** to improve the making of strategic decisions (see **Figure 1–5**):

1. **Evaluate current performance results** in terms of (a) return on investment, profitability, and so forth, and (b) the current mission, objectives, strategies, and policies.

2. **Review corporate governance**, that is, the performance of the firm's board of directors and top management.

3. **Scan and assess the external environment** to determine the strategic factors that pose **O**pportunities and **T**hreats.

4. **Scan and assess the internal corporate environment** to determine the strategic factors that are **S**trengths (especially core competencies) and **W**eaknesses.

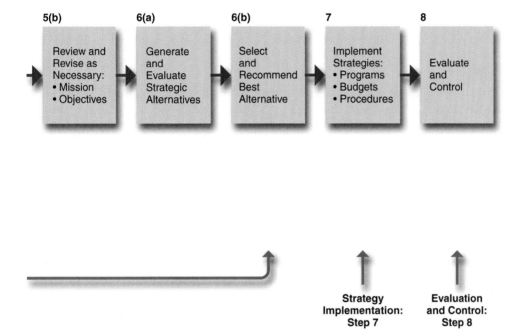

5. **Analyze strategic (SWOT) factors** to (a) pinpoint problem areas, and (b) review and revise the corporate mission and objectives as necessary.

6. **Generate, evaluate, and select the best alternative strategy** in light of the analysis conducted in Step 5.

7. **Implement selected strategies** via programs, budgets, and procedures.

8. **Evaluate implemented strategies** via feedback systems and the control of activities to ensure their minimum deviation from plans.

This rational approach to strategic decision making has been used successfully by corporations like Warner-Lambert, Dayton Hudson, General Electric, Avon Products, Bechtel Group, Inc., and Taisei Corporation. **It is also the basis for the Strategic Audit found in Chapter 10.**

1.8 Impact of the Internet on Strategic Management

Few innovations in history provide as many potential benefits to the strategic management of a corporation as does electronic commerce (e-commerce) via the Internet. The global nature of the technology, low cost, opportunity to reach millions of people, interactive nature, and variety of possibilities result in many potential benefits to strategic managers. E-commerce provides the following benefits to the strategic management of corporations.

- Expands the marketplace to national and international markets. All anyone now needs is a computer to connect buyers and sellers.
- Decreases the cost of creating, processing, distributing, storing, and retrieving information. The cost of electronic payment is $.02, whereas the cost of a paper check is $.43.
- Enables people to create new, highly specialized business ventures. Very narrow market niches can now be reached via special interest chat rooms and Internet search engines.
- Allows smaller inventories, just-in-time manufacturing, and less overhead expenses by facilitating pull-type supply chain management. Dell Computer orders the parts it needs as soon as it receives an order from a customer.
- Enables the customization of products and services to better suit customer needs. Customers are encouraged to select options and styles for the auto of their choice on the BMW Web site ⟨www.bmw.com⟩.
- Provides the stimulus to rethink a firm's strategy and to initiate reengineering projects. The arrival of Amazon.com forced Barnes and Noble to rethink its pure "bricks and mortar" strategy of retail book stores and to begin selling books over its own Web site.
- Increases flexibility, compresses cycle and delivery time, and provides easy access to information on customers, suppliers, and competitors.[43]

Projections for the 21st Century

- From 1994 to 2010, the world economy will grow from $26 trillion to $48 trillion.
- From 1994 to 2010, world trade will increase from $4 trillion to $16.6 trillion.[44]

Discussion Questions

1. Why has strategic management become so important to today's corporations?
2. How does strategic management typically evolve in a corporation?
3. What is a learning organization? Is this approach to strategic management better than the more traditional top-down approach?
4. Why are strategic decisions different from other kinds of decisions?
5. When is the planning mode of strategic decision making superior to the entrepreneurial and adaptive modes?

Strategic Practice Exercise

Mission statements vary widely from one company to another. Why is one mission statement better than another? Develop some criteria for evaluating a mission statement. Then, do one or both of the following exercises:

1. Evaluate the following mission statement of Celestial Seasonings:

   Our mission is to grow and dominate the U.S. specialty tea market by exceeding consumer expectations with the best tasting, 100% natural hot and iced teas, packaged with Celestial art and philosophy, creating the most valued tea experience. Through leadership, inno-vation, focus, and teamwork, we are dedicated to con-tinuously improving value to our consumers, cus-tomers, employees, and stakeholders with a quality-first organization.[45]

2. Using the Internet, find the mission statements of three different organizations, which can be business or not-for-profit. (*Hint*: Check annual reports and 10k forms. They can often be found via a link on a company's Web page or through Hoovers.com.) Which mission statement is best? Why?

Key Terms

adaptive mode (pp. 18–19)
Association of South East Asian Nations (ASEAN) (p. 6)
budget (p. 15)
business policy (p. 2)
business strategy (p. 13)
corporate strategy (p. 13)
electronic commerce (p. 15)
entrepreneurial mode (p. 18)
environmental scanning (p. 9)
European Union (EU) (p. 6)
evaluation and control (p. 16)
external environment (pp. 9–10)
functional strategy (p. 13)
globalization (p. 5)
goal (p. 12)

hierarchy of strategy (p. 13)
institution theory (p. 7)
internal environment (p. 10)
learning organization (p. 8)
logical incrementalism (p. 19)
mission (p. 10)
Mercosur/Mercosul (p. 6)
North American Free Trade Agreement (NAFTA) (p. 6)
objectives (p. 12)
organizational learning theory (p. 8)
performance (p. 16)
performance gap (p. 17)
phases of strategic management (p. 3)
planning mode (p. 19)

policy (p. 14)
population ecology (p. 7)
procedures (p. 15)
program (p. 15)
strategic choice perspective (p. 8)
strategic decision-making process (p. 20)
strategic decisions (p. 18)
strategic factors (p. 9)
strategic inflection point (p. 17)
strategic management (p. 2)
strategy (p. 13)
strategy formulation (p. 10)
strategy implementation (p. 15)
SWOT analysis (p. 9)
triggering event (p. 17)

Notes

1. E. Corcoran, "The E Gang," *Fortune* (July 24, 2000), p. 146.
2. P. L. Moore and G. Smith, "GE Catches Online Fever," *Business Week* (August 14, 2000), pp. 122–123.
3. L. Lee, "Not Just Clicks Anymore," *Business Week* (August 28, 2000), pp. 226–227.
4. For an excellent description of the evolution of business policy into strategic management, see R. E. Hoskisson, M. A. Hitt, W. P. Wan, and D. Yiu, "Theory and Research in Strategic Management: Swings of the Pendulum," *Journal of Management*, Vol. 25, No. 3 (1999), pp. 417–456.
5. F. W. Gluck, S. P. Kaufman, and A. S. Walleck, "The Four Phases of Strategic Management," *Journal of Business Strategy* (Winter 1982), pp. 9–21.
6. M. R. Vaghefi and A. B. Huellmantel, "Strategic Leadership at General Electric," *Long Range Planning* (April 1998), pp. 280–294.
7. T. J. Andersen, "Strategic Planning, Autonomous Actions and Corporate Performance," *Long Range Planning* (April 2000), pp. 184–200; C. C. Miller and L. B. Cardinal, "Strategic Planning and

Firm Performance: A Synthesis of More Than Two Decades of Research," *Academy of Management Journal* (December 1994), pp. 1649–1665; P. Pekar, Jr., and S. Abraham, "Is Strategic Management Living Up to Its Promise?" *Long Range Planning* (October 1995), pp. 32–44.
8. E. J. Zajac, M. S. Kraatz, and R. F. Bresser, "Modeling the Dynamics of Strategic Fit: A Normative Approach to Strategic Change," *Strategic Management Journal* (April 2000), pp. 429–453.
9. K. G. Smith and C. M. Grimm, "Environmental Variation, Strategic Change and Firm Performance: A Study of Railroad Deregulation," *Strategic Management Journal* (July–August 1987), pp. 363–376.
10. I. Wilson, "Strategic Planning Isn't Dead—It Changed," *Long Range Planning* (August 1994), p. 20.
11. R. M. Grant, "Transforming Uncertainty Into Success: Strategic Leadership Forum 1999," *Strategy & Leadership* (July/August/September, 1999), p. 33.

12. L. W. Rue and N. A. Ibrahim, "The Relationship Between Planning Sophistication and Performance in Small Businesses," *Journal of Small Business Management* (October 1998), pp. 24–32; M. A. Lyles, I. S. Baird, J. B. Orris, and D. F. Kuratko, "Formalized Planning in Small Business: Increasing Strategic Choices," *Journal of Small Business Management* (April 1993), pp. 38–50.

13. C. V. Callahan and B. A. Pasternack, "Corporate Strategy in the Digital Age," *Strategy and Business*, Issue 15 (2nd Quarter 1999), pp. 2–6.

14. J. Bowles, "How Digital Marketplaces Are Shaping the Future of B2B Commerce," Special Advertising Section on e Marketmakers, *Forbes* (July 23, 2000).

15. C. V. Callahan and B. A. Pasternack, "Corporate Strategy in the Digital Age," *Strategy & Business*, Issue 15 (2nd Quarter 1999), p. 3.

16. R. M. Kanter, "Managing the Extended Enterprise in a Globally Connected World," *Organizational Dynamics* (Summer 1999), pp. 7–23; C. Havens and E. Knapp, "Easing into Knowledge Management," *Strategy & Leadership* (March/April 1999), pp. 4–9.

17. J. A. C. Baum, "Organizational Ecology," in *Handbook of Organization Studies*, edited by S. R. Clegg, C. Handy, and W. Nord (London: Sage, 1996), pp. 77–114.

18. For more information on these theories, see A. Y. Lewin and H. W. Voloberda, "Prolegomena on Coevolution: A Framework for Research on Strategy and New Organizational Forms," *Organization Science* (October 1999), pp. 519–534, and H. Aldrich, *Organizations Evolving* (London: Sage, 1999), pp. 43–74.

19. C. Gebelein, "Strategic Planning: The Engine of Change," *Planning Review* (September/October 1993), pp. 17–19.

20. R. A. D'Aveni, *Hypercompetition* (New York: Free Press, 1994). Hypercompetition is discussed in more detail in Chapter 3.

21. R. S. M. Lau, "Strategic Flexibility: A New Reality for World-Class Manufacturing," *SAM Advanced Management Journal* (Spring 1996), pp. 11–15.

22. M. A. Hitt, B. W. Keats, and S. M. DeMarie, "Navigating in the New Competitive Landscape: Building Strategic Flexibility and Competitive Advantage in the 21st Century," *Academy of Management Executive* (November 1998), pp. 22–42.

23. D. Lei, J. W. Slocum, and R. A. Pitts, "Designing Organizations for Competitive Advantage: The Power of Unlearning and Learning," *Organizational Dynamics* (Winter 1999), pp. 24–38.

24. D. A. Garvin, "Building a Learning Organization," *Harvard Business Review* (July/August 1993), p. 80. See also P. M. Senge, *The Fifth Discipline: The Art and Practice of the Learning Organization* (New York: Doubleday, 1990).

25. T. T. Baldwin, C. Danielson, and W. Wiggenhorn, "The Evolution of Learning Strategies in Organizations: From Employee Development to Business Redefinition," *Academy of Management Executive* (November 1997), pp. 47–58.

26. W. Mitchell, J. M. Shaver, and B. Yeung, "Getting There in a Global Industry: Impacts on Performance of Changing International Presence," *Strategic Management Journal* (September 1992), pp. 419–432.

27. Research supports the use of this model in examining firm strategies. See J. A. Smith, "Strategies for Start-Ups," *Long Range Planning* (December 1998), pp. 857–872.

28. See A. Campbell and S. Yeung, "Brief Case: Mission, Vision, and Strategic Intent," *Long Range Planning* (August 1991), pp. 145–147; S. Cummings and J. Davies, "Mission, Vision, Fusion," *Long Range Planning* (December 1994), pp. 147–150.

29. J. Cosco, "Down to the Sea in Ships," *Journal of Business Strategy* (November/December 1995), p. 48.

30. W. Ryberg, "Deere Chief Takes 'Double' Aim," *Des Moines Register* (September 9, 2000), p. D1.

31. L. Grant, "Why FedEx Is Flying High," *Fortune* (November 10, 1997), pp. 156–160.

32. D. Welch, "Cadillac Hits the Gas," *Business Week* (September 4, 2000), p. 50.

33. H. A. Simon, *Administrative Behavior*, 2nd edition (NY: Free Press, 1957), p. 231.

34. H. Mintzberg, "Planning on the Left Side and Managing on the Right," *Harvard Business Review* (July–August 1976), p. 56.

35. This phenomenon of "punctuated equilibrium" describes corporations as evolving through relatively long periods of stability (equilibrium periods) punctuated by relatively short bursts of fundamental change (revolutionary periods). See E. Romanelli and M. L. Tushman, "Organizational Transformation as Punctuated Equilibrium: An Empirical Test," *Academy of Management Journal* (October 1994), pp. 1141–1166.

36. Speech to the 1998 Academy of Management. Reported by S. M. Puffer, "Global Executive: Intel's Andrew Grove on Competitiveness," *Academy of Management Executive* (February 1999), pp. 15–24.

37. D. J. Hickson, R. J. Butler, D. Cray, G. R. Mallory, and D. C. Wilson, *Top Decisions: Strategic Decision-Making in Organizations* (San Francisco: Jossey-Bass, 1986), pp. 26–42.

38. L. Grant, "Monsanto's Bet: There's Gold in Going Green," *Fortune* (April 14, 1997), pp. 116–118.

39. H. Mintzberg, "Strategy-Making in Three Modes," *California Management Review* (Winter 1973), pp. 44–53.

40. "Rebuilding the Garage," *Economist* (July 15, 2000), pp. 59–61.

41. J. B. Quinn, *Strategies for Change: Logical Incrementalism* (Homewood, Ill.: Irwin, 1980), p. 58.

42. I. Gold and A. M. A. Rasheed, "Rational Decision-Making and Firm Performance: The Moderating Role of the Environment," *Strategic Management Journal* (August 1997), pp. 583–591; R. L. Priem, A. M. A. Rasheed, and A. G. Kotulic, "Rationality in Strategic Decision Processes, Environmental Dynamism and Firm Performance," *Journal of Management*, Vol. 21, No. 5 (1995), pp. 913–929; J. W. Dean, Jr., and M. P. Sharfman, "Does Decision Process Matter? A Study of Strategic Decision-Making Effectiveness," *Academy of Management Journal* (April 1996), pp. 368–396.

43. E. Turban, J. Lee, D. King, and H. M. Chung, *Electronic Commerce: A Managerial Perspective* (Upper Saddle River, NJ: Prentice Hall, 2000), p. 15. See also M. J. Shaw, "Electronic Commerce: State of the Art," in M. J. Shaw, R. Blanning, T. Strader, and A. Whinston (eds.), *Handbook on Electronic Commerce* (Berlin: Springer, 2000), pp. 3–24.

44. J. Warner, "21st Century Capitalism: Snapshot of the Next Century," *Business Week* (November 18, 1994), p. 194.

45. P. Jones and L. Kahaner, *Say It & Live It: 50 Corporate Mission Statements That Hit the Mark* (New York: Currency Doubleday, 1995), p. 53.

chapter 2

Corporate Governance and Social Responsibility

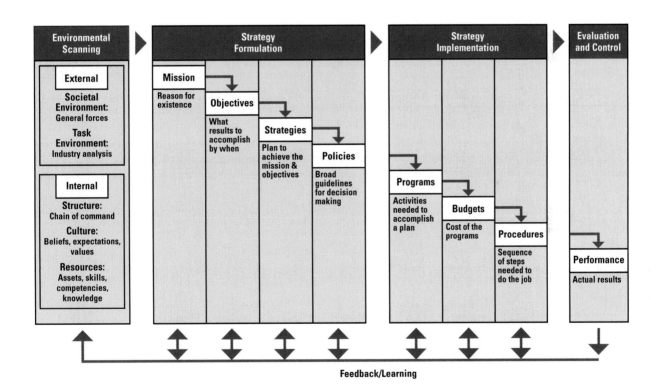

Environmental Scanning	Strategy Formulation	Strategy Implementation	Evaluation and Control

External

Societal Environment: General forces

Task Environment: Industry analysis

Internal

Structure: Chain of command

Culture: Beliefs, expectations, values

Resources: Assets, skills, competencies, knowledge

Mission

Reason for existence

Objectives

What results to accomplish by when

Strategies

Plan to achieve the mission & objectives

Policies

Broad guidelines for decision making

Programs

Activities needed to accomplish a plan

Budgets

Cost of the programs

Procedures

Sequence of steps needed to do the job

Performance

Actual results

Feedback/Learning

Tyco International Ltd. is a diversified manufacturing and service company that operates in more than 100 countries and has annual revenues of over $36 billion. Taking over as CEO in 1992, Dennis Kozlowski transformed Tyco from an obscure U.S. manufacturer into the world's largest provider of undersea telecommunications systems, fire protection systems, and electronic security services. In doing so, Kozlowski treated Tyco as his own personal empire, lavishing hundreds of millions of dollars in unauthorized loans and exorbitant gifts on himself and his top managers. Even though his annual compensation jumped from $8.8 million in 1996 to $136.1 million in 1999, Kozlowski regularly took loans from the company worth hundreds of millions of dollars. Among his purchases were a $2.1 million birthday celebration for his wife plus a $6,000 shower curtain and a $15,000 dog umbrella stand for his $16.8 million New York apartment. By operating without a second-in-command and by hand-picking top mangers who were "smart, poor, and want-to-be-rich," he kept personal control of the corporation. He hand-picked members of the board of directors and filtered all information, such as internal audits, that went to the board. Without board approval, Kozlowski gave $56 million in bonuses to 51 Tyco employees to effectively cancel loans they had earlier taken from the company.

In the wake of the recent Enron scandal, the U.S. Securities and Exchange Commission (SEC), the Internal Revenue Service, and the State of New Hampshire began investigating Tyco for accounting irregularities and its CPA firm for failing to report the questionable practices. Kozlowski resigned as CEO just before being indicted on tax evasion. Subsequent investigation revealed why the board of directors had been so silent during this period of top management excess: Of the company's 10 directors, 3 were Tyco executives who had serious conflicts of interest. Even though board member Joshua Berman had been serving as a Tyco executive since 1997, the company continued to pay millions of dollars in legal fees to his former law firm. John Fort, the Tyco executive who was named the company's interim CEO upon Kozlowski's resignation, had been an investor in a buyout fund that made an $810 million purchase of Tyco operations in 1999, while Fort served as a board member. Tyco's CFO, Mark Swartz, also served as a board member when he received $6.5 million in loans from the company.

In addition, the nonmanagement, or "outside," directors had such deep ties to the company that it raised questions about the board's ability to oversee management. Michael Ashcroft, for example, had previously worked for the company until 1997. Another board member, Stephen Foss, leased an airplane to Tyco. Lead director Frank Walsh, Jr., received $200 million for his services in helping to arrange Tyco's disastrous 2001 acquisition of commercial-finance company CIT Group.

In October 2001, Tyco agreed to pay $5 million to the State of New Hampshire to reimburse shareholders and the public, who had been hurt by the financial misconduct of its former officers. In addition, Tyco's auditing firm was investigated for its failure to identify accounting irregularities. According to Lyn Turner, former chief accountant for the SEC, $41 million of a $96 million loan forgiveness scheme was charged to the balance sheet for "accrued federal income tax." Said Turner, "I can't understand how they missed that one."[1]

2.1 Corporate Governance: Role of the Board of Directors

A **corporation** is a mechanism established to allow different parties to contribute capital, expertise, and labor for their mutual benefit. The investor/shareholder participates in the profits of the enterprise without taking responsibility for the operations. Management runs the company without being responsible for personally providing the funds. To make this possible, laws have been passed so that shareholders have limited liability and, correspondingly, limited involvement in a corporation's activities. That involvement does include, however, the right to elect directors who have a legal duty to represent the shareholders and protect their interests. As representatives of the shareholders, directors have both the authority and the responsibility to establish basic corporate policies and to ensure that they are followed.[2]

The board of directors has, therefore, an obligation to approve all decisions that might affect the long-run performance of the corporation. This means that the corporation is fundamentally governed by the board of directors overseeing top management, with the concurrence of the shareholder. The term **corporate governance** refers to the relationship among these three groups in determining the direction and performance of the corporation.[3]

Over the past decade, shareholders and various interest groups have seriously questioned the role of the board of directors in corporations. They are concerned that inside board members may use their position to feather their own nests and that outside board members often lack sufficient knowledge, involvement, and enthusiasm to do an adequate job of monitoring and providing guidance to top management. Instances of widespread corruption and questionable accounting practices at Enron, Global Crossing, WorldCom, Tyco, and Qwest, among others, seem to justify their concerns. Tyco's board, for example, seemed more interested in keeping CEO Kozlowski happy than in safeguarding shareholder interests. The very passivity of the board (in addition to questionable financial dealings) was one reason the Kozlowski-era directors were forced to resign in 2003.[4]

The general public has not only become more aware and more critical of many boards' apparent lack of responsibility for corporate activities, it has begun to push government to demand accountability. As a result, the board as a rubber stamp of the CEO or as a bastion of the "old-boy" selection system is being replaced by more active, more professional boards.

RESPONSIBILITIES OF THE BOARD

Laws and standards defining the responsibilities of boards of directors vary from country to country. For example, board members in Ontario, Canada, face more than 100 provincial and federal laws governing director liability. The United States, however, has no clear national standards or federal laws. Specific requirements of directors vary, depending on the state in which the corporate charter is issued. There is, nevertheless, a developing worldwide consensus concerning the major responsibilities of a board. Interviews with 200 directors from eight countries (Canada, France, Germany, Finland, Switzerland, The Netherlands, the United Kingdom, and Venezuela) revealed strong agreement on the following five **board of directors responsibilities**, listed in order of importance:

1. Setting corporate strategy, overall direction, mission, or vision
2. Hiring and firing the CEO and top management
3. Controlling, monitoring, or supervising top management
4. Reviewing and approving the use of resources
5. Caring for shareholder interests[5]

Directors in the United States must make certain, in addition to the duties just listed, that the corporation is managed in accordance with the laws of the state in which it is incorporated. They must also ensure management's adherence to laws and regulations, such as those dealing with the issuance of securities, insider trading, and other conflict-of-interest situations. They must also be aware of the needs and demands of constituent groups so that they can achieve a judicious balance among the interests of these diverse groups while ensuring the continued functioning of the corporation.

In a legal sense, the board is required to direct the affairs of the corporation but not to manage them. It is charged by law to act with **due care**. If a director or the board as a whole fails to act with due care and, as a result, the corporation is in some way harmed, the careless director or directors can be held personally liable for the harm done. This is no small concern, given that one survey of outside directors revealed that more than 40% had been named as part of lawsuits against the corporations.[6]

Role of the Board in Strategic Management

How does a board of directors fulfill these many responsibilities? The **role of the board of directors in strategic management** is to carry out three basic tasks:

■ **Monitor:** By acting through its committees, a board can keep abreast of developments inside and outside the corporation, bringing to management's attention developments it might have overlooked. A board should at least carry out this task.

- **Evaluate and influence:** A board can examine management's proposals, decisions, and actions; agree or disagree with them; give advice and offer suggestions; and outline alternatives. Active boards perform this task in addition to the monitoring one.

- **Initiate and determine:** A board can delineate a corporation's mission and specify strategic options to its management. Only the most active boards take on this task in addition to the two previous ones.

Board of Directors Continuum

A board of directors is involved in strategic management to the extent that it carries out the three tasks of monitoring, evaluating and influencing, and initiating and determining. The **board of directors continuum** shown in **Figure 2–1** shows the possible degree of involvement (from low to high) in the strategic management process. As types, boards can range from phantom boards with no real involvement to catalyst boards with very high degrees of involvement. Research suggests that active board involvement in strategic management is positively related to corporate financial performance.[7]

Highly involved boards tend to be very active. They take their tasks of monitoring, evaluating, and influencing, plus initiating and determining, very seriously; they provide advice when necessary and keep management alert. As depicted in **Figure 2–1**, their heavy involvement in the strategic management process places them in the active participation or even catalyst positions. For example, in a survey of directors of large U.S. corporations conducted by Korn/Ferry International, more than 60% indicated that they were deeply involved in the strategy-setting process. In the same survey, 54% of the respondents indicated that their boards participate in annual retreats or special planning sessions to discuss company strategy. Nevertheless, only slightly more than 32% of the boards help develop the strategy. More than two-thirds of the boards review strategy only after it has been first developed by management. Another 1% admit playing no role at all in strategy.[8] These and other studies suggest that most large publicly owned corporations have boards that operate at some point between nominal

Figure 2–1
Board of Directors Continuum

DEGREE OF INVOLVEMENT IN STRATEGIC MANAGEMENT

Low (Passive) ← → High (Active)

Phantom	Rubber Stamp	Minimal Review	Nominal Participation	Active Participation	Catalyst
Never knows what to do, if anything; no degree of involvement.	Permits officers to make all decisions. It votes as the officers recommend on action issues.	Formally reviews selected issues that officers bring to its attention.	Involved to a limited degree in the performance or review of selected key decisions, indicators, or programs of management.	Approves, questions, and makes final decisions on mission, strategy, policies, and objectives. Has active board committees. Performs fiscal and management audits.	Takes the leading role in establishing and modifying the mission, objectives, strategy, and policies. It has a very active strategy committee.

Source: T. L. Wheelen and J. D. Hunger, "Board of Directors Continuum." Copyright © 1994 by Wheelen and Hunger Associates. Reprinted by permission.

and active participation. Some corporations that have actively participating boards are Mead Corporation, Rolm and Haas, Whirlpool, 3M, Apria Healthcare, General Electric, Pfizer, and Texas Instruments.[9]

As a board becomes less involved in the affairs of the corporation, it moves farther to the left on the continuum shown in **Figure 2–1**. On the far left are passive phantom or rubber-stamp boards that typically do not initiate or determine strategy (for example, Tyco) unless a crisis occurs. In these situations, the CEO also serves as Chairman of the Board, personally nominates all directors, and works to keep board members under his or her control by giving them the "mushroom treatment"—throw manure on them and keep them in the dark!

Generally, the smaller the corporation, the less active its board of directors. In an entre-preneurial venture, for example, the privately held corporation may be 100% owned by the founders, who also manage the company. In this case, there is no need for an active board to protect the interests of the owner-manager shareholders—the interests of the owners and the managers are identical. In this instance, a board is really unnecessary and meets only to satisfy legal requirements. If stock is sold to outsiders to finance growth, however, the board becomes more active. Key investors want seats on the board so they can oversee their investment. To the extent that they still control most of the stock, however, the founders dominate the board. Friends, family members, and key shareholders usually become members, but the board acts primarily as a rubber stamp for any proposals put forward by the owner-managers. This cozy relationship between the board and management should change, however, when the corporation goes public and stock is more widely dispersed. The founders, who are still acting as management, may sometimes make decisions that conflict with the needs of the other shareholders (especially if the founders own less than 50% of the common stock). In this instance, problems could occur if the board failed to become more active in terms of its roles and responsibilities.

MEMBERS OF A BOARD OF DIRECTORS

The boards of most publicly owned corporations are composed of both inside and outside directors. **Inside directors** (sometimes called management directors) are typically officers or executives employed by the corporation. **Outside directors** (sometimes called nonmanagement directors) may be executives of other firms but are not employees of the board's corporation. Although there is no clear evidence indicating that a high proportion of outsiders on a board results in improved corporate performance, there is a trend in the United States to increase the number of outsiders on boards. The typical large U.S. corporation has an average of 11 directors, of whom 2 are insiders.[10] Even though outsiders account for slightly more than 80% of the board members in these large U.S. corporations (approximately the same as in Canada), they only account for about 42% of board membership in small U.S. companies.[11] People who favor a high proportion of outsiders state that outside directors are less biased and more likely to evaluate management's performance objectively than are inside directors. This is the main reason the New York Stock Exchange requires that each company listed on the exchange have an audit committee composed entirely of independent, outside members. This view is in agreement with **agency theory**, which states that problems arise in corporations because the agents (top management) are not willing to bear responsibility for their decisions unless they own a substantial amount of stock in the corporation. The theory suggests that a majority of a board needs to be from outside the firm so that top management is prevented from acting selfishly, to the detriment of the shareholders. See the **Theory As It Applies** feature for a discussion of agency theory contrasted with **stewardship theory**.

In contrast, those who prefer inside over outside directors contend that outside directors are less effective than are insiders because the outsiders are less likely to have the necessary interest, availability, or competency. Directors may sometimes serve on so many boards that

Theory As It Applies

Agency Theory Versus Stewardship Theory in Corporate Governance

Managers of large, modern publicly held corporations are typically not the owners. In fact, most of today's top managers own only nominal amounts of stock in the corporations they manage. The real owners (shareholders) elect boards of directors who hire managers as their agents to run the firm's day-to-day activities. Once hired, how trustworthy are these executives? Do they put themselves or the firm first?

Agency Theory

As suggested in the classic study by Berle and Means, top managers are, in effect, "hired hands" who may very likely be more interested in their personal welfare than in that of the shareholders. For example, management might emphasize strategies, such as acquisitions, that increase the size of the firm (to become more powerful and to demand increased pay and benefits) or that diversify the firm into unrelated businesses (to reduce short-term risk and to allow them to put less effort into a core product line that may be facing difficulty) but that result in a reduction in dividends and/or stock price.

Agency theory is concerned with analyzing and resolving two problems that occur in relationships between principals (owners/shareholders) and their agents (top management):

1. The agency problem that arises when (a) the desires or objectives of the owners and the agents conflict or (b) it is difficult or expensive for the owners to verify what the agent is actually doing. One example is when top management is more interested in raising its own salary than in increasing stock dividends.

2. The risk-sharing problem that arises when the owners and agents have different attitudes toward risk. Executives may not select risky strategies because they fear losing their jobs if the strategy fails.

According to agency theory, the likelihood that these problems will occur increases when stock is widely held (no one shareholder owns more than a small percentage of the total common stock), when the board of directors is composed of people who know little of the company or who are personal friends of top management, and when a high percentage of board members are inside (management) directors.

To better align the interests of the agents with those of the owners and to increase the corporation's overall performance, agency theory suggests that top management have a significant degree of ownership in the firm and/or have a strong financial stake in its long-term performance. In support of this argument, research indicates a positive relationship between corporate performance and the amount of stock owned by directors.

Stewardship Theory

In contrast to agency theory, stewardship theory suggests that executives tend to be more motivated to act in the best interests of the corporation than in their own self-interests. Whereas agency theory focuses on extrinsic rewards that serve the lower-level needs, such as pay and security, stewardship theory focuses on the higher-order needs, such as achievement and self-actualization. Stewardship theory argues that senior executives over time tend to view the corporation as an extension of themselves. Rather than use the firm for their own ends, these executives are most interested in guaranteeing the continued life and success of the corporation. The relationship between the board and top management is thus one of principal and steward, not principal and agent ("hired hand"). Stewardship theory notes that in a widely held corporation, the shareholder is free to sell her or his stock at any time. A diversified investor may care little about risk at the company level, preferring that management assume extraordinary risk so long as the return is adequate. Because executives in a firm cannot so easily leave their jobs when in difficulty, they are more interested in a merely satisfactory return and put heavy emphasis on the firm's continued survival. Thus, stewardship theory would argue that in many instances top management may care more about a company's long-term success than do more short-term–oriented shareholders.

Note: For more information about agency theory and stewardship theory, see J. H. Davis, F. D. Schoorman, and L. Donaldson, "Toward a Stewardship Theory of Management," *Academy of Management Review* (January 1997), pp. 20–47. See also P. J. Lane, A. A. Cannella, Jr., and M. H. Lubatkin, "Agency Problems As Antecedents to Unrelated Mergers and Diversification: Amihud and Lev Reconsidered," *Strategic Management Journal* (June 1998), pp. 555–578, and M. L. Hayward and D. C. Hambrick, "Explaining the Premiums Paid for Large Acquisitions: Evidence of CEO Hubris," *Administrative Science Quarterly* (March 1997), pp. 103–127. For background, refer to A. A. Berle, Jr. and G. C. Means, *The Modern Corporation and Private Property* (New York: Macmillan, 1932).

they spread their time and interest too thin to actively fulfill their responsibilities. They could also point out that the term "outsider" is too simplistic—some outsiders are not truly objective and should be considered more as insiders than as outsiders. For example, there can be:

1. **Affiliated directors** who, though not really employed by the corporation, handle the legal or insurance work for the company or are important suppliers (thus dependent on the current management for a key part of their business). These outsiders face a conflict of interest and are not likely to be objective. The number of affiliated directors on Tyco's board was one of the reasons the board was so strongly criticized.

2. **Retired directors** who used to work for the company, such as the past CEO (who is partly responsible for much of the corporation's current strategy and who probably groomed the current CEO as his or her replacement). Many boards of large firms keep the firm's recently retired CEO on the board for one or two years after retirement as a courtesy, especially if he or she performed well as the CEO. It is almost certain, however, that this person will not be able to objectively evaluate the corporation's performance. Nevertheless, a survey by Korn/Ferry International found that only 29% of directors surveyed indicated that their boards required the former CEO to leave the board upon retirement.[12]

3. **Family directors** who are descendants of the founder and own significant blocks of stock (with personal agendas based on a family relationship with the current CEO). The Schlitz Brewing Company, for example, was unable to complete its turnaround strategy with a nonfamily CEO because family members serving on the board wanted their money out of the company, forcing it to be sold.[13]

The majority of outside directors are active or retired CEOs and COOs of other corporations. Others are major investors/shareholders, academicians, attorneys, consultants, former government officials, and bankers. Given that approximately 60% of the outstanding stock in the largest U.S. and U.K. corporations is now owned by institutional investors, such as mutual funds and pension plans, these investors are taking an increasingly active role in board membership and activities.[14] In Germany, bankers are represented on almost every board—primarily because they own large blocks of stock in German corporations. In Denmark, Sweden, Belgium, and Italy, however, investment companies assume this role. For example, the investment company Investor AB casts 42.5% of the Electrolux AB shareholder votes, thus guaranteeing itself positions on the Electrolux board. Surveys of large U.S. corporations found that 73% of the boards have at least one woman director, with 25% having two female directors. Boards having at least one minority member increased from 9% in 1973 to 60% today (African American: 39%; Hispanic: 12%; Asian: 9%).[15]

The globalization of business is having an impact on board membership. By 1998, 10% of all directors of companies surveyed internationally by The Conference Board's Global Corporate Governance Research Center were nonnationals, up from 6% three years earlier. Europe is the most "globalized" region of the world, with 71% of companies reporting having one or more nonnational directors, followed by North America, where the figure was 60% in 1998. Asian and Latin American boards are still predominantly staffed by nationals.[16]

Outside directors serving on the boards of large U.S. corporations annually earned on average (median) $33,000. Almost 90% of large U.S. corporations also provided some form of payment through stock options or grants, raising the median annual total compensation to $43,700.[17] Directors serving on the boards of small companies usually received much less (around $10,000). One study found directors to hold on average 3% of their corporations' outstanding stock.[18]

The vast majority of inside directors are the CEO, COO, and Presidents or Vice Presidents of key operating divisions or functional units. Few, if any, inside directors receive any extra compensation for assuming this extra duty. Very rarely does a U.S. board include any lower-level operating employees.

Codetermination: Should Employees Serve on Boards?

Codetermination, the inclusion of a corporation's workers on its board, began only recently in the United States. Corporations such as Chrysler, Northwest Airlines, United Airlines (UAL), and Wheeling-Pittsburgh Steel have added representatives from employee associations to their boards as part of union agreements or employee stock ownership plans (ESOPs). For example, UAL workers traded 15% in pay cuts for 55% of the company (through an ESOP) and 3 of the firm's 12 board seats. In this instance, workers represent themselves on the board not so much as employees, but primarily as owners. At Chrysler, however, the United Auto Workers union obtained a temporary seat on the board as part of a union contract agreement in exchange for changes in work rules and reductions in benefits. In situations like this, when a director represents an internal stakeholder, critics raise the issue of conflict of interest. Can a member of the board, who is privy to confidential managerial information, function, for example, as a union leader whose primary duty is to fight for the best benefits for his or her members? Although the movement to place employees on the boards of directors of U.S. companies shows little likelihood of increasing (except through employee stock ownership), the European experience reveals an increasing acceptance of worker participation (without ownership) on corporate boards.

Germany pioneered codetermination during the 1950s, with a two-tiered system: a supervisory board elected by shareholders and employees to approve or decide corporate strategy and a policy and management board (composed primarily of top management) appointed by the supervisory board to manage the company's activities. Most other Western European countries have either passed similar codetermination legislation (for example, Sweden, Denmark, Norway, Austria) or use worker councils to work closely with management (for example, Belgium, Luxembourg, France, Italy, Ireland, The Netherlands).

Interlocking Directorates

CEOs often nominate chief executives (as well as board members) from other firms to membership on their own boards in order to create an **interlocking directorate**. A *direct* interlocking directorate occurs when two firms share a director or when an executive of one firm sits on the board of a second firm. An *indirect* interlock occurs when two corporations have directors who also serve on the board of a third firm, such as a bank. Both inside and outside directors at the largest U.S. companies serve on an average of three boards.

Although the Clayton Act and the Banking Act of 1933 prohibit interlocking directorates by U.S. companies competing in the same industry, interlocking continues to occur in almost all corporations, especially large ones. Interlocking occurs because large firms have a large impact on other corporations; these other corporations, in turn, have some control over the firm's inputs and marketplace. For example, most large corporations in the United States, Japan, and Germany are interlocked either directly or indirectly with financial institutions.[19] Interlocking directorates are also a useful method for gaining both inside information about an uncertain environment and objective expertise about potential strategies and tactics. For example, Kleiner Perkins, the high-tech venture capital firm, not only has seats on the boards of the companies in which it invests, but it also has executives (whom Kleiner Perkins hired) from one entrepreneurial venture serve as directors on others. Kleiner Perkins refers to its network of interlocked firms as its *keiretsu*.[20] Family-owned corporations, however, are less likely to have interlocking directorates than are corporations with highly dispersed stock ownership, probably because family-owned corporations do not like to dilute their corporate control by adding outsiders to boardroom discussions. Nevertheless, some evidence indicates that well-interlocked corporations are better able than others to survive in a highly competitive environment.[21]

NOMINATION AND ELECTION OF BOARD MEMBERS

Traditionally the CEO of a corporation decided whom to invite to board membership and merely asked the shareholders for approval in the annual proxy statement. All nominees were usually elected. There are some dangers, however, in allowing the CEO free rein in nominating directors. The CEO might select only board members who, in the CEO's opinion, will not disturb the company's policies and functioning. Given that the average length of service of a U.S. board member is for five 4-year terms, CEO-friendly, passive boards are likely to result. This is especially likely given that 92% of surveyed directors indicated that their company did not have term limits for board members. Directors selected by the CEO often feel that they should go along with any proposal the CEO makes. Thus board members find themselves accountable to the very management they are charged to oversee. Because this is likely to happen, more boards are using a nominating committee to nominate new outside board members for the shareholders to elect. Approximately 74% of large U.S. corporations now use nominating committees to identify potential directors.[22]

Virtually every corporation whose directors serve terms of more than one year divides the board into classes and staggers elections so that only a portion of the board stands for election each year. This is called a **staggered board**. Arguments in favor of this practice are that it provides continuity by reducing the chance of an abrupt turnover in its membership and that it reduces the likelihood of electing people who are unfriendly to management (who might be interested in a hostile takeover) through cumulative voting. An argument against staggered boards is that they make it more difficult for concerned shareholders to curb a CEO's power, especially when that CEO is also Chairman of the Board. For example, out of dissatisfaction with the company's poor performance and their perception that the board was inactive, two unions supported a shareholder proposal in 1996 to cancel Kmart's staggered board so that the entire board would be elected annually.

A survey of directors of U.S. corporations revealed the following criteria for selecting a good director:

- Is willing to challenge management when necessary (95%)
- Has special expertise important to the company (67%)
- Is available outside meetings to advise management (57%)
- Has expertise on global business issues (41%)
- Understands firm's key technologies and processes (39%)
- Brings external contacts that are potentially valuable to the firm (33%)
- Has detailed knowledge of the firm's industry (31%)
- Is highly visible in his or her field (31%)
- Is accomplished at representing the firm to stakeholders (18%)[23]

ORGANIZATION OF THE BOARD

The size of a board in the United States is determined by the corporation's charter and its bylaws, in compliance with state laws. Although some states require a minimum number of board members, most corporations have quite a bit of discretion in determining board size. The average large, publicly held firm has around 11 directors. The average small/medium-size privately held company has approximately seven to eight members.

Sixty-seven percent of the top executives of large U.S. publicly held corporations hold the dual designation of Chairman and CEO. (The percentage of firms having the Chair/CEO position combined in Canada and the United Kingdom is 43% and 20%, respectively.)[24] The combined Chair/CEO position is being increasingly criticized because of the potential for conflict of interest. The CEO is supposed to concentrate on strategy, planning, external relations, and responsibility to the board. The Chairman's responsibility is to ensure that the board and its committees perform their functions as stated in the board's charter. Further, the Chairman schedules board meetings and presides over the annual shareholders' meeting. Critics of combining the two offices in one person ask how the board can properly oversee top management if the Chairman is also top management. For this reason, the Chairman and CEO roles are separated by law in Germany, The Netherlands, and Finland. A similar law has been considered in Britain and Australia. Although research does not clearly indicate either a definite positive or negative effect of combined positions on corporate performance, the stock market does respond negatively to announcements of CEOs also assuming the Chairman position.[25]

Many of those who prefer that the Chairman and CEO positions be combined agree that the outside directors should elect a **lead director**. This person would be consulted by the Chair/CEO regarding board affairs and would coordinate the annual evaluation of the CEO.[26] The lead director position is very popular in the United Kingdom, where it originated. Of those U.S. companies combining the Chair and CEO positions, 30% currently have lead directors.[27] This is one way to give the board more power without undermining the power of the Chair/CEO.

The most effective boards accomplish much of their work through committees. Although they do not usually have legal duties, most committees are granted full power to act with the authority of the board between board meetings. Typical standing committees (in order of prevalence) are the audit (100%), compensation (99%), nominating (74%), and executive (60%) committees. The executive committee is usually composed of two inside and two nearby outside directors who can meet between board meetings to attend to matters that must be settled quickly. This committee acts as an extension of the board and, consequently, may have almost unrestricted authority in certain areas. The audit, compensation, and nominating committees are usually composed only of outside directors.

TRENDS IN CORPORATE GOVERNANCE

The role of the board of directors in the strategic management of the corporation is likely to be more active in the future. Although neither the composition of boards nor the board leadership structure has been consistently linked to firm financial performance, a McKinsey survey reveals that investors are willing to pay 16% more for a corporation's stock if it is known to have good corporate governance. The investors explained that they would pay more because, in their opinion, (1) good governance leads to better performance over time, (2) good governance reduces the risk of the company getting into trouble, and (3) governance is a major strategic issue.[28]

Some of today's **trends in governance** (particularly prevalent in the United States and the United Kingdom) that are likely to continue include the following:[29]

- Boards are getting more involved not only in reviewing and evaluating company strategy but also in shaping it.

- Institutional investors, such as pension funds, mutual funds, and insurance companies, are becoming active on boards and are putting increasing pressure on top management to improve corporate performance. For example, the California Public Employees' Retirement System (CalPERS), the largest pension system in the United States, annually publishes a list of poorly performing companies, hoping to embarrass management into taking remedial action.

- Shareholders are demanding that directors and top managers own more than token amounts of stock in the corporation. Stock is increasingly being used as part of a director's compensation.

- Nonaffiliated outside (nonmanagement) directors are increasing their numbers and power in publicly held corporations as CEOs loosen their grips on boards. Outside members are taking charge of annual CEO evaluations.

- Boards are getting smaller, partially because of the reduction in the number of insiders but also because boards desire new directors to have specialized knowledge and expertise instead of general experience.

- Boards continue to take more control of board functions by either splitting the combined Chair/CEO position into two separate positions or establishing a lead outside director position.

- As corporations become more global, they are increasingly looking for international experience in their board members.

- Society, in the form of special interest groups, increasingly expects boards of directors to balance the economic goal of profitability with the social needs of society. Issues dealing with workforce diversity and the environment are now reaching the board level. For example, the board of Chase Manhattan Corporation recently questioned top management about its efforts to improve the sparse number of women and minorities in senior management.[30]

2.2 Corporate Governance: The Role of Top Management

The top management function is usually conducted by the CEO of the corporation in coordination with the COO or President, Executive Vice President, and Vice Presidents of divisions and functional areas. Even though strategic management involves everyone in the organization, the board of directors holds top management primarily responsible for the strategic management of the firm.[31]

RESPONSIBILITIES OF TOP MANAGEMENT

Top management responsibilities, especially those of the CEO, involve getting things accomplished through and with others in order to meet the corporate objectives. Top management's job is thus multidimensional and is oriented toward the welfare of the total organization. Specific top management tasks vary from firm to firm and are developed from an analysis of the mission, objectives, strategies, and key activities of the corporation. Tasks are typically divided among the members of the top management team. A diversity of skills can thus be very important. Research indicates that top management teams with a diversity of functional and educational backgrounds and length of time with the company tend to be significantly related to improvements in corporate market share and profitability.[32] Nevertheless, the CEO, with the support of the rest of the top management team, must successfully handle two primary responsibilities that are crucial to the effective strategic management of the corporation: (1) provide executive leadership and a strategic vision and (2) manage the strategic planning process.

Provide Executive Leadership and Strategic Vision

Executive leadership is the directing of activities toward the accomplishment of corporate objectives. Executive leadership is important because it sets the tone for the entire corporation. A **strategic vision** is a description of what the company is capable of becoming. It is often communicated in the mission statement. People in an organization want to have a sense of mission, but only top management is in the position to specify and communicate this strategic vision to the general workforce. Top management's enthusiasm (or lack of it) about the corporation tends to be contagious. Entrepreneurs are noted for having a strong passion for their company and for their ability to communicate it to others. The importance of executive leadership is illustrated by John Welch, Jr., the successful Chairman and CEO of General Electric Company (GE). According to Welch, "Good business leaders create a vision, articulate the vision, passionately own the vision, and relentlessly drive it to completion."[33]

CEOs with clear strategic vision are often perceived as dynamic and charismatic leaders. For instance, the positive attitude characterizing many well-known industrial leaders—such as Bill Gates at Microsoft, Anita Roddick at The Body Shop, Ted Turner at CNN, Steve Jobs at Apple Computer, Herb Kelleher at Southwest Airlines, and Andy Grove at Intel—has energized their respective corporations. They are able to command respect and to influence strategy formulation and implementation because they tend to have three key characteristics:

1. **The CEO articulates a strategic vision** for the corporation. The CEO envisions the company not as it currently is, but as it can become. The new perspective that the CEO's vision brings to activities and conflicts gives renewed meaning to everyone's work and enables employees to see beyond the details of their own jobs to the functioning of the total corporation. In a survey of 1,500 senior executives from 20 different countries, when asked the most important behavioral trait a CEO must have, 98% responded that the CEO must convey "a strong sense of vision."[34]

2. **The CEO presents a role** for others to identify with and to follow. The leader sets an example in terms of behavior and dress. The CEO's attitudes and values concerning the corporation's purpose and activities are clear-cut and constantly communicated in words and deeds. People know what to expect and have trust in their CEO. Research indicates that businesses in which the general manager has the trust of the employees have higher sales and profits with lower turnover than do businesses in which there is a lower amount of trust.[35]

3. **The CEO communicates high performance standards and also shows confidence in the followers' abilities** to meet these standards. No leader ever improved performance by setting easily attainable goals that provided no challenge. The CEO must be willing to follow through by coaching people. Selected the "Best CEO" of 2000, John Chambers of Cisco Systems has this characteristic. According to his subordinates, "John treats us like peers. . . . He asks our advice. He gives us power and resources, then sets the sales targets incredibly high, which keeps us challenged. He is an adhesive force keeping us working together and not flying apart."[36]

Manage the Strategic Planning Process

As business corporations adopt more of the characteristics of the learning organization, strategic planning initiatives can now come from any part of an organization. A survey of 90 U.S. global corporations revealed that, in 90% of the firms, strategies are first proposed in the subsidiaries and sent to headquarters for approval.[37] However, unless top management encourages and supports the planning process, strategic management is not likely to result. In most corporations, top management must initiate and manage the strategic planning process. It may do so by first asking business units and functional areas to propose strategic plans for themselves, or it may begin by drafting an overall corporate plan within which the units can then build their own plans. Research suggests that bottom-up strategic planning may be most appropriate in multidivisional corporations operating in relatively stable environments but that top-down strategic planning may be most appropriate for firms operating in turbulent environments.[38] Other organizations engage in concurrent strategic planning, in which all the organization's units draft plans for themselves after they have been provided with the organization's overall mission and objectives.

Regardless of the approach taken, the typical board of directors expects top management to manage the overall strategic planning process so that the plans of all the units and functional areas fit together into an overall corporate plan. Top management's job therefore includes the tasks of evaluating unit plans and providing feedback. To do this, top management may require each unit to justify its proposed objectives, strategies, and programs in terms of how well they satisfy the organization's overall objectives in light of available resources.[39]

Many large organizations have a **strategic planning staff** charged with supporting both top management and the business units in the strategic planning process. This planning staff typically consists of just under 10 people, headed by a Senior Vice President or Director of Corporate Planning. The staff's major responsibilities are to:

1. Identify and analyze companywide strategic issues and suggest corporate strategic alternatives to top management.
2. Work as facilitators with business units to guide them through the strategic planning process.

2.3 Social Responsibilities of Strategic Decision Makers

Should strategic decision makers be responsible only to shareholders, or do they have broader responsibilities? The concept of **social responsibility** proposes that a private corporation has responsibilities to society that extend beyond making a profit. Strategic decisions often affect more than just the corporation. A decision to retrench by closing some plants and discontinuing product lines, for example, affects not only the firm's workforce, but also the communities where the plants are located and the customers that have no other source for the discontinued product. Such situations raise questions of the appropriateness of certain missions, objectives, and strategies of business corporations. Managers must be able to deal with these conflicting interests in an ethical manner to formulate a viable strategic plan.

RESPONSIBILITIES OF A BUSINESS FIRM

What are the responsibilities of a business firm, and how many of them must be fulfilled? Milton Friedman and Archie Carroll offer two contrasting views of the responsibilities of business firms to society.

Friedman's Traditional View of Business Responsibility

Urging a return to a laissez-faire worldwide economy with a minimum of government regulation, Friedman argues against the concept of social responsibility. A business person who acts "responsibly" by cutting the price of the firm's product to prevent inflation or by making expenditures to reduce pollution, or by hiring the hard-core unemployed, according to Friedman, is spending the shareholder's money for a general social interest. Even if the business person has shareholder permission or encouragement to do so, he or she is still acting from motives other than economic and may, in the long run, harm the very society the firm is trying to help. By taking on the burden of these social costs, the business becomes less efficient—either prices go up to pay for the increased costs or investment in new activities and research is postponed. These results negatively affect—perhaps fatally—the long-term efficiency of a business. Friedman thus referred to the social responsibility of business as a "fundamentally subversive doctrine" and stated that:

> There is one and only one social responsibility of business—to use its resources and engage in activities designed to increase its profits so long as it stays within the rules of the game, which is to say, engages in open and free competition without deception or fraud.[40]

Carroll's Four Responsibilities of Business

As shown in Figure 2–2, Archie Carroll proposes that the managers of business organizations have four **responsibilities**:[41]

1. **Economic** responsibilities of a business organization's management are to produce goods and services of value to society so that the firm can repay its creditors and shareholders.

2. **Legal** responsibilities are defined by governments in laws that management is expected to obey. For example, U.S. business firms are required to hire and promote people based on their credentials rather than to discriminate based on non-job-related characteristics such as race, gender, or religion.

3. **Ethical** responsibilities of an organization's management are to follow the generally held beliefs about behavior in a society. For example, society generally expects firms to work with the employees and the community in planning for layoffs, even though no law may require this. The affected people can get very upset if an organization's management fails to act according to generally prevailing ethical values.

4. **Discretionary** responsibilities are the purely voluntary obligations a corporation assumes. Examples are philanthropic contributions, training the hard-core unemployed, and providing day care centers. The difference between ethical and discretionary responsibilities is that few people expect an organization to fulfill discretionary responsibilities, whereas many expect an organization to fulfill ethical ones.[42]

Carroll lists these four responsibilities *in order of priority*. A business firm must first make a profit to satisfy its economic responsibilities. To continue in existence, the firm must follow the laws, thus fulfilling its legal responsibilities. There is evidence that companies found guilty of violating laws have lower profits and sales growth after conviction.[43] To this point Carroll and Friedman are in agreement. Carroll, however, argues that business managers have responsibilities beyond the economic and legal ones.

Having satisfied the two basic responsibilities, according to Carroll, the firm should look to fulfilling its social responsibilities. Social responsibility, therefore, *includes both ethical and discretionary, but not economic and legal, responsibilities*. A firm can fulfill its ethical responsibilities by taking actions that society tends to value but has not yet put into law. When ethical responsibilities are satisfied, a firm can focus on discretionary responsibilities—purely voluntary actions that society has not yet decided are important.

The discretionary responsibilities of today may become the ethical responsibilities of tomorrow. The provision of day care facilities is, for example, moving rapidly from being a discretionary to an ethical responsibility. Carroll suggests that to the extent that business corporations fail to acknowledge discretionary or ethical responsibilities, society, through government, will act, making them legal responsibilities. Government may do this, moreover, without regard to an organization's economic responsibilities. As a result, the organization may have greater difficulty earning a profit than it would have had if it had voluntarily assumed some ethical and discretionary responsibilities.

Both Friedman and Carroll argue their positions based on the impact of socially responsible actions on a firm's profits. Friedman says that socially responsible actions hurt a firm's

Figure 2–2
Responsibilities of Business

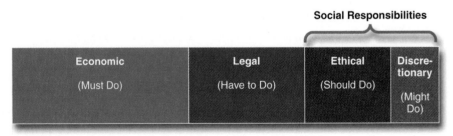

Source: Adapted from A. B. Carroll, "A Three Dimensional Conceptual Model of Corporate Performance," *Academy of Management Review* (October 1979), p. 499. Reprinted with permission.

efficiency. Carroll proposes that a lack of social responsibility results in increased government regulations, which reduce a firm's efficiency.

Research is mixed regarding the effect of social responsibility on a corporation's financial performance. Although a number of research studies find no significant relationship,[44] an increasing number are finding a positive relationship.[45]

Being known as a socially responsible firm may provide a company a competitive advantage. For example, companies that take the lead in being environmentally friendly, such as by using recycled materials, preempt attacks from environmental groups and enhance their corporate image. Programs to reduce pollution, for example, can actually reduce waste and maximize resource productivity. One study that examined 70 ecological initiatives taken by 43 companies found the average payback period to be 18 months.[46] Other examples of benefits received from being socially responsible are:

- Their environmental concerns may enable them to charge premium prices and gain brand loyalty (Ben & Jerry's Homemade, Inc.).
- Their trustworthiness may help them generate enduring relationships with suppliers and distributors without needing to spend a lot of time and money policing contracts (Maytag).
- They can attract outstanding employees who prefer working for a responsible firm (Procter & Gamble).
- They are more likely to be welcomed into a foreign country (Levi Strauss).
- They can utilize the goodwill of public officials for support in difficult times (for example, Minnesota supported Dayton-Hudson's fight to avoid being acquired by Dart Industries of Maryland).
- They are more likely to attract capital infusions from investors who view reputable companies as desirable long-term investments (Rubbermaid).[47]

CORPORATE STAKEHOLDERS

The concept that business must be socially responsible sounds appealing until we ask, "Responsible to whom?" A corporation's task environment includes a large number of groups with interest in a business organization's activities. These groups are referred to as **corporate stakeholders** because they affect or are affected by the achievement of the firm's objectives.[48] Should a corporation be responsible only to some of these groups, or does business have an equal responsibility to all of them?

Recent surveys suggest that the U.S. general public is worried that business is becoming too concerned with profits. A recent survey conducted by Harris Poll found that 66% either strongly or somewhat agreed that large profits are more important to big business than developing safe, reliable, quality products for consumers. Recent revelations of tainted milk in Japan (Snow Brand), flawed child strollers in the United States (Cosco), and unsafe tires globally (Firestone) only add to the public concern that business is ignoring its stakeholders and may be operating unethically or even illegally. According to Harris Poll, 73% of U.S. adults agreed that the compensation of top officers of large U.S. companies is "too much." The survey also found that 95% felt that U.S. corporations owe something to their workers and the communities in which they operate and that they should sometimes sacrifice some profit for the sake of making things better for their workers and communities.[49] Such attitudes become grist for populist politicians who make business people into villains during election campaigns.

In any one strategic decision, the interests of one stakeholder group can conflict with those of another. For example, a business firm's decision to use only recycled materials in its manufacturing process may have a positive effect on environmental groups but a negative effect on shareholder dividends. In another example, Maytag Corporation's top management decided to move dishwasher production from Iowa to a lower-wage location in Tennessee. On the one hand, shareholders were generally pleased with the decision because it would lower costs. On the other hand, Iowa officials and local union people were very unhappy at what they called "community cannibalism." Which group's interests should have priority?

Given the wide range of interests and concerns present in any organization's task environment, one or more groups, at any one time, probably will be dissatisfied with an organization's activities—even if management is trying to be socially responsible. A company may have some stakeholders of which it is only marginally aware. Therefore, before making a strategic decision, strategic managers should consider how each alternative will affect various stakeholder groups. What seems at first to be the best decision because it appears to be the most profitable may actually result in the worst set of consequences to the corporation.

2.4 **Ethical Decision Making**

Some people joke that there is no such thing as "business ethics." They call it an oxymoron—a concept that combines opposite or contradictory ideas. Unfortunately there is some truth to this sarcastic comment. For example, a survey by the Ethics Resource Center of 1,324 employees of 747 U.S. companies found that 48% of employees surveyed said that they had engaged in one or more unethical and/or illegal actions during the past year. The most common questionable behavior involved cutting corners on quality (16%), covering up incidents (14%), abusing or lying about sick days (11%), and lying to or deceiving customers (9%). Some 56% of workers reported pressure to act unethically or illegally on the job.[50] See the **Global Issue** feature for examples of unethical practices at Enron and WorldCom.

Global Issue

Unethical Practices at Enron and WorldCom Exposed by "Whistleblowers"

Corporate scandals at Enron, WorldCom, and Tyco, among other international companies, have caused people around the world to seriously question the ethics of business executives. Enron, in particular, has become infamous for the questionable actions of its top executives in the form of (1) off-balance sheet partnerships used to hide the company's deteriorating finances, (2) revenue from long-term contracts being recorded in its first year instead of being spread over multiple years, (3) financial reports being falsified to inflate executive bonuses, and (4) manipulation of the electricity market, leading to a California energy crisis. Only Sherron Watkins, an Enron accountant, was willing to speak out regarding the questionable nature of these practices. In a now-famous memo to then-CEO Kenneth Lay, Watkins warned:

I realize that we have had a lot of smart people looking at this and a lot of accountants including AA & Co. (Arthur Anderson) have blessed the accounting treatment. None of that will protect Enron if these transactions are ever disclosed in the bright light of day.

At WorldCom, Cynthia Cooper, an internal auditor, noted that some of the company's capital expenditures should have been listed on the second-quarter financial statements as expenses. When she mentioned this to both WorldCom's Controller and its CFO, she was told to stop what she was doing and to delay the audit until the third quarter (when expensing the transactions would not be noticed). Instead, Cooper informed the board of directors' audit committee. Two weeks later, WorldCom announced that it was reducing earnings by $3.9 billion, the largest restatement in history.

Sources: G. Colvin, "Wonder Women of Whistleblowing," *Fortune* (August 12, 2002), p. 56; W. Zellner, "The Deadly Sins of Enron," *Business Week* (October 14, 2002, pp. 26–28, and M. J. Mandel, "And the Enron Award Goes to . . . Enron," *Business Week* (May 20, 2002), p. 46.

SOME REASONS FOR UNETHICAL BEHAVIOR

Why are many business people perceived to be acting unethically? It may be that the involved people are not even aware that they are taking questionable actions. There is no worldwide standard of conduct for business people. Cultural norms and values vary between countries and even between different geographic regions and ethnic groups within a country. For example, what is considered in one country to be a bribe to expedite service is sometimes considered in another country to be normal business practice.

Another possible reason for what is often perceived to be unethical behavior lies in differences in values between business people and key stakeholders. Some business people may believe profit maximization is the key goal of their firm, whereas concerned interest groups may have other priorities, such as the hiring of minorities and women or the safety of their neighborhoods. Of the six values measured by the Allport-Vernon-Lindzey Study of Values test (aesthetic, economic, political, religious, social, and theoretical), both U.S. and British executives consistently score highest on economic and political values and lowest on social and religious ones. This is similar to the value profile of managers from Japan, Korea, India, and Australia, as well as those of U.S. business school students. U.S. Protestant ministers, in contrast, score highest on religious and social values and very low on economic values.[51]

This difference in values can make it difficult for one group of people to understand another's actions. For example, even though some people feel that the advertising of cigarettes (especially to youth) is unethical, the people managing these companies respond that they are simply offering a product; "Let the buyer beware" is a traditional saying in free market capitalism. They argue that customers in a free market democracy have the right to choose how they spend their money and live their lives. Social progressives may contend that business people working in tobacco, alcoholic beverages, and gambling industries are acting unethically by making and advertising products with potentially dangerous and expensive side effects, such as cancer, alcoholism, and addiction. People working in those industries could respond by asking if it is ethical for people who don't smoke, drink, or gamble to reject another person's right to do so.

Moral Relativism

Some people justify their seemingly unethical positions by arguing that there is no one absolute code of ethics and that morality is relative. Simply put, **moral relativism** claims that morality is relative to some personal, social, or cultural standard and that there is no method for deciding whether one decision is better than another.

Adherents of moral relativism may believe that all moral decisions are deeply personal and that individuals have the right to run their own lives; each person should be allowed to interpret situations and act on his or her own moral values. They may also argue that social roles carry with them certain obligations to those roles only. A manager in charge of a department, for example, must put aside his or her personal beliefs and do instead what the role requires—that is, act in the best interests of the department. They could also argue that a decision is legitimate if it is common practice, regardless of other considerations ("Everyone's doing it"). Some propose that morality itself is relative to a particular culture, society, or community. People should therefore understand the practices of other countries but not judge them. If the citizens of another country share certain norms and customs, what right does an outsider have to criticize them?

Although these arguments make some sense, moral relativism could enable a person to justify almost any sort of decision or action, so long as it is not declared illegal.

Kohlberg's Levels of Moral Development

Another reason some business people might be seen as unethical is that they may have no well-developed personal sense of ethics. A person's ethical behavior is affected by his or her level of moral development, certain personality variables, and such situational factors as the job itself, the supervisor, and the organizational culture.[52] Kohlberg proposes that a person progresses through three **levels of moral development**.[53] Similar in some ways to Maslow's hierarchy of needs, Kohlberg's levels of moral development have the individual move from total self-centeredness to a concern for universal values. Kohlberg's three levels are as follows:

1. **The preconventional level** is characterized by a concern for self. Small children and others who have not progressed beyond this stage evaluate behaviors on the basis of personal interest—avoiding punishment or quid pro quo.

2. **The conventional level** is characterized by considerations of society's laws and norms. Actions are justified by an external code of conduct.

3. **The principled level** is characterized by a person's adherence to an internal moral code. The individual at this level looks beyond norms or laws to find universal values or principles.

Kohlberg places most people in the conventional level, with fewer than 20% of U.S. adults in the principled level of development.[54]

ENCOURAGING ETHICAL BEHAVIOR

According to Carroll's work, if business people do not act ethically, government will be forced to pass laws regulating their actions—and usually increasing their costs. For self-interest, if for no other reason, managers should be more ethical in their decision making. One way to do that is by encouraging codes of ethics. Another is by providing guidelines for ethical behavior.

Codes of Ethics

Codes of ethics specify how an organization expects its employees to behave while on the job. Developing codes of ethics can be a useful way to promote ethical behavior, especially for people who are operating at Kohlberg's conventional level of moral development. Such codes are currently being used by about half of U.S. business corporations. According to a report by the Business Roundtable, an association of CEOs from 200 major U.S. corporations, the importance of a code of ethics is that it (1) clarifies company expectations of employee conduct in various situations and (2) makes clear that the company expects its people to recognize the ethical dimensions in decisions and actions.[55]

Various studies indicate that an increasing number of companies are developing codes of ethics and implementing ethics training workshops and seminars. However, research also indicates that when faced with a question of ethics, managers tend to ignore codes of ethics and try to solve their dilemmas on their own.[56] To combat this tendency, the management of a company that wants to improve its employees' ethical behavior should not only develop a comprehensive code of ethics but also communicate the code in its training programs, in its performance appraisal system, its policies and procedures, and through its own actions. It may also want to do the same for the companies with which it does business. For example, Reebok International has developed a set of production standards for the manufacturers that supply the company with its athletic shoes on a contract basis. In response to a report commissioned by Reebok (at a cost of $50,000) that found health and safety problems at two subcontractor plants in Indonesia, the two suppliers were forced to spend $500,000 in factory improvements in order to keep Reebok's business.[57]

Guidelines for Ethical Behavior

Ethics is defined as the consensually accepted standards of behavior for an occupation, a trade, or a profession. **Morality**, in contrast, is the precepts of personal behavior that are based on religious or philosophical grounds. **Law** refers to formal codes that permit or forbid certain behaviors and may or may not enforce ethics or morality.[58] Given these definitions, how do we arrive at a comprehensive statement of ethics to use in making decisions in a specific occupation, trade, or profession? A starting point for such a code of ethics is to consider the three basic approaches to ethical behavior:[59]

1. **Utilitarian approach:** This approach proposes that actions and plans should be judged by their consequences. People should therefore behave in a way that will produce the greatest benefit to society and produce the least harm or the lowest cost. A problem with this approach is the difficulty in recognizing all the benefits and the costs of any particular decision. Research has revealed that only the stakeholders having the most *power* (ability to affect the company), *legitimacy* (legal or moral claim on company resources), and *urgency* (demand for immediate attention) are given priority by CEOs.[60] It is therefore likely that only the most obvious stakeholders will be considered, while others will be ignored.

2. **Individual rights approach:** This approach proposes that human beings have certain fundamental rights that should be respected in all decisions. A particular decision or behavior should be avoided if it interferes with the rights of others. A problem with this approach is in defining "fundamental rights." The U.S. Constitution includes a Bill of Rights that may or may not be accepted throughout the world. This approach can also encourage selfish behavior when a person defines a personal need or want as a right.

3. **Justice approach:** This approach proposes that decision makers be equitable, fair, and impartial in the distribution of costs and benefits to individuals and groups. It follows the principles of *distributive justice* (people who are similar on relevant dimensions such as job seniority should be treated in the same way) and *fairness* (liberty should be equal for all persons). The justice approach can also include the concepts of *retributive justice* (punishment should be proportional to the "crime") and *compensatory justice* (wrongs should be compensated in proportion to the offense). Affirmative action issues such as reverse discrimination are examples of conflicts between distributive and compensatory justice.

Cavanagh proposes that we solve ethical problems by asking the following three questions regarding an act or a decision:[61]

1. **Utility:** Does it optimize the satisfactions of all stakeholders?
2. **Rights:** Does it respect the rights of the individuals involved?
3. **Justice:** Is it consistent with the canons of justice?

For example, is padding an expense account ethical? Using the utility criterion, this action increases the company's costs and thus does not optimize benefits for shareholders or customers. Using the rights approach, a person has no right to the money (otherwise we wouldn't call it "padding"). Using the justice criterion, salary and commissions constitute ordinary compensation, but expense accounts compensate a person only for expenses incurred in doing his or her job—expenses that the person would not normally incur except in doing this job.

Another approach to resolving ethical dilemmas is by applying the logic of the philosopher Immanual Kant. Kant presents two principles (called **categorical imperatives**) to guide our actions:[62]

1. A person's action is ethical only if that person is willing for that same action to be taken by everyone who is in a similar situation. This is the same as the *Golden Rule*: Treat others as you would like them to treat you. For example, padding an expense account would be considered ethical if the person were also willing for everyone to do the same if he or she were the boss. Because it is very doubtful that any manager would be pleased with expense account padding, the action must be considered unethical.

2. A person should never treat another human being simply as a means, but always as an end. This means that an action is morally wrong for a person if that person uses others merely as means for advancing his or her own interests. To be moral, the act should not restrict other people's actions so that they are left disadvantaged in some way.

2.5 Impact of the Internet on Corporate Governance and Social Responsibility

Electronic commerce is offering a great deal of benefits, but it is also raising a number of issues related to social responsibility and stakeholders. Thus far, the Internet has generally been unregulated by governments. To the extent that groups of people find the Internet to have negative effects, government will eventually be called upon to intervene. Europeans are concerned with a user's privacy. Middle Easterners are concerned with decency standards. Americans are concerned with con artists using Web sites and e-mail to take money without providing a service.

In Russia, for example, a recently passed law allows the Federal Security Bureau (FSB) to monitor all Internet, cellular telephone, and pager communication traffic. Directives require all Russian internet service providers (ISPs) to equip their networks with FSB monitors and connect them via high-speed fiber-optic links to FSB headquarters.[63]

A number of problems may make it difficult to keep the Internet unregulated. Some of these are:

- **Cybersquatting:** This occurs when a private speculator purchases the right to a valuable corporate brand name domain, such as businessweek.com, and then sells it to the company at an exorbitant price. Because Web addresses are critical to online branding, companies want to establish a rule that they are entitled to domain names that use their trademarks. In response, consumer advocates say that such a rule would unfairly restrict the rights of schools, museums, religions, and clubs. They argue that an astronomy club should be able to register Saturn.com if the domain is available—and not later lose it to a car company.[64]

- **Fraud:** The Internet is an excellent source of information—information that can be used to defraud innocent people by temporarily stealing their identity. Thanks to personal Web sites and other publicly available information, the Internet can provide all that is needed to charge purchases to someone else's credit cards and to transfer funds out of their bank accounts.

- **Taxation:** In international trade, goods tend to be subject to tariffs, whereas services are not. The Internet is making this distinction difficult. For example, a compact disc (CD) sent from one country to another is a good and thus incurs a tariff as it crosses a border. But what if the music on the CD is sent electronically from a computer in one country to a computer in another country? Because customized data and software, which can also be put on a CD, are usually treated as services, is the music a good or a service?[65]

- **Public interest:** Because most societies have some sort of restrictions on children's access to pornography, should pornographic Web sites also be restricted? If so, by whom? Given that government is often expected to protect its citizens from fraudulent investment schemes and from quack medical treatments, what should it do when these things are offered on the Internet? Governments could impose trade restrictions requiring that financial firms selling on the Internet to residents of a country must also have an office in that country. See the ▨ **Internet Issue** feature for examples of governmental attempts to regulate the Internet.

In addition, the Internet is providing a fast way to communicate a company's mistakes and any unethical or illegal actions to interested people throughout the world. This is making it increasingly difficult for companies undertaking questionable activities to keep things quiet while they cover up the problem with public relations campaigns. Fueled by passion and technical expertise, activists of all kinds have launched sophisticated Web sites that attack individual companies regarding their environmental or labor practices and other issues. For example, the Web site www.corporatewatch.org.uk is operated by Corporate Watch and contains articles on the risks of genetic modification of plants, with case studies targeting leading biotech companies. Interestingly, some companies are beginning to respond by upgrading their Web sites to reflect their shift to a more open dialogue with a wide range of stakeholders. In response to Greenpeace's Shareholders Against New Exploration (SANE) campaign, BP Amoco has added links to environmental information and to its animated explanation of its solar energy research.[66]

Internet Issue

Governments Act to Protect Society by Regulating the Internet

November 20, 2000, a French court ordered Yahoo! to find some way of banning French users from seeing the Nazi memorabilia posted on its U.S. Web sites or face a daily fine of FF100,000 ($13,000). Although Yahoo! appealed the court's decision, it stopped listing sales of Nazi memorabilia on any of its Web sites. France is not alone in regulating the Internet. Myanmar (formerly known as Burma) bans access to the Internet. South Korea outlawed access to gambling Web sites. The United States passed a law requiring schools and libraries that received federal funds for Internet connections to install software on their computers to block material deemed harmful to children. Under a new European Union (EU) law, European consumers can now sue EU-based Internet sites in their own countries. There is some pressure to extend the rule internationally. The United States has endorsed the Council of Europe's cyber-crime treaty, which aims to harmonize international laws against hacking, Internet fraud, and child pornography.

Two tools that can be used to "protect" Internet users are filtering and Internet Protocol (IP) address identification software. Filtering software can be installed on a computer, on an Internet provider's servers, or on gateways that link one country with another. This software acts to block access to certain Web sites. China, for example, has installed this software nationwide to block access to Internet sites that have unwanted content. China has also passed laws requiring Internet companies to apply for licenses and for them to be held accountable for illegal content carried on their Web sites. Web sites can also block users by tracking an Internet server's IP address, the number that identifies computers on the Internet and often reveals where a user is located. A controversial version of IP, called IP/6, was designed by the Internet Engineering Task Force (IETF) to expand the IP address to include the unique serial number of each computer's network connection software. Every data packet would thus contain a user's electronic "fingerprints."

Source: "Stop Signs on the Web," *The Economist* (January 13, 2001), pp. 21–25.

Projections for the 21st Century

- From 1994 to 2010, the world population will grow from 5.607 billion to 7.32 billion.
- From 1994 to 2010, the number of nations will increase from 192 to 202.[67]

Discussion Questions

1. Does a corporation really need a board of directors?
2. What recommendations would you make to improve the effectiveness of today's boards of directors?
3. What is the relationship between corporate governance and social responsibility?
4. What is your opinion of Reebok's production standards of human rights for its suppliers? What would Milton Friedman say? Contrast his view with Archie Carroll's view.
5. Does a company have to act selflessly to be considered socially responsible? For example, when building a new plant, a corporation voluntarily invested in additional equipment that enabled it to reduce its pollution emissions beyond the requirements of any current laws. Knowing that it would be very expensive for its competitors to do the same, the firm lobbied the government to make pollution regulations more restrictive on the entire industry. Is this company socially responsible? Were its managers acting ethically?

Strategic Practice Exercise

How far should people in a business firm go in gathering competitive intelligence? Where do you draw the line?

Evaluate each of the following approaches that a business firm could use to gather information about competition. For each approach, mark your feeling about its appropriateness: 1 (definitely not appropriate), 2 (probably not appropriate), 3 (undecided), 4 (probably appropriate), or 5 (definitely appropriate).

The business firm should try to get useful information about competitors by:

_____ Carefully studying trade journals.

_____ Wiretapping the telephones of competitors.

_____ Posing as a potential customer to competitors.

_____ Getting loyal customers to put out a phony "request for proposal" to solicit competitors' bids.

_____ Buying competitors' products and taking them apart.

_____ Hiring management consultants who have worked for competitors.

_____ Rewarding competitors' employees for useful "tips."

_____ Questioning competitors' customers and/or suppliers.

_____ Buying and analyzing competitors' garbage.

_____ Advertising and interviewing for nonexistent jobs.

_____ Taking public tours of competitors' facilities.

_____ Releasing false information about the company in order to confuse competitors.

_____ Questioning competitors' technical people at trade shows and conferences.

_____ Hiring key people away from competitors.

_____ Analyzing competitors' labor union contracts.

_____ Having employees date persons who work for competitors.

_____ Studying aerial photographs of competitors' facilities.

After you mark each of the preceding approaches, compare your responses to those of other people in your class. For each approach, the people marking **4** or **5** should say why they thought this particular act would be appropriate. Those who marked **1** or **2** should then state why they thought this act would be inappropriate.

What does this tell you about ethics and socially responsible behavior?

Source: Developed from W. A. Jones, Jr., and N. B. Bryan, Jr., "Business Ethics and Business Intelligence: An Empirical Study of Information-Gathering Alternatives," *International Journal of Management* (June 1995), pp. 204–208. For actual examples of some of these activities, see J. Kerstetter, P. Burrows, J. Greene, G. Smith, and M. Conlin, "The Dark Side of the Valley," *Business Week* (July 17, 2000), pp. 42–43.

Key Terms

affiliated directors (p. 31)
agency theory (p. 29)
board of directors continuum (p. 28)
board of directors responsibilities (p. 27)
categorical imperatives (p. 43)
codes of ethics (p. 42)
codetermination (p. 32)
corporate governance (p. 26)
corporate stakeholders (p. 39)
corporation (p. 26)
due care (p. 27)

ethics (p. 42)
executive leadership (p. 35)
family directors (p. 31)
individual rights approach (p. 43)
inside directors (p. 29)
interlocking directorate (p. 32)
justice approach (p. 43)
law (p. 42)
lead director (p. 34)
levels of moral development (p. 42)
moral relativism (p. 41)
morality (p. 42)
outside directors (p. 29)

responsibilities of business (p. 37)
retired directors (p. 31)
role of the board of directors in strategic management (p. 27)
social responsibility (p. 37)
staggered board (p. 33)
stewardship theory (p. 29)
strategic planning staff (p. 37)
strategic vision (p. 35)
top management responsibilities (p. 35)
trends in governance (p. 34)
utilitarian approach (p. 43)

Notes

1. N. Byrnes and W. C. Symonds, "Is the Avalanche Headed for PriceWaterhouse?" *Business Week* (October 14, 2002), pp. 45–46; W. C. Symonds, "Tyco: How Did They Miss a Scam So Big?" *Business Week* (September 30, 2002), pp. 40–42; H. R. Weber, "Questions Arise About Board Reviewing Tyco's Finances," *The (Ames, IA) Tribune* (July 6, 2002), p. C8; N. Varchaver, "The Big Kozlowski," *Fortune* (November 18, 2002), pp. 123–126; H. R. Weber, "The King Is Gone," *Des Moines Register* (September 18, 2002), p. D1; "Tyco Settles," *Des Moines Register* (October 24, 2002), p. 3D.
2. A. G. Monks and N. Minow, *Corporate Governance* (Cambridge, MA: Blackwell Business, 1995), pp. 8–32.
3. Ibid., p. 1.
4. W. Symonds, "Tyco: The Vise Grows Ever-Tighter," *Business Week* (October 7, 2002), pp. 48–49.
5. A. Demb and F. F. Neubauer, "The Corporate Board: Confronting the Paradoxes," *Long Range Planning* (June 1992), p. 13. These results are supported by a 1995 Korn/Ferry International survey in which chairmen and directors agreed that strategy and management succession, in that order, are the most important issues the board expects to face.
6. L. Light, "Why Outside Directors Have Nightmares," *Business Week* (October 23, 1996), p. 6.
7. W. Q. Judge, Jr., and C. P. Zeithaml, "Institutional and Strategic Choice Perspectives on Board Involvement in the Strategic Choice Process," *Academy of Management Journal* (October 1992), 766–794; J. A. Pearce II and S. A. Zahra, "Effective Power-Sharing Between the Board of Directors and the CEO," *Handbook of Business Strategy*, 1992/93 Yearbook (Boston: Warren, Gorham, and Lamont, 1992), pp. 1.1–1.16.
8. *26th Annual Board of Directors Study*, Korn/Ferry International (1999), p. 7.
9. L. Lavelle, "The Best and Worst Boards," *Business Week* (October 7, 2002), pp. 104–114.
10. Statistics on boards of directors are taken from *26th Annual Board of Directors Survey* (New York: Korn/Ferry International, 1999) and *Directors' Compensation and Board Practices in 1999* (New York: Conference Board, 1999).

11. L. L. Carr, "Strategic Determinants of Executive Compensation in Small Publicly Traded Firms," *Journal of Small Business Management* (April 1997), pp. 1–12.
12. *26th Annual Board of Directors Study*, Korn/Ferry International (1999), p. 8.
13. S. Finkelstein and D. C. Hambrick, *Strategic Leadership: Top Executives and Their Impact on Organizations* (St. Paul, MN: West, 1996), p. 213.
14. R. A. G. Monks, "What Will Be the Impact of Acting Shareholders? A Practical Recipe for Constructive Change," *Long Range Planning* (February 1999), p. 20.
15. *26th Annual Board of Directors Study*, Korn/Ferry International (1999), pp. 11–12.
16. *Globalizing the Board of Directors: Trends and Strategies* (New York: The Conference Board, 1999).
17. For additional information on average board retainers, fees, and stock compensation, see *Directors' Compensation and Board Practices in 1999* (New York: The Conference Board, 1999).
18. R. W. Pouder and R. S. Cantrell, "Corporate Governance Reform: Influence on Shareholder Wealth," *Journal of Business Strategies* (Spring 1999), pp. 48–66.
19. M. L. Gerlach, "The Japanese Corporate Network: A Blockmodel Analysis," *Administrative Science Quarterly* (March 1992), pp. 105–139.
20. M. Warner, "Inside the Silicon Valley Money Machine," *Fortune* (October 26, 1998), pp. 128–140.
21. J. A. C. Baum and C. Oliver, "Institutional Linkages and Organizational Mortality," *Administrative Science Quarterly* (June 1991) pp. 187–218; J. P. Sheppard, "Strategy and Bankruptcy: An Exploration into Organizational Death," *Journal of Management* (Winter 1994), pp. 795–833.
22. *26th Annual Board of Directors Study* (New York: Korn/Ferry International, 1999), pp. 7–13.
23. *26th Annual Board of Directors Study* (New York: Korn/Ferry International, 1999), p. 30.
24. The Conference Board reports that although 21% of U.S. firms had outsiders as chairs, 12% had other employees as chair in 1999.

25. D. Harris and C. E. Helfat, "CEO Duality, Succession, Capabilities and Agency Theory: Commentary and Research Agenda," *Strategic Management Journal* (September 1998), pp. 901–904; C. M. Daily and D. R. Dalton, "CEO and Board Chair Roles Held Jointly or Separately: Much Ado About Nothing," *Academy of Management Executive* (August 1997), pp. 11–20; D. L. Worrell, C. Nemec, and W. N. Davidson III, "One Hat Too Many: Key Executive Plurality and Shareholder Wealth," *Strategic Management Journal* (June 1997), pp. 499–507; J. W. Coles and W. S. Hesterly, "Independence of the Chairman and Board Composition: Firm Choices and Shareholder Value," *Journal of Management*, Vol. 26, No. 2 (2000), pp. 195–214.

26. M. Lipton and J. W. Lorsch, "The Lead Director," *Directors & Boards* (Spring 1993), pp. 28–31.

27. The Korn/Ferry and Conference Board reports for 1999 provide different figures regarding combined CEO/Chair positions and lead directors. For example, the Conference Board reported that only 4% of firms had lead directors when the Chairman is also CEO. Korn/Ferry stated that 91% of the firms had a combined CEO/Chair position.

28. D. R. Dalton, C. M. Daily, A. E. Ellstrand, and J. L. Johnson, "Meta-Analytic Reviews of Board Composition, Leadership Structure, and Financial Performance," *Strategic Management Journal* (March 1998), pp. 269–290; G. Beaver, "Competitive Advantage and Corporate Governance—Shop Soiled and Needing Attention!" *Strategic Change* (September–October 1999), p. 330.

29. For governance trends in Europe, see A. Cadbury, "What Are the Trends in Corporate Governance? How Will They Impact Your Company?" *Long Range Planning* (February 1999), pp. 12–19.

30. J. S. Lublin, "Texaco Case Causes a Stir in Boardrooms," *Wall Street Journal* (November 22, 1996), p. B1.

31. S. Finkelstein and D. C. Hambrick, *Strategic Leadership: Top Executives and Their Impact on Organizations* (St. Louis: West, 1996).

32. D. C. Hambrick, T. S. Cho, and M-J Chen, "The Influence of Top Management Team Heterogeneity on Firms' Competitive Moves," *Administrative Science Quarterly* (December 1996), pp. 659–684.

33. N. Tichy and R. Charan, "Speed, Simplicity, Self-Confidence: An Interview with Jack Welch," *Harvard Business Review* (September–October 1989), p. 113.

34. M. Lipton, "Demystifying the Development of an Organizational Vision," *Sloan Management Review* (Summer 1996), p. 84.

35. J. H. David, F. D. Schoorman, R. Mayer, and H. H. Tan, "The Trusted General Manager and Business Unit Performance: Empirical Evidence of a Competitive Advantage," *Strategic Management Journal* (May 2000), pp. 563–576.

36. R. X. Cringely, "The Best CEOs," *Worth* (May 2000), p. 128.

37. M-S. Chae and J. S. Hill, "The Hazards of Strategic Planning for Global Markets," *Long Range Planning* (December 1996), pp. 880–891.

38. T. R. Eisenmann and J. L. Bower, "The Entrepreneurial M-Form: Strategic Integration in Global Media Firms," *Organization Science* (May–June 2000), pp. 348–355.

39. For an in-depth guide to conducting the strategic planning process, see C. D. Fogg, *Team-Based Strategic Planning* (New York: AMACOM, 1994).

40. M. Friedman, "The Social Responsibility of Business Is to Increase Its Profits," *New York Times Magazine* (September 13, 1970), pp. 30, 126–127; M. Friedman, *Capitalism and Freedom* (Chicago: University of Chicago Press, 1963), p. 133.

41. A. B. Carroll, "A Three-Dimensional Conceptual Model of Corporate Performance," *Academy of Management Review* (October 1979), pp. 497–505.

42. Carroll refers to discretionary responsibilities as philanthropic responsibilities in A. B. Carroll, "The Pyramid of Corporate Social Responsibility: Toward the Moral Management of Organizational Stakeholders," *Business Horizons* (July–August 1991), pp. 39–48.

43. M. S. Baucus and D. A. Baucus, "Paying the Piper: An Empirical Examination of Longer-Term Financial Consequences of Illegal Corporate Behavior," *Academy of Management Journal* (February 1997), pp. 129–151.

44. A. McWilliams and D. Siegel, "Corporate Social Responsibility and Financial Performance: Correlation or Misspecification?" *Strategic Management Journal* (May 2000), pp. 603–609; P. Rechner and K. Roth, "Social Responsibility and Financial Performance: A Structural Equation Methodology," *International Journal of Management* (December 1990), pp. 382–391; K. E. Aupperle, A. B. Carroll, and J. D. Hatfield, "An Empirical Examination of the Relationship Between Corporate Social Responsibility and Profitability," *Academy of Management Journal* (June 1985), p. 459.

45. S. A. Waddock and S. B. Graves, "The Corporate Social Performance–Financial Performance Link," *Strategic Management Journal* (April 1997), pp. 303–319; M. V. Russo and P. A. Fouts, "Resource-Based Perspective on Corporate Environmental Performance and Profitability," *Academy of Management Journal* (June 1997), pp. 534–559; H. Meyer, "The Greening of Corporate America," *Journal of Business Strategy* (January/February 2000), pp. 38–43.

46. C. L. Harman and E. R. Stafford, "Green Alliances: Building New Business with Environmental Groups" *Long Range Planning* (April 1997), pp. 184–196.

47. D. B. Turner and D. W. Greening, "Corporate Social Performance and Organizational Attractiveness to Prospective Employees," *Academy of Management Journal* (July 1997), pp. 658–672; S. Preece, C. Fleisher, and J. Toccacelli, "Building a Reputation Along the Value Chain at Levi Strauss," *Long Range Planning* (December 1995), pp. 88–98; J. B. Barney and M. H. Hansen, "Trustworthiness As a Source of Competitive Advantage," *Strategic Management Journal* (Special Winter Issue, 1994), pp. 175–190.

48. R. E. Freeman and D. R. Gilbert, *Corporate Strategy and the Search for Ethics* (Upper Saddle River, NJ: Prentice Hall, 1988), p. 6.

49. M. Arndt, W. Zellner, and P. Coy, "Too Much Corporate Power?" *Business Week* (September 11, 2000), pp. 144–158.

50. "Nearly Half of Workers Take Unethical Actions—Survey," *Des Moines Register* (April 7, 1997), p. 18B.

51. K. Kumar, "Ethical Orientation of Future American Executives: What the Value Profiles of Business School Students Portend," *SAM Advanced Management Journal* (Autumn 1995), pp. 32–36, 47; M. Gable and P. Arlow, "A Comparative Examination of the Value Orientations of British and American Executives," *International Journal of Management* (September 1986), pp. 97–106; W. D. Guth and R. Tagiuri, "Personal Values and Corporate Strategy," *Harvard Business Review* (September–October 1965), pp. 126–127; G. W. England, "Managers and Their Value Systems: A Five Country Comparative Study," *Columbia Journal of World Business* (Summer 1978), p. 35.

52. L. K. Trevino, "Ethical Decision Making in Organizations: A Person-Situation Interactionist Model," *Academy of Management Review* (July 1986), pp. 601–617.

53. L. Kohlberg, "Moral Stage and Moralization: The Cognitive-Development Approach," in *Moral Development and Behavior*, edited by T. Lickona (New York: Holt, Rinehart & Winston, 1976).

54. Trevino, p. 606.

55. J. Keogh, ed., *Corporate Ethics: A Prime Business Asset* (New York: The Business Roundtable, 1988), p. 5.

56. G. F. Kohut and S. E. Corriher, "The Relationship of Age, Gender, Experience and Awareness of Written Ethics Policies to Business Decision Making," *SAM Advanced Management Journal* (Winter 1994), pp. 32–39.

57. "Reebok Finds Bad Conditions in Two Factories," *Des Moines Register* (October 19, 1999), p. 8S.

58. T. J. Von der Embse and R. A. Wagley, "Managerial Ethics: Hard Decisions on Soft Criteria," *SAM Advanced Management Journal* (Winter 1988), p. 6.

59. G. F. Cavanagh, *American Business Values*, 3rd ed. (Upper Saddle River, NJ: Prentice Hall, 1990), pp. 186–199.

60. B. R. Agle, R. K. Mitchell, and J. A. Sonnenfeld, "Who Matters Most to CEOs? An Investigation of Stakeholder Attributes and Salience, Corporate Performance, and CEO Values," *Academy of Management Journal* (October 1999), pp. 507–525.

61. G. F. Cavanagh, pp. 195–196.

62. I. Kant, "The Foundations of the Metaphysic of Morals," in *Ethical Theory: Classical and Contemporary Readings*, 2nd ed., by L. P. Pojman (Belmont, CA: Wadsworth Publishing, 1995), pp. 255–279.

63. M. Coker, "Russia's Stealth Monitoring of Web Traffic," The (Ames, IA) *Daily Tribune* (September 11, 2000), p. C8.

64. M. France, "The Net: How to Head Off Big-Time Regulation," *Business Week* (May 10, 1999), p. 89.

65. "The Wired Trade Organization." *The Economist: Survey of World Trade* (October 3, 1998), p. 16.

66. S. Berkeley, "Web Attack," *Harvard Business Review* (September–October 2000), p. 20.

67. J. Warner, "21st Century Capitalism: Snapshot of the Next Century," *Business Week* (November 18, 1994), p. 194.

PART ENDING VIDEO CASE   PART ONE

ON LOCATION

Newbury Comics, Inc.

STRATEGY BASICS

Newbury Comics was founded in 1978 by MIT roommates, Mike Dreese and John Brusger. With $2,000 and a comic book collection they converted a Newbury Street studio apartment in Boston's trendy Back Bay into the second organized comic book shop in the area. In 1979, Newbury Comics began selling punk and new wave music and quickly became the region's leading specialist in alternative music. By 1982, with a second store open in Harvard Square, the company's revenues were being generated mostly from cutting-edge music and rock-related merchandise.

Newbury Comics consists of 22 stores spanning the New England region and is known to be the place to shop for everything from the best of the underground/independent scene to major label superstars. The chain also stocks a wide variety of non-music related items such as T-shirts, Dr. (doc) Martens shoes, posters, jewelry, cosmetics, books, magazines, and other trendy items.

The video features Cofounders Mike Dreese and John Brusger, as well as Jan Johannet, Manager of one of the New Hampshire stores, talking about the entrepreneurial beginning of Newbury Comics. They point out that the company wants its customers and its employees to "have a good time" in the store. Newbury Comics hires good people who like working in the store. The company attracts creative people because it is different from other retailers. Mike Dreese thinks of the company as expanding out of a comic book retailer into a lifestyle store emphasizing popular culture. He wants Newbury Comics to dominate its product categories and to be the retailer customers seek out in order to obtain what they want. He refers to an expression used throughout the company: "If you can't dominate it, don't do it." He wants the company to grow by looking for "incredible opportunities" (elephant hunting). This approach seems to work at Newbury Comics. The company sustained an annual growth rate of about 80% over the past 7 years resulting in 1000% overall growth.

With some input from others at corporate headquarters, Mike Dreese develops the overall plan for the company by looking at where he would like the company to be in 3, 5, or 10 years. He analyzes the external environment in terms of competition, trends, and customer preferences. John Brusger then puts Mike's plan into action. The company identifies product growth areas by conducting dozens of experiments each month to learn what the customer wants.

Concepts Illustrated in the Video

- The Learning Organization
- Theories of Organizational Adaptation
- Model of Strategic Management
- Modes of Strategic Decision Making
- Strategic Decision Making Process
- Executive Leadership
- Strategic Vision

Study Questions

1. How is Newbury Comics an example of a learning organization?
2. What is the process of strategic management at Newbury Comics? Who is involved in each part?
3. What do you think might be the company's (a) current mission/vision, (b) objectives, (c) strategies, and (d) policies? Give an example of each from the video.
4. What theory of organizational adaptation is being followed by Mike Dreese?
5. Newbury Comics illustrates what mode of strategic decision making? Is it appropriate?

chapter 3

Environmental Scanning and Industry Analysis

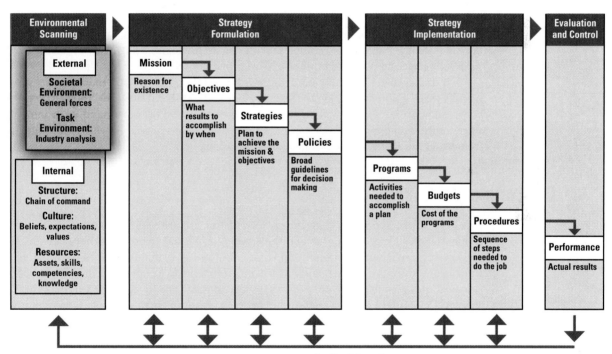

Feedback/Learning

Chefs Unlimited was founded by Dodd and Michelle Aldred of Raleigh, North Carolina. As husband and wife veterans of the restaurant industry, they knew how difficult it was to work long hours and still allow time to prepare home-cooked meals. That was one reason why people were spending more at restaurants. (The percentage of food dollars spent away from home had increased from 36% in 1980 to 44% by the mid-1990s.) The Aldreds felt that many people were beginning to tire of eating out and would be willing to pay for a quality meal eaten in their own home. They offered people the opportunity to order entrees for either a one- or two-week period. Doing their own cooking in a 3,000 square foot commercial kitchen, the Aldreds delivered meals to customers for subsequent reheating. Although more expensive, these meals were of higher quality than the typical frozen dinner. In just four years Chefs Unlimited was so successful catering to modern families that the Aldreds were planning to air express their meals to a nationwide audience the next year. Meanwhile, the U.S. Personal Chef Association was predicting a five-fold increase in the number of personal chef entrepreneurs in the United States and Canada.[1]

Pioneering companies have gone out of business because of their failure to adapt to environmental change or, even worse, by failing to create change. For example, Baldwin Locomotive, the major manufacturer of steam locomotives, was very slow in making the switch to diesel locomotives. General Electric and General Motors soon dominated the diesel locomotive business. The dominant manufacturers of vacuum tubes failed to make the change to transistors and consequently lost this market. Failure to adapt is, however, only one side of the coin. The aforementioned Chefs Unlimited example shows how a changing environment can create new opportunities at the same time it destroys old ones. The lesson is simple: To be successful over time, an organization needs to be in tune with its external environment. There must be a strategic fit between what the environment wants and what the corporation has to offer, as well as between what the corporation needs and what the environment can provide.

Current predictions are that the environment for all organizations will become even more uncertain with every passing year. What is **environmental uncertainty**? It is the *degree of complexity* plus the *degree of change* existing in an organization's external environment. As more and more markets become global, the number of factors a company must consider in any decision become huge—more complex. With new technologies being discovered every year, markets change and products must change with them.

On the one hand, environmental uncertainty is a threat to strategic managers because it hampers their ability to develop long-range plans and to make strategic decisions to keep the corporation in equilibrium with its external environment. On the other hand, environmental uncertainty is an opportunity because it creates a new playing field in which creativity and innovation can have a major part in strategic decisions.

3.1 Environmental Scanning

Before an organization can begin strategy formulation, it must scan the external environment to identify possible opportunities and threats and its internal environment for strengths and weaknesses. **Environmental scanning** is the monitoring, evaluating, and disseminating of information from the external and internal environments to key people within the corporation. A corporation uses this tool to avoid strategic surprise and to ensure its long-term health. Research has found a positive relationship between environmental scanning and profits.[2]

IDENTIFYING EXTERNAL ENVIRONMENTAL VARIABLES

In undertaking environmental scanning, strategic managers must first be aware of the many variables within a corporation's societal and task environments. The **societal environment** includes general forces that do not directly touch on the short-run activities of the organization but that can, and often do, influence its long-run decisions. These, shown in **Figure 1–3**, are as follows:

- **Economic** forces that regulate the exchange of materials, money, energy, and information
- **Technological** forces that generate problem-solving inventions
- **Political-legal** forces that allocate power and provide constraining and protecting laws and regulations
- **Sociocultural** forces that regulate the values, mores, and customs of society

The **task environment** includes those elements or groups that directly affect the corporation and, in turn, are affected by it. These are governments, local communities, suppliers, competitors, customers, creditors, employees/labor unions, special-interest groups, and trade associations. A corporation's task environment is typically the industry within which that firm operates. **Industry analysis** refers to an in-depth examination of key factors within a corporation's task environment. Both the societal and task environments must be monitored to detect the strategic factors that are likely to have a strong impact on corporate success or failure.

Scanning the Societal Environment

The number of possible strategic factors in the societal environment is very high. The number becomes enormous when we realize that, generally speaking, each country in the world can be represented by its own unique set of societal forces—some of which are very similar to neighboring countries and some of which are very different.

For example, even though Korea and China share Asia's Pacific Rim area with Thailand, Taiwan, and Hong Kong (sharing many similar cultural values), they have very different views about the role of business in society. It is generally believed in Korea and China (and to a lesser extent in Japan) that the role of business is primarily to contribute to national development; whereas in Hong Kong, Taiwan, and Thailand (and to a lesser extent in the Philippines, Indonesia, Singapore, and Malaysia), the role of business is primarily to make profits for the shareholders.[3] Such differences may translate into different trade regulations and varying difficulty in the **repatriation of profits** (transferring profits from a foreign subsidiary to a corporation's headquarters) from one group of Pacific Rim countries to another.

Monitoring Societal Trends   As noted in **Table 3–1**, large corporations categorize the societal environment in any one geographic region into four areas and focus their scanning in each area on trends with corporatewide relevance. Obviously trends in any 1 area may be very important to the firms in one industry but of lesser importance to firms in other industries.

Table 3–1   **Some Important Variables in the Societal Environment**

Economic	Technological	Political-Legal	Sociocultural
GDP trends	Total government spending for R&D	Antitrust regulations	Lifestyle changes
Interest rates	Total industry spending for R&D	Environmental protection laws	Career expectations
Money supply	Focus of technological efforts	Tax laws	Consumer activism
Inflation rates	Patent protection	Special incentives	Rate of family formation
Unemployment levels	New products	Foreign trade regulations	Growth rate of population
Wage/price controls	New developments in technology transfer from lab to marketplace	Attitudes toward foreign companies	Age distribution of population
Devaluation/revaluation	Productivity improvements through automation	Laws on hiring and promotion	Regional shifts in population
Energy availability and cost	Internet availability	Stability of government	Life expectancies
Disposable and discretionary income	Telecommunication infrastructure		Birth rates

Trends in the *economic* part of the societal environment can have an obvious impact on business activity. For example, an increase in interest rates means fewer sales of major home appliances. Why? A rising interest rate tends to be reflected in higher mortgage rates. Because higher mortgage rates increase the cost of buying a house, the demand for new and used houses tends to fall. Because most major home appliances are sold when people change houses, a reduction in house sales soon translates into a decline in sales of refrigerators, stoves, and dishwashers and reduced profits for everyone in that industry.

Changes in the *technological* part of the societal environment can also have a great impact on multiple industries. For example, improvements in computer microprocessors have not only led to the widespread use of home computers, but also to better automobile engine performance in terms of power and fuel economy through the use of microprocessors to monitor fuel injection. Researchers at George Washington University have identified a number of breakthrough developments in technology, which they forecast will have a significant impact during the decade from 2000 to 2010:

- **Portable Information Devices and Electronic Networking:** Combining the computing power of the personal computer, the networking of the Internet, the images of the television, and the convenience of the telephone, these appliances will soon be used by over 30% of the population of industrialized nations to make phone calls, send e-mail, and transmit data and documents. Even now, homes, autos, and offices are being connected (via wires and wireless) into intelligent networks that interact with one another. The traditional stand-alone desktop computer may soon join the manual typewriter as a historical curiosity.

- **Fuel Cells and Alternative Energy Sources:** The use of wind, geothermal, hydroelectric, solar, biomass, and other alternative energy sources should increase from their present level of 10% to about 30% by the end of the decade. Once used exclusively to power spacecraft, fuel cells offer the prospect of pollution-free electrical power. Fuel cells chemically combine hydrogen and oxygen to produce electricity with water as a byproduct. Although it will take a number of years before fuel cells replace gas-powered engines or vast power generation plants, this technology is already providing an alternate source of power for large buildings.

- **Precision Farming:** The computerized management of crops to suit variations in land characteristics will make farming more efficient. Farm equipment dealers, such as Case and Deere, add this equipment to tractors for an additional $6,000. It enables farmers to reduce costs, increase yields, and decrease environmental impact. The old system of small, low-tech farming will become less viable as large corporate farms are able to increase crop yields on limited farmland for a growing population.

- **Virtual Personal Assistants:** Very smart computer programs that monitor e-mail, faxes, and phone calls will be able to take over routine tasks, such as writing a letter, retrieving a file, making a phone call, or screening requests. Acting like a secretary, a person's virtual assistant (VA) could substitute for a person at meetings or in dealing with routine actions.

- **Genetically Altered Organisms:** A convergence of biotechnology and agriculture is creating a new field of life sciences. Plant seeds can be genetically modified to produce more needed vitamins or to be less attractive to pests and more able to survive. Animals (and people) could be similarly modified for desirable characteristics and to eliminate genetic disabilities and diseases.

- **Smart, Mobile Robots:** Robot development has been limited by a lack of sensory devices and sophisticated artificial intelligence systems. Improvements in these areas mean that robots will be performing more sophisticated factory work, run errands, do household chores, and assist the handicapped.[4]

Trends in the *political-legal* part of the societal environment have a significant impact not only on the level of competition within an industry, but also on which strategies might be successful.[5] For example, periods of strict enforcement of U.S. antitrust laws directly affect corporate growth strategy. As large companies find it more difficult to acquire another firm in the same or in a related industry, they are typically driven to diversify into unrelated industries.[6] In Europe, the formation of the European Union has led to an increase in merger activity across national boundaries.

Demographic trends are part of the *sociocultural* aspect of the societal environment. The demographic bulge in the U.S. population caused by the "baby boom" in the 1950s strongly affects market demand in many industries. For example, between 1995 and 2005, an average of 4,400 Americans turns 50 every day. This over-50 age group has become the fastest growing age group in all developed countries. Companies with an eye on the future can find many opportunities offering products and services to the growing number of "woofies" (well-off old folks)—defined as people over 50 with money to spend.[7] These people are very likely to purchase recreational vehicles, take ocean cruises, and enjoy leisure sports such as boating, fishing, and bowling, in addition to needing financial services and health care.

This trend can mean increasing sales for firms like Winnebago (RVs), Carnival Cruise Lines, and Brunswick (sports equipment), among others. To attract older customers, retailers will need to place seats in their larger stores so aging shoppers can rest. Washrooms need to be more accessible. Signs need to be larger. Restaurants need to raise the level of lighting so people can read their menus. Home appliances need simpler and larger controls. Already, the market for road bikes is declining as sales for tread mills and massagers for aching muscles increase.

Seven sociocultural trends in the United States that are helping to define what North America and the world will soon look like are:

1. **Increasing environmental awareness:** Recycling and conservation are becoming more than slogans. Busch Gardens, for example, eliminated the use of disposable styrofoam trays in favor of washing and reusing plastic trays.

2. **Growth of the seniors market:** As their numbers increase, people over age 55 will become an even more important market. Already some companies are segmenting the senior population into Young Matures, Older Matures, and the Elderly—each having a different set of attitudes and interests.

3. **Impact of Generation Y boomlet:** Born after 1980 to the boomer and X generations, this cohort may end up being as large as the boomer generation. In 1957, the peak year of the postwar boom, 4.3 million babies were born. In 1990, there were 4.2 million births. By the mid-1990s, elementary schools were becoming overcrowded.[8] As a result, both Republican and Democratic candidates in the 2000 presidential election made "education" a primary issue. The U.S. census bureau projects Generation Y to crest at 30.8 million births by 2005. Expect this cohort to have a strong impact on future products and services.

4. **Decline of the mass market:** Niche markets are beginning to define the marketers' environment. People want products and services that are adapted more to their personal needs. For example, Estee Lauder's "All Skin" and Maybelline's "Shades of You" lines of cosmetic products are specifically made for African American women. "Mass customization"—the making and marketing of products tailored to a person's requirements (e.g., Dell and Gateway Computers)—is replacing the mass production and marketing of the same product in some markets.

5. **Changing pace and location of life:** Instant communication via fax machines, cell phones, and overnight mail enhances efficiency, but it also puts more pressure on people.

Merging the personal computer with the communication and entertainment industry through telephone lines, satellite dishes, and cable television increases consumers' choices and allows workers to leave overcrowded urban areas for small towns and "telecommute" via personal computers and modems.

6. **Changing household composition:** Single-person households could become the most common household type in the United States after the year 2005. By 2005, only households composed of married couples with no children will be larger.[9] Although the Y generation baby boomlet may alter this estimate, a household clearly is no longer the same as it was once portrayed in *The Brady Bunch* in the 1970s or even *The Cosby Show* in the 1980s.

7. **Increasing diversity of workforce and markets:** Minority groups are increasing as a percentage of the total U.S. population. From 1996 to 2050, group percentages are expected by the U.S. Census Bureau to change as follows: whites—from 83% to 75%; African Americans—from 13% to 15%; Asian—from 4% to 9%; American Indian—slight increase. Hispanics, who can be of any race, are projected to grow from 10% to 25% during this time period.[10] Traditional minority groups are increasing their numbers in the workforce and are being identified as desirable target markets. For example, the South Dekalb Mall in Atlanta, Georgia, restyled itself as an "Afrocentric retail center" in response to the rapid growth of the African American 18-to-34 age group.[11]

International Societal Considerations

Each country or group of countries in which a company operates presents a whole new societal environment with a different set of economic, technological, political-legal, and sociocultural variables for the company to face. International societal environments vary so widely that a corporation's internal environment and strategic management process must be very flexible. Cultural trends in Germany, for example, have resulted in the inclusion of worker representatives in corporate strategic planning. Differences in societal environments strongly affect the ways in which a **multinational corporation (MNC)**, a company with significant assets and activities in multiple countries, conducts its marketing, financial, manufacturing, and other functional activities. For example, the existence of regional associations like the European Union, the North American Free Trade Zone, and Mercosur in South America has a significant impact on the competitive "rules of the game" both for those MNCs operating within and for those MNCs wanting to enter these areas.

To account for the many differences among societal environments from one country to another, consider **Table 3–2**. It includes a list of economic, technological, political-legal, and sociocultural variables for any particular country or region. For example, an important economic variable for any firm investing in a foreign country is currency convertibility. Without convertibility, a company operating in Russia cannot convert its profits from rubles to dollars. In terms of sociocultural variables, many Asian cultures (especially China) are less concerned with the value of human rights than are European and North American cultures. Some Asians actually contend that American companies are trying to impose Western human rights requirements on them in an attempt to make Asian products less competitive by raising their costs.[12]

Before planning its strategy for a particular international location, a company must scan the particular country environment(s) in question for opportunities and threats, and compare these with its own organizational strengths and weaknesses. For example, to operate successfully in a global industry such as automobiles, tires, electronics, or watches, a company must be prepared to establish a significant presence in the three developed areas of the world known collectively as the **Triad**. This term was coined by the Japanese management expert, Kenichi Ohmae, and it refers to the three developed markets of Japan, North America, and Western Europe, which now form a single market with common needs.[13] Focusing on the Triad is

Table 3–2   Some Important Variables in *International* Societal Environments

Economic	Technological	Political-Legal	Sociocultural
Economic development	Regulations on technology transfer	Form of government	Customs, norms, values
Per capita income	Energy availability/cost	Political ideology	Language
Climate	Natural resource availability	Tax laws	Demographics
GDP trends	Transportation network	Stability of government	Life expectancies
Monetary and fiscal policies	Skill level of work force	Government attitude toward foreign companies	Social institutions
Unemployment level	Patent-trademark protection		Status symbols
Currency convertibility	Internet availability	Regulations on foreign ownership of assets	Lifestyle
Wage levels	Telecommunication infrastructure		Religious beliefs
Nature of competition		Strength of opposition groups	Attitudes toward foreigners
Membership in regional economic associations		Trade regulations	Literacy level
		Protectionist sentiment	Human rights
		Foreign policies	Environmentalism
		Terrorist activity	
		Legal system	

essential for an MNC pursuing success in a global industry, according to Ohmae, because close to 90% of all high–value-added, high-technology manufactured goods are produced and consumed in North America, Western Europe, and Japan. Ideally a company should have a significant presence in each of these regions so that it can develop, produce, and market its products simultaneously in all three areas. Otherwise, it will lose competitive advantage to Triad-oriented MNCs. No longer can an MNC develop and market a new product in one part of the world before it exports it to other developed countries.

Focusing only on the developed nations, however, causes a corporation to miss important market opportunities in the developing nations of the world. Although these nations may not have developed to the point that they have significant demand for a broad spectrum of products, they may very likely be on the threshold of rapid growth in the demand for specific products. This would be the ideal time for a company to enter this market—before competition is established. The key is to be able to identify the "trigger point" when demand for a particular product or service is ready to boom. See the 🌐 **Global Issue** feature for an in-depth explanation of a technique to identify the optimum time to enter a particular market in a developing nation.

Scanning the Task Environment

As shown in **Figure 3–1**, a corporation's scanning of the environment will include analyses of all the relevant elements in the task environment. These analyses take the form of individual reports written by various people in different parts of the firm. At Procter & Gamble (P&G), for example, people from each of the brand management teams work with key people from the sales and market research departments to research and write a "competitive activity report" each quarter on each of the product categories in which P&G competes. People in purchasing also write similar reports concerning new developments in the industries that supply P&G. These and other reports are then summarized and transmitted up the corporate hierarchy for top management to use in strategic decision making. If a new development is reported regarding a particular product category, top management may then send memos asking peo-

Global Issue

Identifying Potential Markets in Developing Nations

Research by the Deloitte & Touche Consulting Group reveals that the demand for a specific product increases exponentially at certain points in a country's development. Identifying this trigger point of demand is thus critical to entering emerging markets at the best time. A **trigger point** is the time when enough people have enough money to buy what a company has to sell, but before competition is established. This can be done by using the concept of **purchasing power parity (PPP)**, which measures the cost in dollars of the U.S.–produced equivalent volume of goods that an economy produces.

PPP offers an estimate of the material wealth a nation can purchase, rather than the financial wealth it creates as typically measured by Gross Domestic Product (GDP). As a result, restating a nation's GDP in PPP terms reveals much greater spending power than market exchange rates would suggest. For example, a shoe shine costing $5 to $10 in New York City can be purchased for 50¢ in Mexico City. Consequently the

people of Mexico City can enjoy the same standard of living (with respect to shoe shines) as people in New York City with only 5% to 10% of the money. Correcting for PPP restates all Mexican shoe shines at their U.S. purchase value of $5. If one million shoe shines were purchased in Mexico last year, using the PPP model would effectively increase Mexican GDP by $5 million to $10 million. Using PPP, China becomes the world's second largest economy after the United States, with Brazil, Mexico, and India moving ahead of Canada into the top 10 world markets.

Trigger points identify when demand for a particular product is about to rapidly increase in a country. This can be a very useful technique to identify when to enter a new market in a developing nation. Trigger points vary for different products. For example, an apparent trigger point for long-distance telephone services is at $7,500 in GDP per capita—a point when demand for telecommunications services increases rapidly. Once national wealth surpasses $15,000 per capita, demand increases at a much slower rate with further increases in wealth. The trigger point for life insurance is around $8,000 in GDP per capita. At this point, the demand for life insurance increases between 200% and 300% above those countries with GDP per capita below the trigger point.

Source: Summarized from D. Fraser and M. Raynor, "The Power of Parity," *Forecast* (May/June, 1996), pp. 8–12.

Figure 3–1
Scanning the External Environment

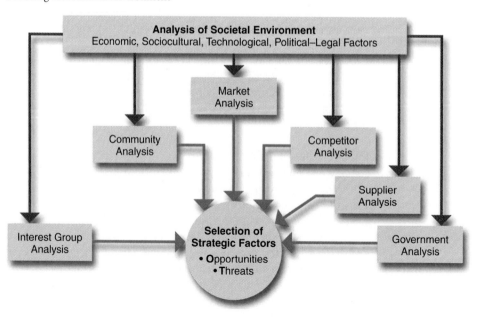

ple throughout the organization to watch for and report on developments in related product areas. The many reports resulting from these scanning efforts, when boiled down to their essentials, act as a detailed list of external strategic factors.

IDENTIFYING EXTERNAL STRATEGIC FACTORS

Why do companies often respond differently to the same environmental changes? One reason is because of differences in the ability of managers to recognize and understand external strategic issues and factors. No firm can successfully monitor all external factors. Choices must be made regarding which factors are important and which are not. Even though managers agree that strategic importance determines what variables are consistently tracked, they sometimes miss or choose to ignore crucial new developments.[14] Personal values and functional experiences of a corporation's managers as well as the success of current strategies are likely to bias both their perception of what is important to monitor in the external environment and their interpretations of what they perceive.[15]

This willingness to reject unfamiliar as well as negative information is called **strategic myopia**.[16] If a firm needs to change its strategy, it might not be gathering the appropriate external information to change strategies successfully.

One way to identify and analyze developments in the external environment is to use the **issues priority matrix (Figure 3–2)** as follows:

1. Identify a number of likely trends emerging in the societal and task environments. These are strategic environmental issues—those important trends that, if they occur, determine what the industry or the world will look like in the near future.

2. Assess the probability of these trends actually occurring from low to high.

3. Attempt to ascertain the likely impact (from low to high) of each of these trends on the corporation being examined.

Figure 3–2
Issues Priority Matrix

Probable Impact on Corporation

	High	Medium	Low
High	High Priority	High Priority	Medium Priority
Medium	High Priority	Medium Priority	Low Priority
Low	Medium Priority	Low Priority	Low Priority

Probability of Occurrence

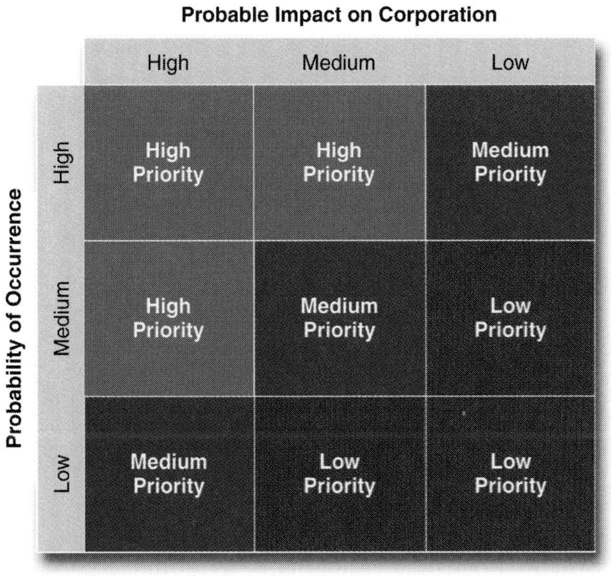

Source: Reprinted from L. L. Lederman, "Foresight Activities in the U.S.A.: Time for a Re-Assessment?" *Long-Range Planning* (June 1984), p. 46. Copyright © 1984. Reprinted with permission from Elsevier Science.

A corporation's **external strategic factors** are those key environmental trends that are judged to have both a medium to high probability of occurrence and a medium to high probability of impact on the corporation. The issues priority matrix can then be used to help managers decide which environmental trends should be merely scanned (low priority) and which should be monitored as strategic factors (high priority). Those environmental trends judged to be a corporation's strategic factors are then categorized as opportunities and threats and are included in strategy formulation.

3.2 Industry Analysis: Analyzing the Task Environment

An **industry** is a group of firms producing a similar product or service, such as soft drinks or financial services. An examination of the important stakeholder groups, such as suppliers and customers, in a particular corporation's task environment is a part of industry analysis.

PORTER'S APPROACH TO INDUSTRY ANALYSIS

Michael Porter, an authority on competitive strategy, contends that a corporation is most concerned with the intensity of competition within its industry. The level of this intensity is determined by basic competitive forces, which are depicted in **Figure 3–3**. "The collective strength of these forces," he contends, "determines the ultimate profit potential in the industry, where profit potential is measured in terms of long-run return on invested capital."[17] In carefully scanning its industry, the corporation must assess the importance to its success of each of the six forces: threat of new entrants, rivalry among existing firms, threat of substitute products or services, bargaining power of buyers, bargaining power of suppliers, and relative power of other stakeholders.[18] The stronger each of these forces, the more limited companies are in their ability to raise prices and earn greater profits. Although Porter mentions only five forces, a sixth—other stakeholders—is added here to reflect the power that governments, local communities, and other groups from the task environment wield over industry activities.

Using the model in **Figure 3–3**, a high force can be regarded as a threat because it is likely to reduce profits. A low force, in contrast, can be viewed as an opportunity because it may allow the company to earn greater profits. In the short run, these forces act as constraints on a company's activities. In the long run, however, it may be possible for a company, through its choice of strategy, to change the strength of one or more of the forces to the company's advantage. For example, in order to pressure its customers (PC makers) to purchase more of Intel's latest microprocessors for use in their PCs, Intel supported the development of sophisticated software needing increasingly larger amounts of processing power. In the mid-1990s Intel began selling 3D graphics chips—not because it wanted to be in that business, but because 3D chips needed large amounts of processing power (provided of course by Intel). Intel also introduced software that made it easier for network administrators to manage PCs on their networks, which Intel believed would help sell more PCs and neutralize a threat from network computers.[19]

A strategist can analyze any industry by rating each competitive force as **high**, **medium**, or **low** in strength. For example, the athletic shoe industry could be currently rated as follows: rivalry is high (Nike, Reebok, Adidas, and Converse are strong competitors worldwide); threat of potential entrants is low (industry has reached maturity; sales growth rate has slowed); threat of substitutes is low (other shoes don't provide support for sports activities); bargaining power of suppliers is medium but rising (suppliers in Asian countries are increasing in size and ability); bargaining power of buyers is medium, but increasing (athletic shoes are dropping in popularity as brown shoes gain); threat of other stakeholders is medium to high (government regulations and human rights concerns are growing). Based on current trends in each of these competitive forces, the industry appears to be increasing in its level of competitive intensity, meaning profit margins will be falling for the industry as a whole.

Figure 3–3
Forces Driving Industry Competition

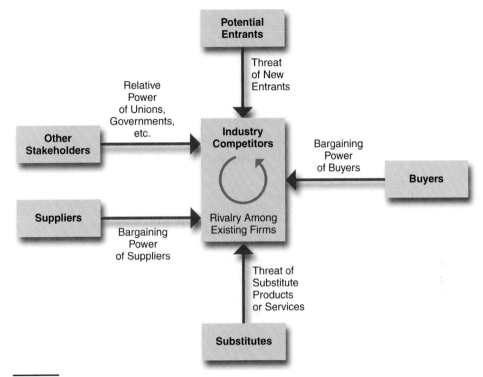

Source: Adapted with permission of The Free Press, a Division of Simon & Schuster, from *Competitive Strategy: Techniques for Analyzing Industries and Competitors* by Michael E. Porter. Copyright © 1980, 1988 by The Free Press.

Threat of New Entrants

New entrants to an industry typically bring to it new capacity, a desire to gain market share, and substantial resources. They are, therefore, threats to an established corporation. The threat of entry depends on the presence of entry barriers and the reaction that can be expected from existing competitors. An **entry barrier** is an obstruction that makes it difficult for a company to enter an industry. For example, no new domestic automobile companies have been successfully established in the United States since the 1930s because of the high capital requirements to build production facilities and to develop a dealer distribution network. Some of the possible barriers to entry are:

- **Economies of Scale:** Scale economies in the production and sale of microprocessors, for example, gave Intel a significant cost advantage over any new rival.

- **Product Differentiation:** Corporations like Procter & Gamble and General Mills, which manufacture products like Tide and Cheerios, create high entry barriers through their high levels of advertising and promotion.

- **Capital Requirements:** The need to invest huge financial resources in manufacturing facilities in order to produce large commercial airplanes creates a significant barrier to entry to any competitor for Boeing and Airbus.

- **Switching Costs:** Once a software program like Excel or Word becomes established in an office, office managers are very reluctant to switch to a new program because of the high training costs.

- **Access to Distribution Channels:** Small entrepreneurs often have difficulty obtaining supermarket shelf space for their goods because large retailers charge for space on their shelves and give priority to the established firms who can pay for the advertising needed to generate high customer demand.

- **Cost Disadvantages Independent of Size:** Once a new product earns sufficient market share to be accepted as the *standard* for that type of product, the maker has a key advantage. Microsoft's development of the first widely adopted operating system (MS-DOS) for the IBM-type personal computer gave it a significant competitive advantage over potential competitors. Its introduction of Windows helped to cement that advantage so that the Microsoft operating system is now on over 90% of personal computers worldwide.

- **Government Policy:** Governments can limit entry into an industry through licensing requirements by restricting access to raw materials, such as oil-drilling sites in protected areas.

Rivalry Among Existing Firms

In most industries, corporations are mutually dependent. A competitive move by one firm can be expected to have a noticeable effect on its competitors and thus may cause retaliation or counterefforts. For example, the entry by mail order companies such as Dell and Gateway into a PC industry previously dominated by IBM, Apple, and Compaq increased the level of competitive activity to such an extent that any price reduction or new product introduction is now quickly followed by similar moves from other PC makers. The same is true of prices in the U.S. airline industry. According to Porter, intense rivalry is related to the presence of several factors, including:

- **Number of Competitors:** When competitors are few and roughly equal in size, such as in the U.S. auto and major home appliance industries, they watch each other carefully to make sure that any move by another firm is matched by an equal countermove.

- **Rate of Industry Growth:** Any slowing in passenger traffic tends to set off price wars in the airline industry because the only path to growth is to take sales away from a competitor.

- **Product or Service Characteristics:** Many people choose a videotape rental store based on location, variety of selection, and pricing because they view videotapes as a commodity—a product whose characteristics are the same regardless of who sells it.

- **Amount of Fixed Costs:** Because airlines must fly their planes on a schedule regardless of the number of paying passengers for any one flight, they offer cheap standby fares whenever a plane has empty seats.

- **Capacity:** If the only way a manufacturer can increase capacity is in a large increment by building a new plant (as in the paper industry), it will run that new plant at full capacity to keep its unit costs as low as possible—thus producing so much that the selling price falls throughout the industry.

- **Height of Exit Barriers: Exit barriers** keep a company from leaving an industry. The brewing industry, for example, has a low percentage of companies that voluntarily leave the industry because breweries are specialized assets with few uses except for making beer.

- **Diversity of Rivals:** Rivals that have very different ideas of how to compete are likely to cross paths often and unknowingly challenge each other's position. This happens often in the retail clothing industry when a number of retailers open outlets in the same location—thus taking sales away from each other.

Threat of Substitute Products or Services

Substitute products are those products that appear to be different but can satisfy the same need as another product. For example, fax machines are a substitute for FedEx, Nutrasweet is a substitute for sugar, and bottled water is a substitute for a cola. According to Porter,

CHAPTER THREE   ENVIRONMENTAL SCANNING AND INDUSTRY ANALYSIS   **63**

"Substitutes limit the potential returns of an industry by placing a ceiling on the prices firms in the industry can profitably charge."[20] To the extent that switching costs are low, substitutes may have a strong effect on an industry. Tea can be considered a substitute for coffee. If the price of coffee goes up high enough, coffee drinkers will slowly begin switching to tea. The price of tea thus puts a price ceiling on the price of coffee. Identifying possible substitute products or services is sometimes a difficult task. It means searching for products or services that can perform the same function, even though they have a different appearance and may not appear to be easily substitutable.

Bargaining Power of Buyers

Buyers affect an industry through their ability to force down prices, bargain for higher quality or more services, and play competitors against each other. A buyer or a group of buyers is powerful if some of the following factors hold true:

- A buyer purchases a large proportion of the seller's product or service (for example, oil filters purchased by a major auto maker).
- A buyer has the potential to integrate backward by producing the product itself (for example, a newspaper chain could make its own paper).
- Alternative suppliers are plentiful because the product is standard or undifferentiated (for example, motorists can choose among many gas stations).
- Changing suppliers costs very little (for example, office supplies are easy to find).
- The purchased product represents a high percentage of a buyer's costs, thus providing an incentive to shop around for a lower price (for example, gasoline purchased for resale by convenience stores makes up half their total costs).
- A buyer earns low profits and is thus very sensitive to costs and service differences (for example, grocery stores have very small margins).
- The purchased product is unimportant to the final quality or price of a buyer's products or services and thus can be easily substituted without affecting the final product adversely (for example, electric wire bought for use in lamps).

Bargaining Power of Suppliers

Suppliers can affect an industry through their ability to raise prices or reduce the quality of purchased goods and services. A supplier or supplier group is powerful if some of the following factors apply:

- The supplier industry is dominated by a few companies, but it sells to many (for example, the petroleum industry).
- Its product or service is unique and/or it has built up switching costs (for example, word processing software).
- Substitutes are not readily available (for example, electricity).
- Suppliers are able to integrate forward and compete directly with their present customers (for example, a microprocessor producer like Intel can make PCs).
- A purchasing industry buys only a small portion of the supplier group's goods and services and is thus unimportant to the supplier (for example, sales of lawn mower tires are less important to the tire industry than are sales of auto tires).

Relative Power of Other Stakeholders

A sixth force should be added to Porter's list to include a variety of stakeholder groups from the task environment. Some of these groups are governments (if not explicitly included elsewhere), local communities, creditors (if not included with suppliers), trade associations, special-interest groups, unions (if not included with suppliers), shareholders, and complementors. According to Andy Grove, ex-CEO of Intel, a **complementor** is a company (e.g., Microsoft) or an industry whose product works well with another industry's or a firm's (e.g., Intel's) product and without which the product would lose much of its value.[21] Another example is the tire and automobile industries.

The importance of these stakeholders varies by industry. For example, environmental groups in Maine, Michigan, Oregon, and Iowa successfully fought to pass bills outlawing disposable bottles and cans, and thus deposits for most drink containers are now required. This effectively raised costs across the board, with the most impact on the marginal producers who could not internally absorb all of these costs. The traditionally strong power of national unions in the U.S. auto and railroad industries has effectively raised costs throughout these industries but are of little importance in computer software.

INDUSTRY EVOLUTION

Over time most industries evolve through a series of stages from growth through maturity to eventual decline. The strength of each of the six forces mentioned earlier varies according to the stage of industry evolution. The industry life cycle is useful for explaining and predicting trends among the six forces driving industry competition. For example, when an industry is new, people often buy the product regardless of price because it fulfills a unique need. This is probably a **fragmented industry**—no firm has large market share and each firm serves only a small piece of the total market in competition with others (for example, Chinese restaurants and cleaning services). As new competitors enter the industry, prices drop as a result of competition. Companies use the experience curve (to be discussed in Chapter 4) and economies of scale to reduce costs faster than the competition. Companies integrate to reduce costs even further by acquiring their suppliers and distributors. Competitors try to differentiate their products from one another's in order to avoid the fierce price competition common to a maturing industry.

By the time an industry enters maturity, products tend to become more like commodities. This is now a **consolidated industry**—dominated by a few large firms, each of which struggles to differentiate its products from the competition. As buyers become more sophisticated over time, purchasing decisions are based on better information. Price becomes a dominant concern, given a minimum level of quality and features. One example of this trend is the videocassette recorder industry. By the 1990s, VCRs had reached the point where there were few major differences among them. Consumers realized that because slight improvements cost significantly more money, it made little sense to pay more than the minimum for a VCR. The same is true of gasoline.

As an industry moves through maturity toward possible decline, its products' growth rate of sales slows and may even begin to decrease. To the extent that exit barriers are low, firms will begin converting their facilities to alternate uses or will sell them to another firm. The industry tends to consolidate around fewer but larger competitors. In the case of the U.S. major home appliance industry, the industry changed from being a fragmented industry (pure competition) composed of hundreds of appliance manufacturers in the industry's early years to a consolidated industry (mature oligopoly) composed of five companies controlling over 98% of U.S. appliance sales. A similar consolidation is occurring now in European major home appliances.

CATEGORIZING INTERNATIONAL INDUSTRIES

According to Porter, world industries vary on a continuum from multidomestic to global (see **Figure 3–4**).[22] **Multidomestic industries** are specific to each country or group of countries. This type of international industry is a collection of essentially domestic industries, like retail-

Figure 3–4

Continuum of International Industries

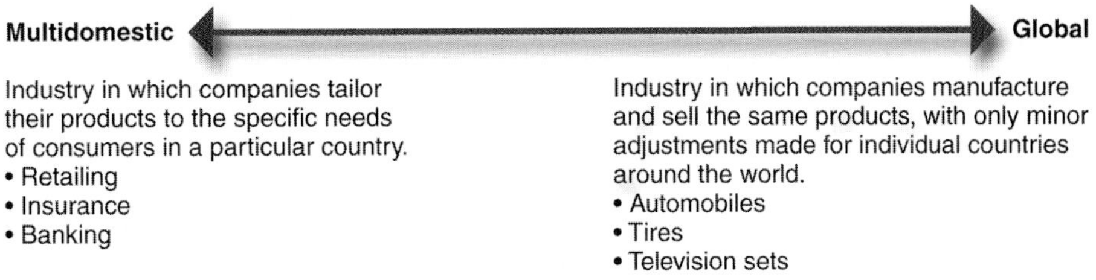

Multidomestic ◄──────────────────────────────────► **Global**

Industry in which companies tailor their products to the specific needs of consumers in a particular country.	Industry in which companies manufacture and sell the same products, with only minor adjustments made for individual countries around the world.
• Retailing	• Automobiles
• Insurance	• Tires
• Banking	• Television sets

ing and insurance. The activities in a subsidiary of a multinational corporation (MNC) in this type of industry are essentially independent of the activities of the MNC's subsidiaries in other countries. Within each country, it has a manufacturing facility to produce goods for sale within that country. The MNC is thus able to tailor its products or services to the very specific needs of consumers in a particular country or group of countries having similar societal environments.

Global industries, in contrast, operate worldwide, with MNCs making only small adjustments for country-specific circumstances. A global industry is one in which an MNC's activities in one country are significantly affected by its activities in other countries. MNCs produce products or services in various locations throughout the world and sell them, making only minor adjustments for specific country requirements. Examples of global industries are commercial aircraft, television sets, semiconductors, copiers, automobiles, watches, and tires. The largest industrial corporations in the world in terms of dollar sales are, for the most part, multinational corporations operating in global industries.

The factors that tend to determine whether an industry will be primarily multidomestic or primarily global are:

1. *Pressure for coordination* within the multinational corporations operating in that industry

2. *Pressure for local responsiveness* on the part of individual country markets

To the extent that the pressure for coordination is strong and the pressure for local responsiveness is weak for multinational corporations within a particular industry, that industry will tend to become global. In contrast, when the pressure for local responsiveness is strong and the pressure for coordination is weak for multinational corporations in an industry, that industry will tend to be multidomestic. Between these two extremes lie a number of industries with varying characteristics of both multidomestic and global industries. The dynamic tension between these two factors is contained in the phrase: *Think globally, but act locally.*

INTERNATIONAL RISK ASSESSMENT

Some firms, such as American Can Company and Mitsubishi Trading Company, develop elaborate information networks and computerized systems to evaluate and rank investment risks. Small companies can hire outside consultants such as Chicago's Associated Consultants International or Boston's Arthur D. Little, Inc., to provide political-risk assessments. Among the many systems that exist to assess political and economic risks are the Political System Stability Index, the Business Environment Risk Index, Business International's Country Assessment Service, and Frost and Sullivan's World Political Risk Forecasts.[23] Business International provides subscribers with continuously updated information on conditions in 63 countries. A Boston company called International Strategies offers an Export Hotline (800 USA-XPORT) that faxes information to callers for only the cost of the call. (Contact

⟨ExportHotline.com⟩ for a free membership.) Regardless of the source of data, a firm must develop its own method of assessing risk. It must decide on its most important risk factors and then assign weights to each.

STRATEGIC GROUPS

A **strategic group** is a set of business units or firms that "pursue similar strategies with similar resources."[24] Categorizing firms in any one industry into a set of strategic groups is very useful as a way of better understanding the competitive environment.[25] Because a corporation's structure and culture tend to reflect the kinds of strategies it follows, companies or business units belonging to a particular strategic group within the same industry tend to be strong rivals and tend to be more similar to each other than to competitors in other strategic groups within the same industry.

For example, although McDonald's and Olive Garden are a part of the same restaurant industry, they have different missions, objectives, and strategies, and thus belong to different strategic groups. They generally have very little in common and pay little attention to each other when planning competitive actions. Burger King and Hardee's, however, have a great deal in common with McDonald's in terms of their similar strategy of producing a high volume of low-priced meals targeted for sale to the average family. Consequently they are strong rivals and are organized to operate similarly.

Strategic groups in a particular industry can be mapped by plotting the market positions of industry competitors on a two-dimensional graph using two strategic variables as the vertical and horizontal axes. (See **Figure 3–5**.)

1. Select two broad characteristics, such as price and menu, that differentiate the companies in an industry from one another.

2. Plot the firms using these two characteristics as the dimensions.

3. Draw a circle around those companies that are closest to one another as one strategic group, varying the size of the circle in proportion to the group's share of total industry sales. (You could also name each strategic group in the restaurant industry with an identifying title, such as quick fast food or buffet style service.)

Other dimensions, such as quality, service, location, or degree of vertical integration, can also be used in additional graphs of the restaurant industry to gain a better understanding of how the various firms in the industry compete. Keep in mind, however, that when choosing the two dimensions, they should not be highly correlated; otherwise, the circles on the map will simply lie along the diagonal, providing very little new information other than the obvious.

STRATEGIC TYPES

In analyzing the level of competitive intensity within a particular industry or strategic group, it is useful to characterize the various competitors for predictive purposes. A **strategic type** is a category of firms based on a common strategic orientation and a combination of structure, culture, and processes consistent with that strategy. According to Miles and Snow, competing firms within a single industry can be categorized on the basis of their general strategic orientation into one of four basic types.[26] This distinction helps explain why companies facing similar situations behave differently and why they continue to do so over a long period of time. These general types have the following characteristics:

- **Defenders** are companies with a limited product line that *focus on improving the efficiency of their existing operations*. This cost orientation makes them unlikely to innovate in new areas.

Figure 3–5

Mapping Strategic Groups in the U.S. Restaurant Chain Industry

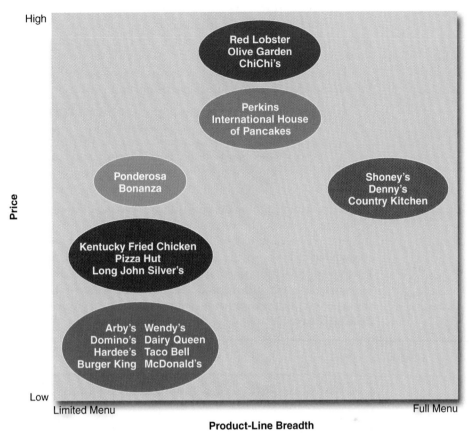

- **Prospectors** are companies with fairly broad product lines that *focus on product innovation and market opportunities*. This sales orientation makes them somewhat inefficient. They tend to emphasize creativity over efficiency.

- **Analyzers** are corporations that *operate in at least two different product–market areas*, one stable and one variable. In the stable areas, efficiency is emphasized. In the variable areas, innovation is emphasized.

- **Reactors** are corporations that *lack a consistent strategy–structure–culture relationship*. Their (often ineffective) responses to environmental pressures tend to be piecemeal strategic changes.

Dividing the competition into these four categories enables the strategic manager not only to monitor the effectiveness of certain strategic orientations, but also to develop scenarios of future industry developments (discussed later in this chapter).

HYPERCOMPETITION

Most industries today are facing an ever-increasing level of environmental uncertainty. They are becoming more complex and more dynamic. Industries that used to be multidomestic are becoming global. New flexible, aggressive, innovative competitors are moving into established markets to erode rapidly the advantages of large previously dominant firms. Distribution channels vary from country to country and are being altered daily through the use of sophisticated information systems. Closer relationships with suppliers are being forged to reduce costs, increase quality, and gain access to new technology. Companies learn to quickly imitate the successful strategies of market leaders, and it becomes harder to sustain any competitive advantage for very long. Consequently, the level of competitive intensity is increasing in most industries.

Richard D'Aveni contends that as this type of environmental turbulence reaches more industries, competition becomes **hypercompetition**. According to D'Aveni:

> In hypercompetition the frequency, boldness, and aggressiveness of dynamic movement by the players accelerates to create a condition of constant disequilibrium and change. Market stability is threatened by short product life cycles, short product design cycles, new technologies, frequent entry by unexpected outsiders, repositioning by incumbents, and tactical redefinitions of market boundaries as diverse industries merge. In other words, environments escalate toward higher and higher levels of uncertainty, dynamism, heterogeneity of the players and hostility.[27]

In hypercompetitive industries such as computers, competitive advantage comes from an up-to-date knowledge of environmental trends and competitive activity coupled with a willingness to risk a current advantage for a possible new advantage. Companies must be willing to **cannibalize** their own products (replacing popular products before competitors do so) in order to sustain their competitive advantage. As a result, industry or competitive intelligence has never been more important. See the boxed example to learn how Microsoft is operating in the hypercompetitive industry of computer software. (Hypercompetition is discussed in more detail in **Chapter 5**.)

Microsoft Operates in a Hypercompetitive Industry

Microsoft is a hypercompetitive firm operating in a hypercompetitive industry. It has used its dominance in operating systems (DOS and Windows) to move into a very strong position in application programs like word processing and spreadsheets (Word and Excel). Even though Microsoft held 90% of the market for personal computer operating systems in 1992, it still invested millions in developing the next generation—Windows 95 and Windows NT. Instead of trying to protect its advantage in the profitable DOS operating system, Microsoft actively sought to replace DOS with various versions of Windows. Before hypercompetition, most experts argued against *cannibalization* of a company's own product line because it destroys a very profitable product instead of harvesting it like a "cash cow." According to this line of thought, a company would be better off defending its older products. New products would be introduced only if it could be proven that they would not take sales away from current products. Microsoft was one of the first companies to disprove this argument against cannibalization.

Bill Gates, Microsoft's Cofounder, Chairman, and CEO, realized that if his company didn't replace its own DOS product line with a better product, someone else would (such as IBM with OS/2 Warp). He knew that success in the software industry depends not so much on company size but on moving aggressively to the next competitive advantage before a competitor does. "This is a hypercompetitive market," explained Gates. "Scale is not all positive in this business. Cleverness is the position in this business." By 2000, Microsoft still controlled over 90% of operating systems software and had achieved a dominant position in applications software as well.

Source: R. A. D'Aveni, *Hypercompetition* (New York: Free Press, 1994), p. 2.

Table 3–3   **Industry Matrix**

Key Success Factors	Weight	Company A Rating	Company A Weighted Score	Company B Rating	Company B Weighted Score
1	2	3	4	5	6
Total	1.00		=		=

Source: T. L. Wheelen and J. D. Hunger, "Industry Matrix." Copyright © 2001 by Wheelen and Hunger Associates. Reprinted by permission.

USING KEY SUCCESS FACTORS TO CREATE AN INDUSTRY MATRIX

Within any industry there usually are certain variables—key success factors—that a company's management must understand in order to be successful. **Key success factors** are those variables that can affect significantly the overall competitive positions of all companies within any particular industry. They typically vary from industry to industry and are crucial to determining a company's ability to succeed within that industry. They are usually determined by the economic and technological characteristics of the industry and by the competitive weapons on which the firms in the industry have built their strategies.[28] For example, in the major home appliance industry, a firm must achieve low costs, typically by building large manufacturing facilities dedicated to making multiple versions of one type of appliance, such as washing machines. Since 60% of major home appliances in the United States are sold through "power retailers" like Sears and Best Buy, a firm must have a strong presence in the mass merchandiser distribution channel. It must offer a full line of appliances and provide a just-in-time delivery system to keep store inventory and ordering costs to a minimum. Because the consumer expects reliability and durability in an appliance, a firm must have excellent process R&D. Any appliance manufacturer that is unable to deal successfully with these key success factors will not long survive in the U.S. market.

Key success factors are different from strategic factors. *Key success factors* deal with an entire industry; whereas, *strategic factors* deal with a particular company.

An **industry matrix** summarizes the key success factors within a particular industry. As shown in **Table 3–3**, the matrix gives a weight for each factor based on how important that factor is for success within the industry. The matrix also specifies how well various competitors in the industry are responding to each factor. To generate an industry matrix using two industry competitors (called A and B), complete the following steps for the industry being analyzed:

1. In **Column 1** (Key Success Factors) list the 8 to 10 factors that appear to determine current and expected success in the industry.

2. In **Column 2** (Weight) assign a weight to each factor from **1.0** (Most Important) to **0.0** (Not Important) based on that factor's probable impact on the overall industry's current and future success. (**All weights must sum to 1.0 regardless of the number of strategic factors.**)

3. In **Column 3** (Company A Rating) examine a particular company within the industry—for example, Company A. Assign a rating to each factor from **5.0** (Outstanding) to **1.0** (Poor) based on Company A's current response to that particular factor. Each rating is a judgment regarding how well that company is currently dealing with each key success factor.

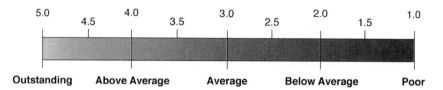

4. In **Column 4** (Company A Weighted Score) multiply the weight in **Column 2** for each factor times its rating in **Column 3** to obtain that factor's weighted score for Company A. This results in a weighted score for each key success factor ranging from **5.0** (Outstanding) to **1.0** (Poor) with **3.0** as the average.

5. In **Column 5** (Company B Rating) examine a second company within the industry—in this case, Company B. Assign a rating to each key success factor from **5.0** (Outstanding) to **1.0** (Poor) based on Company B's current response to each particular factor.

6. In **Column 6** (Company B Weighted Score) multiply the weight in **Column 2** for each factor times its rating in **Column 5** to obtain that factor's weighted score for Company B.

Finally, add the weighted scores for all the factors in **Columns 4** and **6** to determine the total weighted scores for companies A and B. The total weighted score indicates how well each company is responding to current and expected key success factors in the industry's environment. The industry matrix can be expanded to include all the major competitors within an industry simply by adding two additional columns for each additional competitor.

3.3 Competitive Intelligence

Much external environmental scanning is done on an informal and individual basis. Information is obtained from a variety of sources—suppliers, customers, industry publications, employees, industry experts, industry conferences, and the Internet.[29] For example, scientists and engineers working in a firm's R&D lab can learn about new products and competitors' ideas at professional meetings; someone from the purchasing department, speaking with supplier-representatives' personnel, may also uncover valuable bits of information about a competitor. A study of product innovation found that 77% of all product innovations in the scientific instruments and 67% in semiconductors and printed circuit boards were initiated by the customer in the form of inquiries and complaints.[30] In these industries, the sales force and service departments must be especially vigilant.

Competitive intelligence is a formal program of gathering information on a company's competitors. Until recently, few U.S. corporations had fully developed competitive intelligence programs. In contrast, all Japanese corporations involved in international business and most large European companies have active intelligence programs.[31] This situation is changing, however. Competitive intelligence is now one of the fastest growing fields within strategic management.[32] At General Mills, for example, all employees have been trained to recognize and tap sources of competitive information. Janitors no longer simply place orders with suppliers of cleaning materials, they also ask about relevant practices at competing firms! A recent survey of large U.S. corporations revealed that 78% of them reported competitive intelligence activities within their firm.[33]

Most corporations rely on outside organizations to provide them with environmental data. Firms such as A. C. Nielsen Co. provide subscribers with bimonthly data on brand share, retail prices, percentages of stores stocking an item, and percentages of stock-out stores. Strategists can use this data to spot regional and national trends as well as to assess market share. Information on market conditions, government regulations, competitors, and new products can be bought from "information brokers" such as Marketresearch.com and Finsbury Data Services. Company and industry profiles are generally available from the Hoover's Online site on the Internet ⟨www.hoovers.com⟩. Many business corporations have established their own in-house libraries and computerized information systems to deal with the growing mass of available information.

Some companies, however, choose to use industrial espionage or other intelligence-gathering techniques to get their information straight from their competitors. According to the American Society of Industrial Security, there were more than 1,100 documented incidents of illegal economic espionage in 1997 alone.[34] Using current or former competitors' employees and by using private contractors, some firms attempt to steal trade secrets, technology, business plans, and pricing strategies. For example, Avon Products hired private investigators to retrieve from a public dumpster documents (some of them shredded) that Mary Kay Corporation had thrown away. Even Procter & Gamble, which defends itself like a fortress from information leaks, is vulnerable. A competitor was able to learn the precise launch date of a concentrated laundry detergent in Europe when one of its people visited the factory where machinery was being made. Simply asking a few questions about what a certain machine did, whom it was for, and when it would be delivered was all that was necessary.

To combat the increasing theft of company secrets, the U.S. government passed the Economic Espionage Act in 1996. The law makes it illegal (with fines up to $5 million and 10 years in jail) to steal any material that a business has taken "reasonable efforts" to keep secret and if the material derives its value from not being known.[35] The Society of Competitive Intelligence Professionals ⟨www.scip.org⟩ urges strategists to stay within the law and to act ethically when searching for information. The society states that illegal activities are foolish because the vast majority of worthwhile competitive intelligence is available publicly via annual reports, Web sites, and public libraries.

3.4 Forecasting

Environmental scanning provides reasonably hard data on the present situation and current trends, but intuition and luck are needed to predict accurately if these trends will continue. The resulting forecasts are, however, usually based on a set of assumptions that may or may not be valid.

DANGER OF ASSUMPTIONS

Faulty underlying assumptions are the most frequent cause of forecasting errors. Nevertheless many managers who formulate and implement strategic plans rarely consider that their success is based on a series of assumptions. Many long-range plans are simply based on projections of the current situation.

One example of what can happen when a corporate strategy rests on the very questionable assumption that the future will simply be an extension of the present is that of Tupperware, the company that originated air-tight, easy-to-use plastic food storage containers. Much of the company's success had been based on Tupperware parties in the 1950s when housewives gathered in each other's homes to socialize and play games while the local Tupperware lady demonstrated and sold new products. Management assumed during the following decades that Tupperware parties would continue being an excellent distribution channel. Its faith in this assumption blinded it to information about America's changing lifestyle (two-career families) and its likely impact on sales. Even in the 1990s, when Tupperware executives realized that their sales forecasts were no longer justified, they were unable to improve their forecasting techniques until they changed their assumption that the best way to sell Tupperware was at a Tupperware party. Consequently, Rubbermaid and other competitors, who chose to market their containers in grocery and discount stores continued to grow at the expense of Tupperware.[36]

USEFUL FORECASTING TECHNIQUES

Various techniques are used to forecast future situations. Each has its proponents and critics. A study of nearly 500 of the world's largest corporations revealed trend **extrapolation** to be the most widely practiced form of forecasting—over 70% use this technique either occasionally or frequently.[37] Simply stated, extrapolation is the extension of present trends into the future. It rests on the assumption that the world is reasonably consistent and changes slowly in the short run. Time-series methods are approaches of this type; they attempt to carry a series of historical events forward into the future. The basic problem with extrapolation is that a historical trend is based on a series of patterns or relationships among so many different variables that a change in any one can drastically alter the future direction of the trend. As a rule of thumb, the further back into the past you can find relevant data supporting the trend, the more confidence you can have in the prediction.

Brainstorming, expert opinion, and statistical modeling are also very popular forecasting techniques. **Brainstorming** is a nonquantitative approach requiring simply the presence of people with some knowledge of the situation to be predicted. The basic ground rule is to propose ideas without first mentally screening them. No criticism is allowed. Ideas tend to build on previous ideas until a consensus is reached. This is a good technique to use with operating managers who have more faith in "gut feel" than in more quantitative "number crunching" techniques. **Expert opinion** is a nonquantitative technique in which experts in a particular area attempt to forecast likely developments. This type of forecast is based on the ability of a knowledgeable person(s) to construct probable future developments based on the interaction of key variables. One application is the **Delphi technique** in which separated experts independently assess the likelihoods of specified events. These assessments are combined and sent back to each expert for fine tuning until an agreement is reached. **Statistical modeling** is a quantitative technique that attempts to discover causal or at least explanatory factors that link two or more time series together. Examples of statistical modeling are regression analysis and other econometric methods. Although very useful for grasping historic trends, statistical modeling, like trend extrapolation, is based on historical data. As the patterns of relationships change, the accuracy of the forecast deteriorates. Other forecasting techniques, such as *cross-impact analysis (CIA)* and *trend-impact analysis (TIA)*, have not established themselves successfully as regularly employed tools.

Scenario writing appears to be the most widely used forecasting technique after trend extrapolation. Originated by Royal Dutch Shell, scenarios are focused descriptions of different likely futures presented in a narrative fashion. The scenario thus may be merely a written description of some future state, in terms of key variables and issues, or it may be generated in combination with other forecasting techniques.

An **industry scenario** is a forecasted description of a particular industry's likely future. Such a scenario is developed by analyzing the probable impact of future societal forces on key groups in a particular industry. The process may operate as follows.[38]

1. Examine possible shifts in the societal variables globally.
2. Identify uncertainties in each of the six forces of the task environment (for example, potential entrants, competitors, likely substitutes, buyers, suppliers, and other key stakeholders).

3. Make a range of plausible assumptions about future trends.

4. Combine assumptions about individual trends into internally consistent scenarios.

5. Analyze the industry situation that would prevail under each scenario.

6. Determine the sources of competitive advantage under each scenario.

7. Predict competitors' behavior under each scenario.

8. Select the scenarios that are either most likely to occur or most likely to have a strong impact on the future of the company. Use these scenarios in strategy formulation.

3.5 Synthesis of External Factors—EFAS

After strategic managers have scanned the societal and task environments and identified a number of likely external factors for their particular corporation, they may want to refine their analysis of these factors using a form such as that given in **Table 3–4**. The **EFAS** (**E**xternal **F**actors **A**nalysis **S**ummary) **Table** is one way to organize the external factors into the generally accepted categories of opportunities and threats as well as to analyze how well a particular company's management (rating) is responding to these specific factors in light of the perceived importance (weight) of these factors to the company. To generate an EFAS Table for the company being analyzed, complete the following steps:

- In **Column 1** (External Factors), list the 8 to 10 most important opportunities and threats facing the company.

- In **Column 2** (Weight), assign a weight to each factor from **1.0** (Most Important) to **0.0** (Not Important) based on that factor's probable impact on a particular company's current strategic position. The higher the weight, the more important is this factor to the current and future success of the company. (**All weights must sum to 1.0 regardless of the number of factors.**)

- In **Column 3** (Rating), assign a rating to each factor from **5.0** (Outstanding) to **1.0** (Poor) based on management's current response to that particular factor. Each rating is a judgment on how well the company's management is currently dealing with each specific external factor.

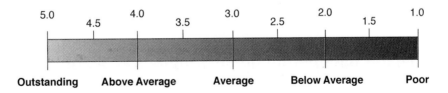

- In **Column 4** (Weighted Score), multiply the weight in **Column 2** for each factor times its rating in **Column 3** to obtain each factor's weighted score. This results in a weighted score for each factor ranging from **5.0** (Outstanding) to **1.0** (Poor) with **3.0** as average.

- In **Column 5** (Comments), note why a particular factor was selected and/or how its weight and rating were estimated.

Finally, add the individual weighted scores for all the external factors in **Column 4** to determine the total weighted score for that particular company. The total weighted **score** indicates how well a particular company is responding to current and expected factors in its external environment. The score can be used to compare that firm to other firms in its industry. The total weighted score for an average firm in an industry is always 3.0.

Table 3–4 External Factor Analysis Summary (EFAS Table): Maytag as Example

External Factors	Weight	Rating	Weighted Score	Comments
	1	2	3	4		5
Opportunities				
• Economic integration of European Community	.20	4.1	.82	Acquisition of Hoover
• Demographics favor quality appliances	.10	5.0	.50	Maytag quality
• Economic development of Asia	.05	1.0	.05	Low Maytag presence
• Opening of Eastern Europe	.05	2.0	.10	Will take time
• Trend to "Super Stores"	.10	1.8	.18	Maytag weak in this channel
Threats				
• Increasing government regulations	.10	4.3	.43	Well positioned
• Strong U.S. competition	.10	4.0	.40	Well positioned
• Whirlpool and Electrolux strong globally	.15	3.0	.45	Hoover weak globally
• New product advances	.05	1.2	.06	Questionable
• Japanese appliance companies	.10	1.6	.16	Only Asian presence is Australia
Total Scores	**1.00**		**3.15**	

Notes:
1. List opportunities and threats (8–10) in column 1.
2. Weight each factor from 1.0 (Most Important) to 0.0 (Not Important) in Column 2 based on that factor's probable impact on the company's strategic position. **The total weights must sum to 1.00**.
3. Rate each factor from 5.0 (Outstanding) to 1.0 (Poor) in Column 3 based on the company's response to that factor.
4. Multiply each factor's weight times its rating to obtain each factor's weighted score in Column 4.
5. Use Column 5 (comments) for rationale used for each factor.
6. Add the individual weighted scores to obtain the total weighted score for the company in Column 4. This tells how well the company is responding to the strategic factors in its external environment.

Source: T. L. Wheelen and J. D. Hunger, "External Factors Analysis Summary (EFAS)." Copyright © 1991 by Wheelen and Hunger Associates. Reprinted by permission.

As an example of this procedure, **Table 3–4** includes a number of external factors for Maytag Corporation with corresponding weights, ratings, and weighted scores provided. This table is appropriate for 1995 before Maytag sold its European and Australian operations. Note that Maytag's total weight is 3.15, meaning that the corporation was slightly above average in the major home appliance industry at that time.

3.6 Impact of the Internet on Environmental Scanning and Industry Analysis

The Internet has changed the way the strategist engages in environmental scanning. It provides the quickest means to obtain data on almost any subject. A recent joint study of 77 companies by the American Productivity & Quality Center and the Society of Competitive Intelligence Professionals reveals that 73% of the firms ranked the Internet as being used to a "great" or "very great" extent. Other mentioned sources of information were competitor offerings & products (66%), industry experts (62%), personal industry contacts (60%), online databases (56%), market research (55%), and the sales force (54%).[39] Although the scope and quality of Internet information is increasing geometrically, it is also littered with "noise," misinformation, and utter nonsense. For example, a number of corporate Web sites are sending unwanted guests to specially constructed bogus Web sites![40]

Unlike the library, the Internet lacks the tight bibliographic control standards that exist in the print world. There is no ISBN or Dewey Decimal System to identify, search, and retrieve a document. Many Web documents lack the name of the author and the date of publication. A Web page providing useful information may be accessible on the Web one day and gone the next! Unhappy ex-employees, far-out environmentalists, and prank-prone hackers create Web sites to attack and discredit an otherwise reputable corporation. Rumors with no basis in fact are spread via chat rooms and personal Web sites. This creates a serious problem for the researcher. How can one evaluate the information found on the Internet?

A basic rule in intelligence gathering is that before a piece of information can be used in any report or briefing, it must first be evaluated in two ways. *First, the source of the information should be judged in terms of its truthfulness and reliability.* How trustworthy is the source? How well can a researcher rely upon it for truthful and correct information? One approach is to rank the reliability of the source on a scale from A (extremely reliable), B (reliable), C (unknown reliability), D (probably unreliable), to E (very questionable reliability). The reliability of a source can be judged on the basis of the author's credentials, the organization sponsoring the information, and past performance, among other factors. *Second, the information or data should be judged in terms of its likelihood of being correct.* The correctness of the data may be ranked on a scale from 1 (correct), 2 (probably correct), 3 (unknown), 4 (doubtful), to 5 (extremely doubtful). The correctness of a piece of data or information can be judged on the basis of its agreement with other bits of separately obtained information or with a general trend supported by previous data. For every piece of information found on the Internet, list not only the Web address of the Web page, but also the evaluation of the information from A1 (good stuff) to E5 (bad doodoo). Information found through library research in sources such as *Moody's Industrials*, *Standard & Poor's*, or *Value Line* can generally be evaluated as having a reliability of A. The correctness of the data can still range anywhere from 1 to 5, but in most instances is likely to be either 1 or 2, but probably no worse than 3 or 4. Other sources may be less reliable.

Sites such as those sponsored by the U.S. Securities and Exchange Commission ⟨www.sec.gov⟩ or Hoovers Online ⟨www.hoovers.com⟩ are extremely reliable. Company sponsored Web sites are generally reliable but are not the place to go for trade secrets, strategic plans, or proprietary information. For one thing, many firms think of their Web sites primarily in terms of marketing, and they provide little data aside from product descriptions and distribution channels. Other companies provide their latest financial statements and links to other useful Web sites. Nevertheless, some companies in very competitive industries may install software on their Web site to ascertain a visitor's Web address. Visitors from a competitor's domain name are thus screened before they are allowed to access certain Web sites. They may not be allowed beyond the product information page or they may be sent to a bogus Web site containing misinformation. Cisco Systems, for example, uses its Web site to send visitors from other high-tech firms to a special Web page asking if they would like to apply for a job at Cisco!

Time searching the Internet can be saved by using search engines—Web sites that search the Internet for names and products typed in by the user. The search engines most used by competitive intelligence professionals are AltaVista (50%), Yahoo! (25%), and Lycos (15%). Others are WebCrawler (7.5%), Switchboard (7.5%), Infoseek (5%), and Metacrawler (5%).[41]

Although information about publicly held corporations is widely available, it is much harder to obtain information on privately held companies. For a comparison of the type of information generally available on publicly and privately held companies, see the Internet Issue feature for competitor information available on the Internet.

Internet Issue

Competitor Information Available on the Internet

Type of Information	Likelihood of Finding Data on the Net for Publicly Held Company	Likelihood of Finding Data on the Net for Privately Held Company
Total Annual Sales	Very high	Very low
Sales and Profitability by Product Line or Distribution Channel	Very low	Very low
Market Sizes in Segments of Interest	Depends on the market: High for large companies, low for small "niche" firms	Same as for publicly held
Trends in Marketing, Technology, Distribution	Same as above	Same as for publicly held
Prices, Including the Lowest Prices to Best Customers	Very low	Very low
Marketing Strategy	Some information available from trade articles and analyst reports, but incomplete and dated	Even less than for publicly held
Sales and Technical Literature on Products	Strong likelihood, but often incomplete; less chance for detailed technical information	Even less than for publicly held
Number of Employees Working on Certain Products or in Particular Departments	Highly unlikely	Highly unlikely
Compensation Levels	Top management generally available; others unlikely	Will not be found
Customer Opinions Regarding Strengths and Weaknesses	Available from trade articles and industry reports; at best, may be incomplete and dated	Less likely than for publicly held
Feedback on Firm's Own Products and Services	Will not be found; look for independent user chat rooms	Same as for publicly held

Source: Adapted from C. Klein, "Overcoming 'Net Disease,'" *Competitive Intelligence Magazine* (July–September 1999), p. 31.

Projections for the 21st Century

- From 1994 to 2010, the number of people living in poverty will increase from 3.7 billion to 3.9 billion.
- From 1994 to 2010, the average number of children per woman will decrease from 3.2 to 2.7.[42]

Discussion Questions

1. Discuss how a development in a corporation's societal environment can affect the corporation through its task environment.

2. According to Porter, what determines the level of competitive intensity in an industry?

3. According to Porter's discussion of industry analysis, is Pepsi-Cola a substitute for Coca-Cola?

4. How can a decision maker identify strategic factors in the corporation's external international environment?

5. Compare and contrast trend extrapolation with the writing of scenarios as forecasting techniques.

Strategic Practice Exercise

What are the forces driving industry competition in the airline industry? Read the following paragraphs. Using Porter's approach to industry analysis, evaluate each of the six forces to ascertain what drives the level of competitive intensity in this industry.

In recent years, the airline industry has become increasingly competitive. Since being deregulated during the 1970s in the United States, long established airlines such as Pan American and Eastern have gone out of business as new upstarts like Midwest Express and Southwest have successfully entered the market. It appeared that almost anyone could buy a few used planes to serve the smaller cities that the larger airlines no longer wanted to serve. These low-cost, small-capacity commuter planes were able to make healthy profits in these markets where it was too expensive to land large jets. Rail and bus transportation either did not exist or was undesirable in many locations. Eventually the low-cost local commuter airlines expanded service to major cities and grabbed market share from the majors by offering cheaper fares with no-frills service. In order to be competitive with these lower cost upstarts, United Airlines and Northwest Airlines offered stock in the company and seats on the Board of Directors to their unionized employees in exchange for wage and benefit reductions. Delta and American Airlines, among other major carriers, reduced their costs by instituting a cap on travel agent commissions. Travel agencies were livid at this cut in their livelihood, but they needed the airlines' business in order to offer customers a total travel package.

Globally it seemed as though every nation had to have its own airline for national prestige. These state-owned airlines were expensive, but the governments subsidized them with money and supporting regulations. For example, a foreign airline was normally allowed to fly only into one of a country's airports, forcing travelers to switch to the national airline to go to other cities. During the 1980s and 1990s, however, many countries began privatizing their airlines as governments tried to improve their budgets. To be viable in an increasingly global industry, national or regional airlines were forced to form alliances and even purchase an airline in another country or region. For example, the Dutch KLM Airline acquired half interest in the U.S Northwest Airlines in order to obtain not only U.S. destinations, but also Northwest's Asian travel routes, thus making it one of the few global airlines.

Costs were still relatively high for all of the world's major airlines because of the high cost of new airplanes. Just one new jet plane costs anywhere from $25 million to $100 million. By 2001, only two airplane manufacturers provided almost all of the large commercial airliners: Boeing and Airbus. Major airlines were forced to purchase new planes because they were more fuel efficient, safer, and easier to maintain. Airlines that chose to stay with an older fleet of planes had to deal with higher fuel and maintenance costs—factors that often made it cheaper to buy new planes.

1. Evaluate each of the forces currently driving competition in the airline industry:

Threat of New Entrants	High, Medium, or Low?	_____
Rivalry Among Existing Firms	High, Medium, or Low?	_____
Threat of Substitutes	High, Medium, or Low?	_____
Bargaining Power of Buyers/Distributors	High, Medium, or Low?	_____
Bargaining Power of Suppliers	High, Medium, or Low?	_____
Relative Power of Other Stakeholders	High, Medium, or Low?	_____
Such as_____		

2. Which of these forces is changing? What will this mean to the overall level of competitive intensity in the airline industry in the future? Would you invest or look for a job in this industry?

Key Terms

brainstorming (p. 72)
cannibalize (p. 68)
competitive intelligence (p. 70)
complementor (p. 64)
consolidated industry (p. 64)
Delphi technique (p. 72)
EFAS Table (p. 73)
entry barrier (p. 61)
environmental scanning (p. 52)
environmental uncertainty (p. 52)
exit barriers (p. 62)
expert opinion (p. 72)
external strategic factors (p. 60)
extrapolation (p. 72)

fragmented industry (p. 64)
global industry (p. 65)
hypercompetition (p. 68)
industry (p. 60)
industry analysis (p. 53)
industry matrix (p. 69)
industry scenario (p. 72)
issues priority matrix (p. 59)
key success factors (p. 69)
multidomestic industry (p. 64)
multinational corporation (MNC) (p. 56)
new entrants (p. 61)

purchasing power parity (PPP) (p. 58)
repatriation of profits (p. 53)
scenario writing (p. 72)
societal environment (p. 52)
statistical modeling (p. 72)
strategic group (p. 66)
strategic myopia (p. 59)
strategic type (p. 66)
substitute products (p. 62)
task environment (p. 53)
Triad (p. 56)
trigger point (p. 58)

Notes

1. D. Phillips, "Special Delivery," *Entrepreneur* (September 1996), pp. 98–100; B. Saporito, "What's for Dinner?" *Fortune* (May 15, 1995), pp. 50–64.
2. J. B. Thomas, S. M. Clark, and D. A. Gioia, "Strategic Sensemaking and Organizational Performance: Linkages Among Scanning, Interpretation, Action, Outcomes," *Academy of Management Journal* (April 1993), pp. 239–270; J. A. Smith, "Strategies for Start-Ups," *Long Range Planning* (December 1998), pp. 857–872.
3. P. Lasserre and J. Probert, "Competing on the Pacific Rim: High Risks and High Returns," *Long Range Planning* (April 1994), pp. 12–35.
4. W. E. Halal, "The Top 10 Emerging Technologies," *Special Report* (World Future Society, 2000).
5. F. Dobbin and T. J. Dowd, "How Policy Shapes Competition: Early Railroad Foundings in Massachusetts," *Administrative Science Quarterly* (September 1997), pp. 501–529.
6. A. Shleifer and R. W. Viskny, "Takeovers in the 1960s and the 1980s: Evidence and Implications," in *Fundamental Issues in Strategy: A Research Agenda*, edited by R. P. Rumelt, D. E. Schendel, and D. J. Teece (Boston: Harvard Business School Press, 1994), pp. 403–418.
7. J. Wyatt, "Playing the Woofie Card," *Fortune* (February 6, 1995), pp. 130–132.
8. J. Greco, "Meet Generation Y," *Forecast* (May/June, 1996), pp. 48–54; J. Fletcher, "A Generation Asks: 'Can the Boom Last?'" *Wall Street Journal* (June 14, 1996), p. B10.
9. "Alone in America," *Futurist* (September–October 1995), pp. 56–57.
10. "Population Growth Slowing as Nation Ages," (Ames, IA) *Daily Tribune* (March 14, 1996), p. A7.
11. L. M. Grossman, "After Demographic Shift, Atlanta Mall Restyles Itself as Black Shopping Center," *Wall Street Journal* (February 26, 1992), p. B1.
12. J. Naisbitt, *Megatrends Asia* (New York: Simon & Schuster, 1996), p. 79.
13. K. Ohmae, "The Triad World View," *Journal of Business Strategy* (Spring 1987), pp. 8–19.
14. B. K. Boyd and J. Fulk, "Executive Scanning and Perceived Uncertainty: A Multidimensional Model," *Journal of Management*, Vol. 22, No. 1 (1996), pp. 1–21.
15. R. A. Bettis and C. K. Prahalad, "The Dominant Logic: Retrospective and Extension," *Strategic Management Journal* (January 1995), pp. 5–14; J. M. Stofford and C. W. F. Baden-Fuller, "Creating Corporate Entrepreneurship," *Strategic Management Journal* (September 1994), pp. 521–536; J. M. Beyer, P. Chattopadhyay, E. George, W. H. Glick, D. Pugliese, "The Selective Perception of Managers Revisited," *Academy of Management Journal* (June 1997), pp. 716–737.
16. H. I. Ansoff, "Strategic Management in a Historical Perspective," in *International Review of Strategic Management*, Vol. 2, No. 1 (1991), edited by D. E. Hussey (Chichester, England: Wiley, 1991), p. 61.
17. M. E. Porter, *Competitive Strategy* (New York: Free Press, 1980), p. 3.
18. This summary of the forces driving competitive intensity is taken from Porter, *Competitive Strategy*, pp. 7–29.
19. P. N. Avakian, "Political Realities in Strategy," *Strategy & Leadership* (October, November, December 1999), pp. 42–48.
20. Porter, *Competitive Strategy*, p. 23.
21. A. S. Grove, "Surviving a 10x Force," *Strategy & Leadership* (January/February 1997), pp. 35–37.
22. M. E. Porter, "Changing Patterns of International Competition," *California Management Review* (Winter 1986), pp. 9–40.
23. T. N. Gladwin, "Assessing the Multinational Environment for Corporate Opportunity," in *Handbook of Business Strategy*, edited by W. D. Guth (Boston: Warren, Gorham and Lamont, 1985), pp. 7.28–7.41.
24. K. J. Hatten and M. L. Hatten, "Strategic Groups, Asymmetrical Mobility Barriers, and Contestability," *Strategic Management Journal* (July–August 1987), p. 329.
25. A. Fiegenbaum and H. Thomas, "Strategic Groups as Reference Groups: Theory, Modeling and Empirical Examination of Industry and Competitive Strategy," *Strategic Management Journal* (September 1995), pp. 461–476; H. R. Greve, "Managerial Cognition and the Mimetic Adoption of Market Positions: What You See Is What You Do," *Strategic Management Journal* (October 1998), pp. 967–988.
26. R. E. Miles and C. C. Snow, *Organizational Strategy, Structure, and Process* (New York: McGraw-Hill, 1978).
27. R. A. D'Aveni, *Hypercompetition* (New York: The Free Press, 1994), pp. xiii–xiv.

28. C. W. Hofer and D. Schendel, *Strategy Formulation: Analytical Concepts* (St. Paul, MN: West Publishing Co., 1978), p. 77.
29. "Information Overload," *Journal of Business Strategy* (January–February 1998), p. 4.
30. E. Von Hipple, *Sources of Innovation* (New York: Oxford University Press, 1988), p. 4.
31. L. Kahaner, *Competitive Intelligence* (New York: Simon & Schuster, 1996).
32. S. M. Shaker and M. P. Gembicki, *WarRoom Guide to Competitive Intelligence* (New York: McGraw-Hill, 1999), p. 10.
33. R. G. Vedder, "CEO and CIO Attitudes about Competitive Intelligence," *Competitive Intelligence Magazine* (October–December 1999), pp. 39–41.
34. S. M. Shaker and M. P. Gembicki, *WarRoom Guide to Competitive Intelligence* (New York: McGraw-Hill, 1999), p. 202.
35. B. Flora, "Ethical Business Intelligence Is NOT Mission Impossible," *Strategy & Leadership* (January/February 1998), pp. 40–41.
36. L. M. Grossman, "Families Have Changed But Tupperware Keeps Holding Its Parties," *Wall Street Journal* (July 21, 1992), pp. A1, A13.
37. H. E. Klein and R. E. Linneman, "Environmental Assessment: An International Study of Corporate Practices," *Journal of Business Strategy* (Summer 1984), p. 72.
38. This process of scenario development is adapted from M. E. Porter, *Competitive Advantage* (New York: Free Press, 1985), pp. 448–470.
39. S. H. Miller, "Developing a Successful CI Program: Preliminary Study Results," *Competitive Intelligence Magazine* (October–December 1999), p. 9.
40. S. H. Miller, "Beware Rival's Web Site Subterfuge," *Competitive Intelligence Magazine* (January–March 2000), p. 8.
41. S. M. Shaker and M. P. Gembicki, *WarRoom Guide to Competitive Intelligence* (New York: McGraw-Hill, 1999), pp. 113–115.
42. J. Warner, "21st Century Capitalism: Snapshot of the Next Century," *Business Week* (November 18, 1994), p. 194

chapter 4

Internal Scanning: Organizational Analysis

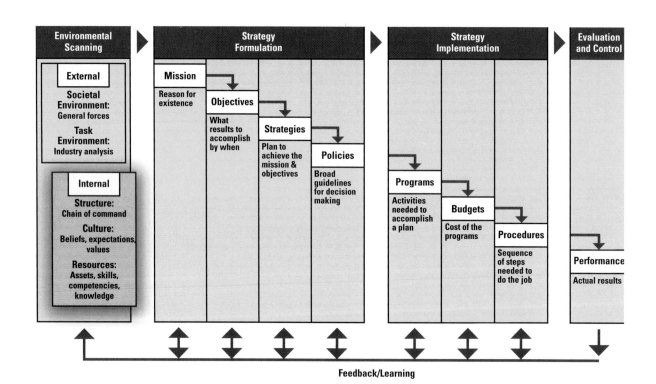

Feedback/Learning

On November 17, 2000, United Airlines increased domestic fares by $50 for trips of less than 1,500 miles and $100 for flights over 1,500 miles. Continental, Delta, and American Airlines quickly followed with their own fare increases. Northwest Airlines and TWA stated that they were considering fare hikes. In contrast (and as usual), Dallas-based Southwest Airlines ignored the increase. "We are aware of it, but we are not taking any action," stated Southwest's spokesman Ed Stewart. He added that management hoped that the price increases by other airlines would drive more traffic to Southwest.[1]

Southwest is the undisputed master of the low fare. It is America's most efficient and profitable airline. Other airlines have tried many times to match or beat Southwest's low fares but have failed. For example, United Airlines used to dominate the California market before Southwest replaced it in the 1990s. To regain this lucrative market, United launched its own low-cost carrier, Shuttle by United. It tried to imitate what it thought were Southwest's advantages. It used a fleet of Boeing 737s, the same plane Southwest used at that time. It was able to obtain looser union work rules and a lower wage scale from those at its United Airlines' parent. To compete effectively, the Shuttle aimed to reduce United's cost of flying from the main airline's 10.5¢ to 7.4¢ per passenger mile. It planned to fly planes longer, speed up passenger boarding and takeoffs, and reduce idle time on the ground. Sixteen months later, however, Shuttle by United had been able to reduce its costs only to 8¢ per passenger mile contrasted with Southwest's 7.1¢ in California. (Southwest's overall cost-per-passenger mile was the lowest in the industry at 6.43¢ compared to American Airlines' 12.95¢ per passenger mile—the highest in the industry.)[2] To keep from losing money, Shuttle by United was forced to raise fares and to pull out of all routes that did not connect with the carrier's hubs in San Francisco and Los Angeles. Even United's most loyal customers were taking Southwest for shorter flights. United's fare from San Francisco to Southern California was often $30 more than Southwest's rate of $69. Southwest had not only regained traffic it had lost initially to the Shuttle, it had actually increased its share of the California market!

In addition to Southwest's reputation for having the lowest costs in the industry, it has a well-earned reputation for flying passengers safely to their destination on time. What gave Southwest Airlines this kind of advantage in a very competitive industry? So far no U.S. airline seems able to copy the secret of its success.

4.1 A Resource-Based Approach to Organizational Analysis

Scanning and analyzing the external environment for opportunities and threats is not enough to provide an organization a competitive advantage. Analysts must also look within the corporation itself to identify **internal strategic factors**—those critical strengths and weaknesses that are likely to determine if the firm will be able to take advantage of opportunities while avoiding threats. This internal scanning is often referred to as **organizational analysis** and is concerned with identifying and developing an organization's resources.

A **resource** is an asset, competency, process, skill, or knowledge controlled by the corporation. A resource is a strength if it provides a company with a competitive advantage. It is something the firm does or has the potential to do particularly well relative to the abilities of existing or potential competitors. A resource is a weakness if it is something the corporation does poorly or doesn't have the capacity to do although its competitors have that capacity. Barney, in his **VRIO framework** of analysis, proposes 4 questions to evaluate each of a firm's key resources:

1. **Value**: Does it provide competitive advantage?
2. **Rareness**: Do other competitors possess it?
3. **Imitability**: Is it costly for others to imitate?
4. **Organization**: Is the firm organized to exploit the resource?

If the answer to these questions is "yes" for a particular resource, that resource is considered a strength and a distinctive competence.[3]

Evaluate the importance of these resources to ascertain if they are internal strategic factors—those particular strengths and weaknesses that will help determine the future of the company. This can be done by comparing measures of these resources with measures of (1) the company's past performance, (2) the company's key competitors, and (3) the industry as a whole. To the extent that a resource (such as a firm's financial situation) is significantly different from the firm's own past, its key competitors, or the industry average, the resource is likely to be a strategic factor and should be considered in strategic decisions.

USING RESOURCES TO GAIN COMPETITIVE ADVANTAGE

Proposing that a company's sustained competitive advantage is primarily determined by its resource endowments, Grant proposes a five-step, resource-based approach to strategy analysis.

1. Identify and classify the firm's resources in terms of strengths and weaknesses.

2. Combine the firm's strengths into specific capabilities. **Corporate capabilities** (often called **core competencies**) are the things that a corporation can do exceedingly well. When these capabilities/competencies are superior to those of competitors, they are often called **distinctive competencies**.

3. Appraise the profit potential of these resources and capabilities in terms of their potential for sustainable competitive advantage and the ability to harvest the profits resulting from the use of these resources and capabilities.

4. Select the strategy that best exploits the firm's resources and capabilities relative to external opportunities.

5. Identify resource gaps and invest in upgrading weaknesses.[4]

As indicated in Step 2, when an organization's resources are combined, they form a number of capabilities. In the earlier example, Southwest Airlines has two identifiable capabilities: low costs per passenger mile, and the capability of energizing its people to provide safe, on-time flight service. To ensure highly motivated employees, Southwest spends an inordinate amount of time and money on hiring and promoting, using a system to identify prospective employees who will fit into the company's corporate culture while retaining their individualism.[5]

DETERMINING THE SUSTAINABILITY OF AN ADVANTAGE

Just because a firm is able to use its resources and capabilities to develop a competitive advantage does not mean it will be able to sustain it. Two characteristics determine the sustainability of a firm's distinctive competency(ies): durability and imitability.

Durability is the rate at which a firm's underlying resources and capabilities (core competencies) depreciate or become obsolete. New technology can make a company's core competency obsolete or irrelevant. For example, Intel's skills in using basic technology developed by others to manufacture and market quality microprocessors was a crucial capability until management realized that the firm had taken current technology as far as possible with the Pentium chip. Without basic R&D of its own, it would slowly lose its competitive advantage to others.

Imitability is the rate at which a firm's underlying resources and capabilities (core competencies) can be duplicated by others. To the extent that a firm's distinctive competency gives it competitive advantage in the marketplace, competitors will do what they can to learn and imitate that set of skills and capabilities. Competitors' efforts may range from **reverse engineering** (taking apart a competitor's product in order to find out how it works), to hiring employees from the competitor, to outright patent infringement. A core competency can be easily imitated to the extent that it is transparent, transferable, and replicable.

- **Transparency** is the speed with which other firms can understand the relationship of resources and capabilities supporting a successful firm's strategy. For example, Gillette has always supported its dominance in the marketing of razors with excellent R&D. A competitor could never understand how the Sensor or Mach 3 razor was produced simply by taking one apart. Gillette's Sensor razor design, in particular, was very difficult to copy, partially because the manufacturing equipment needed to produce it was so expensive and complicated.

- **Transferability** is the ability of competitors to gather the resources and capabilities necessary to support a competitive challenge. For example, it may be very difficult for a wine maker to duplicate a French winery's key resources of land and climate, especially if the imitator is located in Iowa.

- **Replicability** is the ability of competitors to use duplicated resources and capabilities to imitate the other firm's success. For example, even though many companies have tried to imitate Procter & Gamble's success with brand management by hiring brand managers away from P&G, they have often failed to duplicate P&G's success. The competitors failed to identify less visible P&G coordination mechanisms or to realize that P&G's brand management style conflicted with the competitor's own corporate culture. Another example is Wal-Mart's sophisticated cross-docking system, which provides the company a substantial cost advantage by improving its ability to reduce shipping and handling costs. While Wal-Mart has the same resources in terms of retail space, employee skills, and equipment as many other discount chains, it has the unique capability to manage its resources for maximum productivity.[6]

It is relatively easy to learn and imitate another company's core competency or capability if it comes from **explicit knowledge**, that is, knowledge that can be easily articulated and communicated. This is the type of knowledge that competitive intelligence activities can quickly identify and communicate. **Tacit knowledge**, in contrast, is knowledge that is *not* easily communicated because it is deeply rooted in employee experience or in a corporation's culture.[7] Tacit knowledge is more valuable and more likely to lead to a sustainable competitive advantage than is explicit knowledge because it is much harder for competitors to imitate. The knowledge may be complex and combined with other types of knowledge in an unclear fashion in such a way that even management cannot clearly explain the competency.[8] Because Procter & Gamble's successful approach to brand management is primarily composed of tacit knowledge, the firm's top management is very reluctant to make any significant modifications to it, fearing that they might destroy the very thing they are trying to improve!

An organization's resources and capabilities can be placed on a continuum to the extent they are durable and can't be imitated (that is, aren't transparent, transferable, or replicable) by another firm. This **continuum of sustainability** is depicted in **Figure 4–1**. At one extreme are slow-cycle resources, which are sustainable because they are shielded by patents, geography, strong brand names, or tacit knowledge. These resources and capabilities are distinctive competencies because they provide a sustainable competitive advantage. Gillette's Sensor

Figure 4–1
Continuum of Resource Sustainability

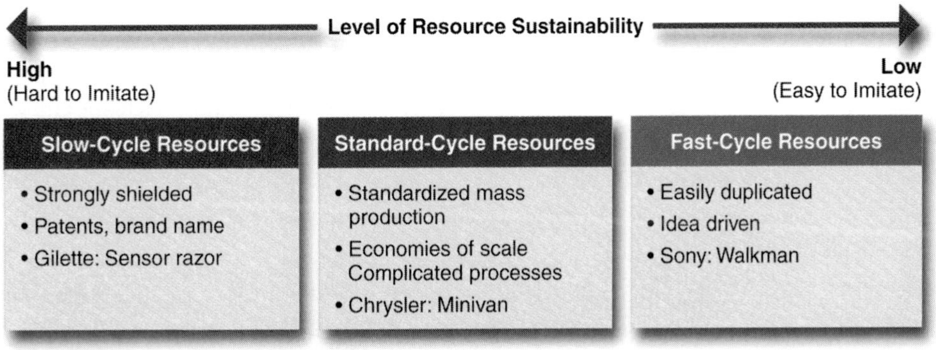

Source: Suggested by J. R. Williams, "How Sustainable Is Your Competitive Advantage?" *California Management Review* (Spring 1992), p. 33. Copyright © 1992 by the Regents of the University of California. Reprinted by permission of the Regents.

razor is a good example of a product built around slow-cycle resources. The other extreme includes fast-cycle resources, which face the highest imitation pressures because they are based on a concept or technology that can be easily duplicated, such as Sony's Walkman. To the extent that a company has fast-cycle resources, the primary way it can compete successfully is through increased speed from lab to marketplace. Otherwise, it has no real sustainable competitive advantage.

With its low-cost position, reputation for safe, on-time flights, and its dedicated workforce, Southwest Airlines has successfully built a sustainable competitive advantage based on relatively slow-cycle resources—resources that are durable and can't be easily imitated because they lack transparency, transferability, and replicability.

4.2 Value Chain Analysis

A good way to begin an organizational analysis is to ascertain where a firm's products are located in the overall value chain. A **value chain** is a linked set of value-creating activities beginning with basic raw materials coming from suppliers, moving on to a series of value-added activities involved in producing and marketing a product or service, and ending with distributors getting the final goods into the hands of the ultimate consumer. See **Figure 4–2** for an example of a typical value chain for a manufactured product. The focus of value chain analysis is to examine the corporation in the context of the overall chain of value-creating activities, of which the firm may be only a small part.

Very few corporations include a product's entire value chain. Ford Motor Company did when it was managed by its founder, Henry Ford I. During the 1920s and 1930s, the company owned its own iron mines, ore-carrying ships, and a small rail line to bring ore to its mile-long River Rouge plant in Detroit. Visitors to the plant would walk along an elevated walkway where they could watch iron ore being dumped from the rail cars into huge furnaces. The resulting steel was poured and rolled out onto a moving belt to be fabricated into auto frames and parts while the visitors watched in awe. As a group of visitors walked along the walkway, they observed an automobile being built piece by piece. Reaching the end of the moving line, the finished automobile was driven out of the plant into a vast adjoining parking lot. Ford trucks would then load the cars for delivery to dealers. Although the Ford dealers were not employees of the company, they had almost no power in the arrangement. Dealerships were awarded by the company and taken away if a dealer was at all disloyal. Ford Motor Company at that time was completely vertically integrated, that is, it controlled (usually by ownership) every stage of the value chain from the iron mines to the retailers.

INDUSTRY VALUE CHAIN ANALYSIS

The value chains of most industries can be split into two segments, *upstream* and *downstream* halves. In the petroleum industry, for example, upstream refers to oil exploration, drilling, and moving the crude oil to the refinery, and downstream refers to refining the oil plus the trans-

Figure 4–2

Typical Value Chain for a Manufactured Product

Source: Suggested by J. R. Galbraith, "Strategy and Organization Planning," in *The Strategy Process: Concepts, Contexts, Cases,* 2nd ed., edited by H. Mintzberg and J. B. Quinn (Upper Saddle River, NJ: Prentice Hall, 1991), p. 316. Reprinted by permission of Pearson Education, Inc., Upper Saddle River, NJ.

porting and marketing of gasoline and refined oil to distributors and gas station retailers. Even though most large oil companies are completely integrated, they often vary in the amount of expertise they at each part of the value chain. Texaco, for example, has its greatest expertise downstream in marketing and retailing. Others, such as British Petroleum (now BP Amoco), are more dominant in upstream activities like exploration.

An industry can be analyzed in terms of the profit margin available at any one point along the value chain. For example, the U.S. auto industry's revenues and profits are divided among many value chain activities, including manufacturing, new and used car sales, gasoline retailing, insurance, after-sales service and parts, and lease financing. From a revenue standpoint, auto manufacturers dominate the industry, accounting for almost 60% of total industry revenues. Profits are, however, a different matter. Auto leasing is the most profitable activity in the value chain, followed by insurance and auto loans. The core activities of manufacturing and distribution, however, earn significantly smaller shares of the total industry profits than they do of total revenues. For example, since auto sales have become marginally profitable, dealerships are now emphasizing service and repair. As a result of various differences along the industry value chain, manufacturers have moved aggressively into auto financing. Ford, for example, generates nearly half its profits from financing, even though financing accounts for less than 20% of the company's revenues.[9]

In analyzing the complete value chain of a product, note that even if a firm operates up and down the entire industry chain, it usually has an area of primary expertise where its primary activities lie. A company's **center of gravity** is the part of the chain that is most important to the company and the point where its greatest expertise and capabilities lie—its core competencies. According to Galbraith, a company's center of gravity is usually the point at which the company started. After a firm successfully establishes itself at this point by obtaining a competitive advantage, one of its first strategic moves is to move forward or backward along the value chain in order to reduce costs, guarantee access to key raw materials, or to guarantee distribution.[10] This process is called *vertical integration* and is discussed in more detail in Chapter 6.

In the paper industry, for example, Weyerhauser's center of gravity is in the raw materials and primary manufacturing parts of the value chain in **Figure 4–2**. Weyerhauser's expertise is in lumbering and pulp mills, which is where the company started. It integrated forward by using its wood pulp to make paper and boxes, but its greatest capability still lay in getting the greatest return from its lumbering activities. In contrast, Procter & Gamble is primarily a consumer products company that also owned timberland and operated pulp mills. Its expertise is in the product producer and marketer distributor parts of the **Figure 4–2** value chain. P&G purchased these assets to guarantee access to the large quantities of wood pulp it needed to expand its disposable diaper, toilet tissue, and napkin products. P&G's strongest capabilities have always been in the downstream activities of product development, marketing, and brand management. It has never been as efficient in upstream paper activities as Weyerhauser. It had no real distinctive competence on that part of the value chain. When paper supplies became more plentiful (and competition got rougher), P&G gladly sold its land and mills to focus more on that part of the value chain where it could provide the greatest value at the lowest cost—creating and marketing innovative consumer products.

CORPORATE VALUE CHAIN ANALYSIS

Each corporation has its own internal value chain of activities. See **Figure 4–3** for an example of a corporate value chain. Porter proposes that a manufacturing firm's **primary activities** usually begin with inbound logistics (raw materials handling and warehousing), go through an operations process in which a product is manufactured, and continue on to outbound logistics (warehousing and distribution), marketing and sales, and finally to service (installa-

Figure 4–3

A Corporation's Value Chain

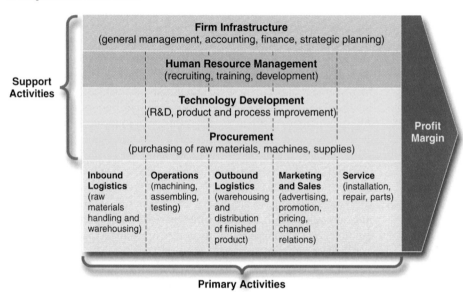

Source: Adapted/reprinted with the permission of The Free Press, an imprint of Simon & Schuster, from *Competitive Advantage: Creating and Sustaining Superior Performance* by Michael E. Porter, p. 37. Copyright © 1985, 1988 by Michael E. Porter.

tion, repair, and sale of parts). Several **support activities**, such as procurement (purchasing), technology development (R&D), human resource management, and firm infrastructure (accounting, finance, strategic planning), ensure that the primary value-chain activities operate effectively and efficiently. Each of a company's product lines has its own distinctive value chain. Because most corporations make several different products or services, an internal analysis of the firm involves analyzing a series of different value chains.

The systematic examination of individual value activities can lead to a better understanding of a corporation's strengths and weaknesses. According to Porter, "Differences among competitor value chains are a key source of competitive advantage."[11] Corporate value chain analysis involves the following three steps:

1. *Examine each product line's value chain in terms of the various activities involved in producing that product or service.* Which activities can be considered strengths (core competencies) or weaknesses (core deficiencies)? Do any of the strengths provide competitive advantage and can thus be labeled distinctive competencies?

2. *Examine the "linkages" within each product line's value chain.* **Linkages** are the connections between the way one value activity (for example, marketing) is performed and the cost of performance of another activity (for example, quality control). In seeking ways for a corporation to gain competitive advantage in the marketplace, the same function can be performed in different ways with different results. For example, quality inspection of 100% of output by the workers themselves instead of the usual 10% by quality control inspectors might increase production costs, but that increase could be more than offset by the savings obtained from reducing the number of repair people needed to fix defective products and increasing the amount of salespeople's time devoted to selling instead of exchanging already-sold, but defective, products.

3. *Examine the potential synergies among the value chains of different product lines or business units.* Each value element, such as advertising or manufacturing, has an inherent economy of scale in which activities are conducted at their lowest possible cost per unit of output. If a particular product is not being produced at a high enough level to reach economies of scale in distribution, another product could be used to share the same distribution channel. This is an example of **economies of scope**, which result when the value chains of two separate products or services share activities, such as the same marketing channels or manufacturing facilities. For example, the cost of joint production of multiple products can be less than the cost of separate production.

4.3 Scanning Functional Resources

The simplest way to begin an analysis of a corporation's value chain is by carefully examining its traditional functional areas for potential strengths and weaknesses. Functional resources include not only the financial, physical, and human assets in each area, but also the ability of the people in each area to formulate and implement the necessary functional objectives, strategies, and policies. The resources include the knowledge of analytical concepts and procedural techniques common to each area as well as the ability of the people in each area to use them effectively. If used properly, these resources serve as strengths to carry out value-added activities and support strategic decisions. In addition to the usual business functions of marketing, finance, R&D, operations, human resources, and information systems, we also discuss structure and culture as key parts of a business corporation's value chain.

BASIC ORGANIZATIONAL STRUCTURES

Although there is an almost infinite variety of structural forms, certain basic types predominate in modern complex organizations. **Figure 4–4** illustrates three basic **organizational structures**. The conglomerate structure is a variant of divisional structure and is thus not depicted as a fourth structure. Generally speaking, each structure tends to support some corporate strategies over others.

- **Simple structure** has no functional or product categories and is appropriate for a small, entrepreneur-dominated company with one or two product lines that operates in a reasonably small, easily identifiable market niche. Employees tend to be generalists and jacks-of-all-trades.
- **Functional structure** is appropriate for a medium-sized firm with several related product lines in one industry. Employees tend to be specialists in the business functions important to that industry, such as manufacturing, marketing, finance, and human resources.
- **Divisional structure** is appropriate for a large corporation with many product lines in several related industries. Employees tend to be functional specialists organized according to product/market distinctions. General Motors, for example, groups its various auto lines into the separate divisions of Chevrolet, Pontiac, Saturn, Oldsmobile, Buick, and Cadillac. Management attempts to find some synergy among divisional activities through the use of committees and horizontal linkages.
- **Strategic business units (SBUs)** are a recent modification to the divisional structure. Strategic business units are divisions or groups of divisions composed of independent product-market segments that are given primary responsibility and authority for the management of their own functional areas. *An SBU may be of any size or level, but it must have (1) a unique mission, (2) identifiable competitors, (3) an external market focus, and (4) control of its business functions.*[12] The idea is to decentralize on the basis of strategic elements rather than on the basis of size, product characteristics, or span of control and to create

Figure 4–4
Basic Organizational Structures

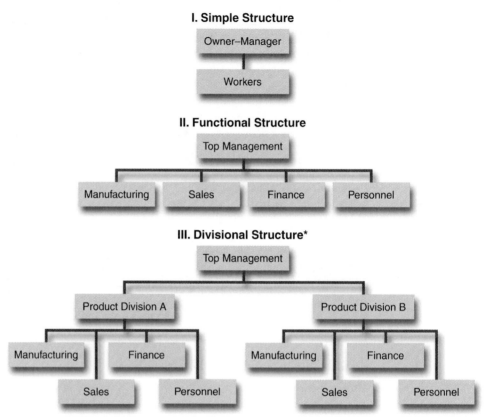

*Conglomerate structure is a variant of the divisional structure.

horizontal linkages among units previously kept separate. For example, rather than organize products on the basis of packaging technology like frozen foods, canned foods, and bagged foods, General Foods organized its products into SBUs on the basis of consumer-oriented menu segments: breakfast food, beverage, main meal, dessert, and pet foods.

■ **Conglomerate structure** is appropriate for a large corporation with many product lines in several unrelated industries. A variant of the divisional structure, the conglomerate structure (sometimes called a holding company) is typically an assemblage of legally independent firms (subsidiaries) operating under one corporate umbrella but controlled through the subsidiaries' boards of directors. The unrelated nature of the subsidiaries prevents any attempt at gaining synergy among them.

If the current basic structure of a corporation does not easily support a strategy under consideration, top management must decide if the proposed strategy is feasible or if the structure should be changed to a more advanced structure such as the matrix or network. (Advanced structural designs such as the matrix and network are discussed in Chapter 7.)

CORPORATE CULTURE: THE COMPANY WAY

There is an oft-told story of a person new to a company asking an experienced coworker what an employee should do when a customer calls. The old-timer responded: "There are three ways to do any job—the right way, the wrong way, and the company way. Around here, we always do things the company way." In most organizations, the "company way" is derived from the corporation's culture. **Corporate culture** is the collection of beliefs, expectations, and values learned and shared by a corporation's members and transmitted from one generation of employees to another. The corporate culture generally reflects the values of the founder(s) and the mission of the firm.[13] It gives a company a sense of identity: *This is who we are. This is what we do. This is what we stand for.* The culture includes the dominant orientation of the company, such as research and development at Hewlett-Packard, customer service at Nordstrom, or product quality at Maytag. It often includes a number of informal work rules (forming the "company way") that employees follow without question. These work practices over time become part of a company's unquestioned tradition.

Corporate culture has two distinct attributes, intensity and integration.[14] **Cultural intensity** is the degree to which members of a unit accept the norms, values, or other culture content associated with the unit. This shows the culture's depth. Organizations with strong norms promoting a particular value, such as quality at Maytag, have intensive cultures, whereas new firms (or those in transition) have weaker, less intensive cultures. Employees in an intensive culture tend to exhibit consistent behavior, that is, they tend to act similarly over time. **Cultural integration** is the extent to which units throughout an organization share a common culture. This is the culture's breadth. Organizations with a pervasive dominant culture may be hierarchically controlled and power oriented, such as a military unit, and have highly integrated cultures. All employees tend to hold the same cultural values and norms. In contrast, a company that is structured into diverse units by functions or divisions usually exhibits some strong subcultures (for example, R&D versus manufacturing) and a less integrated corporate culture.

Corporate culture fulfills several important functions in an organization:

1. Conveys a sense of identity for employees
2. Helps generate employee commitment to something greater than themselves
3. Adds to the stability of the organization as a social system
4. Serves as a frame of reference for employees to use to make sense out of organizational activities and to use as a guide for appropriate behavior[15]

Corporate culture shapes the behavior of people in the corporation. Because these cultures have a powerful influence on the behavior of people at all levels, they can strongly affect a corporation's ability to shift its strategic direction. A strong culture should not only promote survival, but it should also create the basis for a superior competitive position. For example, a culture emphasizing constant renewal may help a company adapt to a changing, hypercompetitive environment.[16] To the extent that a corporation's distinctive competence is embedded in an organization's culture, it will be a form of tacit knowledge and very difficult for a competitor to imitate.[17] See the 🌐 **Global Issue** feature to see how the Swiss company ABB Asea Brown Boveri AG uses its corporate culture to obtain competitive advantage in a global industry.

A change in mission, objectives, strategies, or policies is not likely to be successful if it is in opposition to the accepted culture of the firm. Foot-dragging and even sabotage may result as employees fight to resist a radical change in corporate philosophy. Like structure, if an organization's culture is compatible with a new strategy, it is an internal strength. But if the corporate culture is not compatible with the proposed strategy, it is a serious weakness.

STRATEGIC MARKETING ISSUES

The marketing manager is the company's primary link to the customer and the competition. The manager, therefore, must be especially concerned with the market position and marketing mix of the firm.

Global Issue 🌐

ABB Uses Corporate Culture as a Competitive Advantage

Zurich-based ABB Asea Brown Boveri AG is a worldwide builder of power plants, electrical equipment, and industrial factories in 140 countries. By establishing one set of values throughout its global operations, ABB's management believes that the company will gain an advantage over its rivals Siemens AG of Germany, France's Alcatel-Alsthom NV, and the United State's General Electric Company.

Percy Barnevik, Swedish Chairman of ABB, managed the merger that created ABB from Sweden's Asea AB and Switzerland's BBC Brown Boveri Ltd. At that time both companies were far behind the world leaders in electrical equipment and engineering. Barnevik introduced his concept of a company with no geographic base—one that had many "home" markets that could draw on expertise from around the globe. To do this, he created a set of 500 global managers who could adapt to local cultures while executing ABB's global strategies. These people are multilingual and move around each of ABB's 5,000 profit centers in 140 countries. Their assignment is to cut costs, improve efficiency, and integrate local businesses with the ABB world view.

ABB requires local business units, such as Mexico's motor factory, to report both to one of ABB's traveling global managers and to a business area manager who sets global motor strategy for ABB. When the goals of the local factory conflict with worldwide priorities, it is up to the global manager to resolve it.

Few multinational corporations are as successful as ABB in getting global strategies to work with local operations. In agreement with the resource-based view of the firm, Barnevik states, "Our strength comes from pulling together. . . . If you can make this work real well, then you get a competitive edge out of the organization which is very, very difficult to copy."

Source: J. Guyon, "ABB Fuses Units with One Set of Values," *Wall Street Journal* (October 2, 1996), p. A15. Copyright © 1996 by the *Wall Street Journal.* Reprinted by permission of the *Wall Street Journal* via the Copyright Clearance Center.

Market Position and Segmentation

Market position deals with the question, "Who are our customers?" It refers to the selection of specific areas for marketing concentration and can be expressed in terms of market, product, and geographical locations. Through market research, corporations are able to practice **market segmentation** with various products or services so that managers can discover what niches to seek, which new types of products to develop, and how to ensure that a company's many products do not directly compete with one another.

Marketing Mix

The **marketing mix** refers to the particular combination of key variables under the corporation's control that can be used to affect demand and to gain competitive advantage. These variables are product, place, promotion, and price. Within each of these four variables are several subvariables, listed in **Table 4–1**, that should be analyzed in terms of their effects on divisional and corporate performance.

Product Life Cycle

One of the most useful concepts in marketing, insofar as strategic management is concerned, is that of the **product life cycle.** As depicted in **Figure 4–5**, the product life cycle is a graph showing time plotted against the dollar sales of a product as it moves from introduction through growth and maturity to decline. This concept enables a marketing manager to examine the marketing mix of a particular product or group of products in terms of its position in its life cycle.

Table 4–1   Marketing Mix Variables

Product	Place	Promotion	Price
Quality	Channels	Advertising	List price
Features	Coverage	Personal selling	Discounts
Options	Locations	Sales promotion	Allowances
Style	Inventory	Publicity	Payment periods
Brand name	Transport		Credit items
Packaging			
Sizes			
Services			
Warranties			
Returns			

Source: Philip Kotler, *Marketing Management: Analysis, Planning, and Control*, 4th ed. (Upper Saddle River, NJ: Prentice Hall, 1980), p. 89. Copyright © 1980. Reprinted by permission of Pearson Education, Inc., Upper Saddle River, NJ.

STRATEGIC FINANCIAL ISSUES

The financial manager must ascertain the best sources of funds, uses of funds, and control of funds. Cash must be raised from internal or external (local and global) sources and allocated for different uses. The flow of funds in the operations of the organization must be monitored. To the extent that a corporation is involved in international activities, currency fluctuations must be dealt with to ensure that profits aren't wiped out by the rise or fall of the dollar versus the yen, euro, or other currencies. Benefits in the form of returns, repayments, or products and services must be given to the sources of outside financing. All these tasks must be handled in a way that complements and supports overall corporate strategy. A firm's capital structure (amounts of debt and equity) can influence its strategic choices. For example, increased debt tends to increase risk aversion and decrease the willingness of management to invest in R&D.[18]

Figure 4–5
Product Life Cycle

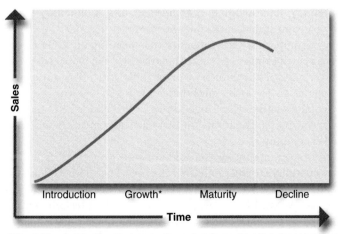

* The right end of the Growth stage is often called Competitive Turbulence because of price and distribution competition that shakes out the weaker competitors. For further information, see C.R. Wasson, *Dynamic Competitive Strategy and Product Life Cycles,* 3rd ed. (Austin, TX: Austin Press, 1978).

Financial Leverage

The mix of externally generated short-term and long-term funds in relation to the amount and timing of internally generated funds should be appropriate to the corporate objectives, strategies, and policies. The concept of **financial leverage** (the ratio of total debt to total assets) is helpful in describing how debt is used to increase the earnings available to common shareholders. When the company finances its activities by sales of bonds or notes instead of through stock, the earnings per share are boosted: The interest paid on the debt reduces taxable income, but fewer shareholders share the profits than if the company had sold more stock to finance its activities. The debt, however, does raise the firm's break-even point above what it would have been if the firm had financed from internally generated funds only. High leverage may therefore be perceived as a corporate strength in times of prosperity and ever-increasing sales, or as a weakness in times of a recession and falling sales. This is because leverage acts to magnify the effect on earnings per share of an increase or decrease in dollar sales. Research indicates that greater leverage has a positive impact on performance for firms in stable environments, but a negative impact for firms in dynamic environments.[19]

Capital Budgeting

Capital budgeting is the analyzing and ranking of possible investments in fixed assets such as land, buildings, and equipment in terms of the additional outlays and additional receipts that will result from each investment. A good finance department will be able to prepare such capital budgets and to rank them on the basis of some accepted criteria or hurdle rate (for example, years to pay back investment, rate of return, or time to break-even point) for the purpose of strategic decision making. Most firms have more than one hurdle rate and vary it as a function of the type of project being considered. Projects with high strategic significance, such as entering new markets or defending market share, will often have low hurdle rates.[20]

STRATEGIC RESEARCH AND DEVELOPMENT (R&D) ISSUES

The R&D manager is responsible for suggesting and implementing a company's technological strategy in light of its corporate objectives and policies. The manager's job, therefore, involves (1) choosing among alternative new technologies to use within the corporation, (2) developing methods of embodying the new technology in new products and processes, and (3) deploying resources so that the new technology can be successfully implemented.

R&D Intensity, Technological Competence, and Technology Transfer

The company must make available the resources necessary for effective research and development. A company's **R&D intensity** (its spending on R&D as a percentage of sales revenue) is a principal means of gaining market share in global competition. The amount spent on R&D often varies by industry. For example, the U.S. computer software industry spends an average of 13.5% of its sales dollar for R&D, whereas the paper and forest products industry spends only 1.0%.[21] A good rule of thumb for R&D spending is that a corporation should spend at a "normal" rate for that particular industry unless its strategic plan calls for unusual expenditures.

Simply spending money on R&D or new projects does not mean, however, that the money will produce useful results. For example, Pharmacia Upjohn spent more of its revenues on research than any other company in any industry (18%), but it was ranked low in innovation.[22] A company's R&D unit should be evaluated for **technological competence** in both the development and the use of innovative technology. Not only should the corporation make a consistent research effort (as measured by reasonably constant corporate expenditures that result in usable innovations), it should also be proficient in managing research personnel and integrating their innovations into its day-to-day operations. If a company is not proficient in

technology transfer, the process of taking a new technology from the laboratory to the marketplace, it will not gain much advantage from new technological advances. For example, Xerox Corporation has been criticized for failing to take advantage of various innovations (such as the mouse and the graphical user interface for personal computers) developed originally in its sophisticated Palo Alto Research Center. See the **boxed example** for a classic example of how Apple Computer's ability to imitate a core competency of Xerox gave it a competitive advantage (sustainable until Microsoft launched Windows 95).

R&D Mix

Basic R&D is conducted by scientists in well-equipped laboratories where the focus is on theoretical problem areas. The best indicators of a company's capability in this area are its patents and research publications. **Product R&D** concentrates on marketing and is concerned with product or product-packaging improvements. The best measurements of ability in this area are the number of successful new products introduced and the percentage of total sales and profits coming from products introduced within the past five years. **Engineering (or process) R&D** is concerned with engineering, concentrating on quality control and the development of design specifications and improved production equipment. A company's capability in this area can be measured by consistent reductions in unit manufacturing costs and by the number of product defects.

Most corporations will have a mix of basic, product, and process R&D, which varies by industry, company, and product line. The balance of these types of research is known as the **R&D mix** and should be appropriate to the strategy being considered and to each product's life cycle. For example, it is generally accepted that product R&D normally dominates the early stages of a product's life cycle (when the product's optimal form and features are still being debated), whereas process R&D becomes especially important in the later stages (when the product's design is solidified and the emphasis is on reducing costs and improving quality).

A Problem of Technology Transfer at Xerox Corporation

In the mid-1970s, Xerox Corporation's Palo Alto Research Center (PARC) had developed Alto, a new type of computer with some innovative features. Although Alto was supposed to serve as a research prototype, it became so popular among PARC personnel that some researchers began to develop Alto as a commercial product. Unfortunately this put PARC into direct conflict with Xerox's product development group, which was at the same time developing a rival machine called the Star. Because the Star was in line with the company's expressed product development strategy, top management, who placed all its emphasis on the Star, ignored Alto.

In 1979, Steve Jobs, Cofounder of Apple Computer, Inc., made a now-legendary tour of the normally very secretive PARC. Researchers gave Jobs a demonstration of the Alto. Unlike the computers that Apple was then building, Alto had the power of a minicomputer. Its user-friendly software generated crisp text and bright graphics. Jobs fell in love with the machine. He promptly asked Apple's engineers to duplicate the look and feel of Alto. The result was the Macintosh—a personal computer that soon revolutionized the industry.

Note: See the 1999 motion picture, *The Pirates of Silicon Valley,* for the full story of how Apple Computer imitated the features of the Alto and how Microsoft, in turn, imitated the "look and feel" of Apple's Macintosh.

Impact of Technological Discontinuity on Strategy

The R&D manager must determine when to abandon present technology and when to develop or adopt new technology. Richard Foster of McKinsey and Company states that the displacement of one technology by another (**technological discontinuity**) is a frequent and strategically important phenomenon. Such a discontinuity occurs when a new technology cannot simply be used to enhance the current technology but actually substitutes for that technology to yield better performance. For each technology within a given field or industry, according to Foster, the plotting of product performance against research effort/expenditures on a graph results in an S-shaped curve. He describes the process depicted in **Figure 4–6**:

> Early in the development of the technology a knowledge base is being built and progress requires a relatively large amount of effort. Later, progress comes more easily. And then, as the limits of that technology are approached, progress becomes slow and expensive. That is when R&D dollars should be allocated to technology with more potential. That is also—not so incidentally—when a competitor who has bet on a new technology can sweep away your business or topple an entire industry.[23]

Computerized information technology is currently on the steep upward slope of its S-curve in which relatively small increments in R&D effort result in significant improvement in performance. This is an example of Moore's Law, which states that silicon chips (microprocessors) double in complexity every 18 months. Proposed by Gordon Moore, Cofounder of Intel, in 1965, the law originally stated that processor complexity would double in one year, but Moore soon changed it to two years. Others changed it to 18 months—the number now generally accepted. In 1965, 16 components could be placed on a silicon chip. By 2000, that number had grown exponentially to 10 million. According to Moore, "Moore's Law has been the name given to everything that changes exponentially in the industry."[24]

Figure 4–6
Technological Discontinuity

What the S-Curves Reveal

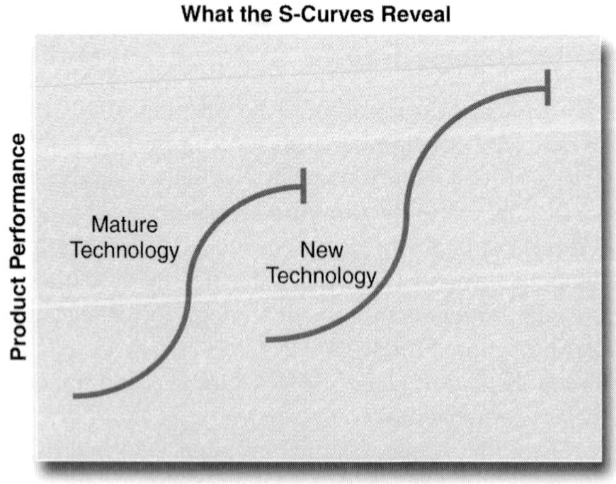

In the corporate planning process, it is generally assumed that incremental progress in technology will occur. But past developments in a given technology cannot be extrapolated into the future because every technology has its limits. The key to competitiveness is to determine when to shift resources to a technology with more potential.

The presence of a technological discontinuity in the world's steel industry during the 1960s explains why the large capital expenditures by U.S. steel companies failed to keep them competitive with the Japanese firms that adopted the new technologies. As Foster points out, "History has shown that as one technology nears the end of its S-curve, competitive leadership in a market generally changes hands."[25]

Christensen explains in *The Innovator's Dilemma* why this transition occurs when a "disruptive technology" enters an industry. In a study of computer disk drive manufacturers, he explains that established market leaders are typically reluctant to move in a timely manner to a new technology. This reluctance to switch technologies (even when the firm is aware of the new technology and may have even invented it!) is because the resource allocation process in most companies gives priority to those projects (typically based on the old technology) with the greatest likelihood of generating a good return on investment—those projects appealing to the firm's current customers (whose products are also based on the characteristics of the old technology). For example, in the 1980s a disk drive manufacturer's customers (PC manufacturers) wanted a better (faster) 5¼″ drive with greater capacity. These PC makers were not interested in the new 3½″ drives based on the new technology because (at that time) the smaller drives were slower and had less capacity. Smaller size was irrelevant since these companies primarily made desktop personal computers that were designed to hold large drives.

The new technology is generally riskier and of little appeal to the current customers of established firms. Products derived from the new technology are more expensive and do not meet the customers' requirements, which are based on the old technology. New entrepreneurial firms are typically more interested in the new technology because it is one way to appeal to a developing market niche in a market currently dominated by established companies. Even though the new technology may be more expensive to develop, it offers performance improvements in areas that are attractive to this small niche, but of no consequence to the customers of the established competitors.

This was the case with the entrepreneurial manufacturers of 3½″ disk drives. These smaller drives appealed to the PC makers who were trying to increase their small PC market share by offering laptop computers. Size and weight were more important to these customers than were capacity and speed. By the time the new technology was developed to the point that the 3½″ drive matched and even surpassed the 5¼″ drive in terms of speed and capacity (in addition to size and weight), it was too late for the established 5¼″ disk drive firms to switch to the new technology. Once their customers begin demanding smaller products using the new technology, the established firms were unable to respond quickly and lost their leadership position in the industry. They were able to remain in the industry (with a much reduced market share) only if they were able to utilize the new technology to be competitive in the new product line.[26]

STRATEGIC OPERATIONS ISSUES

The primary task of the operations (manufacturing or service) manager is to develop and operate a system that will produce the required number of products or services, with a certain quality, at a given cost, within an allotted time. Many of the key concepts and techniques popularly used in manufacturing can be applied to service businesses.

In very general terms, manufacturing can be intermittent or continuous. In **intermittent systems** (job shops), the item is normally processed sequentially, but the work and sequence of the process vary. An example is an auto body repair shop. At each location, the tasks determine the details of processing and the time required for them. These job shops can be very labor intensive. For example, a job shop usually has little automated machinery and thus a small amount of fixed costs. It has a fairly low break-even point, but its variable cost line (composed of wages and costs of special parts) has a relatively steep slope. Because most of the costs associated with the product are variable (many employees earn piece-rate wages), a job shop's variable costs are higher than those of automated firms. Its advantage over other firms is that it can operate at low levels and still be profitable. After a job shop's sales reach breakeven, however, the huge variable costs as a percentage of total costs keep the profit per unit at a relatively low level. In terms of strategy, this firm should look for a niche in the marketplace for which it can produce and sell a reasonably small quantity of goods.

In contrast, **continuous systems** are those laid out as lines on which products can be continuously assembled or processed. An example is an automobile assembly line. A firm using continuous systems invests heavily in fixed investments such as automated processes and highly sophisticated machinery. Its labor force, relatively small but highly skilled, earns salaries rather than piece-rate wages. Consequently this firm has a high amount of fixed costs. It also has a relatively high break-even point, but its variable cost line rises slowly. This is an example of **operating leverage**, the impact of a specific change in sales volume on net operating income. The advantage of high operating leverage is that once the firm reaches breakeven, its profits rise faster than do those of less automated firms having lower operating leverage. Continuous systems reap benefits from economies of scale. In terms of strategy, this firm needs to find a high-demand niche in the marketplace for which it can produce and sell a large quantity of goods. However, a firm with high operating leverage is likely to suffer huge losses during a recession. During an economic downturn, the firm with less automation and thus less leverage is more likely to survive comfortably because a drop in sales primarily affects variable costs. It is often easier to lay off labor than to sell off specialized plants and machines.

Experience Curve

A conceptual framework that many large corporations have used successfully is the experience curve (originally called the learning curve). The **experience curve** suggests that unit production costs decline by some fixed percentage (commonly 20% to 30%) each time the total accumulated volume of production in units doubles. The actual percentage varies by industry and is based on many variables: the amount of time it takes a person to learn a new task, scale economies, product and process improvements, and lower raw materials costs, among others. For example, in an industry with an 85% experience curve, a corporation might expect a 15% reduction in unit costs for every doubling of volume. The total costs per unit can be expected to drop from $100 when the total production is 10 units, to $85 ($100 × 85%) when production increases to 20 units, and to $72.25 ($85 × 85%) when it reaches 40 units. Achieving these results often means investing in R&D and fixed assets; higher fixed costs and less flexibility thus result. Nevertheless the manufacturing strategy is one of building capacity ahead of demand in order to achieve the lower unit costs that develop from the experience curve. On the basis of some future point on the experience curve, the corporation should price the product or service very low to preempt competition and increase market demand. The resulting high number of units sold and high market share should result in high profits, based on the low unit costs.

Management commonly uses the experience curve in estimating the production costs of (1) a product never before made with the present techniques and processes or (2) current products produced by newly introduced techniques or processes. The concept was first applied in the airframe industry and can be applied in the service industry as well. For example, a cleaning company can reduce its costs per employee by having its workers use the same equipment and techniques to clean many adjacent offices in one office building rather than just cleaning a few offices in multiple buildings. Although many firms have used experience curves extensively, an unquestioning acceptance of the industry norm (such as 80% for the airframe industry or 70% for integrated circuits) is very risky. The experience curve of the industry as a whole might not hold true for a particular company for a variety of reasons.

Flexible Manufacturing for Mass Customization

Recently the use of large, continuous, mass-production facilities to take advantage of experience-curve economies has been criticized. The use of Computer-Assisted Design and Computer-Assisted Manufacturing (CAD/CAM) and robot technology means that learning times are shorter and products can be economically manufactured in small, customized batches in a process called **mass customization**—the low-cost production of individually customized goods and services.[27] **Economies of scope** (in which common parts of the manufacturing activities of various products are combined to gain economies even though small numbers of each product are made) replace **economies of scale** (in which unit costs are reduced by making large numbers of the same product) in flexible manufacturing. **Flexible manufacturing** permits the low-volume output of custom-tailored products at relatively low unit costs through economies of scope. It is thus possible to have the cost advantages of continuous systems with the customer-oriented advantages of intermittent systems.

STRATEGIC HUMAN RESOURCE MANAGEMENT (HRM) ISSUES

The primary task of the manager of human resources is to improve the match between individuals and jobs. A good HRM department should know how to use attitude surveys and other feedback devices to assess employees' satisfaction with their jobs and with the corporation as a whole. HRM managers should also use job analysis to obtain job description information about what each job needs to accomplish in terms of quality and quantity. Up-to-date job descriptions are essential not only for proper employee selection, appraisal, training, and development for wage and salary administration, and for labor negotiations, but also for summarizing the corporatewide human resources in terms of employee-skill categories. Just as a company must know the number, type, and quality of its manufacturing facilities, it must also know the kinds of people it employs and the skills they possess. The best strategies are meaningless if employees do not have the skills to carry them out or if jobs cannot be designed to accommodate the available workers. Hewlett-Packard, for example, uses employee profiles to ensure that it has the right mix of talents to implement its planned strategies.

Use of Teams

Management is beginning to realize that it must be more flexible in its utilization of employees in order for human resources to be a strength. Human resource managers, therefore, need to be knowledgeable about work options such as part-time work, job sharing, flex-time, extended leaves, contract work, and especially about the proper use of teams. Over two-thirds of large U.S. companies are successfully using **autonomous (self-managing) work teams** in which a group of people work together without a supervisor to plan, coordinate, and evaluate their own work.[28] Northern Telecom found productivity and quality to increase with work teams to such an extent that it was able to reduce the number of quality inspectors by 40%.[29]

As a way to move a product more quickly through its development stage, companies like Motorola, Chrysler, NCR, Boeing, and General Electric are using **cross-functional work teams**. Instead of developing products in a series of steps—beginning with a request from sales, which leads to design, then to engineering and on to purchasing, and finally to manufacturing (and often resulting in a costly product rejected by the customer)—companies are tearing down the traditional walls separating the departments so that people from each discipline can get involved in projects early on. In a process called **concurrent engineering**, the once-isolated specialists now work side by side and compare notes constantly in an effort to design cost-effective products with features customers want. Taking this approach enabled Chrysler Corporation to reduce its product development cycle from 60 to 36 months.[30] For such cross-functional work teams to be successful, the groups must receive training and coaching.

Otherwise, poorly implemented teams may worsen morale, create divisiveness, and raise the level of cynicism among workers.[31]

Union Relations and Temporary Workers

If the corporation is unionized, a good human resource manager should be able to work closely with the union. Union membership in the United States has dropped to 13.9% overall and to less than 12% of private sector workers in the mid 1990s from more than one-third a few decades earlier.[32] To save jobs, U.S. unions are increasingly willing to support employee involvement programs designed to increase worker participation in decision making.

Outside the United States, the average proportion of unionized workers among major industrialized nations is around 50%. European unions tend to be militant, politically oriented, and much less interested in working with management to increase efficiency. Nationwide strikes can occur quickly. Japanese unions are typically tied to individual companies and are usually supportive of management. These differences among countries have significant implications for the management of multinational corporations.

To increase flexibility, avoid layoffs, and reduce labor costs, corporations are using more temporary workers. From the 1980s to the 1990s, the employment of temporary (also known as contingent) workers in the U.S. increased 250% compared to a 20% increase in overall employment. Ninety percent of U.S. firms use temporary workers in some capacity; 43% now use them in professional and technical functions. Approximately 10% of the U.S. workforce (over 12 million individuals) are now temporary workers.[33] The percentage is even higher in some European countries, such as France. Labor unions are concerned that companies use temps to avoid hiring costlier unionized workers. At United Parcel Service, for example, 80% of the jobs created from 1993 to 1997 were staffed by part-timers, whose pay rates hadn't changed since 1982. Fully 10% of the company's 128,000 part-timers work 30 hours or more per week, but are still paid at a lower rate than are full-time employees.[34] According to John Kinloch, vice-president of Communications Workers of America Local 1058, "Corporations are trying to create a disposable workforce with low wages and no benefits."[35]

Quality of Work Life and Human Diversity

Human resource departments have found that to reduce employee dissatisfaction and unionization efforts (or, conversely, to improve employee satisfaction and existing union relations), they must consider the **quality of work life** in the design of jobs. Partially a reaction to the traditionally heavy emphasis on technical and economic factors in job design, quality of work life emphasizes improving the human dimension of work. The knowledgeable human resource manager, therefore, should be able to improve the corporation's quality of work life by (1) introducing participative problem solving, (2) restructuring work, (3) introducing innovative reward systems, and (4) improving the work environment. It is hoped that these improvements will lead to a more participative corporate culture and thus higher productivity and quality products. Ford Motor Company, for example, is rebuilding and modernizing its famous River Rouge plant using flexible equipment and new processes. Employees will work in teams and use Internet-connected PCs on the shop floor to share their concerns instantly with suppliers or product engineers. Workstations are being redesigned to make them more ergonomic and to reduce repetitive-strain injuries. "If you feel good while you're working, I think quality and productivity will increase, and Ford thinks that too, otherwise, they wouldn't do this," observed Jerry Sullivan, President of United Auto Worker Local 600.[36]

Human diversity refers to the mix in the workplace of people from different races, cultures, and backgrounds. This is a hot issue in HRM. Realizing that the demographics are changing toward an increasing percentage of minorities and women in the U.S. workforce, companies are now concerned with hiring and promoting people without regard to ethnic background. According to a study reported by *Fortune* magazine, companies that pursue diversity outperform the S&P 500.[37] Good human resource managers should be working to ensure that people are treated fairly on the job and not harassed by prejudiced coworkers or managers. Otherwise, they may find themselves subject to lawsuits. Coca-Cola Company, for example, agreed to pay $192.5 million because of discrimination against African American salaried employees in pay, promotions, and evaluations from 1995 and 2000. According to Chairman and CEO Douglas Daft, "Sometimes things happen in an unintentional manner. And I've made it clear that can't happen anymore."[38]

An organization's human resources are especially important in today's world of global communication and transportation systems. For example, on a visit to China during Spring 2000, one of Coca-Cola Company's executives was challenged by Chinese reporters regarding the company's racial problems. Advances in technology are copied almost immediately by competitors around the world. People are not as willing to move to other companies in other countries. This means that the only long-term resource advantage remaining to corporations operating in the industrialized nations may lie in the area of skilled human resources. Research does reveal that competitive strategies are more successfully executed in those companies with a high level of commitment to their employees than in those firms with less commitment.[39]

STRATEGIC INFORMATION SYSTEMS/TECHNOLOGY ISSUES

The primary task of the manager of information systems/technology is to design and manage the flow of information in an organization in ways that improve productivity and decision making. Information must be collected, stored, and synthesized in such a manner that it will answer important operating and strategic questions. The growth of the global Internet economy is forcing corporations to make significant investments in this functional area. (See the **Internet Issue** feature.) Corporate investments in information systems/technology are growing 11% annually even though 70% of all investments are either not completed or exceed cost projections by nearly 200%.[40]

Internet Issue

The Growing Global Internet Economy

Electronic commerce is poised to grow rapidly throughout the world to a total of $6.9 trillion in Internet sales by 2004. According to a report by Forrester Research entitled, *Global eCommerce Approaches Hypergrowth*, Internet sales in the United States should increase to $3.2 trillion by 2004 and account for 46.4% of the global Internet economy. The Asia-Pacific region should grow to $1.6 trillion in sales and account for 23.2% of the total Internet sales. Western Europe should reach $1.5 trillion in sales (21.7% of the total) by 2004. After a slow start, Latin America's Internet sales should total $82.9 billion and account for 1.2% of total world Internet sales. Technologically, Latin America lags behind North America and Western Europe, but is being pushed by trading partners who are sophisticated Internet users to invest in crucial technology infrastructure such as phone lines, computers, Internet hosts, and cell phones. With Brazil and Argentina leading the way in liberalizing trade, the economic climate is rapidly improving. By 2004, Brazil should generate $64 billion on its own in online sales. Eastern Europe, Africa, and the Middle East are still facing the same problems that Latin America is now overcoming and will account for only $68.6 billion in sales, a mere 0.9% of the total world sales. The rest of the world's Internet sales will total $450 billion for the remaining 6.6% of total world sales.

Source: "Hypergrowth for E-Commerce?" *The Futurist* (September–October 2000), p. 15.

A corporation's information system can be a strength or a weakness in all elements of strategic management. It can not only aid in environmental scanning and in controlling a company's many activities, it can also be used as a strategic weapon in gaining competitive advantage. For example, American Hospital Supply (AHS), a leading manufacturer and distributor of a broad line of products for doctors, laboratories, and hospitals, developed an order entry distribution system that directly linked the majority of its customers to AHS computers. The system was successful because it simplified ordering processes for customers, reduced costs for both AHS and the customer, and allowed AHS to provide pricing incentives to the customer. As a result, customer loyalty was high and AHS's share of the market became large.

Information systems/technology offers four main contributions to corporate performance. *First* (beginning in the 1970s with main frame computers), it is used to automate existing back-office processes, such as payroll, human resource records, accounts payable and receivable, and to establish huge databases. *Second* (beginning in the 1980s), it is used to automate individual tasks, such as keeping track of clients and expenses, through the use of personal computers with word processing and spreadsheet software. Corporate databases are accessed to provide sufficient data to analyze the data and create what-if scenarios. These first two contributions tend to focus on reducing costs. *Third* (beginning in the 1990s), it is used to enhance key business functions, such as marketing and operations. This third contribution focuses on productivity improvements. The system provides customer support and help in distribution and logistics. For example, FedEx found that by allowing customers to directly access its package-tracking database via its Internet Web site instead of their having to ask a human operator, the company saved up to $2 million annually.[41] Business processes are analyzed to increase efficiency and productivity via reengineering. Enterprise resource planning application software, by firms such as SAP, PeopleSoft, Oracle, Baan, and J.D. Edwards, are used to integrate worldwide business activities so that employees need to enter information only once and that information is available to all corporate systems (including accounting) around the world. *Fourth* (beginning in 2000), it is used to develop competitive advantage. The focus is now on taking advantage of opportunities via supply chain management, electronic commerce, and knowledge management. Currently, most companies devote 85% of their IS/IT budget to the first two utility functions, 12% to productivity enhancement, and only 3% to efforts to gain competitive advantage.[42]

A current trend in corporate information systems is the increasing use of the Internet for marketing, intranets for internal communication, and extranets for logistics and distribution. An **intranet** is an information network within an organization that also has access to the external worldwide Internet. Intranets typically begin as ways to provide employees with company information such as lists of product prices, fringe benefits, and company policies. They are then converted into extranets for supply chain management. An **extranet** is an information network within an organization that is available to key suppliers and customers. The key issue in building an extranet is the creation of "fire walls" to block extranet users from accessing the firm's or other users' confidential data. Once this is accomplished, companies can allow employees, customers, and suppliers to access information and conduct business on the Internet in a completely automated manner. By connecting these groups, companies hope to obtain a competitive advantage by reducing the time needed to design and bring new products to market, slashing inventories, customizing manufacturing, and entering new markets.[43]

4.4 The Strategic Audit: A Checklist for Organizational Analysis

One way of conducting an organizational analysis to ascertain a company's strengths and weaknesses is by using the Strategic Audit found in **Appendix 10.A of Chapter 10**. The audit provides a checklist of questions by area of concern. For example, Part IV of the audit examines corporate structure, culture, and resources. It looks at resources in terms of the functional areas of marketing, finance, R&D, operations, human resources, and information systems, among others.

4.5 Synthesis of Internal Factors: IFAS

After strategists have scanned the internal organizational environment and identified factors for their particular corporation, they may want to summarize their analysis of these factors using a form such as that given in **Table 4–2**. This **IFAS** (**I**nternal **F**actor **A**nalysis **S**ummary) **Table** is one way to organize the internal factors into the generally accepted categories of strengths and weaknesses as well as to analyze how well a particular company's management is responding to these specific factors in light of the perceived importance of these factors to the company. Use the VRIO framework (**V**alue, **R**areness, **I**mitability, and **O**rganization) to assess the importance of each of the factors that might be considered strengths. Except for its internal orientation, this IFAS Table is built the same way as the EFAS Table described in **Chapter 3** (in **Table 3–4**). To use the IFAS Table, complete the following steps:

- In **Column 1** (Internal Factors), list the 8 to 10 most important strengths and weaknesses facing the company.

- In **Column 2** (Weight), assign a weight to each factor from **1.0** (Most Important) to **0.0** (Not Important) based on that factor's probable impact on a particular company's current strategic position. The higher the weight, the more important is this factor to the current and future success of the company. All weights must sum to 1.0 regardless of the number of factors.

- In **Column 3** (Rating), assign a rating to each factor from **5.0** (Outstanding) to **1.0** (Poor) based on management's current response to that particular factor. Each rating is a judgment regarding how well the company's management is currently dealing with each internal factor.

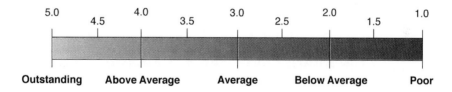

- In **Column 4** (Weighted Score), multiply the weight in **Column 2** for each factor times its rating in **Column 3** to obtain each factor's weighted score. This results in a weighted score for each factor ranging from **5.0** (Outstanding) to **1.0** (Poor) with **3.0** as Average.

- In **Column 5** (Comments), note why a particular factor was selected and/or how its weight and rating were estimated.

Finally, add the individual weighted scores for all the internal factors in **Column 4** to determine the total weighted score for that particular company. The **total weighted score** indicates how well a particular company is responding to current and expected factors in its internal environment. The score can be used to compare that firm to other firms in its industry. The total weighted score for an average firm in an industry is always 3.0.

As an example of this procedure, **Table 4–2** includes a number of internal factors for Maytag Corporation in 1995 (before Maytag sold its European and Australian operations) with corresponding weights, ratings, and weighted scores provided. Note that Maytag's total weighted score was 3.05, meaning that the corporation was about average compared to the strengths and weaknesses of others in the major home appliance industry at that time.

Table 4–2 Internal Factor Analysis Summary (IFAS Table): Maytag as Example

Internal Factors	Weight	Rating	Weighted Score	Comments
	1	2	3	4	5
Strengths				
• Quality Maytag culture	.15	5.0	.75	Quality key to success
• Experienced top management	.05	4.2	.21	Know appliances
• Vertical integration	.10	3.9	.39	Dedicated factories
• Employee relations	.05	3.0	.15	Good, but deteriorating
• Hoover's international orientation	.15	2.8	.42	Hoover name in cleaners
Weaknesses				
• Process-oriented R&D	.05	2.2	.11	Slow on new products
• Distribution channels	.05	2.0	.10	Superstores replacing small dealers
• Financial position	.15	2.0	.30	High debt load
• Global positioning	.20	2.1	.42	Hoover weak outside the United Kingdom and Australia
• Manufacturing facilities	.05	4.0	.20	Investing now
Total Scores	1.00		3.05	

Notes:
1. List strengths and weaknesses (8–10) in Column 1.
2. Weight each factor from 1.0 (Most Important) to 0.0 (Not Important) in Column 2 based on that factor's probable impact on the company's strategic position. **The total weights must sum to 1.00.**
3. Rate each factor from 5.0 (Outstanding) to 1.0 (Poor) in Column 3 based on the company's response to that factor.
4. Multiply each factor's weight times its rating to obtain each factor's weighted score in Column 4.
5. Use Column 5 (comments) for rationale used for each factor.
6. Add the individual weighted scores to obtain the total weighted score for the company in Column 4. This tells how well the company is responding to the strategic factors in its internal environment.

Source: T. L. Wheelen and J. D. Hunger, "Internal Factor Analysis Summary (IFAS)." Copyright © 1991 by Wheelen and Hunger Associates. Reprinted by permission.

4.6 Impact of the Internet on Internal Scanning and Organizational Analysis

The expansion of the marketing-oriented Internet into intranets and extranets is making significant contributions to organizational performance through supply chain management and virtual teams. **Supply chain management** is the forming of networks for sourcing raw materials, manufacturing products or creating services, storing and distributing the goods, and delivering them to customers and consumers.[44] Industry leaders are integrating modern information systems into their corporate value chains to harmonize companywide efforts and to achieve competitive advantage. For example, Heineken Beer distributors input actual depletion figures and replenishment orders to the Netherlands brewer through their linked Web pages. This interactive planning system generates time-phased orders based on actual usage rather than on projected demand. Distributors are then able to modify plans based on local conditions or changes in marketing. Heineken uses these modifications to adjust brewing and supply schedules. As a result of this system, lead times have been reduced from the traditional 10 to 12 weeks to 4 to 6 weeks. This time savings is especially useful in an industry competing on product freshness. In another example, Procter & Gamble participates in an information network to move the company's line of consumer products through Wal-Mart's many stores. As part of the network with Wal-Mart, P&G

knows by cash register and by store what products have passed through the system each day. The network is linked by satellite communications on a real-time basis. With actual point-of-sale information, products are replenished to meet current demand and minimize stockouts while maintaining exceptionally low inventories.[45]

Virtual teams are groups of geographically and/or organizationally dispersed coworkers that are assembled using a combination of telecommunications and information technologies to accomplish an organizational task.[46] Internet, intranet, and extranet systems are combining with other new technologies such as desktop videoconferencing and collaborative software to create a new workplace in which teams of workers are no longer restrained by geography, time, or organizational boundaries. As more companies outsource some of the activities previously conducted internally, the traditional organizational structure is being replaced by a series of virtual teams, which rarely, if ever, meet face-to-face. Such teams may be established as temporary groups to accomplish a specific task or may be more permanent to address continuing issues such as strategic planning. Membership on these teams is often fluid, depending upon the task to be accomplished. They may include not only employees from different functions within a company, but also members of various stakeholder groups, such as suppliers, customers, and law or consulting firms. The use of virtual teams to replace traditional face-to-face work groups is being driven by five trends:

1. Flatter organizational structures with increasing cross-functional coordination needs
2. Turbulent environments requiring more interorganizational cooperation
3. Increasing employee autonomy and participation in decision making
4. Higher knowledge requirements derived from a greater emphasis on service
5. Increasing globalization of trade and corporate activity[47]

Projections for the 21st Century

- From 1994 to 2010, the average income per capita in the developed nations will rise from $16,610 to $22,802.
- From 1994 to 2010, the average income per capita in the developing nations will increase from $950 to $2,563.[48]

Discussion Questions

1. What is the relevance of the resource-based view of the firm to strategic management in a global environment?
2. How can value-chain analysis help identify a company's strengths and weaknesses?
3. In what ways can a corporation's structure and culture be internal strengths or weaknesses?
4. What are the pros and cons of management's using the experience curve to determine strategy?
5. How might a firm's management decide whether it should continue to invest in current known technology or in new, but untested technology? What factors might encourage or discourage such a shift?

Strategic Practice Exercise

Can you analyze a corporation using the Internet? Try the following exercise.

1. Form teams of around five people. Find the Internet 100 Index from the latest copy of *USA Today*. (**Check this publisher's Web site for a recent listing of the**

Internet 100.) The index is divided into the e-Commerce 50 and the e-Business 50. The e-Commerce 50 is composed of four subindustries: e-Retail, e-Finance, e-New Media, and e-Service Providers. The e-Business 50 is composed of three subindustries: e-Infrastructure, e-Services/Solutions, and e-Advertising.

2. Each team selects four companies plus one assigned by the instructor. (The list of companies from which assignments will be made is Amazon.com, E-loan, Cisco Systems, AOL, Yahoo!, and DoubleClick.) Provide the instructor with your list.

3. Conduct research on each of your five companies *using the Internet only.*

4. Write a three to six page double-spaced typed report for each of the five companies. The report should include the following:

   a. Does the firm have any core competencies? Are any of these distinctive (better than the competition)

competencies? Does the firm have any competitive advantage? Provide a SWOT analysis using EFAS and IFAS Tables.

b. What is the likely future of this firm? Will the company survive industry consolidation?

c. Would you buy stock in this company? Assume that your team has $25,000 to invest. Allocate the money among your five companies. Be specific. List the five companies, the number of shares purchased of each, the cost of each share as of a given date, and the total cost for each purchase assuming a typical commission used by an Internet broker, such as E-Trade. (This part of your report will be common to all members of your team.)

Key Terms

autonomous (self-managing) work teams (p. 97)
basic R&D (p. 93)
capital budgeting (p. 92)
center of gravity (p. 85)
concurrent engineering (p. 97)
conglomerate structure (p. 88)
continuous systems (p. 96)
continuum of sustainability (p. 83)
core competencies (p. 82)
corporate capabilities (p. 82)
cross-functional work teams (p. 97)
corporate culture (p. 89)
cultural integration (p. 89)
cultural intensity (p. 89)
distinctive competencies (p. 82)
divisional structure (p. 87)
durability (p. 82)
economies of scale (p. 97)
economies of scope (p. 87)
engineering (or process) R&D (p. 93)
experience curve (p. 96)

explicit knowledge (p. 83)
extranet (p. 100)
financial leverage (p. 92)
flexible manufacturing (p. 97)
functional structure (p. 87)
human diversity (p. 98)
IFAS Table (p. 101)
imitability (p. 82)
intermittent systems (p. 95)
internal strategic factors (p. 81)
intranet (p. 100)
linkages (p. 86)
market position (p. 90)
market segmentation (p. 90)
marketing mix (p. 90)
mass customization (p. 97)
operating leverage (p. 96)
organizational analysis (p. 81)
organizational structures (p. 87)
primary activities (p. 85)
product life cycle (p. 90)
product R&D (p. 93)

quality of work life (p. 98)
R&D intensity (p. 92)
R&D mix (p. 93)
replicability (p. 83)
resource (p. 81)
reverse engineering (p. 82)
simple structure (p. 87)
strategic business units (SBUs) (p. 87)
support activities (p. 86)
supply chain management (p. 102)
tacit knowledge (p. 83)
technological competence (p. 92)
technological discontinuity (p. 94)
technology transfer (p. 93)
transferability (p. 82)
transparency (p. 82)
value chain (p. 84)
VRIO framework (p. 81)
virtual teams (p. 103)

Notes

1. M. Babineck, "United Airlines Increases Fares; Others Follow," *Des Moines Register* (November 18, 2000), p. 6D.
2. R. Roach & Associates, cited in *Air Transport World* (June 1996), p. 1.
3. J. B. Barney, *Gaining and Sustaining Competitive Advantage* (Reading, MA: Addison-Wesley, 1997), pp. 145–164.
4. R. M. Grant, "The Resource-Based Theory of Competitive Advantage: Implications for Strategy Formulation," *California Management Review* (Spring 1991), pp. 114–135.
5. M. Brellis, "Simple Strategy Makes Southwest Successful," (Ames) *Daily Tribune* (November 9, 2000), p. B7.
6. J. E. McGee and L. G. Love, "Sources of Competitive Advantage for Small Independent Retailers: Lessons from the Neighborhood Drugstore," *Association for Small Business & Entrepreneurship*, Houston, Texas (March 10–13, 1999), p. 2.
7. M. Polanyi, *The Tacit Dimension* (London: Routledge & Kegan Paul, 1966).

8. P. E. Bierly III, "Development of a Generic Knowledge Strategy Typology," *Journal of Business Strategies* (Spring 1999), p. 3.

9. O. Gadiesh and J. L. Gilbert, "Profit Pools: A Fresh Look at Strategy," *Harvard Business Review* (May–June, 1998), pp. 139–147.

10. J. R. Galbraith, "Strategy and Organization Planning," in *The Strategy Process: Concepts, Contexts, and Cases*, 2nd ed., edited by H. Mintzberg and J. B. Quinn (Upper Saddle River, NJ: Prentice Hall, 1991), pp. 315–324.

11. M. Porter, *Competitive Advantage: Creating and Sustaining Superior Performance* (New York: The Free Press, 1985), p. 36.

12. M. Leontiades, "A Diagnostic Framework for Planning," *Strategic Management Journal* (January–March 1983), p. 14.

13. E. H. Schein, *The Corporate Culture Survival Guide* (San Francisco: Jossey-Bass, 1999), p. 12; L. C. Harris and E. Ogbonna, "The Strategic Legacy of Company Founders," *Long Range Planning* (June 1999), pp. 333–343.

14. D. M. Rousseau, "Assessing Organizational Culture: The Case for Multiple Methods," in *Organizational Climate and Culture*, edited by B. Schneider (San Francisco: Jossey-Bass, 1990), pp. 153–192.

15. L. Smircich, "Concepts of Culture and Organizational Analysis," *Administrative Science Quarterly* (September 1983), pp. 345–346.

16. K. E. Aupperle, "Spontaneous Organizational Reconfiguration: A Historical Example Based on Xenophon's Anabasis," *Organization Science* (July–August 1996), pp. 445–460.

17. Barney, p. 155.

18. R. L. Simerly and M. Li, "Environmental Dynamism, Capital Structure and Performance: A Theoretical Integration and an Empirical Test," *Strategic Management Journal* (January 2000), pp. 31–49.

19. R. L. Simerly and M. Li, "Environmental Dynamism, Capital Structure and Performance: A Theoretical Integration and an Empirical Test," *Strategic Management Journal* (January 2000), pp. 31–49.

20. J. M. Poterba and L. H. Summers, "A CEO Survey of U.S. Companies' Time Horizons and Hurdle Rates," *Sloan Management Review* (Fall 1995), pp. 43–53.

21. "R&D Scoreboard," *Business Week* (June 27, 1994), pp. 81–103.

22. B. O'Reilly, "The Secrets of America's Most Admired Corporations: New Ideas and New Products," *Fortune* (March 3, 1997), p. 62.

23. P. Pascarella, "Are You Investing in the Wrong Technology?" *Industry Week* (July 25, 1983), p. 37.

24. D. J. Yang, "Leaving Moore's Law in the Dust," *U.S. News & World Report* (July 10, 2000), pp. 37–38; R. Fishburne and M. Malone, "Laying Down the Laws: Gordon Moore and Bob Metcalfe in Conversation," *Forbes ASAP* (February 21, 2000), pp. 97–100.

25. Pascarella., p. 38.

26. C. M. Christensen, *The Innovator's Dilemma* (Boston: Harvard Business School Press, 1997).

27. B. J. Pine, *Mass Customization: The New Frontier in Business Competition* (Boston: Harvard Business School Press, 1993).

28. E. E. Lawler, S. A. Mohrman, and G. E. Ledford, Jr., *Creating High Performance Organizations* (San Francisco: Jossey-Bass, 1995), p. 29.

29. A. Versteeg, "Self-Directed Work Teams Yield Long-Term Benefits," *Journal of Business Strategy* (November/December 1990), pp. 9–12.

30. R. Sanchez, "Strategic Flexibility in Product Competition," *Strategic Management Journal* (Summer 1995), p. 147.

31. A. R. Jassawalla and H. C. Sashittal, "Building Collaborative Cross-Functional New Product Teams," *Academy of Management Executive* (August 1999), pp. 50–63.

32. E. E. Lawler, S. A. Mohrman, and G. E. Ledford, Jr., *Creating High Performance Organizations* (San Francisco: Jossey-Bass, 1995), p. 123. The percentage of unionized government employees is 38.7%. See "Uncle Sam Gompers," *Wall Street Journal* (October 25, 1994), p. A20.

33. S. F. Matusik and C. W. L. Hill, "The Utilization of Contingent Work, Knowledge Creation, and Competitive Advantage," *Academy of Management Executive* (October 1998), pp. 680–697.

34. A. Bewrnstein, "At UPS, Part-Time Work Is a Full-Time Issue," *Business Week* (June 16, 1997), pp. 88–90.

35. D. L. Boroughs, "The New Migrant Workers," *U.S. News & World Report* (July 4, 1994), p. 53.

36. J. Muller, "A Ford Redesign," *Business Week* (November 13, 2000), Special Report.

37. G. Colvin, "The 50 Best Companies for Asians, Blacks, and Hispanics," *Fortune* (July 19, 1999), pp. 53–58.

38. J. Bachman, "Coke to Pay $192.5 Million to Settle Lawsuit," *The (Ames) Tribune* (November 20, 2000), p. D4.

39. J. Lee and D. Miller, "People Matter: Commitment to Employees, Strategy, and Performance in Korean Firms," *Strategic Management Journal* (June 1999), pp. 579–593.

40. B. Rosser, "Making IT Investments Cost Effective," *Executive Edge* (September 1998), pp. 50–54.

41. A. Cortese, "Here Comes the Intranet," *Business Week* (February 26, 1996), p. 76.

42. B. Rosser, "Making IT Investments Cost Effective," *Executive Edge* (September 1998), pp. 50–54.

43. D. Bartholomew, "Blue-Collar Computing," *InformationWeek* (June 19, 1995), pp. 34–43.

44. C. C. Poirier, *Advanced Supply Chain Management* (San Francisco: Berrett-Koehler Publishers, 1999), p. 2.

45. C. C. Poirer, pp. 3–5.

46. A. M. Townsend, S. M. DeMarie, and A. R. Hendrickson, "Virtual Teams" Technology and the Workplace of the Future," *Academy of Management Executive* (August 1998), pp. 17–29.

47. Townsend, DeMarie, and Hendrickson, p. 18.

48. J. Warner, "21st Century Capitalism: Snapshot of the Next Century," *Business Week* (November 18, 1994), p. 194.

Newbury Comics, Inc.

ENVIRONMENTAL SCANNING AND ORGANIZATIONAL ANALYSIS

Newbury Comics Cofounders, Mike Dreese and John Brusger, parlayed $2,000 and a comic book collection into a thriving chain of 22 stores spanning the New England region. Known to be *the* place to shop for everything from the best of the underground/independent scene to major label superstars, the chain also stocks a wide variety of non-music related items such as T-shirts, Dr. (doc) Martens shoes, posters, jewelry, cosmetics, books, magazines, and other trendy items.

In Part Two, "**Scanning the Environment**," the video case addresses the identification of external environmental variables, industry analysis, and organizational analysis. Newbury Comics, Inc., Cofounders Mike and John, and Jan Johannet, Store Manager for one of the New Hampshire stores, reveal more about the development of the company. They discuss factors contributing to the successful growth of Newbury Comics. They describe how their diverse customers plus the emergence of bootlegging (selling illegal copies) and burning discs (copying 1 CD onto another CD) led the company to begin offering used CDs in its stores.

Used CDs have become a very important business for Newbury Comics. Mike Dreese reports that used CDs account for $6 to 7 million in annual sales and $4 million in annual gross profits for the company. This fact is remarkable given that the firm's overall annual sales and pre-tax profits are $75 million and $8 million, respectively. According to John Brusger and Jan Johannet, the new CD market turned "soft" when the mass merchandisers like Target and Best Buy began offering CDs and Internet companies, such as Napster, offered the downloading of music. John and Mike wanted another product to supplement their sales of new CDs. They scanned their environment to learn if it made sense to enter this business.

They asked the owners of local specialty music stores for information. These "mom and pop" retailers had been buying and selling used CDs for years and were very familiar with this product. Mike refers to the local mom and pop retailers as his "strategic alliance of information sources." According to John, surveys of current customers revealed that a large number of Newbury Comics customers wanted the company to be in the used CD business. Management analyzed the competition for used CDs in Newbury Comics' market area. Used CDs appeared to have high sales potential. The immediate competition was composed of mom and pop specialty music retailers; no chain stores offered used CDs at that time. According to Mike Dreese, the local stores weren't doing a good job of marketing used CDs.

According to Mike and Jan, Newbury Comics has several internal strengths which uniquely fit the used CD market. The stores have a wide variety of customers and a staff with "knowledge of the street." The employees live the lifestyle of Newbury Comics' discriminating customers and are thus able to identify trends before the public at large learns of them. Consequently, the stores are able to purchase an excellent selection of underground music in addition to the usual top 50 and older CDs. Mike Dreese states that new entrant specialist shops into the used CD business are "not a threat to us." He is concerned that established chains such as Tower Records, Best Buy, and Music Land might someday enter the used CD business.

Concepts Illustrated in the Video

- Environmental Scanning
- Industry Analysis
- Organizational Analysis
- Identifying Societal Trends
- Rivalry Among Existing Firms

- Threat of New Entrants/Entry Barriers
- Threat of Substitute Products
- Industry Evolution
- Core and Distinctive Competencies
- Corporate Culture

Study Questions

1. How does Newbury Comics conduct environmental scanning? How well is it doing it?
2. Describe the competitors in Newbury Comics's market area. Do they form strategic groups? How do the actions of competitors affect Newbury Comics (and vice versa)?
3. What are the substitutes for CDs? Are they a threat or an opportunity for Newbury Comics?
4. What external factors played a role in the decision to enter the used CD business? What other businesses should the company consider entering?
5. What are the core competencies of Newbury Comics? Are they distinctive? Why?

chapter 5

Strategy Formulation: Situation Analysis and Business Strategy

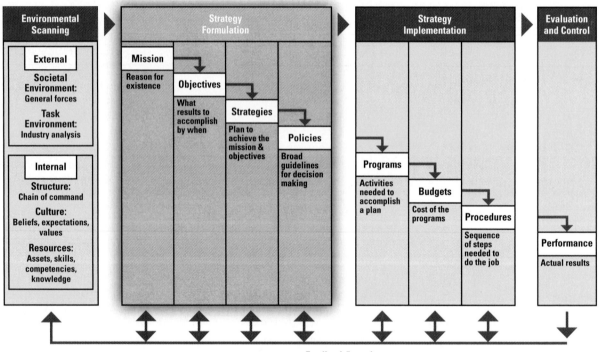

Environmental Scanning	Strategy Formulation	Strategy Implementation	Evaluation and Control
External **Societal Environment:** General forces **Task Environment:** Industry analysis **Internal** **Structure:** Chain of command **Culture:** Beliefs, expectations, values **Resources:** Assets, skills, competencies, knowledge	**Mission** Reason for existence **Objectives** What results to accomplish by when **Strategies** Plan to achieve the mission & objectives **Policies** Broad guidelines for decision making	**Programs** Activities needed to accomplish a plan **Budgets** Cost of the programs **Procedures** Sequence of steps needed to do the job	**Performance** Actual results

Feedback/Learning

When Donald Lamberti incorporated Casey's General Stores in 1967 in Des Moines, Iowa, he formulated a strategy unknown at that time in the convenience store industry. Instead of targeting the large, growing metropolitan areas of the eastern, western, and southern United States where potential sales were high, he chose to focus on the small towns in the agricultural heartland of the Midwest. Contrary to all the conventional wisdom arguing against beginning a business in a declining market, Lamberti avoided direct competition with 7-Eleven and moved into these increasingly ignored small markets. The company expanded its offerings from just gasoline and basic groceries to include fast food and bakeries. In many small Midwestern towns, Casey's was now the only retail business left. These were towns too small for even Wal-Mart to covet. Like any convenience store, prices were somewhat higher than in larger, more specialized stores in the cities. But people from small towns did not want to have to drive 10 to 20 miles for a loaf of bread or a pizza.

By 2001, Casey's had opened over 1,100 stores in the upper midwestern United States. At a time when other convenience stores were struggling to show a profit and avoid bankruptcy, Casey's recorded continuing growth and profitability. (For further information, see <www.caseys.com>.)

Casey's General Stores is successful because its strategic managers formulated a new strategy designed to give it an advantage in a very competitive industry. Casey's is an example of a differentiation focus competitive strategy in which a company focuses on a particular market area to provide a differentiated product or service. This strategy is one of the business competitive strategies discussed in this chapter.

5.1 Situational Analysis: SWOT Analysis

Strategy formulation is often referred to as strategic planning or long-range planning and is concerned with developing a corporation's mission, objectives, strategies, and policies. It begins with situation analysis: the process of finding a strategic fit between external opportunities and internal strengths while working around external threats and internal weaknesses. As shown in the *Strategic Decision-Making Process* in **Figure 1–5** on pages 20–21, this is step 5(a): analyzing strategic factors in light of the current situation using SWOT analysis. **SWOT** is an acronym used to describe the particular **S**trengths, **W**eaknesses, **O**pportunities, and **T**hreats that are strategic factors for a specific company. SWOT analysis should not only result in the identification of a corporation's **distinctive competencies**—the particular capabilities and resources that a firm possesses and the superior way in which they are used—but also in the identification of opportunities that the firm is not currently able to take advantage of due to a lack of appropriate resources. Over the years, SWOT analysis has proven to be the most enduring analytical technique used in strategic management. For example, a survey of 113 manufacturing and service companies in the United Kingdom reported the five most-used tools and techniques in strategic analysis to be (1) spreadsheet "what if" analysis, (2) analysis of key or critical success factors, (3) financial analysis of competitors, (4) SWOT analysis, and (5) core capabilities analysis.[1] It is very likely that these have a similar rate of usage in the rest of the world.

It can be said that the essence of strategy is opportunity divided by capacity.[2] An opportunity by itself has no real value unless a company has the capacity (i.e., resources) to take advantage of that opportunity. This approach, however, considers only opportunities and strengths when considering alternative strategies. By itself, a distinctive competency in a key resource or capability is no guarantee of competitive advantage. Weaknesses in other resource areas can prevent a strategy from being successful. SWOT can thus be used to take a broader view of strategy through the formula SA = O/(S − W) (Strategic Alternative equals Opportunity divided by Strengths minus Weaknesses). This reflects an important issue facing strategic managers: *Should we invest more in our strengths to make them even stronger (a distinctive competence), or should we invest in our weaknesses to at least make them competitive?*

SWOT analysis, by itself, is not a panacea. Some of the primary **criticisms of SWOT** analysis are:

- It generates lengthy lists.
- It uses no weights to reflect priorities.
- It uses ambiguous words and phrases.
- The same factor can be placed in two categories (e.g., a strength may also be a weakness).
- There is no obligation to verify opinions with data or analysis.
- It requires only a single level of analysis.
- There is no logical link to strategy implementation.[3]

Table 4–2 Internal Factor Analysis Summary (IFAS): Maytag as Example (Selection of Strategic Factors)*

Internal Strategic Factors	Weight	Rating	Weighted Score	Comments
	1	2	3	4	5
Strengths				
S1 Quality Maytag culture	.15	5.0	.75	Quality key to success
S2 Experienced top management	.05	4.2	.21	Know appliances
S3 Vertical integration	.10	3.9	.39	Dedicated factories
S4 Employee relations	.05	3.0	.15	Good, but deteriorating
S5 Hoover's international orientation	.15	2.8	.42	Hoover name in cleaners
Weaknesses				
W1 Process-oriented R&D	.05	2.2	.11	Slow on new products
W2 Distribution channels	.05	2.0	.10	Superstores replacing small dealers
W3 Financial position	.15	2.0	.30	High debt load
W4 Global positioning	.20	2.1	.42	Hoover weak outside the United Kingdom and Australia
W5 Manufacturing facilities	.05	4.0	.20	Investing now
Total Scores	1.00		3.05	

Table 3–4 External Factor Analysis Summary (EFAS): Maytag as Example (Selection of Strategic Factors)*

External Strategic Factors	Weight	Rating	Weighted Score	Comments
	1	2	3	4	5
Opportunities				
01 Economic integration of European Community	.20	4.1	.82	Acquisition of Hoover
02 Demographics favor quality appliances	.10	5.0	.50	Maytag quality
03 Economic development of Asia	.05	1.0	.05	Low Maytag presence
04 Opening of Eastern Europe	.05	2.0	.10	Will take time
05 Trend to "Super Stores"	.10	1.8	.18	Maytag weak in this channel
Threats				
T1 Increasing government regulations	.10	4.3	.43	Well positioned
T2 Strong U.S. competition	.10	4.0	.40	Well positioned
T3 Whirlpool and Electrolux strong globally	.15	3.0	.45	Hoover weak globally
T4 New product advances	.05	1.2	.06	Questionable
T5 Japanese appliance companies	.10	1.6	.16	Only Asian presence is Australia
Total Scores	1.00		3.15	

*The most important external and internal factors are identified in the EFAS and IFAS tables as shown here by shading these factors.

GENERATING A STRATEGIC FACTORS ANALYSIS SUMMARY (SFAS) MATRIX

The EFAS and IFAS Tables plus the SFAS Matrix have been developed to deal with the above criticisms of SWOT analysis. When used together, they are a powerful set of analytical tools for strategic analysis. The **SFAS (Strategic Factors Analysis Summary) Matrix** summarizes an organization's strategic factors by combining the external factors from the EFAS Table with the

Figure 5–1
Strategic Factor Analysis Summary (SFAS) Matrix

Strategic Factors (Select the most important opportunities/threats from EFAS, Table 3–4 and the most important strengths and weaknesses from IFAS, Table 4–2)	1 Weight	2 Rating	3 Weighted Score	4 SHORT	Duration INTERMEDIATE	5 LONG	6 Comments
S1 Quality Maytag culture (S)	.10	5.0	.50			X	Quality key to success
S5 Hoover's international orientation (S)	.10	2.8	.28	X	X		Name recognition
W3 Financial position (W)	.10	2.0	.20	X	X		High debt
W4 Global positioning (W)	.15	2.2	.33				Only in N.A., U.K., and Australia
01 Economic integration of European Community (O)	.10	4.1	.41			X X	Acquisition of Hoover
02 Demographics favor quality (O)	.10	5.0	.50		X		Maytag quality
05 Trend to super stores (O + T)	.10	1.8	.18	X			Weak in this channel
T3 Whirlpool and Electrolux (T)	.15	3.0	.45	X			Dominate industry
T5 Japanese appliance companies (T)	.10	1.6	.16			X	Asian presence
Total Scores	1.00		3.01				

Notes:
1. List each of the most important factors developed in your IFAS and EFAS tables in Column 1.
2. Weight each factor from 1.0 (Most Important) to 0.0 (Not Important) in Column 2 based on that factor's probable impact on the company's strategic position. **The total weights must sum to 1.00**.
3. Rate each factor from 5.0 (Outstanding) to 1.0 (Poor) in Column 3 based on the company's response to that factor.
4. Multiply each factor's weight times its rating to obtain each factor's weighted score in Column 4.
5. For duration in Column 5, check appropriate column (short term—less than 1 year; intermediate—1 to 3 years; long term—over 3 years).
6. Use Column 6 (comments) for rationale used for each factor.

Source: T. L. Wheelen and J. D. Hunger, "Strategic Factors Analysis Summary (SFAS)." Copyright © 1997 by Wheelen and Hunger Associates. Reprinted by permission.

internal factors from the IFAS Table. The EFAS and IFAS examples given of Maytag Corporation (as it was in 1995) in **Tables 3–4** and **4–2** list a total of 20 internal and external factors. These are too many factors for most people to use in strategy formulation. The SFAS Matrix requires the strategic decision maker to condense these strengths, weaknesses, opportunities, and threats into fewer than 10 strategic factors. This is done by reviewing and revising the weight given each factor. The revised weights reflect the priority of each factor as a determinant of the company's future success. The highest weighted EFAS and IFAS factors should appear in the SFAS Matrix.

As shown in **Figure 5–1**, you can create an SFAS Matrix by following these steps:

■ In the **Strategic Factors** column (column 1), list the most important (in terms of weight) EFAS and IFAS items. After each factor, indicate whether it is a strength (S), weakness (W), opportunity (O), threat (T), or a combination.

- In the **Weight** column (column 2), enter the weights for all of the internal and external strategic factors. As with the EFAS and IFAS Tables, the **weight column must still total 1.00.** This means that the weights calculated for EFAS and IFAS will probably have to be adjusted.

- In the **Rating** column (column 3), enter the ratings of how the company's management is responding to each of the strategic factors. These ratings will probably (but not always) be the same as those listed in the EFAS and IFAS Tables.

- In the **Weighted Score** column (column 4), calculate the weighted scores as done earlier for EFAS and IFAS.

- In the new **Duration** column (column 5), depicted in **Figure 5–1**, indicate **short-term** *(less than 1 year)*, **intermediate-term** *(1 to 3 years)*, or **long-term** *(3 years and beyond)*.

- In the **Comments** column (column 6), repeat or revise your comments for each strategic factor from the EFAS and IFAS Tables.

The resulting SFAS Matrix is a listing of the firm's external and internal strategic factors in one table. The example given is that of Maytag Corporation in 1995 before the firm sold its European and Australian operations. The SFAS Matrix includes only the most important factors gathered from environmental scanning and thus provides the information essential for strategy formulation. The use of EFAS and IFAS Tables together with the SFAS Matrix deal with many of the criticisms of SWOT analysis.

FINDING A PROPITIOUS NICHE

One desired outcome of analyzing strategic factors is identifying a niche where an organization can use its core competencies to take advantage of a particular market opportunity. A niche is a need in the marketplace that is currently unsatisfied. The goal is to find a **propitious niche**—an extremely favorable niche—that is so well suited to the firm's internal and external environment that other corporations are not likely to challenge or dislodge it.[4] A niche is propitious to the extent that it currently is just large enough for one firm to satisfy its demand. After a firm has found and filled that niche, it is not worth a potential competitor's time or money to also go after the same niche.

Finding such a niche is not always easy. A firm's management must be always looking for a **strategic window**, that is, a unique market opportunity that is available only for a particular time. The first firm through a strategic window can occupy a propitious niche and discourage competition (if the firm has the required internal strengths). One company that has successfully found a propitious niche is Frank J. Zamboni & Company, the manufacturer of the machines that smooth the ice at ice skating rinks. Frank Zamboni invented the unique tractorlike machine in 1949 and no one has found a substitute for what it does. Before the machine was invented, people had to clean and scrape the ice by hand to prepare the surface for skating. Now hockey fans look forward to intermissions just to watch "the Zamboni" slowly drive up and down the ice rink turning rough, scraped ice into a smooth mirror surface—almost like magic. So long as Zamboni's company is able to produce the machines in the quantity and quality desired at a reasonable price, it's not worth another company's time to go after Frank Zamboni & Company's propitious niche.

As the niche grows, so can the company within that niche—by increasing its operations' capacity or through alliances with larger firms. The key is to identify a market opportunity in which the first firm to reach that market segment can obtain and keep dominant market share. For example, Church & Dwight was the first company in the United States to successfully market sodium bicarbonate for use in cooking. Its Arm & Hammer brand baking soda is still found in 95% of all U.S. households. The propitious niche concept is crucial to the software industry. Small initial demand in emerging markets allows new entrepreneurial ventures to go after niches too small to be noticed by established companies. When Microsoft developed its first disk operating system (DOS) in 1980 for IBM's personal computers, for example, the demand for such open systems software was very small—a small niche for a then very small Microsoft. The company was able to fill that niche and to successfully grow with it.

Niches can also change—sometimes faster than a firm can adapt to that change. A company's managers may discover in their situation analysis that they need to invest heavily in the firm's capabilities to keep them competitively strong in a changing niche. South African Breweries (SAB), for example, took this approach when management realized that the only way to keep competitors out of its market was to continuously invest in increased productivity and infrastructure in order to keep its prices very low. See the **Global Issue** feature to see how SAB was able to successfully defend its market niche during significant changes in its environment.

Global Issue

SAB Defends Its Propitious Niche

Out of 50 beers consumed by South Africans, 49 are brewed by South African Breweries (SAB). Founded more than a century ago, SAB controlled most of the local beer market by 1950 with brands like Castle and Lion. When the government repealed the ban on the sale of alcohol to blacks in the 1960s, SAB and other brewers competed for the rapidly growing market. SAB fought successfully to retain its dominance of the market. With the end of apartheid, foreign brewers have been tempted to break SAB's near-monopoly, but have been deterred by the entry barriers SAB has erected.

Entry Barrier #1

Every year for the past two decades SAB has reduced its prices. The "real" (adjusted for inflation) price of its beer is now half what it was during the 1970s. SAB has been able to achieve this through a continuous emphasis on productivity improvements—boosting production while cutting the workforce almost in half. Keeping prices low has been key to SAB's avoiding charges of abusing its monopoly.

Entry Barrier #2

In South Africa's poor and rural areas, roads are rough and electricity is undependable. SAB has long experience in transporting crates to remote villages along bad roads

and making sure that distributors have refrigerators (and electricity generators if needed). Many of its distributors are former employees who have been helped by the company to start their own trucking businesses.

Entry Barrier #3

Most of the beer sold in South Africa is sold through unlicensed pubs called *shebeens*, most of which date back to apartheid when blacks were not allowed licenses. Although the current government of South Africa would be pleased to grant pub licenses to blacks, the shebeen-owners don't want them. They enjoy not paying any taxes. SAB cannot sell directly to the shebeens, but it does so indirectly through wholesalers. The government, in turn, ignores the situation, preferring that people drink SAB beer than potentially deadly moonshine.

To break into South Africa, a new entrant would have to build large breweries and a substantial distribution network. SAB would, in turn, probably reduce its prices still further to defend its market. The difficulties of operating in South Africa are too great, the market is growing too slowly, and (given SAB's low-cost position) the likely profit margin is too low to justify entering the market. Some foreign brewers, such as Heineken, would rather use SAB to distribute their products throughout South Africa. As a result, SAB is now the world's fifth largest brewer by volume. With its home market secure, SAB's management considered acquiring a global brewer such as Bass in June 2000, but decided against it because of the high price.

Source: "Big Lion, Small Cage," *The Economist* (August 12, 2000), p. 56. Reprinted with permission.

5.2 Review of Mission and Objectives

A reexamination of an organization's current mission and objectives must be made before alternative strategies can be generated and evaluated. Even when formulating strategy, decision makers tend to concentrate on the alternatives—the action possibilities—rather than on a mission to be fulfilled and objectives to be achieved. This tendency is so attractive because it is much easier to deal with alternative courses of action that exist right here and now than to really think about what you want to accomplish in the future. The end result is that we often choose strategies that set our objectives for us, rather than having our choices incorporate clear objectives and a mission statement.

Problems in performance can derive from an inappropriate statement of mission, which may be too narrow or too broad. If the mission does not provide a *common thread* (a unifying theme) for a corporation's businesses, managers may be unclear about where the company is heading. Objectives and strategies might be in conflict with each other. Divisions might be competing against one another, rather than against outside competition, to the detriment of the corporation as a whole.

A company's objectives can also be inappropriately stated. They can either focus too much on short-term operational goals or be so general that they provide little real guidance. There may be a gap between planned and achieved objectives. When such a gap occurs, either the strategies have to be changed to improve performance or the objectives need to be adjusted downward to be more realistic. Consequently, objectives should be constantly reviewed to ensure their usefulness. This is what happened at Toyota Motor Corporation when top management realized that its "Global 10" objective of aiming for 10% of the global vehicle market was no longer feasible. Emphasis was then shifted from market share to profits. Interestingly, at the same time that both Toyota and General Motors were de-emphasizing market share as a key corporate objective, Ford Motor Company was stating that it wanted to be Number 1 in sales worldwide. No longer content with being in second place, Alexander Trotman, Ford's Chairman of the Board, contends: "Have you ever seen a team run out on the field and say, 'We're going to be Number 2?'"[5]

5.3 Generating Alternative Strategies Using a TOWS Matrix

Thus far we have discussed how a firm uses SWOT analysis to assess its situation. SWOT can also be used to generate a number of possible alternative strategies. The **TOWS Matrix** (TOWS is just another way of saying SWOT) illustrates how the external opportunities and threats facing a particular corporation can be matched with that company's internal strengths and weaknesses to result in four sets of possible strategic alternatives. (See **Figure 5–2.**) This is a good way to use brainstorming to create alternative strategies that might not otherwise be considered. It forces strategic managers to create various kinds of growth as well as retrenchment strategies. It can be used to generate corporate as well as business strategies.

To generate a TOWS Matrix for Maytag Corporation in 1995, for example, use the *External Factor Analysis Summary* (EFAS) listed in **Table 3–4** from **Chapter 3** and the *Internal Factor Analysis Summary* (IFAS) listed in **Table 4–2** from **Chapter 4**. To build **Figure 5–3**, take the following steps:

1. In the **Opportunities (O)** block, list the external opportunities available in the company's or business unit's current and future environment from the EFAS Table (**Table 3–4**).

2. In the **Threats (T)** block, list the external threats facing the company or unit now and in the future from the EFAS Table (**Table 3–4**).

Figure 5–2
TOWS Matrix

INTERNAL FACTORS (IFAS) / EXTERNAL FACTORS (EFAS)	Strengths (S) List 5 – 10 *internal* strengths here	Weaknesses (W) List 5 – 10 *internal* weaknesses here
Opportunities (O) List 5 – 10 *external* opportunities here	**SO Strategies** Generate strategies here that use **strengths** to take **advantage** of **opportunities**	**WO Strategies** Generate strategies here that take **advantage** of **opportunities** by **overcoming weaknesses**
Threats (T) List 5 – 10 *external* opportunities here	**ST Strategies** Generate strategies here that use **strengths** to **avoid threats**	**WT Strategies** Generate strategies here that **minimize weaknesses** and **avoid threats**

Source: Reprinted from *Long-Range Planning*, April 1982. H. Weihrich, "The TOWS Matrix—A Tool for Situational Analysis," p. 60. Copyright 1982, with permission from Elsevier Science.

3. In the **Strengths (S)** block, list the specific areas of current and future strength for the company or unit from the IFAS Table (**Table 4–2**).

4. In the **Weaknesses (W)** block, list the specific areas of current and future weakness for the company or unit from the IFAS Table (**Table 4–2**).

5. Generate a series of possible strategies for the company or business unit under consideration based on particular combinations of the four sets of factors:

 - **SO Strategies** are generated by thinking of ways in which a company or business unit could use its strengths to take advantage of opportunities.

 - **ST Strategies** consider a company's or unit's strengths as a way to avoid threats.

 - **WO Strategies** attempt to take advantage of opportunities by overcoming weaknesses.

 - **WT Strategies** are basically defensive and primarily act to minimize weaknesses and avoid threats.

The TOWS Matrix is very useful for generating a series of alternatives that the decision makers of a company or business unit might not otherwise have considered. It can be used for the corporation as a whole (as was done in **Figure 5–3** with Maytag Corporation before it sold Hoover Europe), or it can be used for a specific business unit within a corporation (like Hoover's floor-care products). Nevertheless the TOWS Matrix is only one of many ways to generate alternative strategies. Another approach is to evaluate each business unit within a corporation in terms of possible competitive and cooperative strategies.

5.4 Business Strategies

Business strategy focuses on improving the competitive position of a company's or business unit's products or services within the specific industry or market segment that the company or business unit serves. Business strategy can be competitive (battling against all competitors for

Table 4–2 Internal Factor Analysis Summary (IFAS): Maytag as Example (Selection of Strategic Factors)*

Internal Strategic Factors	Weight	Rating	Weighted Score	Comments
	1	2	3	4	5
Strengths				
S1 Quality Maytag culture	.15	5.0	.75	Quality key to success
S2 Experienced top management	.05	4.2	.21	Know appliances
S3 Vertical integration	.10	3.9	.39	Dedicated factories
S4 Employee relations	.05	3.0	.15	Good, but deteriorating
S5 Hoover's international orientation	.15	2.8	.42	Hoover name in cleaners
Weaknesses				
W1 Process-oriented R&D	.05	2.2	.11	Slow on new products
W2 Distribution channels	.05	2.0	.10	Superstores replacing small dealers
W3 Financial position	.15	2.0	.30	High debt load
W4 Global positioning	.20	2.1	.42	Hoover weak outside the United Kingdom and Australia
W5 Manufacturing facilities	.05	4.0	.20	Investing now
Total Scores	1.00		3.05	

Table 3–4 External Factor Analysis Summary (EFAS): Maytag as Example (Selection of Strategic Factors)*

External Strategic Factors	Weight	Rating	Weighted Score	Comments
	1	2	3	4	5
Opportunities				
O1 Economic integration of European Community	.20	4.1	.82	Acquisition of Hoover
O2 Demographics favor quality appliances	.10	5.0	.50	Maytag quality
O3 Economic development of Asia	.05	1.0	.05	Low Maytag presence
O4 Opening of Eastern Europe	.05	2.0	.10	Will take time
O5 Trend to "Super Stores"	.10	1.8	.18	Maytag weak in this channel
Threats				
T1 Increasing government regulations	.10	4.3	.43	Well positioned
T2 Strong U.S. competition	.10	4.0	.40	Well positioned
T3 Whirlpool and Electrolux strong globally	.15	3.0	.45	Hoover weak globally
T4 New product advances	.05	1.2	.06	Questionable
T5 Japanese appliance companies	.10	1.6	.16	Only Asian presence is Australia
Total Scores	1.00		3.15	

*The most important external and internal factors are identified in the EFAS and IFAS tables as shown here by shading these factors.

Figure 5–3

Generating a TOWS Matrix for Maytag Corporation

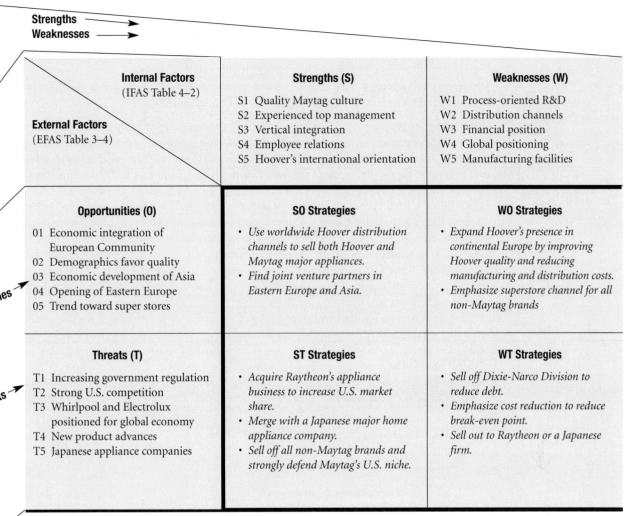

advantage) and/or cooperative (working with one or more competitors to gain advantage against other competitors). Just as corporate strategy asks what industry(ies) the company should be in, business strategy asks how the company or its units should compete or cooperate in each industry.

PORTER'S COMPETITIVE STRATEGIES

Competitive strategy raises the following questions:

- Should we compete on the basis of low cost (and thus price), or should we differentiate our products or services on some basis other than cost, such as quality or service?

- Should we compete head to head with our major competitors for the biggest but most sought-after share of the market, or should we focus on a niche in which we can satisfy a less sought-after but also profitable segment of the market?

Michael Porter proposes two "generic" competitive strategies for outperforming other corporations in a particular industry: lower cost and differentiation.[6] These strategies are called generic because they can be pursued by any type or size of business firm, even by not-for-profit organizations.

- **Lower cost strategy** is the ability of a company or a business unit to design, produce, and market a comparable product more efficiently than its competitors.
- **Differentiation strategy** is the ability to provide unique and superior value to the buyer in terms of product quality, special features, or after-sale service.

Porter further proposes that a firm's competitive advantage in an industry is determined by its **competitive scope**, that is, the breadth of the company's or business unit's target market. Before using one of the two generic competitive strategies (lower cost or differentiation), the firm or unit must choose the range of product varieties it will produce, the distribution channels it will employ, the types of buyers it will serve, the geographic areas in which it will sell, and the array of related industries in which it will also compete. This should reflect an understanding of the firm's unique resources. Simply put, a company or business unit can choose a broad target (that is, aim at the middle of the mass market) or a narrow target (that is, aim at a market niche). Combining these two types of target markets with the two competitive strategies results in the four variations of generic strategies depicted in **Figure 5–4**. When the lower cost and differentiation strategies have a broad mass market target, they are simply called *cost leadership* and *differentiation.* When they are focused on a market niche (narrow target), however, they are called *cost focus* and *differentiation focus.* Although research does indicate that established firms pursuing broad-scope strategies outperform firms following narrow-scope strategies in terms of ROA, new entrepreneurial firms have a better chance of surviving if they follow a narrow-scope over a broad-scope strategy.[7]

Cost leadership is a low-cost competitive strategy that aims at the broad mass market and requires "aggressive construction of efficient-scale facilities, vigorous pursuit of cost reduc-

Figure 5–4
Porter's Generic Competitive Strategies

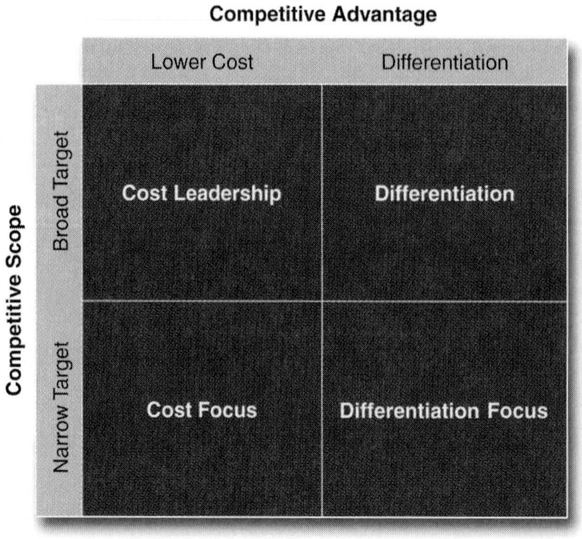

Source: Reprinted with permission of The Free Press, an imprint of Simon & Schuster, from *The Competitive Advantage of Nations* by Michael E. Porter, p. 39. Copyright © 1990 by Michael E. Porter.

tions from experience, tight cost and overhead control, avoidance of marginal customer accounts, and cost minimization in areas like R&D, service, sales force, advertising, and so on."[8] Because of its lower costs, the cost leader is able to charge a lower price for its products than its competitors and still make a satisfactory profit. Some companies successfully following this strategy are Wal-Mart, Alamo Rent-A-Car, Southwest Airlines, Timex, and Gateway 2000. Having a low-cost position also gives a company or business unit a defense against rivals. Its lower costs allow it to continue to earn profits during times of heavy competition. Its high market share means that it will have high bargaining power relative to its suppliers (because it buys in large quantities). Its low price will also serve as a barrier to entry because few new entrants will be able to match the leader's cost advantage. As a result, cost leaders are likely to earn above-average returns on investment.

Differentiation is aimed at the broad mass market and involves the creation of a product or service that is perceived throughout its industry as unique. The company or business unit may then charge a premium for its product. This specialty can be associated with design or brand image, technology, features, dealer network, or customer service. Differentiation is a viable strategy for earning above-average returns in a specific business because the resulting brand loyalty lowers customers' sensitivity to price. Increased costs can usually be passed on to the buyers. Buyer loyalty also serves as an entry barrier—new firms must develop their own distinctive competence to differentiate their products in some way in order to compete successfully. Examples of the successful use of a differentiation strategy are Walt Disney Productions, Maytag appliances, Nike athletic shoes, Apple Computer, and Mercedes-Benz automobiles. Research does suggest that a differentiation strategy is more likely to generate higher profits than is a low-cost strategy because differentiation creates a better entry barrier. A low-cost strategy is more likely, however, to generate increases in market share.[9]

Cost focus is a low-cost competitive strategy that focuses on a particular buyer group or geographic market and attempts to serve only this niche, to the exclusion of others. In using cost focus, the company or business unit seeks a cost advantage in its target segment. A good example of this strategy is Fadal Engineering. Fadal focuses its efforts on building and selling no-frills machine tools to small manufacturers. Fadal achieved cost focus by keeping overhead and R&D to a minimum and by focusing its marketing efforts strictly on its market niche. The cost focus strategy is valued by those who believe that a company or business unit that focuses its efforts is better able to serve its narrow strategic target more efficiently than can its competition. It does, however, require a tradeoff between profitability and overall market share.

Differentiation focus, like cost focus, concentrates on a particular buyer group, product line segment, or geographic market. This is the strategy successfully followed by Casey's General Stores, Morgan Motor Car Company (manufacturer of classic British sports cars), and local health food stores. In using differentiation focus, the company or business unit seeks differentiation in a targeted market segment. This strategy is valued by those who believe that a company or a unit that focuses its efforts is better able to serve the special needs of a narrow strategic target more effectively than can its competition. This is the strategy being effectively used by Inner City Entertainment (ICE), a company focusing on building new high quality movie theaters in inner-city locations aimed primarily at African Americans. Owned and managed by Alisa and Donzell Starks, ICE has successfully opened numerous theaters in Chicago's South Side. The company uses urban radio stations to promote its films and offers special screenings of films with high interest, such as *Amistad*. "I want to be the first black-owned theater chain," states Mr. Starks, the company's CEO. "No ifs, ands, or buts."[10]

Risks in Competitive Strategies

No one competitive strategy is guaranteed to achieve success, and some companies that have successfully implemented one of Porter's competitive strategies have found that they could not sustain the strategy. As shown in **Table 5–1**, each of the generic strategies has its risks. For

Table 5–1 **Risks of Generic Competitive Strategies**

Risks of Cost Leadership	Risks of Differentiation	Risks of Focus
Cost leadership is not sustained: • Competitors intimate. • Technology changes. • Other bases for cost leadership erode. Proximity in differentiation is lost.	Differentiation is not sustained: • Competitors imitate. • Bases for differentiation become less important to buyers. Cost proximity is lost.	The focus strategy is imitated. The target segment becomes structurally unattractive: • Structure erodes. • Demand disappears. Broadly targeted competitors overwhelm the segment: • The segment's differences from other segments narrow. • The advantages of a broad line increase.
Cost focusers achieve even lower cost in segments.	Differentiation focusers achieve even greater differentiation in segments.	New focusers subsegment the industry.

Source: Adapted/reprinted with permission of The Free Press, an imprint of Simon & Schuster, from *Competitive Advantage: Creating and Sustaining Superior Performance* by Michael E. Porter, p. 21. Copyright © 1985 by Michael E. Porter.

example, a company following a differentiation strategy must ensure that the higher price it charges for its higher quality is not priced too far above the competition, otherwise customers will not see the extra quality as worth the extra cost. This is what is meant in **Table 5–1** by the term **cost proximity**. Procter & Gamble's use of R&D and advertising to differentiate its products had been very successful for many years until customers in the value-conscious 1990s turned to cheaper private brands. As a result, P&G was forced to reduce costs until it could get prices back in line with customer expectations.

Issues in Competitive Strategies

Porter argues that to be successful, a company or business unit must achieve one of the preceding generic competitive strategies. It is especially difficult to move between a narrow target strategy and a broad target strategy. Otherwise, the company or business unit is **stuck in the middle** of the competitive marketplace with no competitive advantage and is doomed to below-average performance. An example of a business unit that may be stuck in the middle is Hewlett-Packard's (HP) personal computer division. For years, HP was a niche player following a differentiation focus strategy in personal computers. Its Vectra personal computers were cherished by engineers and scientists for their high quality and for HP's solid service support. The computers were also expensive. HP's management decided in the mid-1990s to leave the niche and to compete instead in the broad-target market. The objective became high market share. In order to compete with its lower cost rivals such as Dell and Gateway, HP reduced prices. The plan worked. With more than 40% sales growth in 2000, it even outpaced Dell, the industry leader. Nevertheless, HP's reputation for high quality and exceptional service support (as reported in *PC Magazine* and *PC World*) declined from the years when it was a quality niche player. HP's switch from a narrow-target to a broad-target competitive strategy had its down side. As of 2000, the computer unit generated 43% of HP's revenues, but only a 4.6% operating margin, the lowest of HP's business units. In contrast, the printer and imaging division, which also accounted for 43% of HP's annual revenues, generated a 12% operating margin.[11] In moving to the mass market, HP had not kept up its quality image (thus losing its differentiation) and had thus far failed to achieve the lower cost position.

Although it may be difficult to move from a narrow- to a broad-target scope strategy (and vice versa) successfully, research does not support the argument that a firm or unit must choose between differentiation and lower cost in order to have success.[12] What of companies that attempt to achieve *both* a low-cost and a high-differentiation position? The Japanese auto

Table 5–2   The Eight Dimensions of Quality

1. **Performance**	Primary operating characteristics, such as a washing machine's cleaning ability
2. **Features**	"Bells and whistles," like cruise control in a car, that supplement the basic functions
3. **Reliability**	Probability that the product will continue functioning without any significant maintenance
4. **Conformance**	Degree to which a product meets standards. When a customer buys a product out of the warehouse, it will perform identically to that viewed on the showroom floor.
5. **Durability**	Number of years of service a consumer can expect from a product before it significantly deteriorates. Differs from reliability in that a product can be durable, but still need a lot of maintenance.
6. **Serviceability**	Product's ease of repair
7. **Aesthetics**	How a product looks, feels, sounds, tastes, or smells
8. **Perceived Quality**	Product's overall reputation. Especially important if there are no objective, easily used measures of quality.

Source: Adapted from D. A. Garvin, *Managing Quality: The Strategic and Competitive Edge* (New York: Free Press, 1988).

companies of Toyota, Nissan, and Honda are often presented as examples of successful firms able to achieve both of these generic strategies. Thanks to advances in technology, a company may be able to design quality into a product or service in such a way that it can achieve both high quality and high market share, thus lowering costs.[13] Although Porter agrees that it is possible for a company or a business unit to achieve low cost and differentiation simultaneously, he continues to argue that this state is often temporary.[14] Porter does admit, however, that many different kinds of potentially profitable competitive strategies exist. Although there is generally room for only one company to successfully pursue the mass market cost leadership strategy (because it is so dependent on achieving dominant market share), there is room for an almost unlimited number of differentiation and focus strategies (depending on the range of possible desirable features and the number of identifiable market niches). Quality, alone, has 8 different dimensions—each with the potential of providing a product with a competitive advantage (see **Table 5–2**).

Most entrepreneurial ventures follow focus strategies. The successful ones differentiate their product from those of other competitors in the areas of quality and service, and they focus the product on customer needs in a segment of the market, thereby achieving a dominant share of that part of the market. Adopting guerrilla warfare tactics, these companies go after opportunities in market niches too small to justify retaliation from the market leaders. Veteran entrepreneur Norm Brodsky argues that it's often much easier for a small company to compete against a big company than against a well-run small company. "We beat the giants on service. We beat them on flexibility. We beat them on location and price."[15]

Industry Structure and Competitive Strategy

Although each of Porter's generic competitive strategies may be used in any industry, certain strategies are more likely to succeed than others in some instances. In a **fragmented industry**, for example, where many small- and medium-sized local companies compete for relatively small shares of the total market, focus strategies will likely predominate. Fragmented industries are typical for products in the early stages of their life cycle. If few economies are to be gained through size, no large firms will emerge and entry barriers will be low, allowing a stream of new entrants into the industry. Chinese restaurants, veterinary care, used-car sales, and funeral homes are examples. As recently as 1996, over 85% of funeral homes in the United States were independently owned.[16]

If a company is able to overcome the limitations of a fragmented market, however, it can reap the benefits of a broadly targeted cost leadership or differentiation strategy. Until Pizza Hut was able to use advertising to differentiate itself from local competitors, the pizza fast-food business was a fragmented industry composed primarily of locally owned pizza parlors, each with its own distinctive product and service offering. Subsequently Domino's used the cost leader strategy to achieve U.S. national market share.

As an industry matures, fragmentation is overcome and the industry tends to become a **consolidated industry** dominated by a few large companies. Although many industries begin fragmented, battles for market share and creative attempts to overcome local or niche market boundaries often increase the market share of a few companies. After product standards become established for minimum quality and features, competition shifts to a greater emphasis on cost and service. Slower growth, overcapacity, and knowledgeable buyers combine to put a premium on a firm's ability to achieve cost leadership or differentiation along the dimensions most desired by the market. Research and development shifts from product to process improvements. Overall product quality improves, and costs are reduced significantly.

The **strategic rollup** was developed in the mid-1990s as an efficient way to quickly consolidate a fragmented industry. With the aid of money from venture capitalists, an entrepreneur acquires hundreds of owner-operated small businesses. The resulting large firm creates economies of scale by building regional or national brands, applies best practices across all aspects of marketing and operations, and hires more sophisticated managers than the small businesses could previously afford. Rollups differ from conventional mergers and acquisitions in three ways: (1) They involve large numbers of firms, (2) the acquired firms are typically owner operated, and (3) the objective is not to gain incremental advantage, but to reinvent an entire industry.[17] Rollups are currently underway in the funeral industry led by Service Corporation International, Stewart Enterprises, the Loewen Group and in the veterinary care industries by Veterinary Centers of America. Of the 16,000 pet hospitals in the United States, Veterinary Centers of American had acquired around 160 by 1997 and was in the process of buying at least 25 more each year for the foreseeable future.[18]

Once consolidated, the industry has become one in which cost leadership and differentiation tend to be combined to various degrees. A firm can no longer gain high market share simply through low price. The buyers are more sophisticated and demand a certain minimum level of quality for price paid. The same is true for firms emphasizing high quality. Either the quality must be high enough and valued by the customer enough to justify the higher price or the price must be dropped (through lowering costs) to compete effectively with the lower priced products. This consolidation is taking place worldwide in the automobile, airline, and home appliance industries.

Hypercompetition and Competitive Strategy

In his book *Hypercompetition*, D'Aveni proposes that it is becoming increasingly difficult to sustain a competitive advantage for very long. "Market stability is threatened by short product life cycles, short product design cycles, new technologies, frequent entry by unexpected outsiders, repositioning by incumbents, and tactical redefinitions of market boundaries as diverse industries merge."[19] Consequently a company or business unit must constantly work to improve its competitive advantage. It is not enough to be just the lowest cost competitor. Through continuous improvement programs, competitors are usually working to lower their costs as well. Firms must find new ways not only to reduce costs further, but also to add value to the product or service being provided.

The same is true of a firm or unit that is following a differentiation strategy. Maytag Company (a unit of Maytag Corporation), for example, was successful for many years by offering the most durable brand in major home appliances. It was able to charge the highest prices for Maytag brand washing machines. When other competitors improved the quality of their products, however, it became increasingly harder for customers to justify Maytag's significantly higher price. Consequently Maytag Company was forced not only to add new features to its products, but also to reduce costs through improved manufacturing processes so that its prices were no longer out of line with those of the competition.

D'Aveni contends that when industries become **hypercompetitive**, they tend to go through escalating stages of competition. Firms initially compete on cost and quality until an abundance of high-quality, low-priced goods result. This occurred in the U.S. major home appliance industry by 1980. In a second stage of competition, the competitors move into untapped markets. Others usually imitate these moves until the moves become too risky or expensive. This epitomized the major home appliance industry during the 1980s and 1990s as firms moved first to Europe and then into Asia and South America.

According to D'Aveni, firms then raise entry barriers to limit competitors. Economies of scale, distribution agreements, and strategic alliances made it all but impossible for a new firm to enter the major home appliance industry by the end of the 20th century. After the established players have entered and consolidated all new markets, the next stage is for the remaining firms to attack and destroy the strongholds of other firms. Maytag's 1995 decision to divest its European division and concentrate on improving its position in North America could be a prelude to building a North American stronghold while Whirlpool, GE, and Electrolux are distracted by European and worldwide investments. Eventually, according to D'Aveni, the remaining large global competitors work their way to a situation of perfect competition in which no one has any advantage and profits are minimal.

Before hypercompetition, strategic initiatives provided competitive advantage for many years, perhaps for decades. This is no longer the case. According to D'Aveni, as industries become hypercompetitive, there is no such thing as a sustainable competitive advantage. Successful strategic initiatives in this type of industry typically last only months to a few years. According to D'Aveni, the only way a firm in this kind of dynamic industry can sustain any competitive advantage is through a continuous series of multiple short-term initiatives aimed at replacing a firm's current successful products with the next generation of products before the competitors can do so. Intel and Microsoft are taking this approach in the hypercompetitive computer industry.

Hypercompetition views competition, in effect, as a distinct series of ocean waves on what used to be a fairly calm stretch of water. As industry competition becomes more intense, the waves grow higher and require more dexterity to handle. Although a strategy is still needed to sail from point A to point B, more turbulent water means that a craft must continually adjust course to suit each new large wave. One danger of D'Aveni's concept of hypercompetition, however, is that it may lead to an overemphasis on short-term tactics (to be discussed in the next section) over long-term strategy. Too much of an orientation on the individual waves of hypercompetition could cause a company to focus too much on short-term temporary advantage and not enough on achieving its long-term objectives through building sustainable competitive advantage.

Which Competitive Strategy Is Best?
Before selecting one of Porter's generic competitive strategies for a company or business unit, management should assess its feasibility in terms of company or business unit resources and capabilities. Porter lists some of the commonly required skills and resources as well as organizational requirements, in **Table 5–3**.

Competitive Tactics
Studies of decision making report that half the decisions made in organizations fail because of poor tactics.[20] A **tactic** is a specific operating plan detailing how a strategy is to be implemented in terms of when and where it is to be put into action. By their nature, tactics are nar-

Table 5–3 Requirements for Generic Competitive Strategies

Generic Strategy	Commonly Required Skills and Resources	Common Organizational Requirements
Overall Cost Leadership	• Sustained capital investment and access to capital • Process engineering skills • Intense supervision of labor • Products designed for ease of manufacture • Low-cost distribution system	• Tight cost control • Frequent, detailed control reports • Structured organization and responsibilities • Incentives based on meeting strict quantitative targets
Differentiation	• Strong marketing abilities • Product engineering • Creative flair • Strong capability in basic research • Corporate reputation for quality or technological leadership • Long tradition in the industry or unique combination of skills drawn from other businesses • Strong cooperation from channels	• Strong coordination among functions in R&D, product development, and marketing • Subjective measurement and incentives instead of quantitative measures • Amenities to attract highly skilled labor, scientists, or creative people
Focus	• Combination of the above policies directed at the particular strategic target	• Combination of the above policies directed at the particular strategic target

Source: Adapted/reprinted with permission of The Free Press, an imprint of Simon & Schuster, from *Competitive Strategy: Techniques for Analyzing Industries and Competitors* by Michael E. Porter, pp. 40–41. Copyright © 1980, 1988 by The Free Press.

rower in their scope and shorter in their time horizon than are strategies. Tactics, therefore, may be viewed (like policies) as a link between the formulation and implementation of strategy. Some of the tactics available to implement competitive strategies are **timing tactics** (when) and **market location tactics** (where).

Timing Tactics: When to Compete

The first company to manufacture and sell a new product or service is called the **first mover** (or **pioneer**). Some of the advantages of being a first mover are that the company is able to establish a reputation as an industry leader, move down the learning curve to assume the cost leader position, and earn temporarily high profits from buyers who value the product or service very highly. A successful first mover can also set the standard for all subsequent products in the industry. A company that sets the standard "locks in" customers and is then able to offer further products based on that standard.[21] Microsoft was able to do this in software with its Windows operating system, and Netscape garnered over 80% share of the Internet browser market by being first to commercialize the product successfully. Research does indicate that moving first or second into a new industry or foreign country results in greater market share and shareholder wealth than does moving later.[22] This is only true, however, if the first mover has sufficient resources to both exploit the new market and to defend its position against later arrivals with greater resources.[23]

Being a first mover does, however, have its disadvantages. These disadvantages can be, conversely, advantages enjoyed by late mover firms. **Late movers** may be able to imitate the technological advances of others (and thus keep R&D costs low), keep risks down by waiting until a new market is established, and take advantage of the first mover's natural inclination to ignore market segments.[24] Once Netscape had established itself as the standard for Internet browsers, Microsoft used its huge resources to directly attack Netscape's position. It did not want Netscape to also set the standard in the developing and highly lucrative intranet market inside corporations. Nevertheless, research suggests that the advantages and disadvantages of first and late movers may not always generalize across industries because of differences in entry barriers and the resources of the specific competitors.[25]

Market Location Tactics: Where to Compete

A company or business unit can implement a competitive strategy either offensively or defensively. An **offensive tactic** usually takes place in an established competitor's market location. A **defensive tactic** usually takes place in the firm's own current market position as a defense against possible attack by a rival.[26]

Offensive Tactics   Some of the methods used to attack a competitor's position are:

- **Frontal Assault**: The attacking firm goes head to head with its competitor. It matches the competitor in every category from price to promotion to distribution channel. To be successful, the attacker must not only have superior resources, but also the willingness to persevere. This is generally a very expensive tactic and may serve to awaken a sleeping giant (as MCI and Sprint did to AT&T in long-distance telephone service), depressing profits for the whole industry.

- **Flanking Maneuver**: Rather than going straight for a competitor's position of strength with a frontal assault, a firm may attack a part of the market where the competitor is weak. Cyrix Corporation followed this tactic with its entry into the microprocessor market—a market then almost totally dominated by Intel. Rather than going directly after Intel's microprocessor business, Cyrix developed a math co-processor for Intel's 386 chip that would run 20 times faster than Intel's microprocessor. To be successful, the flanker must be patient and willing to carefully expand out of the relatively undefended market niche or else face retaliation by an established competitor.

- **Bypass Attack**: Rather than directly attacking the established competitor frontally or on its flanks, a company or business unit may choose to change the rules of the game. This tactic attempts to cut the market out from under the established defender by offering a new type of product that makes the competitor's product unnecessary. For example, instead of competing directly against Microsoft's Windows 95 operating system, Netscape chose to use Java "applets" in its Internet browser so that an operating system and specialized programs were no longer necessary to run applications on a personal computer.

- **Encirclement**: Usually evolving out of a frontal assault or flanking maneuver, encirclement occurs as an attacking company or unit encircles the competitor's position in terms of products or markets or both. The encircler has greater product variety (a complete product line ranging from low to high price) and/or serves more markets (it dominates every secondary market). As a late mover into Internet browsers, Microsoft followed this tactic when it attacked Netscape's business with its "embrace and extend" strategy. By embracing Netscape's use of cross-platform Internet applets and quickly extending it into multiple applications, Microsoft worked to dominate the browser market.

- **Guerrilla Warfare**: Instead of a continual and extensive resource-expensive attack on a competitor, a firm or business unit may choose to "hit and run." Guerrilla warfare is characterized by the use of small, intermittent assaults on different market segments held by the competitor. In this way, a new entrant or small firm can make some gains without seriously threatening a large, established competitor and evoking some form of retaliation. To be successful, the firm or unit conducting guerrilla warfare must be patient enough to accept small gains and to avoid pushing the established competitor to the point that it must respond or else lose face. Microbreweries, which make beer for sale to local customers, use this tactic against national brewers like Anheuser-Busch.

Defensive Tactics According to Porter, defensive tactics aim to lower the probability of attack, divert attacks to less threatening avenues, or lessen the intensity of an attack. Instead of increasing competitive advantage per se, they make a company's or business unit's competitive advantage more sustainable by causing a challenger to conclude that an attack is unattractive. These tactics deliberately reduce short-term profitability to ensure long-term profitability.[27]

- **Raise Structural Barriers**: Entry barriers act to block a challenger's logical avenues of attack. Some of the most important according to Porter are to:

  1. Offer a full line of products in every profitable market segment to close off any entry points (for example, Coca-Cola offers unprofitable noncarbonated beverages to keep competitors off store shelves).
  2. Block channel access by signing exclusive agreements with distributors.
  3. Raise buyer switching costs by offering low-cost training to users.
  4. Raise the cost of gaining trial users by keeping prices low on items new users are most likely to purchase.
  5. Increase scale economies to reduce unit costs.
  6. Foreclose alternative technologies through patenting or licensing.
  7. Limit outside access to facilities and personnel.
  8. Tie up suppliers by obtaining exclusive contracts or purchasing key locations.
  9. Avoid suppliers that also serve competitors.
  10. Encourage the government to raise barriers such as safety and pollution standards or favorable trade policies.

- **Increase Expected Retaliation**: This tactic is any action that increases the perceived threat of retaliation for an attack. For example, management may strongly defend any erosion of market share by drastically cutting prices or matching a challenger's promotion through a policy of accepting any price-reduction coupons for a competitor's product. This counter-attack is especially important in markets that are very important to the defending company or business unit. For example, when Clorox Company challenged Procter & Gamble Company in the detergent market with Clorox Super Detergent, P&G retaliated by test marketing its liquid bleach, Lemon Fresh Comet, in an attempt to scare Clorox into retreating from the detergent market.

- **Lower the Inducement for Attack**: A third type of defensive tactic is to reduce a challenger's expectations of future profits in the industry. Like Southwest Airlines, a company can deliberately keep prices low and constantly invest in cost-reducing measures. With prices kept very low, there is little profit incentive for a new entrant.

COOPERATIVE STRATEGIES

Competitive strategies and tactics are used to gain competitive advantage within an industry by battling against other firms. These are not, however, the only business strategy options available to a company or business unit for competing successfully within an industry. **Cooperative strategies** can also be used to gain competitive advantage within an industry by working with other firms.

Collusion

The two general types of cooperative strategies are collusion and strategic alliances. **Collusion** is the active cooperation of firms within an industry to reduce output and raise prices in order to get around the normal economic law of supply and demand. Collusion may be explicit, in which firms cooperate through direct communication and negotiation, or tacit, in which firms cooperate indirectly through an informal system of signals. Explicit collusion is illegal in most countries. For example, Archer Daniels Midland (ADM), the large U.S. agricultural products firm, has been accused of conspiring with its competitors to limit the sales volume and raise the price of the food additive lysine. Executives from three Japanese and South Korean lysine manufacturers admitted meeting in hotels in major cities throughout the world to form a "lysine trade association." The three companies were fined more than $20 million by the U.S. federal government. Although ADM had earlier agreed to pay $25 million to settle a lawsuit on behalf of 600 lysine customers, U.S. federal prosecutors pursued a grand jury indictment of the company and two of its senior executives.[28]

Collusion can also be tacit, in which there is no direct communication among competing firms. According to Barney, tacit collusion in an industry is most likely to be successful if (1) there are a small number of identifiable competitors, (2) costs are similar among firms, (3) one firm tends to act as the "price leader," (4) there is a common industry culture that accepts cooperation, (5) sales are characterized by a high frequency of small orders, (6) large inventories and order backlogs are normal ways of dealing with fluctuations in demand, and (7) there are high entry barriers to keep out new competitors.[29]

Even tacit collusion can, however, be illegal. For example, when General Electric wanted to ease price competition in the steam turbine industry, it widely advertised its prices and publicly committed not to sell below these prices. Customers were even told that if GE reduced turbine prices in the future, it would give customers a refund equal to the price reduction. GE's message was not lost on Westinghouse, the major competitor in steam turbines. Both prices and profit margins remained stable for the next 10 years in this industry. The U.S. Department of Justice then sued both firms for engaging in "conscious parallelism" (following each other's lead to reduce the level of competition) in order to reduce competition.

Strategic Alliances

A **strategic alliance** is a partnership of two or more corporations or business units to achieve strategically significant objectives that are mutually beneficial.[30] Alliances between companies or business units have become a fact of life in modern business. More than 20,000 alliances occurred between 1992 and 1997, quadruple the total five years earlier.[31] Some alliances are very short term, only lasting long enough for one partner to establish a beachhead in a new market. Over time, conflicts over objectives and control often develop among the partners. For these and other reasons, between 30% and 50% of all alliances perform unsatisfactorily.[32] Others are more long lasting and may even be the prelude to a full merger between two companies. A study by Cooper and Lybrand found that firms involved in strategic alliances had 11% higher revenue and 20% higher growth rate than did companies not involved in alliances.[33]

Companies or business units may form a strategic alliance for a number of reasons, including:

1. **To obtain technology and/or manufacturing capabilities**: For example, Intel formed a partnership with Hewlett-Packard to use HP's capabilities in RISC technology in order to develop the successor to Intel's Pentium microprocessor.

2. **To obtain access to specific markets**: Rather than buy a foreign company or build breweries of its own in other countries, Anheuser-Busch chose to license the right to brew and market Budweiser to other brewers, such as Labatt in Canada, Modelo in Mexico, and Kirin in Japan.

3. **To reduce financial risk**: For example, because the costs of developing a new large jet airplane were becoming too high for any one manufacturer, Boeing, Aerospatiale of France, British Aerospace, Construcciones Aeronáuticas of Spain, and Deutsche Aerospace of Germany planned a joint venture to design such a plane.

4. **To reduce political risk**: To gain access to China while ensuring a positive relationship with the often restrictive Chinese government, Maytag Corporation formed a joint venture with the Chinese appliance maker, RSD.

5. **To achieve or ensure competitive advantage**: General Motors and Toyota formed Nummi Corporation as a joint venture to provide Toyota a manufacturing facility in the United States and GM access to Toyota's low-cost, high-quality manufacturing expertise.[34]

Cooperative arrangements between companies and business units fall along a continuum from weak and distant to strong and close. (See **Figure 5–5**.) The types of alliances range from mutual service consortia to joint ventures and licensing arrangements to value-chain partnerships.[35]

Mutual Service Consortia   A **mutual service consortium** is a partnership of similar companies in similar industries who pool their resources to gain a benefit that is too expensive to develop alone, such as access to advanced technology. For example, IBM of the United States, Toshiba of Japan, and Siemens of Germany formed a consortium to develop new generations of computer chips. As part of this alliance, IBM offered Toshiba its expertise in chemical mechanical polishing to help develop a new manufacturing process using ultraviolet lithography to etch tiny circuits in silicon chips. IBM then transferred the new technology to a facility in the United States.[36] The mutual service consortia is a fairly weak and distant alliance—appropriate for partners who wish to work together but not share their core competencies. There is very little interaction or communication among the partners.

Joint Venture   A **joint venture** is a "cooperative business activity, formed by two or more separate organizations for strategic purposes, that creates an independent business entity and allocates ownership, operational responsibilities, and financial risks and rewards to each member, while preserving their separate identity/autonomy."[37] Along with licensing arrangements, joint ventures lay at the midpoint of the continuum and are formed to pursue an opportunity that needs a capability from two companies or business units, such as the technology of one and the distribution channels of another.

Joint ventures are the most popular form of strategic alliance. They often occur because the companies involved do not want to or cannot legally merge permanently. Joint ventures provide a way to temporarily combine the different strengths of partners to achieve an outcome of value to both. For example, Toys "R" Us and Amazon.com formed a joint venture in August 2000 called Toysrus.com to act as an online toy store. Amazon was to include the joint venture on its Web site, ship the products, and handle customer service. In turn, Toys "R" Us was to choose and buy the toys, using its parent's purchasing power to get the most desired toys at the best price.[38]

Figure 5–5
Continuum of Strategic Alliances

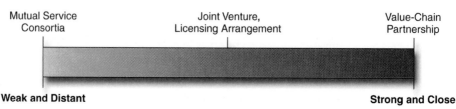

Extremely popular in international undertakings because of financial and political-legal constraints, joint ventures are a convenient way for corporations to work together without losing their independence. Disadvantages of joint ventures include loss of control, lower profits, probability of conflicts with partners, and the likely transfer of technological advantage to the partner. Joint ventures are often meant to be temporary, especially by some companies who may view them as a way to rectify a competitive weakness until they can achieve long-term dominance in the partnership. Partially for this reason, joint ventures have a high failure rate. Research does indicate, however, that joint ventures tend to be more successful when both partners have equal ownership in the venture and are mutually dependent on each other for results.[39]

Licensing Arrangement   A **licensing arrangement** is an agreement in which the licensing firm grants rights to another firm in another country or market to produce and/or sell a product. The licensee pays compensation to the licensing firm in return for technical expertise. Licensing is an especially useful strategy if the trademark or brand name is well known, but the MNC does not have sufficient funds to finance its entering the country directly. Anheuser-Busch uses this strategy to produce and market Budweiser beer in the United Kingdom, Japan, Israel, Australia, Korea, and the Philippines. This strategy also becomes important if the country makes entry via investment either difficult or impossible. The danger always exists, however, that the licensee might develop its competence to the point that it becomes a competitor to the licensing firm. Therefore, a company should never license its distinctive competence, even for some short-run advantage.

Value-Chain Partnership   The **value-chain partnership** is a strong and close alliance in which one company or unit forms a long-term arrangement with a key supplier or distributor for mutual advantage. To improve the quality of parts it purchases, companies in the U.S. auto industry, for example, have decided to work more closely with fewer suppliers and to involve them more in product design decisions. Activities that had been previously done internally by an auto maker are being outsourced to suppliers specializing in those activities.

Such partnerships are also a way for a firm to acquire new technology to use in its own products. For example, Maytag Company was approached by one of its suppliers, Honeywell's Microswitch Division, which offered its expertise in fuzzy logic technology—a technology Maytag did not have at that time. The resulting partnership in product development resulted in Maytag's new IntelliSense™ dishwasher. Unlike previous dishwashers that the operator had to set, Maytag's fuzzy logic dishwasher automatically selected the proper cleaning cycle based on a series of factors such as the amount of dirt and presence of detergent. According to Paul Ludwig, business development manager for Honeywell's Microswitch division, "Had Maytag not included us on the design team, we don't believe the two companies would have achieved the same innovative solution, nor would we have completed the project in such a short amount of time."[40] The benefits of such relationships do not just accrue to the purchasing firm. Research suggests that suppliers who engage in long-term relationships are more profitable than suppliers with multiple short-term contracts.[41] For an example of an Internet value-chain partnership between Cisco Systems and its suppliers, see the ▓ **Internet Issue** feature.

All forms of strategic alliances are filled with uncertainty. There are many issues that need to be dealt with when the alliance is initially formed and others that emerge later. Many problems revolve around the fact that a firm's alliance partners may also be its competitors, either now or in the future. According to Peter Lorange, an authority in strategy, one thorny issue in any strategic alliance is how to cooperate without giving away the company or business unit's core competence. "Particularly when advanced technology is involved, it can be difficult for partners in an alliance to cooperate and openly share strategic know-how, but it is mandatory if the joint venture is to succeed."[42] It is therefore important that a company or business unit that is interested in joining or forming a strategic alliance consider the strategic alliance success factors listed in **Table 5–4**.

Internet Issue

Business to Business at Cisco Systems

Every day Cisco Systems, successful manufacturer of Internet servers, posts its requirements for components on an extranet, the dedicated Internet-based network connecting the company to 32 manufacturing plants. Although Cisco does not own these plants, each plant has completed a lengthy process of certification ensuring that each meets Cisco's quality and other standards. Within hours of the posting, these suppliers respond with a price, a delivery time, and a record of their recent performance in terms of reliability and product quality. Cisco then chooses which bid to select and the deal is finalized.

This process has replaced 50 purchasing agents who used to assemble the same information using telephones and faxes. The operation, which used to take three to four days, now takes only hours. The purchasing agents are instead managing the quality of the components.

Three aspects of Cisco's supply system are especially significant. *One* is the use of the electronic market to set prices. This is characteristic of online auctions and of business to business (B2B) value chain relationships. A *second* is the exchange of information between buyer and seller. The Internet allows the inexpensive flow of information in a way never before realized. *Third* is the extent to which Cisco outsources activities that many other companies do internally. The ability of the Internet to connect multiple departments together with suppliers and distributors in other companies makes outsourcing both effective and efficient.

Source: "Trying to Connect You," *The Economist E-Management Survey* (November 11, 2000), p. 28. Reprinted with permission.

Table 5–4 Strategic Alliance Success Factors

- Have a clear strategic purpose. Integrate the alliance with each partner's strategy. Ensure that mutual value is created for all partners.
- Find a fitting partner with compatible goals and complementary capabilities.
- Identify likely partnering risks and deal with them when the alliance is formed.
- Allocate tasks and responsibilities so that each partner can specialize in what it does best.
- Create incentives for cooperation to minimize differences in corporate culture or organization fit.
- Minimize conflicts among the partners by clarifying objectives and avoiding direct competition in the marketplace.
- If an international alliance, ensure that those managing it should have comprehensive cross-cultural knowledge.
- Exchange human resources to maintain communication and trust. Don't allow individual egos to dominate.
- Operate with long-term time horizons. The expectation of future gains can minimize short-term conflicts.
- Develop multiple joint projects so that any failures are counterbalanced by successes.
- Agree upon a monitoring process. Share information to build trust and keep projects on target. Monitor customer responses and service complaints.
- Be flexible in terms of willingness to renegotiate the relationship in terms of environmental changes and new opportunities.
- Agree upon an exit strategy for when the partners' objectives are achieved or the alliance is judged a failure.

Sources: Compiled from B. Gomes-Casseres, "Do You Really Have an Alliance Strategy?" *Strategy & Leadership* (September/October 1998), pp. 6–11; L. Segil, "Strategic Alliances for the 21st Century," *Strategy & Leadership* (September/October 1998), pp. 12–16; A. C. Inkpen and K-Q Li, "Joint Venture Formation: Planning and Knowledge Gathering for Success," *Organizational Dynamics* (Spring 1999), pp. 33–47. Inkpen and Li provide a checklist of 17 questions on p. 46.

5.5 Impact of the Internet on Business Strategy

The initial impact of the Internet was on marketing. **Business to consumer (B2C)** described the many dot-com start-ups selling items directly to consumers via their Web sites. The most well-known of these first entrants or pioneers was Amazon.com, the successful marketer of books and related merchandise. Not wanting to be disadvantaged late entrants, established manufacturers became active participants on the Internet. They supplemented their current distribution network with direct selling through their own Internet site or formed marketing alliances with technologically competent Web-based businesses. One such alliance is the joint venture between Toys "R" Us and Amazon.com to form Toysrus.com.

Business to business (B2B) describes the launching of Web portals aimed at electronically connecting buyers with suppliers, strengthening collective purchasing activities, and auctioning inventory. Dick Hunter, head of Dell Computer's supply chain management, states that one purpose of B2B is for information to replace inventory. For example, the companies supplying Dell with metal and plastic boxes for Dell's computers are located within 90 miles of Dell's assembly plant. They have access to Dell's real-time information on its use of their products. On the basis of Dell's usage of their parts, they make more and ship them as needed to Dell's plant. In turn, the suppliers keep only a day's worth of finished stock on hand. "If our information was 100% right," asserts Hunter, "the only inventory that would exist would be in transit."[43]

The B2B consortium is a recent example of the use of cooperative strategies to obtain competitive advantage. Traditional competitors are forming Internet consortia to centralize many activities, such as purchasing, which had been previously done internally. General Motors, Ford, and Chrysler have established an auto parts exchange called Covisint. Boeing, Lockheed Martin, Raytheon, and BAE Systems have formed the Global Aerospace & Defense Trading Exchange. Hewlett-Packard, Compaq, and 10 other computer makers have created Ehitex.com. Goodyear, Michelin, Bridgestone, and 4 other tire makers have formed Rubbernetwork.com. Although these consortia are being formed with great expectations, the reality has problems. For example, Covisint has three project leaders (one for each auto maker) who are battling over what to charge and how much trading data to allow users to access. The U. S. Federal Trade Commission is reviewing these consortia among erstwhile competitors for antitrust issues. Since Covisint's owners collectively dominate the North American automobile market, there could easily be collusion. According to Dana Corporation, an auto components supplier, "We're concerned about how big this gorilla is going to be. There's only so much room to squeeze prices."[44]

Although B2B is still in its initial stages, Hau Lee, director of the Global Supply Chain Management Forum at Stanford University proposes that business-to-business commerce will move through 4 stages of development.

Stage 1: *Information, such as demand forecasts and sales data, is exchanged.* Companies work to define common standards for inventory and point-of-sale to allow better planning.

Stage 2: *Companies move beyond data transfer to exchanging information.* For example, when Wal-Mart's Florida stores ran out of mosquito repellant during a heat wave, the company discovered that Warner Lambert, its supplier, was able to track weather forecasts to predict future peaks in demand. The sharing of this information enabled both companies to do better.

Stage 3: *Companies exchange the right to make decisions.* For example, since Wal-Mart sells disposable diapers made by P&G, which use sticky tape made by 3M, the three companies are experimenting with a system allowing one person instead of three to make the ordering decision for all three companies.

Stage 4: *Companies exchange work and roles.* The manufacturer becomes a retailer and the retailer moves to a support role. For example, companies such as VooDooCycles and Cannondale, makers of sport bicycles, are increasingly taking customers' orders directly and only then building the bicycles. Since a high quality bike needs last minute adjustments before it is ready for the customer, bicycle retailers are needed to perform this crucial service as well as to offer last minute purchases of helmets or other paraphernalia.[45]

Projections for the 21st Century

- From 1994 to 2010, the average life expectancy for women will rise from 67 to 71 and for men will increase from 63 to 67.
- From 1994 to 2010, the number of AIDS cases worldwide will increase from 20 million to 38 million.[46]

Discussion Questions

1. What industry forces might cause a propitious niche to disappear?

2. Is it possible for a company or business unit to follow a cost leadership strategy and a differentiation strategy simultaneously? Why or why not?

3. Is it possible for a company to have a sustainable competitive advantage when its industry becomes hyper-competitive?

4. What are the advantages and disadvantages of being a first mover in an industry? Give some examples of first mover and late mover firms. Were they successful?

5. Why are many strategic alliances temporary?

Strategic Practice Exercise

Following is an Internet case focusing upon strategic alliances. To begin the exercise, you will need a computer with Internet access. The rest is up to you!

Amy's Bread at Chelsea Market: A Web Discovery Case

CATHLEEN S. BURNS, UNIVERSITY OF MISSOURI, AND PAULA S. WEBER, ST. CLOUD STATE UNIVERSITY

COMPANY BACKGROUND AND HISTORY

In 1992, Amy Scherber opened her own business, "Amy's Bread." Amy's Bread is a retail and wholesale bakery in the Hell's Kitchen area of Manhattan. Amy's Bread has now expanded to a second Manhattan location in Chelsea Market, an innovative mall full of other entrepreneurs selling both food and nonfood items.

AMY'S DILEMMA

While Amy's Bread is doing well in Chelsea Market, profits are less than desired and the bakery has excess capacity. Amy is trying to decide what strategic alliances with other tenants in the mall would help her boost profits and absorb excess production capacity. You will help formulate Amy's emerging marketing strategy during your Web-based search process.

First Activity: Get familiar with Internet searches (if you are not already).

1. Check out a Web site that provides information on search engines and searching:
   - ⟨www.pbs.org/uti/begin.html⟩
   - ⟨www.microsoft.com/insider/internet/default.htm⟩
   - ⟨www.itrc.ucf.edu⟩ [search "search engines"]
   - ⟨www.zdnet.com/pccomp/features/fea1096/sub2.html⟩

- ⟨www.cl.ais.net/egsmlib/crawler.html⟩
- ⟨www.hamline.edu/library/bush/handouts/worms.html⟩

2. Search the Internet for Amy's Bread using at least three search engines:
   - ⟨yahoo.com⟩
   - ⟨altavista.com⟩
   - ⟨excite.com⟩
   - ⟨infoseek.com⟩
   - your choice

3. Search the Internet for Amy's Bread using one mega-search engine:
   - ⟨askjeeves.com⟩
   - ⟨metacrawler.com⟩

4. **Class discussion opportunity**: Share with the class (or your team) what you discovered about how search engines search the Internet. What differences exist in the data accessed by each search engine?

Second Activity: Get familiar with Amy's Bread's homepage.

   Class discussion opportunity: Share with the class (or your team) what information is included in Amy's Bread's Web site.
   - ⟨amysbread.com/sitemap.htm⟩

Third Activity: Prepare a brief Strengths/Weaknesses/Opportunities/Threats (SWOT) analysis for Amy's Bread.

1. **The Owner**: How did Amy prepare herself to be an entrepreneur?
   - ⟨amysbread.com/bio/htm⟩

2. **The Products**: How does Amy differentiate her bread products from low cost breads?
   - ⟨amysbread.com/chelsea.htm⟩

3. **The Media**: How does the media differentiate Amy's bread products from other bakeries' products?
   - ⟨amysbread.com/news.htm⟩

4. **The Locations**: How many Amy's Bread locations are there and how are they different or the same?
   - ⟨amysbread.com/locate.htm⟩
   - ⟨library.northernlight.com/SG19990714170000046.html?cb=13&sc=0⟩

     [The Web site above has some interesting history on Oreo cookies and the Chelsea Market location.]

5. **The Competition**: How many competitors does Amy's Bread have in the Manhattan area?
   - ⟨go-newyork.city.com/food/index.html⟩
   - ⟨www.womenshands.com/artisans/chelsea_market/related_story.htm⟩
   - ⟨www.womenshands.com/artisans/chelsea_market⟩

- ⟨store.yahoo.com/cmb/aboutcm.html⟩
- ⟨www.chelseamarketbaskets.com⟩
- ⟨www.elizabar.com⟩

6. **The Customers**: What can you discover about Chelsea Market customers? What do you think pedestrian traffic is like in that area? What are some of the demographics of New York City citizens that would affect their bakery purchases? For example, New Yorkers tend to walk or use public transportation; how does this impact their grocery shopping? New Yorkers tend to live in small apartments or condos; how does this impact their interest in dining out? What options exist for dining out in New York as opposed to a medium-sized city in your area?
   - ⟨www.demographia.com/dm-nyc.htm⟩ [Population density in NYC]
   - ⟨stats.bls.gov/csxmsa.htm⟩ [Consumer Expenditure Data by Metropolitan Statistical Area]

Fourth Activity: Consider strategic alliances that would be appropriate for Amy's Bread to pursue.

1. Using the textbook or Web resources, define what is meant by "strategic alliances." What are the advantages and disadvantages of strategic alliances?
   - ⟨www.e-marketing.com.au/documents/strategicalliances.htm⟩

2. On a macro level, what businesses has the developer, Irwin Cohen, included in the Chelsea Market commercial development?
   - ⟨store.yahoo.cmb/aboutcm.html⟩
   - ⟨westvillage.about.com/cities/midatlanticus/westvillage/library/weekly/aa050499.htm⟩
   - ⟨www.womenshands.com/artisans/chelsea_market/related_story.htm⟩

3. Use the information in #2 above and your creativity to answer this question. On a more micro level, which of the Chelsea Market tenants appear to have potential for strategic alliances with Amy's Bread? Why?

4. Using the information in #2 above and your creativity, what other businesses (non-Chelsea Market tenants) can you imagine would have potential for strategic alliances with Amy's Bread? Why?

5. If the Chelsea Market developer asked you, Amy Scherber, for input on potential new mall tenants, what mall tenants would you recommend that the developer add to the mall? Why? What would be some of the decision factors the developer would consider in selecting tenants?

Source: This exercise was written as a case by Cathleen S. Burns of the University of Missouri, Columbia, and Paula S. Weber of St. Cloud State University and presented to the North American Research Association, October 2000. Copyright © 2000 by Cathleen S. Burns and Paula S. Weber. Reprinted by permission.

Key Terms

business strategy (p. 115)
business to business (B2B) (p. 131)
business to consumer (B2C) (p. 131)
collusion (p. 126)
competitive scope (p. 118)
competitive strategy (p. 117)
consolidated industry (p. 122)
cooperative strategies (p. 126)
cost focus (p. 119)
cost leadership (p. 118)
cost proximity (p. 120)
criticism of SWOT (p. 109)
defensive tactic (p. 125)
differentiation (p. 119)

differentiation focus (p. 119)
differentiation strategy (p. 118)
distinctive competencies (p. 109)
first movers (p. 124)
fragmented industry (p. 121)
hypercompetitive (p. 123)
joint venture (p. 128)
late movers (p. 124)
licensing arrangement (p. 129)
lower cost strategy (p. 118)
market location tactics (p. 124)
mutual service consortium (p. 128)
offensive tactic (p. 125)
pioneer (p. 124)

propitious niche (p. 112)
SFAS (Strategic Factors Analysis
    Summary) Matrix (p. 110)
SO, ST, WO, WT Strategies (p. 115)
strategic alliance (p. 127)
strategic rollup (p. 122)
strategic window (p. 112)
stuck in the middle (p. 120)
SWOT (p. 109)
tactic (p. 123)
timing tactics (p. 124)
TOWS Matrix (p. 114)
value-chain partnership (p. 129)

Notes

1. K. W. Glaister and J. R. Falshaw, "Strategic Planning: Still Going Strong?" *Long Range Planning* (February 1999), pp. 107–116.
2. T. Brown, "The Essence of Strategy," *Management Review* (April 1997), pp. 8–13.
3. T. Hill and R. Westbrook, "SWOT Analysis: It's Time for a Product Recall," *Long Range Planning* (February 1997), pp. 46–52.
4. W. H. Newman, "Shaping the Master Strategy of Your Firm," *California Management Review*, Vol. 9, No. 3 (1967), pp. 77–88.
5. R. L. Simpson and O. Suris, "Alex Trotman's Goal: To Make Ford No. 1 in World Auto Sales," *Wall Street Journal* (July 18, 1995), p. A5.
6. M. E. Porter, *Competitive Strategy* (New York: The Free Press, 1980), pp. 34–41 as revised in M. E. Porter, *The Competitive Advantage of Nations* (New York: The Free Press, 1990), pp. 37–40.
7. J. O. DeCastro and J. J. Chrisman, "Narrow-Scope Strategies and Firm Performance: An Empirical Investigation," *Journal of Business Strategies* (Spring 1998), pp. 1–16; T. M. Stearns, N. M. Carter, P. D. Reynolds, and M. L. Williams, "New Firm Survival: Industry, Strategy, and Location," *Journal of Business Venturing* (January 1995), pp. 23–42.
8. Porter, *Competitive Strategy*, p. 35.
9. R. E. Caves and P. Ghemawat, "Identifying Mobility Barriers," *Strategic Management Journal* (January 1992), pp. 1–12.
10. R. O. Crockett, "They're Lining Up for Flicks in the 'Hood," *Business Week* (June 8, 1998), pp. 75–76.
11. D. P. Hamilton, "H-P's First Breakdown of Profit Shows Under 25% Is from Computer Business," *Wall Street Journal* (November 28, 2000), p. B8; P. Burrows, "Can Fiorina Reboot HP?" *Business Week* (November 27, 2000), p. 59.
12. C. Campbell-Hunt, "What Have We Learned About Generic Competitive Strategy? A Meta Analysis," *Strategic Management Journal* (February 2000), pp. 127–154.
13. M. Kroll, P. Wright, and R. A. Heiens, "The Contribution of Product Quality to Competitive Advantage: Impacts on Systematic Variance and Unexplained Variance in Returns," *Strategic Management Journal* (April 1999), pp. 375–384.
14. R. M. Hodgetts, "A Conversation with Michael E. Porter: A 'Significant Extension' Toward Operational Improvement and Positioning," *Organizational Dynamics* (Summer 1999), pp. 24–33.

15. N. Brodsky, "Size Matters," *INC.* (September 1998), pp. 31–32.
16. R. Tomsho, "Funeral Parlors Become Big Business," *Wall Street Journal* (September 18, 1996), pp. B1, B4.
17. P. F. Kocourek, S. Y. Chung, and M. G. McKenna, "Strategic Rollups: Overhauling the Multi-Merger Machine," *Strategy + Business* (2nd Qtr 2000), pp. 45–53.
18. J. A. Tannenbaum, "Acquisitive Companies Set Out to 'Roll Up' Fragmented Industries," *Wall Street Journal* (March 3, 1997), pp. P. A1, A6.
19. R. A. D'Aveni, *Hypercompetition* (New York: The Free Press, 1994), pp. xiii–xiv.
20. P. C. Nutt, "Surprising But True: Half the Decisions in Organizations Fail," *Academy of Management Executive* (November 1999), pp. 75–90.
21. Some refer to this as the economic concept of "increasing returns." Instead of reaching a point of diminishing returns when a product saturates a market and the curve levels off, the curve continues to go up as the company takes advantage of setting the standard to spin off new products that use the new standard to achieve higher performance than competitors. See J. Alley, "The Theory That Made Microsoft," *Fortune* (April 29, 1996), pp. 65–66.
22. H. Lee, K. G. Smith, C. M. Grimm, and A. Schomburg, "Timing, Order and Durability of New Product Advantages with Imitation," *Strategic Management Journal* (January 2000), pp. 23–30; Y. Pan and P. C. K. Chi, "Financial Performance and Survival of Multinational Corporations in China," *Strategic Management Journal* (April 1999), pp. 359–374; R. Makadok, "Can First-Mover and Early-Mover Advantages Be Sustained in an Industry with Low Barriers to Entry/Imitation?" *Strategic Management Journal* (July 1998), pp. 683–696; B. Mascarenhas, "The Order and Size of Entry Into International Markets," *Journal of Business Venturing* (July 1997), pp. 287–299.
23. G. J. Tellis and P. N. Golder, "First to Market, First to Fail? Real Causes of Enduring Market Leadership," *Sloan Management Review* (Winter 1996), pp. 65–75.
24. For an in-depth discussion of first and late mover advantages and disadvantages, see D-S. Cho, D-J. Kim, and D. K. Rhee, "Latecomer Strategies: Evidence from the Semiconductor Industry in Japan and Korea," *Organization Science* (July–August 1998), pp. 489–505.

25. T. S. Schoenecker and A. C. Cooper, "The Role of Firm Resources and Organizational Attributes in Determining Entry Timing: A Cross-Industry Study," *Strategic Management Journal* (December 1998), pp. 1127–1143.

26. Summarized from various articles by L. Fahey in *The Strategic Management Reader*, edited by L. Fahey (Englewood Cliffs, N.J.: Prentice-Hall, 1989), pp. 178–205.

27. This information on defensive tactics is summarized from M. E. Porter, *Competitive Advantage* (New York: Free Press, 1985), pp. 482–512.

28. T. M. Burton, "Archer-Daniels Faces a Potential Blow as Three Firms Admit Price-Fixing Plot," *Wall Street Journal* (August 28, 1996), pp. A3, A6; R. Henkoff, "The ADM Tale Gets Even Stranger," *Fortune* (May 13, 1996), pp. 113–120.

29. Much of the content on cooperative strategies was summarized from J. B. Barney, *Gaining and Sustaining Competitive Advantage* (Reading, Mass.: Addison-Wesley, 1997), pp. 255–278.

30. E. A. Murray, Jr., and J. F. Mahon, "Strategic Alliances: Gateway to the New Europe," *Long Range Planning* (August 1993), p. 103.

31. H. Meyer, "My Enemy, My Friend," *Journal of Business Strategy* (September–October 1998), pp. 42–46.

32. T. K. Das and B-S Teng, "Instabilities of Strategic Alliances: An Internal Tensions Perspective," *Organization Science* (January–February 2000), pp. 77–101.

33. L. Segil, "Strategic Alliances for the 21st Century," *Strategy & Leadership* (September/October 1998), pp. 12–16.

34. E. A. Murray, Jr., and J. F. Mahon, "Strategic Alliances: Gateway to the New Europe?" *Long Range Planning* (August 1993), pp. 105–106.

35. R. M. Kanter, "Collaborative Advantage: The Art of Alliances," *Harvard Business Review* (July–August 1994), pp. 96–108.

36. B. Bremner, Z. Schiller, T. Smart, and W. J. Holstein, "Keiretsu Connections," *Business Week* (July 22, 1996), pp. 52–54.

37. R. P. Lynch, *The Practical Guide to Joint Ventures and Corporate Alliances* (New York: John Wiley and Sons, 1989), p. 7.

38. H. Green, "Double Play," *Business Week E-Biz* (October 23, 2000), pp. EB42–EB46.

39. L. L. Blodgett, "Factors in the Instability of International Joint Ventures: An Event History Analysis," *Strategic Management Journal* (September 1992), pp. 475–481; J. Bleeke and D. Ernst, "The Way to Win in Cross-Border Alliances," *Harvard Business Review* (November–December 1991), pp. 127–135; J. M. Geringer, "Partner Selection Criteria for Developed Country Joint Ventures," in *International Management Behavior*, 2nd ed., edited by H. W. Lane, and J. J. DiStephano (Boston: PWS-Kent, 1992), pp. 206–216.

40. S. Stevens, "Speeding the Signals of Change," *Appliance* (February 1995), p. 7.

41. K. Z. Andrews, "Manufacturer/Supplier Relationships: The Supplier Payoff," *Harvard Business Review* (September–October 1995), pp. 14–15.

42. P. Lorange, "Black-Box Protection of Your Core Competencies in Strategic Alliances," in *Cooperative Strategies: European Perspectives*, edited by P. W. Beamish and J. P. Killing (San Francisco: The New Lexington Press, 1997), pp. 59–99.

43. "Enter the Eco-System," *The Economist E-Management Survey* (November 11, 2000), p. 30.

44. N. Weinberg, "Herding Cats," *Forbes* (July 24, 2000), pp. 108–110.

45. "Enter the Eco-System," *The Economist E-Management Survey* (November 11, 2000), p. 34.

46. J. Warner, "21st Century Capitalism: Snapshot of the Next Century," *Business Week* (November 18, 1994), p. 194.

chapter 6

Strategy Formulation: Corporate Strategy

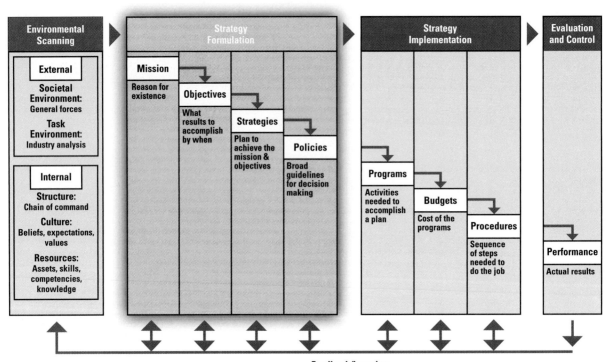

Environmental Scanning	Strategy Formulation	Strategy Implementation	Evaluation and Control

External

Societal Environment:
General forces

Task Environment:
Industry analysis

Internal

Structure:
Chain of command

Culture:
Beliefs, expectations, values

Resources:
Assets, skills, competencies, knowledge

Mission

Reason for existence

Objectives

What results to accomplish by when

Strategies

Plan to achieve the mission & objectives

Policies

Broad guidelines for decision making

Programs

Activities needed to accomplish a plan

Budgets

Cost of the programs

Procedures

Sequence of steps needed to do the job

Performance

Actual results

Feedback/Learning

D eregulation and antitrust decisions by the U.S. federal government forced American Telephone and Telegraph (AT&T) to sell its local telephone business. This presented AT&T with some serious problems. For one thing, it no longer had any direct access to the individual households. It could no longer sell local service to its long-distance customers. The so-called "Baby Bells," such as US West and Bell South, controlled the telephone lines as well as the local phone business. Thanks to deregulation, upstarts like MCI and Sprint entered the long-distance business and began a price war to cut into AT&T's dominance of this market. As if this wasn't bad enough, the Baby Bells began talking about also entering the long-distance business. AT&T's market research revealed that consumers preferred to buy local and long-distance service from one source and get just one bill. The company had to either create a way to offer local phone service or watch its current long-distance customers be taken by competitors.

AT&T's top management established a new objective to obtain local access for its long-distance customers. How could it achieve this objective? One possibility, becoming a wholesaler by reselling local Bell service, didn't allow the company to control its costs or provide innovative services. The firm still needed its own local lines. It could buy a local phone system, such as Bell South, but for financial and antitrust reasons it could not purchase all of the Baby Bells. In a drastic change to the company's corporate strategy, AT&T chose to acquire the country's biggest cable operators, TCI and Media One, for $110 billion. With cable modems offering faster service than standard modems using phone lines, these acquisitions put AT&T directly into the booming Internet business. This was a significant advantage of the strategy. Unfortunately, the cable companies served only about half of AT&T's long-distance customers. To achieve its corporate objective, should the company purchase more cable companies (very expensive), form strategic alliances with cable companies (many cable companies were not interested), or should it try something different?[1]

AT&T's solution was to offer the tens of millions of U.S. households not served by AT&T Cable Services a new technology called "fixed wireless." This new technology would be able to beam both phone and Internet service from existing AT&T cell phone towers. This would enable the company to offer not only local and long-distance services, but also digital television, interactive TV, and high-speed Internet access. The hope was that this new strategy would provide AT&T with significant growth potential and sizable profits for many years to come.

6.1 Corporate Strategy

The vignette about AT&T illustrates the importance of corporate strategy to a firm's survival and success. **Corporate strategy** deals with three key issues facing the corporation as a whole:

1. The firm's overall orientation toward growth, stability, or retrenchment (*directional strategy*)
2. The industries or markets in which the firm competes through its products and business units (*portfolio strategy*)
3. The manner in which management coordinates activities, transfers resources, and cultivates capabilities among product lines and business units (*parenting strategy*)

Corporate strategy is primarily about the choice of direction for the firm as a whole.[2] This is true whether the firm is a small, one-product company or a large multinational corporation. In a large multibusiness company, however, corporate strategy is also about managing various product lines and business units for maximum value. In this instance, corporate headquarters must play the role of the organizational "parent," in that it must deal with various product and business unit "children." Even though each product line or business unit has its own competitive or cooperative strategy that it uses to obtain its own competitive advantage in the marketplace, the corporation must coordinate these different business strategies so that the corporation as a whole succeeds as a "family."[3]

Corporate strategy, therefore, includes decisions regarding the flow of financial and other resources to and from a company's product lines and business units. Through a series of coordinating devices, a company transfers skills and capabilities developed in one unit to other units that need such resources. In this way, it attempts to obtain synergies among numerous product lines and business units so that the corporate whole is greater than the sum of its individual business unit parts.[4] All corporations, from the smallest company offering one product in only one industry to the largest conglomerate operating in many industries with many products must, at one time or another, consider one or more of these issues.

To deal with each of the key issues, this chapter is organized into three parts that examine corporate strategy in terms of *directional strategy* (orientation toward growth), *portfolio analysis* (coordination of cash flow among units), and *corporate parenting* (building corporate synergies through resource sharing and development).

6.2 Directional Strategy

Just as every product or business unit must follow a business strategy to improve its competitive position, every corporation must decide its orientation toward growth by asking the following three questions:

1. Should we expand, cut back, or continue our operations unchanged?

2. Should we concentrate our activities within our current industry or should we diversify into other industries?

3. If we want to grow and expand nationally and/or globally, should we do so through internal development or through external acquisitions, mergers, or strategic alliances?

A corporation's **directional strategy** is composed of three general orientations (sometimes called grand strategies):

- **Growth strategies** expand the company's activities.

- **Stability strategies** make no change to the company's current activities.

- **Retrenchment strategies** reduce the company's level of activities.

Having chosen the general orientation (such as growth), a company's managers can select from several more specific corporate strategies such as concentration within one product line/industry or diversification into other products/industries. (See **Figure 6–1.**) These strategies are useful both to corporations operating in only one industry with one product line and to those operating in many industries with many product lines.

GROWTH STRATEGIES

By far the most widely pursued corporate directional strategies are those designed to achieve growth in sales, assets, profits, or some combination. Companies that do business in expanding industries must grow to survive. Continuing growth means increasing sales and a chance to take advantage of the experience curve to reduce the per-unit cost of products sold, thereby increasing profits. This cost reduction becomes extremely important if a corporation's industry is growing quickly and competitors are engaging in price wars in attempts to increase their shares of the market. Firms that have not reached "critical mass" (that is, gained the necessary economy of large-scale production) will face large losses unless they can find and fill a small,

Figure 6–1
Corporate Directional Strategies

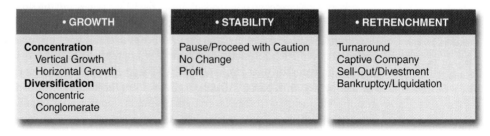

• GROWTH	• STABILITY	• RETRENCHMENT

Concentration
  Vertical Growth
  Horizontal Growth
Diversification
  Concentric
  Conglomerate
	Pause/Proceed with Caution
	No Change
	Profit
		Turnaround
		Captive Company
		Sell-Out/Divestment
		Bankruptcy/Liquidation

but profitable, niche where higher prices can be offset by special product or service features. That is why Motorola, Inc., continued to spend large sums on the product development of cellular phones, pagers, and two-way radios, despite a serious drop in market share and profits. According to Motorola's Chairman George Fisher, "What's at stake here is leadership." Even though the industry was changing quickly, the company was working to avoid the erosion of its market share by jumping into new wireless markets as quickly as possible. Being one of the market leaders in this industry would almost guarantee Motorola enormous future returns.

A corporation can grow internally by expanding its operations both globally and domestically, or it can grow externally through mergers, acquisitions, and strategic alliances. A **merger** is a transaction involving two or more corporations in which stock is exchanged, but from which only one corporation survives. Mergers usually occur between firms of somewhat similar size and are usually "friendly." The resulting firm is likely to have a name derived from its composite firms. One example is the merging of Allied Corporation and Signal Companies to form Allied Signal. An **acquisition** is the purchase of a company that is completely absorbed as an operating subsidiary or division of the acquiring corporation. Examples are Procter & Gamble's acquisition of Richardson-Vicks, known for its Oil of Olay and Vidal Sassoon brands, and Noxell Corporation, known for Noxzema and Cover Girl.

Acquisitions usually occur between firms of different sizes and can be either friendly or hostile. Hostile acquisitions are often called takeovers. A **strategic alliance** is a partnership of two or more corporations or business units to achieve strategically significant objectives that are mutually beneficial. See **Chapter 5** for a detailed discussion of strategic alliances.

Growth is a very attractive strategy for two key reasons:

■ Growth based on increasing market demand may mask flaws in a company—flaws that would be immediately evident in a stable or declining market. A growing flow of revenue into a highly leveraged corporation can create a large amount of **organization slack** (unused resources) that can be used to quickly resolve problems and conflicts between departments and divisions. Growth also provides a big cushion for a turnaround in case a strategic error is made. Larger firms also have more bargaining power than do small firms and are more likely to obtain support from key stakeholders in case of difficulty.

■ A growing firm offers more opportunities for advancement, promotion, and interesting jobs. Growth itself is exciting and ego-enhancing for CEOs. The marketplace and potential investors tend to view a growing corporation as a "winner" or "on the move." Executive compensation tends to get bigger as an organization increases in size. Large firms are also more difficult to acquire than are smaller ones; thus an executive's job is more secure.

The two basic growth strategies are **concentration** on the current product line(s) in one industry and **diversification** into other product lines in other industries.

Concentration

If a company's current product lines have real growth potential, concentration of resources on those product lines makes sense as a strategy for growth. The two basic concentration strategies are vertical growth and horizontal growth. Growing firms in a growing industry tend to choose these strategies before they try diversification.

Vertical Growth   **Vertical growth** can be achieved by taking over a function previously provided by a supplier or by a distributor. The company, in effect, grows by making its own supplies and/or by distributing its own products. This may be done in order to reduce costs, gain control over a scarce resource, guarantee quality of a key input, or obtain access to potential customers. This growth can be achieved either internally by expanding current operations or externally through acquisitions. Henry Ford, for example, used internal company resources to build his River Rouge Plant outside Detroit. The manufacturing process was integrated to the point that iron ore entered one end of the long plant and finished automobiles rolled out the other end into a huge parking lot. In contrast, Cisco Systems, the maker of Internet hardware, chose the external route to vertical growth by purchasing Radiata, Inc., a maker of chip sets for wireless networks. This acquisition gave Cisco access to technology permitting wireless communications at speeds previously possible only with wired connections.[5]

Vertical growth results in **vertical integration**—the degree to which a firm operates vertically in multiple locations on an industry's value chain from extracting raw materials to manufacturing to retailing. More specifically, assuming a function previously provided by a supplier is called **backward integration** (going backward on an industry's value chain). The purchase of Carroll's Foods for its hog-growing facilities by Smithfield Foods, the world's largest pork processor, is an example of backward integration.[6] Assuming a function previously provided by a distributor is labeled **forward integration** (going forward on an industry's value chain). Micron, for example, used forward integration when it expanded out of its successful memory manufacturing business to make and market its own personal computers.

Vertical growth is a logical strategy for a corporation or business unit with a strong competitive position in a highly attractive industry—especially when technology is predictable and markets are growing.[7] To keep and even improve its competitive position, the company may use backward integration to minimize resource acquisition costs and inefficient operations as well as forward integration to gain more control over product distribution. The firm, in effect, builds on its distinctive competence by expanding along the industry's value chain to gain greater competitive advantage.

Although backward integration is usually more profitable than forward integration, it can reduce a corporation's strategic flexibility. The resulting encumbrance of expensive assets that might be hard to sell could create an *exit barrier*, preventing the corporation from leaving that particular industry. When sales of its autos were declining, General Motors, for example, resorted to offering outside parts suppliers the use of its idle factories and workers.

Transaction cost economics proposes that vertical integration is more efficient than contracting for goods and services in the marketplace when the transaction costs of buying goods on the open market become too great. When highly vertically integrated firms become excessively large and bureaucratic, however, the costs of managing the internal transactions may become greater than simply purchasing the needed goods externally, thus justifying outsourcing over vertical integration. See the **Theory As It Applies** feature on how transaction cost economics helps explain why firms vertically integrate.

Harrigan proposes that a company's degree of vertical integration can range from total ownership of the value chain needed to make and sell a product to no ownership at all.[8] (**See Figure 6–2**.) Under **full integration**, a firm internally makes 100% of its key supplies and completely controls its distributors. Large oil companies, such as BP Amoco and Royal Dutch Shell, are fully integrated. They own the oil rigs that pump the oil out of the ground, the ships and pipelines that transport the oil, the refineries that convert the oil to gasoline, and the trucks that deliver the gasoline to company-owned and franchised gas stations. If a corporation does not want the disadvantages of full vertical integration, it may choose either taper or

Figure 6–2
Vertical Integration Continuum

Full Integration	Taper Integration	Quasi-Integration	Long-Term Contract

Source: Suggested by K. R. Harrigan, *Strategies for Vertical Integration* (Lexington, MA: Lexington Books, D.C. Heath, 1983), pp. 16–21.

Theory As It Applies

Transaction Cost Economics Analyzes Vertical Growth Strategy

Why do corporations use vertical growth to permanently own suppliers or distributors when they could simply purchase individual items when needed on the open market? Transaction cost economics is a branch of institutional economics that attempts to answer this question. Beginning with work by Coase and extended by Williamson, transaction cost economics proposes that ownership of resources through vertical growth is more efficient than contracting for goods and services in the marketplace when the transaction costs of buying goods on the open market become too great. Transaction costs include the basic costs of drafting, negotiating, and safeguarding a market agreement (a contract) as well as the later managerial costs when the agreement is creating problems (goods aren't being delivered on time or quality is lower than needed), renegotiation costs (costs of meetings and phone calls), and the costs of settling disputes (lawyers' fees and court costs).

According to Williamson, three conditions must be met before a corporation will prefer internalizing a vertical transaction through ownership over contracting for the transaction in the marketplace: (1) a high level of uncertainty must surround the transaction, (2) assets involved in the transaction must be highly specialized to the transaction, and (3) the transaction must occur frequently. If there is a high level of uncertainty, it will be impossible to write a contract covering all contingencies and it is likely that the contractor will act opportunistically to exploit any gaps in the written agreement, thus creating problems and increasing costs. If the assets

being contracted for are highly specialized (goods or services with few alternate uses), there are likely to be few alternative suppliers, thus allowing the contractor to take advantage of the situation and increase costs. The more frequent the transactions, the more opportunity for the contractor to demand special treatment and thus increase costs further.

Vertical integration is not always more efficient than the marketplace, however. When highly vertically integrated firms become excessively large and bureaucratic, the costs of managing the internal transactions may become greater than simply purchasing the needed goods externally, thus justifying outsourcing over ownership. The usually hidden management costs (excessive layers of management, endless committee meetings needed for interdepartmental coordination, and delayed decision making due to excessively detailed rules and policies) add to the internal transaction costs, thus reducing the effectiveness and efficiency of vertical integration. The decision to own or to contract is, therefore, based on the particular situation surrounding the transaction and the ability of the corporation to manage the transaction internally both effectively and efficiently.

Sources: O. E. Williamson and S. G. Winter, eds., *The Nature of the Firm: Origins, Evolution, and Development* (New York: Oxford University Press, 1991); E. Mosakowski, "Organizational Boundaries and Economic Performance: An Empirical Study of Entrepreneurial Computer Firms," *Strategic Management Journal* (February 1991), pp. 115–133; P. S. Ring and A. H. Van De Ven, "Structuring Cooperative Relationships Between Organizations," *Strategic Management Journal* (October 1992), pp. 483–498.

quasi-integration strategies. With **taper integration**, a firm internally produces less than half of its own requirements and buys the rest from outside suppliers. In case of Smithfield Foods, its purchase of Carroll's allows it to produce 27% of the hogs it needs to process into pork. In terms of distributors, a firm sells part of its goods through company-owned stores and the rest through general wholesalers. Both Xerox and IBM have experimented (unsuccessfully) with selling their products through their own stores. With **quasi-integration**, a company does not make any of its key supplies but purchases most of its requirements from outside suppliers that are under its partial control. For example, by purchasing 20% of the common stock of a key supplier, In Focus Systems, Motorola guaranteed its access to In Focus' technology and enabled Motorola to establish a joint venture with In Focus to manufacture flat-panel video displays.[9] An example of forward quasi-integration would be a large pharmaceutical firm that acquires part interest in a drugstore chain in order to guarantee that its drugs have access to the distribution channel. Purchasing part interest in a key supplier or distributor usually provides a company with a seat on the other firm's board of directors, thus guaranteeing the acquiring firm both information and control. A company may not want to invest in suppliers or distributors, but it still wants to guarantee access to needed supplies or distribution channels. In this case, it may use contractual agreements. **Long-term contracts** are agreements between two separate firms to provide agreed-upon goods and services to each other for a specified period of time. This cannot really be considered to be vertical integration unless the contract specifies that the supplier or distributor cannot have a similar relationship with a competitive firm. In this case, the supplier or distributor is really a *captive company* that, although officially independent, does most of its business with the contracted firm and is formally tied to the other company through a long-term contract.

Recently there has been a movement away from vertical growth strategies (and thus vertical integration) toward cooperative contractual relationships with suppliers and even with competitors. These relationships range from **outsourcing**, in which resources are purchased from outsiders through long-term contracts instead of being made in-house (for example, Hewlett-Packard buys all its laser engines from Canon for HP's laser jet printers), to strategic alliances, in which partnerships, technology licensing agreements, and joint ventures supplement a firm's capabilities (for example, Toshiba has used strategic alliances with GE, Siemens, Motorola, and Ericsson to become one of the world's leading electronic companies).[10]

Horizontal Growth   **Horizontal growth** can be achieved by expanding the firm's products into other geographic locations and/or by increasing the range of products and services offered to current markets. In this case, the company expands sideways at the same location on the industry's value chain. For example, Dell Computers followed a horizontal growth strategy when it extended its mail order business to Europe and to China. A company can grow horizontally through internal development or externally through acquisitions or strategic alliances with another firm in the same industry.

Horizontal growth results in **horizontal integration**—the degree to which a firm operates in multiple geographic locations at the same point in an industry's value chain. Horizontal integration for a firm may range from full to partial ownership to long-term contracts. For example, KLM, the Dutch airline, purchased a controlling stake (partial ownership) in Northwest Airlines to obtain access to American and Asian markets. KLM was unable to acquire all of Northwest's stock because of U.S. government regulations forbidding foreign ownership of a domestic airline (for defense reasons). Many small commuter airlines engage in long-term contracts with major airlines in order to offer a complete arrangement for travelers. For example, Mesa Airlines arranged a five-year agreement with United Airlines to be listed on United's computer reservations as United Express through the Denver airport.

Diversification Strategies

When an industry consolidates and becomes mature, most of the surviving firms have reached the limits of growth using vertical and horizontal growth strategies. Unless the competitors are able to expand internationally into less mature markets, they may have no choice but to diversify into different industries if they want to continue growing. The two basic diversification strategies are concentric and conglomerate.

Concentric (Related) Diversification   Growth through **concentric diversification** into a related industry may be a very appropriate corporate strategy when a firm has a strong competitive position but industry attractiveness is low. By focusing on the characteristics that have given the company its distinctive competence, the company uses those very strengths as its means of diversification. The firm attempts to secure strategic fit in a new industry where the firm's product knowledge, its manufacturing capabilities, and the marketing skills it used so effectively in the original industry can be put to good use.[11] The corporation's products or processes are related in some way: They possess some common thread. The search is for **synergy**, the concept that two businesses will generate more profits together than they could separately. The point of commonality may be similar technology, customer usage, distribution, managerial skills, or product similarity.

This is the rationale taken by Toro Company when it diversified out of lawn mowers into snow blowers, recycling products, and irrigation equipment. According to CEO Kendrick Melrose, the company is changing from a lawn mower company to "an outdoor environmental problem-solver."[12]

The firm may choose to diversify concentrically through either internal or external means. American Airlines, for example, has diversified both internally and externally out of the unpredictable airline business into a series of related businesses run by the parent company, AMR Corporation. Building on the expertise of its SABRE Travel Information Network, it built a computerized reservations system for the French high-speed rail network and for the tunnel under the English Channel.

Conglomerate (Unrelated) Diversification   When management realizes that the current industry is unattractive and that the firm lacks outstanding abilities or skills that it could easily transfer to related products or services in other industries, the most likely strategy is **conglomerate diversification**—diversifying into an industry unrelated to its current one. Rather than maintaining a common thread throughout their organization, strategic managers who adopt this strategy are primarily concerned with financial considerations of cash flow or risk reduction.

The emphasis in conglomerate diversification is on financial considerations rather than on the product–market synergy common to concentric diversification. A cash-rich company with few opportunities for growth in its industry might, for example, move into another industry where opportunities are great but cash is hard to find. Another instance of conglomerate diversification might be when a company with a seasonal and, therefore, uneven cash flow purchases a firm in an unrelated industry with complementing seasonal sales that will level out the cash flow. CSX management considered the purchase of a natural gas transmission business (Texas Gas Resources) by CSX Corporation (a railroad-dominated transportation company) to be a good fit because most of the gas transmission revenue was realized in the winter months—the railroads' lean period.

INTERNATIONAL ENTRY OPTIONS

In today's world, growth usually has international implications. Research indicates that going international is positively associated with firm profitability.[13] A corporation can select from several strategic options the most appropriate method for it to use in entering a foreign market or establishing manufacturing facilities in another country. The options vary from simple exporting to acquisitions to management contracts. As in the case of KLM's purchase of stock in Northwest Airlines, this can be a part of the corporate strategies previously discussed. See the ⊕ **Global Issue** feature to see how Wal-Mart is using international entry options in a horizontal growth strategy to expand in Europe. Some of the more popular options for international entry are as follows:

- **Exporting:** A good way to minimize risk and experiment with a specific product is **exporting**, shipping goods produced in the company's home country to other countries for marketing. The company could choose to handle all critical functions itself, or it could contract these functions to an export management company. Exporting is becoming increasingly popular for small businesses because of the Internet, fax machines, 800 numbers, and overnight air express services, which reduce the once formidable costs of going international.

Global Issue

Wal-Mart Enters International Markets

How can Wal-Mart continue to grow? From its humble beginnings in Bentonville, Arkansas, the company has successfully grown such that its discount stores can now be found in most every corner of the United States. Wal-Mart long ago surpassed Sears as the largest retailer in the country. Over the next few years most of the company's growth will likely continue to come from expansion within the U.S., but an increasing percentage will be coming from international markets. The company's first attempts to expand outside the country in the early 1990s had flopped miserably. It offered the wrong products, such as tennis balls that wouldn't bounce in high-altitude Mexico City and 110-volt appliances in Argentina where 220 volts is the norm. Learning from those early attempts, Wal-Mart opened profitable stores in Canada, Mexico, China, Brazil, and Britain. Of the company's total 1998 sales, 9% came from international operations. Management wanted to raise that amount to 20% by 2001.

After closing a losing operation in Indonesia, management altered its strategy to focus on becoming a major retailer in Europe. In December 1997, Wal-Mart purchased the 21-store German Tertkauf chain. A year later, it strengthened its hold in Germany by acquiring 74 Interspar stores. It took months of remodeling the stores with wider aisles, better lighting, and more check-out counters before the stores were rechristened Wal-Mart. In 1999, Wal-Mart bought Britain's 229-store Asda Group, the country's third largest grocery chain. Nevertheless, according to Hubertus Pellengahr of the Association of German Retailers, "They will have to grow a lot to gain critical mass."

Not content to grow by acquisition, Wal-Mart's management announced in July 2000 a three-year plan to open 50 new locations in Germany and to double its share of the European discount market to 20%. Given difficulties in obtaining building permits from the German bureaucracy, management negotiated with Germany's largest retailer, Metro AG, to swap subsidiaries. This would give Wal-Mart two additional German chains. Given that nonunionized Wal-Mart was now dealing with German unions, analysts wondered if management could turn the money-losing German operation into a profitable one.

Sources: L. Kim, "Crossing the Rhine," *U.S. News & World Report* (August 14, 2000; "Wal-Mart to Buy British Food Chain," *Des Moines Register* (June 15, 1999), p. 9S; P. Geitner, "Wal-Mart Rises in Germany," *Des Moines Register* (December 11, 1999), p. 12S; *Money* (December, 1999), p. 162.

- **Licensing:** Under a **licensing** agreement, the licensing firm grants rights to another firm in the host country to produce and/or sell a product. The licensee pays compensation to the licensing firm in return for technical expertise. This is an especially useful strategy if the trademark or brand name is well known, but the company does not have sufficient funds to finance its entering the country directly. Anheuser-Busch uses this strategy to produce and market Budweiser beer in the United Kingdom, Japan, Israel, Australia, Korea, and the Philippines. This strategy also becomes important if the country makes entry via investment either difficult or impossible. The danger always exists, however, that the licensee might develop its competence to the point that it becomes a competitor to the licensing firm. Therefore, a company should never license its distinctive competence, even for some short-run advantage.

- **Franchising:** Under a **franchising** agreement, the franchiser grants rights to another company to open a retail store using the franchiser's name and operating system. In exchange, the franchisee pays the franchiser a percentage of its sales as a royalty. Franchising provides an opportunity for firms to establish a presence in countries where the population or per capita spending is not sufficient to support a major expansion effort.[14] Franchising accounts for 40% of total U.S. retail sales. Approximately 44% of U.S. franchisers, such as Toys "R" Us, are currently franchising internationally while an additional 31% are planning to do so.[15]

- **Joint Ventures:** The rate of **joint venture** formation between U.S. companies and international partners has been growing 27% annually since 1985.[16] It is the most popular strategy used to enter a new country.[17] Companies often form joint ventures to combine the resources and expertise needed to develop new products or technologies. It also enables a firm to enter a country that restricts foreign ownership. The corporation can enter another country with fewer assets at stake and thus lower risk. For example, when Mexico privatized its railroads in 1996 (two years after the North American Trade Agreement was ratified), the Kansas City Southern (KCS) saw an opportunity to form one complete railroad from Mexico's industrialized northeast to Canada. KCS jointly bid with the Mexican shipping line Transportacion Maritima Mexicana (with whom it would jointly operate the Mexican rail system) to purchase 80% of Grupo Transportacion Ferroviaria Mexicana (TFM). KCS then formed an alliance with Canadian National Railway to complete the route.[18] A joint venture may be an association between a company and a firm in the host country or a government agency in that country. A quick method of obtaining local management, it also reduces the risks of expropriation and harassment by host country officials.

- **Acquisitions:** A relatively quick way to move into an international area is through **acquisitions**—purchasing another company already operating in that area. Synergistic benefits can result if the company acquires a firm with strong complementary product lines and a good distribution network. Maytag Corporation's acquisition of Hoover gave it entry into Europe through Hoover's strength in home appliances in the United Kingdom and in its vacuum cleaner distribution centers on the European continent. To expand into North America, the Swedish appliance maker, A.B. Electrolux, purchased the major home appliance operations of White Consolidated Industries and renamed the unit Frigidaire. Research does suggest that wholly owned subsidiaries are more successful in international undertakings than are strategic alliances, such as joint ventures.[19] This is one reason why firms more experienced in international markets take a higher ownership position when making a foreign investment.[20] In some countries, however, acquisitions can be difficult to arrange because of a lack of available information about potential candidates. Government restrictions on ownership, such as the U.S. requirement that limits foreign ownership of U.S. airlines to 49% of nonvoting and 25% of voting stock, can also discourage acquisitions.

- **Green-Field Development:** If a company doesn't want to purchase another company's problems along with its assets (as Japan's Bridgestone did when it acquired Firestone in the United States) it may choose **green-field development**—building its own manufacturing plant and distribution system. This is usually a far more complicated and expensive operation than acquisition, but it allows a company more freedom in designing the plant, choosing suppliers, and hiring a workforce. For example, Nissan, Honda, and Toyota built auto factories in rural areas of Great Britain and then hired a young workforce with no experience in the industry.

- **Production Sharing:** Coined by Peter Drucker, the term **production sharing** means the process of combining the higher labor skills and technology available in the developed countries with the lower cost labor available in developing countries. The current trend is to move data processing and programming activities "offshore" to places such as Ireland, India, Barbados, Jamaica, the Philippines, and Singapore where wages are lower, English is spoken, and telecommunications are in place.

- **Turnkey Operations: Turnkey operations** are typically contracts for the construction of operating facilities in exchange for a fee. The facilities are transferred to the host country or firm when they are complete. The customer is usually a government agency of, for example, a Middle Eastern country that has decreed that a particular product must be produced locally and under its control. For example, Fiat built an auto plant in Russia to produce an older model of Fiat under a Russian brand name. MNCs that perform turnkey operations are frequently industrial equipment manufacturers that supply some of their own equipment for the project and that commonly sell replacement parts and maintenance services to the host country. They thereby create customers as well as future competitors.

- **BOT Concept:** The **BOT** (**B**uild, **O**perate, **T**ransfer) **concept** is a variation of the turnkey operation. Instead of turning the facility (usually a power plant or toll road) over to the host country when completed, the company operates the facility for a fixed period of time during which it earns back its investment, plus a profit. It then turns the facility over to the government at little or no cost to the host country.[21]

- **Management Contracts:** A large corporation operating throughout the world is likely to have a large amount of management talent at its disposal. **Management contracts** offer a means through which a corporation may use some of its personnel to assist a firm in a host country for a specified fee and period of time. Management contracts are common when a host government expropriates part or all of a foreign-owned company's holdings in its country. The contracts allow the firm to continue to earn some income from its investment and keep the operations going until local management is trained.

CONTROVERSIES IN DIRECTIONAL GROWTH STRATEGIES

Is vertical growth better than horizontal growth? Is concentric diversification better than conglomerate diversification? Although the research is not in complete agreement, growth into areas related to a company's current product lines is generally more successful than is growth into completely unrelated areas.[22] For example, one study of various growth projects examined how many were considered successful, that is, still in existence after 22 years. The results were: vertical growth, 80%; horizontal growth, 50%; concentric diversification, 35%; and conglomerate diversification, 28%.[23]

In terms of diversification strategies, research suggests that the relationship between relatedness and performance is curvilinear in the shape of an inverted U-shaped curve. If a new business is very similar to that of the acquiring firm, it adds little new to the corporation and only marginally improves performance. If the new business is completely different from the acquiring company's businesses, there may be very little potential for any synergy. If, however, the new business provides new resources and capabilities in a different, but similar, business, the likelihood of a significant performance improvement is high.[24]

Is internal growth better than external growth? Corporations can follow the growth strategies of either concentration or diversification through the internal development of new products and services or through external acquisitions, mergers, and strategic alliances. The value of global acquisitions and mergers has steadily increased from around $300,000 billion in 1991 to $3.5 trillion in 2000.[25] Although not yet conclusive, the research indicates that firms that grow through acquisitions do not perform financially as well as firms that grow through internal means.[26] Studies do reveal that over two-thirds of acquisitions are failures primarily because the premiums paid were too high for them to earn their cost of capital.[27] Other research indicates, however, that acquisitions have a higher survival rate than do new internally generated business ventures.[28] It is likely that neither strategy is best by itself and that some combination of internal and external growth strategies is better than using one or the other exclusively.[29]

STABILITY STRATEGIES

A corporation may choose stability over growth by continuing its current activities without any significant change in direction. Although sometimes viewed as a lack of strategy, the stability family of corporate strategies can be appropriate for a successful corporation operating in a reasonably predictable environment.[30] They are very popular with small business owners who have found a niche and are happy with their success and the manageable size of their firms. Stability strategies can be very useful in the short run, but they can be dangerous if followed for too long (as many small-town businesses discovered when Wal-Mart came to town). Some of the more popular of these strategies are the pause/proceed with caution, no change, and profit strategies.

Pause/Proceed with Caution Strategy

A **pause/proceed with caution strategy** is, in effect, a timeout—an opportunity to rest before continuing a growth or retrenchment strategy. It is a very deliberate attempt to make only incremental improvements until a particular environmental situation changes. It is typically conceived as a temporary strategy to be used until the environment becomes more hospitable or to enable a company to consolidate its resources after prolonged rapid growth. This was the strategy Dell Computer Corporation followed in 1993 after its growth strategy had resulted in more growth than it could handle. Explained CEO Michael Dell, "We grew 285% in two years, and we're having some growing pains." Selling personal computers by mail enabled it to underprice Compaq Computer and IBM, but it could not keep up with the needs of the $2 billion, 5,600-employee company selling PCs in 95 countries. Dell did not give up on its growth strategy; it merely put it temporarily in limbo until the company was able to hire new managers, improve the structure, and build new facilities.

No Change Strategy

A **no change strategy** is a decision to do nothing new—a choice to continue current operations and policies for the foreseeable future. Rarely articulated as a definite strategy, a no change strategy's success depends on a lack of significant change in a corporation's situation. The relative stability created by the firm's modest competitive position in an industry facing little or no growth encourages the company to continue on its current course, making only small adjustments for inflation in its sales and profit objectives. There are no obvious opportunities or threats nor much in the way of significant strengths or weaknesses. Few aggressive new competitors are likely to enter such an industry. The corporation has probably found a reasonably profitable and stable niche for its products. Unless the industry is undergoing consolidation, the relative comfort a company in this situation experiences is likely to encourage the company to follow a no change strategy in which the future is expected to continue as an extension of the present. Most small-town businesses probably follow this strategy before Wal-Mart moves into their areas.

Profit Strategy

A **profit strategy** is a decision to do nothing new in a worsening situation but instead to act as though the company's problems are only temporary. The profit strategy is an attempt to artificially support profits when a company's sales are declining by reducing investment and short-term discretionary expenditures. Rather than announcing the company's poor position to shareholders and the investment community at large, top management may be tempted to follow this very seductive strategy. Blaming the company's problems on a hostile environment (such as antibusiness government policies, unethical competitors, finicky customers, and/or greedy lenders), management defers investments and/or cuts expenses (such as R&D, maintenance, and advertising) to stabilize profits during this period. It may even sell one of its product lines for the cash flow benefits. Obviously the profit strategy is useful only to help a company get through a temporary difficulty. Unfortunately the strategy is seductive and if continued long enough will lead to a serious deterioration in a corporation's competitive position. The profit strategy is thus usually top management's passive, short-term, and often self-serving response to the situation.

RETRENCHMENT STRATEGIES

A company may pursue retrenchment strategies when it has a weak competitive position in some or all of its product lines resulting in poor performance—sales are down and profits are becoming losses. These strategies impose a great deal of pressure to improve performance. In an attempt to eliminate the weaknesses that are dragging the company down, management may follow one of several retrenchment strategies ranging from turnaround or becoming a captive company to selling out, bankruptcy, or liquidation.

Turnaround Strategy

The **turnaround strategy** emphasizes the improvement of operational efficiency and is probably most appropriate when a corporation's problems are pervasive but not yet critical. Analogous to a weight reduction diet, the two basic phases of a turnaround strategy are contraction and consolidation.[31]

Contraction is the initial effort to quickly "stop the bleeding" with a general across-the-board cutback in size and costs. The second phase, **consolidation**, implements a program to stabilize the now-leaner corporation. To streamline the company, plans are developed to reduce unnecessary overhead and to make functional activities cost-justified. This is a crucial time for the organization. If the consolidation phase is not conducted in a positive manner, many of the best people leave the organization. An overemphasis on downsizing and cutting costs coupled with a heavy hand by top management is usually counterproductive and can actually hurt performance.[32] If, however, all employees are encouraged to get involved in productivity improvements, the firm is likely to emerge from this retrenchment period a much stronger and better organized company. It has improved its competitive position and is able once again to expand the business. See the **boxed feature** for a description of IBM's effective use of the turnaround strategy.

Captive Company Strategy

A **captive company strategy** is the giving up of independence in exchange for security. A company with a weak competitive position may not be able to engage in a full-blown turnaround strategy. The industry may not be sufficiently attractive to justify such an effort from either the current management or from investors. Nevertheless a company in this situation faces poor sales and increasing losses unless it takes some action. Management desperately searches for an "angel" by offering to be a captive company to one of its larger customers in order to guarantee the company's continued existence with a long-term contract. In this way, the corporation may be able to reduce the scope of some of its functional activities, such as marketing, thus reducing costs significantly. The weaker company gains certainty of sales and production in return for becoming heavily dependent on one firm for at least 75% of its sales. For example, to become the sole supplier of an auto part to General Motors, Simpson Industries of Birmingham, Michigan, agreed to let a special team from GM inspect its engine parts facilities and books and interview its employees. In return, nearly 80% of the company's production was sold to GM through long-term contracts.[33]

Sell-Out/Divestment Strategy

If a corporation with a weak competitive position in its industry is unable either to pull itself up by its bootstraps or to find a customer to which it can become a captive company, it may have no choice but to **sell out**. The sell-out strategy makes sense if management can still obtain a good price for its shareholders and the employees can keep their jobs by selling the entire company to another firm. The hope is that another company will have the necessary resources and determination to return the company to profitability. This is why Rover, the venerable British car manufacturer, was sold to BMW (Bayerische Motoren Werke AG) for $1.2 billion in 1994.

Turnaround Strategy: IBM Becomes "Internet Business Machines"

During the 1970s and 1980s, IBM dominated the computer industry worldwide. It was the market leader in both large mainframe and small personal computers. Along with Apple Computer, IBM set the standard for all personal computers. Even until recently—when IBM no longer dominates the field—personal computers are still identified as being either Apple or IBM-style PCs.

IBM's problems came to a head in the early 1990s. The company's computer sales were falling. More companies were choosing to replace their large, expensive mainframe computers with personal computers, but they weren't buying the PCs from IBM. An increasing number of firms like Hewlett-Packard, Dell, Gateway, and Compaq had entered the industry. They offered IBM-style PC "clones" that were considerably cheaper and often more advanced than IBM's PCs. IBM's falling revenues meant corporate losses—$15 billion in cumulative losses from 1991 through 1993. Industry experts perceived the company as a bureaucratic dinosaur that could no longer adapt to changing conditions. Its stock price fell to $40 with no end in sight.

IBM's Board of Directors in 1993 hired a new CEO, Louis Gerstner, to lead a corporate turnaround strategy at "Big Blue" (the nickname IBM earned from its rigid dress code policies). To stop the flow of red ink, the company violated its long-held "no layoffs" policy by reducing its workforce 40%. Under Gerstner, IBM reorganized its sales force around specific industries such as retailing and banking. Decision making was made easier. Previously, according to Joseph Formichelli, a top executive with the PC division, he "had to go through seven layers to get things done." Firing incompetent employees could take a year, "so you pawned them off on another group." Strategy presentations were hashed over so many times "they got watered down to nothing." Under Gerstner, however, formal presentations were no longer desired. The emphasis switched to quicker decision making and a stronger customer orientation.

At the same time that Gerstner was beginning his turnaround strategy in 1994, David Grossman, a recently hired IBM programmer, was arguing that the future of the computer lay in the developing Internet. According to Grossman, "I came from a progressive computing environment and was telling people at IBM that there was this thing called UNIX—there was an Internet. No one knew what I was talking about." Teamed with John Patrick, a career person with IBM who also served on a strategy task force, and David Singer, a researcher who had written one of the first Gopher programs, Grossman began building a corporate intranet and eventually created a formal Internet group with Patrick as Chief Technical Officer. Recalled Patrick, "A lot of people were saying, 'How do you make money at this?' I said, 'I have no idea. All I know is that this is the most powerful, important form of communication both inside and outside the company that has ever existed . . . .' From the beginning, our goal was to help IBM become the Internet Business Machines company."

From 1994 to 2000, the company transformed itself from being a besieged computer maker to a dominant service provider. Its Global Services unit has grown from almost nothing to a $30 billion business with more than 135,000 employees. By the end of 1998, IBM had completed 18,000 e-business consulting engagements—a third of which were Internet-related. In a 1999 report to financial analysts, CEO Gerstner stated, ". . . IBM is already generating more (e-business) revenue and certainly more profits than all of the top Internet companies combined."

Sources: G. Hamel, "Waking Up IBM," *Harvard Business Review* (July–August 2000), pp. 137–146; I. Sager, "Inside IBM: Internet Business Machines," *Business Week E.Biz* (December 13, 1999), pp. EB20–EB40; B. Ziegler, "Gerstner's IBM Revival: Impressive, Incomplete," *Wall Street Journal* (March 25, 1997), pp. B1, B4.

If the corporation has multiple business lines and it chooses to sell off a division with low growth potential, this is called **divestment**. This was the strategy used by BMW in 2000. After investing $3.4 billion in Rover over six years and failing to make it profitable, BMW sold Land Rover to Ford Motors for $2.9 billion and the rest of the car unit to Alchemy (renamed as the MG Car Company) for a nominal $15.[34] As another example, when Quaker Oats purchased Snapple, the premium soft drink in 1994, Quaker's management believed that they would be able to use Quaker's resources to continue Snapple's phenomenal growth. They had hoped to transform the stately old oatmeal company into a soft-drink power. Unfortunately for Quaker, the soft drink market was changing rapidly. New entrants, like Arizona Iced Tea, Mystic, and Nantucket Nectars, imitated Snapple while Coke and Pepsi formed alliances with Nestea and Lipton to enter the market. After three years of losses, Quaker sold its struggling Snapple beverage unit for $300 million, which was $1.4 billion less than it had paid for the business.[35]

Bankruptcy/Liquidation Strategy

When a company finds itself in the worst possible situation with a poor competitive position in an industry with few prospects, management has only a few alternatives—all of them distasteful. Because no one is interested in buying a weak company in an unattractive industry, the firm must pursue a bankruptcy or liquidation strategy. **Bankruptcy** involves giving up management of the firm to the courts in return for some settlement of the corporation's obligations. Top management hopes that once the court decides the claims on the company, the company will be stronger and better able to compete in a more attractive industry. L.A. Gear, once the third-largest athletic shoe company in the United States, fell on hard times when it paid $20 million to singer Michael Jackson for an endorsement tied to an album that was never made. Strong competition from Nike and Reebok coupled with a trend toward "brown shoes" drove L.A. Gear into a string of losses and eventual bankruptcy in 1998.[36]

In contrast to bankruptcy, which seeks to perpetuate the corporation, **liquidation** is the termination of the firm. Because the industry is unattractive and the company too weak to be sold as a going concern, management may choose to convert as many saleable assets as possible to cash, which is then distributed to the shareholders after all obligations are paid. The benefit of liquidation over bankruptcy is that the board of directors, as representatives of the shareholders, together with top management make the decisions instead of turning them over to the court, which may choose to ignore shareholders completely. As an example, Precision Thermoforming & Packaging (PTP) was a successful company whose main business had been making, assembling, and mailing computer disks to prospective customers of America Online (AOL). When AOL failed to pay $2.2 million for the 170 million disks it had ordered, PTP was unable to pay its debtors and went out of business. Although the company sued AOL for its money, management raised $3 million by auctioning off the firm's $6.2 million worth of equipment to partially pay the creditors. The PTP facility stood vacant while its owners awaited the result of the lawsuit.[37]

At times, top management must be willing to select one of these less desirable retrenchment strategies. Unfortunately, many top managers are unwilling to admit that their company has serious weaknesses for fear that they may be personally blamed. Even worse, top management may not even perceive that crises are developing. When these top managers do eventually notice trouble, they are prone to attribute the problems to temporary environmental disturbances and tend to follow profit strategies. Even when things are going terribly wrong, top management is greatly tempted to avoid liquidation in the hope of a miracle. Thus, a corporation needs a strong board of directors who, to safeguard shareholders' interests, can tell top management when to quit.

6.3 **Portfolio Analysis**

Chapter 5 dealt with how individual product lines and business units can gain competitive advantage in the marketplace by using competitive and cooperative strategies. Companies with multiple product lines or business units must also ask themselves how these various products and business units should be managed to boost overall corporate performance.

- How much of our time and money should we spend on our best products and business units to ensure that they continue to be successful?

- How much of our time and money should we spend developing new costly products, most of which will never be successful?

One of the most popular aids to developing corporate strategy in a multibusiness corporation is portfolio analysis. Although its popularity has dropped since the 1970s and 1980s, when over half of the largest business corporations used portfolio analysis, it is still used by around 27% of *Fortune 500* firms in corporate strategy formulation.[38] Portfolio analysis puts corporate headquarters into the role of an internal banker. In **portfolio analysis**, top management views its product lines and business units as a series of investments from which it expects a profitable return. The product lines/business units form a portfolio of investments that top management must constantly juggle to ensure the best return on the corporation's invested money. Two of the most popular approaches are the BCG Growth-Share Matrix and GE Business Screen. This concept can also be used to develop strategies for international markets.

BCG GROWTH-SHARE MATRIX

The **BCG (Boston Consulting Group) Growth-Share Matrix** depicted in **Figure 6–3** is the simplest way to portray a corporation's portfolio of investments. Each of the corporation's product lines or business units is plotted on the matrix according to both the growth rate of the industry in which it competes and its relative market share. A unit's relative competitive position is defined as its market share in the industry divided by that of the largest other competitor. By this calculation, a relative market share above 1.0 belongs to the market leader. The business growth rate is the percentage of market growth, that is, the percentage by which sales of a particular business unit classification of products have increased. The matrix assumes that, other things being equal, a growing market is attractive.

The line separating areas of high and low relative competitive position is set at 1.5 times. A product line or business unit must have relative strengths of this magnitude to ensure that it will have the dominant position needed to be a "star" or "cash cow." On the other hand, a product line or unit having a relative competitive position less than 1.0 has "dog" status.[39] Each product or unit is represented in **Figure 6–3** by a circle. The area of the circle represents the relative significance of each business unit or product line to the corporation in terms of assets used or sales generated.

The BCG Growth-Share Matrix has a lot in common with the product life cycle. As a product moves through its life cycle, it is categorized into one of four types for the purpose of funding decisions:

- **Question marks** (sometimes called "problem children" or "wildcats") are new products with the potential for success, but they need a lot of cash for development. If such a product is to gain enough market share to become a market leader and thus a star, money must be taken from more mature products and spent on a question mark.

- **Stars** are market leaders typically at the peak of their product life cycle and are usually able to generate enough cash to maintain their high share of the market. When their market growth rate slows, stars become cash cows.

Figure 6–3
BCG Growth-Share Matrix

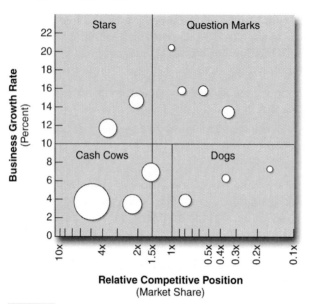

Relative Competitive Position
(Market Share)

Source: B. Hedley, "Strategy and the Business Portfolio," *Long Range Planning* (February 1977), p. 12. Reprinted with permission from Elsevier Science.

- **Cash cows** typically bring in far more money than is needed to maintain their market share. In this declining stage of their life cycle, these products are "milked" for cash that will be invested in new question marks.

- **Dogs** have low market share and do not have the potential (because they are in an un-attractive industry) to bring in much cash. Question marks unable to obtain a dominant market share (and thus become stars) by the time the industry growth rate inevitably slows become dogs. According to the BCG Growth-Share Matrix, dogs should be either sold off or managed carefully for the small amount of cash they can generate.

Underlying the BCG Growth-Share Matrix is the concept of the experience curve (discussed in **Chapter 4**). The key to success is assumed to be market share. Firms with the highest market share tend to have a cost leadership position based on economies of scale, among other things. If a company is able to use the experience curve to its advantage, it should be able to manufacture and sell new products at a price low enough to garner early market share leadership (assuming no successful imitation by competitors). Once the product becomes a star, it is destined to be very profitable, considering its inevitable future as a cash cow.

Having plotted the current positions of its product lines or business units on a matrix, a company can project their future positions, assuming no change in strategy. Present and pro-jected matrixes can thus be used to help identify major strategic issues facing the organization. The goal of any company is to maintain a balanced portfolio so it can be self-sufficient in cash and always working to harvest mature products in declining industries to support new ones in growing industries.

The BCG Growth-Share Matrix is a very well-known portfolio concept with some clear *advantages*. It is quantifiable and easy to use. Cash cows, dogs, and stars are an easy-to-remember way to refer to a corporation's business units or products. Unfortunately the BCG Growth-Share Matrix also has some serious *limitations*:

- The use of highs and lows to form four categories is too simplistic.
- The link between market share and profitability is questionable.[40] Low-share businesses can also be profitable. For example, Olivetti is still profitably selling manual typewriters through mail order catalogues.
- Growth rate is only one aspect of industry attractiveness.
- Product lines or business units are considered only in relation to one competitor: the market leader. Small competitors with fast-growing market shares are ignored.
- Market share is only one aspect of overall competitive position.

GE BUSINESS SCREEN

General Electric, with the assistance of the McKinsey and Company consulting firm, developed a more complicated matrix. As depicted in **Figure 6–4**, the **GE Business Screen** includes 9 cells based on long-term industry attractiveness and business strength/competitive position. The GE Business Screen, in contrast to the BCG Growth-Share Matrix, includes much more data in its 2 key factors than just business growth rate and comparable market share. For example, at GE, industry attractiveness includes market growth rate, industry profitability, size, and pricing practices, among other possible opportunities and threats. Business strength or competitive position includes market share as well as technological position, profitability, and size, among other possible strengths and weaknesses.[41]

Figure 6–4
General Electric's Business Screen

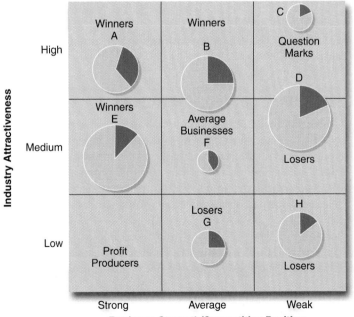

Source: Adapted from *Strategic Management in GE*, Corporate Planning and Development, General Electric Corporation. Used by permission of General Electric Company.

The individual product lines or business units are identified by a letter and plotted as circles on the GE Business Screen. The area of each circle is in proportion to the size of the industry in terms of sales. The pie slices within the circles depict the market share of each product line or business unit.

To plot product lines or business units on the GE Business Screen, follow these 4 steps:

Step 1: Select criteria to rate the industry for each product line or business unit. Assess overall industry attractiveness for each product line or business unit on a scale from 1 (very unattractive) to 5 (very attractive).

Step 2: Select the key factors needed for success in each product line or business unit. Assess business strength/competitive position for each product line or business unit on a scale of 1 (very weak) to 5 (very strong).

Step 3: Plot each product line's or business unit's current position on a matrix like that depicted in **Figure 6–4**.

Step 4: Plot the firm's future portfolio assuming that present corporate and business strategies remain unchanged. Is there a performance gap between projected and desired portfolios? If so, this gap should serve as a stimulus to seriously review the corporation's current mission, objectives, strategies, and policies.

Overall the nine-cell GE Business Screen is an improvement over the BCG Growth-Share Matrix. The GE Business Screen considers many more variables and does not lead to such simplistic conclusions. It recognizes, for example, that the attractiveness of an industry can be assessed in many different ways (other than simply using growth rate), and it thus allows users to select whatever criteria they feel are most appropriate to their situation. This portfolio matrix, however, does have some *shortcomings*:

■ It can get quite complicated and cumbersome.

■ The numerical estimates of industry attractiveness and business strength/competitive position give the appearance of objectivity, but they are in reality subjective judgments that may vary from one person to another.

■ It cannot effectively depict the positions of new products or business units in developing industries.

INTERNATIONAL PORTFOLIO ANALYSIS

To aid international strategic planning, portfolio analysis can be applied to international markets.[42] Two factors form the axes of the matrix in **Figure 6–5**. A **country's attractiveness** is composed of its market size, the market rate of growth, the extent and type of government regulation, and economic and political factors. A **product's competitive strength** is composed of its market share, product fit, contribution margin, and market support. Depending on where a product fits on the matrix, it should either receive more funding or be harvested for cash.

Portfolio analysis might not be useful, however, to corporations operating in a global industry rather than a multidomestic one. In discussing the importance of global industries, Porter argues against the use of portfolio analysis on a country-by-country basis:

> In a global industry, however, managing international activities like a portfolio will undermine the possibility of achieving competitive advantage. In a global industry, a firm must in some way integrate its activities on a worldwide basis to capture the linkage among countries.[43]

Figure 6–5
Portfolio Matrix for Plotting Products by Country

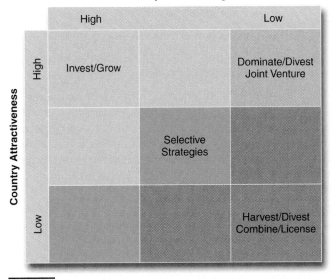

Source: G. D. Harrell and R. O. Kiefer, "Multinational Strategic Market Portfolios," *MSU Business Topics* (Winter 1981), p. 7. Reprinted by permission.

ADVANTAGES AND LIMITATIONS OF PORTFOLIO ANALYSIS

Portfolio analysis is commonly used in strategy formulation because it offers certain *advantages*:

- It encourages top management to evaluate each of the corporation's businesses individually and to set objectives and allocate resources for each.
- It stimulates the use of externally oriented data to supplement management's judgment.
- It raises the issue of cash flow availability for use in expansion and growth.
- Its graphic depiction facilitates communication.

Portfolio analysis does, however, have some very real *limitations* that have caused some companies to reduce their use of this approach:

- It is not easy to define product/market segments.
- It suggests the use of standard strategies that can miss opportunities or be impractical.
- It provides an illusion of scientific rigor when in reality positions are based on subjective judgments.
- Its value-laden terms like cash cow and dog can lead to self-fulfilling prophecies.
- It is not always clear what makes an industry attractive or where a product is in its life cycle.
- Naively following the prescriptions of a portfolio model may actually reduce corporate profits if they are used inappropriately. For example, General Mills' Chief Executive H. Brewster Atwater cites his company's Bisquick brand of flour as a product that would have been written off years ago based on portfolio analysis. "This product is 57 years old. By all rights it should have been overtaken by newer products. But with the proper research to improve the product and promotion to keep customers excited, it's doing very well."[44]

6.4 Corporate Parenting

Campbell, Goold, and Alexander, authors of *Corporate-Level Strategy: Creating Value in the Multibusiness Company*, contend that corporate strategists must address two crucial questions:

- What businesses should this company own and why?
- What organizational structure, management processes, and philosophy will foster superior performance from the company's business units?[45]

Portfolio analysis attempts to answer these questions by examining the attractiveness of various industries and by managing business units for cash flow, that is, by using cash generated from mature units to build new product lines. Unfortunately portfolio analysis fails to deal with the question of what industries a corporation should enter or with how a corporation can attain synergy among its product lines and business units. As suggested by its name, portfolio analysis tends to primarily view matters financially, regarding business units and product lines as separate and independent investments.

Corporate parenting, in contrast, views the corporation in terms of resources and capabilities that can be used to build business unit value as well as generate synergies across business units. According to Campbell, Goold, and Alexander:

> *Multibusiness companies create value by influencing—or parenting—the businesses they own. The best parent companies create more value than any of their rivals would if they owned the same businesses. Those companies have what we call parenting advantage.*[46]

Corporate parenting generates corporate strategy by focusing on the core competencies of the parent corporation and on the value created from the relationship between the parent and its businesses. In the form of corporate headquarters, the parent has a great deal of power in this relationship. If there is a good fit between the parent's skills and resources and the needs and opportunities of the business units, the corporation is likely to create value. If, however, there is not a good fit, the corporation is likely to destroy value.[47] This approach to corporate strategy is useful not only in deciding what new businesses to acquire, but also in choosing how each existing business unit should be best managed. This appears to be the secret to the success of General Electric under CEO Jack Welch. According to one analyst, ". . . he and his managers really add value by imposing tough standards of profitability and by disseminating knowledge and best practice quickly around the GE empire. If some manufacturing trick cuts costs in GE's aero-engine repair shops in Wales, he insists it be applied across the group."[48]

The primary job of corporate headquarters is, therefore, to obtain synergy among the business units by providing needed resources to units, transferring skills and capabilities among the units, and by coordinating the activities of shared unit functions to attain economies of scope (as in centralized purchasing).[49] This is in agreement with the concept of the learning organization discussed in Chapter 1 in which the role of the large firm is to facilitate and transfer the knowledge assets and services throughout the corporation.[50] This is especially important given that ¾ of a modern company's market value stems from its intangible assets—the organization's knowledge.[51]

DEVELOPING A CORPORATE PARENTING STRATEGY

Campbell, Goold, and Alexander recommend that the search for appropriate corporate strategy involves three analytical steps.

First, examine each business unit (or target firm in the case of acquisition) in terms of its strategic factors. People in the business units probably identified the strategic factors when they were generating business strategies for their units.

Second, examine each business unit (or target firm) in terms of areas in which performance can be improved. These are considered to be parenting opportunities. For example, two business units might be able to gain economies of scope by combining their sales forces. In another instance, a unit may have good, but not great, manufacturing and logistics skills. A parent company having world-class expertise in these areas can improve that unit's performance. The corporate parent could also transfer some people from one business unit having the desired skills to another unit in need of those skills. People at corporate headquarters may, because of their experience in many industries, spot areas where improvements are possible that even people in the business unit may not have noticed. Unless specific areas are significantly weaker than the competition, people in the business units may not even be aware that these areas could be improved, especially if each business unit only monitors its own particular industry.

Third, analyze how well the parent corporation fits with the business unit (or target firm). Corporate headquarters must be aware of its own strengths and weaknesses in terms of resources, skills, and capabilities. To do this, the corporate parent must ask if it has the characteristics that fit the parenting opportunities in each business unit. It must also ask if there is a misfit between the parent's characteristics and the critical success factors of each business unit.

PARENTING-FIT MATRIX

Campbell, Goold, and Alexander further recommend the use of a **parenting-fit matrix** that summarizes the various judgments regarding corporate/business unit fit for the corporation as a whole. Instead of describing business units in terms of their growth potential, competitive position, or industry structure, such a matrix emphasizes their fit with the corporate parent. As shown in **Figure 6–6**, the parenting-fit matrix is composed of two dimensions: the positive contributions that the parent can make and the negative effects the parent can make. The combination of these two dimensions creates five different positions—each with its own implications for corporate strategy.

Figure 6–6
Parenting-Fit Matrix

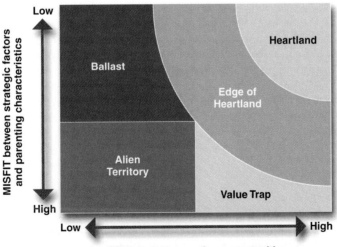

Source: Adapted from M. Alexander, A. Campbell, and M. Goold, "A New Model for Reforming the Planning Review Process," *Planning Review* (January/ February 1995), p. 17. Copyright © MCB University Press Ltd. Reprinted with permission.

Heartland Businesses

According to Campbell, Goold, and Alexander, business units that lie in the top right corner of the matrix should be at the heart of the corporation's future. These **heartland businesses** have opportunities for improvement by the parent, and the parent understands their strategic factors well. These businesses should have priority for all corporate activities.

Edge-of-Heartland Businesses

For **edge-of-heartland businesses**, some parenting characteristics fit the business, but others do not. The parent may not have all the characteristics needed by a unit, or the parent may not really understand all of the unit's strategic factors. For example, a unit in this area may be very strong in creating its own image through advertising—a critical success factor in its industry (such as in perfumes). The corporate parent may, however, not have this strength and tends to leave this to its advertising agency. If the parent forced the unit to abandon its own creative efforts in favor of using the corporation's favorite ad agency, the unit may flounder. Such business units are likely to consume much of the parent's attention, as the parent tries to understand them better and transform them into heartland businesses. In this instance, the parent needs to know when to interfere in business unit activities and strategies and when to keep at arm's length.

Ballast Businesses

Ballast businesses fit very comfortably with the parent corporation but contain very few opportunities to be improved by the parent. This is likely to be the case in units that have been with the corporation for many years and have been very successful. The parent may have added value in the past, but it can no longer find further parenting opportunities. Like cash cows, ballast businesses may be important sources of stability and earnings. They can, however, also be a drag on the corporation as a whole by slowing growth and distracting the parent from more productive activities. Some analysts might put IBM's mainframe business units in this category. Because there is always a danger that environmental changes could move a ballast business unit into alien territory, corporate decision makers should consider divesting this unit as soon as they can get a price that exceeds the expected value of future cash flows.

Alien Territory Businesses

Alien territory businesses have little opportunity to be improved by the corporate parent, and a misfit exists between the parenting characteristics and the units' strategic factors. There is little potential for value creation but high potential for value destruction on the part of the parent. These units are usually small and are often remnants of past experiments with diversification, businesses acquired as part of a larger purchase, or pet projects of senior managers. Even though corporate headquarters may admit that there is little fit, there may be reasons for keeping a unit: It is currently profitable, there are few buyers, the parent has made commitments to the unit's managers, or it is a favorite of the chairman. Because the corporate parent is probably destroying value in its attempts to improve fit, Campbell, Goold, and Alexander recommend that the corporation divest this unit while it still has value.

Value Trap Businesses

Value trap businesses fit well with parenting opportunities, but they are a misfit with the parent's understanding of the units' strategic factors. This is where corporate headquarters can make its biggest error. It mistakes what it sees as opportunities for ways to improve the business unit's profitability or competitive position. For example, in its zeal to make the unit a world-class manufacturer (because the parent has world-class manufacturing skills), it may not notice that the unit is primarily successful because of its unique product development and niche marketing expertise. The potential for possible gain blinds the parent to the downside risks of doing the wrong thing and destroying the unit's core competencies.

HORIZONTAL STRATEGY AND MULTIPOINT COMPETITION

A **horizontal strategy** is a corporate strategy that cuts across business unit boundaries to build synergy across business units and to improve the competitive position of one or more business units. When used to build synergy, it acts like a parenting strategy. When used to improve the competitive position of one or more business units, it can be thought of as a corporate competitive strategy. In **multipoint competition**, large multibusiness corporations compete against other large multibusiness firms in a number of markets. These multipoint competitors are firms that compete with each other not only in one business unit, but also in a number of business units. At one time or another, a cash-rich competitor may choose to build its own market share in a particular market to the disadvantage of another corporation's business unit. Although each business unit has primary responsibility for its own business strategy, it may sometimes need some help from its corporate parent, especially if the competitor business unit is getting heavy financial support from its corporate parent. In this instance, corporate headquarters develops a horizontal strategy to coordinate the various goals and strategies of related business units.[52]

For example, Procter & Gamble, Kimberly-Clark, Scott Paper, and Johnson and Johnson compete with one another in varying combinations of consumer paper products, from disposable diapers to facial tissue. If (purely hypothetically) Johnson and Johnson had just developed a toilet tissue with which it chose to challenge Procter & Gamble's high-share Charmin brand in a particular district, it might charge a low price for its new brand to build sales quickly. Procter & Gamble might not choose to respond to this attack on its share by cutting prices on Charmin. Because of Charmin's high market share, Procter & Gamble would lose significantly more sales dollars in a price war than Johnson and Johnson would with its initially low-share brand. To retaliate, Procter & Gamble might thus challenge Johnson and Johnson's high-share baby shampoo with Procter & Gamble's own low-share brand of baby shampoo in a different district. Once Johnson and Johnson had perceived Procter & Gamble's response, it might choose to stop challenging Charmin so that Procter & Gamble would stop challenging Johnson and Johnson's baby shampoo.

Multipoint competition and the resulting use of horizontal strategy may actually slow the development of hypercompetition in an industry. The realization that an attack on a market leader's position could result in a response in another market leads to mutual forbearance in which managers behave more conservatively toward multimarket rivals and competitive rivalry is reduced.[53] In one industry, for example, multipoint competition resulted in firms being less likely to exit a market. "Live and let live" replaced strong competitive rivalry.[54] Multipoint competition is likely to become even more prevalent in the future as corporations become global competitors and expand into more markets through strategic alliances.[55]

6.5 Impact of the Internet on Corporate Strategy

One impact of the growth of the Internet is that corporations are rethinking what businesses they should be in. For example, Emerson Electric, the 110-year-old St. Louis manufacturer of electrical motors, refrigeration components, and industrial tools, is now positioning itself in power backup systems for computers. In January 2000, Emerson purchased Jordan Industries Inc.'s telecommunications-products business. Three months later, Emerson bought the power supply division of Swedish phone maker Ericsson. With the power grid reaching its capacity, electrical outages are becoming more commonplace in the United States. For example, the state of California suffered under "rolling blackouts" in 2001 because of insufficient power generation capacity.

Emerson's acquisitions mean that the company could now provide reliable power backup capability for its customers. When the power goes out, Emerson's components act to switch the power from one source to another and regulate the voltage. Emerson provides the generators and fuel cells to generate the temporary electricity. These products have become crucial for any company that relies on the Internet for conducting business. Intira Corp., a St. Louis Web-hosting company, suffered a seven-hour outage due to a malfunctioning transformer but was able to stay online thanks to Emerson equipment. According to John Steensen, Intira's chief technology officer, "All of our affected customers would have gotten a month of free service if we had gone down, costing us hundreds of thousands of dollars." The acquisitions significantly increased Emerson's sales and made the power unit the largest and fastest growing of Emerson's five SBUs. Cisco Systems, WorldCom, and Intel are Emerson customers. Emerson's management is estimating that its high-tech power-systems business will grow at 15% to 20% annually for the foreseeable future.[56]

Any company considering entering international markets must consider the impact of the Internet. Simply creating a Web site is likely to result in inquiries from people in foreign countries where the company may have no experience. (See the **Internet Issue** feature for Internet usage by country and by language.) A few years ago, The Doll Collection was a barely profitable neighborhood retail shop in Louisville, Kentucky, with a staff of three people. Looking for an inexpensive way to boost its sales, one of the employees, Jason Walters, suggested putting a Web page ⟨www.dollpage.com⟩ on the Internet. After spending two weeks learning the Internet computer language, html, Walters designed a simple site showcasing well-known dolls like Barbie and Madam Alexander to attract buyers. Employees of The Doll Collection were amazed by the response—much of which came from outside North America. Sales jumped 375%. In one year the shop had become a global retailer, marketing Barbie and Madam Alexander dolls to people in almost every country, including Japan, China, and Australia.[57]

Internet Issue

Global Online Population

By 2002, 490 million people throughout the world will have achieved Internet access. For every 1,000 people, 80 will be using the Web. By the end of 2005, the number is expected to rise to 118 per 1,000 people. Fifteen countries will account for nearly 82% of these worldwide Internet users. The United States in 2000 accounted for 43% of the total 259 million worldwide. This percentage will drop to 33% in 2002 and only 27% in 2005. The top 10 nations with the most Internet users in 2000 were:

Country	Internet Users (in thousands)
1. United States	110,825
2. Japan	18,156
3. United Kingdom	13,156
4. Canada	12,277
5. Germany	12,285
6. Australia	6,837
7. Brazil	6,790
8. China	6,308
9. France	5,696
10. South Korea	5,688

Given that 4 of the top 10 countries using the Internet speak English, it is no surprise that English has become the dominant language of the Internet. In 1996, it was the first language of 80% of Internet users. As other countries become active in the Internet, that figure is changing. By 2000, only 49.9% of Internet users had English as their first language. Chinese was second with 7.6%, followed by Japanese at 7.2%, German at 5.9%, and Spanish at 5%.

Source: J. Kirchner, "Global Online Population," *PC Magazine* (June 6, 2000), p. 23; R. O. Crockett, "Surfing in Tongues," *Business Week E.Biz* (December 11, 2000), p. EB 18.

Projections for the 21st Century

- From 1994 to 2010, the number of wired telephone lines in the world will increase from 607 million to 1.4 billion.
- From 1994 to 2010, the number of wireless telephone lines in the world will increase from 34 million to 1.3 billion.[58]

Discussion Questions

1. How does horizontal growth differ from vertical growth as a corporate strategy? From concentric diversification?
2. What are the tradeoffs between an internal and an external growth strategy? Which approach is best as an international entry strategy?
3. Is stability really a strategy or just a term for no strategy?
4. Compare and contrast SWOT analysis with portfolio analysis.
5. How is corporate parenting different from portfolio analysis? How is it alike? Is it a useful concept in a global industry?

Strategic Practice Exercise

On March 14, 2000, Stephen King, the horror writer, published his new book, *Riding the Bullet*, on the Internet before it appeared in print. Within 24 hours, around 400,000 people had downloaded the book—even though most of them needed to download the software in order to read the book. The unexpected demand crashed servers. According to Jack Romanos, President of Simon & Schuster, "I don't think anybody could have anticipated how many people were out there who are willing to accept the written word in a paperless format." To many, this announced the coming of the electronic novel. Environmentalists applauded that e-books would soon replace paper books and newspapers, thus reducing pollution coming from paper mills and landfills. The King book was easy to download and took less time than a trip to the bookstore. Critics argued that the King book used the Internet because at 66 pages, it was too short to be a standard printed novel. It was also free, so there was nothing to discourage natural curiosity. Some people in the industry remarked that 75% of those who downloaded the book did not read it.[59]

1. Form into small groups in the class to discuss the future of Internet publishing.
2. Consider the following questions as discussion guides:
   - What are the *pros* and *cons* of electronic publishing?
   - Should newspaper and book publishers convert to electronic publishing over paper?
   - The *Wall Street Journal* and others publish in both paper and electronic formats. Has this been a success?
   - Would you prefer this textbook and others in an electronic format?
   - How would publishers distribute books and textbooks?
3. Present your group's conclusions to the class.

Key Terms

acquisition (pp. 139, 145)
alien territory businesses (p. 158)
backward integration (p. 140)
ballast businesses (p. 158)
bankruptcy (p. 150)
BCG (Boston Consulting Group) Growth-Share Matrix (p. 151)
BOT concept (p. 146)
captive company strategy (p. 148)
cash cows (p. 152)

concentration (p. 139)
concentric diversification (p. 142)
conglomerate diversification (p. 143)
consolidation (p. 148)
contraction (p. 148)
corporate parenting (p. 156)
corporate strategy (p. 137)
country's attractiveness (p. 154)
directional strategy (p. 138)
diversification (p. 139)

divestment (p. 150)
dogs (p. 152)
edge-of-heartland businesses (p. 158)
exporting (p. 143)
forward integration (p. 140)
franchising (p. 144)
full integration (p. 140)
GE Business Screen (p. 153)
green-field development (p. 145)
growth strategies (p. 138)

heartland businesses (p. 158)
horizontal growth (p. 142)
horizontal integration (p. 142)
horizontal strategy (p. 159)
joint ventures (p. 145)
licensing (p. 144)
liquidation (p. 150)
long-term contracts (p. 142)
management contracts (p. 146)
merger (p. 139)
multipoint competition (p. 159)
no change strategy (p. 147)
organization slack (p. 139)

outsourcing (p. 142)
parenting-fit matrix (p. 157)
pause/proceed with caution strategy (p. 147)
portfolio analysis (p. 151)
product's competitive strength (p. 154)
production sharing (p. 145)
profit strategy (p. 147)
quasi-integration (p. 141)
question marks (p. 151)
retrenchment strategies (p. 138)
sell out (p. 148)

stability strategies (p. 138)
stars (p. 151)
strategic alliance (p. 139)
synergy (p. 143)
taper integration (p. 141)
transaction cost economics (p. 140)
turnaround strategy (p. 148)
turnkey operations (p. 145)
value trap businesses (p. 158)
vertical growth (p. 139)
vertical integration (p. 140)

Notes

1. J. Guyon, "AT&T's Big Bet Keeps Getting Dicier," *Fortune* (January 10, 2000): 126–129.
2. R. P. Rumelt, D. E. Schendel, and D. J. Teece, "Fundamental Issues in Strategy," in *Fundamental Issues in Strategy: A Research Agenda*, edited by R. P. Rumelt, D. E. Schendel, and D. J. Teece (Boston: HBS Press, 1994), p. 42.
3. This analogy of corporate parent and business unit children was initially proposed by A. Campbell, M. Goold, and M. Alexander. See "Corporate Strategy: The Quest for Parenting Advantage," *Harvard Business Review* (March–April, 1995), pp. 120–132.
4. M. E. Porter, "From Competitive Strategy to Corporate Strategy," in *International Review of Strategic Management*, Vol. 1, edited by D. E. Husey (Chicester, England: John Wiley & Sons, 1990), p. 29.
5. "Cisco Buys Wireless Chip-Set Maker," *The (Ames) Tribune* (November 11, 2000), p. B7.
6. J. Perkins, "It's a Hog Predicament," *Des Moines Register* (April 11, 1999), pp. J1–J2.
7. J. W. Slocum, Jr., M. McGill, and D. T. Lei, "The New Learning Strategy: Anytime, Anything, Anywhere," *Organizational Dynamics* (Autumn 1994), p. 36.
8. K. R. Harrigan, *Strategies for Vertical Integration* (Lexington, MA: Lexington Books, D. C. Heath, 1983), pp. 16–21.
9. L. Grant, "Partners in Profit," *U. S. News and World Report* (September 20, 1993), pp. 65–66.
10. For a discussion of the pros and cons of contracting versus vertical integration, see J. T. Mahoney, "The Choice of Organizational Form: Vertical Financial Ownership Versus Other Methods of Vertical Integration," *Strategic Management Journal* (November 1992), pp. 559–584.
11. A. Y. Ilinich and C. P. Zeithaml, "Operationalizing and Testing Galbraith's Center of Gravity Theory," *Strategic Management Journal* (June 1995), pp. 401–410.
12. R. Gibson, "Toro Charges into Greener Fields with New Products," *Wall Street Journal* (July 22, 1997), p. B4.
13. A. Delios and P. W. Beamish, "Geographic Scope, Product Diversification, and the Corporate Performance of Japanese Firms," *Strategic Management Journal* (August 1999), pp. 711–727.
14. E. Elango and V. H. Fried, "Franchising Research: A Literature Review and Synthesis," *Journal of Small Business Management* (July 1997), pp. 68–81.
15. T. Thilgen, "Corporate Clout Replaces 'Small Is Beautiful,'" *Wall Street Journal* (March 27, 1997), p. B14.
16. S. Sherman, "Are Strategic Alliances Working?" *Fortune* (September 21, 1992), p. 77.
17. J. E. McCann, III, "The Growth of Acquisitions in Services," *Long Range Planning* (December 1996), pp. 835–841.

18. P. Gogoi and G. Smith, "The Way to Run a Railroad," *Business Week* (October 23, 2000), pp. 106–110.
19. B. Voss, "Strategic Federations Frequently Falter in Far East," *Journal of Business Strategy* (July/August 1993), p. 6; S. Douma, "Success and Failure in New Ventures," *Long Range Planning* (April 1991), pp. 54–60.
20. A. Delios and P. W. Beamish, "Ownership Strategy of Japanese Firms: Transactional, Institutional, and Experience Approaches," *Strategic Management Journal* (October 1999), pp. 915–933.
21. J. Naisbitt, *Megatrends Asia* (New York: Simon & Schuster, 1996), p. 143.
22. K. Ramaswamy, "The Performance Impact of Strategic Similarity in Horizontal Mergers: Evidence from the U.S. Banking Industry," *Academy of Management Journal* (July 1997), pp. 697–715; D. J. Flanagan, "Announcements of Purely Related and Purely Unrelated Mergers and Shareholder Returns: Reconciling the Relatedness Paradox," *Journal of Management*, Vol. 22, No. 6 (1996), pp. 823–835; D. D. Bergh, "Predicting Diversification of Unrelated Acquisitions: An Integrated Model of Ex Ante Conditions," *Strategic Management Journal* (October 1997), pp. 715–731.
23. J. M. Pennings, H. Barkema, and S. Douma, "Organizational Learning and Diversification," *Academy of Management Journal* (June 1994), pp. 608–640.
24. L. E. Palich, L. B. Cardinal, and C. C. Miller, "Curvilinearity in the Diversification-Performance Linkage: An Examination of Over Three Decades of Research," *Strategic Management Journal* (February 2000), pp. 155–174.
25. "The Great Merger Wave Breaks," *The Economist* (January 27, 2001), pp. 59–60.
26. W. B. Carper, "Corporate Acquisitions and Shareholder Wealth: A Review and Exploratory Analysis," *Journal of Management* (December 1990), pp. 807–823; P. G. Simmonds, "Using Diversification as a Tool for Effective Performance," *Handbook of Business Strategy, 1992/93 Yearbook*, edited by H. E. Glass and M. A. Hovde (Boston: Warren, Gorham & Lamont, 1992), pp. 3.1–3.7; B. T. Lamont and C. A. Anderson, "Mode of Corporate Diversification and Economic Performance," *Academy of Management Journal* (December 1985), pp. 926–936.
27. M. L. Sirower, *The Synergy Trap* (NY: Free Press, 1997); B. Jensen, "Make It Simple! How Simplicity Could Become Your Ultimate Strategy," *Strategy & Leadership* (March/April 1997), p. 35.
28. J. M. Pennings, H. Barkema, and S. Douma, "Organizational Learning and Diversification," *Academy of Management Journal* (June 1994), pp. 608–640.

29. E. C. Busija, H. M. O'Neill, and C. P. Zeithaml, "Diversification Strategy, Entry Mode, and Performance: Evidence of Choice and Constraints," *Strategic Management Journal* (April 1997), pp. 321–327; A. Sharma, "Mode of Entry and Ex-Post Performance," *Strategic Management Journal* (September 1998), pp. 879–900.

30. A. Inkpen and N. Choudhury, "The Seeking of Strategy Where It Is Not: Towards a Theory of Strategy Absence," *Strategic Management Journal* (May 1995), pp. 313–323.

31. J. A. Pearce II and D. K. Robbins, "Retrenchment Remains the Foundation of Business Turnaround," *Strategic Management Journal* (June 1994), pp. 407–417.

32. J. R. Morris, W. F. Cascio, and C. E. Young, "Downsizing After All These Years," *Organizational Dynamics* (Winter 1999), pp. 78–87; P. H. Mirvis, "Human Resource Management: Leaders, Laggards, and Followers," *Academy of Management Executive* (May 1997), pp. 43–56; J. K. DeDee and D. W. Vorhies, "Retrenchment Activities of Small Firms During Economic Downturn: An Empirical Investigation," *Journal of Small Business Management* (July 1998), pp. 46–61.

33. J. B. Treece, "U.S. Parts Makers Just Won't Say 'Uncle,'" *Business Week* (August 10, 1987), pp. 76–77.

34. S. Miller and M. Champion, "BMW Sells Rover Cars to Phoenix Group of U.K.," *Wall Street Journal* (May 10, 2000), p. A23.

35. "Quaker Oats Gives Up on Snapple, Sells It at a $1.4 Billion Loss," *Des Moines Register* (March 28, 1997), p. 8S.

36. S. P. Dinnen, "Common Shareholders Lose in Bankruptcy of L. A. Gear," *Des Moines Register* (June 18, 2000), p. 1D.

37. K. L. McQuaid, "Packaging Company Diss-ked by AOL," *INC.* (September 1997), p. 31.

38. B. C. Reimann and A. Reichert, "Portfolio Planning Methods for Strategic Capital Allocation: A Survey of Fortune 500 Firms," *International Journal of Management* (March 1996), pp. 84–93; D. K. Sinha, "Strategic Planning in the Fortune 500," *Handbook of Business Strategy, 1991/92 Yearbook*, edited by H. E. Glass and M. A. Hovde (Boston: Warren Gorham & Lamont, 1991), p. 9.6.

39. B. Hedley, "Strategy and the Business Portfolio," *Long Range Planning* (February 1977), p. 9.

40. C. Anterasian, J. L. Graham, and R. B. Money, "Are U.S. Managers Superstitious About Market Share," *Sloan Management Review* (Summer 1996), pp. 67–77.

41. R. G. Hamermesh, *Making Strategy Work* (New York: John Wiley & Sons, 1986), p. 14.

42. G. D. Harrell and R. O. Kiefer, "Multinational Strategic Market Portfolios," *MSU Business Topics* (Winter 1981), p. 5.

43. M. E. Porter, "Changing Patterns of International Competition," *California Management Review* (Winter 1986), p. 12.

44. J. J. Curran, "Companies That Rob the Future," *Fortune* (July 4, 1988), p. 84.

45. A. Campbell, M. Goold, and M. Alexander, *Corporate-Level Strategy: Creating Value in the Multibusiness Company* (New York: John Wiley & Sons, 1994). See also M. Goold, A. Campbell, and M. Alexander, "Corporate Strategy and Parenting Theory," *Long Range Planning* (April 1998), pp. 308–318.

46. A. Campbell, M. Goold, and M. Alexander, "Corporate Strategy: The Quest for Parenting Advantage," *Harvard Business Review* (March–April 1995), p. 121.

47. Campbell, Goold, and Alexander, p. 122.

48. "Jack's Gamble," *The Economist* (October 28, 2000), pp. 13–14.

49. D. J. Collis, "Corporate Strategy in Multibusiness Firms," *Long Range Planning* (June 1996), pp. 416–418; D. Lei, M. A. Hitt, and R. Bettis, "Dynamic Core Competencies Through Meta-Learning and Strategic Context," *Journal of Management*, Vol. 22, No. 4 (1996), pp. 549–569.

50. D. J. Teece, "Strategies for Managing Knowledge Assets: The Role of Firm Structure and Industrial Context," *Long Range Planning* (February 2000), pp. 35–54.

51. C. Havens and E. Knapp, "Easing into Knowledge Management," *Strategy & Leadership* (March/April 1999), pp. 4–9.

52. M. E. Porter, *Competitive Advantage* (New York: Free Press, 1985), pp. 317–382.

53. J. Gimeno and C. Y. Woo, "Hypercompetition in a Multimarket Environment: The Role of Strategic Similarity and Multimarket Contact in Competitive De-Escalation," *Organization Science* (May/June 1996), pp. 322–341.

54. W. Boeker, J. Goodstein, J. Stephan, and J. P. Murmann, "Competition in a Multimarket Environment: The Case of Market Exit," *Organization Science* (March/April 1997), pp. 126–142.

55. J. Gimeno and C. Y. Woo, "Multimarket Contact, Economies of Scope, and Firm Performance," *Academy of Management Journal* (June 1999), pp. 239–259.

56. D. Little, "Emerson Electric Jump-Starts Itself," *Business Week* (July 24, 2000), pp. 78–80.

57. L. Beresford, "Global Smarts, Toy Story," *Entrepreneur* (February 1997), p. 38.

58. J. Warner, "21st Century Capitalism: Snapshot of the Next Century," *Business Week* (November 18, 1994), p. 194.

59. "Learning to E-Read," *The Economist Survey E-Entertainment* (October 7, 2000), p. 22.

chapter 7

Strategy Formulation: Functional Strategy and Strategic Choice

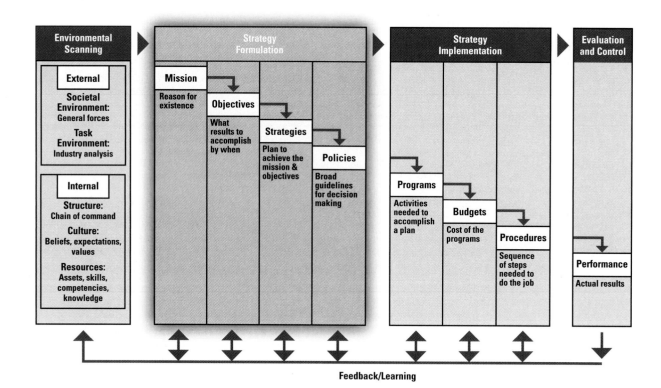

| Environmental Scanning | Strategy Formulation | Strategy Implementation | Evaluation and Control |

Feedback/Learning

For almost 150 years, the Church & Dwight Company has been building market share on a brand name whose products are in 95% of all U.S. households. Yet if you asked the average person what products this company made, few would know. Although Church & Dwight may not be a household name, the company's ubiquitous orange box of Arm & Hammer[1] brand baking soda is cherished throughout North America. Church & Dwight is a classic example of a marketing functional strategy called product development. Shortly after its introduction in 1878, Arm & Hammer Baking Soda became a fundamental item on the pantry shelf as people found many uses for sodium bicarbonate other than baking, such as cleaning, deodorizing, and tooth brushing. Hearing of the many uses people were finding for its product, the company advertised that its baking soda was good not only for baking, but also for deodorizing refrigerators—simply by leaving an open box in the refrigerator. In a brilliant marketing move, the firm then suggested that consumers buy the product and throw it away—deodorize a kitchen sink by dumping Arm & Hammer baking soda down the drain! The company did not stop here. It looked for other uses of its sodium bicarbonate in new products. Church & Dwight has achieved consistent growth in sales and earnings through the use of "line extensions"—putting the Arm & Hammer brand first on baking soda, then on laundry detergents, toothpaste, and deodorants. By the beginning of the 21st century, Church & Dwight had become a significant competitor in markets previously dominated only by giants like Procter & Gamble, Lever Brothers, and Colgate, using only one brand name. Was there a limit to this growth? Was there a point at which these continuous line extensions would begin to eat away at the integrity of the Arm & Hammer name?

7.1 Functional Strategy

Functional strategy is the approach a functional area takes to achieve corporate and business unit objectives and strategies by maximizing resource productivity. It is concerned with developing and nurturing a distinctive competence to provide a company or business unit with a competitive advantage. Just as a multidivisional corporation has several business units, each with its own business strategy, each business unit has its own set of departments, each with its own functional strategy.

The orientation of the functional strategy is dictated by its parent business unit's strategy. For example, a business unit following a competitive strategy of differentiation through high quality needs a manufacturing functional strategy that emphasizes expensive, quality assurance processes over cheaper, high-volume production; a human resource functional strategy that emphasizes the hiring and training of a highly skilled, but costly, workforce; and a marketing functional strategy that emphasizes distribution channel "pull" using advertising to increase consumer demand over "push" using promotional allowances to retailers. If a business unit were to follow a low-cost competitive strategy, however, a different set of functional strategies would be needed to support the business strategy.

Just as a competitive strategy may need to vary from one region of the world to another, functional strategies may need to vary from region to region. When Mr. Donut expanded into Japan, for example, it had to market donuts not as breakfast, but as snack food. Because the Japanese had no breakfast coffee-and-donut custom, they preferred to eat the donuts in the afternoon or evening. Mr. Donut restaurants were thus located near railroad stations and supermarkets. All signs were in English to appeal to the Western interests of the Japanese.

CORE COMPETENCIES

As defined earlier in **Chapter 4**, a **core competency** is something that a corporation can do exceedingly well. It is a key strength. It may also be called a **core capability** because it includes a number of constituent skills. For example, a core competency of Avon Products is its expertise in door-to-door selling. FedEx has a core competency in information technology. A company must continually reinvest in its core competencies or risk losing them.[2] When these competencies or capabilities are superior to those of the competition, they are called **distinctive competencies**. Although it is typically not an asset in the accounting sense, a core competency is a very valuable resource—it does not "wear out." In general, the more core competencies are used, the more refined they get and the more valuable they become. To be considered a *distinctive competency*, the competency must meet three tests:

1. **Customer Value**: It must make a disproportionate contribution to customer-perceived value.

2. **Competitor Unique**: It must be unique and superior to competitor capabilities.

3. **Extendibility:** It must be something that can be used to develop new products/services or enter new markets.[3]

Even though a distinctive competency is certainly considered a corporation's key strength, a key strength may not always be a distinctive competency. As competitors attempt to imitate another company's competence in a particular functional area, what was once a distinctive competency becomes a minimum requirement to compete in the industry.[4] Even though the competency may still be a core competency and thus a strength, it is no longer unique. For example, when Maytag Company alone had high-quality products, Maytag's ability to make exceedingly reliable and durable washing machines was a distinctive competency. As other appliance makers imitated its quality control and design processes, this continued to be a key strength (that is, a core competency) of Maytag, but it was less and less a distinctive competency.

Where do these competencies come from? A corporation can gain access to a distinctive competency in four ways:

- It may be an asset endowment, such as a key patent, coming from the founding of the company—Xerox grew on the basis of its original copying patent.

- It may be acquired from someone else—Whirlpool bought a worldwide distribution system when it purchased Philips's appliance division.

- It may be shared with another business unit or alliance partner—Apple Computer worked with a design firm to create the special appeal of its Apple II and Mac computers.

- It may be carefully built and accumulated over time within the company—Honda carefully extended its expertise in small motor manufacturing from motorcycles to autos and lawnmowers.[5]

For core competencies to be distinctive competencies, they must be superior to those of the competition. As more industries become hypercompetitive (discussed in **Chapter 3**), it will be increasingly difficult to keep a core competence distinctive. These resources are likely either to be imitated or made obsolete by new technologies.

For a functional strategy to have the best chance of success, it should be built on a distinctive competency residing within that functional area. If a corporation does not have a distinctive competency in a particular functional area, that functional area could be a candidate for outsourcing.

THE SOURCING DECISION: WHERE SHOULD FUNCTIONS BE HOUSED?

Where should a function be housed? Should it be integrated within the organization or purchased from an outside contractor? **Outsourcing** is purchasing from someone else a product or service that had been previously provided internally. For example, DuPont contracted out project engineering and design to Morrison Knudsen; AT&T outsourced its credit card processing to Total System Services; and Northern Telecom outsourced its electronic component manufacturing to Comptronix. Outsourcing is becoming an increasingly important part of strategic decision making and an important way to increase efficiency and often quality. Firms competing in global industries must in particular search worldwide for the most appropriate suppliers.

In a study of 30 firms, outsourcing resulted on average in a 9% reduction in costs and a 15% increase in capacity and quality.[6] For example, Motorola sold its factories in Iowa and Ireland to Celestica, Inc., for $70 million. Motorola then agreed to pay Celestica more than $1 billion over three years to make handsets, pagers, two-way radios, and other accessories for Motorola. Celestica, which was once a factory of IBM in Toronto, Canada, offered jobs to many of Motorola's employees in Iowa and Ireland. Motorola then shifted manufacturing from its plant in Florida to the Ireland plant it just sold Celestica so that its Florida facility could concentrate on software design and administration. According to Motorola's management, this was part of a broad effort to make the corporation's supply chain more efficient, consolidate its manufacturing operations, and improve financial performance.[7]

According to an American Management Association survey of member companies, 94% of the firms outsource at least one activity. The outsourced activities are general and administrative (78%), human resources (77%), transportation and distribution (66%), information systems (63%), manufacturing (56%), marketing (51%), and finance and accounting (18%). The survey also reveals that 25% of the respondents have been disappointed in their outsourcing results. Fifty-one percent of the firms reported bringing an outsourced activity back in-house. Nevertheless, authorities expect the number of companies engaging in outsourcing to not only increase, but also to outsource an increasing number of functions, especially in customer service, bookkeeping, financial clerical, sales/telemarketing, and mailroom.[8]

Sophisticated strategists, according to Quinn, are no longer thinking just of market share or vertical integration as the keys to strategic planning:

> *Instead they concentrate on identifying those few core service activities where the company has or can develop: (1) a continuing strategic edge and (2) long-term streams of new products to satisfy future customer demands. They develop these competencies in greater depth than anyone else in the world. Then they seek to eliminate, minimize, or outsource activities where the company cannot be preeminent, unless those activities are essential to support or protect the chosen areas of strategic focus.[9]*

The key to outsourcing is to purchase from outside only those activities that are not key to the company's distinctive competencies. Otherwise, the company may give up the very capabilities that made it successful in the first place—thus putting itself on the road to eventual decline. Therefore, in determining functional strategy, the strategist must:

- Identify the company's or business unit's core competencies.
- Ensure that the competencies are continually being strengthened.
- Manage the competencies in such a way that best preserves the competitive advantage they create.

An outsourcing decision depends on the fraction of total value added that the activity under consideration represents and by the amount of potential competitive advantage in that activity for the company or business unit. See the outsourcing matrix in **Figure 7-1**. A firm should consider outsourcing any activity or function that has low potential for competitive advantage. If that activity constitutes only a small part of the total value of the firm's products or services, it should be purchased on the open market (assuming that quality providers of the activity are plentiful). If, however, the activity contributes highly to the company's products or services, the firm should purchase it through long-term contracts with trusted suppliers or distributors. A firm should always produce at least some of the activity or function (taper vertical integration) if that activity has the potential for providing the company some competitive advantage. Full vertical integration should only be considered, however, when that activity or function adds significant value to the company's products or services in addition to providing competitive advantage.

Outsourcing does, however, have some disadvantages. For example, GE's introduction of a new washing machine was delayed three weeks by production problems at a supplier's company to whom it had contracted out key work. Some companies have found themselves locked into long-term contracts with outside suppliers that are no longer competitive.[10] Some authorities propose that the cumulative effects of continued outsourcing steadily reduces a firm's ability to learn new skills and to develop new core competencies.[11] A study of 30 firms

Figure 7–1
Proposed Outsourcing Matrix

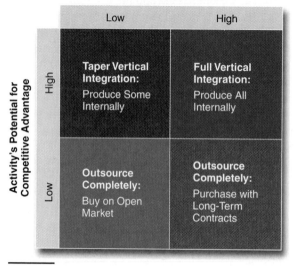

Source: J. D. Hunger and T. L. Wheelen, "Proposed Outsourcing Matrix." Copyright © 1996 by Wheelen and Hunger Associates. Reprinted by permission.

with outsourcing experience revealed that *unsuccessful* outsourcing efforts had three common characteristics:

- The firms' finance and legal departments and their vendors dominated the decision process.
- Vendors were not prequalified based on total capabilities.
- Short-term benefits dominated decision making.[12]

Outsourcing has become an important issue in all industries, especially in global industries such as automobiles where cost competition is fierce. General Motors, for example, was faced with a strike by its Canadian unions when it wanted to outsource some operations. The Canadian unions were very concerned that such outsourcing would reduce union employment and increase the number of low-paying jobs. Expect this issue to continue in importance throughout the world as more industries become global.

MARKETING STRATEGY

Marketing strategy deals with pricing, selling, and distributing a product. Using a **market development** strategy, a company or business unit can (1) capture a larger share of an existing market for current products through market saturation and market penetration or (2) develop new markets for current products. Consumer product giants such as Procter & Gamble, Colgate-Palmolive, and Unilever are experts at using advertising and promotion to implement a market saturation/penetration strategy to gain the dominant market share in a product category. As seeming masters of the product life cycle, these companies are able to extend product life almost indefinitely through "new and improved" variations of product and packaging that appeal to most market niches. These companies also follow the second market development strategy by taking a successful product they market in one part of the world and marketing it elsewhere. Noting the success of their presoak detergents in Europe, for example, both P&G and Colgate successfully introduced this type of laundry product to North America under the trade names of Biz and Axion.

Using the **product development** strategy, a company or unit can (1) develop new products for *existing markets* or (2) develop new products for *new markets*. Church & Dwight has had great success following the first product development strategy by developing new products to sell to its current customers. Acknowledging the widespread appeal of its Arm & Hammer brand baking soda, the company generated new uses for its sodium bicarbonate by reformulating it as toothpaste, deodorant, and detergent. Using a successful brand name to market other products is called *line extension* and is a good way to appeal to a company's current customers. Sara Lee Corporation (famous for its frozen cheesecake) is taking the same approach by putting the Sara Lee name on various new food products, such as premium meats and fresh baked goods. Arm & Hammer successfully followed the second product development strategy by developing new pollution reduction products (using sodium bicarbonate compounds) for sale to coal-fired electric utility plants—a very different market from grocery stores.

There are numerous other marketing strategies. For advertising and promotion, for example, a company or business unit can choose between a "push" or a "pull" marketing strategy. Many large food and consumer products companies in the United States and Canada have followed a **push strategy** by spending a large amount of money on trade promotion in order to gain or hold shelf space in retail outlets. Trade promotion includes discounts, in-store special offers, and advertising allowances designed to "push" products through the distribution system. The Kellogg Company recently decided to change its emphasis from a push to a **pull strategy**, in which advertising "pulls" the products through the distribution channels. The company now spends more money on consumer advertising designed to build brand awareness so that shoppers will ask for the products. Research has indicated that a high level of advertising (a key part of a pull strategy) is most beneficial to leading brands in a market.[13]

Other marketing strategies deal with distribution and pricing. Should a company use distributors and dealers to sell its products or should it sell directly to mass merchandisers? Using both channels simultaneously can lead to problems. In order to increase the sales of its lawn tractors and mowers, for example, John Deere decided to sell the products not only through its current dealer network, but also through mass merchandisers like Home Depot. Deere's dealers, however, were furious. They considered Home Depot to be a key competitor. The dealers were concerned that Home Depot's ability to underprice them would eventually lead to their becoming little more than repair facilities for their competition and left with insufficient sales to stay in business.[14]

When pricing a new product, a company or business unit can follow one of two strategies. For new-product pioneers, **skim pricing** offers the opportunity to "skim the cream" from the top of the demand curve with a high price while the product is novel and competitors are few. **Penetration pricing**, in contrast, attempts to hasten market development and offers the pioneer the opportunity to use the experience curve to gain market share with a low price and dominate the industry. Depending on corporate and business unit objectives and strategies, either of these choices may be desirable to a particular company or unit. Penetration pricing is, however, more likely than skim pricing to raise a unit's operating profit in the long term.[15]

FINANCIAL STRATEGY

Financial strategy examines the financial implications of corporate and business-level strategic options and identifies the best financial course of action. It can also provide competitive advantage through a lower cost of funds and a flexible ability to raise capital to support a business strategy. Financial strategy usually attempts to maximize the financial value of the firm.

The tradeoff between achieving the desired debt-to-equity ratio and relying on internal long-term financing via cash flow is a key issue in financial strategy. Many small- and medium-sized companies such as Urschel Laboratories try to avoid all external sources of funds in order to avoid outside entanglements and to keep control of the company within the family. Many financial analysts believe, however, that only by financing through long-term debt can a corporation use financial leverage to boost earnings per share, thus raising stock price and the overall value of the company. Research indicates that higher debt levels not only deter takeover by other firms (by making the company less attractive), but also leads to improved productivity and improved cash flows by forcing management to focus on core businesses.[16]

Research reveals that a firm's financial strategy is influenced by its corporate diversification strategy. Equity financing, for example, is preferred for related diversification while debt financing is preferred for unrelated diversification.[17] The recent trend away from unrelated to related acquisitions explains why the number of acquisitions being paid for entirely with stock increased from only 2% in 1988 to 50% in 1998.[18]

A very popular financial strategy is the leveraged buy out (LBO). In a **leveraged buy out**, a company is acquired in a transaction financed largely by debt—usually obtained from a third party, such as an insurance company or an investment banker. Ultimately the debt is paid with money generated from the acquired company's operations or by sales of its assets. The acquired company, in effect, pays for its own acquisition! Management of the LBO is then under tremendous pressure to keep the highly leveraged company profitable. Unfortunately the huge amount of debt on the acquired company's books may actually cause its eventual decline by focusing management's attention on short-term matters. One study of LBOs (also called MBOs—**M**anagement **B**uy **O**uts) revealed that the financial performance of the typical LBO usually falls below the industry average in the fourth year after the buy out. The firm declines because of inflated expectations, utilization of all slack, management burnout, and a lack of strategic management.[19] Often the only solution is to go public once again by selling stock to finance growth.

The management of dividends to shareholders is an important part of a corporation's financial strategy. Corporations in fast-growing industries such as computers and computer software often do not declare dividends. They use the money they might have spent on dividends to finance rapid growth. If the company is successful, its growth in sales and profits is reflected in a higher stock price—eventually resulting in a hefty capital gain when shareholders sell their common stock. Other corporations that do not face rapid growth must support the value of their stock by offering generous and consistent dividends.

A recent financial strategy being used by large established corporations to highlight a high-growth business unit in a popular sector of the stock market is to establish a tracking stock. A **tracking stock** is a type of common stock tied to one portion of a corporation's business. This strategy allows established companies to highlight a high-growth business unit without selling the business. By keeping the unit as a subsidiary with its common stock separately identified, the corporation is able to keep control of the subsidiary and yet allow the subsidiary the ability to fund its own growth with outside money. It goes public as an IPO and pays dividends based on the unit's performance. Because the tracking stock is actually an equity interest in the parent company (not the subsidiary), another company cannot acquire the subsidiary by buying its shares. Examples of corporations using tracking stocks as part of their financial strategy are AT&T (AT&T Wireless), Sprint (Sprint PCS), J.C. Penney (Eckerd Drugs), and Staples (Staples.com).[20]

RESEARCH AND DEVELOPMENT (R&D) STRATEGY

R&D strategy deals with product and process innovation and improvement. It also deals with the appropriate mix of different types of R&D (basic, product, or process) and with the question of how new technology should be accessed—internal development, external acquisition, or through strategic alliances.

Table 7–1   Research and Development Strategy and Competitive Advantage

	Technological Leadership	Technological Followership
Cost Advantage	Pioneer the lowest cost product design. Be the first firm down the learning curve. Create low-cost ways of performing value activities.	Lower the cost of the product or value activities by learning from the leader's experience. Avoid R&D costs through imitation.
Differentiation	Pioneer a unique product that increases buyer value. Innovate in other activities to increase buyer value.	Adapt the product or delivery system more closely to buyer needs by learning from the leader's experience.

Source: Adapted/reprinted with the permission of The Free Press, an imprint of Simon & Schuster, from *Competitive Advantage: Creating and Sustaining Superior Performance* by Michael E. Porter, p. 181. Copyright © 1985 by Michael E. Porter.

One of the R&D choices is to be either a **technological leader** in which one pioneers an innovation or a **technological follower** in which one imitates the products of competitors. Porter suggests that deciding to become a technological leader or follower can be a way of achieving either overall low cost or differentiation. (See **Table 7–1**.)

One example of an effective use of the *leader* R&D functional strategy to achieve a differentiation competitive advantage is Nike, Inc. Nike spends more than most in the industry on R&D to differentiate the performance of its athletic shoes from that of its competitors. As a result, its products have become the favorite of the serious athlete. An example of the use of the *follower* R&D functional strategy to achieve a low-cost competitive advantage is Dean Foods Company. "We're able to have the customer come to us and say, 'If you can produce X, Y, and Z product for the same quality and service, but at a lower price and without that expensive label on it, you can have the business,'" says Howard Dean, President of the company.[21]

An increasing number of companies are working with their suppliers to help them keep up with changing technology. They are beginning to realize that a firm cannot be competitive technologically only through internal development. For example, Chrysler Corporation's skillful use of parts suppliers to design everything from car seats to drive shafts has enabled it to spend consistently less money than its competitors to develop new car models. Strategic technology alliances are one way to combine the R&D capabilities of two companies. Maytag Company worked with one of its suppliers to apply fuzzy logic technology to its new IntelliSense™ dishwasher. The partnership enabled Maytag to complete the project in a shorter amount of time than if it had tried to do it alone.[22]

OPERATIONS STRATEGY

Operations strategy determines how and where a product or service is to be manufactured, the level of vertical integration in the production process, and the deployment of physical resources. It should also deal with the optimum level of technology the firm should use in its operations processes. See the 🌐 **Global Issue** feature to see how differences in national conditions can lead to differences in product design and manufacturing facilities from one country to another.

Advanced **M**anufacturing **T**echnology (AMT) is revolutionizing operations worldwide and should continue to have a major impact as corporations strive to integrate diverse business activities using computer-integrated design and manufacturing (CAD/CAM) principles. The use of CAD/CAM, flexible manufacturing systems, computer numerically controlled systems, automatically guided vehicles, robotics, manufacturing resource planning (MRP II), optimized production technology, and just-in-time contribute to increased flexibility, quick response time, and higher productivity. Such investments also act to increase the company's

Global Issue

International Differences Alter Whirlpool's Operations Strategy

To better penetrate the growing markets in developing nations, Whirlpool decided to build a "world washer." This new type of washing machine was to be produced in Brazil, Mexico, and India. Lightweight, with substantially fewer parts than its U.S. counterpart, its performance was to be equal to or better than anything on the world market while being competitive in price with the most popular models in these markets. The goal was to develop a complete product, process, and facility design package that could be used in different countries with low initial investment. Originally the plan had been to make the same low-cost washer in identical plants in each of the three countries.

Significant differences in each of the three countries forced Whirlpool to change its product design to suit each nation's situation. According to Lawrence Kremer, Senior Vice-President of Global Technology and Operations, "Our Mexican affiliate, Vitromatic, has porcelain and glassmaking capabilities. Porcelain baskets made sense for them. Stainless steel became the preferred material for the others." Costs also affected decisions. "In India, for example, material costs may run as much as 200% to 800% higher than elsewhere, while labor and overhead costs are comparatively minimal," added Kremer. Another consideration were the garments to be washed in each country. For example, saris—the 18-foot lengths of cotton or silk with which Indian women drape themselves—needed special treatment in an Indian washing machine, forcing additional modifications.

Manufacturing facilities also varied from country to country. Brastemp, Whirlpool's Brazilian partner, built its plant of precast concrete to address the problems of high humidity. In India, however, the construction crew cast the concrete, allowed it to cure, and then using chain, block, and tackle, five or six men raised each three-ton slab into place. Instead of using one building, Mexican operations used two, one housing the flexible assembly lines and stamping operations and an adjacent facility housing the injection molding and extrusion processes.

Source: A. A. Ullmann, "Whirlpool Corporation, 1993: A Metamorphosis," in Wheelen and Hunger, *Strategic Management and Business Policy*, 5th ed. (Reading, MA: Addison-Wesley, 1995), pp. 713–715.

fixed costs and could cause significant problems if the company is unable to achieve economies of scale or scope.

A firm's manufacturing strategy is often affected by a product's life cycle. As the sales of a product increase, there will be an increase in production volume ranging from lot sizes as low as one in a **job shop** (one-of-a-kind production using skilled labor) through **connected line batch flow** (components are standardized; each machine functions like a job shop but is positioned in the same order as the parts are processed) to lot sizes as high as 100,000 or more per year for **flexible manufacturing systems** (parts are grouped into manufacturing families to produce a wide variety of mass-produced items) and **dedicated transfer lines** (highly automated assembly lines making one mass-produced product using little human labor). According to this concept, the product becomes standardized into a commodity over time in conjunction with increasing demand. Flexibility thus gives way to efficiency.[23]

Increasing competitive intensity in many industries has forced companies to switch from traditional mass production using dedicated transfer lines to a continuous improvement production strategy. A **mass production** system was an excellent method to produce a large amount of low-cost, standard goods and services. Employees worked on narrowly defined, repetitive tasks under close supervision in a bureaucratic and hierarchical structure. Quality, however, often tended to be fairly low. Learning how to do something better was the prerogative of management; workers were expected only to learn what was assigned to them. This system tended to dominate manufacturing until the 1970s. Under the **continuous improvement** system developed by Japanese firms, empowered cross-functional teams strive constantly to improve production processes. Managers become more like coaches. The result is a large quantity of low-cost, standard goods and services, but with high quality. The key to continuous improvement is the acknowledgment that workers' experience and knowledge can help managers solve production problems and contribute toward tightening variances and reducing errors. Because continuous improvement enables firms to use the same low-cost competitive strategy as do mass production firms but at a significantly higher level of quality, it is rapidly replacing mass production as an operations strategy.

The automobile industry is currently experimenting with the strategy of **modular manufacturing** in which preassembled subassemblies are delivered as they are needed *(Just-in-Time)* to a company's assembly line workers, who quickly piece the modules together into a finished product. For example, General Motors built a new automotive complex in Brazil to make its new subcompact, the Celta. Sixteen of the 17 buildings are occupied by suppliers, including Delphi, Lear, and Goodyear. These suppliers deliver preassembled modules (which comprise 85% of the final value of each car) to GM's building for assembly. In a process new to the industry, the suppliers act as a team to build a single module comprising the motor, transmission, fuel lines, rear axle, brake-fluid lines, and exhaust system, which is then installed as one piece. GM is hoping that this manufacturing strategy will enable it to produce 100 vehicles annually per worker compared to standard rate of 30 to 50 autos.[24] Ford and Chrysler have also opened similar modular facilities in Brazil.

The concept of a product's life cycle eventually leading to one-size-fits-all mass production is being increasingly challenged by the new concept of mass customization. Appropriate for an ever-changing environment, **mass customization** requires that people, processes, units, and technology reconfigure themselves to give customers exactly what they want, when they want it. In contrast to continuous improvement, mass customization requires flexibility and quick responsiveness. Managers coordinate independent, capable individuals. An efficient linkage system is crucial. The result is low-cost, high-quality, customized goods and services. Mass customization is having a significant impact on product development. Under a true mass customization system, no one knows exactly what the next customer will want. Therefore, no one can know exactly what product the company will be creating/producing next. Because it is becoming increasingly difficult to predict what product–market opportunity will open up next, it is harder to create a long-term vision of the company's products.

One example of mass customization is the "Personal Pair" system Levi Strauss introduced to combat the growing competition from private label jeans. The customer is measured at one of the company's Personal Pair outlets, the measurements are sent to Levi's by computer, and the made-to-order jeans arrive a few days later. The jeans cost more than an off-the-shelf pair. Levi Strauss then launched Original Spin, offering more options plus men's jeans. More choices are now available to the customer without any increase in store inventory. For example, a fully stocked Levi's store carries approximately 130 pairs of jeans for any given waist and inseam. That number virtually increases to 430 with Personal Pair and to 750 with Original Spin. Lands' End is currently working to develop special body scanning booths that will create an electronic 3D model of a person's body that will sit in memory at a Web site. Mattel is hoping to soon allow people to customize the manufacturing of their own Barbie doll. According to Mattel's marketing vice president, Anne Parducci, "We are going to build a database of children's names to develop a one-to-one relationship with these girls."[25]

PURCHASING STRATEGY

Purchasing strategy deals with obtaining the raw materials, parts, and supplies needed to perform the operations function. The basic purchasing choices are multiple, sole, and parallel sourcing. Under **multiple sourcing**, the purchasing company orders a particular part from several vendors. Multiple sourcing has traditionally been considered superior to other purchasing approaches because (1) it forces suppliers to compete for the business of an important buyer, thus reducing purchasing costs; and (2) if one supplier could not deliver, another usually could, thus guaranteeing that parts and supplies would always be on hand when needed. Multiple sourcing was one way a purchasing firm could control the relationship with its suppliers. So long as suppliers could provide evidence that they could meet the product specifications, they were kept on the purchaser's list of acceptable vendors for specific parts and supplies. Unfortunately the common practice of accepting the lowest bid often compromised quality.

W. Edward Deming, a well-known management consultant, strongly recommended **sole sourcing** as the only manageable way to obtain high supplier quality. Sole sourcing relies on only one supplier for a particular part. Given his concern with designing quality into a product in its early stages of development, Deming argued that the buyer should work closely with the supplier at all stages. This reduces both cost and time spent on product design as well as improving quality. It can also simplify the purchasing company's production process by using the **Just-In-Time (JIT)** concept of the purchased parts arriving at the plant just when they are needed rather than keeping inventories. The concept of sole sourcing is being taken one step further in JIT II, in which vendor sales representatives actually have desks next to the purchasing company's factory floor, attend production status meetings, visit the R&D lab, and analyze the purchasing company's sales forecasts. These in-house suppliers then write sales orders for which the purchasing company is billed. Developed by Lance Dixon at Bose Corporation, JIT II is also being used at IBM, Honeywell, and Ingersoll-Rand. Karen Dale, Purchasing Manager for Honeywell's office supplies, said she was very concerned about confidentiality when JIT II was first suggested to her. Now she has 5 suppliers working with her 20 buyers and reports few problems.[26]

Sole sourcing reduces transaction costs and builds quality by having purchaser and supplier work together as partners rather than as adversaries. Sole sourcing means that more companies are going to have longer relationships with fewer suppliers. Sole sourcing does, however, have its limitations. If a supplier is unable to deliver a part, the purchaser has no alternative but to delay production. Multiple suppliers can provide the purchaser with better information about new technology and performance capabilities. The limitations of sole sourcing have led to the development of parallel sourcing. In **parallel sourcing**, two suppliers are the sole suppliers of two different parts, but they are also backup suppliers for each other's parts. In case one vendor cannot supply all of its parts on time, the other vendor would be asked to make up the difference.[27]

The Internet is being increasingly used both to find new sources of supply and to keep inventories replenished. For example, Hewlett-Packard introduced a Web-based procurement system to enable its 84,000 employees to buy office supplies from a standard set of suppliers. The new system enabled the company to save $60 to $100 million annually in purchasing costs.[28] See the **Internet Issue** feature to learn how David Crosier, Vice President for supply-chain management at Staples, uses the Internet to keep the retailer in Post-it notes and Scotch tape from 3M.

LOGISTICS STRATEGY

Logistics strategy deals with the flow of products into and out of the manufacturing process. Three trends are evident: centralization, outsourcing, and the use of the Internet. To gain logistical synergies across business units, corporations began centralizing logistics in the headquarters group. This centralized logistics group usually contains specialists with expertise in different transportation modes such as rail or trucking. They work to aggregate shipping volumes across the entire corporation to gain better contracts with shippers. Companies like Amoco Chemical, Georgia-Pacific, Marriott, and Union Carbide view the logistics function as an important way to differentiate themselves from the competition, to add value, and to reduce costs.

Internet Issue

Staples Uses Internet to Replenish Inventory from 3M

David Crosier was mad. As the Vice President for supply-chain management for Staples, the office supplies retailer, Crosier couldn't even find a Post-it Note to write down the complaint that his stores were consistently low on 3M products. Crosier would send an order to the Minnesota Mining & Manufacturing Company (3M) for 10,000 rolls of Scotch tape and receive only 8,000. Even worse, the supplies from 3M often arrived late causing "stock outs" of popular products. Crosier then discovered 3M's new online ordering system for office supplies. The Web site enabled 3M to reduce customer frustration caused by paper forms and last minute phone calls by eliminating error-prone steps in purchasing. Since using 3M's Web site, Staples' Crosier reports that 3M's fill rate has improved by 20% and that its on-time performance has almost doubled. "The technology takes a lot of inefficiencies out of the supply-chain process," says Crosier.

This improvement at 3M was initiated by Allen Messerli, Information Manager at 3M, over a five-year period. Since 1997, 3M has invested $30 million in the project. Ongoing maintenance costs of keeping the system current are $2.6 million. Previous to implementing this online system, 3M had serious problems with its finished goods inventory, distribution, and customer service. For example, nearly 40% of its customer records (in the United States alone) have invalid addresses. Bloated finished goods inventory in 1998 caused a 45% drop in earnings. With more than 70,000 employees around the world, 3M had difficulty linking employees, managers, and customers because of incompatible networks. With its new Global Enterprise Data Warehouse, 3M is now delivering customer, product, sales, inventory, and financial data directly to its employees and partners, who can access the information via the Internet ⟨www.3m.com⟩. The company reports saving $10 million annually in maintenance and customer-service costs. More accurate and current sales reporting is saving an additional $2.5 million per year. The new technology improved productivity, boosting global sales. Supply-chain managers like David Crosier at Staples are pleased with making the Internet an important part of their purchasing strategy.

Source: D. Little, "3M: Glued to the Web," *Business Week E.Biz* (November 2000), pp. EB65–EB70. Reprinted by special permission, copyright © 2000 by The McGraw-Hill Companies, Inc.

Many companies have found that outsourcing of logistics reduces costs and improves delivery time. For example, Hewlett-Packard (HP) contracted with Roadway Logistics to manage its inbound raw materials warehousing in Vancouver, Canada. Nearly 140 Roadway employees replaced 250 HP workers, who were transferred to other HP activities.[29]

Many companies are using the Internet to simplify their logistical system. For example, Ace Hardware created an online system for its retailers and suppliers. An individual hardware store can now see on the Web site that ordering 210 cases of wrenches is cheaper than ordering 200 cases. Since a full pallet is composed of 210 cases of wrenches, an order for a full pallet means that the supplier doesn't have to pull 10 cases off a pallet and repackage them for storage. There is less chance for loose cases to be lost in delivery and the paperwork doesn't have to be redone. As a result, Ace's transportation costs are down 18% and warehouse costs have been cut 28%.[30] As shown in the 📡 **Internet Issue** feature, 3M's new system enabled it to save $10 million annually in maintenance and customer-service costs.

HUMAN RESOURCE MANAGEMENT (HRM) STRATEGY

HRM strategy, among other things, addresses the issue of whether a company or business unit should hire a large number of low-skilled employees who receive low pay, perform repetitive jobs, and most likely quit after a short time (the McDonald's restaurant strategy) or hire skilled employees who receive relatively high pay and are cross-trained to participate in *self-managing work teams*. As work increases in complexity, the more suited it is for teams, especially in the case of innovative product development efforts. Multinational corporations are increasingly using self-managing work teams in their foreign affiliates as well as in home country operations.[31] Research indicates that the use of work teams leads to increased quality and productivity as well as to higher employee satisfaction and commitment.[32]

Many North American and European companies are not only using an increasing amount of part-time and temporary employees, they are also experimenting with leasing *temporary employees* from employee leasing companies. The percentage of the U.S. workforce employed by personnel supply agencies has increased from half a percent in 1980 to almost 3%—more than 3 million people—by 2000. An additional 10% of the U.S. workforce are either independent contractors or temporary workers hired directly by companies.[33] Around 90% of U.S. corporations use temporary workers in some capacity—even as managers. Temporary managers accounted for $2.8 billion of the total temporary worker payroll of $43.4 billion in 1998.[34]

The number of employees who work only part-time is steadily increasing. Part-timers are attractive to a company because the firm does not need to pay fringe benefits, such as health insurance and pension plans. In the United States, the percentage of part-time regular employees (defined as those working for less than 35 hours per week) has risen from 10.2% in 1955 to 17.7% in 2000.[35] In the European Union, the number of part-time workers increased from 13.3% in 1990 to 16.4% in 1999. At the same time, overall part-time employment in all the developed (OECD) countries of the world increased from 14.3% to 15.8%.[36]

Companies are finding that having a *diverse workforce* can be a competitive advantage. Research reveals that firms with a high degree of racial diversity following a growth strategy have higher productivity than do firms with less racial diversity.[37] Avon Company, for example, was able to turn around its unprofitable inner-city markets by putting African American and Hispanic managers in charge of marketing to these markets.[38] Diversity in terms of age and national origin also offers benefits. DuPont's use of multinational teams has helped the company develop and market products internationally. McDonald's has discovered that older workers perform as well as, if not better than, younger employees. According to Edward Rensi, CEO of McDonald's USA: "We find these people to be particularly well motivated, with a sort of discipline and work habits hard to find in younger employees."[39]

INFORMATION SYSTEMS STRATEGY

Corporations are increasingly adopting **information systems strategies** in that they are turning to information systems technology to provide business units with competitive advantage. When FedEx first provided its customers with *PowerShip* computer software to store addresses, print shipping labels, and track package location, its sales jumped significantly. UPS soon followed with its own *MaxiShips* software. Viewing its information system as a distinctive competency, FedEx continued to push for further advantage against UPS by using its Web site to enable customers to track their packages. FedEx uses this competency in its advertisements by showing how customers can track the progress of their shipments.

Multinational corporations are finding that the use of a sophisticated intranet for the use of its employees allows them to practice *follow-the-sun management*, in which project team members living in one country can pass their work to team members in another country in which the work day is just beginning. Thus, night shifts are no longer needed.[40] The development of instant translation software is also enabling workers to have online communication with coworkers in other countries who use a different language. Lotus Translation Services for Sametime is a Java-based application that can deliver translated text during a chat session or an instant message in 17 languages. Another software, e-lingo ⟨www.e-lingo.com⟩ offers a multilingual search function and Web surfing as well as text and e-mail translation.[41]

Many companies are also attempting to use information systems to form closer relationships with both their customers and suppliers through sophisticated extranets. For example,

General Electric's Trading Process Network allows suppliers to electronically download GE's requests for proposals, view diagrams of parts specifications, and communicate with GE purchasing managers. According to Robert Livingston, GE's head of worldwide sourcing for the Lighting Division, going on the Web reduces processing time by one-third.[42]

7.2 Strategies to Avoid

Several strategies, which could be considered corporate, business, or functional, are very dangerous. Managers who have made a poor analysis or lack creativity may be trapped into considering some of the following **strategies to avoid**:

- **Follow the Leader:** Imitating a leading competitor's strategy might seem to be a good idea, but it ignores a firm's particular strengths and weaknesses and the possibility that the leader may be wrong. Fujitsu Ltd., the world's second-largest computer maker, was driven since the 1960s by the sole ambition of catching up to IBM. Like IBM, Fujitsu competed primarily as a mainframe computer maker. So devoted was it to catching IBM, however, that it failed to notice that the mainframe business had reached maturity by 1990 and was no longer growing.

- **Hit Another Home Run:** If a company is successful because it pioneered an extremely successful product, it tends to search for another super product that will ensure growth and prosperity. Like betting on long shots at the horse races, the probability of finding a second winner is slight. Polaroid spent a lot of money developing an "instant" movie camera, but the public ignored it in favor of the camcorder.

- **Arms Race:** Entering into a spirited battle with another firm for increased market share might increase sales revenue, but that increase will probably be more than offset by increases in advertising, promotion, R&D, and manufacturing costs. Since the deregulation of airlines, price wars and rate "specials" have contributed to the low profit margins or bankruptcy of many major airlines such as Eastern and Continental.

- **Do Everything:** When faced with several interesting opportunities, management might tend to leap at all of them. At first, a corporation might have enough resources to develop each idea into a project, but money, time, and energy are soon exhausted as the many projects demand large infusions of resources. The Walt Disney Company's expertise in the entertainment industry led it to acquire the ABC network. As the company churned out new motion pictures and television programs like *Who Wants To Be a Millionaire*, it spent $750 million to build new theme parks and buy a cruise line (as well as a hockey team). By 2000, even though corporate sales continued to increase, net income was falling.[43]

- **Losing Hand:** A corporation might have invested so much in a particular strategy that top management is unwilling to accept its failure. Believing that it has too much invested to quit, the corporation continues to throw "good money after bad." Pan American Airlines, for example, chose to sell its Pan Am Building and Intercontinental Hotels, the most profitable parts of the corporation, to keep its money-losing airline flying. Continuing to suffer losses, the company followed this strategy of shedding assets for cash, until it had sold off everything and went bankrupt.

7.3 Strategic Choice: Selection of the Best Strategy

After the pros and cons of the potential strategic alternatives have been identified and evaluated, one must be selected for implementation. By now, it is likely that many feasible alternatives will have emerged. How is the best strategy determined?

Perhaps the most important criterion is the ability of the proposed strategy to deal with the specific strategic factors developed earlier in the SWOT analysis. If the alternative doesn't take advantage of environmental opportunities and corporate strengths/competencies, and lead away from environmental threats and corporate weaknesses, it will probably fail.

Another important consideration in the selection of a strategy is the ability of each alternative to satisfy agreed-on objectives with the least resources and the fewest negative side effects. It is, therefore, important to develop a tentative implementation plan so that the difficulties that management is likely to face are addressed. This should be done in light of societal trends, the industry, and the company's situation based on the construction of scenarios.

CONSTRUCTING CORPORATE SCENARIOS

Corporate scenarios are *pro forma* balance sheets and income statements that forecast the effect each alternative strategy and its various programs will likely have on division and corporate return on investment. In a survey of *Fortune* 500 firms, 84% reported using computer simulation models in strategic planning. Most of these were simply spreadsheet-based simulation models dealing with "what if" questions.[44]

The recommended scenarios are simply extensions of the industry scenarios discussed in **Chapter 3**. If, for example, industry scenarios suggest the probable emergence of a strong market demand in a specific country for certain products, a series of alternative strategy scenarios can be developed. The alternative of acquiring another firm having these products in that country can be compared with the alternative of a green-field development (building new operations in that country). Using three sets of estimated sales figures (optimistic, pessimistic, and most likely) for the new products over the next five years, the two alternatives can be evaluated in terms of their effect on future company performance as reflected in its probable future financial statements. Pro forma (estimated future) balance sheets and income statements can be generated with spreadsheet software, such as Lotus 1-2-3 or Excel, on a personal computer.

To construct a scenario, follow these steps:

- **First**, *use industry scenarios* (discussed earlier in **Chapter 3**) to develop a set of assumptions about the task environment (in the specific country under consideration). For example, 3M requires the general manager of each business unit to describe annually what his or her industry will look like in 15 years. List *optimistic, pessimistic,* and *most likely* assumptions for key economic factors such as the GDP (Gross Domestic Product), CPI (Consumer Price Index), and prime interest rate, and for other key external strategic factors such as governmental regulation and industry trends. *This should be done for every country/region in which the corporation has significant operations that will be affected by each strategic alternative.* These same underlying assumptions should be listed for each of the alternative scenarios to be developed.

- **Second**, *develop common-size financial statements* (to be discussed in **Chapter 10**) for the company's or business unit's previous years, to serve as the basis for the trend analysis projections of **pro forma financial statements**. Use the *Scenario Box* form in **Table 7–2**.
  - **a.** Use the historical common-size percentages to estimate the level of revenues, expenses, and other categories in pro forma statements for future years.
  - **b.** Develop for each strategic alternative a set of *optimistic, pessimistic,* and *most likely* assumptions about the impact of key variables on the company's future financial statements.
  - **c.** Forecast three sets of sales and cost of goods sold figures for at least five years into the future.
  - **d.** Analyze historical data and make adjustments based on the environmental assumptions listed earlier. Do the same for other figures that can vary significantly.

Table 7-2   Scenario Box for Use in Generating Financial Pro Forma Statements

Factor	Last Year	Historical Average	Trend Analysis	Projections[1] 200-			200-			200-			Comments
				O	P	ML	O	P	ML	O	P	ML	
GDP													
CPI													
Other													
Sales units													
Dollars													
COGS													
Advertising and marketing													
Interest expense													
Plant expansion													
Dividends													
Net profits													
EPS													
ROI													
ROE													
Other													

Note:
1. **O** = Optimistic; **P** = Pessimistic; **ML** = Most Likely.

Source: T. L. Wheelen and J. D. Hunger. Copyright © 1993 by Wheelen and Hunger Associates. Reprinted by permission.

e. Assume for other figures that they will continue in their historical relationship to sales or some other key determining factor. Plug in expected inventory levels, accounts receivable, accounts payable, R&D expenses, advertising and promotion expenses, capital expenditures, and debt payments (assuming that debt is used to finance the strategy), among others.

f. Consider not only historical trends, but also programs that might be needed to implement each alternative strategy (such as building a new manufacturing facility or expanding the sales force).

■ **Third**, *construct detailed pro forma financial statements* for each strategic alternative.

a. List the actual figures from this year's financial statements in the left column of the spreadsheet.

b. List to the right of this column the optimistic figures for years one through five.

c. Go through this same process with the same strategic alternative, but now list the pessimistic figures for the next five years.

d. Do the same with the most likely figures.

e. Develop a similar set of *optimistic* (O), *pessimistic* (P), and *most likely* (ML) pro forma statements for the second strategic alternative. This process generates six different pro forma scenarios reflecting three different situations (O, P, and ML) for two strategic alternatives.

f. Calculate financial ratios and common-size income statements, and balance sheets to accompany the pro forma statements.

g. Compare the assumptions underlying the scenarios with these financial statements and ratios to determine the feasibility of the scenarios. For example, if cost of goods sold drops from 70% to 50% of total sales revenue in the pro forma income statements, this drop should result from a change in the production process or a shift to cheaper raw materials or labor costs, rather than from a failure to keep the cost of goods sold in its usual percentage relationship to sales revenue when the predicted statement was developed.

The result of this detailed scenario construction should be anticipated net profits, cash flow, and net working capital for each of three versions of the two alternatives for five years into the future. A strategist might want to go further into the future if the strategy is expected to have a major impact on the company's financial statements beyond five years. The result of this work should provide sufficient information on which forecasts of the likely feasibility and probable profitability of each of the strategic alternatives could be based.

Obviously these scenarios can quickly become very complicated, especially if three sets of acquisition prices and development costs are calculated. Nevertheless this sort of detailed "what if" analysis is needed to realistically compare the projected outcome of each reasonable alternative strategy and its attendant programs, budgets, and procedures. Regardless of the quantifiable pros and cons of each alternative, the actual decision will probably be influenced by several subjective factors like those described in the following sections.

Management's Attitude Toward Risk

The attractiveness of a particular strategic alternative is partially a function of the amount of risk it entails. **Risk** is composed not only of the *probability* that the strategy will be effective, but also of the *amount of assets* the corporation must allocate to that strategy and the *length of time* the assets will be unavailable for other uses. Because of variation among countries in terms of customs, regulations, and resources, companies operating in global industries must deal with a greater amount of risk than firms operating only in one country. The greater the assets involved and the longer they are committed, the more likely top management is to demand a high probability of success. Do not expect managers with no ownership position in a company to have much interest in putting their jobs in danger with a risky decision. Research does indicate that managers who own a significant amount of stock in their firms are more likely to engage in risk-taking actions than are managers with no stock.[45]

A high level of risk was why Intel's Board of Directors found it difficult to vote for a proposal in the early 1990s to commit $5 billion to making the Pentium microprocessor chip—five times the amount needed for its previous chip. In looking back on that board meeting, then-CEO Andy Grove remarked, "I remember people's eyes looking at that chart and getting big. I wasn't even sure I believed those numbers at the time." The proposal committed the company to building new factories, something Intel had been reluctant to do. A wrong decision would mean that the company would end up with a killing amount of overcapacity. Based on Grove's presentation, the board decided to take the gamble. Intel's resulting manufacturing expansion eventually cost $10 billion, but resulted in Intel's obtaining 75% of the microprocessor business and huge cash profits.[46]

Risk might be one reason that significant innovations occur more often in small firms than in large, established corporations. The small firm managed by an entrepreneur is willing to accept greater risk than would a large firm of diversified ownership run by professional managers.[47] It is one thing to take a chance if you are the primary shareholder and are not concerned with periodic changes in the value of the company's common stock. It is something else if the corporation's stock is widely held and acquisition-hungry competitors or takeover artists surround the company like sharks every time the company's stock price falls below some external assessment of the firm's value!

A new approach to evaluating alternatives under conditions of high environmental uncertainty is to use real-options theory. According to the **real options** approach, when the future is highly uncertain, it pays to have a broad range of options open. This is in contrast to using **net present value** (npv) to calculate the value of a project by predicting its payouts, adjusting them for risk, and subtracting the amount invested. By boiling everything down to one scenario, npv doesn't provide any flexibility in case circumstances change. Npv is also difficult to apply to projects in which the potential payoffs are currently unknown. The real options approach, however, deals with these issues by breaking the investment into stages. Management allocates a small amount of funding to initiate multiple projects, monitors their development, and then cancels the projects that aren't successful and funds those that are doing well. This approach is very similar to the way venture capitalists fund an entrepreneurial venture in stages of funding based upon the venture's performance. Corporations using the real options approach are Chevron for bidding on petroleum reserves, Airbus for calculating the costs of airlines changing their orders at the last minute, and the Tennessee Valley Authority for outsourcing electricity generation instead of building its own plant. Because of its complexity, the real options approach is not worthwhile for minor decisions or for projects requiring a full commitment at the beginning.[48]

Pressures from Stakeholders

The attractiveness of a strategic alternative is affected by its perceived compatibility with the key stakeholders in a corporation's task environment. Creditors want to be paid on time. Unions exert pressure for comparable wage and employment security. Governments and interest groups demand social responsibility. Shareholders want dividends. All of these pressures must be given some consideration in the selection of the best alternative.

Stakeholders can be categorized in terms of their (1) interest in the corporation's activities and (2) relative power to influence the corporation's activities.[49] Using the **Stakeholder Priority Matrix** depicted in **Figure 7-2**, each stakeholder group may be placed in one of the nine cells.

Strategic managers should ask four questions to assess the importance of stakeholder concerns in a particular decision:

1. How will this decision affect each stakeholder, especially those given high and medium priority?
2. How much of what each stakeholder wants are they likely to get under this alternative?
3. What are they likely to do if they don't get what they want?
4. What is the probability that they will do it?

Strategy makers should be better able to choose strategic alternatives that minimize external pressures and maximize the probability of gaining stakeholder support. In addition, top management can propose a **political strategy** to influence its key stakeholders. Some of the most commonly used political strategies are constituency building, political action committee contributions, advocacy advertising, lobbying, and coalition building.

Pressures from the Corporate Culture

If a strategy is incompatible with the corporate culture, the likelihood of its success is very low. Foot-dragging and even sabotage will result as employees fight to resist a radical change in corporate philosophy. Precedents from the past tend to restrict the kinds of objectives and strategies that can be seriously considered.[50] The "aura" of the founders of a corporation can linger long past their lifetimes because their values have been imprinted on a corporation's members.

Figure 7–2
Stakeholder Priority Matrix

	Low Power	**Medium Power**	**High Power**
High Interest	Medium Priority	High Priority	High Priority
Medium Interest	Low Priority	Medium Priority	High Priority
Low Interest	Low Priority	Low Priority	Medium Priority

Source: Suggested by C. Anderson, "Values-Based Management," *Academy of Management Executive* (November 1997), p, 31. Reprinted by permission of *Academy of Management Executive* via the Copyright Clearance Center.

In evaluating a strategic alternative, the strategy makers must consider **corporate culture pressures** and assess the strategy's compatibility with the corporate culture. If there is little fit, management must decide if it should:

- Take a chance on ignoring the culture.
- Manage around the culture and change the implementation plan.
- Try to change the culture to fit the strategy.
- Change the strategy to fit the culture.

Further, a decision to proceed with a particular strategy without a commitment to change the culture or manage around the culture (both very tricky and time consuming) is dangerous. Nevertheless restricting a corporation to only those strategies that are completely compatible with its culture might eliminate from consideration the most profitable alternatives. (See **Chapter 9** for more information on managing corporate culture.)

Needs and Desires of Key Managers

Even the most attractive alternative might not be selected if it is contrary to the needs and desires of important top managers. Personal characteristics and experience do affect a person's assessment of an alternative's attractiveness.[51] A person's ego may be tied to a particular proposal to the extent that all other alternatives are strongly lobbied against. As a result, he or she may have unfavorable forecasts altered so that they are more in agreement with the desired alternative.[52] A key executive might influence other people in top management to favor a particular alternative so that objections to it are ignored. For example, Nextel's CEO, Daniel Akerson, decided that the best place to locate the corporation's 500-person national headquarters would be the Washington, DC, area, close to his own home.[53]

Industry and cultural backgrounds affect strategic choice. For example, executives with strong ties within an industry tend to choose strategies commonly used in that industry. Other executives who have come to the firm from another industry and have strong ties outside the industry tend to choose different strategies from what is being currently used in their industry.[54] Research reveals that executives from Korea, the United States, Japan, and Germany tend to make different strategic choices in similar situations because they use different decision criteria and weights. For example, Korean executives emphasize industry attractiveness, sales, and market share in their decisions; whereas, U.S. executives emphasize projected demand, discounted cash flow, and ROI.[55]

There is a tendency to maintain the status quo, which means that decision makers continue with existing goals and plans beyond the point when an objective observer would recommend a change in course. Some executives show a self-serving tendency to attribute the firm's problems not to their own poor decisions, but to environmental events out of their control such as government policies or a poor economic climate.[56] Negative information about a particular course of action to which a person is committed may be ignored because of a desire to appear competent or because of strongly held values regarding consistency. It may take a crisis or an unlikely event to cause strategic decision makers to seriously consider an alternative they had previously ignored or discounted.[57] For example, it wasn't until the CEO of ConAgra, a multinational food products company, had a heart attack that ConAgra started producing the Healthy Choice line of low-fat, low-cholesterol, low-sodium frozen-food entrees.

PROCESS OF STRATEGIC CHOICE

There is an old story at General Motors:

> At a meeting with his key executives, CEO Alfred Sloan proposed a controversial strategic decision. When asked for comments, each executive responded with supportive comments and praise. After announcing that they were all in apparent agreement, Sloan stated that they were not going to proceed with the decision. Either his executives didn't know enough to point out potential downsides of the decision, or they were agreeing to avoid upsetting the boss and disrupting the cohesion of the group. The decision was delayed until a debate could occur over the pros and cons.[58]

Strategic choice is the evaluation of alternative strategies and selection of the best alternative. There is mounting evidence that when an organization is facing a dynamic environment, the best strategic decisions are not arrived at through **consensus** when everyone agrees on one alternative. They actually involve a certain amount of heated disagreement and even conflict. This is certainly the case for firms operating in a global industry. Because unmanaged conflict often carries a high emotional cost, authorities in decision making propose that strategic managers use "programmed conflict" to raise different opinions regardless of the personal feelings of the people involved.[59] Two techniques help strategic managers avoid the consensus trap that Alfred Sloan found:

1. **Devil's Advocate:** The devil's advocate originated in the medieval Roman Catholic Church as a way of ensuring that impostors were not canonized as saints. One trusted person was selected to find and present all reasons why the person should not be canonized. When applied to strategic decision making, the **devil's advocate** (who may be an individual or a group) is assigned to identify potential pitfalls and problems with a proposed alternative strategy in a formal presentation.

2. **Dialectical Inquiry:** The dialectic philosophy, which can be traced back to Plato and Aristotle and more recently to Hegel, involves combining two conflicting views—the thesis and the antithesis—into a synthesis. When applied to strategic decision making, **dialectical inquiry** requires that two proposals using different assumptions be generated for each alternative strategy under consideration. After advocates of each position present and debate the merits of their arguments before key decision makers, either one of the alternatives or a new compromise alternative is selected as the strategy to be implemented.

Research generally supports the conclusion that both the devil's advocate and dialectical inquiry are equally superior to consensus in decision making, especially when the firm's environment is dynamic. The debate itself, rather than its particular format, appears to improve the quality of decisions by formalizing and legitimizing constructive conflict and by encouraging critical evaluation. Both lead to better assumptions and recommendations and to a higher level of critical thinking among the people involved.[60]

Another approach to generating a series of diverse and creative strategic alternatives is to use a **strategy shadow committee**. At Anheuser-Busch, top management established such a committee composed of employees at least two to three echelons below the executive-level strategy committee. Members of the shadow committee serve for two years. During that time they see all materials and attend all meetings of the executive strategy committee. One year the shadow committee was taken off site and asked what was wrong with management and to propose what the company should be doing differently. The group's report was then given to the Board of Directors.[61]

Regardless of the process used to generate strategic alternatives, each resulting alternative must be rigorously evaluated in terms of its ability to meet four criteria:

1. **Mutual Exclusivity:** Doing any one would preclude doing any other.
2. **Success:** It must be doable and have a good probability of success.
3. **Completeness:** It must take into account all the key strategic issues.
4. **Internal Consistency:** It must make sense on its own as a strategic decision for the entire firm and not contradict key goals, policies, and strategies currently being pursued by the firm or its units.[62]

7.4 Development of Policies

The selection of the best strategic alternative is not the end of strategy formulation. The organization must now engage in **developing policies**. Policies define the broad guidelines for implementation. Flowing from the selected strategy, policies provide guidance for decision making and actions throughout the organization. At General Electric, for example, Chairman Jack Welch initiated the policy that any GE business unit be number one or number two wherever it competes. This policy gives clear guidance to managers throughout the organization. Another example of such a policy is Casey's General Stores' policy that a new service or product line may be added to its stores only when the product or service can be justified in terms of increasing store traffic.

Policies tend to be rather long lived and can even outlast the particular strategy that created them. Interestingly these general policies—such as "The customer is always right" or "Research and development should get first priority on all budget requests"—can become, in time, part of a corporation's culture. Such policies can make the implementation of specific strategies easier. They can also restrict top management's strategic options in the future. Thus a change in strategy should be followed quickly by a change in policies. Managing policy is one way to manage the corporate culture.

7.5 **Impact of the Internet on Functional Strategy**

Every time a person clicks on a banner or views a product on the Internet, Web site operators add this information to that person's digital trail. The user doesn't have to purchase anything because a decision not to buy is almost as important as a decision to buy. The data is used to answer questions such as, "Why did the customer visit our site but not buy our products? Is our checkout process too long? Did the customer come from an affiliate site? Should we have offered this person a discount or special offer?" The answers to these questions can strongly influence a company's marketing functional strategy.

Tracking potential online customers is the rationale for **electronic customer relationship management (e-CRM) software**. Divided into the three areas of marketing, services, and sales, e-CRM is the fastest growing area of the software industry. The marketing part of e-CRM is growing at a rate of 50% annually and is divided into the fields of analytics, e-marketing, and personalization. According to Phil Fernandez, Executive Vice President of E.piphany, an e-CRM developer, "*Analytics* helps you to understand the customer. *E-marketing* helps structure how you reach out to that customer, and *personalization* is about using all that knowledge to create a personalized experience."

Analytics software creates information from data gathered from a number of customer *touch points*, both online and off-line. Combining demographic data with sales information from customer records can indicate how purchases vary by demographic group. Online activity records can tell what particular groups of customers buy, what Web pages they tend to visit, and their tastes. Companies such as Accrue, digiMine, Coremetrics, NetGenesis, Personify, and MicroStrategy offer software that can analyze customer data and turn it into usable reports. Hoover's Online used analytics software to analyze Web site traffic, create customer profiles, and classify users by market segment. According to Craig Lakey, vice president of marketing for Hoover's Online, "Using Personify's technology, we were able to analyze where people were going and promote areas that they were ignoring. We were able to cross-promote other aspects of the site. Just by virtue of analyzing what we found, we tripled the traffic on the business travel channel."

E-marketing software is used to keep track of which marketing campaigns succeed and which fail as well as to plan future marketing programs. The analytics stage answers questions such as "Of the people who bought Gucci bags, how many also bought Calvin Klein shirts?" In the e-marketing stage, companies use the answers to allow a firm to offer discounts on Gucci bags via e-mail to customers who bought Calvin Klein shirts. Companies offering e-marketing software are Annuncio, Broadbase Software, E.piphany, and Responsys.com.

Personalization software allows businesses to offer products uniquely relevant to the individual visitor to a Web site by creating a Web experience tailored to that individual's taste. Amazon.com uses this software to inform people who purchase a book or CD that people who previously bought that book or CD also bought books by another author/artist. Like Amazon.com, statistical correlation techniques are used to find other Web site visitors with similar patterns of behavior and use the behavior of these like-minded people to make recommendations for further purchases. Personalization software also uses neural network-based artificial intelligence to model Web site visitors on the basis of their "clickstream" (a sequence of Web pages selected by a visitor) and purchase behavior. Personalization is superior to blindly e-mailing coupons to potential customers because it is more closely connected to that person's interests. Personalization software is still in the development stage but has a lot of appeal to companies with an Internet presence. Some of the companies offering personalization software are Net Perceptions,

Angara, the Art Technology Group, Blaze Software, and BroadVision. According to Lynne Harvey, Senior Consultant with the Patricia Seybold Group, "The number of touch points is expanding, so there will be an increased demand by the customers for companies to be more responsive, as opposed to the old way, where you had a predefined offer and you hoped that someone would be attracted enough to buy it."[63]

Thanks to e-CRM software, firms are now able to practice *dynamic pricing*, a controversial pricing practice in which different customers pay different prices for the same product or service. Tried by Amazon.com, the company uses a customer's address, record of previous purchases, sites visited, and other information to decide if the customer is price-sensitive. If the software puts the customer in a price-sensitive category, the customer is offered a low price. Otherwise, the customer pays a premium. Other firms practice *dynamic service*, in which they offer varying levels of service for the same price. Customers are coded based on the profitability of their business. Using a customer's code, phone centers or Web sites route customers to different queues. The most profitable customers have fees waived and receive special offers the typical customer doesn't know exist.[64] Gambling casinos have used this marketing strategy for years to encourage "high rollers" who are prone to spend (and lose) a large amount of money in gambling establishments.

Projections for the 21st Century

- From 1994 to 2010, the number of desktop PCs worldwide will double from 132 million to 278 million.
- From 1994 to 2010, the number of mobile PCs worldwide will increase from 18 million to 47 million.[63]

Discussion Questions

1. How can a corporation identify its core competencies? Its distinctive competencies?

2. When should a corporation or business unit outsource a function or activity?

3. Why is penetration pricing more likely than skim pricing to raise a company's or a business unit's operating profit in the long run?

4. How does mass customization support a business unit's competitive strategy?

5. What is the relationship of policies to strategies?

Strategic Practice Exercise

Wal-Mart is a very successful mass marketing retailer with stores throughout North America and an increasing presence in Europe, South America, and Asia. The company is known for its distinctive competency in information systems and distribution logistics. According to Michael Campbell, CEO of Campbell Software, "Wal-Mart is so far ahead of the (technology) curve because they were the first ones to embrace the fact that they are in the information business."[66]

In 1996, management decided to establish a position for the company on the Internet. During this period of time when its brick and mortar stores were registering double-digit sales and earnings growth, its virtual store on the Internet had continual problems. For example, in 1999 the company was forced to warn Web customers that it couldn't guarantee Christmas delivery of goods ordered after December 14. A redesigned and expanded Web site debuted in February 2000 but was criticized for its cumbersome design, slow downloading time, and poor search engine. In September 2000, it was ranked 47th out of 50 retail sites by Media Metrix.[67]

Timothy Mullaney, a columnist for *Business Week's* e-biz section, compared Wal-Mart's Web site during September 2000 with that of Amazon.com. He found that Wal-Mart's Web site didn't measure up to its own brick and mortar stores, much less to Amazon. He rated Walmart.com a failure on content, convenience, and fun. Among its faults were the following: Walmart.com settled for taking orders rather than enticing visitors (as Amazon did) to consider things they hadn't thought of buying. Compared to Amazon.com, he found the site boring. Its home page was composed of a long list of categories. The site provided basic data on each product offered but failed to provide any reviews of the products or show them in use. In contrast, Amazon.com's Web site provided reviews by both Amazon and 33 users supplemented by a table that let the user compare the features of one CD player with those of other players. Simple one-click boxes referred the user to accessories and batteries. Amazon.com tailored its recommendations to the visitor's tastes and interests; whereas, Walmart.com made generic suggestions that fit few visitors. Walmart.com's navigation features were poor. The site contained a number of broken or poorly designed links. For example, a request for romantic comedies starring Tom Hanks led to *Nightmare at 43 Hillcrest*, a Hanks' drama about drug-dealing. Prices and shipping costs were, however, about the same at both sites. The columnist summed up his experience with the statement, "Right now,

Amazon.com is a very good store, and Walmart.com is still learning the online fundamentals."[68]

Reacting to the poor performance of its Web site, Wal-Mart's management hired Jeanne Jackson as the new CEO of Walmart.com Hired during the Spring of 2000 from Banana Republic where she had been CEO as well as head of the company's catalogue and Web operations, Jackson vowed to make the largest brick and mortar retailer into a successful virtual retailer. She closed the Web site in late September for remodeling and opened it a few weeks later as a much leaner site without personalized promotions or 3D graphics. Although the site had a more streamlined and intuitive layout in 2001, critics found it dull. CEO Jackson continued to be optimistic. The online efforts of Sears, Kmart, and Target were still in their infancy. Jackson commented, "This is a marathon. It's not a sprint."

1. Given that Wal-Mart has a distinctive competence in information technology, why has it done so poorly on the Internet?
2. Considering that as of early 2001, almost no dot.com retailer (including Amazon.com) had yet to show a profit, why all the fuss about Internet retailing?
3. Is the marriage of "bricks" and "clicks" the right formula for marketing success on the Internet?
4. Should Wal-Mart be investing in the Internet at a time when it has so many alternative growth opportunities throughout the world?
5. What advice would you give Jeanne Jackson regarding Walmart.com?

Key Terms

connected line batch flow (p. 172)
consensus (p. 183)
continuous improvement (p. 172)
core capability (p. 165)
core competency (p. 165)
corporate culture pressures (p. 182)
corporate scenarios (p. 178)
dedicated transfer lines (p. 172)
developing policies (p. 184)
devil's advocate (p. 183)
dialectical inquiry (p. 184)
distinctive competency (p. 165)
electronic customer relationship management (e-CRM) software (p. 185)
financial strategy (p. 169)
flexible manufacturing systems (p. 172)
functional strategy (p. 165)

HRM strategy (p. 175)
information systems strategy (p. 176)
job shop (p. 172)
Just-In-Time (p. 174)
leveraged buy out (p. 170)
logistics strategy (p. 174)
market development (p. 168)
marketing strategy (p. 168)
mass customization (p. 173)
mass production (p. 172)
modular manufacturing (p. 173)
multiple sourcing (p. 173)
net present value (p. 181)
operations strategy (p. 171)
outsourcing (p. 166)
parallel sourcing (p. 174)
penetration pricing (p. 169)
political strategy (p. 181)

pro forma financial statements (p. 178)
product development (p. 169)
pull strategy (p. 169)
purchasing strategy (p. 173)
push strategy (p. 169)
R&D strategy (p. 170)
real options (p. 181)
risk (p. 180)
skim pricing (p. 169)
sole sourcing (p. 174)
stakeholder priority matrix (p. 181)
strategic choice (p. 183)
strategies to avoid (p. 177)
strategy shadow committee (p. 184)
technological follower (p. 171)
technological leader (p. 171)
tracking stock (p. 170)

Notes

1. Arm & Hammer is a registered trademark of Church & Dwight Company, Inc.
2. M. A. Hitt, B. W. Keats, and S. M. DeMarie, "Navigating in the New Competitive Landscape: Building Strategic Flexibility and Competitive Advantage in the 21st Century," *Academy of Management Executive* (November 1998), pp. 22–42. According to the authors, failure to reinvest in a core competency will result in its becoming a "core rigidity."
3. G. Hamel and S. K. Prahalad, *Competing for the Future* (Boston: Harvard Business School Press, 1994), pp. 202–207.
4. Ibid, p. 211.
5. P. J. Verdin and P. J. Williamson, "Core Competencies, Competitive Advantage and Market Analysis: Forging the Links," in *Competence-Based Competition*, edited by G. Hamel and A. Heene (New York: John Wiley and Sons, 1994), pp. 83–84.
6. B. Kelley, "Outsourcing Marches On," *Journal of Business Strategy* (July/August 1995), p. 40.
7. BridgeNews, "Motorola Will Cut 2,870 Jobs in Outsourcing Deal," *The (Ames) Tribune* (December 11, 2000), p. D4.
8. J. Greco, "Outsourcing: The New Partnership," *Journal of Business Strategy* (July/August 1997), pp. 48–54.
9. J. B. Quinn, "The Intelligent Enterprise: A New Paradigm," *Academy of Management Executive* (November 1992), pp. 48–63.
10. J. A. Byrne, "Has Outsourcing Gone Too Far?" *Business Week* (April 1, 1996), pp. 26–28.
11. D. Lei and M. A. Hitt, "Strategic Restructuring and Outsourcing: The Effect of Mergers and Acquisitions and LBOs on Building Firm Skills and Capabilities," *Journal of Management*, Vol. 21, No. 5 (1995), pp. 835–859.
12. Kelley, "Outsourcing Marches On," p. 40.
13. S. M. Oster, *Modern Competitive Analysis*, 2d ed. (New York: Oxford University Press, 1994), p. 93.
14. M. Springer, "Plowed Under," *Forbes* (February 21, 2000), p. 56.
15. W. Redmond, "The Strategic Pricing of Innovative Products," *Handbook of Business Strategy, 1992/1993 Yearbook*, edited by H. E. Glass and M. A. Hovde (Boston: Warren, Gorham and Lamont, 1992), pp. 16.1–16.13.
16. A. Safieddine and S. Titman in April 1999 *Journal of Finance* as summarized by D. Champion, "The Joy of Leverage," *Harvard Business Review* (July–August 1999), pp. 19–22.
17. R. Kochhar and M. A. Hitt, "Linking Corporate Strategy to Capital Structure: Diversification Strategy, Type and Source of Financing," *Strategic Management Journal* (June 1998), pp. 601–610.
18. A. Rappaport and M. L. Sirower, "Stock or Cash?" *Harvard Business Review* (November–December 1999), pp. 147–158.
19. D. Angwin and I. Contardo, "Unleashing Cerberus: Don't Let Your MBOs Turn on Themselves," *Long Range Strategy* (October 1999), pp. 494–504.
20. S. Scherreik, "Tread Carefully When You Buy Tracking Stocks," *Business Week* (March 6, 2000), pp. 182–184.
21. T. Due, "Dean Foods Thrives on Regional Off-Brand Products," *Wall Street Journal* (September 17, 1987), p. A6.
22. S. Stevens, "Speeding the Signals of Change," *Appliance* (February 1995), p. 7.
23. J. R. Williams and R. S. Novak, "Aligning CIM Strategies to Different Markets," *Long Range Planning* (February 1990), pp. 126–135.
24. J. Wheatley, "Super Factory—or Super Headache," *Business Week* (July 31, 2000), p. 66.
25. G. Hamel, "Strategy as Revolution," *Harvard Business Review* (July–August, 1996), p. 73 and E. Schonfeld, "The Customized, Digitized, Have-It-Your-Way Economy," *Fortune* (September 28, 1998), pp. 115–124.

26. F. R. Bleakley, "Some Companies Let Supplier Work on Site and Even Place Orders," *Wall Street Journal* (January 13, 1995), pp. A1, A6.
27. J. Richardson, "Parallel Sourcing and Supplier Performance in the Japanese Automobile Industry," *Strategic Management Journal* (July 1993), pp. 339–350.
28. S. Roberts-Witt, "Procurement: The HP Way," *PC Magazine* (November 21, 2000), pp. iBiz 21–22.
29. J. Bigness, "In Today's Economy, There Is Big Money to Be Made in Logistics," *Wall Street Journal* (September 6, 1995), pp. A1, A9.
30. F. Keenan, "Logistics Gets a Little Respect," *Business Week* (November 20, 2000), pp. E.Biz 112–116.
31. B. L. Kirkman and D. L. Shapiro, "The Impact of Cultural Values on Employee Resistance to Teams: Toward a Model of Globalized Self-Managing Work Team Effectiveness," *Academy of Management Review* (July 1997), pp. 730–757.
32. R. D. Banker, J. M. Field, R. G. Schroeder, and K. K. Sinha, "Impact of Work Teams on Manufacturing Performance: A Longitudinal Field Study," *Academy of Management Journal* (August 1996), pp. 867–890; B. L. Kirkman and B. Rosen, "Beyond Self-Management: Antecedents and Consequences of Team Empowerment," *Academy of Management Journal* (February 1999), pp. 58–74.
33. M. J. Mandel, "The Risk that Boom Will Turn to Bust," *Business Week* (February 14, 2000), pp. 120–122; "Economic Indicators," *The Economist* (June 24, 2000), p. 120.
34. P. Johnson, "Temporary Executives Score Big," *Des Moines Register* (October 30, 2000), pp. 1D, 4D.
35. P. Brimelow, "Part-Time U.S.A.," *Forbes* (January 22, 2001), p. 81.
36. "Economic Indicators," *The Economist* (June 24, 2000), p. 120.
37. O. C. Richard, "Racial Diversity, Business Strategy, and Firm Performance: A Resource-Based View," *Academy of Management Journal* (April 2000), pp. 164–177.
38. G. Robinson and K. Dechant, "Building a Business Case for Diversity," *Academy of Management Executive* (August 1997), pp. 21–31.
39. K. Labich, "Making Diversity Pay," *Fortune* (September 9, 1996), pp. 177–180.
40. J. Greco, "Good Day Sunshine," *Journal of Business Strategy* (July/August 1998), pp. 4–5.
41. W. Howard, "Translate Now," *PC Magazine* (September 19, 2000), p. 81.
42. T. Smart, "Jack Welch's Cyber-Czar," *Business Week* (August 5, 1996), p. 83.
43. R. Grover and D. Polek, "Millionaire Buys Disney Time," *Business Week* (June 26, 2000), pp. 141–144.
44. D. K. Sinha, "Strategic Planning in the Fortune 500," *Handbook of Business Strategy, 1991/1992 Yearbook*, edited by H. E. Glass and M. A. Hovde (Boston: Warren, Gorham and Lamont, 1991), pp. 9.6–9.8.
45. T. B. Palmer and R. M. Wiseman, "Decoupling Risk Taking from Income Stream Uncertainty: A Holistic Model of Risk," *Strategic Management Journal* (November 1999), pp. 1037–1062.
46. D. Clark, "All the Chips: A Big Bet Made Intel What It Is Today; Now It Wagers Again," *Wall Street Journal* (June 6, 1995), pp. A1, A5.
47. L. W. Busenitz and J. B. Barney, "Differences Between Entrepreneurs and Managers in Large Organizations: Biases and Heuristics in Strategic Decision-Making," *Journal of Business Venturing* (January 1997), pp. 9–30.
48. P. Coy, "Exploiting Uncertainty," *Business Week* (June 7, 1999), pp. 118–124. For further information on real options, see M. Amram and N. Kulatilaka, "Uncertainty: The New Rules for Strategy," *Journal of Business Strategy* (May/June 1999), pp. 25–29; M. Amram and N. Kulatilaka, "Disciplined Decisions: Aligning Strategy with the Financial Markets," *Harvard Business Review* (January–February 1999), pp. 95–104; T. A. Luehrman, "Strategy

as a Portfolio of Real Options," *Harvard Business Review* (September–October 1998), pp. 89–99; T. A. Luehrman, "Investment Opportunities as Real Options: Getting Started with the Numbers," *Harvard Business Review* (July-August 1998), pp. 51–67; R. G. McGrath, "Falling Forward: Real Options Reasoning and Entrepreneurial Failure," *Academy of Management Review* (January 1999), pp. 13–30.

49. C. Anderson, "Values-Based Management," *Academy of Management Executive* (November 1997), pp. 25–46.

50. H. M. O'Neill, R. W. Pouder, and A. K. Buchholtz, "Patterns in the Diffusion of Strategies Across Organizations: Insights from the Innovation Diffusion Literature," *Academy of Management Executive* (January 1998), pp. 98–114.

51. B. B. Tyler and H. K. Steensma, "Evaluating Technological Collaborative Opportunities: A Cognitive Modeling Perspective," *Strategic Management Journal* (Summer 1995), pp. 43–70; D. Duchan, D. P. Ashman, and M. Nathan, "Mavericks, Visionaries, Protestors, and Sages: Toward a Typology of Cognitive Structures for Decision Making in Organizations," *Journal of Business Strategies* (Fall 1997), pp. 106–125; P. Chattopadhyay, W. H. Glick, C. C. Miller, and G. P. Huber, "Determinants of Executive Beliefs: Comparing Functional Conditioning and Social Influence," *Strategic Management Journal* (August 1999), pp. 763–789; B. Katey and G. G. Meredith, "Relationship Among Owner/Manager Personal Values, Business Strategies, and Enterprise Performance," *Journal of Small Business Management* (April 1997), pp. 37–64.

52. C. S. Galbraith and G. B. Merrill, "The Politics of Forecasting: Managing the Truth," *California Management Review* (Winter 1996), pp. 29–43.

53. M. Leuchter, "The Rules of the Game," *Forecast* (May/June 1996), pp. 16–23.

54. M. A. Geletkanycz and D. C. Hambrick, "The External Ties of Top Executives: Implications for Strategic Choice and Performance," *Administrative Science Quarterly* (December 1997), pp. 654–681.

55. M. A. Hitt, M. T. Dacin, B. B. Tyler, and D. Park, "Understanding the Differences in Korean and U.S. Executives' Strategic Orientation," *Strategic Management Journal* (February 1997), pp. 159–167; L. G. Thomas III and G. Waring, "Competing Capitalisms: Capital Investment in American, German, and Japanese Firms," *Strategic Management Journal* (August 1999), pp. 729–748.

56. J. A. Wagner III and R. Z. Gooding, "Equivocal Information and Attribution: An Investigation of Patterns of Managerial Sensemaking," *Strategic Management Journal* (April 1997), pp. 275–286.

57. J. Ross and B. M. Staw, "Organizational Escalation and Exit: Lessons from the Shoreham Nuclear Power Plant," *Academy of Management Journal* (August 1993), pp. 701–732; P. W. Mulvey, J. F. Veiga, and P. M. Elsass, "When Teammates Raise a White Flag," *Academy of Management Executive* (February 1996), pp. 40–49.

58. R. A. Cosier and C. R. Schwenk, "Agreement and Thinking Alike: Ingredients for Poor Decisions," *Academy of Management Executive* (February 1990), p. 69.

59. A. C. Amason, "Distinguishing the Effects of Functional and Dysfunctional Conflict on Strategic Decision Making: Resolving a Paradox for Top Management Teams," *Academy of Management Journal* (February 1996), pp. 123–148; A. C. Amason and H. J. Sapienza, "The Effects of Top Management Team Size and Interaction Norms on Cognitive and Affective Conflict," *Journal of Management*, Vol. 23, No. 4 (1997), pp. 495–516.

60. D. M. Schweiger, W. R. Sandberg, and P. L. Rechner, "Experiential Effects of Dialectical Inquiry, Devil's Advocacy, and Consensus Approaches to Strategic Decision Making," *Academy of Management Journal* (December 1989), pp. 745–772; G. Whyte, "Decision Failures: Why They Occur and How to Prevent Them," *Academy of Management Executive* (August 1991), pp. 23–31; R. L. Priem, D. A. Harrison, and N. K. Muir, "Structured Conflict and Consensus Outcomes in Group Decision Making," *Journal of Management*, Vol. 21, No. 4 (1995), pp. 691–710.

61. G. Hamel, "Turning Your Business Upside Down," *Fortune* (June 23, 1997), p. 87.

62. S. C. Abraham, "Using Bundles to Find the Best Strategy," *Strategy & Leadership* (July/August/September 1999), pp. 53–55.

63. C. Medford, "Know Who I Am," *PC Magazine* (January 16, 2001), pp. 136–148, S. L. Roberts-Witt, "Personalization: Is It Worth It?" *PC Magazine* (December 19, 2000), pp. iBiz 8–12.

64. P. Krugman, "The Cost of Convenience," *The (Ames) Tribune* (October 5, 2000), p. A6; D. Brady, "Customer Service?" *Business Week* (October 23, 2000), pp. 119–128.

65. J. Warner, "21st Century Capitalism: Snapshot of the Next Century," *Business Week* (November 18, 1994), p. 194.

66. J. Jordan and D. Svetcov, "Data-Crunching Santa," *U.S. News & World Report* (December 21, 1998), pp. 44–48.

67. W. Zellner, "Will Walmart.com Get It Right This Time?" *Business Week* (November 6, 2000), pp. 104–112.

68. T. J. Mullaney, "This Race Isn't Even Close," *Business Week* (December 18, 2000), pp. 208–210.

PART ENDING VIDEO CASE   PART THREE

Newbury Comics, Inc.

STRATEGY FORMULATION

*N*ewbury Comics Cofounders, Mike Dreese and John Brusger parlayed $2,000 and a comic book collection into a thriving chain of 22 stores spanning the New England region, known to be *the* place to shop for everything from the best of the underground/independent scene to major label superstars. The chain also stocks a wide variety of non-music related items such as T-shirts, Dr. (doc) Martens shoes, posters, jewelry, cosmetics, books, magazines, and other trendy items.

In Part Three, **"Strategy Formulation,"** the video addresses strategy formulation in terms of situation analysis, business, corporate, and functional strategy. Mike, John, and Jan conduct a SWOT analysis of Newbury Comics in terms of Strengths, Weaknesses, Opportunities and Threats and how strategy is formulated. They are very much aware of how the company's core competencies provide competitive advantage.

Mike explains that he dislikes setting three-year revenue targets (objectives), but prefers to formulate strategy on an experimental basis. Note that even when discussing strategy formulation, Mike talks about implementation. He tells how he assigned the development of the used CD implementation plan to Duncan Brown, Senior Vice President. Brown was to look for long-run roadblocks in case the strategy was successful in the short run.

Newbury Comics is a good example of the value of SWOT analysis when formulating strategy. Most of the information, such as the employees' knowledge and competition, was presented in the earlier video dealing with environmental scanning. Some of the threats, however, are mentioned for the first time. Mike notes that the vendor community (suppliers of new CDs) may decide to make it difficult for any retailer to buy new CDs if that retailer sells used ones. He also notes that in four to five years, Napster-type operators who deal in digit-to-digit downloads instead of CDs may dominate the business of music distribution.

The management of Newbury Comics definitely believes that the company has a competitive advantage (edge) in its market. Jan states that the company's prices are cheaper than the mall music stores plus it offers used CDs. Even when competitors like Best Buy have similar prices, Newbury Comics has a better selection plus used CDs. Mike again points out that the company's corporate culture attracts employees with a "knowledge of the street." One-third of the employees play in bands. John adds that Newbury Comics offers hard-to-find material that is sold in "onesies" and "twosies" to the discriminating buyer.

Concepts Illustrated in the Video

- Strategy Formulation
- SWOT Analysis
- Propitious Niche
- Competitive Strategy
- Competitive Tactics (timing)
- Corporate Growth Strategy
- Marketing Strategy
- Human Resource Management Strategy
- Information Systems Strategy
- Management's Attitude Toward Risk

Study Questions

1. Has Newbury Comics found a "propitious niche"?
2. Conduct a SWOT analysis of Newbury Comics. Did you list anything that management failed to list?
3. The video casually mentions mission and objectives for the company. Formulate a mission statement for Newbury Comics.
4. What competitive strategy is being followed by Newbury Comics?
5. What corporate strategy is being followed by Newbury Comics?

chapter 8

Strategy Implementation: Organizing for Action

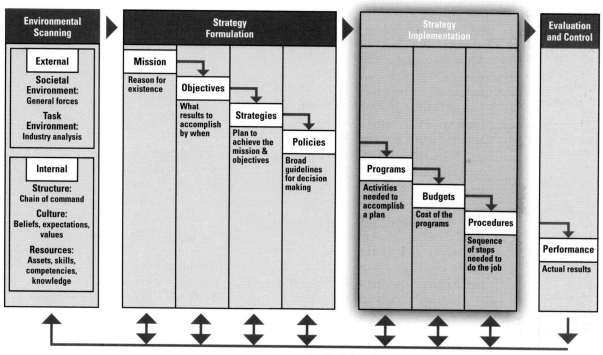

In 1998, Fingerhut Company had been a thriving mail order retailer with annual revenues of $2 billion. It was making a successful transition to electronic commerce. This venerable catalogue company was rapidly opening Internet Web sites and buying equity stakes in other online retailers. With its expertise in filling and shipping catalogue orders, Fingerhut successfully marketed its order-fulfillment competency on a contract basis to other companies, such as eToys and Wal-Mart. Business analysts were impressed by Fingerhut's diversification strategy. *Fortune* magazine declared Fingerhut one of the "10 companies that get it." Impressed with the company's performance, Federated Department Stores acquired Fingerhut in February

1999 for $1.7 billion. Federated's management confidently predicted that the corporation's overall Internet sales would reach $2 to $3 billion by 2004 with the addition of Fingerhut.

Twenty months after purchasing Fingerhut, Federated discovered that its Internet sales had reached only $180 million and were not likely to go much higher anytime soon. Management found that while Fingerhut had an excellent strategy for the Internet and its catalogue businesses, its implementation of that strategy had been dismal. Fingerhut's fulfillment contracts had dropped from 22 to 8 after allegations of poor service and a very visible dispute with eToys. The company had also mismanaged its plan to provide additional credit to its catalogue customers. The result was a number of special charges and layoffs totaling $795 million in expenses plus losses from unpaid credit card bills totaling around $400 million in 2000. As a result, Federated's stock dropped 35% in value. What went wrong?

According to a former Fingerhut executive, "The infrastructure was always a step-and-a-half behind." The company didn't have sufficient knowledge of the technology needed to operate successfully as an Internet retailer. With growth, its operations had become sluggish, and management failed to hire enough competent people to run its Web sites and fulfillment software. For example, Fingerhut found it too difficult to modify its existing software to communicate with fulfillment customers and its warehouse. Instead, the company created another version of the software to handle orders from other companies. Unfortunately, the software was so buggy that notices of a customer's purchase would get lost between the company's central computers and its warehouses, causing days of delay. At other times, the software lost track of inventory so Fingerhut didn't have an accurate measure of what was in stock at a warehouse. Its fulfillment customers, like eToys and Children's Place, complained that Fingerhut was, in some cases, sending out partial orders, forcing them to pay for two separate shipments instead of one. In other instances, Fingerhut took so long to assemble orders that the customer had to pay for express shipments. According to Mark Amodio, head of e-commerce at Children's Place, because of Fingerhut's inability to track shipments, his company was forced to cancel orders and try again!

Fingerhut failed to properly manage its credits and collections. To boost sales, the company offered credit cards to its current (generally low income) customers who had been previously purchasing Fingerhut products on the installment plan. It offered large lines of credit to even its riskier customers. Many of these customers ran up large bills but were unable to pay them. The company also failed to think through its acquisitions. After the company had purchased the Popular Club catalogue, it moved the catalogue's operations from New Jersey to its Minnesota facility. On the surface this move made sense. Nevertheless, the move tripled the time it took to get mailings to Popular Club's mainly Northeast-based customers, causing sales to plummet. Fingerhut was eventually forced to move the operation back to New Jersey.

Federated's management was furious. It closed five of Fingerhut's eight Web sites and stopped investing in a sixth site, Garage.com, a clearance retailer. It also cut 550 positions, 24% of the Fingerhut workforce. Management stated that Federated would no longer invest in e-commerce companies and that it will stop pursuing new third party fulfillment contracts.[1]

8.1 Strategy Implementation

Strategy implementation is the sum total of the activities and choices required for the execution of a strategic plan. It is the process by which strategies and policies are put into action through the development of programs, budgets, and procedures. Although implementation is usually considered after strategy has been formulated, implementation is a key part of strategic management. Strategy formulation and strategy implementation should thus be considered as two sides of the same coin. Poor implementation has been blamed for a number of strategic failures. For example, studies show that half of all acquisitions fail to achieve what was expected of them, and one out of four international ventures do not succeed.[2] A study by KPMG of the 700 largest mergers from 1996 to 1998 found that 83% of the mergers failed to increase the acquirer's shareholder value within a year of completing the merger.[3] Fingerhut Company is one example of how a good strategy can result in a disaster through poor strategy implementation.

To begin the implementation process, strategy makers must consider these questions:

- *Who* are the people who will carry out the strategic plan?

- *What* must be done to align the company's operations in the new intended direction?

- *How* is everyone going to work together to do what is needed?

These questions and similar ones should have been addressed initially when the pros and cons of strategic alternatives were analyzed. They must also be addressed again before appropriate implementation plans can be made. Unless top management can answer these basic questions satisfactorily, even the best planned strategy is unlikely to provide the desired outcome.

A survey of 93 *Fortune* 500 U.S. firms revealed that over half of the corporations experienced the following 10 problems when they attempted to implement a strategic change. These problems are listed in order of frequency.

1. Implementation took more time than originally planned.
2. Unanticipated major problems arose.
3. Activities were ineffectively coordinated.
4. Competing activities and crises took attention away from implementation.
5. The involved employees had insufficient capabilities to perform their jobs.
6. Lower-level employees were inadequately trained.
7. Uncontrollable external environmental factors created problems.
8. Departmental managers provided inadequate leadership and direction.
9. Key implementation tasks and activities were poorly defined.
10. The information system inadequately monitored activities.[4]

Fingerhut experienced almost all of these problems in its Internet expansion—all except the first one. Fingerhut's President, William Lansing, had been hired in the spring of 1998 to remake the catalogue company into an e-commerce player. Within months he started so many Web initiatives that the firm was soon unable to keep up with them. He started new Web sites and catalogues and acquired others. He offered unused warehouse space plus packaging and shipping services to other catalogue and Web companies. To boost sales faster, Lansing pushed giving credit cards to four million low-income customers over a two-year period instead of the originally planned three-year period.

8.2 Who Implements Strategy?

Depending on how the corporation is organized, those who implement strategy will probably be a much more diverse set of people than those who formulate it. In most large, multi-industry corporations, the implementers are everyone in the organization. Vice presidents of functional areas and directors of divisions or SBUs work with their subordinates to put together large-scale implementation plans. Plant managers, project managers, and unit heads put together plans for their specific plants, departments, and units. Therefore, every operational manager down to the first-line supervisor and every employee is involved in some way in implementing corporate, business, and functional strategies.

Many of the people in the organization who are crucial to successful strategy implementation probably have little to do with the development of the corporate and even business strategy. Therefore, they might be entirely ignorant of the vast amount of data and work that went into the formulation process. Unless changes in mission, objectives, strategies, and policies and their importance to the company are communicated clearly to all operational managers, there can be a lot of resistance and foot-dragging. Managers might hope to influence top management into abandoning its new plans and returning to its old ways. This is one reason why involving people from all organizational levels in the formulation and in the implementation of strategy tends to result in better organizational performance.

8.3 What Must Be Done?

The managers of divisions and functional areas work with their fellow managers to develop programs, budgets, and procedures for the implementation of strategy. They also work to achieve synergy among the divisions and functional areas in order to establish and maintain a company's distinctive competence.

DEVELOPING PROGRAMS, BUDGETS, AND PROCEDURES

Strategy implementation is composed of establishing programs to create a series of new organizational activities, budgets to allocate funds to the new activities, and procedures to handle the day-to-day details.

Programs

The purpose of a **program** is to make the strategy action-oriented. For example, PepsiCo recently made a strategic decision to grow in areas where the company could dominate. Instead of competing with Coca-Cola in every market, PepsiCo decided to concentrate on supermarkets where Pepsi had its greatest sales. To implement this strategy, the company developed a program called the "Power of One." The purpose of the strategy was to move Pepsi soft drinks next to Frito-Lay chips so that shoppers would be tempted to pick up both when they chose one. Since PepsiCo products accounted for 3% of total supermarket sales, 29% of supermarket cash flow, and offered 9% operating margins compared to the usual 2% margin for other goods, the supermarket managers were happy to put the PepsiCo's products together—especially since PepsiCo people delivered and stocked the shelves for them. As a result of this program, Frito-Lay increased its market share from 54% to 56% and Pepsi-Cola's volumes rose 0.6%. PepsiCo expanded the program into Mexico where its Sabritas brand had an 81% market share of the salty snack market. Management planned to initiate the program in other developing nations from India to China.[5]

One way to examine the likely impact new programs will have on an existing organization is to compare proposed programs and activities with current programs and activities. Brynjolfsson, Renshaw, and Van Alstyne propose a **matrix of change** to help managers decide how quickly change should proceed, in what order changes should take place, whether to start at a new site, and whether the proposed systems are stable and coherent. As shown in **Figure 8–1**, target practices (new programs) for a manufacturing plant are drawn on the vertical axis and existing practices (current activities) are drawn on the horizontal axis. As shown, any new strategy will likely involve a sequence of new programs and activities. Any one of these may conflict with existing practices/activities, creating implementation problems. Use the following steps to create the matrix:

1. Compare each of the new programs/target practices with each other to see if they are complementary (+), interfering (−), or have no effect on each other (leave blank).

2. Examine existing practices/activities for their interactions with each other using the same symbols.

3. Compare each new program/target practice with each existing practice/activity for any interaction effects. Place the appropriate symbols in the cells in the lower right part of the matrix.

4. Evaluate each program/activity in terms of its relative importance to achieving the strategy or getting the job accomplished.

5. Examine the overall matrix to identify problem areas where proposed programs are likely to either interfere with each other or with existing practices/activities. Note in **Figure 8–1** that the proposed program of installing flexible equipment interferes with the proposed program of assembly line rationalization. The two new programs need to be changed so that they no longer conflict with each other. Note also that the amount of change necessary to carry out the proposed implementation programs (target practices) is a function of the number of times each program interferes with existing practices/activities. That is, the more minus signs and the less plus signs exist in the matrix, the more implementation problems can be expected.

Figure 8–1
The Matrix of Change

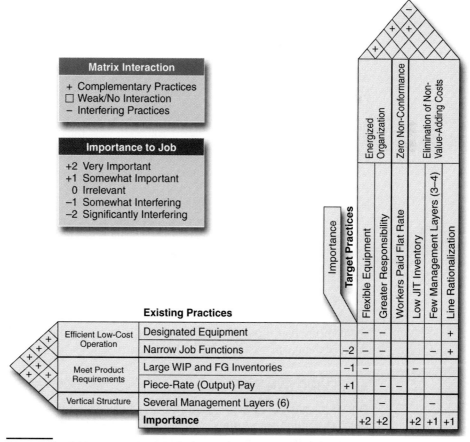

Source: E. Brynjolfsson, A. A. Renshaw, and M. Van Alstyne, "The Matrix of Change," *Sloan Management Review* (Winter 1997), p. 43. Reprinted by permission of publisher. Copyright © 1997 by Massachusetts Institute of Technology. All rights reserved.

The matrix of change can be used to address the following types of questions:

- **Feasibility:** Do the proposed programs and activities constitute a coherent, stable system? Are the current activities coherent and stable? Is the transition likely to be difficult?
- **Sequence of Execution:** Where should the change begin? How does the sequence affect success? Are there reasonable stopping points?
- **Location:** Are we better off instituting the new programs at a new site or can we reorganize the existing facilities at a reasonable cost?
- **Pace and Nature of Change:** Should the change be slow or fast, incremental or radical? Which blocks of current activities must be changed at the same time?
- **Stakeholder Evaluations:** Have we overlooked any important activities or interactions? Should we get further input from interested stakeholders? Which new programs and current activities offer the greatest sources of value?

The matrix offers useful guidelines on where, when, and how fast to implement change.[6] A matrix of change could have been very useful for Fingerhut's William Lansing in developing his implementation programs of creating new Web sites, changing credit policies, offering fulfillment contracts, and acquiring other companies.

Budgets

After programs have been developed, the **budget** process begins. Planning a budget is the last real check a corporation has on the feasibility of its selected strategy. An ideal strategy might be found to be completely impractical only after specific implementation programs are costed in detail.

Procedures

After the program, divisional, and corporate budgets are approved, **procedures** must be developed. Often called **Standard Operating Procedures (SOPs)**, they typically detail the various activities that must be carried out to complete a corporation's programs. Once in place, they must be updated to reflect any changes in technology as well as in strategy. These procedures ensure that the day-to-day operations will be consistent over time (that is, next week's work activities will be the same as this week's) and consistent among locations (that is, each retail store will operate in the same manner as the others). For example, to ensure that its policies are carried out to the letter in every one of its fast-food retail outlets, McDonald's has done an excellent job of developing very detailed procedures (and policing them!).

In the case of PepsiCo's "Power of One" program, the company's sales people developed a set of procedures to persuade supermarket managers to add shelf space and displays in poorer performing locations, display snack foods with soft drinks, and to bring the two products together at end-of-aisle displays. They wrote a series of procedures to ensure the ideal display of snack foods and soft drinks in supermarkets given various types of store layouts. These procedures were incorporated in sales aids and information sheets given to the sales force and explained in monthly sales meetings. Logistics people developed procedures for the truck drivers to ensure that PepsiCo products were actually placed on the shelves as needed, not just dropped in the supermarket's back room.

ACHIEVING SYNERGY

One of the goals to be achieved in strategy implementation is synergy between and among functions and business units. This is the reason why corporations commonly reorganize after an acquisition. **Synergy** is said to exist for a divisional corporation if the return on investment (ROI) of each division is greater than what the return would be if each division were an independent business. According to Goold and Campbell, synergy can take place in one of six forms:

- **Shared Know-How:** Combined units often benefit from sharing knowledge or skills. This is a leveraging of core competencies.

- **Coordinated Strategies:** Aligning the business strategies of two or more business units may provide a corporation significant advantage by reducing interunit competition and developing a coordinated response to common competitors (horizontal strategy).

- **Shared Tangible Resources:** Combined units can sometimes save money by sharing resources, such as a common manufacturing facility or R&D lab.

- **Economies of Scale or Scope:** Coordinating the flow of products or services of one unit with that of another unit can reduce inventory, increase capacity utilization, and improve market access.

- **Pooled Negotiating Power:** Combined units can combine their purchasing to gain bargaining power over common suppliers to reduce costs and improve quality. The same can be done with common distributors.

- **New Business Creation:** Exchanging knowledge and skills can facilitate new products or services by extracting discrete activities from various units and combining them in a new unit or by establishing joint ventures among internal business units.[7]

For example, Federated Department Stores' purchase of Fingerhut was justified on the basis that Fingerhut would help Federated bolster its own Internet and catalogue operations. Since the acquisition, Fingerhut has successfully taken over control of Federated's order-fulfillment center and was starting to handle some of Federated's catalogue and Internet sales from its own warehouses.

8.4 How Is Strategy to Be Implemented? Organizing for Action

Before plans can lead to actual performance, a corporation should be appropriately organized, programs should be adequately staffed, and activities should be directed toward achieving desired objectives. (Organizing activities are reviewed briefly in this chapter; staffing, directing, and control activities are covered in **Chapters 9** and **10**.)

Any change in corporate strategy is very likely to require some sort of change in the way an organization is structured and in the kind of skills needed in particular positions. Managers must, therefore, closely examine the way their company is structured in order to decide what, if any, changes should be made in the way work is accomplished. Should activities be grouped differently? Should the authority to make key decisions be centralized at headquarters or decentralized to managers in distant locations? Should the company be managed like a "tight ship" with many rules and controls, or "loosely" with few rules and controls? Should the corporation be organized into a "tall" structure with many layers of managers, each having a narrow span of control (that is, few employees per supervisor) to better control his or her subordinates; or should it be organized into a "flat" structure with fewer layers of managers, each having a wide span of control (that is, more employees per supervisor) to give more freedom to his or her subordinates?

STRUCTURE FOLLOWS STRATEGY

In a classic study of large U.S. corporations such as DuPont, General Motors, Sears, and Standard Oil, Alfred Chandler concluded that **structure follows strategy**—that is, changes in corporate strategy lead to changes in organizational structure.[8] He also concluded that organizations follow a pattern of development from one kind of structural arrangement to another as they expand. According to Chandler, these structural changes occur because the old structure, having been pushed too far, has caused inefficiencies that have become too obviously detrimental to bear. Chandler, therefore, proposed the following as the sequence of what occurs:

1. New strategy is created.
2. New administrative problems emerge.
3. Economic performance declines.
4. New appropriate structure is invented.
5. Profit returns to its previous level.

Chandler found that in their early years, corporations such as DuPont tend to have a centralized functional organizational structure that is well suited to producing and selling a limited range of products. As they add new product lines, purchase their own sources of supply, and create their own distribution networks, they become too complex for highly centralized structures. To remain successful, this type of organization needs to shift to a decentralized structure with several semiautonomous divisions (referred to in **Chapter 4** as divisional structure).

Alfred P. Sloan, past CEO of General Motors, detailed how GM conducted such structural changes in the 1920s.[9] He saw decentralization of structure as "centralized policy determination coupled with decentralized operating management." After top management had developed a strategy for the total corporation, the individual divisions (Chevrolet, Buick, and so on) were free to choose how to implement that strategy. Patterned after DuPont, GM found the decentralized multidivisional structure to be extremely effective in allowing the maximum amount of freedom for product development. Return on investment (ROI) was used as a financial control. (*ROI is discussed in more detail in* **Chapter 10.**)

Research generally supports Chandler's proposition that structure follows strategy (as well as the reverse proposition that structure influences strategy).[10] As mentioned earlier, changes in the environment tend to be reflected in changes in a corporation's strategy, thus leading to changes in a corporation's structure. Strategy, structure, and the environment need to be closely aligned; otherwise, organizational performance will likely suffer.[11] For example, a business unit following a differentiation strategy needs more freedom from headquarters to be successful than does another unit following a low-cost strategy.[12]

Although it is agreed that organizational structure must vary with different environmental conditions, which, in turn, affect an organization's strategy, there is no agreement about an optimal organizational design. What was appropriate for DuPont and General Motors in the 1920s might not be appropriate today. Firms in the same industry do, however, tend to organize themselves similarly. For example, automobile manufacturers tend to emulate General Motors' divisional concept, whereas consumer-goods producers tend to emulate the brand-management concept (a type of matrix structure) pioneered by Procter & Gamble Company. The general conclusion seems to be that firms following similar strategies in similar industries tend to adopt similar structures.

STAGES OF CORPORATE DEVELOPMENT

Successful corporations tend to follow a pattern of structural development as they grow and expand. Beginning with the simple structure of the entrepreneurial firm (in which everybody does everything), they usually (if they are successful) get larger and organize along functional lines with marketing, production, and finance departments. With continuing success, the company adds new product lines in different industries and organizes itself into interconnected divisions. The differences among these three structural **stages of corporate development** in terms of typical problems, objectives, strategies, reward systems and other characteristics are specified in detail in **Table 8–1.**

T a b l e 8 – 1   Factors Differentiating Stage I, II, and III Companies

Function	Stage I	Stage II	Stage III
1. Sizing up: Major problems	Survival and growth dealing with short-term operating problems.	Growth, rationalization, and expansion of resources, providing for adequate attention to product problems.	Trusteeship in management and investment and control of large, increasing, and diversified resources. Also, important to diagnose and take action on problems at division level.
2. Objectives	Personal and subjective.	Profits and meeting functionally oriented budgets and performance targets.	ROI, profits, earnings per share.
3. Strategy	Implicit and personal; exploitation of immediate opportunities seen by owner-manager.	Functionally oriented moves restricted to "one product" scope; exploitation of one basic product or service field.	Growth and product diversification; exploitation of general business opportunities.
4. Organization: Major characteristic of structure	One unit, "one-man show."	One unit, functionally specialized group.	Multiunit general staff office and decentralized operating divisions.
5. (a) Measurement and control	Personal, subjective control based on simple accounting system and daily communication and observation.	Control grows beyond one person; assessment of functional operations necessary; structured control systems evolve.	Complex formal system geared to comparative assessment of performance measures, indicating problems and opportunities and assessing management ability of division managers.
5. (b) Key performance indicators	Personal criteria, relationships with owner, operating efficiency, ability to solve operating problems.	Functional and internal criteria such as sales, performance compared to budget, size of empire, status in group, personal relationships, etc.	More impersonal application of comparisons such as profits, ROI, P/E ratio, sales, market share, productivity, product leadership, personnel development, employee attitudes, public responsibility.
6. Reward-punishment system	Informal, personal, subjective; used to maintain control and divide small pool of resources to provide personal incentives for key performers.	More structured; usually based to a greater extent on agreed policies as opposed to personal opinion and relationships.	Allotment by "due process" of a wide variety of different rewards and punishments on a formal and systematic basis. Companywide policies usually apply to many different classes of managers and workers with few major exceptions for individual cases.

Source: D. H. Thain, "Stages of Corporate Development," *Ivey Business Journal* (formerly *Ivey Business Quarterly*), (Winter 1969), p. 37. Copyright © 1969 by Ivey Management Services.

Stage I: Simple Structure

Stage I is typified by the entrepreneur, who founds the company to promote an idea (product or service). The entrepreneur tends to make all the important decisions personally and is involved in every detail and phase of the organization. The Stage I company has little formal structure, which allows the entrepreneur to directly supervise the activities of every employee (see **Figure 4–4** for an illustration of the simple, functional, and divisional structures). Planning is usually short range or reactive. The typical managerial functions of planning, organizing, directing, staffing, and controlling are usually performed to a very limited degree, if at all. The greatest strengths of a Stage I corporation are its flexibility and dynamism. The drive of the entrepreneur energizes the organization in its struggle for growth. Its greatest weakness is its extreme reliance on the entrepreneur to decide general strategies as well as detailed procedures. If the entrepreneur falters, the company usually flounders. This is labeled by Greiner as a **crisis of leadership**.[13]

Stage I describes Oracle Corporation, the computer software firm, under the management of its Cofounder and CEO Lawrence Ellison. The company adopted a pioneering approach to retrieving data called structured query language (SQL). When IBM made SQL its standard, Oracle's success was assured. Unfortunately Ellison's technical wizardry was not sufficient to manage the company. Often working at home, he lost sight of details outside his technical interests. Although the company's sales were rapidly increasing, its financial controls were so weak that management had to restate an entire year's results to rectify irregularities. After the company recorded its first loss, Ellison hired a set of functional managers to run the company while he retreated to focus on new product development.

Stage II: Functional Structure

Stage II is the point when the entrepreneur is replaced by a team of managers who have functional specializations. The transition to this stage requires a substantial managerial style change for the chief officer of the company, especially if he or she was the Stage I entrepreneur. He or she must learn to delegate; otherwise, having additional staff members yields no benefits to the organization. The previous example of Ellison's retreat from top management at Oracle Corporation to new product development manager is one way that technically brilliant founders are able to get out of the way of the newly empowered functional managers. Once into Stage II, the corporate strategy favors protectionism through dominance of the industry, often through vertical and horizontal growth. The great strength of a Stage II corporation lies in its concentration and specialization in one industry. Its great weakness is that all of its eggs are in one basket.

By concentrating on one industry while that industry remains attractive, a Stage II company, like Oracle Corporation in computer software, can be very successful. Once a functionally structured firm diversifies into other products in different industries, however, the advantages of the functional structure break down. A **crisis of autonomy** can now develop in which people managing diversified product lines need more decision-making freedom than top management is willing to delegate to them. The company needs to move to a different structure.

Stage III: Divisional Structure

Stage III is typified by the corporation's managing diverse product lines in numerous industries; it decentralizes the decision-making authority. These organizations grow by diversifying their product lines and expanding to cover wider geographical areas. They move to a divisional structure with a central headquarters and decentralized operating divisions—each division or business unit is a functionally organized Stage II company. They may also use a conglomerate structure if top management chooses to keep its collection of Stage II subsidiaries operating autonomously. A **crisis of control** can now develop in which the various units act to optimize their own sales and profits without regard to the overall corporation, whose headquarters seems so far away and almost irrelevant.

Recently divisions have been evolving into Strategic Business Units (SBUs) to better reflect product–market considerations. Headquarters attempts to coordinate the activities of its operating divisions or SBUs through performance- and results-oriented control and reporting systems, and by stressing corporate planning techniques. The units are not tightly controlled but are held responsible for their own performance results. Therefore, to be effective, the company has to have a decentralized decision process. The greatest strength of a Stage III corporation is its almost unlimited resources. Its most significant weakness is that it is usually so large and complex that it tends to become relatively inflexible. General Electric, DuPont, and General Motors are Stage III corporations.

Stage IV: Beyond SBUs

Even with its evolution into strategic business units during the 1970s and 1980s, the divisional form is not the last word in organization structure. The use of SBUs may result in a **red tape crisis** in which the corporation has grown too large and complex to be managed through formal programs and rigid systems and procedures take precedence over problem-solving. Under conditions of (1) increasing environmental uncertainty, (2) greater use of sophisticated technological production methods and information systems, (3) the increasing size and scope of worldwide business corporations, (4) a greater emphasis on multi-industry competitive strategy, and (5) a more educated cadre of managers and employees, new advanced forms of organizational structure have emerged and are continuing to emerge. These structures attempt to emphasize collaboration over competition in the managing of an organization's multiple overlapping projects and developing businesses.

The *matrix* and the *network* are two possible candidates for a fourth stage in corporate development—a stage that not only emphasizes horizontal over vertical connections between people and groups, but also organizes work around temporary projects in which sophisticated information systems support collaborative activities. According to Greiner, it is likely that this stage of development will have its own crisis as well—a sort of **pressure-cooker crisis**. He predicts that employees in these collaborative organizations will eventually grow emotionally and physically exhausted from the intensity of teamwork and the heavy pressure for innovative solutions.[14]

Blocks to Changing Stages

Corporations often find themselves in difficulty because they are blocked from moving into the next logical stage of development. Blocks to development may be internal (such as lack of resources, lack of ability, or a refusal of top management to delegate decision making to others) or they may be external (such as economic conditions, labor shortages, and lack of market growth). For example, Chandler noted in his study that the successful founder/CEO in one stage was rarely the person who created the new structure to fit the new strategy, and that, as a result, the transition from one stage to another was often painful. This was true of General Motors Corporation under the management of William Durant, Ford Motor Company under Henry Ford I, Polaroid Corporation under Edwin Land, Apple Computer under Steven Jobs, and Hayes Microcomputer Products under Dennis Hayes. (See the 🗷 **Internet Issue** feature for what happened to the company founded by the inventor of the modern modem.)

This difficulty in moving to a new stage is compounded by the founder's tendency to maneuver around the need to delegate by carefully hiring, training, and grooming his or her own team of managers. The team tends to maintain the founder's influence throughout the organization long after the founder is gone. This is what happened at Walt Disney Productions when the family continued to emphasize Walt's policies and plans long after he was dead. Although this may often be an organization's strength, it may also be a weakness—to the extent that the culture supports the status quo and blocks needed change.

ORGANIZATIONAL LIFE CYCLE

Instead of considering stages of development in terms of structure, the organizational life cycle approach places the primary emphasis on the dominant issue facing the corporation. Organizational structure is only a secondary concern. The **organizational life cycle** describes

Internet Issue

The Founder of the Modem Blocks Transition to Stage II

Would there be an Internet without the modem? Although most large organizations now rent digital T1 lines for fast Internet access, most individuals and small business owners still access the World Wide Web using the same type of modem and command set invented by Dennis Hayes.

Dennis Hayes is legendary not only for inventing the personal computer modem, but also for driving his company into bankruptcy—not once but twice. Hayes and retired partner Dale Heatherington founded Hayes Microcomputer Products 20 years ago when they invented a device called the Hayes Smartmodem, which allowed personal computers to communicate with each other through telephone lines via the Hayes Standard AT Command Set. The modem was needed to convert voice analogue data into the digital data needed by computers. Modem sales boomed from $4.8 million in 1981 to $150 million in 1985. When competitors developed low-cost modems, Hayes delayed until the early 1990s to respond with its own low-priced version. Sales and profits plummeted. Hayes lost its dominant position to U.S. Robotics. Management problems mounted. Creditors and potential investors looking into the company's books and operations found them a shambles. According to one investment banker, "The factory was in complete disarray." The company reported its first

loss in 1994, by which time the company had nearly $70 million in debt. In November 1994, Hayes applied for protection from creditors under Chapter 11 of the U.S. Bankruptcy Code.

Under the leadership of its founder, the company underwent a turnaround during 1995. Still in second place with a 9.3% market share of modem sales in North America, Dennis Hayes put his company up for sale. He turned down a bid of $140 million from rival Diamond Multimedia Systems and instead accepted only $30 million for 49% of the company from Asian investors. Although the offer required Mr. Hayes to relinquish the title of CEO, Hayes would still be Chairman of the Board. He explained his decision as deriving from his unwillingness to completely let go of his baby. "I'll be able to have input, through the board and as chairman, that will best use my abilities. What I was concerned about was that someone would come in and . . . slash a part of the company without understanding how it fit in."

The company, renamed Hayes Corporation, continued to suffer losses. On October 9, 1998, the company declared Chapter 11 bankruptcy for the last time. Unable to find further financing to turn things around, the company was forced to sell its brands, manufacturing facilities, and distribution offices to the Canadian firm, Zoom Telephonics ⟨www.zoomtel.com⟩, for $5.3 million. It sold its Web site domain name, Hayes.com, service center, and spare parts inventories to Modem Express ⟨www.modemexpress.com⟩, a seller of refurbished "orphan" products. The company founded by Dennis Hayes now exists only as a division of another company.

Sources: D. McDermott, "Asians Rejuvenate Hayes Microcomputer," *Wall Street Journal* (May 6, 1996), p. A10 plus information gathered from company Web sites and Hayes Company documents within the SEC's Edgar database.

how organizations grow, develop, and eventually decline. It is the organizational equivalent of the product life cycle in marketing. These stages are Birth (Stage I), Growth (Stage II), Maturity (Stage III), Decline (Stage IV), and Death (Stage V). The impact of these stages on corporate strategy and structure is summarized in **Table 8–2**. Note that the first three stages of the organizational life cycle are similar to the three commonly accepted stages of corporate development mentioned previously. The only significant difference is the addition of Decline and Death stages to complete the cycle. Even though a company's strategy may still be sound, its aging structure, culture, and processes may be such that they prevent the strategy from being executed properly. Its core competencies become core rigidities no longer able to adapt to changing conditions—thus the company moves into Decline.[15]

Movement from Growth to Maturity to Decline and finally to Death is not, however, inevitable. A Revival phase may occur sometime during the Maturity or Decline stages. The corporation's life cycle can be extended by managerial and product innovations.[16] Revival often occurs during the implementation of a turnaround strategy. This is what happened at Lionel, the maker of toy electric trains. Founded by Joshua Lionel Cowen in 1900 to make

Table 8–2   Organizational Life Cycle

	Stage I	Stage II	Stage III*	Stage IV	Stage V
Dominant Issue	Birth	Growth	Maturity	Decline	Death
Popular Stategies	Concentration in a niche	Horizontal and vertical growth	Concentric and conglomerate diversification	Profit strategy followed by retrenchment	Liquidation or bankruptcy
Likely Structure	Entrepreneur-dominated	Functional management emphasized	Decentralization into profit or investment centers	Structural surgery	Dismemberment of structure

Note: *An organization may enter a *Revival Phase* either during the Maturity or Decline Stages and thus extend the organization's life.

electrical devices, Lionel came to define the toy "electric train." In 1953, Lionel sold three million engines and freight cars, making it the biggest toy manufacturer in the world. By the mid-1960s, the company was in decline. Electric trains were becoming a historical curiosity. Slot cars and space toys were in demand. Train hobbyists preferred the smaller HO gauge electric train over Lionel's larger train because HO gauge trains were more realistic and used less space. The company barely managed to remain in business over the next three decades. In 1999, Lionel's new owners hired Richard Maddox, a lifelong train enthusiast and an executive close to retirement at toy company Bachmann Industries. Maddox and his executive team worked to update Lionel's trains with new models and the latest technology. He improved the catalogue and established dozens of licensing agreements. "We're trying to excel in things whimsical, clever," says Maddox. The unofficial Lionel historian, Todd Wagner, discovered long-forgotten blueprints of trains from the 1920s and 1930s that were gathering dust in old Lionel storerooms. The company is now using those plans to build more authentic historical models. The reinvigorated company's sales increased 15% in 2000 and were expected to increase by the same amount in 2001.[17]

Unless a company is able to resolve the critical issues facing it in the Decline stage, it is likely to move into Stage V, corporate death—also known as bankruptcy. This is what happened to Montgomery Ward, Pan American Airlines, Macy's Department Stores, Baldwin-United, Eastern Airlines, Colt's Manufacturing, Orion Pictures, and Wheeling-Pittsburgh Steel, as well as to many other firms. So many Internet ventures went bankrupt during 2000 that *Fortune* magazine listed 135 Internet companies on its "Dot-Com Deathwatch."[18] As in the cases of Johns-Manville, International Harvester, and Macy's—all of which went bankrupt—a corporation might nevertheless rise like a phoenix from its own ashes and live again under the same or a different name. The company may be reorganized or liquidated, depending on individual circumstances. For example, Fashionmall.com spent $4,000 for all rights to Boo.com, which had gone bankrupt in May 2000 (and listed on Fortune's Dot-Com Deathwatch), and relaunched it five months later as a high-fashion Web site with links to the hottest stores throughout the world.[19] Unfortunately fewer than 20% of firms entering Chapter 11 bankruptcy in the United States emerge as going concerns; the rest are forced into liquidation.[20]

Few corporations will move through these five stages in order. Some corporations, for example, might never move past Stage II. Others, like General Motors, might go directly from Stage I to Stage III. A large number of entrepreneurial ventures jump from Stage I or II directly into Stage IV or V. Hayes Microcomputer Products, for example, went from the Growth to Decline stage under its founder Dennis Hayes. The key is to be able to identify indications that a firm is in the process of changing stages and to make the appropriate strategic and structural adjustments to ensure that corporate performance is maintained or even improved. This is what the successful Internet auction firm eBay did when it hired Meg Whitman from Hasbro as CEO to professionalize its management and to improve its marketing.

Table 8–3 **Changing Structural Characteristics of Modern Corporations**

Old Organizational Design	New Organizational Design
One large corporation	Minibusiness units and cooperative relationships
Vertical communication	Horizontal communication
Centralized top-down decision making	Decentralized participative decision making
Vertical integration	Outsourcing and virtual organizations
Work/quality teams	Autonomous work teams
Functional work teams	Cross-functional work teams
Minimal training	Extensive training
Specialized job design focused on individual	Value-chain team-focused job design

Source: Adapted from B. Macy and H. Izumi, "Organizational Change, Design, and Work Innovation: A Meta-Analysis of 131 North American Field Studies—1961–1991," in Woodman: *Research in Organizational Change and Development,* Vol. 7, JAI Press (1993), p. 298. Copyright © 1993 with permission from Elsevier Science.

ADVANCED TYPES OF ORGANIZATIONAL STRUCTURES

The basic structures (simple, functional, divisional, and conglomerate) were discussed earlier in **Chapter 4** and summarized under the first three stages of corporate development. A new strategy may require more flexible characteristics than the traditional functional or divisional structure can offer. Today's business organizations are becoming less centralized with a greater use of cross-functional work teams. **Table 8–3** depicts some of the changing structural characteristics of modern corporations. Although many variations and hybrid structures contain these characteristics, two forms stand out: the matrix structure and the network structure.

Matrix Structure

Most organizations find that organizing around either functions (in the functional structure) or around products and geography (in the divisional structure) provides an appropriate organizational structure. The matrix structure, in contrast, may be very appropriate when organizations conclude that neither functional nor divisional forms, even when combined with horizontal linking mechanisms like strategic business units, are right for their situations. In **matrix structures**, functional and product forms are combined simultaneously at the same level of the organization. (See **Figure 8–2**.) Employees have two superiors, a product or project manager and a functional manager. The "home" department—that is, engineering, manufacturing, or sales—is usually functional and is reasonably permanent. People from these functional units are often assigned temporarily to one or more product units or projects. The product units or projects are usually temporary and act like divisions in that they are differentiated on a product–market basis.

Pioneered in the aerospace industry, the matrix structure was developed to combine the stability of the functional structure with the flexibility of the product form. The matrix structure is very useful when the external environment (especially its technological and market aspects) is very complex and changeable. It does, however, produce conflicts revolving around duties, authority, and resource allocation. To the extent that the goals to be achieved are vague and the technology used is poorly understood, a continuous battle for power between product and functional managers is likely. The matrix structure is often found in an organization or within an SBU when the following three conditions exist:

■ Ideas need to be cross-fertilized across projects or products.

■ Resources are scarce.

■ Abilities to process information and to make decisions need to be improved.[21]

Figure 8–2
Matrix and Network Structures

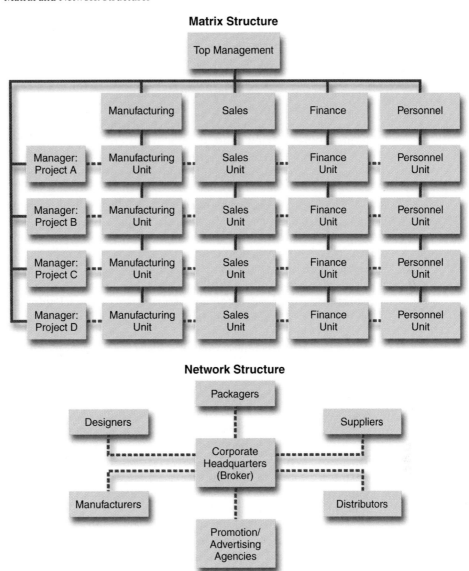

Davis and Lawrence, authorities on the matrix form of organization, propose that *three distinct phases* exist in the development of the matrix structure.[22]

1. **Temporary Cross-Functional Task Forces:** These are initially used when a new product line is being introduced. A project manager is in charge as the key horizontal link. Chrysler has extensively used this approach in product development.

2. **Product/Brand Management:** If the cross-functional task forces become more permanent, the project manager becomes a product or brand manager and a second phase begins. In this arrangement, function is still the primary organizational structure, but product or brand managers act as the integrators of semipermanent products or brands. Considered by many a key to the success of Procter & Gamble, brand management has been widely imitated by other consumer products firms around the world.

3. **Mature Matrix:** The third and final phase of matrix development involves a true dual-authority structure. Both the functional and product structures are permanent. All employees are connected to both a vertical functional superior and a horizontal product manager. Functional and product managers have equal authority and must work well together to resolve disagreements over resources and priorities. Boeing and TRW Systems are example of companies that use a mature matrix.

Network Structure—The Virtual Organization

A newer and somewhat more radical organizational design, the **network structure** (see **Figure 8–2**) is an example of what could be termed a "nonstructure" by its virtual elimination of in-house business functions. Many activities are outsourced. A corporation organized in this manner is often called a **virtual organization** because it is composed of a series of project groups or collaborations linked by constantly changing nonhierarchical, cobweblike networks.[23]

The network structure becomes most useful when the environment of a firm is unstable and is expected to remain so. Under such conditions, there is usually a strong need for innovation and quick response. Instead of having salaried employees, it may contract with people for a specific project or length of time. Long-term contracts with suppliers and distributors replace services that the company could provide for itself through vertical integration. Electronic markets and sophisticated information systems reduce the transaction costs of the marketplace, thus justifying a "buy" over a "make" decision. Rather than being located in a single building or area, an organization's business functions are scattered worldwide. The organization is, in effect, only a shell, with a small headquarters acting as a "broker," electronically connected to some completely owned divisions, partially owned subsidiaries, and other independent companies. In its ultimate form, the network organization is a series of independent firms or business units linked together by computers in an information system that designs, produces, and markets a product or service.[24]

An example of a complete network organization is Just Toys. The New York City company licenses characters like Disney's Little Mermaid, Hanna-Barbera's Flintstones, and Marvel Entertainment's Spiderman to make bendable polyvinyl chloride figures called Bend-Ems. The manufacturing and administrative work for Bend-Ems is contracted out. The company has only 30 employees. If a toy isn't selling well, production can be reduced and shipments stopped almost immediately. It would take Mattel and Hasbro months to react in a similar situation.

Other companies like Nike, Reebok, and Benetton use the network structure in their operations function by subcontracting manufacturing to other companies in low-cost locations around the world. For control purposes, the Italian-based Benetton maintains what it calls an "umbilical cord" by assuring production planning for all its subcontractors, planning materials requirements for them, and providing them with bills of labor and standard prices and costs, as well as technical assistance to make sure their quality is up to Benetton's standards.

The network organization structure provides an organization with increased flexibility and adaptability to cope with rapid technological change and shifting patterns of international trade and competition. It allows a company to concentrate on its distinctive competencies, while gathering efficiencies from other firms who are concentrating their efforts in their areas of expertise. The network does, however, have disadvantages. Some believe that the network is really only a transitional structure because it is inherently unstable and subject to tensions.[25] The availability of numerous potential partners can be a source of trouble. Contracting out functions to separate suppliers/distributors may keep the firm from discovering any synergies by combining activities. If a particular firm overspecializes on only a few functions, it runs the risk of choosing the wrong functions and thus becoming noncompetitive.

Cellular Organization: A New Type of Structure?

Miles and Snow et al. propose that the evolution of organizational forms is leading from the matrix and the network to the cellular. According to them, "a **cellular organization** is composed of cells (self-managing teams, autonomous business units, etc.) that can operate alone but that can interact with other cells to produce a more potent and competent business mechanism." It is this combination of independence and interdependence that allows the cellular organizational form to generate and share the knowledge and expertise to produce continuous innovation. The cellular form includes the dispersed entrepreneurship of the divisional structure, customer responsiveness of the matrix, and self-organizing knowledge and asset sharing of the network.[26] As proposed, the cellular structure is similar to a current trend in industry of using internal joint ventures to temporarily combine specialized expertise and skills within a corporation to accomplish a task individual units alone could not accomplish.[27]

According to the authors of the cellular organization, the impetus for such a new structure is the pressure for a continuous process of innovation in all industries. Each cell has an entrepreneurial responsibility to the larger organization. Beyond knowledge creation and sharing, the cellular form adds value by keeping the firm's total knowledge assets more fully in use than any other type of structure. It is beginning to appear in those firms focused on rapid product and service innovation—providing unique or state-of-the-art offerings.

REENGINEERING AND STRATEGY IMPLEMENTATION

Reengineering is the radical redesign of business processes to achieve major gains in cost, service, or time. It is not in itself a type of structure, but it is an effective way to implement a turnaround strategy.

Reengineering strives to break away from the old rules and procedures that develop and become ingrained in every organization over the years. These may be a combination of policies, rules, and procedures that have never been seriously questioned because they were established years earlier. These may range from "Credit decisions are made by the credit department" to "Local inventory is needed for good customer service." These rules of organization and work design were based on assumptions about technology, people, and organizational goals that may no longer be relevant. Rather than attempting to fix existing problems through minor adjustments and fine-tuning existing processes, the key to reengineering is to ask "If this were a new company, how would we run this place?"

Michael Hammer, who popularized the concept, suggests the following principles for reengineering:

- **Organize around outcomes, not tasks.** Design a person's or a department's job around an objective or outcome instead of a single task or series of tasks.
- **Have those who use the output of the process perform the process.** With computer-based information systems, processes can now be reengineered so that the people who need the result of the process can do it themselves.
- **Subsume information-processing work into the real work that produces the information.** People or departments that produce information can also process it for use instead of just sending raw data to others in the organization to interpret.
- **Treat geographically dispersed resources as though they were centralized.** With modern information systems, companies can provide flexible service locally while keeping the actual resources in a centralized location for coordination purposes.
- **Link parallel activities instead of integrating their results.** Instead of having separate units perform different activities that must eventually come together, have them communicate while they work so that they can do the integrating.

- **Put the decision point where the work is performed, and build control into the process.** The people who do the work should make the decisions and be self-controlling.
- **Capture information once and at the source.** Instead of having each unit develop its own database and information processing activities, the information can be put on a network so that all can access it.[28]

Studies of the performance of reengineering programs show mixed results. Several companies have had success with reengineering. For example, the Mossville Engine Center, a business unit of Caterpillar, Inc., used reengineering to decrease process cycle times by 50%, reduce the number of process steps by 45%, reduce manpower by 8%, and improve cross-divisional interactions and overall employee decision making.[29] One study of North American financial firms found: "The average reengineering project took 15 months, consumed 66 person-months of effort, and delivered cost savings of 24%."[30] In a survey of 782 corporations using reengineering, 75% of the executives said their companies had succeeded in reducing operating expenses and increasing productivity. Although only 47% stated that their companies had succeeded in generating revenue growth and 37% at raising market share, 70% of the respondents stated that their companies planned to use reengineering in the future.[31] Nevertheless, other studies report that anywhere from 50% to 70% of reengineering programs fail to achieve their objectives.[32]

DESIGNING JOBS TO IMPLEMENT STRATEGY

Organizing a company's activities and people to implement strategy involves more than simply redesigning a corporation's overall structure; it also involves redesigning the way jobs are done. With the increasing emphasis on reengineering, many companies are beginning to rethink their work processes with an eye toward phasing unnecessary people and activities out of the process. Process steps that had traditionally been performed sequentially can be improved by performing them concurrently using cross-functional work teams. Harley-Davidson, for example, has managed to reduce total plant employment by 25% while reducing by 50% the time needed to build a motorcycle. Restructuring through fewer people requires broadening the scope of jobs and encouraging teamwork. The design of jobs and subsequent job performance are, therefore, increasingly being considered as sources of competitive advantage.

Job design refers to the design of individual tasks in an attempt to make them more relevant to the company and to the employee(s). To minimize some of the adverse consequences of task specialization, corporations have turned to new job design techniques: **job enlargement** (combining tasks to give a worker more of the same type of duties to perform), **job rotation** (moving workers through several jobs to increase variety), and **job enrichment** (altering the jobs by giving the worker more autonomy and control over activities). The job characteristics model is a good example of job enrichment. (See the **Theory As It Applies** feature.) Although each of these methods has its adherents, no one method seems to work in all situations.

A good example of modern job design is the introduction of team-based production by Corning, Inc., the glass manufacturer, in its Blacksburg, Virginia, plant. With union approval, Corning reduced job classifications from 47 to 4 to enable production workers to rotate jobs after learning new skills. The workers were divided into 14-member teams that, in effect, managed themselves. The plant had only two levels of management: Plant Manager Robert Hoover and two line leaders who only advised the teams. Employees worked demanding 12½ hour shifts, alternating three-day and four-day weeks. The teams made managerial decisions, imposed discipline on fellow workers, and were required to learn three "skill modules" within two years or else lose their jobs. As a result of this new job design, a Blacksburg team, made up of workers with interchangeable skills, can retool a line to produce a different type of filter in only 10 minutes—six times faster than workers in a traditionally designed filter plant. The Blacksburg plant earned

Theory As It Applies

Designing Jobs with the Job Characteristics Model

The **job characteristics model** is an advanced approach to job design based on the belief that tasks can be described in terms of certain objective characteristics and that these characteristics affect employee motivation. In order for the job to be motivating, (1) the worker needs to feel a sense of responsibility, feel the task to be meaningful, and receive useful feedback on his or her performance; and (2) the job has to satisfy needs that are important to the worker. The model proposes that managers follow five principles for redesigning work:

1. Combine tasks to increase task variety and to enable workers to identify with what they are doing.

2. Form natural work units to make a worker more responsible and accountable for the performance of the job.

3. Establish client relationships so the worker will know what performance is required and why.

4. Vertically load the job by giving workers increased authority and responsibility over their activities.

5. Open feedback channels by providing workers with information on how they are performing.

Research supports the job characteristics model as a way to improve job performance through job enrichment. Although there are several other approaches to job design, practicing managers seem increasingly to follow the prescriptions of this model as a way of improving productivity and product quality.

Sources: J. R. Hackman and G. R. Oldham, *Work Redesign* (Reading, MA: Addison-Wesley, 1980), pp. 135–141; G. Johns, J. L. Xie, and Y. Fang, "Mediating and Moderating Effects in Job Design," *Journal of Management* (December 1992), pp. 657–676; R. W. Griffin, "Effects of Work Redesign on Employee Perceptions, Attitudes, and Behaviors: A Long-Term Investigation," *Academy of Management Journal* (June 1991), pp. 425–435.

a $2 million profit in its first eight months of production, instead of losing the $2.3 million projected for the start-up period. The plant performed so well that Corning's top management acted to convert the company's 27 other factories to team-based production.[33]

8.5 International Issues in Strategy Implementation

An international company is one that engages in any combination of activities, from exporting/importing to full-scale manufacturing, in foreign countries. The **multinational corporation (MNC)**, in contrast, is a highly developed international company with a deep involvement throughout the world, plus a worldwide perspective in its management and decision making. For a multinational corporation to be considered global, it must manage its worldwide operations as if they were totally interconnected. This approach works best when the industry has moved from being *multidomestic* (each country's industry is essentially separate from the same industry in other countries; an example is retailing) to *global* (each country is a part of one worldwide industry; an example is consumer electronics).

Strategic alliances, such as joint ventures and licensing agreements, between a multinational company (MNC) and a local partner in a host country are becoming increasingly popular as a means by which a corporation can gain entry into other countries, especially less developed countries. The key to the successful implementation of these strategies is the selection of the local partner. Each party needs to assess not only the strategic fit of each company's project strategy, but also the fit of each company's respective resources. A successful joint venture may require as much as two years of prior contacts between both parties.

The design of an organization's structure is strongly affected by the company's stage of development in international activities and the types of industries in which the company is involved. The issue of centralization versus decentralization becomes especially important for a multinational corporation operating in both multidomestic and global industries.

STAGES OF INTERNATIONAL DEVELOPMENT

Corporations operating internationally tend to evolve through five common stages, both in their relationships with widely dispersed geographic markets and in the manner in which they structure their operations and programs. These **stages of international development** are:

- **Stage 1 (Domestic Company):** The primarily domestic company exports some of its products through local dealers and distributors in the foreign countries. The impact on the organization's structure is minimal because an export department at corporate headquarters handles everything.

- **Stage 2 (Domestic Company with Export Division):** Success in Stage 1 leads the company to establish its own sales company with offices in other countries to eliminate the middlemen and to better control marketing. Because exports have now become more important, the company establishes an export division to oversee foreign sales offices.

- **Stage 3 (Primarily Domestic Company with International Division):** Success in earlier stages leads the company to establish manufacturing facilities in addition to sales and service offices in key countries. The company now adds an international division with responsibilities for most of the business functions conducted in other countries.

- **Stage 4 (Multinational Corporation with Multidomestic Emphasis):** Now a full-fledged multinational corporation, the company increases its investments in other countries. The company establishes a local operating division or company in the host country, such as Ford of Britain, to better serve the market. The product line is expanded, and local manufacturing capacity is established. Managerial functions (product development, finance, marketing, and so on) are organized locally. Over time, the parent company acquires other related businesses, broadening the base of the local operating division. As the subsidiary in the host country successfully develops a strong regional presence, it achieves greater autonomy and self-sufficiency. The operations in each country are, nevertheless, managed separately as if each is a domestic company.

- **Stage 5 (Multinational Corporation with Global Emphasis):** The most successful multinational corporations move into a fifth stage in which they have worldwide personnel, R&D, and financing strategies. Typically operating in a global industry, the MNC denationalizes its operations and plans product design, manufacturing, and marketing around worldwide considerations. Global considerations now dominate organizational design. The global MNC structures itself in a matrix form around some combination of geographic areas, product lines, and functions. All managers are now responsible for dealing with international as well as domestic issues.

Research provides some support for the stages of international development concept, but it does not necessarily support the preceding sequence of stages. For example, a company may initiate production and sales in multiple countries without having gone through the steps of exporting or having local sales subsidiaries. In addition, any one corporation can be at different stages simultaneously with different products in different markets at different levels. Firms may also leapfrog across stages to a global emphasis. Developments in information technology are changing the way business is being done internationally. See the 🌐 **Global Issue** feature to see how FedEx is using its expertise in information technology to help customers sidestep the building of a costly logistical infrastructure to take advantage of global markets. Nevertheless the stages concept provides a useful way to illustrate some of the structural changes corporations undergo when they increase their involvement in international activities.

CENTRALIZATION VERSUS DECENTRALIZATION

A basic dilemma a multinational corporation faces is how to organize authority centrally so that it operates as a vast interlocking system that achieves synergy, and at the same time decentralize authority so that local managers can make the decisions necessary to meet the demands

Global Issue

FedEx Provides the Infrastructure for Companies to Become Global

Globalization is becoming a permanent and irreversible part of economic life. A key reason is the use of information system technology to connect operations around the world. The Internet via e-mail, chat rooms, and Web sites in multiple languages provides instantaneous communication 24 hours a day. *Enterprise resource planning (ERP) systems*, such as SAP's R/3 software, can manage all of a corporation's internal operations (including international) in a single powerful network. ERP is able to unite customers and suppliers so that they can transact business with each other online. Retailers like Wal-Mart are going global and are pressuring suppliers to have global sourcing and pricing.

FedEx is a key force behind globalization, but not just because it delivers 2.8 million packages in 210 countries each day. It is using information technology to remake its clients' worldwide supply and distribution systems. FedEx is becoming the global logistical backbone for many of its customers. Using its technology, FedEx manages its customers' worldwide inventory, warehousing, distribution, and customs clearance. It can help a customer assemble and make products by securing supplies globally in a reliable and cost-effective manner. It is able to do this because it is able to electronically track any of its shipments at any point in time. This provides FedEx with a distinctive competency, which it is able to use to provide valuable service to others. With a guarantee of on-time delivery, customers are able to reduce costly inventories and institute just-in-time systems. According to CEO and Chairman Frederick Smith, "We decided years ago that the most important element in this business is information technology, and we have geared everything to that philosophy—recruitment, training, and compensation. Fail-safe precision is the key to it all."

Dell Computer Corporation eliminated its costly distribution infrastructure in favor of using FedEx to coordinate the assembly of computers and their customs clearance and shipping from a manufacturing center in Malaysia to customers in Japan and Taiwan. By managing National Semiconductor Corporation's global warehousing and distribution systems, FedEx was able to reduce its customer's total costs of logistics from 3% to 1.9% of revenues.

Source: J. E. Garten, "Why the Global Economy Is Here to Stay," *Business Week* (March 23, 1998), p. 21. By special permission, copyright © 1998 by The McGraw-Hill Companies, Inc.

of the local market or host government.[34] To deal with this problem, MNCs tend to structure themselves either along product groups or geographic areas. They may even combine both in a matrix structure—the design chosen by 3M Corporation and Asea Brown Boveri (ABB), among others.[35] One side of 3M's matrix represents the company's product divisions; the other side includes the company's international country and regional subsidiaries.

Two examples of the usual international structures are Nestlé and American Cyanamid. Nestlé's structure is one in which significant power and authority have been decentralized to geographic entities. This structure is similar to that depicted in **Figure 8–3**, in which each geographic set of operating companies has a different group of products. In contrast, American Cyanamid has a series of centralized product groups with worldwide responsibilities. To depict Cyanamid's structure, the geographical entities in **Figure 8–3** would have to be replaced by product groups or strategic business units.

The **product-group structure** of American Cyanamid enables the company to introduce and manage a similar line of products around the world. This enables the corporation to centralize decision making along product lines and to reduce costs. The **geographic-area structure** of Nestlé, in contrast, allows the company to tailor products to regional differences and to achieve regional coordination. This decentralizes decision making to the local subsidiaries. As industries move from being multidomestic to more globally integrated, multinational corporations are increasingly switching from the geographic-area to the product-group structure. Texaco, Inc., for example, changed to a product-group structure by consolidating its international, U.S., and new business opportunities under each line of business at its White Plains,

Figure 8–3
Geographic Area Structure for a Multinational Corporation

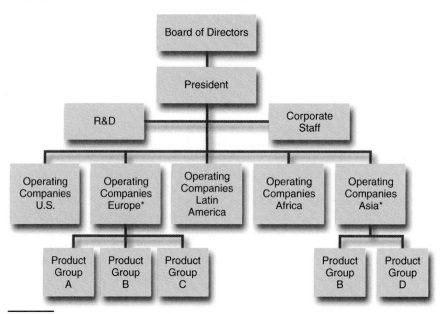

*Note: Because of space limitations, product groups for only Europe and Asia are shown here.

New York, headquarters. According to Chairman Peter Bijur, "By placing groups which will perform similar work in the same location, they will be able to share information, ideas, and resources more readily—and move critical information throughout the organization."[36]

Simultaneous pressures for decentralization to be locally responsive and centralization to be maximally efficient are causing interesting structural adjustments in most large corporations. Companies are attempting to decentralize those operations that are culturally oriented and closest to the customers—manufacturing, marketing, and human resources. At the same time, the companies are consolidating less visible internal functions, such as research and development, finance, and information systems, where there can be significant economies of scale.

8.6 Impact of the Internet on Organizational Design and Structure

The Cluetrain Manifesto written by Levine, Locke, Searls, and Weinberger, proposes 95 theses about how the Internet is changing the world and the way it does business. Many of today's companies are still stuck in traditional, conservative mindsets, creating virtual barriers between themselves and the people they hope to reach. The book argues that the Internet has "something special" about it, which the **Cluetrain Manifesto** calls "voice" that sets it apart from any other medium. The Internet connects people to each other allowing them to have conversations and comment on things in a forum that joins a wealth of knowledge from different resources. The **hyperlinked organization** is a new type of developing organization, which provides all employees easy access to one another and to people outside the organization in a rich variety of ways from e-mail to personal Web sites. Workers and markets speak the same language.

According to Levine et al., bringing the Internet into a corporation changes things in unpredictable ways. The new hyperlinked organization contains several major themes.

- **Hyperlinked and Decentralized:** There is no central authority on the Web; it consists of hundreds of millions of pages linked together by the author of each individual page. Organizations become hyperlinked when they decentralize their teams, committees, task forces, and individuals. Official structure is set aside in favor of networks of trusted colleagues.

- **Hypertime:** With the Internet, people can look for information and connections at their own pace and under their own control any time of the day or week without having to search for a parking place and obtaining a library card. In a hyperlinked organization, schedules are driven locally, not centrally, created by local groups and individuals. Traditional deadlines are replaced by a team's motivation to help a customer or coworker.

- **Directly Accessible:** The Internet provides direct access to everyone on the planet to every piece of information made available. Hyperlinked organizations replace the old mindset of hoarding information with new, wide-open policies that encourage collaboration over intranets, moving individual tasks to group tasks, and bringing in people because they have the necessary skills and shared interests, not because of their position in the hierarchy.

- **Full of Rich Data:** The currency of the Internet is pages of information. The various types of Internet communication (especially e-mail) allow the hyperlinked organization to link staff, management, and customers who can tell stories, create valuable narratives, and explore the many ways to translate ideas using each participant's distinctive voice.

- **Broken:** Because the Internet is a large, complex network controlled by no one, it will always be somewhat "broken." Any search of the Internet is bound to find many dead links and dead ends (those "sticky" sites that refuse to allow the visitor to use the browser to go back to a previous Web page). While the traditional hierarchy demanded predictability and consistency, the hyperlinked organization looks for innovation and expects mistakes and slightly broken systems and structures, which are always in a state of repair and rebuilding.

- **Borderless:** Traditional organizations and networks were concerned as much with security as with access. They were usually very clear where one department ended and another began—even within the same company. People had access to important information only if they "had a need to know." In contrast, the Internet was designed so that one page could be linked to another without obtaining the author's permission. Because of the way links work, it is often hard to tell if one is still on the same Web page or on another page located in another part of the world. Hyperlinked organizations accept that borders between units are permeable and changing. Intranets and extranets allow companies to share previously unknown processes with customers and to solicit ideas and suggestions from them. They also allow internal communications to flow easier, replacing closed meeting rooms with e-mail discussion groups and group intranet sites. As the hurdles to membership lower, the boundaries begin to blur.[37]

According to *The Cluetrain Manifesto*, the structures of corporations must change if they are to be effective in a changing, global, Internet-linked environment. This suggests that traditional organization structures must adopt more of the characteristics of the matrix, the network, and the cellular forms of organization.

Projections for the 21st Century

- From 1994 to 2010, the number of automobiles produced in the developed countries will increase from 20 million to 30 million vehicles.

- From 1994 to 2010, the number of automobiles produced in the emerging market nations will jump from 8 million to 30 million vehicles.[38]

Discussion Questions

1. How should a corporation attempt to achieve synergy among functions and business units?

2. How should an owner-manager prepare a company for its movement from Stage I to Stage II?

3. How can a corporation keep from sliding into the Decline stage of the organizational life cycle?

4. Is reengineering just another management fad or does it offer something of lasting value?

5. How is the cellular organization different from the network structure?

Strategic Practice Exercise

The Synergy Game

YOLANDA SARASON AND CATHERINE BANBURY

SETUP
Put three to five chairs on either side of a room facing each other in the front of the class. Put a table in the middle with a bell in the middle of the table.

PROCEDURE
The instructor/moderator divides the class into teams of three to five people. Each team selects a name for itself. The instructor/moderator lists the team names on the board. The first two teams come to the front and sit in the chairs facing each other. The instructor/moderator reads a list of products or services being provided by an actual company. The winning team must identify (1) possible sources of synergy and (2) the actual company being described. For example, if the products/services listed are family restaurants, airline catering, hotels, and retirement centers, the synergy is **standardized food service and hospitality settings** and the company is **The Marriott Corporation**. The first team to successfully name the company *and* the synergy wins the round.

After one practice session, the game begins. Each of the teams is free to discuss the question with other team members. Once one of the two teams thinks that it has the answer to both parts of the question, it must be the first to ring the bell in order to announce their answer. If it gives the correct answer, it is deemed the winner of round one. Both parts of the answer must be given for a team to have the correct answer. If a team correctly provides only one part, that answer is still wrong—no partial credit. The instructor/moderator does not say which part of the answer, if either,

was correct. The second team then has the opportunity to state the answer. If the second team is wrong, both teams may try once more. If neither chooses to try again, the instructor/moderator may (1) declare no round winner and both teams sit down, (2) allow the next two teams to provide the answer to round one, or (3) go on to the next round with the same two teams. Two new teams then come to the front for the next round. Once all groups have played once, the winning teams play each other. Rounds continue until there is a grand champion. The instructor should provide a suitable prize, such as candy bars, for the winning team.

Source: This exercise was developed by Professors Yolanda Sarason of Colorado State University and Catherine Banbury of St. Mary's College and Purdue University and presented at the Organizational Behavior Teaching Conference, June 1999. Copyright © 1999 by Yolanda Sarason and Catherine Banbury. Adapted with permission.

Note from Wheelen and Hunger
The *Instructors' Manual* for this book contains a list of products and services with their synergy and the name of the company. In case your instructor does not use this exercise, try the following examples.

1. Motorcycles, autos, lawn mowers, generators

2. Athletic footwear, Rockport shoes, Greg Norman clothing, sportswear

Did you guess the company providing these products/services and the synergy obtained? The answers are printed here upside down:

1. *Engine technology by Honda*

2. *Marketing and distribution for athletic conscious by Reebok*

Key Terms

budget (p. 196)
cellular organization (p. 207)
Cluetrain Manifesto (p. 212)
crisis of autonomy (p. 200)
crisis of control (p. 200)
crisis of leadership (p. 200)
geographic-area structure (p. 211)
hyperlinked organization (p. 212)
job characteristics model (p. 209)
job design (p. 208)
job enlargement (p. 208)
job enrichment (p. 208)

job rotation (p. 208)
matrix of change (p. 194)
matrix structure (p. 204)
multinational corporation (MNC) (p. 209)
network structure (p. 206)
organizational life cycle (p. 201)
pressure-cooker crisis (p. 201)
procedures (p. 196)
product-group structure (p. 211)
program (p. 194)
red tape crises (p. 201)

reengineering (p. 207)
stages of corporate development (p. 198)
stages of international development (p. 210)
standard operating procedures (SOPs) (p. 196)
strategy implementation (p. 192)
structure follows strategy (p. 197)
synergy (p. 196)
virtual organization (p. 206)

Notes

1. C. Edwards, "Federated's Fingerhut Fiasco," *Business Week* (December 18, 2000), pp. 198–202.
2. J. W. Gadella, "Avoiding Expensive Mistakes in Capital Investment," *Long Range Planning* (April 1994), pp. 103–110; B. Voss, "World Market Is Not for Everyone," *Journal of Business Strategy* (July/August 1993), p. 4.
3. J. I. Rigdon, "The Integration Game," *Red Herring* (July 2000), pp. 356–366.
4. L. D. Alexander, "Strategy Implementation: Nature of the Problem," *International Review of Strategic Management*, Vol. 2, No. 1, edited by D. E. Hussey (New York: John Wiley & Sons, 1991), pp. 73–113.
5. J. A. Byrne, "PepsiCo's New Formula," *Business Week* (April 10, 2000), pp. 172–184.
6. E. Brynjolfsson, A. A. Renshaw, and M. Van Alstyne, "The Matrix of Change," *Sloan Management Review* (Winter 1997), pp. 37–54.
7. M. Goold and A. Campbell, "Desperately Seeking Synergy," *Harvard Business Review* (September–October 1998), pp. 131–143.
8. A. D. Chandler, *Strategy and Structure* (Cambridge, MA: MIT Press, 1962).
9. A. P. Sloan, Jr., *My Years with General Motors* (Garden City, NY: Doubleday, 1964).
10. T. L. Amburgey and T. Dacin, "As the Left Foot Follows the Right? The Dynamics of Strategic and Structural Change," *Academy of Management Journal* (December 1994), pp. 1427–1452; M. Ollinger, "The Limits of Growth of the Multidivisional Firm: A Case Study of the U.S. Oil Industry from 1930–90," *Strategic Management Journal* (September 1994), pp. 503–520.
11. D. F. Jennings and S. L. Seaman, "High and Low Levels of Organizational Adaptation: An Empirical Analysis of Strategy, Structure, and Performance," *Strategic Management Journal* (July 1994), pp. 459–475; L. Donaldson, "The Normal Science of Structured Contingency Theory," in *Handbook of Organization Studies*, edited by S. R. Clegg, C. Hardy, and W. R. Nord (London: Sage Publications, 1996), pp. 57–76.
12. A. K. Gupta, "SBU Strategies, Corporate-SBU Relations, and SBU Effectiveness in Strategy Implementation," *Academy of Management Journal* (September 1987), pp. 477–500.
13. L. E. Greiner, "Evolution and Revolution as Organizations Grow," *Harvard Business Review* (May–June 1998), pp. 55–67. This is an updated version of Greiner's classic 1972 article.

14. Greiner, p. 64. Although Greiner simply labeled this as the "?" crisis, the term "pressure-cooker" seems apt.
15. W. P. Barnett, "The Dynamics of Competitive Intensity," *Administrative Science Quarterly* (March 1997), pp. 128–160; D. Miller, *The Icarus Paradox: How Exceptional Companies Bring About Their Own Downfall* (New York: Harper Business, 1990).
16. D. Miller and P. H. Friesen, "A Longitudinal Study of the Corporate Life Cycle," *Management Science* (October 1984), pp. 1161–1183.
17. J. Green, "The Toy-Train Company that Thinks It Can," *Business Week* (December 4, 2000), pp. 64–69.
18. G. David, F. Garcia, and I. Gashurov, "Welcome to the Valley of the Damned.Com," *Fortune* (January 22, 2001), p. 52.
19. "First Dot-Com Casualty Is Back," *The (Ames) Tribune* (November 29, 2000), p. B7.
20. H. Tavakolian, "Bankruptcy: An Emerging Corporate Strategy," *SAM Advanced Management Journal* (Spring 1995), p. 19.
21. L. G. Hrebiniak and W. F. Joyce, *Implementing Strategy* (New York: Macmillan, 1984), pp. 85–86.
22. S. M. Davis and P. R. Lawrence, *Matrix* (Reading, MA: Addison-Wesley, 1977), pp. 11–24.
23. J. G. March, "The Future Disposable Organizations and the Rigidities of Imagination," *Organization* (August/November 1995), p. 434.
24. M. P. Koza and A. Y. Lewin, "The Coevolution of Network Alliances: A Longitudinal Analysis of an International Professional Service Network," *Organization Science* (September/October 1999), pp. 638–653.
25. For more information on managing a network organization, see G. Lorenzoni and C. Baden-Fuller, "Creating a Strategic Center to Manage a Web of Partners," *California Management Review* (Spring 1995), pp. 146–163.
26. R. E. Miles, C. C. Snow, J. A. Mathews, G. Miles, and H. J. Coleman, Jr., "Organizing in the Knowledge Age: Anticipating the Cellular Form," *Academy of Management Executive* (November 1997), pp. 7–24.
27. J. Naylor and M. Lewis, "Internal Alliances: Using Joint Ventures in a Diversified Company," *Long Range Planning* (October 1997), pp. 678–688.
28. Summarized from M. Hammer, "Reengineering Work: Don't Automate, Obliterate," *Harvard Business Review* (July–August 1990), pp. 104–112.

29. D. Paper, "BPR: Creating the Conditions for Success," *Long Range Planning* (June 1998), pp. 426–435.

30. S. Drew, "BPR in Financial Services: Factors for Success," *Long Range Planning* (October 1994), pp. 25–41.

31. "Do as I Say, Not as I Do," *Journal of Business Strategy* (May/June 1997), pp. 3–4.

32. K. Grint, Reengineering History: Social Resonances and Business Process Reengineering," *Organization* ((July 1994), pp. 179–201; A. Kleiner, "Revisiting Reengineering," *Strategy + Business* (3rd Quarter 2000), pp. 27–31.

33. J. Hoerr, "Sharpening Minds for a Competitive Edge," *Business Week* (December 17, 1990), pp. 72–78.

34. J. H. Taggart, "Strategy Shifts in MNC Subsidiaries," *Strategic Management Journal* (July 1998), pp. 663–681.

35. C. A. Bartlett and S. Ghoshal, "Beyond the M-Form: Toward a Managerial Theory of the Firm," *Strategic Management Journal* (Winter 1993), pp. 23–46.

36. A. Sullivan, "Texaco Revamps Executive Structure to Focus on Business, Not Geography," *Wall Street Journal* (October 3, 1996), p. B15.

37. R. Levine, C. Locke, D. Searls, and D. Weinberger, *The Cluetrain Manifesto* (Cambridge, MA: Perseus Books, 2000). Originally posted on a Web site ⟨www.cluetrain.com⟩, *The Cluetrain Manifesto* has now reached the status of a cult book within the Internet community.

38. J. Warner, "21st Century Capitalism: Snapshot of the Next Century," *Business Week* (November 18, 1994), p. 194.

chapter 9

Strategy Implementation: Staffing and Directing

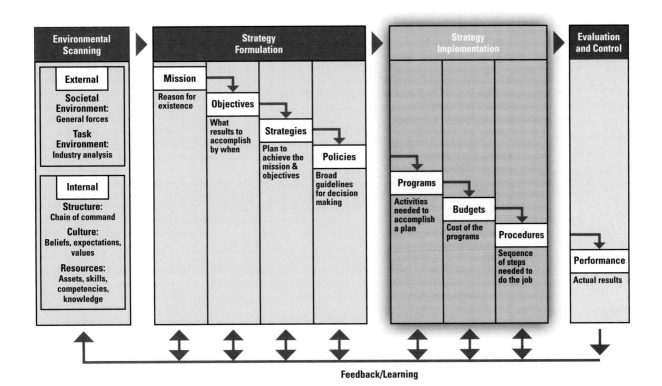

Feedback/Learning

Have you heard of Enterprise Rent-A-Car? You won't find it at the airport with Hertz, Avis, or National car rental operations. Yet Enterprise owns more cars and operates in more locations than Hertz. The company accounts for over 20% of the $15 billion per year U.S. car rental market compared to 17% for Hertz and 12% for Avis. In ignoring the highly competitive airport market, Enterprise has chosen a differentiation competitive strategy by marketing to people in need of a spare car. Instead of locating many cars at a few high-priced locations at airports, Enterprise sets up inexpensive offices throughout metropolitan areas. As a result, cars are rented for 30% less than they cost at airports. As soon as one branch office grows to about 150 cars, the company opens another rental office a few miles away. People are increasingly renting from Enterprise even when their current car works fine. According to CEO Andy

Taylor, "We call it a 'virtual car.' Small-business people who have to pick up clients call us when they want something better than their own car." Why is Enterprise able to follow this competitive strategy so successfully without attracting Hertz and Avis into its market?

The secret to Enterprise's success is its well-executed strategy implementation. Clearly laid out programs, budgets, and procedures support the company's competitive strategy by making Enterprise stand out in the mind of the consumer. When a new rental office opens, employees spend time developing relationships with the service managers of every auto dealership and body shop in the area. Enterprise employees bring pizza and doughnuts to workers at the auto garages across the country. Enterprise forms agreements with dealers to provide replacements for cars brought in for service. At major accounts, the company actually staffs an office at the dealership and has cars parked outside so customers don't have to go to an Enterprise office to complete paperwork.

One key to implementation at Enterprise is staffing—through hiring and promoting a certain kind of person. Virtually every Enterprise employee is a college graduate, usually from the bottom half of the class. According to COO Donald Ross, "We hire from the half of the college class that makes the upper half possible. We want athletes, fraternity types—especially fraternity presidents and social directors. People people." These new employees begin as management trainees in the $20,000 to $25,000 salary range. Instead of regular raises, their pay is tied to branch office profits.

Another key to implementation at Enterprise is leading—through specifying clear performance objectives and promoting a team-oriented corporate culture. The company stresses promotion from within. Every Enterprise employee, including top executives, starts at the bottom. As a result, a bond of shared experience connects all employees and managers. To reinforce a cohesive culture of camaraderie, senior executives routinely do "grunt work" at branch offices. Even Andy Taylor, the CEO, joins the work. "We were visiting an office in Berkeley and it was mobbed, so I started cleaning cars," says Taylor. "As it was happening, I wondered if it was a good use of my time, but the effect on morale was tremendous." Because the financial results of every branch office and every region are available to all, the collegial culture stimulates good-natured competition. "We're this close to beating out Middlesex," grins Woody Erhardt, an area manager in New Jersey. "I want to pound them into the ground. If they lose, they have to throw a party for us, and we get to decide what they wear."[1]

This example from Enterprise Rent-A-Car illustrates how a strategy must be implemented with carefully considered programs in order to succeed. This chapter discusses strategy implementation in terms of staffing and leading. *Staffing* focuses on the selection and use of employees. *Leading* emphasizes the use of programs to better align employee interests and attitudes with a new strategy.

9.1 Staffing

The implementation of new strategies and policies often calls for new human resource management priorities and a different use of personnel. Such **staffing** issues can involve hiring new people with new skills, firing people with inappropriate or substandard skills, and/or training existing employees to learn new skills.

If growth strategies are to be implemented, new people may need to be hired and trained. Experienced people with the necessary skills need to be found for promotion to newly created managerial positions. When a corporation follows a growth through acquisition strategy, it may find that it needs to replace several managers in the acquired company. The percentage of an acquired company's top management team that either quit or was asked to leave is around 25% after the first year, 35% after the second year, 48% after the third year, 55% after the fourth year, and 61% after five years.[2] It is one thing to lose excess employees after a merger, but it is something else to lose highly skilled people who are difficult to replace. To deal with problems such as this, some companies are appointing special integration managers to shepherd companies through the implementation process of an acquisition. To be a successful integration manager, a person should have (1) a deep knowledge of the acquiring company, (2) a flexible management style, (3) an ability to work in cross-functional project teams, (4) a willingness to work independently, and (5) sufficient emotional and cultural intelligence to work well with people from all backgrounds.[3]

If a corporation adopts a retrenchment strategy, however, a large number of people may need to be laid off or fired; and top management, as well as the divisional managers, needs to specify the criteria to be used in making these personnel decisions. Should employees be fired on the basis of low seniority or on the basis of poor performance? Sometimes corporations find it easier to close or sell off an entire division than to choose which individuals to fire.

STAFFING FOLLOWS STRATEGY

As in the case of structure, staffing requirements are likely to follow a change in strategy. For example, promotions should be based not only on current job performance, but also on whether a person has the skills and abilities to do what is needed to implement the new strategy.

Hiring and Training Requirements Change

Having formulated a new strategy, a corporation may find that it needs to either hire different people or retrain current employees to implement the new strategy. Consider the introduction of team-based production at Corning's filter plant mentioned earlier in **Chapter 8**. Employee selection and training were crucial to the success of the new manufacturing strategy. Plant Manager Robert Hoover sorted through 8,000 job applications before hiring 150 people with the best problem-solving ability and a willingness to work in a team setting. Those selected received extensive training in technical and interpersonal skills. During the first year of production, 25% of all hours worked were devoted to training at a cost of $750,000.[4]

One way to implement a company's business strategy, such as overall low cost, is through training and development. A study of 51 corporations in the United Kingdom found that 71% of "leading" companies rated staff learning and training as important or very important compared to 62% of the other companies.[5] Another study of 155 U.S. manufacturing firms revealed that those with training programs had 19% higher productivity than did those without such a program. Another study found that a doubling of formal training per employee resulted in a 7% reduction in scrap.[6] Training is especially important for a differentiation strategy emphasizing quality or customer service. For example, Motorola, with annual sales of $17 billion, spends 4% of its payroll on training by providing at least 40 hours of training a year to each employee. There is a very strong connection between strategy and training at Motorola. For example, after setting a goal to reduce product development cycle time, Motorola created a two-week course to teach its employees how to accomplish that goal. It brought together marketing, product development, and manufacturing managers to create an action learning format in which the managers worked together instead of separately. The company is especially concerned with attaining the highest quality possible in all its operations. Realizing that it couldn't hit quality targets with poor parts, Motorola developed a class for its suppliers on statistical process control. The company estimates that every $1 it spends on training delivers $30 in productivity gains within three years.[7]

Training is also important when implementing a retrenchment strategy. As suggested earlier, successful downsizing means that the company has to invest in its remaining employees. General Electric's Aircraft Engine Group used training to maintain its share of the market even though it had cut its workforce from 42,000 to 33,000 in the 1990s.[8]

Matching the Manager to the Strategy

The most appropriate type of general manager needed to effectively implement a new corporate or business strategy depends on the desired strategic direction of that firm or business unit. Executives with a particular mix of skills and experiences may be classified as an **executive type** and paired with a specific corporate strategy. For example, a corporation following a concentration strategy emphasizing vertical or horizontal growth would probably want an aggressive new chief executive with a great deal of experience in that particular industry—a *dynamic industry expert*. A diversification strategy, in contrast, might call for someone with an analytical mind who is highly knowledgeable in other industries and can manage diverse product lines—an *analytical portfolio manager*. A corporation choosing to follow a stability strategy would probably want as its CEO a *cautious profit planner*, a person with a conservative style, a production or engineering background, and experience with controlling budgets, capital expenditures, inventories, and standardization procedures. Weak companies in a relatively attractive industry tend to turn to a type of challenge-oriented executive known as the **turnaround specialist** to save the company. Albert J. Dunlap, known as "Chainsaw Al" or "Rambo in Pinstripes," was a premier example of a turnaround "artist" who saved troubled corporations by trimming expenses and downsizing the workforce. After restoring Scott Paper to profitability, Dunlap successfully did the same to Sunbeam Corporation. Unfortunately, Dunlap was unable to build a company once he had turned it around, so he chose to acquire three companies—each showing losses and needing to be "turned around." Dunlap was soon fired by the board in favor of an executive with a less mercurial management style who could regain the confidence of both investors and the employees.[9]

If a company cannot be saved, a *professional liquidator* might be called on by a bankruptcy court to close the firm and liquidate its assets. This is what happened to Montgomery Ward, Inc., the nation's first catalogue retailer, which closed its stores for good in 2001 after declaring bankruptcy for the second time. Research tends to support the conclusion that as a firm's environment changes, it tends to change the type of top executive to implement a new strategy.[10] For example, during the 1990s when the emphasis was on growth in a company's core products/services, the most desired background for a U.S. CEO was either in marketing or international, contrasted with finance during the 1980s when conglomerate diversification was popular.[11]

This approach is in agreement with Chandler, who proposed in **Chapter 8** that the most appropriate CEO of a company changes as a firm moves from one stage of development to another. Because priorities certainly change over an organization's life, successful corporations need to select managers who have skills and characteristics appropriate to the organization's particular stage of development and position in its life cycle. For example, founders of firms tend to have functional backgrounds in technological specialties; whereas successors tend to have backgrounds in marketing and administration.[12] A change in the environment leading to a change in a company's strategy also leads to a change in the top management team. For example, a change in the U.S. utility industry's environment in 1992 supporting internally focused, efficiency-oriented strategies, led to the top management teams being dominated by older managers with longer company and industry tenure with efficiency-oriented backgrounds in operations, engineering, and accounting.[13]

Other studies have found a link between the type of CEO and the firm's overall strategic type. (Strategic types were presented in **Chapter 3**.) For example, successful prospector firms tend to be headed by CEOs from research/engineering and general management backgrounds. High performance defenders tend to have CEOs with accounting/finance, manufacturing/production, and general management experience. Analyzers tend to have CEOs with a marketing/sales background.[14]

A study of 173 firms over a 25-year period revealed that CEOs in these companies tended to have the same functional specialization as the former CEO, especially when the past CEO's strategy continued to be successful. This may be a pattern for successful corporations.[15] In particular, it explains why so many prosperous companies tend to recruit their top executives from one particular area. At Procter & Gamble (a good example of an analyzer firm), the route to the CEO's position has traditionally been through brand management with a strong emphasis on marketing—and more recently international experience. In other firms, the route may be through manufacturing, marketing, accounting, or finance, depending on what the corporation has always considered its key area (and its overall strategic orientation).

SELECTION AND MANAGEMENT DEVELOPMENT

Selection and development are important not only to ensure that people with the right mix of skills and experiences are initially hired, but also to help them grow on the job so that they might be prepared for future promotions.

Executive Succession: Insiders Versus Outsiders

Executive succession is the process of replacing a key top manager. Given that two-thirds of all major corporations worldwide have replaced their CEO at least once between 1995 and 2000, it is important that the firm plan for this eventuality.[16] It is especially important for a company that usually promotes from within to prepare its current managers for promotion. Companies known for being excellent training grounds for executive talent are AlliedSignal, Bain & Company, Bankers Trust, Bristol Myers Squibb, Cititcorp, General Electric, Hewlett-Packard, McDonalds, McKinsey & Company, Microsoft, Nike, PepsiCo, Pfizer, and Procter & Gamble. For example, approximately 10,000 of GE's 276,000 employees take at least one class at the company's famous Leadership Development Center in Crotonville, New York.[17] Some of the best practices for top management succession are encouraging boards to help the CEO create a succession plan, identifying succession candidates below the top layer, measuring internal candidates against outside candidates to ensure the development of a comprehensive set of skills, and providing appropriate financial incentives.[18] See the **boxed feature** to see how Hewlett-Packard identifies those with potential for executive leadership positions.

Prosperous firms tend to look outside for CEO candidates only if they have no obvious internal candidates. Firms in trouble, however, tend to choose outsiders to lead them.[19] For example, one study of 22 firms undertaking a turnaround strategy over a 13-year period found that the CEO was replaced in all but two companies. Of 27 changes of CEO (several firms had more than one CEO during this period), only 7 were insiders—20 were outsiders.[20] The probability of an outsider being chosen to lead a firm in difficulty increases if there is no internal heir apparent, the last CEO was fired, and if the board of directors is composed of a large percentage of outsiders.[21] Boards realize that the best way to force a change in strategy is to hire a new CEO with no connections to the current strategy.[22]

Identifying Abilities and Potential

A company can identify and prepare its people for important positions in several ways. One approach is to establish a sound **performance appraisal system** to identify good performers with promotion potential. A survey of 34 corporate planners and human resource executives from 24 large U.S. corporations revealed that approximately 80% made some attempt to identify managers' talents and behavioral tendencies so that they could place a manager with a likely fit to a given competitive strategy.[23] A company should examine its human resource system to ensure not only that people are being hired without regard to their racial, ethnic, or religious background, but also that they are being identified for training and promotion in the same manner. Management diversity could be a competitive advantage in a multiethnic world. With more women in the workplace, an increasing number are moving into top management. Recent studies are suggesting that female executives score higher than men on motivating oth-

---

How Hewlett-Packard Identifies Potential Executives

Hewlett-Packard identifies those with high potential for executive leadership by looking for six broad competencies that the company believes are necessary.

1. *Practice the HP way* by building trust and respect, focusing on achievement, demonstrating integrity, being innovative with customers, contributing to the community, and developing organizational decision making.

2. *Lead change and learning* by recognizing and acting on signals for change, leading organizational change, learning from organizational experience, removing barriers to change, developing self, and challenging and developing others.

3. *Know the internal and external environments* by anticipating global trends, acting on trends, and learning from others.

4. *Lead strategy setting* by inspiring breakthrough business strategy, leading the strategy-making process, committing to business vision, creating long-range strategies, building financial strategies, and defining a business-planning system.

5. *Align the organization* by working across boundaries, implementing competitive cost structures, developing alliances and partnerships, planning and managing core business, and designing the organization.

6. *Achieve results* by building a track record, establishing accountability, supporting calculated risks, making tough individual decisions, and resolving performance problems.

Source: R. M. Fulmer, P. A. Gibbs, and M. Goldsmith, "The New HP Way: Leveraging Strategy with Diversity, Leadership Development and Decentralization," *Strategy & Leadership* (October/November/December, 1999), pp. 21–29.

---

ers, fostering communication, producing high-quality work, and listening to others, while there is no difference in strategic planning or in analyzing issues.[24]

Many large organizations are using **assessment centers** to evaluate a person's suitability for an advanced position. Corporations such as AT&T, Standard Oil, IBM, Sears, and GE have successfully used assessment centers. Because each is specifically tailored to its corporation, these assessment centers are unique. They use special interviews, management games, in-basket exercises, leaderless group discussions, case analyses, decision-making exercises, and oral presentations to assess the potential of employees for specific positions. Promotions into these positions are based on performance levels in the assessment center. Many assessment centers have been able to accurately predict subsequent job performance.

Job rotation—moving people from one job to another—is also used in many large corporations to ensure that employees are gaining the appropriate mix of experiences to prepare them for future responsibilities. Rotating people among divisions is one way that the corporation can improve the level of organizational learning. For example, companies that pursue related diversification strategies through internal development make greater use of interdivisional transfers of people than do companies that grow through unrelated acquisitions. Apparently the companies that grow internally attempt to transfer important knowledge and skills throughout the corporation in order to achieve some sort of synergy.[25]

PROBLEMS IN RETRENCHMENT

Downsizing (sometimes called "rightsizing") refers to the planned elimination of positions or jobs. This program is often used to implement retrenchment strategies. Because the financial community is likely to react favorably to announcements of downsizing from a company in difficulty, such a program may provide some short-term benefits such as raising the company's stock price. If not done properly, however, downsizing may result in less, rather than more, productivity. One study found that a 10% reduction in people resulted in only a 1.5% reduction in costs, profits increased in only half the firms downsizing, and that the stock price of downsized firms increased over three years, but not as much as did that of firms which did not downsize.[26] Why were the results so marginal? Another study of downsizing revealed that at 20 out of 30 automobile-related U.S. industrial companies, either the wrong jobs were eliminated or blanket offers of early retirement prompted managers, even those considered invaluable, to leave. After the layoffs, the remaining employees had to do not only their work, but also the work of the people who had gone. Because the survivors often didn't know how to do the departeds' work, morale and productivity plummeted.[27] Creativity drops significantly (affecting new product development) and it becomes very difficult to keep high performers from leaving the company.[28] In addition, cost-conscious executives tend to defer maintenance, skimp on training, delay new product introductions, and avoid risky new businesses—all of which leads to lower sales and eventually to lower profits.

A good retrenchment strategy can thus be implemented well in terms of organizing but poorly in terms of staffing. A situation can develop in which retrenchment feeds on itself and acts to further weaken instead of strengthening the company. Research indicates that companies undertaking cost-cutting programs are four times more likely than others to cut costs again, typically by reducing staff.[29] This happened at Eastman Kodak and Xerox during the 1990s, but the companies were still having difficulty in 2001. In contrast, successful downsizing firms undertake a strategic reorientation, not just a bloodletting of employees. Research shows that when companies use downsizing as part of a larger restructuring program to narrow company focus, they enjoy better performance.[30]

Consider the following guidelines that have been proposed for successful downsizing:

- **Eliminate unnecessary work instead of making across-the-board cuts.** Spend the time to research where money is going and eliminate the task, not the workers, if it doesn't add value to what the firm is producing. Reduce the number of administrative levels rather than the number of individual positions. Look for interdependent relationships before eliminating activities. Identify and protect core competencies.

- **Contract out work that others can do cheaper.** For example, Bankers Trust of New York has contracted out its mail room and printing services and some of its payroll and accounts payable activities to a division of Xerox. Outsourcing may be cheaper than vertical integration.

- **Plan for long-run efficiencies.** Don't simply eliminate all postponable expenses, such as maintenance, R&D, and advertising, in the unjustifiable hope that the environment will become more supportive. Continue to hire, grow, and develop—particularly in critical areas.

- **Communicate the reasons for actions.** Tell employees not only why the company is downsizing, but also what the company is trying to achieve. Promote educational programs.

- **Invest in the remaining employees.** Because most "survivors" in a corporate downsizing will probably be doing different tasks from what they were doing before the change, firms need to draft new job specifications, performance standards, appraisal techniques, and compensation packages. Additional training is needed to ensure that everyone has the proper skills to deal with expanded jobs and responsibilities. Empower key individuals/groups and emphasize team building. Identify, protect, and mentor people with leadership talent.

- **Develop value-added jobs to balance out job elimination.** When no other jobs are currently available within the organization to transfer employees to, management must consider other staffing alternatives. Harley-Davidson, for example, worked with the company's unions to find other work for surplus employees by moving work into Harley plants that was previously done by suppliers.[31]

INTERNATIONAL ISSUES IN STAFFING

Implementing a strategy of international expansion takes a lot of planning and can be very expensive. Nearly 80% of midsize and larger companies send their employees abroad and 45% plan to increase the number they have on foreign assignment. A complete package for one executive working in another country costs from $300,000 to $1 million annually. Nevertheless, between 10% and 20% of all U.S. managers sent abroad returned early because of job dissatisfaction or difficulties in adjusting to a foreign country. Of those who stayed for the duration of their assignment, nearly one-third did not perform as well as expected. One-fourth of those completing an assignment left their company within one year of returning home—often leaving to join a competitor.[32] One common mistake is failing to educate the person about the customs in other countries.

Because of cultural differences, managerial style and human resource practices must be tailored to fit the particular situations in other countries. Since only 11% of human resource managers have ever worked abroad, most have little understanding of a global assignment's unique personal and professional challenges and thus fail to develop the training necessary for such an assignment.[33] Ninety percent of companies select employees for an international assignment based on their technical expertise while ignoring other areas.[34] This situation is, however, improving. Multinational corporations are now putting more emphasis on intercultural training for those managers being sent on an assignment to a foreign country. This training is one of the commonly cited reasons for the lower expatriate failure rates—6% or less—for European and Japanese MNCs, which have emphasized cross-cultural experiences, compared with a 35% failure rate for U.S.-based MNCs.[35]

To improve organizational learning, many multinational corporations are providing their managers with international assignments lasting as long as five years. Upon their return to headquarters, these expatriates have an in-depth understanding of the company's operations in another part of the world. This has value to the extent that these employees communicate this understanding to others in decision-making positions. Unfortunately, not all corporations appropriately manage international assignments. While out of the country, a person may be overlooked for an important promotion (out of sight, out of mind). Upon his or her return to the home country, coworkers may deprecate the out-of-country experience as a waste of time.

Out of their study of 750 U.S., Japanese, and European companies, Black and Gregersen found that the companies that do a good job of managing foreign assignments follow three general practices.

- When making international assignments, they focus on transferring knowledge and developing global leadership.
- They make foreign assignments to people whose technical skills are matched or exceeded by their cross-cultural abilities.
- They end foreign assignments with a deliberate repatriation process with career guidance and jobs where the employees can apply what they learned in their assignments.[36]

Once a corporation has established itself in another country, it hires and promotes people from the host country into higher level positions. For example, most large multinational corporations (MNCs) attempt to fill managerial positions in their subsidiaries with well-qualified citizens of the host countries. Unilever and IBM take this approach to international staffing. This policy serves to placate nationalistic governments and to better attune management practices to the host country's culture. The danger in using primarily foreign nationals to staff managerial positions in subsidiaries is the increased likelihood of suboptimization (the local subsidiary ignores the needs of the larger parent corporation). This makes it difficult for a multinational corporation to meet its long-term, worldwide objectives. To a local national in an MNC subsidiary, the corporation as a whole is an abstraction. Communication and coordination across subsidiaries become more difficult. As it becomes harder to coordinate the activities of several international subsidiaries, an MNC will have serious problems operating in a global industry.

Another approach to staffing the managerial positions of multinational corporations is to use people with an "international" orientation, regardless of their country of origin or host country assignment. This is a widespread practice among European firms. For example, Electrolux, a Swedish firm, had a French director in its Singapore factory. Using third-country "nationals" can allow for more opportunities for promotion than does Unilever's policy of hiring local people, but it can also result in more misunderstandings and conflicts with the local employees and with the host country's government.

Some U.S. corporations take advantage of immigrants and their children to staff key positions when negotiating entry into another country and when selecting an executive to manage the company's new foreign operations. For example, when General Motors wanted to learn more about business opportunities in China, it turned to Shirley Young, a Vice-President of Marketing at GM. Born in Shanghai and fluent in Chinese language and customs, Young was instrumental in helping GM negotiate a $1 billion joint venture with Shanghai Automotive to build a Buick plant in China. With other Chinese Americans, Young formed a committee to advise GM on relations with China. Although just a part of a larger team of GM employees working on the joint venture, Young coached GM employees on Chinese customs and traditions.[37]

Multinational corporations with a high level of international interdependence among activities need to provide their managers with significant international assignments and experiences as part of their training and development. Such assignments provide future corporate leaders with a series of valuable international contacts in addition to a better personal understanding of international issues and global linkages among corporate activities.[38] Executive recruiters report that more major corporations are now requiring candidates to have international experience.[39]

9.2 Leading

Implementation also involves **leading** people to use their abilities and skills most effectively and efficiently to achieve organizational objectives. Without direction, people tend to do their work according to their personal view of what tasks should be done, how, and in what order. They may approach their work as they have in the past or emphasize those tasks that they most enjoy—regardless of the corporation's priorities. This can create real problems, particularly if the company is operating internationally and must adjust to customs and traditions in other countries. This direction may take the form of management leadership, communicated norms of behavior from the corporate culture, or agreements among workers in autonomous work groups. It may also be accomplished more formally through action planning or through programs such as Management By Objectives and Total Quality Management.

MANAGING CORPORATE CULTURE

Because an organization's culture can exert a powerful influence on the behavior of all employees, it can strongly affect a company's ability to shift its strategic direction. A problem for a strong culture is that a change in mission, objectives, strategies, or policies is not likely to be successful if it is in opposition to the accepted culture of the company. Corporate culture has a strong tendency to resist change because its very reason for existence often rests on preserving stable relationships and patterns of behavior. For example, the male-dominated, Japanese-centered corporate culture of the giant Mitsubishi Corporation created problems for the company when it implemented its growth strategy in North America. The alleged sexual harassment of its female employees by male supervisors resulted in a lawsuit by the U.S. Equal Employment Opportunity Commission and a boycott of the company's automobiles by the National Organization for Women.[40]

Figure 9–1
Assessing Strategy–Culture Compatibility

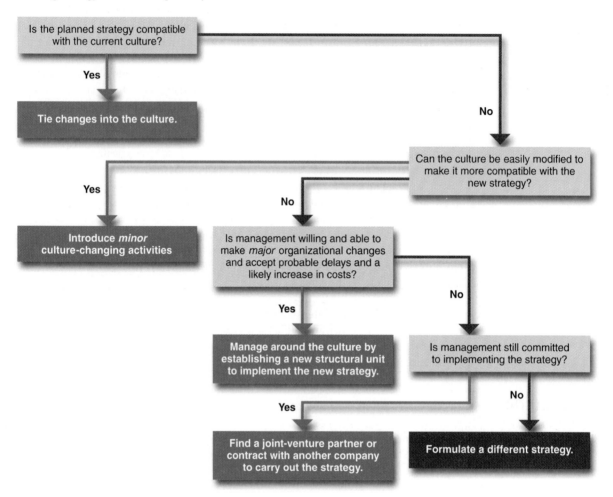

There is no one best corporate culture. An optimal culture is one that best supports the mission and strategy of the company of which it is a part. This means that, like structure and staffing, *corporate culture should support the strategy.* Unless strategy is in complete agreement with the culture, any significant change in strategy should be followed by a modification of the organization's culture. Although corporate culture can be changed, it may often take a long time and it requires much effort. A key job of management involves **managing corporate culture**. In doing so, management must evaluate what a particular change in strategy means to the corporate culture, assess if a change in culture is needed, and decide if an attempt to change the culture is worth the likely costs.

Assessing Strategy-Culture Compatibility

When implementing a new strategy, a company should take the time to assess **strategy–culture compatibility.** (See **Figure 9–1.**) Consider the following questions regarding the corporation's culture:

1. **Is the planned strategy compatible with the company's current culture?** *If yes*, full steam ahead. Tie organizational changes into the company's culture by identifying how the new strategy will achieve the mission better than the current strategy does. *If not . . .*

2. **Can the culture be easily modified to make it more compatible with the new strategy?** *If yes,* move forward carefully by introducing a set of culture-changing activities such as minor structural modifications, training and development activities, and/or hiring new managers who are more compatible with the new strategy. When Procter & Gamble's top management decided to implement a strategy aimed at reducing costs, for example, it made some changes in how things were done, but it did not eliminate its brand-management system. The culture adapted to these modifications over a couple years and productivity increased. *If not . . .*

3. **Is management willing and able to make major organizational changes and accept probable delays and a likely increase in costs?** *If yes,* manage around the culture by establishing a new structural unit to implement the new strategy. At General Motors, for example, top management realized the company had to make some radical changes to be more competitive. Because the current structure, culture, and procedures were very inflexible, management decided to establish a completely new division (GM's first new division since 1918) called Saturn to build its new auto. In cooperation with the United Auto Workers, an entirely new labor agreement was developed, based on decisions reached by consensus. Carefully selected employees received from 100 to 750 hours of training, and a whole new culture was built piece by piece. *If not . . .*

4. **Is management still committed to implementing the strategy?** *If yes,* find a joint-venture partner or contract with another company to carry out the strategy. *If not,* formulate a different strategy.

Managing Cultural Change Through Communication

Communication is key to the effective management of change. Rationale for strategic changes should be communicated to workers not only in newsletters and speeches, but also in training and development programs. Companies in which major cultural changes have taken place successfully had the following characteristics in common:

- The CEO and other top managers had a strategic vision of what the company could become and communicated this vision to employees at all levels. The current performance of the company was compared to that of its competition and constantly updated.

- The vision was translated into the key elements necessary to accomplish that vision. For example, if the vision called for the company to become a leader in quality or service, aspects of quality and service were pinpointed for improvement and appropriate measurement systems were developed to monitor them. These measures were communicated widely through contests, formal and informal recognition, and monetary rewards, among other devices.[41]

Managing Diverse Cultures Following an Acquisition

When merging with or acquiring another company, top management must give some consideration to a potential clash of corporate cultures. According to a Hewitt Associates survey of 218 major U.S. corporations, integrating culture was a top challenge for 69% of the reporting companies.[42] It's dangerous to assume that the firms can simply be integrated into the same reporting structure. The greater the gap between the cultures of the acquired firm and the acquiring firm, the faster executives in the acquired firm quit their jobs and valuable talent is lost.

There are four general methods of managing two different cultures. (See **Figure 9–2**.) The choice of which method to use should be based on (1) *how much members of the acquired firm value preserving their own culture* and (2) *how attractive they perceive the culture of the acquirer to be.*[43]

1. **Integration** involves a relatively balanced give-and-take of cultural and managerial practices between the merger partners, and no strong imposition of cultural change on either company. It merges the two cultures in such a way that the separate cultures of both firms

Figure 9–2
Methods of Managing the Culture of an Acquired Firm

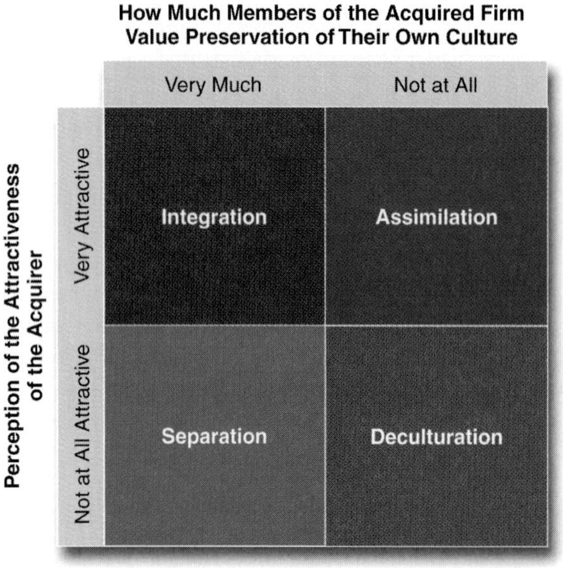

How Much Members of the Acquired Firm Value Preservation of Their Own Culture

	Very Much	Not at All
Very Attractive	Integration	Assimilation
Not at All Attractive	Separation	Deculturation

(*Perception of the Attractiveness of the Acquirer*)

Source: A. Nahavardi and A. R. Malekzadeh, "Acculturation in Mergers and Acquisitions," *Academy of Management Review* (January 1988), p. 83. Copyright © 1988 by the Academy of Management. Reprinted by permission of Academy of Management via the Copyright Clearance Center.

are preserved in the resulting culture. This is what occurred when the Seaboard and Chesapeake & Ohio railroads merged to form CSX Corporation. The top executives were so concerned that both cultures be equally respected that they kept referring to the company as a "partnership of equals."

2. **Assimilation** involves the domination of one organization over the other. The domination is not forced, but it is welcomed by members of the acquired firm, who may feel for many reasons that their culture and managerial practices have not produced success. The acquired firm surrenders its culture and adopts the culture of the acquiring company. See the **boxed feature** describing this method of acculturation when Admiral was acquired by Maytag Corporation.

3. **Separation** is characterized by a separation of the two companies' cultures. They are structurally separated, without cultural exchange. In the Shearson-American Express merger, both parties agreed to keep the fast-paced Shearson completely separate from the planning-oriented American Express. This approach allowed American Express to easily divest Shearson once it discovered that the merger was not working.

4. **Deculturation** involves the disintegration of one company's culture resulting from unwanted and extreme pressure from the other to impose its culture and practices. This is the most common and most destructive method of dealing with two different cultures. It is often accompanied by much confusion, conflict, resentment, and stress. This is a primary reason why so many executives tend to leave after their firm is acquired.[44] Such a merger typically results in poor performance by the acquired company and its eventual divestment. This is what happened when AT&T acquired NCR Corporation in 1990 for its computer business. It replaced NCR managers with an AT&T management team, reor-

Admiral Assimilates Maytag's Culture

Maytag's corporate culture had been dominated almost from the beginning of the company by the concept of quality. Maytag employees took great pride in being known as the "dependability people." Over the years, Maytag Company consistently advertised that their repairmen were "lonely" because Maytag products rarely, if ever, needed repair.

Admiral's history had, however, been quite different. Prior to Maytag's purchase of Magic Chef (and thus Admiral) in 1986, Admiral had been owned by three different corporations. Its manufacturing plant in Galesburg, Illinois, had deteriorated to a dismal level by the time Maytag acquired it. Refrigerators sometimes rolled off the assembly line with screws driven in crooked and temperature balances askew!

Maytag's management had always wanted to have its own Maytag brand refrigerator. That was one reason why it purchased Admiral. But it was worried that Admiral might not be able to produce a quality product to Maytag's specifications. To improve Admiral's quality, Maytag's top management decided to integrate Admiral directly into Maytag Company operations. As a result, all Admiral functional departments, except marketing, reported directly to the Maytag Company president.

Under the direction of Leonard Hadley, while he was serving as Maytag Company President, a project was initiated to design and manufacture a refrigerator for the Maytag brand at the Admiral plant. When Hadley first visited Admiral's facilities to discuss the design of a Maytag line of refrigerators, Admiral personnel asked Hadley when the name on their plant's water tower would be changed from Admiral to Maytag. Hadley (acknowledging Maytag's cultural concerns regarding quality) responded: "*When you earn it.*"

The refrigerator resulting from the Maytag–Admiral collaboration was a huge success. The project crystallized corporate management's philosophy for forging synergies among the Maytag companies while simultaneously allowing the individual expertise of those units to flourish. Admiral's employees were willing to accept the dominance of Maytag's strong quality-oriented culture because they respected it. In turn, they expected to be treated with some respect for their tradition of skill in refrigeration technology.

ganized sales, forced employees to adhere to the AT&T code of values (called the "Common Bond"), and even dropped the proud NCR name (successor to National Cash Register) in favor of a sterile GIS (Global Information Solutions) nonidentity. By 1995, AT&T was forced to take a $1.2 billion loss and lay off 10,000 people.[45] The NCR unit was put up for sale in 1996.

ACTION PLANNING

Activities can be directed toward accomplishing strategic goals through action planning. At a minimum, an **action plan** states what actions are going to be taken, by whom, during what timeframe, and with what expected results. After a program has been selected to implement a particular strategy, an action plan should be developed to put the program in place.

Take the example of a company choosing forward vertical integration through the acquisition of a retailing chain as its growth strategy. Now that it owns its own retail outlets, it must integrate the stores into the company. One of the many programs it would have to develop is a new advertising program for the stores. See **Table 9–1** for an example of an action plan for a

Table 9–1 Example of an Action Plan

Action Plan for Jan Lewis, Advertising Manager, and Rick Carter, Advertising Assistant, Ajax Continental

Program Objective: To Run a New Advertising and Promotion Campaign for the Combined Jones Surplus/Ajax Continental Retail Stores for the Coming Christmas Season Within a Budget of $XX.

Program Activities:
1. Identify three Best Ad Agencies for New Campaign.
2. Ask three Ad Agencies to Submit a Proposal for a New Advertising and Promotion Campaign for Combined Stores.
3. Agencies Present Proposals to Marketing Manager.
4. Select Best Proposal and Inform Agencies of Decision.
5. Agency Presents Winning Proposal to Top Management.
6. Ads Air on TV and Promotions Appear in Stores.
7. Measure Results of Campaign in Terms of Viewer Recall and Increase in Store Sales.

Action Steps	Responsibility	Start–End
1. A. Review previous programs	Lewis & Carter	1/1–2/1
B. Discuss with boss	Lewis & Smith	2/1–2/3
C. Decide on three agencies	Lewis	2/4
2. A. Write specifications for ad	Lewis	1/15–1/20
B. Assistant writes ad request	Carter	1/20–1/30
C. Contact ad agencies	Lewis	2/5–2/8
D. Send request to three agencies	Carter	2/10
E. Meet with agency acct. execs	Lewis & Carter	2/16–2/20
3. A. Agencies work on proposals	Acct. Execs	2/23–5/1
B. Agencies present proposals	Carter	5/1–5/15
4. A. Select best proposal	Lewis	5/15–5/20
B. Meet with winning agency	Lewis	5/22–5/30
C. Inform losers	Carter	6/1
5. A. Fine-tune proposal	Acct. Exec	6/1–7/1
B. Presentation to management	Lewis	7/1–7/3
6. A. Ads air on TV	Lewis	9/1–12/24
B. Floor displays in stores	Carter	8/20–8/30
7. A. Gather recall measures of ads	Carter	9/1–12/24
B. Evaluate sales data	Carter	1/1–1/10
C. Prepare analysis of campaign	Carter	1/10–2/15

new advertising and promotion program. The resulting action plan to develop a new advertising program should include much of the following information:

1. **Specific actions to be taken to make the program operational:** One action might be to contact three reputable advertising agencies and ask them to prepare a proposal for a new radio and newspaper ad campaign based on the theme "Jones Surplus is now a part of Ajax Continental. Prices are lower. Selection is better."

2. **Dates to begin and end each action:** Time would have to be allotted not only to select and contact three agencies, but also to allow them sufficient time to prepare a detailed proposal. For example, allow one week to select and contact the agencies plus three months for them to prepare detailed proposals to present to the company's marketing director. Also allow some time to decide which proposal to accept.

3. **Person (identified by name and title) responsible for carrying out each action:** List someone—such as Jan Lewis, advertising manager, or Rick Carter, advertising assistant—who can be put in charge of each action.

4. **Person responsible for monitoring the timeliness and effectiveness of each action:** Indicate that Jan Lewis is responsible for ensuring that the proposals are of good quality and are priced within the planned program budget. She will be the primary company contact for the ad agencies and will report on the progress of the program once a week to the company's marketing director.

5. **Expected financial and physical consequences of each action:** Estimate when a completed ad campaign will be ready to show top management and how long it will take after approval to begin to air the ads. Estimate also the expected increase in store sales over the six-month period after the ads are first aired. Indicate if "recall" measures will be used to help assess the ad campaign's effectiveness plus how, when, and by whom the recall data will be collected and analyzed.

6. **Contingency plans:** Indicate how long it will take to get an acceptable ad campaign to show top management if none of the initial proposals is acceptable.

Action plans are important for several reasons. First, action plans serve as a link between strategy formulation and evaluation and control. Second, the action plan specifies what needs to be done differently from the way operations are currently carried out. Third, during the evaluation and control process that comes later, an action plan helps in both the appraisal of performance and in the identification of any remedial actions, as needed. In addition, the explicit assignment of responsibilities for implementing and monitoring the programs may contribute to better motivation.

MANAGEMENT BY OBJECTIVES

Management By Objectives (MBO) is an organization-wide approach to help ensure purposeful action toward desired objectives. MBO links organizational objectives and the behavior of individuals. Because it is a system that links plans with performance, it is a powerful implementation technique.

The MBO process involves:

1. Establishing and communicating organizational objectives

2. Setting individual objectives (through superior-subordinate interaction) that help implement organizational ones

3. Developing an action plan of activities needed to achieve the objectives

4. Periodically (at least quarterly) reviewing performance as it relates to the objectives and including the results in the annual performance appraisal

MBO provides an opportunity for the corporation to connect the objectives of people at each level to those at the next higher level. MBO, therefore, acts to tie together corporate, business, and functional objectives, as well as the strategies developed to achieve them.

One of the real benefits of MBO is that it can reduce the amount of internal politics operating within a large corporation. Political actions within a firm can cause conflict and create divisions between the very people and groups who should be working together to implement strategy. People are less likely to jockey for position if the company's mission and objectives are clear and they know that the reward system is based not on game playing, but on achieving clearly communicated, measurable objectives.

TOTAL QUALITY MANAGEMENT

Total Quality Management (TQM) is an operational philosophy committed to *customer satisfaction* and *continuous improvement*. TQM is committed to quality/excellence and to being the best in all functions. Because TQM aims to reduce costs and improve quality, it can be used as a program to implement both an overall low-cost or a differentiation business strategy. About 92% of manufacturing companies and 69% of service firms have implemented some form of quality management practices.[46] Nevertheless, a report by McKinsey & Company reported that two-thirds of the TQM programs it examined had failed to produce expected improvements. An analysis of the successes and failures of TQM concluded that the key is top management. Successful TQM programs occur in those companies in which "top managers move beyond defensive and tactical orientations to embrace a developmental orientation."[47]

TQM has four objectives:

1. Better, less variable quality of the product and service
2. Quicker, less variable response in processes to customer needs
3. Greater flexibility in adjusting to customers' shifting requirements
4. Lower cost through quality improvement and elimination of non–value-adding work[48]

According to TQM, faulty processes, not poorly motivated employees, are the cause of defects in quality. The program involves a significant change in corporate culture, requiring strong leadership from top management, employee training, empowerment of lower level employees (giving people more control over their work), and teamwork for it to succeed in a company. TQM emphasizes prevention, not correction. Inspection for quality still takes place, but the emphasis is on improving the process to prevent errors and deficiencies. Thus quality circles or quality improvement teams are formed to identify problems and to suggest how to improve the processes that may be causing the problems.

TQM's *essential ingredients* are:

- **An intense focus on customer satisfaction:** Everyone (not just people in the sales and marketing departments) understands that their jobs exist only because of customer needs. Thus all jobs must be approached in terms of how it will affect customer satisfaction.

- **Internal as well as external customers:** An employee in the shipping department may be the internal customer of another employee who completes the assembly of a product, just as a person who buys the product is a customer of the entire company. An employee must be just as concerned with pleasing the internal customer as in satisfying the external customer.

- **Accurate measurement of every critical variable in a company's operations:** This means that employees have to be trained in what to measure, how to measure, and how to interpret the data. A rule of TQM is "you only improve what you measure."

- **Continuous improvement of products and services:** Everyone realizes that operations need to be continuously monitored to find ways to improve products and services.

- **New work relationships based on trust and teamwork:** Important is the idea of empowerment—giving employees wide latitude in how they go about achieving the company's goals. Research indicates that the key to TQM success lies in executive commitment, an open organizational culture, and employee empowerment.[49]

INTERNATIONAL CONSIDERATIONS IN LEADING

In a study of 53 different national cultures, Hofstede found that each nation's unique culture could be identified using five dimensions. He found that national culture is so influential that it tends to overwhelm even a strong corporate culture. In measuring the differences among these **dimensions of national culture** from country to country, he was able to explain why a certain management practice might be successful in one nation, but fail in another.[50]

1. **Power distance (PD)** is the *extent to which a society accepts an unequal distribution of power* in organizations. Malaysia and Mexico scored highest, whereas Germany and Austria scored lowest. People in those countries scoring high on this dimension tend to prefer autocratic to more participative managers.

2. **Uncertainty avoidance (UA)** is the *extent to which a society feels threatened by uncertain and ambiguous situations*. Greece and Japan scored highest on disliking ambiguity, whereas the United States and Singapore scored lowest. People in those nations scoring high on this dimension tend to want career stability, formal rules, and clear-cut measures of performance.

3. **Individualism–collectivism (I–C)** is the *extent to which a society values individual freedom and independence of action compared with a tight social framework and loyalty to the group*. The United States and Canada scored highest on individualism, whereas Mexico and Guatemala scored lowest. People in those nations scoring high on individualism tend to value individual success through competition, whereas people scoring low on individualism (thus high on collectivism) tend to value group success through collective cooperation.

4. **Masculinity–femininity (M–F)** is the *extent to which society is oriented toward money and things* (which Hofstede labels masculine) *or toward people* (which Hofstede labels feminine). Japan and Mexico scored highest on masculinity, whereas France and Sweden scored lowest (thus highest on femininity). People in those nations scoring high on masculinity tend to value clearly defined sex roles where men dominate and to emphasize performance and independence, whereas people scoring low on masculinity (and thus high on femininity) tend to value equality of the sexes where power is shared and to emphasize the quality of life and interdependence.

5. **Long-term orientation (LT)** is the *extent to which society is oriented toward the long versus the short term*. Hong Kong and Japan scored highest on long-term orientation, whereas Pakistan scored the lowest. A long-term time orientation emphasizes the importance of hard work, education, and persistence as well as the importance of thrift. Nations with a long-term time orientation should value strategic planning and other management techniques with a long-term payback.

These dimensions of national culture may help to explain why some management practices work well in some countries, but not in others. For example, Management By Objectives (MBO), which originated in the United States, has succeeded in Germany, according to Hofstede, because the idea of replacing the arbitrary authority of the boss with the impersonal authority of mutually agreed-upon objectives fits the low power distance that is a dimension of the German culture. It has failed in France, however, because the French are used to high power distances—to accepting orders from a highly personalized authority. In addition, some of the difficulties experienced by U.S. companies in using Japanese-style quality circles in TQM may stem from the extremely high value U.S. culture places on individualism. The differences between the U.S and Mexico on power distance (Mexico 104 versus U.S. 46) and individualism–collectivism (U.S. 91 versus Mexico 30) dimensions may help explain why some companies operating in both countries have difficulty adapting to the differences in customs.[51]

When one successful company in one country merges with another successful company in another country, the clash of corporate cultures is compounded by the clash of national cultures. With the value of cross-border mergers and acquisitions totaling $720 billion in 1999, the management of cultures is becoming a key issue in strategy implementation.[52]

See the **Global Issue** feature to learn how differences in national and corporate cultures created conflict when Upjohn Company of the United States and Pharmacia AB of Sweden merged.

Multinational corporations must pay attention to the many differences in cultural dimensions around the world and adjust their management practices accordingly. Cultural differences can easily go unrecognized by a headquarters staff that may interpret these differences as personality defects, whether the people in the subsidiaries are locals or expatriates. When conducting strategic planning in a multinational corporation, top management must be aware that the process will vary based upon the national culture where a subsidiary is located. For example, in one MNC, the French expect concepts and key questions and answers. North American managers provide heavy financial analysis. Germans give precise dates and financial analysis. Information is usually late from Spanish and Moroccan operations and quotas are typically inflated. It is up to management to adapt to the differences.[53] Hofstede and Bond conclude: "Whether they like it or not, the headquarters of multinationals are in the business of multicultural management."[54]

Global Issue

Cultural Differences Create Implementation Problems in Merger

When Upjohn Pharmaceuticals of Kalamazoo, Michigan, and Pharmacia AB of Stockholm, Sweden, merged in 1995, employees of both sides were optimistic for the newly formed Pharmacia & Upjohn, Inc. Both companies were second-tier competitors fighting for survival in a global industry. Together, the firms would create a global company that could compete scientifically with its bigger rivals.

Because Pharmacia had acquired an Italian firm in 1993, it also had a large operation in Milan. American executives scheduled meetings throughout the summer of 1996, only to cancel them when their European counterparts could not attend. Although it was common knowledge in Europe that most Swedes take the entire month of July for vacation and that Italians take off all of August, this was not common knowledge in Michigan. Differences in management styles became a special irritant. Swedes were used to an open system with autonomous work teams. Executives sought the whole group's approval before making an important decision. Upjohn executives followed the more traditional American top-down approach. Upon taking command of the newly merged firm, Dr. Zabriskie (who had been Upjohn's CEO), divided the company into departments reporting to the new London headquarters. He required frequent reports, budgets, and staffing updates. The Swedes reacted negatively to this top-down management hierarchical style. "It was degrading," said Stener Kvinnsland, head of Pharmacia's cancer research in Italy before he quit the new company.

The Italian operations baffled the Americans, even though the Italians felt comfortable with a hierarchical management style. Italy's laws and unions made layoffs difficult. Italian data and accounting were often inaccurate. Because the Americans didn't trust the data, they were constantly asking for verification. In turn, the Italians were concerned that the Americans were trying to take over Italian operations. At Upjohn, all workers were subject to testing for drug and alcohol abuse. Upjohn also banned smoking. At Pharmacia's Italian business center, however, waiters poured wine freely every afternoon in the company dining room. Pharmacia's boardrooms were stocked with humidors for executives who smoked cigars during long meetings. After a brief attempt to enforce Upjohn's policies, the company dropped both of the no-drinking and no-smoking policies for European workers.

Although the combined company had cut annual costs by $200 million, overall costs of the merger reached $800 million, some $200 million more than projected. Nevertheless, Jan Eckberg, CEO of Pharmacia before the merger, remained confident of the new company's ability to succeed. He admitted, however, that "we have to make some smaller changes to release the full power of the two companies."

Source: R. Frank and T. M. Burton, "Cross-Border Merger Results in Headaches for a Drug Company," *Wall Street Journal* (February 4, 1997), pp. A1, A12. Copyright © 1997 by the *Wall Street Journal.* Reprinted by permission of the *Wall Street Journal* via the Copyright Clearance Center.

9.3 Impact of the Internet on Staffing and Leading in Organizations

The widespread acceptance of the Internet has created demand for the development of intranets in most large organizations. An **intranet** is an *internal Internet created for the use of a corporation's employees.* The availability of the World Wide Web, servers, chat rooms, bulletin boards, and electronic mail allows companies to use their existing technologies to build intranets without needing additional investment in hardware or software. Intranets support the development of virtual teams, disseminate information about the company's products and services, provide information about internal job openings and health benefits, plus offer e-mail and file transfer services so that people can transfer project information from one personal computer to another. Unlike the Internet, an intranet is owned entirely by the corporation. Information posted on them cannot be accessed by the general public without being provided explicit access privileges. Intranets are protected from unauthorized entry through "firewalls," software programs that check and verify the credentials of potential users. Unlike other technologies, intranets don't need standard hardware platforms, such as IBM or Macintosh, on which an application resides. The vast majority of companies report a positive return from their intranet investment.[55]

Intranets can be either *static* (updated periodically) or *dynamic* (updated continuously). Examples of static information are phone directories, internal job openings, employee benefits information, company news releases, corporate events, technical documents, and company policies and procedures. Examples of dynamic information are sales, inventory, and expense account transactions.

Static Intranet Applications

The primary goal of static intranet applications is to provide information when and if people need it. For example, a number of large corporations are installing internal *Yellow Pages* in which an employee can type key skills, knowledge, or experience into the computer and get back the names and resumes of other employees within the firm who have those skills, knowledge, or experiences. Deere & Company uses a "People Who Know" database to help people with questions find people with answers. Bruce Boardman, head of metals research at Deere, states that the cost of the system is "less than the salary of one engineer—it pays for itself at least half a dozen times a year," especially when the production line stops and someone needs help immediately.

When Bechtel Corporation created a new division called Bechtel Systems & Infrastructure (BSII), it developed a Yellow Pages for the unit. The division was a combination of all Bechtel's work for governments around the world and included 6,000 people. According to Mary O'Donnell of BSII's human resource department, "We didn't know all the skills we had." The Yellow Pages, based on Lotus Notes, contains employee resumes listing a person's skills, current project and when it will be completed, past projects, military, international, and supervisory experience, and other information. Together with online Notes forums called "twigs" (technical working groups), the system provides a way to find answers to technical questions. It also enables the division to staff jobs more quickly.

NatWest Markets, the investment banking division of Britain's NatWest Group, developed a Green Book containing the names of 800 people arranged by area of expertise within the five categories of financial products, industry sectors, geography, support, and business intelligence. About 100 of the people are "knowledge coordinators" who have volunteered to direct other people not only to other people, but to legal documents or files. Interestingly, the people are not listed by titles. According to Victoria Ward, NatWest

Markets Chief Knowledge Officer: "I'm not interested in titles. It might turn out that one of our best experts in securitization works in the equities unit, not in the debt unit. This is about function, not form."[56]

Dynamic Intranet Applications

Intranets can also be used effectively to process and exchange dynamic information by linking employees with company databases and proprietary transaction systems such as inventory and purchasing systems. Software, such as HotOffice, allows project coworkers to access folders and read posted documents. The HotOffice system includes a bulletin board, group calendar, personal calendars, virtual meeting rooms for real-time discussions, and private e-mail. For real-time collaboration over a LAN (local area network), Lotus Sametime is a software package that includes text chat and whiteboard applications as well as application sharing.[57] (See the **Internet Issue** feature for an example of how business people use the net to interact over long distances.)

Ford Motor Company's intranet connects 120,000 workstations at offices and factories worldwide to thousands of Ford Web sites containing proprietary information like market research, analyses of competitors' components, and rankings of the most efficient suppliers of parts. Its product development system allows engineers, designers, and suppliers to work from the same data. Every vehicle team has a Web site where team members can post questions and progress reports, note bottlenecks, and resolve issues. According to Paul Blumberg, Director of Product Development, sharing such information widely has helped Ford reduce the time to get new models into production from 36 to 24 months. The company links its dealers into the intranet so they can order vehicles from the assembly plant, check on production status, and change orders up to seven days before a car is finished. The dealers are then able to offer custom ordering and delivery on every car or truck.[58]

Internet Issue

Virtual Teams Use the Net to Operate at Long Distance

Christine Martin, President and CEO of TLCi, tells how her company uses the net for both the internal and external transaction of business.

My company is a virtual company in three ways:

First, our CFO and Ops Director works from eastern Canada, while the company is headquartered in Southern California. We meet every morning over the Internet, employing a videocam along with audio. If the Internet connection is not satisfactory, we work over the telephone. We regularly address our strategic plan and work on our various client projects together. This is a highly productive and beneficial arrangement.

Second, TLCi has various strategic partners with whom we are connected virtually. We use e-mail on a regular basis. We send important links and information, and exchange drafts and final documents (such as business plans) over the Internet. We find e-mail to be the best vehicle for exchanging working documents, saving time and ensuring accuracy.

Third, to ensure ourselves against catastrophe, we regularly update our virus-protection software and back up files religiously. We also manage our own Web site, to make sure that company information is always current. Future projects include videoconferencing with clients worldwide.

Source: C. Martin, "Virtual Companies: A Reality," *EntreWorld Discussion ListServe* (December 18, 2000). Reprinted by permission.

Advantages and Disadvantages of Intranets

Intranets have many *advantages*. Among them are:

- **Speed, effectiveness, and relatively low cost:** Less time and money is spent on printing reams of paper and disseminating it to employees who often just dump it in the trash.
- **Elimination of time and space barriers:** People can find answers to their questions regardless of the time or the location.
- **Can use existing infrastructure:** Once a firm has the hardware in place to use the Internet, it is very easy to create an intranet.
- **Ease of use:** Accessing information on an intranet is much simpler and faster than digging into file cabinets to find policy folders or calling friends to find an expert on a particular problem.
- **Enhances productivity:** The time spent in searching for information is significantly reduced.

Intranets also have some *disadvantages*. Among them are:

- **Information and hyperlinks need to be continually updated.** Nothing is more frustrating than being sent to a site that is no longer operating or one that contains out-of-date information. Employees need to be periodically reminded to update their resumes.
- **Technology is continually changing and must be updated often.** The increasing use of virtual work teams is pushing the development of video and voice systems on computers, requiring investments in newer, more powerful, and faster personal computers and workstations.
- **Technical support is needed to maintain the system.** People must be trained on how to use it. Someone must monitor what people put on the intranet, such as resumes, to ensure that the information is correct.
- **Security is a critical issue.** Even well-constructed firewalls cannot keep out serious hackers who like to meddle with confidential documents. Industrial espionage is always a concern for companies in highly competitive or defense-related industries.
- **Access is an issue.** Unless all employees have access to the intranet, many of the advantages may be lost.[59]

Projections for the 21st Century

- From 1994 to 2010, movie screens will increase in the United States from 25,105 to 74,114.
- From 1994 to 2010, movie screens will grow worldwide from 86,902 to 162,766.[60]

Discussion Questions

1. What skills should a person have for managing a business unit following a differentiation strategy? Why? What should a company do if no one is available internally and the company has a policy of promotion from within?

2. When should someone from outside the company be hired to manage the company or one of its business units?

3. What are some ways to implement a retrenchment strategy without creating a lot of resentment and conflict with labor unions?

4. How can corporate culture be changed?

5. Why is an understanding of national cultures important in strategic management?

Strategic Practice Exercise

Staffing involves finding the person with the right blend of characteristics, such as personality, training, and experience, to implement a particular strategy. The Keirsey Temperament Sorter is designed to identify different kinds of personality temperament. It is similar to other instruments derived from Carl Jung's theory of psychological types, such as the Myers-Briggs, the Singer-Loomis, and the Grey-Wheelright. The questionnaire identifies four temperament types: **Guardian (SJ)**, **Artisan (SP)**, **Idealist (NF)**, and **Rational (NT)**. *Guardians* have natural talent in managing goods and services. They are dependable and trustworthy. *Artisans* have keen senses and are at home with tools, instruments, and vehicles. They are risk-takers and like action. *Idealists* are concerned with growth and development and like to work with people. They prefer friendly cooperation over confrontation and conflict. *Rationalists* are problem solvers who like to know how things work. They work tirelessly to accomplish their goals. Each of these four types has four variants.[61]

Keirsey challenges the assumption that people are basically the same in the ways that we think, feel, and approach problems. Keirsey argues that it is far less desirable to attempt to change others (because it has little likelihood of success) than to attempt to understand, work with, and take advantage of normal differences. Companies can use this type of questionnaire to help team members understand how each person can contribute to team performance. For example, Lucent Technology used the Myers-Briggs Type Indicator to help build trust and understanding among 500 engineers in 13 time zones and 3 continents in a distributed development project.

1. Access the Keirsey Temperament Sorter using your Internet browser. Type in the following url:

   ⟨www.keirsey.com/cgi-bin/keirsey/newkts.cgi⟩.

2. Once you complete and score the questionnaire, print the description of your personality type.

3. Read the information on the Web site about each personality type. Become familiar with each.

4. Bring to class a sheet of paper containing your name and your personality type: Guardian, Artisan, Idealist, or Rational. Your instructor will either put you into a group containing people with the same predominant style or into a group with representatives from each type. She or he may then give each group a number. The instructor will then give the teams a project to accomplish. Each group will have approximately 30 minutes to do the project. It may be to solve a problem, analyze a short case, or propose a new entrepreneurial venture. The instructor will provide you with very little guidance other than to form and number the groups, give them the project, and keep track of time. He or she may move from group to group to sit in on each team's progress. When the time is up, the instructor will ask a spokesperson from each group to (1) describe the process the group went through and (2) present orally each group's ideas. After each group makes its presentation, the instructor may choose one or more of the following:

   ■ On a sheet of paper, each person in the class identifies his or her personality type and votes which team did the best on the project.

   ■ The class as a whole tries to identify each group's dominant decision-making style in terms of how they did their assignment. See how many people vote for one of the four types for each team.

   ■ Each member of a group guesses if she or he was put into a team composed of the same personality types or in one composed of all four personality types.

Key Terms

action plan (p. 229)
assessment centers (p. 222)
assimilation (p. 228)
deculturation (p. 228)
dimensions of national culture (p. 233)
downsizing (p. 222)
executive succession (p. 221)
executive type (p. 220)
individualism–collectivism (I–C) (p. 233)
integration (p. 227)

intranet (p. 235)
job rotation (p. 222)
leading (p. 225)
long-term orientation (LT) (p. 233)
management by objectives (MBO) (p. 231)
managing corporate culture (p. 226)
masculinity–femininity (M–F) (p. 233)
performance appraisal system (p. 221)

power distance (PD) (p. 233)
separation (p. 228)
staffing (p. 218)
staffing follows strategy (p. 219)
strategy–culture compatibility (p. 226)
total quality management (TQM) (p. 232)
turnaround specialist (p. 220)
uncertainty avoidance (UA) (p. 233)

Notes

1. B. O'Reilly, "The Rent-A-Car Jocks Who Made Enterprise #1," *Fortune* (October 28, 1996), pp. 125–128.

2. The numbers are approximate averages from 3 separate studies of top management turnover after mergers. See M. Lubatkin, D. Schweiger, and Y. Weber, "Top Management Turnover in Related M&Ss: An Additional Test of the Theory of Relative Standing," *Journal of Management* 25, 1 (1999), pp. 55–73.

3. R. N. Ashkenas and S. C. Francis, "Integration Managers: Special Leaders for Special Times," *Harvard Business Review* (November–December 2000), pp. 108–116.

4. J. Hoerr, "Sharpening Minds for a Competitive Edge," *Business Week* (December 17, 1990), pp. 72–78.

5. "Training and Human Resources," *Business Strategy News Review* (July 2000), p. 6.

6. *High Performance Work Practices and Firm Performance* (Washington, DC: U.S. Department of Labor, Office of the American Workplace, 1993), pp. i, 4.

7. T. T. Baldwin, C. Danielson, and W. Wiggenhorn, "The Evolution of Learning Strategies in Organizations: From Employee Development to Business Redefinition," *Academy of Management Executive* (November 1997), pp. 47–58; K. Kelly, "Motorola: Training for the Millennium," *Business Week* (March 28, 1996), pp. 158–161.

8. R. Henkoff, "Companies That Train Best," *Fortune* (March 22, 1993), pp. 62–75.

9. For further details, see J. A. Byrne, *Chainsaw: The Notorious Career of Al Dunlap in the Era of Profit-at-Any-Price* (NY: HarperBusiness, 1999).

10. D. K. Datta and N. Rajagopalan, "Industry Structure and CEO Characteristics: An Empirical Study of Succession Events," *Strategic Management Journal* (September 1998), pp. 833–852; A. S. Thomas and K. Ramaswamy, "Environmental Change and Management Staffing: A Comment," *Journal of Management* (Winter 1993), pp. 877–887; J. P. Guthrie, C. M. Grimm, and K. G. Smith, "Environmental Change and Management Staffing: An Empirical Study," *Journal of Management* (December 1991), pp. 735–748.

11. J. Greco, "The Search Goes On," *Journal of Business Strategy* (September/October 1997), pp. 22–25; W. Ocasio and H. Kim, "The Circulation of Corporate Control: Selection of Functional Backgrounds on New CEOs in Large U.S. Manufacturing Firms, 1981–1992," *Administrative Science Quarterly* (September 1999), pp. 532–562.

12. R. Drazin and R. K. Kazanjian, "Applying the Del Technique to the Analysis of Cross-Classification Data: A Test of CEO Succession and Top Management Team Development," *Academy of Management Journal* (December 1993), pp. 1374–1399; W. E. Rothschild, "A Portfolio of Strategic Leaders," *Planning Review* (January/February 1996), pp. 16–19.

13. R. Subramanian and C. M. Sanchez, "Environmental Change and Management Staffing: An Empirical Examination of the Electric Utilities Industry," *Journal of Business Strategies* (Spring 1998), pp. 17–34.

14. J. A. Parnell, "Functional Background and Business Strategy: The Impact of Executive-Strategy Fit on Performance," *Journal of Business Strategies* (Spring 1994), pp. 49–62.

15. M. Smith and M. C. White, "Strategy, CEO Specialization, and Succession," *Administrative Science Quarterly* (June 1987), pp. 263–280.

16. A. Bianco, L. Lavelle, J. Merrit, and A. Barrett, "The CEO Trap," *Business Week* (December 11, 2000), pp. 86–92.

17. M. Leuchter, "Management Farm Teams," *Journal of Business Strategy* (May/June 1998), pp. 29–32.

18. D. C. Carey and D. Ogden, *CEO Succession: A Window on How Boards Do It Right When Choosing a New Chief Executive* (NY: Oxford University Press, 2000).

19. A. A. Buchko and D. DiVerde, "Antecedents, Moderators, and Consequences of CEO Turnover: A Review and Reconceptualization," Paper presented to *Midwest Academy of Management* (Lincoln, NE: 1997), p. 10; W. Ocasio, "Institutionalized Action and Corporate Governance: The Reliance on Rules of CEO Succession," *Administrative Science Quarterly* (June 1999), pp. 384–416.

20. C. Gopinath, "Turnaround: Recognizing Decline and Initiating Intervention," *Long Range Planning* (December 1991), pp. 96–101.

21. K. B. Schwartz and K. Menon, "Executive Succession in Failing Firms," *Academy of Management Journal* (September 1985), pp. 680–686; A. A. Cannella, Jr., and M. Lubatkin, "Succession as a Sociopolitical Process: Internal Impediments to Outsider Selection," *Academy of Management Journal* (August 1993), pp. 763–793; W. Boeker and J. Goodstein, "Performance and Succession Choice: The Moderating Effects of Governance and Ownership," *Academy of Management Journal* (February 1993), pp. 172–186.

22. W. Boeker, "Executive Migration and Strategic Change: The Effect of Top Manager Movement on Product-Market Entry," *Administrative Science Quarterly* (June 1997), pp. 213–236.

23. P. Lorange and D. Murphy, "Bringing Human Resources Into Strategic Planning: System Design Characteristics," in *Strategic Human Resource Management*, edited by C. J. Fombrun, N. M. Tichy, and M. A. Devanna (New York: John Wiley & Sons, 1984), pp. 281–283.

24. R. Sharpe, "As Leaders, Women Rule," *Business Week* (November 20, 2000), pp. 75–84.

25. R. A. Pitts, "Strategies and Structures for Diversification," *Academy of Management Journal* (June 1997), pp. 197–208.

26. K. E. Mishra, G. M. Spreitzer, and A. K. Mishra, "Preserving Employee Morale During Downsizing," *Sloan Management Review* (Winter 1998), pp. 83–95.

27. B. O'Reilly, "Is Your Company Asking Too Much?" *Fortune* (March 12, 1990), p. 41. For more information on the emotional reactions of survivors of downsizing, see C. R. Stoner and R. I. Hartman, "Organizational Therapy: Building Survivor Health & Competitiveness," *SAM Advanced Management Journal* (Summer 1997), pp. 15–31, 41.

28. T. M. Amabile and R. Conti, "Changes in the Work Environment for Creativity During Downsizing," *Academy of Management Journal* (December 1999), pp. 630–640; A. G. Bedeian and A. A. Armenakis, "The Cesspool Syndrome: How Dreck Floats to the Top of Declining Organizations," *Academy of Management Executive* (February 1998), pp. 58–67.

29. *Wall Street Journal* (December 22, 1992), p. B1.

30. G. D. Bruton, J. K. Keels, and C. L. Shook, "Downsizing the Firm: Answering the Strategic Questions," *Academy of Management Executive* (May 1996), pp. 38–45.

31. M. A. Hitt, B. W. Keats, H. F. Harback, and R. D. Nixon, "Rightsizing: Building and Maintaining Strategic Leadership and Long-Term Competitiveness," *Organizational Dynamics* (Autumn 1994), pp. 18–32. For additional suggestions, see T. Mroczkowski and M. Hanaoka, "Effective Rightsizing Strategies in Japan and America: Is There a Convergence of Employment Practices?" *Academy of Management Executive* (May 1997), pp. 57–67.

32. J. S. Black and H. B. Gregersen, "The Right Way to Manage Expats," *Harvard Business Review* (March–April 1999), pp. 52–61.

33. Black and Gregersen, p. 54.

34. J. I. Sanchez, P. E. Spector, and C. L. Cooper, "Adapting to a Boundaryless World: A Developmental Expatriate Model," *Academy of Management Executive* (May 2000), pp. 96–106.

35. R. L. Tung, *The New Expatriates* (Cambridge, MA: Ballinger, 1988); J. S. Black, M. Mendenhall, and G. Oddou, "Toward a Comprehensive Model of International Adjustment: An Integration of Multiple Theoretical Perspectives," *Academy of Management Review* (April 1991), pp. 291–317.

36. Black and Gregersen, p. 54.

37. G. Stern, "GM Executive's Ties to Native Country Help Auto Maker Clinch Deal in China," *Wall Street Journal* (November 2, 1995), p. B7.

38. K. Roth, "Managing International Interdependence: CEO Characteristics in a Resource-Based Framework," *Academy of Management Journal* (February 1995), pp. 200–231.

39. J. S. Lublin, "An Overseas Stint Can Be a Ticket to the Top," *Wall Street Journal* (January 29, 1996), pp. B1, B2.

40. P. Elstrom and S. V. Brull, "Mitsubishi's Morass," *Business Week* (June 3, 1996), p. 35.

41. G. G. Gordon, "The Relationship of Corporate Culture to Industry Sector and Corporate Performance," in *Gaining Control of the Corporate Culture,* edited by R. H. Kilmann, M. J. Saxton, R. Serpa, and Associates (San Francisco: Jossey-Bass, 1985), p. 123; T. Kono, "Corporate Culture and Long-Range Planning," *Long Range Planning* (August 1990), pp. 9–19.

42. T. J. Tetenbaum, "Seven Key Practices that Improve the Chance for Expected Integration and Synergies," *Organizational Dynamics* (Autumn 1999), pp. 22–35.

43. A. R. Malekzadeh and A. Nahavandi, "Making Mergers Work by Managing Cultures," *Journal of Business Strategy* (May/June 1990), pp. 53–57; A. Nahavandi and A. R. Malekzadeh, "Acculturation in Mergers and Acquisitions," *Academy of Management Review* (January 1988), pp. 79–90.

44. Lubatkin, Schweiger, and Weber, pp. 55–73.

45. J. J. Keller, "Why AT&T Takeover of NCR Hasn't Been a Real Bell Ringer," *Wall Street Journal* (September 19, 1995), pp. A1, A5.

46. S. S. Masterson and M. S. Taylor, "Total Quality Management and Performance Appraisal: An Integrative Perspective," *Journal of Quality Management 1,* No. 1 (1996), pp. 67–89.

47. T. Y. Choi and O. C. Behling, "Top Managers and TQM Success: One More Look After All These Years," *Academy of Management Executive* (February 1997), pp. 37–47.

48. R. J. Schonberger, "Total Quality Management Cuts a Broad Swath—Through Manufacturing and Beyond," *Organizational Dynamics* (Spring 1992), pp. 16–28.

49. T. C. Powell, "Total Quality Management as Competitive Advantage: A Review and Empirical Study," *Strategic Management Journal* (January 1995), pp. 15–37.

50. G. Hofstede, *Cultures and Organizations: Software of the Mind* (London: McGraw-Hill, 1991); G. Hofstede and M. H. Bond, "The Confucius Connection: From Cultural Roots to Economic Growth," *Organizational Dynamics* (Spring 1988), pp. 5–21; R. Hodgetts, "A Conversation with Geert Hofstede," *Organizational Dynamics* (Spring 1993), pp. 53–61.

51. See Hofstede and Bond, "The Confucius Connection," pp. 12–13.

52. "Emerging-Market Indicators," *The Economist* (October 7, 2000), p. 124.

53. T. T. Herbert, "Multinational Strategic Planning: Matching Central Expectations to Local Realities," *Long Range Planning* (February 1999), pp. 81–87.

54. Hofstede and Bond, "The Confucius Connection," p. 20.

55. U. G. Gupta and F. J. Hebert, "Is Your Company Ready for an Intranet?" *SAM Advanced Management Journal* (Autumn 1998), pp. 11–17, 26.

56. T. A. Stewart, "Does Anyone Around Here Know . . . ?" *Fortune* (September 29, 1997), pp. 279–280.

57. C. Metz, "Work Together," *PC Magazine* (July 2000), pp. 171–172.

58. M. J. Cronin, "Ford's Intranet Success," *Fortune* (March 30, 1998), p. 158.

59. Gupta and Hebert, p. 16.

60. J. Warner, "21st Century Capitalism: Snapshot of the Next Century," *Business Week* (November 18, 1994), p. 194.

61. D. Keirsey, *Please Understand Me II* (Del Mar, CA: Prometheus Nemesis Book Co., 1998).

chapter 10

Evaluation and Control

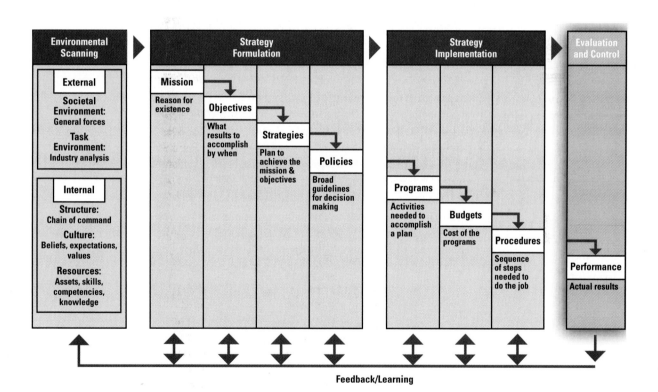

Feedback/Learning

Nucor Corporation, one of the most successful steel firms operating in the United States, keeps its evaluation and control process simple and easy to manage. According to Kenneth Iverson, Chairman of the Board:

> We try to keep our focus on what really matters—bottom-line performance and long-term survival. That's what we want our people to be thinking about. Management takes care not to distract the company with a lot of talk about other issues. We don't clutter the picture with lofty vision statements or ask employees to pursue vague, intermediate objectives like "excellence" or burden them with complex business strategies. Our competitive strategy is to build manufacturing facilities

economically and to operate them efficiently. Period. Basically, we ask our employees to produce more product for less money. Then we reward them for doing that well.[1]

The **evaluation and control process** ensures that the company is achieving what it set out to accomplish. It compares performance with desired results and provides the feedback necessary for management to evaluate results and take corrective action, as needed. This process can be viewed as a five-step feedback model, as depicted in **Figure 10–1**.

1. **Determine what to measure**. Top managers and operational managers need to specify what implementation processes and results will be monitored and evaluated. The processes and results must be capable of being measured in a reasonably objective and consistent manner. The focus should be on the most significant elements in a process—the ones that account for the highest proportion of expense or the greatest number of problems. Measurements must be found for all important areas, regardless of difficulty.

2. **Establish standards of performance**. Standards used to measure performance are detailed expressions of strategic objectives. They are measures of acceptable performance results. Each standard usually includes a tolerance range, which defines acceptable deviations. Standards can be set not only for final output, but also for intermediate stages of production output.

3. **Measure actual performance**. Measurements must be made at predetermined times.

4. **Compare actual performance with the standard.** If actual performance results are within the desired tolerance range, the measurement process stops here.

5. **Take corrective action**. If actual results fall outside the desired tolerance range, action must be taken to correct the deviation. The following questions must be answered:
   a. Is the deviation only a chance fluctuation?
   b. Are the processes being carried out incorrectly?
   c. Are the processes appropriate to the achievement of the desired standard? Action must be taken that will not only correct the deviation, but will also prevent its happening again.
   d. Who is the best person to take corrective action?

Top management is often better at the first two steps of the control model than it is in the last three follow-through steps. It tends to establish a control system and then delegate the implementation to others. This can have unfortunate results. Nucor is unusual in its ability to deal with the entire evaluation and control process.

Figure 10–1
Evaluation and Control Process

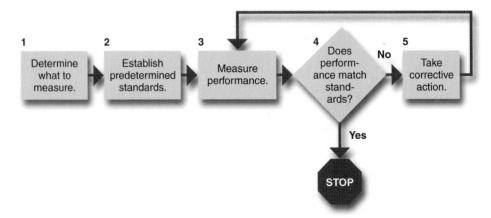

10.1 Evaluation and Control in Strategic Management

Evaluation and control information consists of performance data and activity reports (gathered in Step 3 of **Figure 10–1**). If undesired performance results because the strategic management processes were inappropriately used, operational managers must know about it so that they can correct the employee activity. Top management need not be involved. If, however, undesired performance results from the processes themselves, top managers, as well as operational managers, must know about it so that they can develop new implementation programs or procedures. Evaluation and control information must be relevant to what is being monitored. One of the obstacles to effective control is the difficulty in developing appropriate measures of important activities and outputs.

An application of the control process to strategic management is depicted in **Figure 10–2**. It provides strategic managers with a series of questions to use in evaluating an implemented strategy. Such a strategy review is usually initiated when a gap appears between a company's financial objectives and the expected results of current activities. After answering the proposed set of questions, a manager should have a good idea of where the problem originated and what must be done to correct the situation.

10.2 Measuring Performance

Performance is the end result of activity. Which measures to select to assess performance depends on the organizational unit to be appraised and the objectives to be achieved. The objectives that were established earlier in the strategy formulation part of the strategic management process (dealing with profitability, market share, and cost reduction, among others) should certainly be used to measure corporate performance once the strategies have been implemented.

APPROPRIATE MEASURES

Some measures, such as return on investment (ROI), are appropriate for evaluating the corporation's or division's ability to achieve a profitability objective. This type of measure, however, is inadequate for evaluating additional corporate objectives such as social responsibility or employee development. Even though profitability is a corporation's major objective, ROI can be computed only after profits are totaled for a period. It tells what happened after the fact— not what is happening or what will happen. A firm, therefore, needs to develop measures that predict likely profitability. These are referred to as **steering controls** because they measure variables that influence future profitability. One example of this type of control is the use of control charts in Statistical Process Control (SPC). In SPC, workers and managers maintain charts and graphs detailing quality and productivity on a daily basis. They are thus able to make adjustments to the system before it gets out of control.[2]

TYPES OF CONTROLS

Controls can be established to focus on actual performance results (output), the activities that generate the performance (behavior), or on resources that are used in performance (input). **Behavior controls** specify how something is to be done through policies, rules, standard operating procedures, and orders from a superior. **Output controls** specify what is to be accomplished by focusing on the end result of the behaviors through the use of objectives and performance targets or milestones. **Input controls** focus on resources, such as knowledge, skills, abilities, values, and motives of employees.[3]

Figure 10–2
Evaluating an Implemented Strategy

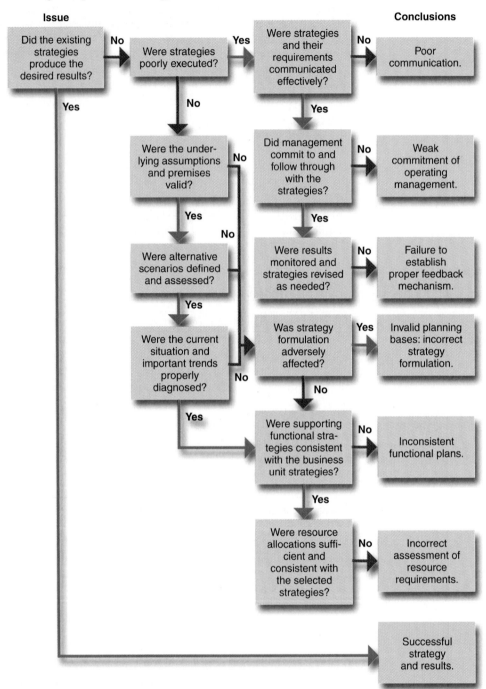

Source: Jeffery A. Schmidt, "The Strategic Review," *Planning Review* (July/August 1988), p. 15. Copyright © 1988 by MCB University Press Ltd. Reprinted with permission.

Behavior, output, and input controls are not interchangeable. Behavior controls (such as following company procedures, making sales calls to potential customers, and getting to work on time) are most appropriate when performance results are hard to measure but the cause–effect connection between activities and results is clear. Output controls (such as sales quotas, specific cost reduction or profit objectives, and surveys of customer satisfaction) are most appropriate when specific output measures have been agreed on but the cause–effect connection between activities and results is not clear. Input controls (such as number of years of education and experience) are most appropriate when output is difficult to measure and there is no clear cause–effect relationship between behavior and performance (such as in college teaching). Corporations following the strategy of conglomerate diversification tend to emphasize output controls with their divisions and subsidiaries (presumably because they are managed independently of each other); whereas, corporations following concentric diversification use all three types of controls (presumably because synergy is desired).[4] Even if all three types of control are used, one or two of them may be emphasized more than another depending on the circumstances. For example, Muralidharan and Hamilton propose that as a multinational corporation moves through its stages of development, its emphasis on control should shift from being primarily output at first, to behavioral, and finally to input control.[5]

One example of an increasingly popular behavior control is the **ISO 9000 Standards Series** on quality management and assurance developed by the International Standards Association of Geneva, Switzerland. The ISO 9000 series (composed of five sections from 9000 to 9004) is a way of objectively documenting a company's high level of quality operations. ISO 9000 and 9004 contain guidelines for use with the other sections; 9001 is the most comprehensive standard; 9002 is less stringent; 9003 is used only for inspecting and testing procedures. A company wanting certification would probably document its process for product introductions, among other things. ISO 9001 would require this firm to separately document design input, design process, design output, and design verification—a large amount of work. Although the average total cost for a company to be certified is close to $250,000, the annual savings are around $175,000 per company.[6]

Many corporations view ISO 9000 certification as assurance that a supplier sells quality products. Firms such as DuPont, Hewlett-Packard, and 3M have facilities registered to ISO standards. Companies in over 60 countries, including Canada, Mexico, Japan, the United States (including the entire U.S. auto industry), and the European Union (EU), are requiring ISO 9000 certification of their suppliers. By 1996, close to 100,000 firms were registered worldwide.[7] In one survey of manufacturing executives, 51% of the executives found that certification increased their international competitiveness. Other executives noted that it signaled their commitment to quality and gave them a strategic advantage over noncertified competitors.[8]

ACTIVITY-BASED COSTING

Activity-based costing (ABC) is a new accounting method for allocating indirect and fixed costs to individual products or product lines based on the value-added activities going into that product.[9] This accounting method is thus very useful in doing a value-chain analysis of a firm's activities for making outsourcing decisions. Traditional cost accounting, in contrast, focuses on valuing a company's inventory for financial reporting purposes. To obtain a unit's cost, cost accountants typically add direct labor to the cost of materials. Then they compute overhead from rent to R&D expenses, based on the number of direct labor hours it takes to make a product. To obtain unit cost, they divide the total by the number of items made during the period under consideration.

Traditional cost accounting is useful when direct labor accounts for most of total costs and a company produces just a few products requiring the same processes. This may have been true of companies during the early part of the twentieth century, but it is no longer relevant today when overhead may account for as much as 70% of manufacturing costs. According to Bob Van Der Linde, CEO of a contract manufacturing services firm in San Diego, California: "Overhead is 80% to 90% in our industry, so allocation errors lead to pricing errors, which could easily bankrupt the company."[10] The appropriate allocation of indirect costs and overhead has thus become crucial for decision making. The traditional volume-based cost-driven system systematically understates the cost per unit of products with low sales volumes and products with a high degree of complexity. Similarly, it overstates the cost per unit of products with high sales volumes and with a low degree of complexity.[11]

ABC accounting allows accountants to charge costs more accurately than the traditional method because it allocates overhead far more precisely. For example, imagine a production line in a pen factory where black pens are made in high volume and blue pens in low volume. Assume it takes eight hours to retool (reprogram the machinery) to shift production from one kind of pen to the other. The total costs include supplies (the same for both pens), the direct labor of the line workers, and factory overhead. In this instance, a very significant part of the overhead cost is the cost of reprogramming the machinery to switch from one pen to another. If the company produces 10 times as many black pens as blue pens, 10 times the cost of the reprogramming expenses will be allocated to the black pens as to the blue pens under traditional cost accounting methods. This approach underestimates, however, the true cost of making the blue pens.

ABC accounting, in contrast, first breaks down pen manufacturing into its activities. It is then very easy to see that it is the activity of changing pens that triggers the cost of retooling. The ABC accountant calculates an average cost of setting up the machinery and charges it against each batch of pens that requires retooling regardless of the size of the run. Thus a product carries only those costs for the overhead it actually consumes. Management is now able to discover that its blue pens cost almost twice as much as do the black pens. Unless the company is able to charge a higher price for its blue pens, it cannot make a profit on these pens. Unless there is a strategic reason why it must offer blue pens (such as a key customer who must have a small number of blue pens with every large order of black pens or a marketing trend away from black to blue pens), the company will earn significantly greater profits if it completely stops making blue pens.[12]

PRIMARY MEASURES OF CORPORATE PERFORMANCE

The days when simple financial measures such as ROI or EPS were used alone to assess overall corporate performance are coming to an end. Analysts now recommend a broad range of methods to evaluate the success or failure of a strategy. Some of these methods are stakeholder measures, shareholder value, and the balanced scorecard approach. Even though each of these methods has its supporters as well as detractors, the current trend is clearly toward more complicated financial measures and an increasing use of nonfinancial measures of corporate performance.[13] For example, research indicates that companies pursuing strategies founded on innovation and new product development now tend to favor nonfinancial over financial measures.[14]

Traditional Financial Measures
The most commonly used measure of corporate performance (in terms of profits) is **return on investment (ROI)**. It is simply the result of dividing net income before taxes by total assets. Although using ROI has several advantages, it also has several distinct limitations. (See **Table 10–1**.) Although ROI gives the impression of objectivity and precision, it can be easily manipulated.

Earnings per share (EPS), dividing net earnings by the number of shares of common stock issued, also has several deficiencies as an evaluation of past and future performance.

Table 10–1 Advantages and Limitations of Using ROI as a Measure of Corporate Performance

Advantages

1. ROI is a single comprehensive figure influenced by everything that happens.
2. It measures how well the division manager uses the property of the company to generate profits. It is also a good way to check on the accuracy of capital investment proposals.
3. It is a common denominator that can be compared with many entities.
4. It provides an incentive to use existing assets efficiently.
5. It provides an incentive to acquire new assets only when doing so would increase the return.

Limitations

1. ROI is very sensitive to depreciation policy. Depreciation write-off variances between divisions affect ROI performance. Accelerated depreciation techniques increase ROI, conflicting with capital budgeting discounted cash-flow analysis.
2. ROI is sensitive to book value. Older plants with more depreciated assets have relatively lower investment bases than newer plants (note also the effect of inflation), thus increasing ROI. Note that asset investment may be held down or assets disposed of in order to increase ROI performance.
3. In many firms that use ROI, one division sells to another. As a result, transfer pricing must occur. Expenses incurred affect profit. Since, in theory, the transfer price should be based on the total impact on firm profit, some investment center managers are bound to suffer. Equitable transfer prices are difficult to determine.
4. If one division operates in an industry that has favorable conditions and another division operates in an industry that has unfavorable conditions, the former division will automatically "look" better than the other.
5. The time span of concern here is short range. The performance of division managers should be measured in the long run. This is top management's timespan capacity.
6. The business cycle strongly affects ROI performance, often despite managerial performance.

Source: "Advantages and Limitations of ROI as a Measure of Corporate Performance" from *Organizational Policy and Strategic Management: Text and Cases*, 2nd ed. by James M. Higgins, copyright © 1983. Reproduced by permission of South-Western College Publishing, a division of Thomson Learning.

First, because alternative accounting principles are available, EPS can have several different but equally acceptable values, depending on the principle selected for its computation. Second, because EPS is based on accrual income, the conversion of income to cash can be near term or delayed. Therefore, EPS does not consider the time value of money. **Return on equity (ROE)**, dividing net income by total equity, also has its share of limitations because it is also derived from accounting-based data. In addition, EPS and ROE are often unrelated to a company's stock price. Because of these and other limitations, ROI, EPS and ROE by themselves are not adequate measures of corporate performance. Nevertheless, they are still better than the measures proposed by Internet startups during the 1990s. (See the ▨ **Internet Issue** feature for an example of how Amazon.com used "eyeballs" as its primary measure of performance.)

Stakeholder Measures

Each stakeholder has its own set of criteria to determine how well the corporation is performing. These criteria typically deal with the direct and indirect impact of corporate activities on stakeholder interests. Top management should establish one or more simple **stakeholder measures** for each stakeholder category so that it can keep track of stakeholder concerns. (See **Table 10–2**.)

Internet Issue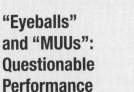

"Eyeballs" and "MUUs": Questionable Performance Measures

When Amazon.com's investor-relations team went to Denver in September, 2000, to seek funding from Marsico Capital Management, a mutual fund company, it presented its usual performance story. Even though the company had never shown a profit, the team told how Amazon.com had a "first to market" advantage and that its Web site received an extremely high number of "monthly unique visitors" and "eyeballs." Although such presentations had in the past raised millions of dollars for the company in stock purchases, it failed this time. Marsico was more concerned with when the company would become profitable. The Amazon.com team left empty-handed.

Until 2000, investors had been so enamored with new Internet firms that they made decisions based on novel measures of performance and firm valuation. They looked at measures such as "stickiness" (length of Web site visit), "eyeballs" (number of people who visit a Web site), and "mindshare" (brand awareness). Mergers and acquisitions were priced on multiples of "MUUs" (monthly unique users) or even on registered users. Since practically all the dot.com (Internet) firms failed to earn a profit, investors and analysts used these mea-

sures to estimate what the firms might be worth sometime in the future. By 2000, however, "the market concluded the (Net stock) valuations were insane," commented Charles Wolf, analyst with UBS Warburg.

With $2.1 billion in debt, Amazon.com's accumulated net loss from 1994 through 2000 was $1.75 billion. Its management had proposed that as the company grew in scale, its operations would become more efficient, and its gross margin per customer would improve. The question from investors was—when? For example, Amazon.com in 2000 averaged $160.01 annually in revenue from each of its 17 million customers for books and CDs. The annual cost of these books and CDs was $139.22, leaving a gross profit of $20.79 per customer. Annual marketing expenses amounted to $42.47 per customer. Using the traditional profit measure, Amazon.com was losing $21.68 per person. This didn't include an additional $19.83 per person for warehousing, shipping, customer service, and other operating expenses. The company did sell prominent positions on its Web site to firms such as drugstore.com for $105 million and car-dealer Greenlight.com for $145 million. With sufficient sales of space on its Web site, it could become profitable soon. Since Amazon.com realized an 80% margin from this sort of advertising, it was not so much an Internet retailer as a newspaper or television station existing off advertising.

Sources: E. Schonfeld, "How Much Are Your Eyeballs Worth?" *Fortune* (February 21, 2000), pp. 197–204; N. Byrnes, "Eyeballs, Bah! Figuring Dot-Coms' Real Worth," *Business Week* (October 30, 2000), p. 62; R. Barker, "Amazon: Cheaper—But Cheap Enough?" *Business Week* (December 4, 2000), p. 172.

Shareholder Value

Because of the belief that accounting-based numbers such as return on investment, return on equity, and earnings per share are not reliable indicators of a corporation's economic value, many corporations are using shareholder value as a better measure of corporate performance and strategic management effectiveness. **Shareholder value** can be defined as the present value of the anticipated future stream of cash flows from the business plus the value of the company if liquidated. Arguing that the purpose of a company is to increase shareholder wealth, shareholder value analysis concentrates on cash flow as the key measure of performance. The value of a corporation is thus the value of its cash flows discounted back to their present value, using the business's cost of capital as the discount rate. As long as the returns from a business exceed its cost of capital, the business will create value and be worth more than the capital invested in it.

The New York consulting firm Stern Stewart & Company devised and popularized two shareholder value measures: economic value added (EVA) and market value added (MVA). Well-known companies, such as Coca-Cola, General Electric, AT&T, Whirlpool, Quaker Oats, Eli Lilly, Georgia-Pacific, Polaroid, Sprint, Teledyne, and Tenneco have adopted MVA and/or

Table 10–2 A Sample Scorecard for "Keeping Score" with Stakeholders

Stakeholder Category	Possible Near-Term Measures	Possible Long-Term Measures
Customers	Sales ($ and volume) New customers Number of new customer needs met ("tries")	Growth in sales Turnover of customer base Ability to control price
Suppliers	Cost of raw material Delivery time Inventory Availability of raw material	Growth rates of: Raw material costs Delivery time Inventory New ideas from suppliers
Financial community	EPS Stock price Number of "buy" lists ROE	Ability to convince Wall Street of strategy Growth in ROE
Employees	Number of suggestions Productivity Number of grievances	Number of internal promotions Turnover
Congress	Number of new pieces of legislation that affect the firm Access to key members and staff	Number of new regulations that affect industry Ratio of "cooperative" vs. "competitive" encounters
Consumer advocate (CA)	Number of meetings Number of "hostile" encounters Number of times coalitions formed Number of legal actions	Number of changes in policy due to C.A. Number of C.A.-initiated "calls for help"
Environmentalists	Number of meetings Number of hostile encounters Number of times coalitions formed Number of EPA complaints Number of legal actions	Number of changes in policy due to environmentalists Number of environmentalist "calls for help"

Source: R. E. Freeman, *Strategic Management: A Stakeholder Approach* (Boston: Ballinger Publishing Company, 1984), p. 179. Copyright © 1984 by R. E. Freeman. Reprinted by permission.

EVA as the best yardstick for corporate performance. According to Sprint's CFO, Art Krause, "Unlike EPS, which measures accounting results, MVA gauges true economic performance."[15]

Economic value added (EVA) has become an extremely popular shareholder value method of measuring corporate and divisional performance and may be on its way to replacing ROI as the standard performance measure. EVA measures the difference between the prestrategy and poststrategy value for the business. Simply put, EVA is after-tax operating income minus the total annual cost of capital. The formula to measure EVA is:

EVA = After tax operating income – (investment in assets × weighted average cost of capital)[16]

The cost of capital combines the cost of debt and equity. The annual cost of borrowed capital is the interest charged by the firm's banks and bondholders. To calculate the cost of equity, assume that shareholders generally earn about 6% more on stocks than on government bonds. If long-term treasury bills are selling at 7.5%, the firm's cost of equity should be 13.5%—more if the firm is in a risky industry. A corporation's overall cost of capital is the weighted-average cost of the firm's debt and equity capital. The investment in assets is the total the amount of capital invested in the business, including buildings, machines, computers, and investments in

R&D and training (allocating costs annually over their useful life). Since the typical balance sheet understates the investment made in a company, Stern Stewart has identified 150 possible adjustments, before EVA is calculated.[17] Multiply the firm's total investment in assets by the weighted-average cost of capital. Subtract that figure from after-tax operating income. If the difference is positive, the strategy (and the management employing it) is generating value for the shareholders. If it is negative, the strategy is destroying shareholder value.[18]

Roberto Goizueta, CEO of Coca-Cola, explains, "We raise capital to make concentrate, and sell it at an operating profit. Then we pay the cost of that capital. Shareholders pocket the difference."[19] Managers can improve their company's or business unit's EVA by: (1) earning more profit without using more capital, (2) using less capital, and (3) investing capital in high-return projects. Studies have found that companies using EVA outperform their median competitor by an average of 8.43% of total return annually.[20] EVA does, however, have some limitations. For one thing, it does not control for size differences across plants or divisions. Like ROI, managers can manipulate the numbers. Like ROI, EVA is an after-the-fact measure and cannot be used like a steering control.[21] Although proponents of EVA argue that EVA (unlike ROI, ROE, and/or ROS) has a strong relationship to stock price, other studies do not support this contention.[22]

Market value added (MVA) is the difference between the market value of a corporation and the capital contributed by shareholders and lenders. Like net present value, it measures the stock market's estimate of the net present value of a firm's past and expected capital investment projects. As such, MVA is the present value of future EVA.[23] To calculate MVA:

1. First add all the capital that has been put into a company—from shareholders, bondholders, and retained earnings.

2. Reclassify certain accounting expenses, such as R&D, to reflect that they are actually investments in future earnings. This provides the firm's total capital. So far, this is the same approach taken in calculating EVA.

3. Using the current stock price, total the value of all outstanding stock, adding it to the company's debt. This is the company's market value. If the company's market value is greater than all the capital invested in it, the firm has a positive MVA—meaning that management (and the strategy it is following) has created wealth. In some cases, however, the market value of the company is actually less than the capital put into it—shareholder wealth is being destroyed.

Microsoft, General Electric, Intel, and Coca-Cola tend to have high MVAs in the United States, whereas General Motors and RJR Nabisco have low ones.[24] Studies have shown that EVA is a predictor of MVA. Consecutive years of positive EVA generally lead to a soaring MVA.[25] Research also reveals that CEO turnover is significantly correlated with MVA and EVA, whereas ROA and ROE are not. This suggests that EVA and MVA may be more appropriate measures of the market's evaluation of a firm's strategy and its management than are the traditional measures of corporate performance.[26] Nevertheless, these measures consider only the financial interests of the shareholder and ignore other stakeholders, such as environmentalists and employees.

Balanced Scorecard Approach: Using Key Performance Measures

Rather than evaluate a corporation using a few financial measures, Kaplan and Norton argue for a "balanced scorecard," including nonfinancial as well as financial measures.[27] This approach is especially useful given that research indicates that nonfinancial assets explain 50% to 80% of a firm's value.[28] The **balanced scorecard** combines financial measures that tell the results of actions already taken with operational measures on customer satisfaction, internal processes, and the corporation's innovation and improvement activities—the drivers of future financial performance. Management should develop goals or objectives in each of four areas:

1. **Financial**: How do we appear to shareholders?
2. **Customer**: How do customers view us?
3. **Internal Business Perspective**: What must we excel at?
4. **Innovation and Learning**: Can we continue to improve and create value?

Each goal in each area (for example, avoiding bankruptcy in the financial area) is then assigned one or more measures, as well as a target and an initiative. These measures can be thought of as **key performance measures**—measures that are essential for achieving a desired strategic option.[29] For example, a company could include cash flow, quarterly sales growth, and ROE as measures for success in the financial area. It could include market share (competitive position goal) and percentage of new sales coming from new products (customer acceptance goal) as measures under the customer perspective. It could include cycle time and unit cost (manufacturing excellence goal) as measures under the internal business perspective. It could include time to develop next generation products (technology leadership objective) under the innovation and learning perspective.

Several companies are starting to use one or more variations of the scorecard and view it as complementary to its knowledge management activities. A study of the *Fortune 500* firms in the United States and the *Post 300* firms in Canada revealed the most popular nonfinancial measures to be customer satisfaction, customer service, product quality, market share, productivity, service quality, and core competencies. New product development, corporate culture, and market growth were not far behind.[30] CIGNA, for example, uses the balanced scorecard to determine employee bonuses. Moving cautiously, financial measures still account for half of the bonus at CIGNA.[31]

Evaluating Top Management

Through its strategy, audit, and compensation committees, a board of directors closely evaluates the job performance of the CEO and the top management team. Of course, it is concerned primarily with overall corporate profitability as measured quantitatively by return on investment, return on equity, earnings per share, and shareholder value. The absence of short-run profitability certainly contributes to the firing of any CEO. The board, however, is also concerned with other factors.

Members of the compensation committees of today's boards of directors generally agree that a CEO's ability to establish strategic direction, build a management team, and provide leadership are more critical in the long run than are a few quantitative measures. The board should evaluate top management not only on the typical output-oriented quantitative measures, but also on behavioral measures—factors relating to its strategic management practices. The specific items that a board uses to evaluate its top management should be derived from the objectives that both the board and top management agreed on earlier. If better relations with the local community and improved safety practices in work areas were selected as objectives for the year (or for five years), these items should be included in the evaluation. In addition, other factors that tend to lead to profitability might be included, such as market share, product quality, or investment intensity. Although the number of boards conducting systematic evaluations of their CEO are increasing in number, it is estimated that no more than half of the boards do so.

An increasing number of companies are using a 17-item questionnaire developed by Charan that focuses on the four key areas of company performance, leadership of the organization, team-building and management succession, and leadership of external constituencies.[32] After taking an hour to complete the questionnaire, the board of KeraVision, Inc., used it as a basis for a lengthy discussion with the CEO, Thomas Loarie. The board criticized Loarie for "not tempering enthusiasm with reality" and urged Loarie to develop a clear management succession plan. The evaluation caused Loarie to involve the board more closely in setting the company's primary objectives and discussing "where we are, where we want to go, and the operating environment."[33]

Management audits are very useful to boards of directors in evaluating management's handling of various corporate activities. Management audits have been developed to evaluate activities such as corporate social responsibility, functional areas such as the marketing department, and divisions such as the international division, as well as to evaluate the corporation itself in a strategic audit. The strategic audit is explained in detail later in this chapter.

PRIMARY MEASURES OF DIVISIONAL AND FUNCTIONAL PERFORMANCE

Companies use a variety of techniques to evaluate and control performance in divisions, SBUs, and functional areas. If a corporation is composed of SBUs or divisions, it will use many of the same performance measures (ROI or EVA, for instance) that it uses to assess overall corporate performance. To the extent that it can isolate specific functional units such as R&D, the corporation may develop responsibility centers. It will also use typical functional measures such as market share and sales per employee (marketing), unit costs and percentage of defects (operations), percentage of sales from new products and number of patents (R&D), and turnover and job satisfaction (HRM). For example, FedEx uses Enhanced Tracker software with its COSMOS database to track the progress of its 2.5 to 3.5 million shipments daily. As a courier is completing her or his day's activities, the Enhanced Tracker asks if the person's package count equals the Enhanced Tracker's count. If the count is off, the software helps reconcile the differences.[34]

During strategy formulation and implementation, top management approves a series of programs and supporting **operating budgets** from its business units. During evaluation and control, actual expenses are contrasted with planned expenditures and the degree of variance is assessed. This is typically done on a monthly basis. In addition, top management will probably require **periodic statistical reports** summarizing data on such key factors as the number of new customer contracts, volume of received orders, and productivity figures.

Responsibility Centers

Control systems can be established to monitor specific functions, projects, or divisions. Budgets are one type of control system that is typically used to control the financial indicators of performance. **Responsibility centers** are used to isolate a unit so that it can be evaluated separately from the rest of the corporation. Each responsibility center, therefore, has its own budget and is evaluated on its use of budgeted resources. It is headed by the manager responsible for the center's performance. The center uses resources (measured in terms of costs or expenses) to produce a service or a product (measured in terms of volume or revenues). There are five major types of responsibility centers. The type is determined by the way the corporation's control system measures these resources and services or products.

1. **Standard Cost Centers:** Primarily used in manufacturing facilities, standard (or expected) costs are computed for each operation on the basis of historical data. In evaluating the center's performance, its total standard costs are multiplied by the units produced. The result is the expected cost of production, which is then compared to the actual cost of production.

2. **Revenue Centers:** Production, usually in terms of unit or dollar sales, is measured without consideration of resource costs (for example, salaries). The center is thus judged in terms of effectiveness rather than efficiency. The effectiveness of a sales region, for exam-

ple, is determined by comparing its actual sales to its projected or previous year's sales. Profits are not considered because sales departments have very limited influence over the cost of the products they sell.

3. **Expense Centers:** Resources are measured in dollars without consideration for service or product costs. Thus budgets will have been prepared for *engineered expenses* (those costs that can be calculated) and for *discretionary expenses* (those costs that can be only estimated). Typical expense centers are administrative, service, and research departments. They cost an organization money, but they only indirectly contribute to revenues.

4. **Profit Centers:** Performance is measured in terms of the difference between revenues (which measure production) and expenditures (which measure resources). A profit center is typically established whenever an organizational unit has control over both its resources and its products or services. By having such centers, a company can be organized into divisions of separate product lines. The manager of each division is given autonomy to the extent that she or he is able to keep profits at a satisfactory (or better) level.

   Some organizational units that are not usually considered potentially autonomous can, for the purpose of profit center evaluations, be made so. A manufacturing department, for example, can be converted from a standard cost center (or expense center) into a profit center; it is allowed to charge a transfer price for each product it "sells" to the sales department. The difference between the manufacturing cost per unit and the agreed-upon transfer price is the unit's "profit."

   Transfer pricing is commonly used in vertically integrated corporations and can work well when a price can be easily determined for a designated amount of product. Even though most experts agree that market-based transfer prices are the best choice, only 30% to 40% of companies use market price to set the transfer price. (Of the rest, 50% use cost; 10% to 20% use negotiation.)[35] When a price cannot be set easily, however, the relative bargaining power of the centers, rather than strategic considerations, tends to influence the agreed-upon price. Top management has an obligation to make sure that these political considerations do not overwhelm the strategic ones. Otherwise, profit figures for each center will be biased and provide poor information for strategic decisions at both corporate and divisional levels.

5. **Investment Centers:** Because many divisions in large manufacturing corporations use significant assets to make their products, their asset base should be factored into their performance evaluation. Thus it is insufficient to focus only on profits, as in the case of profit centers. An investment center's performance is measured in terms of the difference between its resources and its services or products. For example, two divisions in a corporation made identical profits, but one division owns a $3 million plant, whereas the other owns a $1 million plant. Both make the same profits, but one is obviously more efficient; the smaller plant provides the shareholders with a better return on their investment. The most widely used measure of investment center performance is return on investment (ROI).

Most single-business corporations, such as Apple Computer, tend to use a combination of cost, expense, and revenue centers. In these corporations, most managers are functional specialists and manage against a budget. Total profitability is integrated at the corporate level. Multidivisional corporations with one dominating product line, such as Anheuser-Busch, which have diversified into a few businesses but that still depend on a single product line (such as beer) for most of their revenue and income, generally use a combination of cost, expense, revenue, plus profit centers. Multidivisional corporations, such as General Electric, tend to emphasize investment centers—although in various units throughout the corporation other types of responsibility centers are also used. One problem with using responsibility centers, however, is that the separation needed to measure and evaluate a division's performance can diminish the level of cooperation among divisions that is needed to attain synergy for the corporation as a whole. (This problem is discussed later in this chapter under "Suboptimization.")

Using Benchmarking to Evaluate Performance

According to Xerox Corporation, the company that pioneered this concept in the United States, **benchmarking** is "the continual process of measuring products, services, and practices against the toughest competitors or those companies recognized as industry leaders."[36] Benchmarking, an increasingly popular program, is based on the concept that it makes no sense to reinvent something that someone else is already using. It involves openly learning how others do something better than one's own company so that one not only can imitate, but perhaps even improve on their current techniques. The benchmarking process usually involves the following steps:

- **Identify the area or process to be examined.** It should be an activity that has the potential to determine a business unit's competitive advantage.

- **Find behavioral and output measures of the area or process and obtain measurements.**

- **Select an accessible set of competitors and best-in-class companies against which to benchmark.** These may very often be companies that are in completely different industries, but perform similar activities. For example, when Xerox wanted to improve its order fulfillment, it went to L. L. Bean, the successful mail-order firm, to learn how it achieved excellence in this area.

- **Calculate the differences among the company's performance measurements and those of the best-in-class and determine why the differences exist.**

- **Develop tactical programs for closing performance gaps.**

- **Implement the programs and then compare the resulting new measurements with those of the best-in-class companies.**

Benchmarking has been found to produce best results in companies that are already well managed. Apparently poorer performing firms tend to be overwhelmed by the discrepancy between their performance and the benchmark, and they tend to view the benchmark as too difficult to reach.[37] Nevertheless, a survey by Bain & Company of 460 companies of various sizes across all U.S. industries indicated that over 70% were using benchmarking in either a major or limited manner.[38] Cost reductions range from 15% to 45%.[39] Benchmarking can also increase sales, improve goal setting, and boost employee motivation.[40] The average cost of a benchmarking study is around $100,000 involving 30 weeks of effort.[41] Manco, Inc., a small Cleveland-area producer of duct tape regularly benchmarks itself against Wal-Mart, Rubbermaid, and PepsiCo to enable it to better compete with giant 3M. The American Productivity & Quality Center, a Houston research group, established the International Benchmarking Clearinghouse composed of 600 leading techniques from over 250 companies (see ⟨www.apqc.org⟩).

INTERNATIONAL MEASUREMENT ISSUES

The three most widely used techniques for international performance evaluation are return on investment, budget analysis, and historical comparisons. In one study, 95% of the corporate officers interviewed stated that they use the same evaluation techniques for foreign and domestic operations. Rate of return was mentioned as the single most important measure.[42] However, ROI can cause problems when it is applied to international operations: Because of foreign currencies, different rates of inflation, different tax laws, and the use of transfer pricing, both the net income figure and the investment base may be seriously distorted.[43]

A study of 79 MNCs revealed that **international transfer pricing** from one country unit to another is primarily used not to evaluate performance but to minimize taxes.[44] Taxes are an important issue for MNCs given that corporate tax rates vary from over 40% in Canada, Japan, Italy, and the United States to 25% in Bolivia, 15% in Chile, and 10% to 15% in Zambia.[45] For example, the U.S. Internal Revenue Service contends that many Japanese firms doing business in the United States have artificially inflated the value of U.S. deliveries in order to reduce the profits and thus the taxes of their American subsidiaries.[46] Parts made in a subsidiary of a Japanese MNC in a low-tax country like Singapore can be shipped to its subsidiary in a high-tax country like the United States at such a high price that the U.S. subsidiary reports very little profit (and thus pays few taxes), while the Singapore subsidiary reports a very high profit (but also pays few taxes because of the lower tax rate). A Japanese MNC can, therefore, earn more profit worldwide by reporting less profit in high-tax countries and more profit in low-tax countries. Transfer pricing is an important factor, given that 56% of all trade in the triad and one-third of all international trade is composed of intercompany transactions.[47] Transfer pricing can thus be one way the parent company can reduce taxes and "capture profits" from a subsidiary. Other common ways of transferring profits to the parent company (often referred to as the **repatriation of profits**) are through dividends, royalties, and management fees.[48]

An important issue in international trade is **piracy**. Firms in developing nations around the world make money by making counterfeit copies of well-known name brand products and selling them globally. See the **Global Issue** feature to learn how this is being done.

Global Issue

The Impact of Piracy on International Trade

Many foreign manufacturers in China conservatively estimate that 30% of their products in the mainland are counterfeits. This includes products from Tide detergent and Budweiser beer to Marlboro cigarettes. Yamaha estimates that five out of every six bikes bearing its brand name are fake. Procter & Gamble estimates that 15% of the soaps and detergents under its Head & Shoulders, Vidal Sassoon, Safeguard, and Tide brands in China are counterfeit, costing the company $150 million in lost sales. According to Joseph M. Johnson, President of the China division of Bestfoods Asia Ltd, "We are spending millions of dollars to combat counterfeiting." The trend in counterfeiting seems to be increasing. In the first four months of 2000, for example, Gillette seized more fake products than it did in the past two years combined.

Tens of thousands of counterfeiters are currently active in China. They range from factories mixing shampoo and soap in back rooms to large state-owned enterprises making copies of soft drinks and beer. Other factories make everything from car batteries to automobiles. Mobile CD factories with optical disk-mastering machines counterfeit music and software. These factories in southern Guangdong or Fujian provinces truck their products to a central distribution center, such as the one in Yiwu (five hours by train from Shanghai). They may also be shipped across the border into Russia, Pakistan, Vietnam, or Burma. Chinese counterfeiters have developed a global reach through their connections with organized crime.

According to the market research firm, Automotive Resources, the profit margins on counterfeit shock absorbers can reach 80% versus only 15% for the real ones. Counterfeiters charge up to 80% less for an oil filter for a Mercedes than the $24 for an authentic filter.

Counterfeit products can be found around the world—not just in China. The worldwide cost of software piracy is around $12 million annually. For example, 27% of the software sold in the United States is pirated. That figure increases to around 50% in Brazil, Singapore, and Poland, and to over 90% in Russia, Indonesia, China, and Vietnam. Thanks to Napster and others, the music and book industries are in serious danger from piracy sites, according to Forrester Research, Inc. "As piracy increases and artists and authors break away from the publishers to go independent, record labels and book publishers will lose $3.1 billion and $1.5 billion, respectively, by 2005," warns the report by Forrester Research.

Sources: D. Roberts, F. Balfour, P. Magnusson, P. Engardio, and J. Lee, "China's Piracy Plague," *Business Week* (June 5, 2000), pp. 44–48; "Emerging Market Indicators: Software Piracy," *The Economist* (June 27, 1998), p. 108; "Piracy's Big-Business Victims," *Futurist Update* (December 2000).

Authorities in international business recommend that the control and reward systems used by a global MNC be different from those used by a multidomestic MNC.[49] The *multidomestic MNC* should use loose controls on its foreign units. The management of each geographic unit should be given considerable operational latitude, but it should be expected to meet some performance targets. Because profit and ROI measures are often unreliable in international operations, it is recommended that the MNC's top management, in this instance, emphasize budgets and nonfinancial measures of performance such as market share, productivity, public image, employee morale, and relations with the host country government.[50] Multiple measures should be used to differentiate between the worth of the subsidiary and the performance of its management.

The *global MNC*, however, needs tight controls over its many units. To reduce costs and gain competitive advantage, it is trying to spread the manufacturing and marketing operations of a few fairly uniform products around the world. Therefore, its key operational decisions must be centralized. Its environmental scanning must include research not only into each of the national markets in which the MNC competes, but also into the "global arena" of the interaction between markets. Foreign units are thus evaluated more as cost centers, revenue centers, or expense centers than as investment or profit centers because MNCs operating in a global industry do not often make the entire product in the country in which it is sold.

10.3 Strategic Information Systems

Before performance measures can have any impact on strategic management, they must first be communicated to those people responsible for formulating and implementing strategic plans. Strategic information systems can perform this function. They can be computer-based or manual, formal or informal. One of the key reasons given for the bankruptcy of International Harvester was the inability of the corporation's top management to precisely determine its income by major class of similar products. Because of this inability, management kept trying to fix ailing businesses and was unable to respond flexibly to major changes and unexpected events. In contrast, one of the key reasons for the success of Toys "R" Us and Wal-Mart has been management's use of the company's sophisticated information system to control purchasing decisions. Cash registers in the many U.S. Toys "R" Us and Wal-Mart retail stores transmit information daily to computers at each company's headquarters. Consequently managers know every morning exactly how many of each item have been sold the day before, how many have been sold so far in the year, and how this year's sales compare to last year's. The information system allows all reordering to be done automatically by computers without any managerial input. It also allows the company to experiment with new products without committing to big orders in advance. In effect, the system allows the customers to decide through their purchases what gets reordered.

ENTERPRISE RESOURCE PLANNING (ERP)

Many corporations around the world have adopted or are adopting **enterprise resource planning (ERP)** software. ERP unites all of a company's major business activities from order processing to production within a single family of software modules. The system provides instant access to critical information to everyone in the organization from the CEO to the factory floor worker. Because of the ability of ERP software to use a common information system throughout a company's many operations around the world, it is becoming the business information systems' global standard. The major providers of this software are SAP AG, Oracle, J. D. Edwards, Peoplesoft, Baan, and SSA.

The German company SAP AG originated the concept with its R/3 software system. Microsoft, for example, used R/3 to replace a tangle of 33 financial tracking systems in 26 subsidiaries. Even though it cost the company $25 million and took 10 months to install, R/3 annually saves Microsoft $18 million. Coca-Cola uses the R/3 system to enable a manager in Atlanta to use her personal computer to check the latest sales of 20-ounce bottles of Coke Classic in India. Owens-Corning envisions that its R/3 system will allow sales people to learn what is available at any plant or warehouse and to quickly assemble orders for customers.

ERP is, nevertheless, not for every company. The system is extremely complicated and demands a high level of standardization throughout a corporation. Its demanding nature often forces companies to change the way they do business. There are three reasons why ERP could fail: (1) insufficient tailoring of the software to fit the company, (2) inadequate training, and (3) insufficient implementation support.[51] Over the two-year period of installing R/3, Owens-Corning had to completely overhaul its operations. Because R/3 was incompatible with Apple Computer's very organic corporate culture, the company was only able to apply it to its order management and financial operations, but not to manufacturing. Other companies having difficulty installing and using ERP are Whirlpool, Hershey Foods, and Stanley Works. At Whirlpool, SAP's software led to missed and delayed shipments, causing Home Depot to cancel its agreement for selling Whirlpool products.[52]

DIVISIONAL AND FUNCTIONAL IS SUPPORT

At the divisional or SBU level of a corporation, the information system should be used to support, reinforce, or enlarge its business-level strategy through its decision support system. An SBU pursuing a strategy of overall cost leadership could use its information system to reduce costs either by improving labor productivity or improving the use of other resources such as inventory or machinery. Merrill Lynch took this approach when it developed PRISM software to provide its 500 U.S. retail offices with quick access to financial information in order to boost brokers' efficiency. Another SBU, in contrast, might want to pursue a differentiation strategy. It could use its information system to add uniqueness to the product or service and contribute to quality, service, or image through the functional areas. FedEx wanted to use superior service to gain a competitive advantage. It invested significantly in several types of information systems to measure and track the performance of its delivery service. Together, these information systems gave FedEx the fastest error-response time in the overnight delivery business.

Increasingly, corporations are connecting their intranets to other firms via extranets to implement strategic decisions and monitor their results. For example, Chicago-based Navistar no longer maintains a tire-and-rim inventory at its Springfield, Ohio, truck assembly plant. That responsibility is now being handled electronically by Goodyear Tire & Rubber, one of Navistar's suppliers. A Goodyear office in New York receives Navistar's manufacturing schedule and tire-and-rim requirements by electronic data interchange. The information is then sent to a Goodyear plant in Ohio where tires are mounted on rims. The completed assemblies are shipped to Navistar's Springfield plant—arriving just eight hours ahead of when they are needed. [53]

10.4 Problems in Measuring Performance

The measurement of performance is a crucial part of evaluation and control. The lack of quantifiable objectives or performance standards and the inability of the information system to provide timely and valid information are two obvious control problems. Without objective and timely measurements, it would be extremely difficult to make operational, let alone strategic, decisions. Nevertheless, the use of timely, quantifiable standards does not guarantee good performance. The very act of monitoring and measuring performance can cause side effects that interfere with overall corporate performance. Among the most frequent negative side effects are a short-term orientation and goal displacement.

SHORT-TERM ORIENTATION

Top executives report that in many situations they analyze neither the long-term implications of present operations on the strategy they have adopted nor the operational impact of a strategy on the corporate mission. Long-run evaluations are often not conducted because executives (1) don't realize their importance, (2) believe that short-run considerations are more important than long-run considerations, (3) aren't personally evaluated on a long-term basis, or (4) don't have the time to make a long-run analysis.[54] There is no real justification for the first and last "reasons." If executives realize the importance of long-run evaluations, they make the time needed to conduct them. Even though many chief executives point to immediate pressures from the investment community and to short-term incentive and promotion plans to support the second and third reasons, evidence does not always support their claims.[55]

Many accounting-based measures do, however, encourage a **short-term orientation**. Table 10–1 indicates that one of the limitations of ROI as a performance measure is its short-term nature. In theory, ROI is not limited to the short run, but in practice it is often difficult to use this measure to realize long-term benefits for the company. Because managers can often manipulate both the numerator (earnings) and the denominator (investment), the resulting ROI figure can be meaningless. Advertising, maintenance, and research efforts can be reduced. Mergers can be undertaken that will do more for this year's earnings (and next year's paycheck) than for the division's or corporation's future profits. Research of 55 firms that engaged in major acquisitions revealed that even though the firms performed poorly after the acquisition, the acquiring firms' top management still received significant increases in compensation![56] Expensive retooling and plant modernization can be delayed as long as a manager can manipulate figures on production defects and absenteeism.

Research supports the conclusion that many CEOs and their friends on the board of directors compensation committee manipulate information to provide themselves a pay raise. For example, CEOs tend to announce bad news—thus reducing the company's stock price—just before the issuance of stock options. Once the options are issued, the CEOs tend to announce good news—thus raising the stock price and making their options more valuable.[57] Board compensation committees tend to expand the peer group comparison outside of their industry to include lower performing firms to justify a high raise to the CEO. They tend to do this when the company performs poorly, the industry performs well, the CEO is already highly paid, and when shareholders are powerful and active.[58]

GOAL DISPLACEMENT

Monitoring and measuring performance (if not carefully done) can actually result in a decline in overall corporate performance. **Goal displacement** is the *confusion of means with ends* and occurs when activities originally intended to help managers attain corporate objectives become ends in themselves—or are adapted to meet ends other than those for which they were intended. Two types of goal displacement are behavior substitution and suboptimization.

Behavior Substitution

Behavior substitution refers to a phenomenon when people substitute activities that do not lead to goal accomplishment for activities that do lead to goal accomplishment because the wrong activities are being rewarded. Managers, like most people, tend to focus more of their attention on those behaviors that are clearly measurable than on those that are not. Employees often receive little to no reward for engaging in hard-to-measure activities such as cooperation and initiative. However, easy-to-measure activities might have little to no relationship to the desired good performance. Rational people, nevertheless, tend to work for the rewards that the system has to offer. Therefore, people tend to substitute behaviors that are recognized and rewarded for those behaviors that are ignored, without regard to their contribution to goal accomplishment. A U.S. Navy quip sums up this situation: "What you inspect (or reward) is what you get." Sears, Roebuck & Co. thought that it would improve employee productivity by tying performance to rewards. It, therefore, paid commissions to its auto shop employees as a percentage of each repair bill. Behavior substitution resulted as employees altered their behavior to fit the reward system. The result was over-billed customers, charges for work never done, and a scandal that tarnished Sears' reputation for many years.[59]

The law governing the effect of measurement on behavior seems to be that *quantifiable measures drive out nonquantifiable measures.*

Suboptimization

Suboptimization refers to the phenomenon when a unit optimizes its goal accomplishment to the detriment of the organization as a whole. The emphasis in large corporations on developing separate responsibility centers can create some problems for the corporation as a whole. To the extent that a division or functional unit views itself as a separate entity, it might refuse to cooperate with other units or divisions in the same corporation if cooperation could in some way negatively affect its performance evaluation. The competition between divisions to achieve a high ROI can result in one division's refusal to share its new technology or work process improvements. One division's attempt to optimize the accomplishment of its goals can cause other divisions to fall behind and thus negatively affect overall corporate performance. One common example of suboptimization occurs when a marketing department approves an early shipment date to a customer as a means of getting an order and forces the manufacturing department into overtime production for this one order. Production costs are raised, which reduces the manufacturing department's overall efficiency. The end result might be that, although marketing achieves its sales goal, the corporation as a whole fails to achieve its expected profitability.

10.5 Guidelines for Proper Control

In designing a control system, top management should remember that *controls should follow strategy.* Unless controls ensure the use of the proper strategy to achieve objectives, there is a strong likelihood that dysfunctional side effects will completely undermine the implementation of the objectives. The following guidelines are recommended:

1. **Control should involve only the minimum amount of information** needed to give a reliable picture of events. Too many controls create confusion. *Focus on the strategic factors by following the 80/20 rule: monitor those 20% of the factors that determine 80% of the results.*

2. **Controls should monitor only meaningful activities and results**, regardless of measurement difficulty. If cooperation between divisions is important to corporate performance, some form of qualitative or quantitative measure should be established to monitor cooperation.

3. **Controls should be timely** so that corrective action can be taken before it is too late. Steering controls, controls that monitor or measure the factors influencing performance, should be stressed so that advance notice of problems is given.

4. **Long-term and short-term controls should be used**. If only short-term measures are emphasized, a short-term managerial orientation is likely.

5. **Controls should aim at pinpointing exceptions.** Only those activities or results that fall outside a predetermined tolerance range should call for action.

6. **Emphasize the reward of meeting or exceeding standards** rather than punishment for failing to meet standards. Heavy punishment of failure typically results in goal displacement. Managers will "fudge" reports and lobby for lower standards.

To the extent that the culture complements and reinforces the strategic orientation of the firm, there is less need for an extensive formal control system. In their book *In Search of Excellence*, Peters and Waterman state that "the stronger the culture and the more it was directed toward the marketplace, the less need was there for policy manuals, organization charts, or detailed procedures and rules. In these companies, people way down the line know what they are supposed to do in most situations because the handful of guiding values is crystal clear."[60] For example, at Eaton Corporation, the employees are expected to enforce the rules themselves. If someone misses too much work or picks fights with coworkers, other members of the production team point out the problem. According to Randy Savage, a long-time Eaton employee, "They say there are no bosses here, but if you screw up, you find one pretty fast."[61]

10.6 Strategic Incentive Management

To ensure congruence between the needs of the corporation as a whole and the needs of the employees as individuals, management and the board of directors should develop an incentive program that rewards desired performance. This reduces the likelihood of agency problems (when employees act to feather their own nest instead of building shareholder value) mentioned earlier in **Chapter 2**. Incentive plans should be linked in some way to corporate and divisional strategy. For example, a survey of 600 business units indicates that the pay mix associated with a growth strategy emphasizes bonuses and other incentives over salary and benefits, whereas the pay mix associated with a stability strategy has the reverse emphasis.[62] Research does indicate that SBU managers having long-term performance elements in their compensation program favor a long-term perspective and thus greater investments in R&D, capital equipment, and employee training.[63] The typical CEO pay package is composed of 21% salary, 27% short-term annual incentives, 16% long-term incentives, and 36% stock options.[64]

The following three approaches are tailored to help match measurements and rewards with explicit strategic objectives and timeframes.[65]

1. **Weighted-Factor Method:** This method is particularly appropriate for measuring and rewarding the performance of top SBU managers and group level executives when performance factors and their importance vary from one SBU to another. One corporation's measurements might contain the following variations: the performance of high-growth SBUs is measured in terms of market share, sales growth, designated future payoff, and progress on several future-oriented strategic projects; the performance of low-growth SBUs, in contrast, is measured in terms of ROI and cash generation; and the performance of medium-growth SBUs is measured for a combination of these factors. (Refer to **Table 10–3**.)

2. **Long-Term Evaluation Method:** This method compensates managers for achieving objectives set over a multiyear period. An executive is promised some company stock or "performance units" (convertible into money) in amounts to be based on long-term performance. An executive committee, for example, might set a particular objective in terms of growth in earnings per share during a five-year period. The giving of awards would be contingent on the corporation's meeting that objective within the designated time. Any executive who leaves the corporation before the objective is met receives nothing. The typical emphasis on stock price makes this approach more applicable to top management than to business unit managers. Because rising stock markets tend to raise the stock price of mediocre companies, there is a developing trend to index stock options to competitors or to the Standard & Poor's 500.[66]

3. **Strategic-Funds Method:** This method encourages executives to look at developmental expenses as being different from expenses required for current operations. The accounting statement for a corporate unit enters strategic funds as a separate entry below the current ROI. It is, therefore, possible to distinguish between those expense dollars consumed

Table 10–3 Weighted-Factor Approach to Strategic Incentive Management

Strategic Business Unit Category	Factor	Weight
High Growth	Return on assets	10%
	Cash flow	0%
	Strategic-funds programs (developmental expenses)	45%
	Market-share increase	45%
	Total	100%
Medium Growth	Return on assets	25%
	Cash flow	25%
	Strategic-funds programs (developmental expenses)	25%
	Market-share increase	25%
	Total	100%
Low Growth	Return on assets	50%
	Cash flow	50%
	Strategic-funds programs (developmental expenses)	0%
	Market-share increase	0%
	Total	100%

Source: Reprinted by permission of the publisher from "The Performance Measurement and Reward System: Critical to Strategic Management," by Paul J. Stonich, from *Organizational Dynamics* (Winter 1984), p. 51. Copyright © 1984 with permission from Elsevier Science.

in the generation of current revenues and those invested in the future of the business. Therefore, the manager can be evaluated on both a short- and a long-term basis and has an incentive to invest strategic funds in the future. (See **Table 10–4.**)

An effective way to achieve the desired strategic results through a reward system is to combine the three approaches:

1. Segregate strategic funds from short-term funds as is done in the strategic-funds method.
2. Develop a weighted-factor chart for each SBU.
3. Measure performance on three bases: The pretax profit indicated by the strategic-funds approach, the weighted factors, and the long-term evaluation of the SBUs' and the corporation's performance.

Genentech, General Electric, and Textron are some of the firms in which CEO compensation is contingent upon the company's achieving strategic objectives.[67]

Table 10–4 Strategic Funds Approach to an SBU's Profit-and-Loss Statement

Sales	$12,300,000
Cost of sales	−6,900,000
Gross margin	$ 5,400,000
General and administrative expenses	−3,700,000
Operating profit (return on sales)	$ 1,700,000
Strategic funds (development expenses)	−1,000,000
Pretax profit	$ 700,000

Source: Reprinted by permission of the publisher from "The Performance Measurement and Reward System: Critical to Strategic Management," by Paul J. Stonich, from *Organizational Dynamics* (Winter 1984), p. 52. Copyright © 1984 with permission from Elsevier Science.

10.7 Using the Strategic Audit to Evaluate Corporate Performance

The **strategic audit** provides a checklist of questions, by area or issue, that enables a systematic analysis of various corporate functions and activities to be made. (See **Appendix 10.A** at the end of this chapter.) It is a type of management' audit and is extremely useful as a diagnostic tool to pinpoint corporatewide problem areas and to highlight organizational strengths and weaknesses.[68] The strategic audit can help determine why a certain area is creating problems for a corporation and help generate solutions to the problem.

The strategic audit is not an all-inclusive list, but it presents many of the critical questions needed for a detailed strategic analysis of any business corporation. Some questions or even some areas might be inappropriate for a particular company; in other cases, the questions may be insufficient for a complete analysis. However, each question in a particular area of the strategic audit can be broken down into an additional series of sub-questions. Develop these sub-questions when they are needed.

The strategic audit summarizes the key topics in the Strategic Management Model discussed in **Chapters 1** through **10**. As you look through the major headings of the audit in **Appendix 10.A**, note that it identifies by chapter, section, and page numbers where information about each topic can be found. The strategic audit puts into action the strategic decision-making process illustrated in **Figure 1–5**. The headings in the audit are the same as those shown in **Figure 1–5**:

1. Evaluate Current Performance Results
2. Review Corporate Governance
3. Scan and Assess the External Environment
4. Scan and Assess the Internal Environment
5. Analyze Strategic Factors Using SWOT
6. Generate and Evaluate Strategic Alternatives
7. Implement Strategies
8. Evaluate and Control

10.8 Impact of the Internet on Evaluation and Control

Privacy is becoming a major issue with the use of the Internet. According to the American Management Association, nearly 75% of U. S. companies actively monitored their workers' communications and on-the-job activities in 2000—more than double the number four years earlier. Around 54% tracked individual employees' Internet connections and 38% admitted storing and reviewing their employees' e-mail. About 45% of the companies surveyed had disciplined workers (16% fired them). For example, Xerox fired 40 employees for visiting pornographic Web sites.[69] New desktop software products now allow anyone—boss, business partner, or spouse—to track a person's Internet activities. One software firm advertises: "Secretly record everything your spouse, children, and employees do online." The U.S. Congress was considering in late 2000 several bills regarding computer surveillance, but none would make monitoring illegal.[70] According to Paul Saffo, Director, Institute of the Future,

> *What will end up happening—and it already is happening—is that privacy becomes an increasingly scarce good that you will pay increasingly more for. That is, if you want an unlisted phone number, you pay for that privilege. If you don't want your transactions tracked. . . . (you know,*

theoretically an electronic transaction could be tracked. In fact, the system's so screwed up I don't think anyone can find anything.) But, in theory, if you didn't want your transactions tracked, you would get cash and put up with the inconvenience of doing that. . . .

Well, I think the fact is there's a multiplicity of players in this. And everybody's trying to have their role. The problem is that the boundaries between the roles are not clear. The legislative process is a very heavy club and not a precise tool. On the other hand, high-tech in particular has a dreadful history about protecting privacy. Companies just can't help but put unique serial numbers in chips or unique serial numbers in software. This is an industry that still calls its customers "users." As far as I know, there are only two high-growth industries on this planet that reserve such a scornful term for their customers. The other one's in Columbia.[71]

Privacy is also an issue for companies wanting to safeguard confidential information from unwanted visitors. Computer hackers are seemingly able to get into almost any company through their Internet Web sites. In October 2000, hackers were able to view Microsoft's source code. They entered the giant software company by infecting the company's network with a Trojan horse program. This was probably done by sliding past disabled antivirus programs, static IP addresses at Microsoft (a problem with any site constantly connected to the Internet via a T-1, cable, or DSL line), and employee laptops used while telecommuting. With this program, hackers obtained Microsoft IP addresses, user names, and passwords in order to access the corporate network from somewhere in Russia.[72]

Intelligence agencies from America, Britain, Canada, Australia and New Zealand jointly monitor all international satellite communications traffic via a system called "Echelon" that can identify specific words or phrases from hundreds of thousand of messages. The National Security Agency (NSA) of the United States and its partners have been accused in the European Parliament of tapping into billions of messages per minutes ranging from telephone calls to e-mail. The NSA was said to have used the Echelon system to assist U.S. corporations to win two large business contracts in the mid-1990s.[73]

Even though the U.S. Congress passed a law allowing digital signature in July 2000, many people are still concerned that the Internet is not a secure means of communicating important or confidential information. Don't expect the Internet to replace FedEx or UPS anytime soon.

Projections for the 21st Century

- From 1994 to 2010, the number of miles traveled by air will double from 1.5 trillion to 3 trillion.
- From 1994 to 2010, the number of credit card transactions will increase from 1.5 trillion to 2 trillion.[74]

Discussion Questions

1. Is **Figure 10–1** a realistic model of the evaluation and control process?

2. What are some examples of behavior controls? Output controls? Input controls?

3. Is EVA an improvement over ROI, ROE, or EPS?

4. How much faith can a manager place in a transfer price as a substitute for a market price in measuring a profit center's performance?

5. Is the evaluation and control process appropriate for a corporation that emphasizes creativity? Are control and creativity compatible?

Strategic Practice Exercise

Each year, *Fortune* magazine publishes an article entitled, "America's Most Admired Companies." It lists the 10 most admired and the 10 least admired. *Fortune's* rankings are based on scoring publicly held U.S. companies on what it calls "eight key attributes of reputation": innovativeness, quality of management, employee talent, quality of products/services, long-term investment value, financial soundness, social responsibility, and use of corporate assets. *Fortune* asks Clark, Martire & Bartolomeo to survey more than 10,000 executives, directors, and securities analysts. Respondents are asked to choose the companies they admire most, regardless of industry. *Fortune* has been publishing this list since 1982. The 2000 *Fortune* listing of the top 10 most admired were (starting with #1): GE, Microsoft, Dell Computer, Cisco Systems, Wal-Mart Stores, Southwest Airlines, Berkshire Hathaway, Intel, Home Depot, and Lucent Technologies. The bottom 10 were: Humana, Revlon, Trans World Airlines, CKE Restaurants, CHS Electronics, Rite Aid, Trump Resorts, Fruit of the Loom, Amerco, and Caremark Rx (least admired).

TRY ONE OF THESE EXERCISES:

1. Go to the library and find a "Most Admired Companies" article from the 1980s or early 1990s and compare that list to the latest one. (See ⟨www.fortune.com⟩ for latest list.) Which companies have fallen out of the top 10? Pick one of the companies to investigate why it is no longer "admired."

2. How much of the evaluation is dominated by the profitability of the company? See how many of the top 10 are very profitable and how many of the bottom 10 are losing money. How many of these companies also appear in *Fortune's* "The 100 Best Companies to Work For"?

3. Pick one of the least admired companies in any year of the survey (such as Trump Resorts) and find out why that company has such a poor reputation. How many of the least admired had received bad publicity the previous year? How many of the least admired companies were listed in multiple years compared to the most admired companies?

Key Terms

80/20 rule (p. 259)
activity-based costing (ABC) (p. 245)
balanced scorecard (p. 250)
behavior controls (p. 243)
behavior substitution (p. 258)
benchmarking (p. 254)
earnings per share (EPS) (p. 246)
economic value added (EVA) (p. 249)
enterprise resource planning (ERP) (p. 256)
evaluation and control information (p. 243)
evaluation and control process (p. 242)
expense center (p. 253)

goal displacement (p. 258)
input controls (p. 243)
international transfer pricing (p. 255)
investment center (p. 253)
ISO 9000 Standards Series (p. 245)
key performance measures (p. 251)
long-term evaluation method (p. 260)
management audits (p. 252)
market value added (MVA) (p. 250)
operating budgets (p. 252)
output controls (p. 243)
performance (p. 243)
periodic statistical reports (p. 252)
piracy (p. 255)

profit center (p. 253)
repatriation of profits (p. 255)
responsibility centers (p. 252)
return on equity (ROE) (p. 247)
return on investment (ROI) (p. 246)
revenue center (p. 252)
shareholder value (p. 248)
short-term orientation (p. 258)
stakeholder measures (p. 247)
standard cost center (p. 252)
steering controls (p. 243)
strategic audit (pp. 252, 262)
strategic-funds method (p. 260)
suboptimization (p. 259)
transfer pricing (p. 253)
weighted-factor method (p. 260)

Strategic Audit of a Corporation

I. Current Situation

A. Current Performance
See Section 10.2 on pages 243–256.

How did the corporation perform the past year overall in terms of return on investment, market share, and profitability?

B. Strategic Posture
See Section 1.3 on pages 7–8.

1. What are the corporation's current mission, objectives, strategies, and policies? Are they clearly stated or are they merely implied from performance?
2. **Mission:** What business(es) is the corporation in? Is the mission statement appropriate?
3. **Objectives:** What are the corporate, business, and functional objectives? Are they consistent with each other, with the mission, and with the internal and external environments?
4. **Strategies:** What are the current corporate, business, and functional strategies? Are they consistent with each other, with the mission and objectives, and with the internal and external environments?
5. **Policies:** What are they? Are they consistent with each other, with the mission, objectives, and strategies, and with the internal and external environments?
6. Do the current mission, objectives, strategies, and policies reflect the corporation's international operations—whether global or multidomestic?

II. Corporate Governance

A. Board of Directors
See Section 2.1 on pages 26–36.

1. Who are the directors? Are they internal or external?
2. Do they own significant shares of stock?
3. Is the stock privately held or publicly traded? Are there different classes of stock with different voting rights?
4. What do they contribute to the corporation in terms of knowledge, skills, background, and connections? If the corporation has international operations, do board members have international experience?
5. How long have they served on the board?
6. What is their level of involvement in strategic management? Do they merely rubber-stamp top management's proposals or do they actively participate and suggest future directions?

Source: T. L. Wheelen and J. D. Hunger, *Strategic Audit of a Corporation.* Copyright © 1982 by Wheelen and Hunger Associates. Reprinted by permission. Revised 1988, 1991, 1994, 1997, and 2001.

B. Top Management — See Sections 2.2 to 2.4 on pages 35–43.

1. What person or group constitutes top management?

2. What are top management's chief characteristics in terms of knowledge, skills, background, and style? If the corporation has international operations, does top management have international experience? Are executives from acquired companies considered part of the top management team?

3. Has top management been responsible for the corporation's performance over the past few years? How many managers have been in their current position for less than three years? Were they internal promotions or external hires?

4. Has it established a systematic approach to strategic management?

5. What is its level of involvement in the strategic management process?

6. How well does top management interact with lower level managers and with the board of directors?

7. Are strategic decisions made ethically in a socially responsible manner?

8. What role do stock options play in executive compensation?

9. Is top management sufficiently skilled to cope with likely future challenges?

III. External Environment: Opportunities and Threats (SW<u>OT</u>)

A. Societal Environment — See Section 3.1 on pages 52–60.

1. What general environmental forces are currently affecting both the corporation and the industries in which it competes? Which present current or future threats? Opportunities? See **Table 3–1** on page 53.

   a) Economic

   b) Technological

   c) Political-legal

   d) Sociocultural

2. Are these forces different in other regions of the world?

B. Task Environment (Industry) — See Section 3.2 on pages 60–70.

1. What forces drive industry competition? Are these forces the same globally or do they vary from country to country?

   a) Threat of new entrants

   b) Bargaining power of buyers

   c) Threat of substitute products or services

   d) Bargaining power of suppliers

   e) Rivalry among competing firms

   f) Relative power of unions, governments, special interest groups, etc.

2. What key factors in the immediate environment (that is, customers, competitors, suppliers, creditors, labor unions, governments, trade associations, interest groups, local communities, and shareholders) are currently affecting the corporation? Which are current or future threats? Opportunities?

C. Summary of External Factors — See EFAS Table on pages 73–74.

Which of these forces and factors are the most important to the corporation and to the industries in which it competes at the present time? Which will be important in the future?

IV. Internal Environment: Strengths and Weaknesses (S<u>W</u>OT)

A. Corporate Structure   See Sections 4.3 and 8.4 on pages 87–100 and 197–209.

1. How is the corporation structured at present?
   a) Is the decision-making authority centralized around one group or decentralized to many units?
   b) Is it organized on the basis of functions, projects, geography, or some combination of these?
2. Is the structure clearly understood by everyone in the corporation?
3. Is the present structure consistent with current corporate objectives, strategies, policies, and programs as well as with the firm's international operations?
4. In what ways does this structure compare with those of similar corporations?

B. Corporate Culture   See Section 4.3 on pages 87–100.

1. Is there a well-defined or emerging culture composed of shared beliefs, expectations, and values?
2. Is the culture consistent with the current objectives, strategies, policies, and programs?
3. What is the culture's position on important issues facing the corporation (that is, on productivity, quality of performance, adaptability to changing conditions, and internationalization)?
4. Is the culture compatible with the employees' diversity of backgrounds?
5. Does the company take into consideration the values of each nation's culture in which the firm operates?

C. Corporate Resources

1. **Marketing**   See Section 4.3 on pages 87–100.
   a) What are the corporation's current marketing objectives, strategies, policies, and programs?
      i. Are they clearly stated, or merely implied from performance and/or budgets?
      ii. Are they consistent with the corporation's mission, objectives, strategies, policies, and with internal and external environments?
   b) How well is the corporation performing in terms of analysis of market position and marketing mix (that is, product, price, place, and promotion) in both domestic and international markets? What percentage of sales comes from foreign operations? Where are current products in product life cycle?
      i. What trends emerge from this analysis?
      ii. What impact have these trends had on past performance and how will they probably affect future performance?
      iii. Does this analysis support the corporation's past and pending strategic decisions?
      iv. Does marketing provide the company with a **competitive advantage**?
   c) How well does this corporation's marketing performance compare with that of similar corporations?
   d) Are marketing managers using accepted marketing concepts and techniques to evaluate and improve product performance? (Consider product life cycle, market segmentation, market research, and product portfolios.)
   e) Does marketing adjust to the conditions in each country in which it operates?
   f) What is the role of the marketing manager in the strategic management process?

2. Finance   **See Sections 4.3 and 14.3 on pages 91–92 and 342–348.**

a) What are the corporation's current financial objectives, strategies, policies, and programs?

     i. Are they clearly stated or merely implied from performance and/or budgets?

     ii. Are they consistent with the corporation's mission, objectives, strategies, policies, and with internal and external environments?

b) How well is the corporation performing in terms of financial analysis? (Consider ratios, common size statements, and capitalization structure.) How balanced, in terms of cash flow, is the company's portfolio of products and businesses?

     i. What trends emerge from this analysis?

     ii. Are there any significant differences when statements are calculated in constant versus reported dollars?

     iii. What impact have these trends had on past performance and how will they probably affect future performance?

     iv. Does this analysis support the corporation's past and pending strategic decisions?

     v. Does finance provide the company with a **competitive advantage**?

c) How well does this corporation's financial performance compare with that of similar corporations?

d) Are financial managers using accepted financial concepts and techniques to evaluate and improve current corporate and divisional performance? (Consider financial leverage, capital budgeting, ratio analysis, and managing foreign currencies.)

e) Does finance adjust to the conditions in each country in which the company operates?

f) What is the role of the financial manager in the strategic management process?

3. Research and Development (R&D)   **See Section 4.3 on pages 92–95.**

a) What are the corporation's current R&D objectives, strategies, policies, and programs?

     i. Are they clearly stated, or merely implied from performance and/or budgets?

     ii. Are they consistent with the corporation's mission, objectives, strategies, policies, and with internal and external environments?

     iii. What is the role of technology in corporate performance?

     iv. Is the mix of basic, applied, and engineering research appropriate given the corporate mission and strategies?

     v. Does R&D provide the company with a **competitive advantage**?

b) What return is the corporation receiving from its investment in R&D?

c) Is the corporation competent in technology transfer? Does it use concurrent engineering and cross-functional work teams in product and process design?

d) What role does technological discontinuity play in the company's products?

e) How well does the corporation's investment in R&D compare with the investments of similar corporations?

f) Does R&D adjust to the conditions in each country in which the company operates?

g) What is the role of the R&D manager in the strategic management process?

4. Operations and Logistics   **See Section 4.3 on pages 95–97.**

a) What are the corporation's current manufacturing/service objectives, strategies, policies, and programs?

     i. Are they clearly stated, or merely implied from performance and/or budgets?

     ii. Are they consistent with the corporation's mission, objectives, strategies, policies, and with internal and external environments?

b) What is the type and extent of operations capabilities of the corporation? How much is done domestically versus internationally? Is the amount of outsourcing appropriate to be competitive? Is purchasing being handled appropriately?

   i. If product-oriented, consider plant facilities, type of manufacturing system (continuous mass production, intermittent job shop, or flexible manufacturing), age and type of equipment, degree and role of automation and/or robots, plant capacities and utilization, productivity ratings, availability and type of transportation.

   ii. If service-oriented, consider service facilities (hospital, theater, or school buildings), type of operations systems (continuous service over time to same clientele or intermittent service over time to varied clientele), age and type of supporting equipment, degree and role of automation and/or use of mass communication devices (diagnostic machinery, videotape machines), facility capacities and utilization rates, efficiency ratings of professional/service personnel, availability and type of transportation to bring service staff and clientele together.

c) Are manufacturing or service facilities vulnerable to natural disasters, local or national strikes, reduction or limitation of resources from suppliers, substantial cost increases of materials, or nationalization by governments?

d) Is there an appropriate mix of people and machines in manufacturing firms, or of support staff to professionals in service firms?

e) How well does the corporation perform relative to the competition? Is it balancing inventory costs (warehousing) with logistical costs (just-in-time)? Consider costs per unit of labor, material, and overhead; downtime; inventory control management and/or scheduling of service staff; production ratings; facility utilization percentages; and number of clients successfully treated by category (if service firm) or percentage of orders shipped on time (if product firm).

   i. What trends emerge from this analysis?

   ii. What impact have these trends had on past performance and how will they probably affect future performance?

   iii. Does this analysis support the corporation's past and pending strategic decisions?

   iv. Does operations provide the company with a **competitive advantage**?

f) Are operations managers using appropriate concepts and techniques to evaluate and improve current performance? Consider cost systems, quality control and reliability systems, inventory control management, personnel scheduling, TQM, learning curves, safety programs, and engineering programs that can improve efficiency of manufacturing or of service.

g) Do operations and logistics adjust to the conditions in each country in which it has facilities?

h) What is the role of the operations manager in the strategic management process?

5. **Human Resources Management (HRM)**   **See Section 4.3 on pages 97–99.**

a) What are the corporation's current HRM objectives, strategies, policies, and programs?

   i. Are they clearly stated, or merely implied from performance and/or budgets?

   ii. Are they consistent with the corporation's mission, objectives, strategies, policies, and with internal and external environments?

b) How well is the corporation's HRM performing in terms of improving the fit between the individual employee and the job? Consider turnover, grievances, strikes, layoffs, employee training, and quality of work life.

   i. What trends emerge from this analysis?

   ii. What impact have these trends had on past performance and how will they probably affect future performance?

      iii. Does this analysis support the corporation's past and pending strategic decisions?

      iv. Does HRM provide the company with a **competitive advantage**?

      v. Do the company's employees (skills, education, knowledge) provide the company with a **competitive advantage**?

c) How does this corporation's HRM performance compare with that of similar corporations?

d) Are HRM managers using appropriate concepts and techniques to evaluate and improve corporate performance? Consider the job analysis program, performance appraisal system, up-to-date job descriptions, training and development programs, attitude surveys, job design programs, quality of relationship with unions, and use of autonomous work teams.

e) How well is the company managing the diversity of its workforce? What is the company's position and record on human rights?

f) Does HRM adjust to the conditions in each country in which the company operates? Does the company have a code of conduct for HRM in developing nations? Are employees receiving international assignments to prepare them for managerial positions?

g) What is the role of the HRM manager in the strategic management process?

6. **Information Systems (IS)**   See Section 4.3 on pages 99–100.

a) What are the corporation's current IS objectives, strategies, policies, and programs?

      i. Are they clearly stated, or merely implied from performance and/or budgets?

      ii. Are they consistent with the corporation's mission, objectives, strategies, policies, and with internal and external environments?

b) How well is the corporation's IS performing in terms of providing a useful database, offering Internet access and Web sites, automating routine clerical operations, assisting managers in making routine decisions, and providing information necessary for strategic decisions?

      i. What trends emerge from this analysis?

      ii. What impact have these trends had on past performance and how will they probably affect future performance?

      iii. Does this analysis support the corporation's past and pending strategic decisions?

      iv. Does IS provide the company with a **competitive advantage**?

c) How does this corporation's IS performance and stage of development compare with that of similar corporations? Is it appropriately using the Internet?

d) Are IS managers using appropriate concepts and techniques to evaluate and improve corporate performance? Do they know how to build and manage a complex database, establish Web sites with firewalls, conduct system analyses, and implement interactive decision-support systems?

e) Does the company have a global IS and Internet presence? Does it have difficulty with getting data across national boundaries?

f) What is the role of the IS manager in the strategic management process?

D. Summary of Internal Factors   See IFAS Table on pages 101–102.

Which of these factors are *core competencies*? Which are *distinctive competencies*? Which of these factors are the most important to the corporation and to the industries in which it competes at the present time? Which of these factors will be important in the future?

V. Analysis of Strategic Factors (SWOT)
See Sections 5.1 and 5.2 on pages 109–114.

A. Situational Analysis   See SFAS Table on pages 110–112.

What are the most important internal and external factors (*Strengths, Weaknesses, Opportunities, Threats*) that strongly affect the corporation's present and future performance? List 8 to 10 strategic factors.

B. Review of Mission and Objectives   See Section 5.2 on page 114.

1. Are the current mission and objectives appropriate in light of the key strategic factors and problems?
2. Should the mission and objectives be changed? If so, how?
3. If changed, what will be the effects on the firm?

VI. Strategic Alternatives and Recommended Strategy

A. Strategic Alternatives   See Sections 5.3, 5.4, 6.2, and 7.1 on pages 114–115, 115–130, 138–150, and 165–177.

1. Can the current or revised **objectives** be met by the simple, more careful implementing of those strategies presently in use (for example, fine-tuning the strategies)?
2. What are the major feasible alternative **strategies** available to this corporation? What are the pros and cons of each? Can corporate scenarios be developed and agreed upon? **(Alternatives must fit societal environment, industry, and company for next 3–5 years.)**
   a) Consider *cost leadership* and *differentiation* as business strategies.
   b) Consider *stability, growth*, and *retrenchment* as corporate strategies.
   c) Consider any functional strategic alternatives that might be needed for reinforcement of an important corporate or business strategic alternative.

B. Recommended Strategy   See Sections 7.3 and 7.4 on pages 177–184.

1. Specify which of the strategic alternatives you are recommending for the corporate, business, and functional levels of the corporation. Do you recommend different business or functional strategies for different units of the corporation?
2. Justify your recommendation in terms of its ability to resolve both long- and short-term problems and effectively deal with the strategic factors.
3. What **policies** should be developed or revised to guide effective implementation?
4. What is the impact of recommended strategy on the company's core and distinctive competencies?

VII. Implementation   See Chapters 8 and 9.

A. What kinds of programs (for example, restructuring the corporation or instituting TQM) should be developed to implement the recommended strategy?

1. Who should develop these programs?
2. Who should be in charge of these programs?

B. Are the programs financially feasible? Can pro forma budgets be developed and agreed upon? Are priorities and timetables appropriate to individual programs?

C. Will new standard operating procedures need to be developed?

VIII. Evaluation and Control   See Chapter 10.

A. Is the current information system capable of providing sufficient feedback on implementation activities and performance? Can it measure strategic factors?

1. Can performance results be pinpointed by area, unit, project, or function?
2. Is the information timely?

B. Are adequate control measures in place to ensure conformance with the recommended strategic plan?

1. Are appropriate standards and measures being used?
2. Are reward systems capable of recognizing and rewarding good performance?
3. Who takes corrective action?

Notes

1. K. F. Iverson with T. Varian, "Plain Talk," *INC.* (October 1997), p. 81. Excerpted from Iverson's book, *Plain Talk: Lessons from a Business Maverick*, published by John Wiley, 1997.
2. D. Pickton, M. Starkey, and M. Bradford, "Understand Business Variation for Improved Business Performance," *Long Range Planning* (June 1996), pp. 412–415.
3. R. Muralidharan and R. D. Hamilton III, "Aligning Multinational Control Systems," *Long Range Planning* (June 1999), pp. 352–361. These types are based on W. G. Ouchi, "The Relationship Between Organizational Structure and Organizational Control," *Administrative Science Quarterly*, Vol. 20 (1977), pp. 95–113, and W. G. Ouchi, "A Conceptual Framework for the Design of Organizational Control Mechanisms," *Management Science*, Vol. 25 (1979), pp. 833–848. Muralidhara and Hamilton refer to Ouchi's clan control as input control.
4. W. G. Rowe and P. M. Wright, "Related and Unrelated Diversification and Their Effect on Human Resource Management Controls," *Strategic Management Journal* (April 1997), pp. 329–338.
5. Muralidharan and Hamilton, pp. 356–359.
6. F. C. Barnes, "ISO 9000 Myth and Reality: A Reasonable Approach to ISO 9000," *SAM Advanced Management Journal* (Spring 1998), pp. 23–30.
7. M. V. Uzumeri, "ISO 9000 and Other Metastandards: Principles for Management Practice?" *Academy of Management Executive* (February 1997), pp. 21–36.
8. A. M. Hormozi, "Understanding and Implementing ISO 9000: A Manager's Guide," *SAM Advanced Management Journal* (Autumn 1995), pp. 4–11.
9. J. K. Shank and V. Govindarajan, *Strategic Cost Management* (New York: The Free Press, 1993).
10. S. S. Rao, "ABCs of Cost Control," *Inc. Technology*, No. 2 (1997), pp. 79–81.
11. R. Gruber, "Why You Should Consider Activity-Based Costing," *Small Business Forum* (Spring 1994), pp. 20–36.
12. T. P. Pare, "A New Tool For Managing Costs," *Fortune* (June 14, 1993), pp. 124–129.
13. C. K. Brancato, *New Corporate Performance Measures* (New York: The Conference Board, 1995).
14. C. D. Ittner, D. F. Larcker, and M. V. Rajan, "The Choice of Performance Measures in Annual Bonus Contracts," Working paper reported by K. Z. Andrews in "Executive Bonuses," *Harvard Business Review* (January–February 1996), pp. 8–9; J. Low and T. Siesfeld, "Measures that Matter: Wall Street Considers Non-Financial Performance More than You Think," *Strategy & Leadership* (March/April 1998), pp. 24–30.
15. S. Tully, "America's Best Wealth Creators," *Fortune* (November 28, 1994), p. 143.
16. P. C. Brewer, G. Chandra, and C. A. Hock, "Economic Value Added (EVA): Its Uses and Limitations," *SAM Advanced Management Journal* (Spring 1999), pp. 4–11.
17. D. J. Skyrme and D. M. Amidon, "New Measures of Success," *Journal of Business Strategy* (January/February 1998), p. 23.
18. G. B. Stewart III, "EVA Works—But Not If You Make These Common Mistakes," *Fortune* (May 1, 1995), pp. 117–118.
19. S. Tully, "The Real Key to Creating Wealth," *Fortune* (September 20, 1993), p. 38.
20. A. Ehrbar, "Using EVA to Measure Performance and Assess Strategy," *Strategy & Leadership* (May/June 1999), pp. 20–24.
21. Brewer, Chandra, and Hock, pp. 7–9.
22. PRO: K. Lehn and A. K. Makhija, "EVA & MVA as Performance Measures and Signals for Strategic Change," *Strategy & Leadership* (May/June 1996), pp. 34–38. CON: D. I. Goldenberg, "Shareholder Value Debunked," *Strategy & Leadership* (January/February 2000), pp. 30–36.
23. Ehrbar, p. 21.

24. S. Tully, "America's Wealth Creators," *Fortune* (November 22, 1999), pp. 275–284, and A. B. Fisher, "Creating Stockholder Wealth: Market Value Added," *Fortune* (December 11, 1995), pp. 105–116.
25. A. B. Fisher, "Creating Stockholder Wealth: Market Value Added," *Fortune* (December 11, 1995), pp. 105–116.
26. Lehn and Makhija, p. 37.
27. R. S. Kaplan and D. P. Norton, "Using the Balanced Scorecard as a Strategic Management System," *Harvard Business Review* (January–February 1996), pp. 75–85; R. S. Kaplan and D. P. Norton, "The Balanced Scorecard—Measures that Drive Performance," *Harvard Business Review* (January–February, 1992), pp. 71–79.
28. D. I. Goldenberg, p. 34.
29. C. K. Brancato, *New Performance Measures* (New York: The Conference Board, 1995).
30. B. P. Stivers and T. Joyce, "Building a Balanced Performance Management System," *SAM Advanced Management Journal* (Spring 2000), pp. 22–29.
31. D. J. Skyrme and D. M. Amidon, p. 22.
32. R. Charan, *Boards At Work* (San Francisco, CA: Jossey-Bass, 1998), pp. 176–177.
33. T. D. Schellhardt, "Directors Get Tough: Inside a CEO Performance Review," *Wall Street Journal Interactive Edition* (April 27, 1998).
34. H. Threat, "Measurement Is Free," *Strategy & Leadership* (May/June 1999), pp. 16–19.
35. Z. U. Khan, S. K. Chawla, M. F. Smith, and M. F. Sharif, "Transfer Pricing Policy Issues in Europe 1992," *International Journal of Management* (September 1992), pp. 230–241.
36. H. Rothman, "You Need Not Be Big to Benchmark," *Nation's Business* (December 1992), p. 64.
37. C. W. Von Bergen and B. Soper, "A Problem with Benchmarking: Using Shaping as a Solution," *SAM Advanced Management Journal* (Autumn 1995), pp. 16–19.
38. "Tool Usage Rates," *Journal of Business Strategy* (March/April 1995), p. 12.
39. R. J. Kennedy, "Benchmarking and Its Myths," *Competitive Intelligence Magazine* (April–June 2000), pp. 28–33.
40. L. Mann, D. Samson, and D. Dow, "A Field Experiment on the Effects of Benchmarking & Goal Setting on Company Sales Performance," *Journal of Management*, Vol. 24, No. 1 (1998), pp. 73–96.
41. S. A. W. Drew, "From Knowledge to Action: The Impact of Benchmarking on Organizational Performance," *Long Range Planning* (June 1997), pp. 427–441.
42. S. M. Robbins and R. B. Stobaugh, "The Bent Measuring Stick for Foreign Subsidiaries," *Harvard Business Review* (September–October 1973), p. 82.
43. J. D. Daniels and L. H. Radebaugh, *International Business*, 5th ed. (Reading, Mass.: Addison-Wesley, 1989), pp. 673–674.
44. W. A. Johnson and R. J. Kirsch, "International Transfer Pricing and Decision Making in United States Multinationals," *International Journal of Management* (June 1991), pp. 554–561.
45. "Global Economy Makes Taxing Harder," *The Futurist* (March–April 2000), p. 11; "Financial Indicators," *The Economist* (August 26, 2000), p. 89.
46. "Fixing the Bottom Line," *Time* (November 23, 1992), p. 20.
47. T. A. Stewart, "The New Face of American Power," *Fortune* (July 26, 1993), p. 72; G. P. Zachary, "Behind Stocks' Surge Is an Economy in Which Big U.S. Firms Thrive," *Wall Street Journal* (November 22, 1995), pp. A1, A5.
48. J. M. L. Poon, R. Ainuddin, and H. Affrim, "Management Policies and Practices of American, British, European, and Japanese Subsidiaries in Malaysia: A Comparative Study," *International Journal of Management* (December 1990), pp. 467–474.
49. C. W. L. Hill, P. Hwang, and W. C. Kim, "An Eclectic Theory of the Choice of International Entry Mode," *Strategic Management*

Journal (February 1990), pp. 117–128; D. Lei, J. W. Slocum, Jr., and R. W. Slater, "Global Strategy and Reward Systems: The Key Roles of Management Development and Corporate Culture," *Organizational Dynamics* (Autumn 1990), pp. 27–41; W. R. Fannin and A. F. Rodriques, "National or Global?—Control vs. Flexibility," *Long Range Planning* (October 1986), pp. 84–88.
50. A. V. Phatak, *International Dimensions of Management*, 2nd ed. (Boston: Kent, 1989), pp. 155–157.
51. S. McAlary, "Three Pitfalls in ERP Implementation," *Strategy & Leadership* (October/November/December 1999), pp. 49–50.
52. J. B. White, D. Clark, and S. Ascarelli, "This German Software Is Complex, Expensive—and Wildly Popular," *Wall Street Journal* (March 14, 1997), pp. A1, A8; D. Ward, "Whirlpool Takes a Dive with Software Snarl," *Des Moines Register* (April 29, 2000), p. 8D.
53. B. Richards, "The Business Plan," *Wall Street Journal* (November 11, 1996), p. R10.
54. R. M. Hodgetts and M. S. Wortman, *Administrative Policy*, 2nd ed. (New York: John Wiley & Sons, 1980), p. 128.
55. J. R. Wooldridge and C. C. Snow, "Stock Market Reaction to Strategic Investment Decisions," *Strategic Management Journal* (September 1990), pp. 353–363.
56. D. R. Schmidt and K. L. Fowler, "Post-Acquisition Financial Performance and Executive Compensation," *Strategic Management Journal* (November–December 1990), pp. 559–569.
57. D. Jones, "Bad News Can Enrich Executives," *Des Moines Register* (November 26, 1999), p. 8S.
58. J. F. Porac, J. B. Wade, and T. G. Pollock, "Industry Categories and the Politics of the Comparable Firm in CEO Compensation," *Administrative Science Quarterly* (March 1999), pp. 112–144.
59. W. Zellner, E. Schine, and G. Smith, "Trickle-Down Is Trickling Down at Work," *Business Week* (March 18, 1996), p. 34.
60. T. J. Peters and R. H. Waterman, *In Search of Excellence* (New York: HarperCollins, 1982), pp. 75–76.
61. T. Aeppel, "Not All Workers Find Idea of Empowerment as Neat as It Sounds," *Wall Street Journal* (September 8, 1997), pp. A1, A13.
62. D. B. Balkin and L. R. Gomez-Mejia, "Matching Compensation and Organizational Strategies," *Strategic Management Journal* (February 1990), pp. 153–169.
63. C. S. Galbraith, "The Effect of Compensation Programs and Structure on SBU Competitive Strategy: A Study of Technology-Intensive Firms," *Strategic Management Journal* (July 1991), pp. 353–370.
64. T. A. Stewart, "CEO Pay: Mom Wouldn't Approve," *Fortune* (March 31, 1997), pp. 119–120.
65. P. J. Stonich, "The Performance Measurement and Reward System: Critical to Strategic Management," *Organizational Dynamics* (Winter 1984), pp. 45–57.
66. A. Rappaport, "New Thinking on How to Link Executive Pay with Performance," *Harvard Business Review* (March–April 1999), pp. 91–101.
67. W. Grossman and R. E. Hoskisson, "CEO Pay at the Crossroads of Wall Street and Main: Toward the Strategic Design of Executive Compensation," *Academy of Management Executive* (February 1998), pp. 43–57.
68. T. L. Wheelen and J. D. Hunger, "Using the Strategic Audit," *SAM Advanced Management Journal* (Winter 1987), pp. 4–12; G. Donaldson, "A New Tool for Boards: The Strategic Audit," *Harvard Business Review* (July–August 1995), pp. 99–107.
69. L. Armstrong, "Someone to Watch Over You," *Business Week* (July 10, 2000), pp. 189–190.
70. B. Wallace and J. Fenton, "Is Your PC Watching You?" *PC World* (December 2000), pp. 59–63.
71. *The Charlie Rose Show* on PBS, transcript of May 24, 1999.
72. C. Machrone, "Security," *PC Magazine* (February 6, 2001), p. 159.
73. "The Surveillance Society," *The Economist*, May 1, 1999, p. 22.
74. J. Warner, "21st Century Capitalism: Snapshot of the Next Century," *Business Week* (November 18, 1994), p. 194.

Newbury Comics, Inc

IMPLEMENTATION AND CONTROL

Newbury Comics Cofounders Mike Dreese and John Brusger parlayed $2,000 and a comic book collection into a thriving chain of 22 stores spanning the New England region, known to be *the* place to shop for everything from the best of the underground/independent scene to major label superstars. The chain also stocks a wide variety of non-music related items such as T-shirts, Dr. (doc) Martens shoes, posters, jewelry, cosmetics, books, magazines, and other trendy items.

In Part Four, "**Strategy Implementation and Control**," the video focuses on Newbury Comics' used CD business. Mike, John, and Jan discuss the development of procedures and control processes for introducing the used CD program. Budgeting is indirectly mentioned in terms of huge expenditures made at the six-month point to greatly expand the program. The video also highlights the importance of having the right staff to implement a strategy.

As pointed out in Part 3 of the Video Case, the project of developing an implementation plan was assigned to Duncan Brown, Senior Vice President. Part of this plan was to begin the used CD program in a few stores and then evaluate how well the program was working. This was a very ad hoc approach to implementation, but it fit the very loose entrepreneurial approach Newbury Comics takes toward strategy formulation. Mike tells us that he is more interested in "continuous improvement" than in setting specific sales or profit objectives. He admits that one reason he wanted to enter the used CD business was because he likes being a "pioneer" (i.e., first mover). But being a pioneer has its problems.

Jan points out that when the used CD program was started, a store would just put up signs saying that it now bought and sold used CDs. It was then up to the manager to set both the buying and selling price for each CD (with no help from any computer). The headquarters office would then print tags for that store. As a result, stores (even the same store) would offer the same CD for a different price. Following Mike's belief in encouraging creativity and individual initiative, there were no attempts to place blame during this implementation period.

Mike points out that the used CD business is much more complicated than dealing with new CDs. Although management saw it as a risky business, they also believed that its potential for the company outweighed the risk. Because of the many complications of the used CD business, it resulted in a series of new activities in implementation, evaluation, and control, such as choosing what CDs to buy at what price, cleaning, and packaging them. These new activities resulted in adding new job duties at the store level, warehouse, and main office—thus changing the structure of the organization from one of being fairly decentralized at the store level to one with much more centralization of decision making at headquarters. The main office took control of pricing. The IBM AS-400 computer was part of the information system developed for the used CD bar code program to integrate information from all the stores. Duties were expanded and positions were added at the headquarters office and warehouse to deal with finding sources of bulk shipments, setting prices, and sorting, cleaning, and packaging used CDs. Special relationships were developed with some bulk suppliers of used CDs to make sure that Newbury Comics would get the first look at a new batch in return for paying more than other purchasers. A system of procedures was developed to sell non-selling used CDs to other retailers.

- Strategy Implementation: Programs, Budgets, and Procedures
- Achieving Synergy
- Job Design
- Staffing Follows Strategy
- Evaluation and Control: Measuring Performance
- Strategic Information Systems

Study Questions

1. Why was the used CD program at Newbury Comics a success?
2. What programs and procedures did management use to implement the growth strategy?
3. How important is staffing to this company's success?
4. How does the structure of Newbury Comics help or hinder the company's growth?
5. How is synergy achieved throughout the company?

chapter 11

Strategic Issues in Managing Technology and Innovation

Trilogy Software, Inc., is in the business of creating new businesses by properly managing new technology and innovative concepts. A private company with more than $200 million in revenues, Trilogy recruits the best engineers directly from campus by offering them a direct chance to build the company. The new employees attend a three-month intensive training program, called Trilogy University, taught by senior managers. Joe Liemandt, Cofounder and President of Trilogy, challenges every class to create at least 20% of new revenues within two years. Since the company is private, it doesn't motivate by offering stock options. Instead, it offers employees the chance to create and run new businesses. Thus far, Trilogy has spun off six new companies.

Liemandt uses the Internet to establish conversations with Trilogy's 1,500 employees. He asks them not only to respond to mission statements drafted by top management, but also to periodically assess managers online. According to President Liemandt, "Energy and excitement is why people do start-ups. But as the company gets larger, people don't feel as engaged. They feel as if they are spoken to instead of being engaged in a collaboration. The net provides a 10-to-20-fold increase in the level of interaction you can have."[1]

Trilogy is a good example of a company successfully energizing its people to create new products and services. Properly managing technology and innovation is crucial in a fast-moving interconnected world. Over the past 15 years, the top 20% of firms in an annual innovation poll conducted by *Fortune* magazine achieved double the shareholder returns of their peers.[2] Nevertheless, many large firms find it difficult to be continually innovative. A recent

Table 11–1 Executives Fear Their Companies Are Becoming Less Innovative

A survey of business executives conducted by *Fortune* with the consulting firm, Integral, Inc., revealed the percentages of those responding either **agree** or **strongly agree** to the following five statements:

■ Your company has recently lost relatively low-value customers in small market niches or low-end market segments.	55%
■ Your organization passes up growth opportunities it would have pursued when the company was smaller because the opportunities are now "too small to be interesting."	60%
■ There is a disconnect between the kind of innovations your frontline troops suggest and the types of innovations upper management invests in.	64%
■ When your organization sees a potentially disruptive technology, it defines it as a technical problem ("Will our customers accept the product?") instead of a market problem.	58%
■ New entrants have exploited opportunities where uncertainty over market size and customer needs resulted in inaction by your company.	68%

Source: "Don't Leave Us Behind," *Fortune* (April 3, 2000), p. 250. Copyright © 2000 Time, Inc. All rights reserved.

survey of business executives reveals that a significant majority are concerned that their companies are losing growth opportunities because they are not able to properly manage new technology (see **Table 11–1**).[3] Even innovative established companies, such as 3M, Procter & Gamble, and Rubbermaid, have had a recent slowing in their rate of successful new product introductions.[4]

In this chapter, we examine strategic issues in technology and innovation as they impact environmental scanning, strategy formulation, strategy implementation, and evaluation and control.

11.1 Role of Management

Due to increased competition and accelerated product development cycles, innovation and the management of technology is becoming crucial to corporate success. Research conducted by *Forbes*, Ernst & Young, and the Wharton School of Business found the most important driver of corporate value for both durable and nondurable companies to be innovation.[5] Approximately half the profits of all U.S. companies come from products launched in the previous 10 years.[6] What is less obvious is how a company can generate a significant return from investment in R&D as well as an overall sense of enthusiasm for innovative behavior and risk taking. One way is to include innovation in the corporation's mission statement. See the **boxed example** for mission statements from well-known companies. Another way is by establishing policies that support the innovative process. For

Examples of Innovation Emphasis in Mission Statements

To emphasize the importance of technology, creativity, and innovation to overall future corporate success, some well-known firms have added sections to this effect in their published mission statements. Some of these are listed here.

AT&T: "We believe innovation is the engine that will keep us vital and growing. Our culture embraces creativity, seeks different perspectives and risks pursuing new opportunities. We create and rapidly convert technology into products and services, constantly searching for new ways to make technology more useful to customers."

General Mills: "Innovation is the principal driver of growth. . . . To be first among our competitors, we must constantly challenge the status quo and be willing to experiment. . . . Our motivation system will strongly reward successful risk taking, while not penalizing an innovative idea that did not work."

Gerber: "[The mission will be achieved by] investing in continued product and body-of-knowledge, innovation, and research in the areas of infant nutrition, care, and development."

Gillette: "We will invest in and master the key technologies vital to category success."

Hallmark: "[We believe] that creativity and quality—in our concept, products and services—are essential to our success."

Intel: "To succeed we must maintain our innovative environment. We strive to embrace change, challenge the status quo, listen to all ideas and viewpoints, encourage and reward informed risk taking, and learn from our successes and mistakes."

Merck & Co.: "We are dedicated to achieving the highest level of scientific excellence and commit our research to maintaining human health and improving the quality of life."

Source: P. Jones and L. Kahaner, *Say It and Live It: The 50 Corporate Mission Statements That Hit the Mark* (New York: Currency Doubleday, 1995).

example, 3M has set a policy of generating at least 25% of its revenue from products introduced in the preceding three years. To support this policy, this $13 billion corporation annually spends nearly $1 billion in R&D.[7]

The importance of technology and innovation must be emphasized by people at the very top and reinforced by people throughout the corporation. If top management and the board are not interested in these topics, managers below them tend to echo their lack of interest. When Akio Morita, Chairman of Sony Corporation, visited the United Kingdom a number of years ago, he expressed disbelief at the number of accountants leading that country's companies. Uncomfortable because they lacked familiarity with science or technology, these top managers too often limited their role to approving next year's budget. Constrained by what the company could afford and guided by how much the competition was spending, they perceived R&D as a line expense item instead of as an investment in the future.[8]

Management has an obligation to not only encourage new product development, but also to develop a system to ensure that technology is being used most effectively with the consumer in mind. Between 33% and 60% of all new products that reach the market fail to make a profit.[9] A study by Chicago consultants Kuczmarski & Associates of 11,000 new products marketed by 77 manufacturing, service, and consumer-product firms revealed that only 56% of all newly introduced products were still being sold five years later. Only 1 in 13 new product ideas ever made it into test markets. Although some authorities argue that this percentage of successful new products needs to be improved, others contend that too high a percentage means that a company isn't taking the risks necessary to develop a really new product.[10]

The importance of top management's providing appropriate direction is exemplified by Chairman Morita's statement of his philosophy for Sony Corporation:

> The key to success for Sony, and to everything in business, science, and technology for that matter, is never to follow the others . . . . Our basic concept has always been this—to give new convenience, or new methods, or new benefits, to the general public with our technology.

Morita and his Cofounder, Masuru Ibuka, always looked for ways to turn ideas into clear targets. Says Morita, "When Ibuka was first describing his idea for the Betamax videocassette, he gave the engineers a paperback book and said, 'Make it this size.' Those were his only instructions."[11]

11.2 Environmental Scanning

EXTERNAL SCANNING

Corporations need to continually scan their external societal and task environments for new developments in technology that may have some application to their current or potential products. Stakeholders, especially customers, can be important participants in the new product development process.

Technological Developments

Motorola, a company well known for its ability to invest in profitable new technologies and manufacturing improvements, has a sophisticated scanning system. Its intelligence department monitors the latest technology developments introduced at scientific conferences, in journals, and in trade gossip. This information helps it build "technology roadmaps" that assess where breakthroughs are likely to occur, when they can be incorporated into new products, how much money their development will cost, and which of the developments is being worked on by the competition.[12]

Focusing one's scanning efforts too closely on one's own industry is dangerous. Most new developments that threaten existing business practices and technologies do not come from existing competitors or even from within traditional industries.[13] A new technology that can substitute for an existing technology at a lower cost and provide higher quality can change the very basis for competition in an industry. Consider, for example, the impact of Internet technology on the personal computer software industry. Microsoft Corporation had ignored the developing Internet technology while the company battled successfully with IBM, Lotus, and WordPerfect to dominate operating system software via Windows 95 as well as word processing and spreadsheet programs via Microsoft Office. Ironically, just as Microsoft introduced its new Windows 95 operating system, newcomer Netscape used Java applets in its user-friendly, graphically oriented browser program with the potential to make operating systems unnecessary. By the time Microsoft realized this threat to its business, Netscape had already established itself as the industry standard for browsers. Microsoft was forced to spend huge amounts of time and resources trying to catch up to Netscape's dominant market share with its own Internet Explorer browser.

One way to learn about new technological developments in an industry is to locate part of a company's R&D or manufacturing in those locations making a strong impact on product development. Large multinational corporations undertake between 5% and 25% of their R&D outside their home country.[14] For example, automobile companies like to have design centers in Southern California and in Italy, key areas for automotive styling. Software companies throughout the world know that they must have a programming presence in Silicon Valley if they are to compete on the leading edge of technology. The same is true of the semiconductor industry in terms of manufacturing.[15]

Impact of Stakeholders on Innovation

A company should look to its stakeholders, especially its customers, suppliers, and distributors, for sources of product and service improvements. These groups of people have the most to gain from innovative new products or services. Under certain circumstances, they may propose new directions for product development. Some of the methods of gathering information from key stakeholders are using lead users, market research, and new product experimentation.

Lead Users

Research by Von Hippel indicates customers are a key source of innovation in many industries. For example, 77% of the innovations developed in the scientific instruments industry came from the users of the products. Suppliers are often important sources as well. Suppliers accounted for 36% of innovations in the thermoplastics industry, according to Von Hippel.[16] One way to commercialize a new technology is through early and in-depth involvement with a firm's customer in a process called co-development.[17] This type of customer can be called a "lead user."

Von Hippel proposes that companies should look to lead users for help in product development, especially in high technology industries where things move so quickly that a product is becoming obsolete by the time it arrives on the market. These **lead users** are "companies, organizations, or individuals that are well ahead of market trends and have needs that go far beyond those of the average user."[18] They are the first to adopt a product because they benefit significantly from its use—even if it is not fully developed.

At 3M, for example, a product development team in 3M's Medical Surgical Markets Division was charged with creating a breakthrough in the area of surgical drapes—the material that prevents infections from spreading during surgery. At the time, 3M dominated the market but had not developed a new product improvement in almost a decade. After spending six weeks learning about the cause and prevention of infections, the project team spent six more weeks investigating trends in infection control. The team then worked to identify lead users—doctors in developing nations and veterinarians who couldn't afford the current expensive drapes. The team invited several lead users to a 2½-day workshop focused on "Can we find a revolutionary, low-cost approach to infection control?" The workshop generated concepts for six new product lines and a radical new approach to infection control. The team chose the three strongest concepts for presentation to senior management. 3M has successfully applied the lead user method in 8 of its 55 divisions.

Lead user teams are typically composed of four to six people from marketing and technical departments with one person serving as project leader. Team members usually spend 12 to 15 hours per week on the project for its duration. For planning purposes, a team should allow 4 to 6 weeks for each phase and four to six months for the entire project. The *four phases of the lead user process* are:

1. **Laying the Foundation:** Identify target markets and the type and level of innovations desired.
2. **Determining the Trends:** Research the field and talk with experts with a broad view of emerging technologies and leading-edge applications.

3. **Identify Lead Users:** Talk with users at the leading edge of the target and related markets to understand their needs.

4. **Develop the Breakthrough:** Host a two- to three-day workshop with several lead users and a half dozen marketing and technical people. Participants first work in small groups and then as a whole to design the final concepts that fit the company's and the users' needs.[19]

Market Research

A more traditional method of obtaining new product ideas is to use **market research** to survey current users regarding what they would like in a new product. This method has been successfully used by companies such as Procter & Gamble to identify consumer preferences. It is especially useful in directing incremental improvements to existing products. For example, the auto maker BMW solicits suggestions from BMW owners to improve its current offerings and to obtain ideas for new products.

Market research may not, however, necessarily provide the information needed for truly innovative products or services (radical innovation). According to Sony executive Kozo Ohsone, "When you introduce products that have never been invented before, what good is market research?" For example, Hal Sperlich took the concept of the minivan from Ford to Chrysler when Ford refused to develop the concept. According to Sperlich,

> [Ford] lacked confidence that a market existed because the product didn't exist. The auto industry places great value on historical studies of market segments. Well, we couldn't prove there was a market for the minivan because there was no historical segment to cite. In Detroit most product-development dollars are spent on modest improvements to existing products, and most market research money is spent on studying what customers like among available products. In 10 years of developing the minivan we never once got a letter from a housewife asking us to invent one. To the skeptics, that proved there wasn't a market out there.[20]

A heavy emphasis on being customer-driven could actually prevent companies from developing innovative new products. A study of the impact of **technological discontinuity** (explained earlier in **Chapter 4**) in various industries revealed that the leading firms failed to switch to the new technology not because management was ignorant of the new development, but rather because they listened too closely to their current customers. In all of these firms, a key task of management was to decide which of the many product and development programs continually being proposed to them should receive financial resources. The criterion used for the decision was the total return perceived in each project, adjusted by the perceived riskiness of the project. Projects targeted at the known needs of key customers in established markets consistently won the most resources. Sophisticated systems for planning and compensation favored this type of project every time. As a result, the leading companies continued to use the established technology to make the products its current customers demanded, allowing smaller entrepreneurial competitors to develop the new, more risky technology.[21]

Because the market for the innovative products based on the new technology was fairly small at first, new ventures had time to fine-tune product design, build sufficient manufacturing capacity, and establish the product as the industry standard (as Netscape did with its Internet browser). As the marketplace began to embrace the new standard, the customers of the leading companies began to ask for products based on the new technology. Although some established manufacturers were able to defend their market share positions through aggressive product development and marketing activity (as Microsoft did against Netscape), many firms, finding that the new entrants had developed insurmountable advantages in manufacturing cost and design experience, were forced out of the market. Even the established manufacturers that converted to the new technology were unable to win a significant share of the new market.[22]

New Product Experimentation   Instead of using lead users or market research to test the potential of innovative products, some successful companies are using speed and flexibility to gain market information. These companies developed their products by "probing" potential markets with early versions of the products, learning from the probes, and probing again.[23] For example, Seiko's only market research is surprisingly simple. The company introduces hundreds of new models of watches into the marketplace. It makes more of the models that sell; it drops those that don't.

The consulting firm Arthur D. Little found that the use of standard market research techniques has only resulted in a success rate of 8% for new cereals—92% of all new cereals fail. As a result, innovative firms, such as Keebler and the leading cereal makers, are reducing their expenditures for market research and working to reduce the cost of launching new products by making their manufacturing processes more flexible.[24]

From its beginning as a software company, Microsoft has successfully followed a strategy of monitoring the competition for new developments. It follows an *embrace and extend* strategy of imitating new products developed by pioneers, refining them, and outmarketing the competition. (This approach is nothing new. Procter & Gamble did this to *Lestoil* when P&G introduced *Mr. Clean.*) Microsoft's distinctive competency is its ability to change directions and adjust priorities when the market changes.[25] The company purchased the rights to a program that formed the basis for PC DOS, which it sold to IBM for its personal computers. It then imitated the "look and feel" of Apple's graphical user interface (which Steve Jobs had first seen at Xerox's Palo Alto Research Center) with its Windows operating system. Once the company realized the importance of the Internet browser, it developed its own Internet Explorer and has successfully battled Netscape for market share.

INTERNAL SCANNING

In addition to scanning the external environment, strategists should also assess their company's ability to innovate effectively by asking the following questions:

1. Has the company developed the resources needed to try new ideas?
2. Do the managers allow experimentation with new products or services?
3. Does the corporation encourage risk taking and tolerate mistakes?
4. Are people more concerned with new ideas or with defending their turf?
5. Is it easy to form autonomous project teams?[26]

In addition to answering these questions, strategists should assess how well company resources are internally allocated and evaluate the organization's ability to develop and transfer new technology in a timely manner into the generation of innovative products and services. These issues are important given that it takes on average seven ideas to generate a new commercial product, according to the Product and Development and Management Association.[27]

RESOURCE ALLOCATION ISSUES

The company must make available the resources necessary for effective research and development. Research indicates that a company's **R&D intensity** (its spending on R&D as a percentage of sales revenue) is a principal means of gaining market share in global competition.[28] The amount of money spent on R&D often varies by industry. For example, the computer software and drug industries spend an average of 11% to 13% of their sales dollar for R&D. Others, such as the food and the containers and packaging industries, spend less than 1%. A good rule of thumb for R&D spending is that a corporation should spend at a "normal" rate for that particular industry, unless its competitive strategy dictates otherwise.[29] Research indicates that consistency in R&D strategy and resource allocation across lines of business improves corporate performance by enabling the firm to better develop synergies among product lines and business units.[30]

Simply spending money on R&D or new projects does not, however, guarantee useful results. One study found that although large firms spent almost twice as much per R&D patent than did smaller firms, the smaller firms used more of their patents. The innovation rate of small businesses was 322 innovations per million employees versus 225 per million for large companies.[31] One explanation for this phenomenon is that large (especially older) firms tend to spend development money on extensions of their current products (incremental innovation) or to increase the efficiency of existing performance.[32] In contrast, small firms tend to apply technology to improving effectiveness through developing completely new products (radical innovation).[33] Other studies reveal that the maximum innovator in various industries often was the middle-sized firm. These firms were generally more effective and efficient in technology transfer. Very small firms often do not have sufficient resources to exploit new concepts (unless supported by venture capitalists with deep pockets), whereas the bureaucracy present in large firms rewards consistency over creativity.[34] From these studies, Hitt, Hoskisson, and Harrison propose the existence of an inverted U-shaped relationship between size and innovation. According to Hitt et al., "This suggests that organizations are flexible and responsive up to some threshold size but encounter inertia after that point."[35]

Sometimes most of the firms in an industry can waste their R&D spending. For example, between 1950 and 1979, the U.S. steel industry spent 20% more on plant maintenance and upgrading for each ton of production capacity added or replaced than did the Japanese steel industry. Nevertheless the top management of U.S. steel firms failed to recognize and adopt two breakthroughs in steelmaking—the basic oxygen furnace and continuous casting. Their hesitancy to adopt new technology caused them to lose the world steel market.[36]

Time to Market Issues

In addition to money, another important consideration in the effective management of research and development is **time to market**. A decade ago, the time from inception to profitability of a specific R&D program was generally accepted to be 7 to 11 years. According to Karlheinz Kaske, CEO of Siemens AG, however, the time available to complete the cycle is getting shorter. Companies no longer can assume that competitors will allow them the number of years needed to recoup their investment. In the past, Kaske says, "10 to 15 years went by before old products were replaced by new ones . . . now, it takes only 4 or 5 years."[37] Time to market is an important issue because *60% of patented innovations are generally imitated within 4 years at 65% of the cost of innovation.*[38] In the 1980s, Japanese auto manufacturers gained incredible competitive advantage over U.S. manufacturers by reducing new products' time to market to only 3 years (U.S. auto companies needed 5 years).[39]

11.3 Strategy Formulation

Research and development strategy deals not only with the decision to be a leader or a follower in terms of technology and market entry (discussed earlier in **Chapter 7** under R&D strategy), but also with the source of the technology. Should a company develop its own technology or purchase it from others? The strategy also takes into account a company's particular mix of basic versus applied and product versus process R&D (discussed earlier in **Chapter 4**). The particular mix should suit the level of industry development and the firm's particular corporate and business strategies. The **Global Issue** feature illustrates how a company's com-

Global Issue

Impact of R&D on Competitive Advantage in China

China is one of the 10 largest economies in the world. Average income has tripled since 1978 for most rural people. Urban incomes have risen even faster as the country's economy has grown at an annual rate of 9% in real terms for the past 15 years. As income increases, people are using it to improve their standard of living.

China is the world's fastest growing and potentially most profitable market for bathroom fixture manufacturers. Western-style toilets, which are easier to keep clean and use less water than the traditional Chinese fixtures, have become the standard in thousands of new apartment and office buildings. Two globally oriented companies attempting to dominate this lucrative market are American Standard of the United States and Toto Ltd. of Japan. Both design their products in their home country, manufacture them in Thailand using low-cost labor, and then ship the products to China for sale.

Product design has a significant impact on each company's competitive strategy in China. Toto has an advantage in one part of the design process because its designers in Japan use computers to generate models from blocks of foam. Engineering design is its distinctive competency. Blueprints can be in the hands of factory engineers in four weeks. In contrast, American Standard's process takes two months, on average. Models are crafted by hand by Jack Kaiser, an acknowledged design expert, and six associates. The personal touch is part of Standard's distinctive competency. Although the designers dominate the process, they work closely with marketing and production to develop a product to suit consumers' needs. In contrast, Toto's engineers dominate the process—building for production, but limiting creativity and neglecting markets in other countries. This limits Toto's ability to successfully enter a new market with unusual needs.

Toto dominates the luxury bathroom market in China, but it has been slow to adapt to the fast-growing low end of the market. "To ask a Japanese engineer to make something cheaper is harder than to ask him to make something better," explained Thibault Danjou, a Toto Marketing Manager. American Standard has another advantage in its flexible manufacturing facility in Thailand. It stocks only 14 days' worth of inventory. Its production process is flexible enough to produce to order. Toto, in contrast, has a much more rigid production process and must keep two months' inventory on hand. American Standard can also fill odd size orders that Toto finds too difficult to fill. In selling new-style toilets to China, manufacturers must customize toilets to line up with existing sewage pipes. Selling close to half of the bathroom fixtures imported into China, American Standard is certainly cleaning up!

Source: S. Glain, "Top Toilet Makers from U.S. and Japan Vie for Chinese Market," *Wall Street Journal* (December 19, 1996), pp. A1, A11; "Deng's China: The Last Emperor," *The Economist* (February 22, 1997), pp. 21–25.

petence in different aspects of R&D can affect its competitive strategy and its ability to successfully enter new markets. It shows not only how distinctive competencies in R&D can affect a company's competitive strategy, but also how emerging markets, such as China, are crucial to corporate growth strategies. Toto Ltd. is able to get from design to market quickly, but American Standard is able to design a product to better suit the needs of a new market.

In addition, R&D strategy in a large corporation deals with the proper balance of its product portfolio based on the life cycle of the products.

PRODUCT VERSUS PROCESS R&D

As illustrated in **Figure 11–1**, the proportion of product and process R&D tends to vary as a product moves along its life cycle. In the early stages, **product innovations** are most important because the product's physical attributes and capabilities most affect financial performance. Later, **process innovations** such as improved manufacturing facilities, increasing product quality, and faster distribution become important to maintaining the product's economic returns. Generally product R&D has been key to achieving differentiation strategies, whereas process R&D has been at the core of successful cost leadership strategies.

Figure 11–1

Product and Process R&D in the Innovation Life Cycle

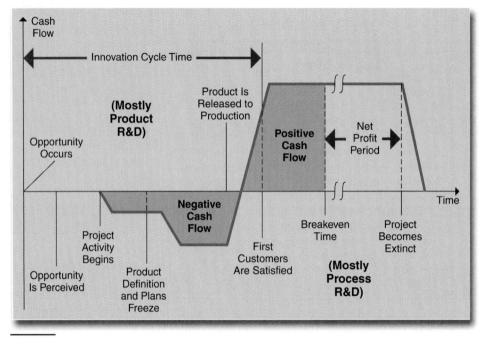

Source: Adapted from M. L. Patterson, "Lessons from the Assembly Line," *Journal of Business Strategy* (May/June 1993), p. 43. Permission granted by Faulkner & Gray, Eleven Penn Plaza, NY, NY 10001.

Historically, U.S. corporations have not been as skillful at process innovations as have German and Japanese companies. The primary reason has been a function of the amount of money invested in each form of R&D. U.S. firms spend, on the average, 70% of their R&D budgets on product R&D and only 30% on process R&D; German firms spend 50% on each form; and Japanese firms spend 30% on product and 70% on process R&D.[40] The traditionally heavy emphasis by U.S. major home appliance manufacturers on process R&D is one reason why they continue to have a strong position in the North American market. (See the **boxed example** on the U.S. major home appliance industry.)

To be competitive, companies must find the proper mix of product and process R&D. Even though the key to the success of the U.S. major home appliance industry has been its emphasis on process innovation, significant product innovation is more likely to result in a first mover advantage. For example, the first company to successfully use sound waves to clean clothes (instead of water and detergent) may very likely change the entire dynamics of the industry.

TECHNOLOGY SOURCING

Technology sourcing, typically a make-or-buy decision, can be important in a firm's R&D strategy. Although in-house R&D has traditionally been an important source of technical knowledge for companies, firms can also tap the R&D capabilities of competitors, suppliers, and other organizations through contractual agreements (such as licensing, R&D agreements, and joint ventures). One example is Matsushita's licensing of Iomega's Zip drive technology in 1996 so that Matsushita could also manufacture and sell removable cartridges for personal computers. When technological cycles were longer, a company was more likely to choose an independent R&D strategy not only because it gave the firm a longer lead time before com-

Product and Process Innovation in the Major Home Appliance Industry

Product innovation is being used in the major home appliance industry to provide consumers with new products as well as to add newer functions and features to existing products. The microwave oven was the last completely new product in this industry. Fuzzy logic technology is now being used to provide more effective, consumer-friendly appliances. Japanese appliance makers were the first to use this new technology to replace the many selector switches on an appliance with one start button. With fuzzy logic, a sophisticated set of electronic sensors and self-diagnostic software can measure the amount of detergent placed in a washing machine, check water temperature, gauge the amount of dirt on clothes, and decide not only how long the wash and rinse cycles should run, but also how vigorously the agitator should swish the water to get the clothes clean. Most major home appliance manufacturers have added fuzzy logic technology to top-end appliances in at least one of their product categories. Whirlpool added fuzzy logic to its VIP series of microwave ovens. Maytag did the same to its Intellisense™ line of dishwashers.

Process innovation for more efficient manufacturing of current products (as compared to new product development) has dominated research and development efforts in the U.S. major home appliance industry since the 1950s. Even though a refrigerator or a washing machine still looks and acts very much the same today as it did in the 1950s, it is built in a far different and more efficient manner. The components inside the appliances are being produced in highly automated plants using computer-integrated manufacturing processes. An example of this emphasis on product simplification was Maytag's "Dependable Drive" washer transmission, which was designed to have 40.6% fewer parts than the transmission it replaced. Fewer parts meant simplified manufacturing and less chance of a breakdown. The result was lower manufacturing costs and higher product quality.

Most industry analysts agreed that continual process improvements have kept U.S. major home appliance manufacturers dominant in the North American market. The emphasis on quality and durability, coupled with a reluctance to make major design changes simply for the sake of change, resulted in products with an average life expectancy of 20 years for refrigerators and 15 years for washers and dryers. Even though quality has improved significantly over the past 20 years, the average washer, dryer, and refrigerator cost no more than they did 20 years ago and yet last almost twice as long. If only the same could be said of the U.S. automobile industry!

petitors copied it, but also because it was more profitable in the long run. In today's world of shorter innovation life cycles and global competition, a company may no longer have the luxury of waiting to reap a long-term profit.

During a time of technological discontinuity in an industry, a company may have no choice but to purchase the new technology from others if it wants to remain competitive. For example, Ford Motor Company paid $100 million for 10.8% of the common stock of Cummins Engine Co., an expert in diesel engine technology. In return for its money, Ford got exclusive access to Cummins's truck engine technology. This allowed Ford to forgo the $300 million expense of designing a new engine on its own to meet U.S. emission standards.[41]

Firms that are unable to finance alone the huge costs of developing a new technology may coordinate their R&D with other firms through a **strategic R&D alliance**. By the 1990s, more than 150 cooperative alliances involving 1,000 companies were operating in the United States and many more were operating throughout Europe and Asia.[42] These alliances can be (a) joint programs or contracts to develop a new technology, (b) joint ventures establishing a separate company to take a new product to market, or (c) minority investments in innovative firms wherein the innovator obtains needed capital and the investor obtains access to valuable research. For example, Intel formed an alliance with Hewlett-Packard (HP) in 1994 to develop the Merced, a microprocessor combining elements of CISC (Complex Instruction Set Computing) and RISC (Reduced Instruction Set Computing) architecture. Up to this time Intel had little experience with designing general-purpose RISC chips. Since HP was already producing its own highly regarded RISC processor, Intel proposed the technology alliance. This alliance combined HP's knowledge of RISC with Intel's knowledge of CISC and Intel's manufacturing capabilities.[43]

When should a company buy or license technology from others instead of developing it internally? Following the resource-based view of the firm discussed previously in **Chapter 4**, a company should buy technologies that are commonly available but should make (and protect) those that are rare, valuable, hard to imitate, and have no close substitutes. In addition, *outsourcing technology may be appropriate when*:

- The technology is of low significance to competitive advantage.
- The supplier has proprietary technology.
- The supplier's technology is better and/or cheaper and reasonably easy to integrate into the current system.
- The company's strategy is based on system design, marketing, distribution, and service—not on development and manufacturing.
- The technology development process requires special expertise.
- The technology development process requires new people and new resources.[44]

Licensing technology to other companies may be an excellent R&D strategy—especially in a turbulent high tech environment where being the first firm to establish the standard dominant design may bring competitive advantage.[45] Matsushita successfully used this strategy to overcome the technologically superior Sony beta format with its VHS format for VCRs. By freely licensing the VHS format to all other VCR makers, Matsushita (through its Panasonic brand) became one of the dominant VCR manufacturers and Sony was relegated to a minority position in the market.[46]

IMPORTANCE OF TECHNOLOGICAL COMPETENCE

Firms that emphasize growth through acquisitions over internal development tend to be less innovative in the long run.[47] Research suggests that companies must have at least a minimal R&D capability if they are to correctly assess the value of technology developed by others. R&D creates a capacity in a firm to assimilate and exploit new knowledge. This is called a company's "absorptive capacity" and is a valuable by-product of routine in-house R&D activity.[48] **Absorptive capacity** is a firm's ability to value, assimilate, and utilize new external knowledge.[49] Firms having absorptive capacity are able to use knowledge obtained externally to increase the productivity of their research expenditures.[50] Further, without this capacity, firms could become locked out in their ability to assimilate the technology at a later time.

Those corporations that do purchase an innovative technology must have the **technological competence** to make good use of it. Some companies that introduce the latest technology into their processes do not adequately assess the competence of their people to handle it. For example, a survey conducted in the United Kingdom found that 44% of all companies that started to use robots met with initial failure and that 22% of these firms abandoned the use of robots altogether, mainly because of inadequate technological knowledge and skills.[51] One U.S. company built a new plant equipped with computer-integrated manufacturing and statistical process controls, but the employees could not operate the equipment because 25% of them were illiterate.[52]

A corporation may acquire a smaller high technology company in order to learn not only the new technology, but also a new way of managing its business. For example, Northern

Telecom, the Canadian telecommunications equipment manufacturer, was looking for renewal in 1998. CEO John Roth had identified the need for a cultural "right-angle turn." To become involved in the Internet, the company purchased Bay Networks. Roth made it clear from the beginning that the renamed company, Nortel Networks, would be culturally closer to Bay Networks than to the former Northern Telecom. Roth made Bay's CEO, Dave House, President of the entire company and installed House's people in key positions in development, operations, and customer service. Bay's Chief Technology Officer was promoted to the same position over all of Nortel. Together, Roth and House remade Nortel's planning and product development around the idea of shortened product life cycles and innovative new products.[53]

PRODUCT PORTFOLIO

Developed by Hofer and based on the product life cycle, the 15-cell **product/market evolution matrix** (shown in **Figure 11–2**) depicts the types of developing products that cannot be easily shown on other portfolio matrixes. Products are plotted in terms of their competitive

Figure 11–2
Product/Market Evolution Portfolio Matrix

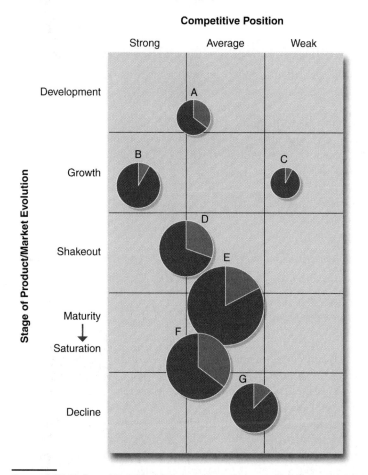

Source: C. W. Hofer and D. Schendel, *Strategy Formulation: Analytical Concepts* (St. Paul, MN: West Publishing Co., 1978), p. 34. From C. W. Hofer, "Conceptual Constructs for Formulating Corporate and Business Strategies" (Dover, MA: Case Publishing), no. BP-0041, p. 3. Copyright © 1977 by Charles W. Hofer. Reprinted by permission.

positions and their stages of product/market evolution. As on the GE Business Screen (depicted in **Figure 6.4** in **Chapter 6**), the circles represent the sizes of the industries involved, and the pie wedges represent the market shares of the firm's business product lines. Present and future matrixes can be developed to identify strategic issues. In response to **Figure 11–2**, for example, we could ask why product B does not have a greater share of the market, given its strong competitive position. We could also ask why the company has only one product in the developmental stage. A limitation of this matrix is that the product life cycle does not always hold for every product. Many products, for example, do not inevitably fall into decline but (like Tide detergent and Colgate toothpaste) are revitalized and put back on a growth track.

11.4 Strategy Implementation

If a corporation decides to develop innovations internally, it must make sure that its corporate system and culture are suitable for such a strategy. It must make sufficient resources available for new products, provide collaborative structures and processes, and incorporate innovation into its overall corporate strategy.[54] It must ensure that its R&D operations are managed appropriately. It must establish procedures to support all six **stages of new product development**. (See **Table 11–2**.) If, like most large corporations, the culture is too bureaucratic and rigid to support entrepreneurial projects, top management must reorganize so that innovative projects can be free to develop.

DEVELOPING AN INNOVATIVE ENTREPRENEURIAL CULTURE

To create a more innovative corporation, top management must develop an entrepreneurial culture—one that is open to the transfer of new technology into company activities and products and services. The company must be flexible and accepting of change. It should include a willingness to withstand a certain percentage of product failures on the way to success. Largeness is not a disadvantage. In his classic book, *Diffusion of Innovations*, Rogers reveals that innovative organizations tend to have the following characteristics:

- Positive attitude toward change
- Decentralized decision making
- Complexity
- Informal structure
- Interconnectedness
- Organizational slack (unused resources)
- Large size
- System openness[55]

Such a culture has been noted in 3M Corporation and Texas Instruments, among others. Research and development in these companies is managed quite differently from traditional methods. *First*, employees are dedicated to a particular project outcome rather than to innovation in general. *Second*, employees are often responsible for all functional activities and for all phases of the innovation process. Time is allowed to be sacrificed from regular duties to spend on innovative ideas. If the ideas are feasible, employees are temporarily reassigned to help develop them. They may become project champions who fight for resources to make the project a success. *Third*, these internal ventures are often separated from the rest of the company to provide them with greater independence, freedom from short-term pressures, different rewards, improved visibility, and access to key decision makers.[56]

The innovative process often involves individuals at different organizational levels who fulfill three different types of entrepreneurial roles: product champion, sponsor, and orchestrator.

Table 11–2 Six Stages of New Product Development

1. **Idea Generation:** New product concepts are identified and refined.
2. **Concept Evaluation:** Screening techniques are used to determine the concept's validity and market opportunity. Preliminary market research is conducted and a strategy is developed. A business plan is developed to present to management.
3. **Preliminary Design:** A new venture team is formed to prepare desired product specifications.
4. **Prototype Build and Test:** A functioning model of the product is built and subjected to numerous tests.
5. **Final Design and Pilot Production:** Final product and process designs are developed to produce small numbers of the product for use in test marketing. Suggestions from the users are fed back to the design team for possible inclusion in the final product.
6. **New Business Development:** The entire company is energized to launch the product.

Source: H.W. Oden, *Managing Corporate Culture, Innovation, and Intrapreneurship* (Westport, CT: Quorum Books, 1997).

A **product champion** is a person who generates a new idea and supports it through many organizational obstacles. A **sponsor** is usually a department manager who recognizes the value of the idea, helps obtain funding to develop the innovation, and facilitates its implementation. An **orchestrator** is someone in top management who articulates the need for innovation, provides funding for innovating activities, creates incentives for middle managers to sponsor new ideas, and protects idea/product champions from suspicious or jealous executives. Unless all of these roles are present in a company, major innovations are less likely to occur.[57]

Companies are finding that one way to overcome the barriers to successful product innovation is by using multifunctional teams with significant autonomy dedicated to a project. In a survey of 701 companies from Europe, the United States, and Japan, 85% of the respondents have used this approach with 62% rating it as successful.[58] Research reveals that cross-functional teams are best for designing and developing innovative new products, whereas the more traditional bureaucratic structures seem to be best for developing modifications to existing products, line extensions, and me-too products.[59] Chrysler Corporation was able to reduce the development time for new vehicles by 40% by using cross-functional teams and by developing a partnership approach to new projects.[60] International Specialty Products, a maker of polymers, used "product express" teams composed of chemists and representatives from manufacturing and engineering to cut development time in half. "Instead of passing a baton, we bring everyone into the commercialization process at the same time," explained John Tancredi, Vice-President for R&D. "We are moving laterally, like rugby players, instead of like runners in a relay race."[61] Companies throughout the world are beginning to realize the benefits from cross-functional teams in product development activities.

ORGANIZING FOR INNOVATION: CORPORATE ENTREPRENEURSHIP

Corporate entrepreneurship (also called intrapreneurship) is defined by Guth and Ginsburg as "the birth of new businesses within existing organizations, that is, internal innovation or venturing; and the transformation of organizations through renewal of the key ideas on which they are built, that is, strategic renewal."[62] A large corporation that wants to encourage innovation and creativity within its firm must choose a structure that will give the new business unit an appropriate amount of freedom while maintaining some degree of control at headquarters. Research reveals that corporate entrepreneurship has a positive impact on a company's financial performance.[63] Burgelman proposes (see **Figure 11–3**) that the use of a particular organizational design should be determined by (1) *the strategic importance of the new business to the corporation* and (2) *the relatedness of the unit's operations to those of the corpora-*

Figure 11–3
Organizational Designs for Corporate Entrepreneurship

Strategic Importance

	Very Important	Uncertain	Not Important
Unrelated	**3** Special Business Units	**6** Independent Business Units	**9** Complete Spin-Off
Partly Related	**2** New Product Business Department	**5** New Venture Division	**8** Contracting
Strongly Related	**1** Direct Integration	**4** Micro New Ventures Department	**7** Nurturing and Contracting

Operational Relatedness

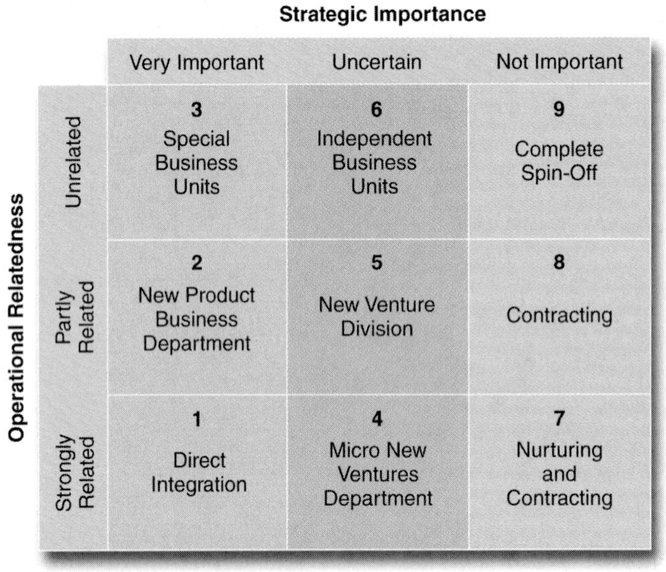

Source: Reprinted from R. A. Burgelman, "Designs for Corporate Entrepreneurship in Established Firms." Copyright © 1984 by the Regents of the University of California. Reprinted/condensed from *California Management Review*, Vol. 26, No. 3, p. 161. By permission of The Regents.

tion.[64] The combination of these two factors results in nine organizational designs for corporate entrepreneurship.

1. **Direct Integration:** A new business with a great deal of strategic importance and operational relatedness must be a part of the corporation's mainstream. Product champions—people who are respected by others in the corporation and who know how to work the system—are needed to manage these projects. Janiece Webb championed the incorporation of Internet Web browsers in Motorola's mobile phones and is now in charge of Motorola's Personal Networks Group. Since Webb's unit makes only software, she works with other divisions to shape their "product maps" that show what they hope to bring to market and when.[65]

2. **New Product Business Department:** A new business with a great deal of strategic importance and partial operational relatedness should be a separate department organized around an entrepreneurial project in the division where skills and capabilities can be shared. Maytag Corporation did this when it built a new plant near its current Newton, Iowa, washer plant to manufacture a wholly new *Neptune* line of energy and water efficient front-loading dishwashers.

3. **Special Business Units:** A new business with a great deal of strategic importance and low operational relatedness should be a special new business unit with specific objectives and time horizons. Teradyne tried this with a new product called Integra. The new product was based on a new, low-cost technology—something that might be good enough in a few years to replace Teradyne's current technology. Since the technology wasn't good enough for Teradyne's high-end applications, Teradyne's management treated Integra like an entrepreneurial venture. Integra's General Manager, Marc Levine, reported to a board of directors composed of Teradyne's top executives. Instead of a budget, Levine had a busi-

ness plan and venture capital (from Teradyne). This governance structure allowed Integra to operate autonomously by recruiting and purchasing from outside the company. According to Levine, "The idea was to think of this as a business from the start, not an R&D project. The board setup allows more of a coaching attitude." Says Teradyne's Rogas, "A division is always pressed to do the next logical thing—and make it compatible with the existing line. We told Marc: Be aggressive on the technology; do something no one else has done."[66]

4. **Micro New Ventures Department:** A new business with uncertain strategic importance and high operational relatedness should be a peripheral project, which is likely to emerge in the operating divisions on a continuous basis. Each division thus has its own new ventures department. Xerox Corporation, for example, uses its SBUs to generate and nurture new ideas. Small product-synthesis teams within each SBU test the feasibility of new ideas. Those concepts receiving a "go" are managed by an SBU product-delivery team, headed by a chief engineer, that takes the prototype from development through manufacturing.

5. **New Venture Division:** A new business with uncertain strategic importance that is only partly related to present corporate operations belongs in a new venture division. It brings together projects that either exist in various parts of the corporation or can be acquired externally; sizable new businesses are built. Lucent established an internal venture capital operation to fund the ideas of researchers from its Bell Labs R&D unit that didn't fit into existing business units. One new venture, Visual Insights, sells software that can detect billing fraud by analyzing patterns in large amounts of data. Another, Veridicom, does fingerprint authentication.[67]

6. **Independent Business Units:** Uncertain strategic importance coupled with no relationship to present corporate activities can make external arrangements attractive. Hewlett-Packard established printers as an independent business unit in Boise, Idaho (far from its Palo Alto, California, headquarters) because management was unsure of the desktop printer's future. According to Richard Belluzzo, head of HP's printer business, "We had the resources of a big company, but we were off on our own. There wasn't central planning . . . , so we could make decisions really fast."[68]

7. **Nurturing and Contracting:** When an entrepreneurial proposal might not be important strategically to the corporation but is strongly related to present operations, top management might help the entrepreneurial unit to spin off from the corporation. This allows a friendly competitor, instead of one of the corporation's major rivals, to capture a small niche. Techtronix has extensively used this approach. Because of research revealing that related spin-offs tend to be poorer performers than nonrelated spin-offs (presumably owing to the loss of benefits enjoyed with a larger company), it is especially important that the parent company continue to support the development of the spun-off unit in this cell.[69]

8. **Contracting:** As the required capabilities and skills of the new business are less related to those of the corporation, the parent corporation may spin off the strategically unimportant unit yet keep some relationship through a contractual arrangement with the new firm. The connection is useful in case the new firm eventually develops something of value to the corporation. For example, B.F. Goodrich offered manufacturing rights plus a long-term purchasing agreement to a couple of its managers for a specific raw material Goodrich still used (in declining quantities) in its production process but no longer wanted to manufacture internally.

9. **Complete Spin-Off:** If both the strategic importance and the operational relatedness of the new business are negligible, the corporation is likely to completely sell off the business to another firm or to the present employees in some form of ESOP (Employee Stock

Ownership Plan). The corporation also could sell off the unit through a leveraged buy-out (executives of the unit buy the unit from the parent company with money from a third source, to be repaid out of the unit's anticipated earnings). Because 3M wanted to focus its development money on areas with more profit potential, it decided to spin off its money-losing data storage and medical imaging divisions as a new company called Imation.

Organizing for innovation has become especially important for those corporations that want to become more innovative, but their age and size have made them highly bureaucratic with a culture that discourages creative thinking. These new structural designs for corporate entrepreneurship cannot work by themselves, however; they must have the support of management and sufficient resources. They must also have employees who are risk takers, willing to purchase an ownership interest in the new venture, and a corporate culture that supports new ventures.

11.5 Evaluation and Control

Companies want to gain more productivity at a faster pace from their research and development activities. But how do we measure the effectiveness or efficiency of a company's R&D? This is a problem given that a company shouldn't expect more than one in seven product ideas from basic research to make it to the marketplace. Some companies measure the proportion of their sales attributable to new products. For example, Hewlett-Packard measures how much of its revenues come from products introduced in the past three years.[70] At BellCore, the research part of seven regional Bell telephone companies, the effectiveness of basic research is measured by how often the lab's research is cited in other scientists' work. This measure is compiled and published by the Institute for Scientific Information. Other companies judge the quality of research by counting how many patents are filed annually.

A novel way of both evaluating and marketing new software products is to use potential consumers to sample the product. Microsoft routinely offers information systems people and other software users the opportunity to try beta (not quite ready for prime time) versions of its software. A cheap way to do quality control, users e-mail Microsoft about any problems they had with a program. At one time, beta testing was so popular that Microsoft actually charged people for the use of its betas! An even more novel approach to evaluation and control is that being used by Argus Systems Group, maker of PitBull computer security software. See the 🖼 **Internet Issue** feature to see how the company actually challenged hackers to attack its product.

Pittiglio Rabin Todd McGrath (PRTM), a high-tech consulting firm, proposes an **index of R&D effectiveness**. The index is calculated by dividing the percentage of total revenue spent on R&D into new product profitability, which is expressed as a percentage. When applying this measure to 45 large electronics manufacturers, only 9 companies scored 1.0 or higher, indicating that only 20% received a positive payback from their R&D spending. The top companies kept spending on marginal products to a minimum by running frequent checks on product versus market opportunities and canceling questionable products quickly. They also moved new products to market in half the time of the others. As a result, revenue growth among the top 20% of the companies was double the average of all 45 companies.[71]

A study of 15 multinational companies with successful R&D operations focused on three measures of R&D success: (1) improving technology transfer from R&D to business units, (2) accelerating time to market for new products and processes, and (3) institutionalizing cross-functional participation in R&D. The companies participated in basic, applied, and developmental research activities. The study revealed 13 **best practices** that all of the companies followed.[72] Listed in **Table 11–3**, they provide a benchmark for a company's R&D activities.

Internet Issue

Software Company Challenges Hackers to Attack Its Product

A key problem with the Internet is computer security. The Web sites of companies like Yahoo!, eBay, and even Microsoft have been successfully attacked by hackers. Given time and patience, a software expert could get past most corporations' computer security systems. As a way of testing and marketing its PitBull software, Argus Systems Groups joined with *eWeek* magazine in 2001 to challenge computer hackers to penetrate its computer security product. Although hacking contests have been taking place since the mid-1980s, Argus raised the stakes to validate a product it contends is the Fort Knox of computer security. Hackers were given two weeks to complete four tasks relating to corrupting a Web site protected by PitBull. There were prizes for being the first to complete each task with a grand prize of $50,000 for being the first to complete all four. (Argus had originally thought to give away a car, but then realized that a significant number of the participants were not old enough to drive.)

In previous contests in Las Vegas and Munich, hackers had failed to break into Argus-protected systems. Argus joined the contest as a way of proving the worth of its product. Many in the computer industry argue that hacking contests such as this one prove little. "If you have the skills to break into a product that's secure, are you going to announce it to the world, or are you going to keep those skills to yourself?" asks Jeff Moss, a hacker and security expert at Blackhat, a computer company firm. For example, Riley Eller, known as "caezar" to fellow computer hackers known as the Ghetto Hackers, stated that he would not take part in the OpenHackIII competition. Randy Sandone, CEO of Argus, acknowledged that the test was imperfect. "Even if we survive the two weeks without breaches, we're not going to claim that our system is fundamentally impenetrable." Nevertheless, the contest provided some incentive to "some pretty serious people to give (the system) a good thrashing."

Source: J. Pope, "Computer Hacking Competition Begins," *The (Ames) Tribune* (January 16, 2001), p. A2.

Table 11–3 Thirteen "Best Practices" for Improving R&D

1. Corporate and business unit strategies are well defined and clearly communicated.
2. Core technologies are defined and communicated to R&D.
3. Investments are made in developing multinational R&D capabilities to tap ideas throughout the world.
4. Funding for basic research comes from corporate sources to ensure a long-term focus; funding for development comes from business units to ensure accountability.
5. Basic and applied research are performed either at a central facility or at a small number of labs, each focused on a particular discipline of science or technology. Development work is usually performed at business unit sites.
6. Formal, cross-functional teams are created for basic, applied, and developmental projects.
7. Formal mechanisms exist for regular interaction among scientists, and between R&D and other functions.
8. Analytical tools are used for selecting projects as well as for on-going project evaluation.
9. The transfer of technology to business units is the most important measure of R&D performance.
10. Effective measures of career development are in place at all levels of R&D.
11. Recruiting of new people is from diverse universities and from other companies when specific experience or skills are required that would take long to develop internally.
12. Some basic research is performed internally, but there are also many university and third-party relationships.
13. Formal mechanisms are used for monitoring external technological developments.

Source: I. Krause and J. Liu, "Benchmarking R&D Productivity," *Planning Review* (January/February 1993), pp. 16–21, 52–53. Copyright © MCB University Press Ltd. Reprinted with permission.

Impact of the Internet on Managing Technology and Innovation

The Internet is becoming essential for research and development in today's world. Cross-functional collaboration with colleagues around the world is possible only with modern communication. At the Royal Dutch/Shell Group, six teams of six people each meet every week at the Exploration and Production Divisions in Houston, Texas, and in Rijswijk, Netherlands, to consider ideas that have been sent to them by e-mail. Out of these "GameChanger" teams came four of the five top business initiatives for the corporation in 1999. One of them was Shell's new "Light Touch" oil-discovery method—a way of using lasers to sense hydrocarbon emissions released naturally into the air from underground reserves. Increasing numbers of companies are using the Internet to stimulate and manage innovation. The concept is for small entrepreneurial teams to drive innovation at a rate never before experienced in large corporations. According to Christensen, author of *The Innovator's Dilemma*, "The trend now is to decentralize operations, to build idea factories, or idea markets. This is a way to bring the startup mentality inside."[73]

Companies like Nortel Networks and Procter & Gamble are adopting this "knowledge market" approach to innovation. Nortel allocates *phantom stock* to those who volunteer for special high-risk innovative projects. Nortel buys the stock as if the project was an IPO. Employees are paid in chits redeemable for cash once when the project is finished and again after it has been on the market about a year. P&G has created a Corporate New Ventures (CNV) unit as an autonomous idea lab with a mission of encouraging new ideas for products and putting them into speedy production. Ideas bubbling up from P&G's worldwide workforce of 110,000 people are routed to the CNV innovation panel via *My Idea*, a corporate collaboration network. Employees submitting winning ideas are rewarded with stock options. CNV teams then analyze the ideas using the Internet to analyze markets, demographics, and cost information to learn if the idea is a feasible opportunity. Once the team agrees on an idea, a project is launched within days. The CNV has the authority to tap any resources in the company to bring a product to market. So far, CNV has generated 58 marketable products. One of these, a cleaning product called *Swiffer*, was commercialized in just 10 months, less than half the usual time. Swiffer is a disposable cloth that generates static electricity to attract dust and dirt. The idea for it was generated by P&G's paper and cleaning-agent experts during a discussion on the Internet. According to Craig Wynett, CNV President, "It was an exercise in speed, in breaking down the company's traditional division-by-division territories to come up with new ideas."[74]

Projections for the 21st Century

- From 1994 to 2010, the number of communications satellites worldwide will grow from 1,100 to 2,260.
- From 1994 to 2010, the number of McDonald's fast food restaurants will increase from 14,000 to 31,000—many of them outside the United States.[75]

Discussion Questions

1. How should a corporation scan the external environment for new technological developments? Who should be responsible?

2. What is technology research and how does it differ from market research?

3. What is the importance of product and process R&D to competitive strategy?

4. What factors help determine whether a company should outsource a technology?

5. How can a company develop an entrepreneurial culture?

Strategic Practice Exercise

HOW CREATIVE IS YOUR ORGANIZATION?

One of the keys to managing technology and innovation is to have a creative organization in which people are free to propose and try new ideas. The following questionnaire is taken from "Building a Creative Hothouse" by Barton Kunstler in the January–February, 2001, issue of *The Futurist.* It is a simplified version of the Hothouse Assessment Instrument presented in greater detail in the Spring 2000 issue of *Futures Research Quarterly.* This version describes many of the elements of a highly creative organization.

If you work or have worked full time in an organization, answer this questionnaire in light of your experience with that organization. If you have not worked full time anywhere, find someone who is working full time and ask them to complete this questionnaire. Then discuss their answers with them.

To assess the level of creativity in your organization's culture, score your level of agreement or disagreement with the statements below as follows: **Strongly Agree** (5 points), **Mildly Agree** (4 points), **Neutral** (3 points), **Mildly Disagree** (2 points), **Strongly Disagree** (1 point).

Values

_____ 1. We believe that our work can change the world.

_____ 2. The organization actively promotes a positive quality of life in our surrounding communities.

_____ 3. People here really believe our products and services are vital to others' well-being.

_____ 4. Virtually all who work here continually study and question the basic nature of their job and the technologies—human, organizational, technical—they work with.

_____ 5. Working here fills me with a sense of personal well-being and commitment to my higher values.

Mission and Vision

_____ 6. Principles of justice and compassion directly and significantly influence strategy, design, and development.

_____ 7. We explore the fundamental practices and principles of our industry and its disciplines as a source of creativity, values, and purpose.

_____ 8. We can fail without fear for our jobs.

_____ 9. My organization takes the long view.

_____ 10. Employees are free to develop their own vision of what their jobs entail.

Ideas

_____ 11. This organization cultivates the growth of knowledge into wisdom and views wisdom as a guide to action.

_____ 12. Organizational structure is shaped by innovative, idea-driven approaches to our challenges and tasks.

_____ 13. Organizational responses to crises are thoughtful and imaginative, not reactive and typical.

_____ 14. The organization respects thinkers.

_____ 15. I am respected for all my talents, whether or not they contribute to the bottom line.

Exchange

_____ 16. My organization rewards those who display mastery at their jobs and seeks their advice, whatever their title or position.

_____ 17. Institutionalized procedures enable anyone to make suggestions or raise objections.

_____ 18. Intellectually exciting and stimulating conversation directly influences product development and delivery.

_____ 19. "Idea people" share their vision with other employees and invite feedback.

_____ 20. The group uses conflict as an opportunity for personal and organizational growth.

Perception

_____ 21. How we perceive our tasks, our expertise, and the group itself is a legitimate object of inquiry.

_____ 22. Whole-minded thinking, including activities based on movement and heightening awareness of the five senses, is encouraged.

_____ 23. Employees are taught and encouraged to think creatively.

_____ 24. We continually re-vision our group's place within its industry and society as a whole.

_____ 25. Clear problem-solving algorithms are taught, practiced, developed, and applied wherever a need is perceived, without regard to concerns of status, tradition, or company politics.

Learning

_____ 26. To be viewed as a "continuous learner" at work benefits one's career.

_____ 27. We regularly challenge group norms, and anyone can initiate this process.

_____ 28. My organization is constantly engaged in learning about itself and the environments in which it operates.

_____ 29. The organization allocates resources toward employee involvement in cultural events as attendees, participants, or learners.

_____ 30. Projects are undertaken by integrated teams whose members bring multiple disciplines and diverse perspectives to the task.

Social

_____ 31. Our relationships at work are relaxed, irreverent, warm, and crackling with ideas.

_____ 32. People from different departments and organizational levels socialize together, either during or after work.

_____ 33. Committee meetings are reasonably productive and amicable.

_____ 34. When we form teams to work on special projects, the work is integrated into our day-to-day schedules.

_____ 35. We always produce effective leadership when and where we need it.

Festiva

_____ 36. Social occasions are planned and designed in highly creative ways.

_____ 37. The line between work and play is virtually nonexistent.

_____ 38. Developments in art, politics, science, and other fields not directly related to our work are discussed in relation to their impact upon our organization and industry.

_____ 39. We have a strong group vocabulary of terms and symbols that promotes communication, community, and creativity.

_____ 40. We are encouraged to play whimsically with ideas, materials, and objects as well as with new ways of doing things.

_____ **TOTAL POINTS**

SCORING YOUR ORGANIZATION'S CREATIVITY

If you Scored:	Organization Is in the Creative...
40–79	**Dead Zone**—a place where it is virtually impossible for creativity to flourish
80–159	**I-Zone**—where management thinks in terms of the next quarter and creativity is seldom transmitted from one person or department to another* OR... **O-Zone**—where creativity is valued but not consistently incorporated into the organization's strategy*
160–200	**Hot Zone**—where creativity is intense and productive

*Note: I-Zone organizations score higher on Values, Ideas, Perception, and Social questions. O-Zone organizations score higher on Mission and Vision, Learning, Exchange, and Festiva questions.

Source: B. Kunstler, "Building a Creative Hothouse," *The Futurist* (January–February 2001), pp. 22–29. Reprinted by permission.

Key Terms

absorptive capacity (p. 288)
best practices (p. 294)
corporate entrepreneurship (p. 291)
index of R&D effectiveness (p. 294)
lead user (p. 281)
market research (p. 282)
new product experimentation (p. 283)

orchestrator (p. 291)
process innovations (p. 285)
product champion (p. 291)
product innovations (p. 285)
product/market evolution matrix (p. 289)
R&D intensity (p. 283)
sponsor (p. 291)

stages of new product development (p. 290)
strategic R&D alliance (p. 287)
technological competence (p. 288)
technological discontinuity (p. 282)
technology sourcing (p. 286)
time to market (p. 284)

Notes

1. J. A. Byrne, "Management by Web," *Business Week* (August 28, 2000), p. 96.
2. R. Jonash and T. Sommerlatte, *The Innovation Premium* (Perseus Books, 1999).
3. G. Getz and C. Christensen, "Should You Fear Disruptive Technology?" *Fortune* (April 3, 2000), pp. 249–250.
4. "Fear of the Unknown," *The Economist* (December 4, 1999), pp. 61–62.
5. M. S. Malone, "Which Are the Most Valuable Companies in the New Economy?" *Forbes ASAP* (May 29, 2000), pp. 212–214.
6. S. J. Towner, "Four Ways to Accelerate New Product Development," *Long Range Planning* (April 1994), p. 57.
7. R. Garud and P. R. Nayyar, "Transformative Capacity: Continual Structuring by Intertemporal Technology Transfer," *Strategic Management Journal* (June 1994), p. 379.
8. C. A. Ferland, book review of *Third Generation R&D—Managing the Link to Corporate Strategy* by P. A. Roussel, K. N. Saad, and T. J. Erickson, in *Long Range Planning* (April 1993), p. 128.
9. M. A. Schilling and C. W. L. Hill, "Managing the New Product Development Process: Strategic Imperatives," *Academy of Management Executive* (August 1998), pp. 67–81.
10. C. Power, K. Kerwin, R. Grover, K. Alexander, and R. D. Hof, "Flops," *Business Week* (August 16, 1993), pp. 76–82.
11. B. R. Schlender, "How Sony Keeps the Magic Going," *Fortune* (February 24, 1992), p. 77.
12. G. C. Hill and K. Yamada, "Motorola Illustrates How an Aged Giant Can Remain Vibrant," *Wall Street Journal* (December 9, 1992), pp. A1, A14.
13. N. Snyder, "Environmental Volatility, Scanning Intensity and Organizational Performance," *Journal of Contemporary Business* (September 1981), p. 16.
14. R. Nobel and J. Birkinshaw, "Innovations in MNCs: Control and Communication Patterns in International R&D Operations," *Strategic Management Journal* (May 1998), pp. 479–496.
15. P. Almeida, "Knowledge Sourcing by Foreign Multinationals: Patent Citation Analysis in the U.S. Semiconductor Industry," *Strategic Management Journal* (December 1996), pp. 155–165.
16. E. Von Hippel, *The Sources of Innovation* (Oxford: Oxford University Press, 1988), p. 4.
17. M. R. Neale and D. R. Corkindale, "Co-Developing Products: Involving Customer Earlier and More Deeply," *Long Range Planning* (June 1998), pp. 418–425.
18. E. Von Hippel, *The Sources of Innovation*, p. 107; E. Von Hippel, S. Thomke, and M. Sonnack, "Creating Breakthroughs at 3M," *Harvard Business Review* (September–October 1999), p. 48.
19. Von Hippel, Thomke, and Sonnack, p. 52.
20. G. Hamel and C. K. Prahalad, "Seeing the Future First," *Fortune* (September 5, 1995), p. 70.
21. C. M. Christensen, *The Innovator's Dilemma* (Boston: HBS Press, 1997); J. Wade, "A Community-Level Analysis of Sources and Rates of Technological Variation in the Microprocessor Market," *Academy of Management Journal* (October 1996), pp. 1218–1244.
22. C. M. Christensen and J. L. Bower, "Customer Power, Strategic Investment, and the Failure of Leading Firms," *Strategic Management Journal* (March 1996), pp. 197–218.
23. G. S. Lynn, J. G. Morone, and A. S. Paulson, "Marketing and Discontinuous Innovation: The Probe and Learn Process," *California Management Review* (Spring 1996), pp. 8–37.
24. W. I. Zangwill, "When Customer Research Is a Lousy Idea," *Wall Street Journal* (March 8, 1993), p. A10.
25. S. Baker, "What Every Business Should Learn from Microsoft," *Journal of Business Strategy* (September/October 1998), pp. 36–41.
26. D. F. Kuratko, J. S. Hornsby, D. W. Naffziger, and R. V. Montagno, "Implement Entrepreneurial Thinking in Established Organizations," *SAM Advanced Management Journal* (Winter 1993), p. 29.
27. "Business Bulletin," *Wall Street Journal* (May 1, 1997), p. A1. The number has improved from 58 ideas in 1967 to 11 in 1990, to 7 in 1995.
28. L. G. Franko, "Global Corporate Competition: Who's Winning, Who's Losing, and the R&D Factor as One Reason Why," *Strategic Management Journal* (September–October 1989), pp. 449–474. See also P. S. Chan, E. J. Flynn, and R. Chinta, "The Strategies of Growing and Turnaround Firms: A Multiple Discriminant Analysis," *International Journal of Management* (September 1991), pp. 669–675.
29. M. J. Chussil, "How Much to Spend on R&D?" *The PIMS-letter of Business Strategy*, No. 13 (Cambridge, Mass.: The Strategic Planning Institute, 1978), p. 5.
30. J. S. Harrison, E. H. Hall, Jr., and R. Nargundkar, "Resource Allocation as an Outcropping of Strategic Consistency: Performance Implications," *Academy of Management Journal* (October 1993), pp. 1026–1051.
31. S. B. Graves and N. S. Langowitz, "Innovative Productivity and Returns to Scale in the Pharmaceutical Industry," *Strategic Management Journal* (November 1993), pp. 593–605; A. Brady, "Small Is as Small Does," *Journal of Business Strategy* (March/April 1995), pp. 44–52.
32. J. B. Sorensen and T. E. Stuart, "Aging, Obsolescence, and Organizational Innovation," *Administrative Science Quarterly* (March 2000), pp. 81–112.
33. D. H. Freedman, "Through the Looking Glass," in "The State of Small Business," *INC.* (May 21, 1996), pp. 48–54.
34. N. Nohria and R. Gulati, "Is Slack Good or Bad for Innovation?" *Academy of Management Journal* (October 1996), pp. 1245–1264.
35. M. A. Hitt, R. E. Hoskisson, and J. S. Harrison, "Strategic Competitiveness in the 1990s: Challenges and Opportunities for U.S. Executives," *Academy of Management Executive* (May 1991), p. 13.
36. T. F. O'Boyle, "Steel's Management Has Itself to Blame," *Wall Street Journal* (May 17, 1983), p. 32.
37. M. Silva and B. Sjögren, *Europe 1992 and the New World Power Game* (New York: John Wiley & Sons, 1990), p. 231.
38. E. Mansfield, M. Schwartz, and S. Wagner, "Imitation Costs and Patents: An Empirical Study," *Economic Journal* (December 1981), pp. 907–918.
39. G. Stalk, Jr., and A. M. Webber, "Japan's Dark Side of Time," *Harvard Business Review* (July–August 1993), p. 99.
40. M. Robert, "Market Fragmentation Versus Market Segmentation," *Journal of Business Strategy* (September/October 1992), p. 52.
41. K. Kelly and M. Ivey, "Turning Cummins into the Engine Maker That Could," *Business Week* (July 30, 1990), pp. 20–21.
42. Silva and Sjögren, *Europe 1992 and the New World Power Game*, pp. 239–241. See also P. Nueno and J. Oosterveld, "Managing Technology Alliances," *Long Range Planning* (June 1988), pp. 11–17.
43. B. Schlender, "Killer Chip," *Fortune* (November 10, 1997), pp. 70–80.
44. P. R. Nayak, "Should You Outsource Product Development?" *Journal of Business Strategy* (May/June 1993), pp. 44–45.
45. C. W. L. Hill, "Establishing a Standard: Competitive Strategy and Technological Standards in Winner-Take-All Industries," *Academy of Management Executive* (May 1997), pp. 7–25.
46. M. H. Roy and S. S. Dugal, "The Effect of Technological Environment and Competitive Strategy on Licensing Decisions," *American Business Review* (June 1999), pp. 112–118.

47. M. A. Hitt, R. E. Hoskisson, R. A. Johnson, and D. D. Moesel, "The Market for Corporate Control and Firm Innovation," *Academy of Management Journal* (October 1996), pp. 1084–1119.

48. W. M. Cohen and D. A. Levinthal, "Absorptive Capacity: A New Perspective on Learning and Innovation," *Administrative Science Quarterly* (March 1990), pp. 128–152.

49. P. J. Lane and M. Lubatkin, "Absorptive Capacity and Inter-organizational Learning," *Strategic Management Journal* (May 1998), pp. 461–477.

50. M. B. Heeley, "Appropriating Rents from External Knowledge: The Impact of Absorptive Capacity on Firm Sales Growth and Research Productivity," paper presented to *Babson Entrepreneurship Research Conference* (Wellesley, MA), 1997.

51. "The Impact of Industrial Robotics on the World of Work," *International Labour Review*, Vol. 125, No. 1 (1986). Summarized in "The Risks of Robotization," *The Futurist* (May–June 1987), p. 56.

52. Hitt, Hoskisson, and Harrison, "Strategic Competitiveness in the 1990s: Challenges and Opportunities for U.S. Executives," p. 9.

53. S. Chaudhuri and B. Tabrizi, "Capturing the Real Value in High-Tech Acquisitions," *Harvard Business Review* (September/October 1999), pp. 123–130.

54. D. Dougherty and C. Hardy, "Sustained Product Innovation in Large, Mature Organizations: Overcoming Innovation-to-Organization Problems," *Academy of Management* (October 1996), pp. 1120–1153.

55. E. M. Rogers, *Diffusion of Innovations*, 4th edition (New York: Free Press, 1995).

56. C. A. Lengnick-Hall, "Innovation and Competitive Advantage: What We Know and What We Need to Know," *Journal of Management* (June 1992), pp. 399–429.

57. J. R. Galbraith, "Designing the Innovative Organization," *Organizational Dynamics* (Winter 1982), pp. 5–25.

58. P. R. Nayak, "Product Innovation Practices in Europe, Japan, and the U.S.," *Journal of Business Strategy* (May/June 1992), pp. 62–63.

59. E. M. Olson, "Organizing for Effective New Product Development: The Moderating Role of Product Innovativeness," *Journal of Marketing* (January 1995) as reported by K. Z. Andrews in *Harvard Business Review* (November–December 1995), pp. 12–13.

60. D. Rowe, "Up and Running," *Journal of Business Strategy* (May/June 1993), pp. 48–50.

61. N. Freundlich and M. Schroeder, "Getting Everybody Into the Act," *Business Week* (Quality 1991 edition), p. 152.

62. W. D. Guth and A. Ginsberg, "Corporate Entrepreneurship," *Strategic Management Journal* (Summer 1990), p. 5.

63. S. A. Zahra and J. G. Covin, "Contextual Measures on the Corporate Entrepreneurship–Performance Relationship: A Longitudinal Analysis," *Journal of Business Venturing*, Vol. 10 (1995), pp. 43–58.

64. R. A. Burgelman, "Designs for Corporate Entrepreneurship," *California Management Review* (Spring 1984), pp. 154–166; R. A. Burgelman and L. R. Sayles, *Inside Corporate Innovation* (New York: The Free Press, 1986).

65. W. J. Holstein, "Remaking Motorola Isn't Easy," *U.S. News & World Report* (October 23, 2000), p. 52; R. O. Crockett, "A New Company Called Motorola," *Business Week* (April 17, 2000), pp. 86–92.

66. T. A. Stewart, "How Teradyne Solved the Innovator's Dilemma," *Fortune* (June 10, 2000), pp. 188–190.

67. J. Carey, "An Ivory Tower That Spins Pure Gold," *Business Week* (April 19, 1999), pp. 167–170.

68. S. K. Yoder, "How H-P Used Tactics of the Japanese to Beat Them at Their Game," *Wall Street Journal* (September 8, 1994), pp. A1, A6.

69. C. Y. Woo, G. E. Willard, and S. M. Beckstead, "Spin-Offs: What Are the Gains?" *Journal of Business Strategy* (March–April 1989), pp. 29–32.

70. J. B. Levin and R. D. Hof, "Has Philips Found Its Wizard?" *Business Week* (September 6, 1993), pp. 82–84.

71. O. Port, "Rating R&D: How Companies Get the Biggest Bang for the Buck," *Business Week* (July 5, 1993), p. 98.

72. I. Krause and J. Liu, "Benchmarking R&D Productivity," *Planning Review* (January/February 1993), pp. 16–21, 52–53.

73. M. Stepanek, "Using the Net for Brainstorming," *Business Week E.Biz* (December 13, 1999), p. EB55.

74. Stepanek, pp. EB55–EB59.

75. J. Warner, "21st Century Capitalism: Snapshots of the Next Century," *Business Week* (November 18, 1994), p. 194.

chapter 12

Strategic Issues in Entrepreneurial Ventures and Small Businesses

Debbie Giampapa was at a party juggling her food plate and drink. "This is ridiculous," she thought. "Why doesn't somebody make something to hold this?" When she got home she pulled a piece of cardboard out of the trash and cut a hole large enough to hold a standard 10-ounce plastic cup. Then she added a smaller hole for a wine glass. After much trial and error and a lot of perseverance in obtaining funding, plus deciding how to make and market her product, she established her own company, FunZone. She went to die cutters and machinists to learn how machines could make her product. She told them she was doing door hangers because she didn't want them to steal her idea. Said Giampapa, "The more I understand what the machine can do, the better I can design the product." Giampapa is now selling thousands of "Party HOLDems" to customers like American Express, Walt Disney Company, and Coopers and Lybrand. When asked the secret of her success, she responded:

> It's not having the idea. It's believing in yourself and your product enough to put up the money and time for that. I've put in 16-hour days, seven-day weeks for two years.[1]

12.1 Importance of Small Business and Entrepreneurial Ventures

Strategic management as a field of study typically deals with large, established business corporations. However, small business cannot be ignored. There are 22 million small businesses—over 95% of all businesses in the United States. During the 1990s, 85% of all new jobs in the United States were created by small firms and 70% of these by the fastest growing entrepreneurial firms.[2] Research reveals that not only do small firms spend almost twice as much of their R&D dollars on fundamental research as do large firms, but also that small companies are responsible for a high proportion of innovations in products and services.[3] For example, new small firms produce 24 times more innovation per research dollar than do the much larger *Fortune* 500 firms.[4] The National Science Foundation estimates that 98% of "radical" product developments result from the research done in the labs of small companies.[5] Nevertheless, not every country is as supportive of new ventures as is the United States. See the **Global Issue** feature to learn how different countries support entrepreneurship.

Despite the overall success of small businesses, however, every year tens of thousands of small companies fail. Figures from the U.S. Small Business Administration generally support the rule of thumb that 50% of businesses founded in any one year are not in business

Global Issue

Entrepreneurship: Some Countries Are More Supportive Than Others

Entrepreneurship is becoming increasingly important throughout the world. True to economist Joseph Schumpeter's view of entrepreneurship as "creative destruction," much of the world from Eastern Europe to South America to Asia envisions entrepreneurial ventures as the means to build successful free market economies. New entrepreneurial ventures are emerging daily in these countries. Unfortunately, not every country makes it easy to start a new business.

According to the World Economic Forum's *Global Competitiveness Report*, countries range from easy (7) to difficult (1) in terms of the ease of starting an entrepreneurial venture. The easiest is the United States with a rating of 6.06, followed by New Zealand, Iceland, Canada, Finland, Britain, and The Netherlands at 5.5. The most difficult countries listed are Austria at 3.96, followed by Japan, Italy, Spain, Belgium, France, and Germany at 4.5. A separate *Economic Creativity Index* developed by the World Economic Forum gauges countries' involvement in innovation. Based on observed data and survey results, the index measures the level of technology and the conditions favoring new business start-ups. Highest marks go to the United States (+2.1) followed by Finland, Singapore, Israel, Britain, Hong Kong, Germany, and Taiwan (+1.0). The lowest marks go to Columbia (−1.3) followed by Venezuela, Russia, Peru, China, Argentina, and Indonesia (−0.4).

Even though entrepreneurship is more difficult in many other parts of the world than in the United States, the situation is changing. For example, investors are flocking to young, fast-growing companies in Europe. The number of European entrepreneurs has been gradually increasing through the 1990s. Politicians are beginning to see entrepreneurs as part of a solution to unemployment rather than as grasping exploiters. In 1997, European venture capital firms accounted for $23 billion in new venture capital. The total amount spent by private equity firms increased by 42% to $11.3 billion. The EASDAQ, founded in 1996, is Europe's version of the NASDAQ. Companies can be listed on the EASDAQ regardless of size or history so long as they agree to international accounting standards and U.S. style financial reporting.

There is still an ingrained cultural aversion to the risk taking so necessary to entrepreneurship. The contradiction between the Marxist ideology and private ownership in China means that business entrepreneurs are not perceived as legitimate. The social stigma attached to business failure is deeply entrenched in many countries. According to Christophe Sapet, the French founder of a computer game company called Infogrames, "When you earn money, (French) people are jealous. They think you have done something wrong." From 1984 to 1991, the OECD estimates that the United States established new businesses at four times the rate of France.

Sources: J. Kahn, "Suddenly, Startups Are Chic," *Fortune* (February 15, 1999), p. 110; "Financial Indicators," *The Economist* (October 16, 1999), p. 109; "Emerging-Market Indicators," *The Economist* (September 23, 2000), p. 128; E. W. K. Tsang, "In Search of Legitimacy: The Private Entrepreneur in China," *Entrepreneurship Theory and Practice* (Fall 1996), pp. 21–30.

five years later.[6] Similar rates occur in the United Kingdom, The Netherlands, Japan, Taiwan, and Hong Kong.[7] Although an increasing number of studies are more positive regarding the survival rate of new entrepreneurial ventures, new businesses are definitely considered risky.[8] The causes of small-business failure (depending on the study cited) range from inadequate accounting systems to inability to cope with growth. The underlying problem appears to be an overall lack of strategic management—beginning with an inability to plan a strategy to reach the customer and ending with a failure to develop a system of controls to keep track of performance.[9]

DEFINITION OF SMALL-BUSINESS FIRMS AND ENTREPRENEURIAL VENTURES

The most commonly accepted definition of a small-business firm in the United States is one that employs fewer than 500 people and that generates sales of less than $20 million annually.

Although the meanings of the terms "small business" and "entrepreneurship" overlap considerably, the concepts are different. The **small-business firm** is independently owned and operated, not dominant in its field, and does not engage in innovative practices. The **entrepreneurial venture**, in contrast, is any business whose primary goals are profitability and growth and that can be characterized by innovative strategic practices.[10] The basic difference between the small-business firm and the entrepreneurial venture, therefore, lies not in the type of goods or services provided but in their fundamental views on growth and innovation. According to Donald Sexton, an authority on entrepreneurship, this explains why strategic planning is more likely to be present in an entrepreneurial venture than in the typical small-business firm:

> Most firms start with just a single product. Those oriented toward growth immediately start looking for another one. It's that planning approach that separates the entrepreneur from the small-business owner.[11]

THE ENTREPRENEUR AS STRATEGIST

Often defined as a person who organizes and manages a business undertaking and who assumes risk for the sake of a profit, the **entrepreneur** is the ultimate strategist. He or she makes all the strategic as well as operational decisions. All three levels of strategy—corporate, business, and functional—are the concerns of this founder and owner/manager of a company. As one entrepreneur puts it: "Entrepreneurs are strategic planners without realizing it."

The founding of FunZone described earlier captures the key elements of the entrepreneurial venture: a basic business idea that has not yet been successfully tried and a gutsy entrepreneur who, while working on borrowed capital and a shoestring budget, creates a new business through a lot of trial and error and persistent hard work. Similar stories can be told of other people, such as Debbie Fields, who created Mrs. Fields Cookies, and Will Parish, who founded National Energy Associates. Both were ridiculed at one time or another for their desire to start a business. Friends and family told Debbie Fields that starting a business to sell chocolate chip cookies "was a stupid idea." Will Parish, who built a power plant in California's Imperial Valley that burns "pasture patties," was called an "entre-manure." Every day the plant burned 900 tons of manure collected from nearby feedlots to generate 15 megawatts of electricity—enough to light 20,000 homes. The power was sold to Southern California Edison. Parish got the idea from a trip to India where the fuel used to heat a meal was cow dung. Once the plant was earning a profit, Parish planned to build a larger plant nearby that would burn wheat straw and other crop wastes. The plants provide an environmentally sound as well as profitable way to dispose of waste. Very interested in conservation, Parish says, "I wanted to combine doing well with doing good."[12]

Successful new ventures often propose an entirely new approach to doing business, called a "new business model." A **business model** describes the mix of activities a company performs to deliver goods and services to customers. Coined in the 1990s, the term is used to show how the Internet and global trade are changing how companies must do business today.

12.2 Use of Strategic Planning and Strategic Management

Research shows that strategic planning is strongly related to small-business financial performance.[13] A survey of the high growth *Inc.* 500 firms revealed that 86% performed strategic planning. Of those performing strategic planning, 94% reported improved profits.[14] Nevertheless, many small companies still do not use the process. The reasons often cited for the apparent lack of strategic planning practices in many small-business firms are fourfold:

- **Not enough time:** Day-to-day operating problems take up the time necessary for long-term planning. It's relatively easy to justify avoiding strategic planning on the basis of day-to-day crisis management. Some will ask: "How can I be expected to do strategic planning when I don't know if I'm going to be in business next week?"
- **Unfamiliar with strategic planning:** The small-business CEO may be unaware of strategic planning or may view it as irrelevant to the small-business situation. Planning may be viewed as a straitjacket that limits flexibility.
- **Lack of skills:** Small-business managers often lack the skills necessary to begin strategic planning and do not have or want to spend the money necessary to import trained consultants. Future uncertainty may be used to justify a lack of planning. One entrepreneur admits, "Deep down, I know I should plan. But I don't know what to do. I'm the leader but I don't know how to lead the planning process."
- **Lack of trust and openness:** Many small-business owner/managers are very sensitive regarding key information about the business and are thus unwilling to share strategic planning with employees or outsiders. For this reason, boards of directors are often composed only of close friends and relatives of the owner/manager—people unlikely to provide an objective viewpoint or professional advice.

DEGREE OF FORMALITY

Research generally concludes that the strategic planning process can be far more informal in small companies than it is in large corporations.[15] Some studies have even found that too much formalization of the strategic planning process may actually result in reduced performance.[16] It is possible that a heavy emphasis on structured, written plans can be dysfunctional to the small entrepreneurial firm because it detracts from the very flexibility that is a benefit of small size. *The process of strategic planning, not the plan itself, is probably the key to improving business performance.* Research does show, however, that as an entrepreneurial firm matures, its strategic planning process tends to become more formal.[17]

These observations suggest that new entrepreneurial ventures begin life in Mintzberg's *entrepreneurial mode* of strategic planning (explained in **Chapter 1**) and move toward the *planning mode* as the company becomes established and wants to continue its strong growth. If, after becoming successfully established, the entrepreneur instead chooses stability over growth, the venture moves more toward the *adaptive mode* so common to many small businesses.

USEFULNESS OF STRATEGIC MANAGEMENT MODEL

The model of strategic management (presented in **Figure 1–2** of **Chapter 1**) is also relevant to entrepreneurial ventures and small businesses. This basic model holds for both an established small company and a new entrepreneurial venture. As the research mentioned earlier concluded, small and developing companies increase their chances of success if they make a serious attempt to work through the strategic issues embedded in the strategic management model. The key is to focus on what's important—the set of managerial decisions and actions that determines the long-run performance of the company. The list of informal questions presented in **Table 12–1** may be more useful to a small entrepreneurial company than their more formal counterparts used by large established corporations.

USEFULNESS OF STRATEGIC DECISION-MAKING PROCESS

As mentioned in **Chapter 1**, one way in which the strategic management model can be made action oriented is to follow the strategic decision-making model presented in **Figure 1–5**. The eight steps presented in that model are just as appropriate for small companies as they are for large corporations. Unfortunately the process does not fit new entrepreneurial ventures. These companies must develop new missions, objectives, strategies, and policies out of a comparison of their external opportunities and threats to their potential strengths and weaknesses. Consequently we propose in **Figure 12–1** a modified version of the strategic decision-making process; this version more closely suits the new entrepreneurial business.

The proposed **strategic decision-making process for entrepreneurial ventures** is composed of the following eight interrelated steps:

1. **Develop the basic business idea**—a product and/or service having target customers and/or markets. The idea can be developed from a person's experience or generated in a moment of creative insight. For example, Debbie Giampapa conceived of the beverage-holding party tray long before such a product was feasible.

Table 12–1 Informal Questions to Begin the Strategic Management Process in a Small Company or Entrepreneurial Venture

Formal	Informal
Define mission	What do we stand for?
Set objectives	What are we trying to achieve?
Formulate strategy	How are we going to get there? How can we beat the competition?
Determine policies	What sort of ground rules should we all be following to get the job done right?
Establish programs	How should we organize this operation to get what we want done as cheaply as possible with the highest quality possible?
Prepare *pro forma* budgets	How much is it going to cost us and where can we get the cash?
Specify procedures	In how much detail do we have to lay things out, so that everybody knows what to do?
Determine performance measures	What are those few key things that will determine whether we can make it? How can we keep track of them?

Figure 12–1
Strategic Decision-Making Process for New Ventures

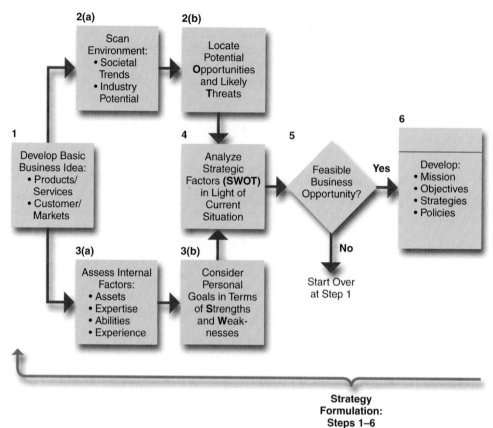

2. **Scan and assess the external environment** to locate factors in the societal and task environments that pose opportunities and threats. The scanning should focus particularly on market potential and resource accessibility.

3. **Scan and assess the internal factors** relevant to the new business. The entrepreneur should objectively consider personal assets, areas of expertise, abilities, and experience, all in terms of the organizational needs of the new venture.

4. **Analyze the strategic factors** in light of the current situation using SWOT. The venture's potential strengths and weaknesses must be evaluated in light of opportunities and threats. Develop a SFAS Table (**Figure 5–1**) of the strategic factors.

5. **Decide go or no go.** If the basic business idea appears to be a feasible business opportunity, the process should be continued. Otherwise, further development of the idea should be canceled unless the strategic factors change.

6. **Generate a business plan** specifying how the idea will be transformed into reality. See **Table 12–2** for the suggested contents of a strategic **business plan**. The proposed venture's mission, objectives, strategies, and policies, as well as its likely board of directors (if a corporation) and key managers should be developed. Key internal factors should be specified and performance projections generated. The business plan serves as a vehicle through which financial support is obtained from potential investors and creditors. Research indicates that new ventures with business plans tend to have higher revenue and sales growth than do those without a business plan.[18] Starting a business without a busi-

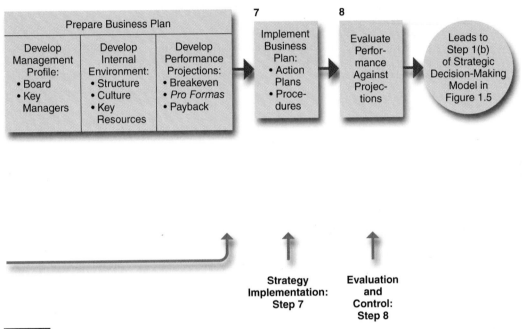

Source: T. L. Wheelen and C. E. Michaels, Jr., "Model for Strategic Decision-Making Process for New Ventures." Copyright © 1987 by T. L. Wheelen. Reprinted by permission.

ness plan is the quickest way to kill a new venture. For example, one study of 270 clothing retailers found that 80% of the successful stores had written a business plan, whereas 65% of the failed businesses had not.[19]

The strategic audit (see **Appendix 10.A at the end of Chapter 10**) can be used to develop a formal business plan. The audit's sections and subsections, along with the questions within them, provide a useful framework. Instead of analyzing the historical events of an existing company, use the questions to project the proposed company's future. The questions can be reoriented to follow the outline in **Appendix 10.A**. A crucial building block of a sound business plan is the construction of realistic scenarios for the pro forma financials. The pro formas must reflect the impact of seasonality on the cash flows of the proposed new venture.

7. **Implement the business plan** through the use of action plans and procedures.

8. **Evaluate the implemented business plan** through comparison of actual performance against projected performance results. This step leads to Step 1(b) of the strategic decision-making process shown in **Figure 1–5**. To the extent that actual results are less than or much greater than the anticipated results, the entrepreneur needs to reconsider the company's current mission, objectives, strategies, policies, and programs, and possibly make changes to the original business plan.

**Table 12–2 Contents of a Strategic Business Plan
for an Entrepreneurial Venture**

I.	Table of Contents	X.	Human Resources Plan
II.	Executive Summary	XI.	Ownership
III.	Nature of the Business	XII.	Risk Analysis
IV.	Strategy Formulation	XIII.	Timetables and Milestones
V.	Market Analysis	XIV.	Strategy Implementation—Action Plans
VI.	Marketing Plan	XV.	Evaluation and Control
VII.	Operational Plans—Service/Product	XVI.	Summary
VIII.	Financial Plans	XVII.	Appendixes
IX.	Organization and Management		

Note: The Strategic Audit in Appendix 10A can be used to develop a business plan. It provides detailed questions to serve as a checklist.

Source: Thomas L. Wheelen, "Contents of a Strategic Business Plan for an Entrepreneurial Venture." Copyright © 1988 by Thomas L. Wheelen. Reprinted by permission.

12.3 Issues in Corporate Governance

Corporate governance is much simpler in small entrepreneurial ventures than in large, established corporations. For one thing, the owners and the managers are usually the same people—the company founders (or their close relatives). If a venture is not incorporated, there is no need for a board of directors. It may be a sole proprietorship or a simple partnership. Those entrepreneurial ventures wishing to grow quickly or wishing to limit the liability of the owners often incorporate the business. Once incorporated, the company can sell shares of stock to others (such as venture capitalists) to finance its growth. Once the company is owned by shareholders (even if the shareholders are composed of only the founding owners who also manage the firm), the company must have a board of directors.

The boards of directors of entrepreneurial firms are likely to be either very passive or very active. Passive boards exist when the stock is closely held by the founding owners (and their immediate families) who manage the company on a day-to-day basis. As the only stockholders, they elect themselves to board offices and call meetings only when the law requires it—usually as a social occasion. There is no need for an active board, since there are no other stockholders and thus no agency problems. The board typically has no external directors. In most instances, the primary role of the board is simply to be a figurehead to satisfy the law.

Those entrepreneurial ventures financed by venture capitalists (VCs) will typically have very active boards of directors. The venture capitalists expect to obtain seats on the board in exchange for their investment.[20] Once on the board, VCs tend to be very powerful members of the board and are highly involved in strategic management.[21] The boards of directors of fast-growth entrepreneurial firms have around five directors, of whom about three are external. Almost 80% of them have written strategic plans with a time horizon of 12 to 24 months.[22]

Since closely held entrepreneurial ventures and small businesses tend to have relatively passive boards composed primarily of insiders, these types of businesses should use an advisory board to provide advice to the owner/managers. An **advisory board** is a group of external business people who voluntarily meet periodically with the owner/managers of the firm to discuss strategic and other issues. The members are usually invited to join the board by the president of the company. The advisory board has no official capacity but is expected to provide management with useful suggestions and act as a sounding board.

Since the members typically receive no compensation for serving, quarterly business meetings are often followed by cocktails and dinner at a nearby country club, hotel, or prestigious restaurant. It is important to staff the advisory board with knowledgeable people with significant business experience or skills who can complement the background and skills of the company's owner/managers. Advisory boards are an easy way to obtain free professional consulting advice. Research does indicate that advisory boards improve the performance of small businesses.[23]

12.4 Issues in Environmental Scanning and Strategy Formulation

Environmental scanning in small businesses is much less sophisticated than it is in large corporations. The business is usually too small to justify hiring someone to do only environmental scanning or strategic planning. Top managers, especially if they are the founders, tend to believe that they know the business and can follow it better than anyone else. A study of 220 small rapid-growth companies revealed that the majority of CEOs were actively and personally involved in all phases of the planning process but especially in the setting of objectives. Only 15% of the companies used a planning officer or formed a planning group to assist in the planning process. In the rest of the firms, operating managers who participated in strategic planning provided input only to the CEO, who then formulated the plan.[24] Unfortunately, the literature suggests that most small business owner/managers rely more on internal as opposed to external sources of information.[25] Few small businesses do much competitor analysis.

A fundamental reason for differences in strategy formulation between large and small entrepreneurial companies lies in the relationship between owners and managers. The CEO of a large corporation has to consider and balance the varied needs of the corporation's many stakeholders. The CEO of a small business, however, is very likely also to be the owner—the company's primary stakeholder. Personal and family needs can thus strongly affect the company's mission and objectives and can overrule other considerations.[26]

Size can affect the selection of an appropriate corporate strategy. Large corporations often choose growth strategies for their many side benefits for management as well as for shareholders. A small company may, however, choose a stability strategy because the entrepreneur is interested mostly in (1) generating employment for family members, (2) providing the family a "decent living," and (3) being the "boss" of a firm small enough that he or she can manage it comfortably. Thus the goals of a small business are likely to be the same as the goals of the owner/manager.

Basic SWOT analysis is just as relevant to small entrepreneurial businesses as it is to established large ones. Both the greatest strength and the greatest weakness of the small firm, at least in the beginning, rest with the entrepreneur—the owner/manager of the business. The entrepreneur is *the manager*, the source of product/market strategy, and the dynamo who energizes the company. That is why the internal assessment of a new venture's strengths and weaknesses focuses in **Figure 12–1** on the founder's personal characteristics—his or her assets, expertise, abilities, and experience. Just as an entrepreneur's strengths can be the key to company success, personal weaknesses can be a primary cause of failure. For example, the study of clothing retailers mentioned earlier showed that the owner/managers of 85% of the failed stores had no prior retailing experience.

SOURCES OF INNOVATION

Peter Drucker, in his book *Innovation and Entrepreneurship*, proposes seven sources for innovative opportunity that should be monitored by those interested in starting an entrepreneurial venture, either within an established company or as an independent small business.[27] The first four **sources of innovation** lie within the industry itself; the last three arise in the societal environment. These seven sources are:

1. **The Unexpected:** An unexpected success, an unexpected failure, or an unexpected outside event can be a symptom of a unique opportunity. When Don Cullen of Transmet Corporation spilled a box of very fine aluminum flakes onto his company's parking lot, he discovered that their presence in the asphalt prevented it from turning sticky in high temperatures. His company now produces aluminum chips for use in roofing. Sales have doubled every year since the product's introduction and his company will soon dominate the business.

2. **The Incongruity:** A discrepancy between reality and what everyone assumes it to be, or between what is and what ought to be, can create an opportunity for innovation. For example, a side effect of retailing via the Internet is the increasing number of packages being delivered to the home. Since neither FedEx nor UPS can leave a package unless someone is home to sign for it, many deliveries are delayed. Tony Paikeday founded zBox Company to make and sell a hard-plastic container that would receive deliveries from any delivery service and would be accessible only by the owner and the delivery services. "We're amazed that it doesn't exist yet," says Paikeday. "We think it will be the next great appliance of the century."[28]

3. **Innovation Based on Process Need:** When a weak link is evident in a particular process, but people work around it instead of doing something about it, an opportunity is present for the person or company willing to forge a stronger one. Tired of having to strain to use a too-small keyboard on his personal computer, David Levy invented a keyboard with 64 normal-sized keys cleverly put into an area the size of a credit card.[29]

4. **Changes in Industry or Market Structure:** A business is ready for an innovative product, service, or approach to the business when the underlying foundation of the industry or market shifts. Black Entertainment Television, Inc. (BET) was born when Robert Johnson noticed that no television programmer was targeting the increasing number of black viewers. The BET brand has expanded into magazines and is now known by over 90% of African Americans.[30]

5. **Demographics:** Changes in the population's size, age structure, composition, employment, level of education, and income can create opportunities for innovation. For example, Pam Henderson started a company called Kids Kab to shuttle children and teenagers to private schools, doctor and dental appointments, lessons, and extracurricular activities. With the trend to dual careers, parents were no longer always available to provide personal transportation for their own children and needed such a service.

6. **Changes in Perception, Mood, and Meaning:** Opportunities for innovation can develop when a society's general assumptions, attitudes, and beliefs change. For example, the increasing dominance of a few national brewers have caused beer drinkers to look for alternatives to the same old national brands. By positioning Yuengling, a local Pennsylvania beer, as a full-flavored beer and providing it with an artsy, nostalgic-looking label, the small company was able to catch the fancy of young, trendy consumers who viewed it as Pennsylvania's version of Anchor Steam, the successful San Francisco beer.

7. **New Knowledge:** Advances in scientific and nonscientific knowledge can create new products and new markets. Advances in two different areas can sometimes be integrated to form the basis of a new product. For example, Medical Foods was formed to make foods that act like medicine to treat conditions from diabetes to arthritis. Its first product,

NiteBite is a chocolate-flavored snack bar designed to help diabetics manage nocturnal hypoglycemia, caused by low blood sugar. NiteBite gradually releases glucose into the bloodstream, where it lasts for six hours or more.[31]

FACTORS AFFECTING A NEW VENTURE'S SUCCESS

According to Hofer and Sandberg, three factors have a substantial impact on a new venture's performance. In order of importance, these **factors affecting new venture success** are (1) the structure of the industry entered, (2) the new venture's business strategy, and (3) behavioral characteristics of the entrepreneur.[32]

Industry Structure

Research shows that the chances for success are greater for entrepreneurial ventures that enter rapidly changing industries than for those that enter stable industries. In addition, prospects are better in industries that are in the early, high-growth stages of development.[33] Competition is often less intense. Fast market growth also allows new ventures to make some mistakes without serious penalty. New ventures also increase their chances of success when they enter markets in which they can erect entry barriers to keep out competitors.

Contrary to popular wisdom, patents may not always provide competitive advantage, especially for new ventures in a high-tech or hypercompetitive industry. A well-financed competitor could examine a newly filed application for a patent, work around the patent, and beat the pioneering firm to market with a similar product. In addition, the time and cost of filing and defending a patent may not be worth the effort. According to Connie Bagley, author of *The Entrepreneur's Guide to Business Law*:

> It might take 18 months to get a patent on a product that has a 12-month life cycle. By the time you finally get the damn thing litigated, it's meaningless. So people are focusing less on proprietary assurance and more on first-mover advantage. . . . The law is just too slow for this high-speed economy.[34]

Most new ventures enter industries having a low degree of industry concentration (that is, no dominant competitors).[35] Industry concentration is not necessarily bad. It may create market niches being ignored by large firms.[36] Hofer and Sandberg found that a new venture is more likely to be successful entering an industry in which one dominant competitor has a 50% or more market share than entering an industry in which the largest competitor has less than a 25% market share. To explain this phenomenon, Hofer and Sandberg point out that when an industry has one dominant firm, the remaining competitors are relatively weak and are easy prey for an aggressive entrepreneur. To avoid direct competition with a major rival, the new venture can focus on a market segment that is being ignored.

Industry product characteristics also have a significant impact on a new venture's success. First, a new venture is more likely to be successful when it enters an industry with heterogeneous (different) products than when it enters one with homogeneous (similar) products. In a heterogeneous industry, a new venture can differentiate itself from competitors with a unique product; or, by focusing on the unique needs of a market segment, it can find a market niche. Second, a new venture is, according to research data, more likely to be successful if the product is relatively unimportant to the customer's total purchasing needs than if it is important. Customers are more likely to experiment with a new product if its cost is low and product failure will not create a problem.

Business Strategy

According to Hofer and Sandberg, the key to success for most new ventures is (1) to differentiate the product from those of other competitors in the areas of quality and service and (2) to focus the product on customer needs in a segment of the market in order to achieve a domi-

Internet Issue

Web Site Provides Local Business a Global Presence

A few years ago, The Doll Collection was a barely profitable neighborhood retail shop in Louisville, Kentucky, with a staff of three people. Looking for an inexpensive way to boost its sales, one of the employees,

Jason Walters, suggested putting a Web page on the Internet. After spending two weeks learning the Internet computer language, html, Walters designed a simple site showcasing well-known dolls like Barbie and Madam Alexander to attract buyers. Employees of The Doll Collection were amazed by the response—much of which came from outside North America. Sales jumped 375%. By 1997, the shop had become a global retailer, marketing Barbie and Madam Alexander dolls to people in almost every country, including Japan, China, and Australia. Try its Web site at ⟨www.dollpage.com⟩.

Source: L. Beresford, "Global Smarts: Toy Story," *Entrepreneur* (February 1997), p. 38.

---

nant share of that part of the market (Porter's focused differentiation competitive strategy). Adopting guerrilla-warfare tactics, these companies go after opportunities in market niches too small or too localized to justify retaliation from the market leaders.[37]

To continue its growth once it has found a niche, the entrepreneurial firm can emphasize continued innovation and pursue natural growth in its current markets. It can expand into related markets in which the company's core skills, resources, and facilities offer the keys to further success.

Some studies do indicate, however, that new ventures can also be successful following strategies other than going after an undefended niche with a focus strategy. A narrow market approach may leave the new firm vulnerable and preordained to only limited sales. One possible approach would be to offer products that are substitutable to, but differentiated from, those offered by bigger firms.[38] As noted in the ▨ **Internet Issue** feature, small businesses are finding it easy to enter global markets simply by developing a Web site on the Internet.

Entrepreneurial Characteristics

Four **entrepreneurial characteristics** are key to a new venture's success. Successful entrepreneurs have:

1. The *ability to identify potential venture opportunities* better than most people. They focus on opportunities—not on problems—and try to learn from failure. Entrepreneurs are goal oriented and have a strong impact on the emerging culture of an organization. They are able to envision where the company is going and are thus able to provide a strong overall sense of strategic direction.

2. A *sense of urgency* that makes them action oriented. They have a high need for achievement, which motivates them to put their ideas into action. They tend to have an internal locus of control that leads them to believe that they can determine their own fate through their own behavior. They also have a significantly greater capacity to tolerate ambiguity and stress than do many in established organizations.[39] They also have a strong need for control and may even be viewed as "misfits who need to create their own environment." They tend to distrust others and often have a need "to show others that they amount to something, that they cannot be ignored."[40]

3. A *detailed knowledge of the keys to success in the industry and the physical stamina* to make their work their lives. They have better than average education and significant work experience in the industry in which they start their business. They often work with partners to

Table 12–3 Some Guidelines for New Venture Success

- Focus on industries facing substantial technological or regulatory changes, especially those with recent exits by established competitors.
- Seek industries whose smaller firms have relatively weak competitive positions.
- Seek industries that are in early, high-growth stages of evolution.
- Seek industries in which it is possible to create high barriers to subsequent entry.
- Seek industries with heterogeneous products that are relatively unimportant to the customer's overall success.
- Seek to differentiate your products from those of your competitors in ways that are meaningful to your customers.
- Focus such differentiation efforts on product quality, marketing approaches, and customer service—and charge enough to cover the costs of doing so.
- Seek to dominate the market segments in which you compete. If necessary, either segment the market differently or change the nature and focus of your differentiation efforts to increase your domination of the segments you serve.
- Stress innovation, especially new product innovation, that is built on existing organizational capabilities.
- Seek natural, organic growth through flexibility and opportunism that builds on existing organizational strengths.

Source: C. W. Hofer and W. R. Sandberg, "Improving New Venture Performance: Some Guidelines for Success," *American Journal of Small Business* (Summer 1987), pp. 17, 19. Copyright © 1987 by C. W. Hofer and W. R. Sandberg. Reprinted by permission.

form a new venture (70% of new high-tech ventures are started by more than one founder).[41] More than half of all entrepreneurs work at least 60 hours a week in the start-up year, according to a National Federation of Independent Business study.[42]

4. *Access to outside help* to supplement their skills, knowledge, and abilities. Over time, they develop a network of people having key skills and knowledge whom the entrepreneurs can call upon for support. Through their enthusiasm, these entrepreneurs are able to attract key investors, partners, creditors, and employees. For example, the founders of eBay did not hesitate to bring in Meg Whitman as CEO because Whitman had the managerial skills that eBay needed to expand.

In summarizing their conclusions regarding factors affecting the success of entrepreneurial ventures, Hofer and Sandberg propose the guidelines presented in **Table 12–3**.

12.5 Issues in Strategy Implementation

Two key implementation issues in small companies are organizing and staffing the growing company and transferring ownership of the company to the next generation.

SUBSTAGES OF SMALL BUSINESS DEVELOPMENT

The implementation problems of a small business change as the company grows and develops over time. Just as the decision-making process for entrepreneurial ventures is different from that of established businesses, the managerial systems in small companies often vary from those of large corporations. Those variations are based on their stage of development. The stages of corporate growth and development discussed in **Chapter 8** suggest that all small businesses are either in Stage I or trying to move into Stage II. These models imply that all successful new ventures eventually become Stage II, functionally organized companies. This is not always true, however. In attempting to show clearly how small businesses develop, Churchill and Lewis propose five **substages of small business development**: (a) existence, (b) survival, (c) success, (d) take-off, and (e) resource maturity.[43] A review of these small business substages shows in more detail how a company can move through the entrepreneurial Stage I into a functionally oriented, professionally managed Stage II.

Stage A: Existence

At this point, the entrepreneurial venture faces the problems of obtaining customers and delivering the promised product or service. The organizational structure is simple. The entrepreneur does everything and directly supervises subordinates. Systems are minimal. The owner is the business.

Stage B: Survival

Those ventures able to satisfy a sufficient number of customers enter this stage; the rest close when their owners run out of start-up capital. Those reaching the survival stage are concerned about generating the cash flow needed to repair and replace capital assets as they wear out and to finance the growth to continue satisfying the market segment they have found.

At this stage, the organizational structure is still simple, but it probably has a sales manager or general supervisor to carry out the owner's well-defined orders. A major problem of many small businesses at this stage is finding a person who is qualified to supervise the business when the owner can't be present but who is still willing to work for a very modest salary. Entrepreneurs usually try to use family members rather than hiring an outsider who lacks the entrepreneur's dedication to the business and (in the words of one owner/manager) "steals them blind." A company that remains in this stage for a long time is often called a "mom and pop" firm. It earns marginal returns on invested time and capital (with lots of psychic income!) and eventually goes out of business when "mom and pop" give up or retire. This type of small business is viewed more as a **lifestyle company** in which the firm is purely an extension of the owner's lifestyle. Over 94% of small private companies are in this category.[44]

Stage C: Success

By this point, the company's sales have reached a level where the firm is not only profitable, but also has sufficient cash flow to reinvest in itself. The key issue at this stage is whether the company should be used as a platform for growth or as a means of support for the owners as they completely or partially disengage from the company. The company is transforming into a functionally structured organization, but it still relies on the entrepreneur for all key decisions. The two options are disengagement and growth.

C(1) Disengagement   The company can now successfully follow a stability strategy and remain at this stage almost indefinitely—provided that environmental change does not destroy its niche or poor management reduce its competitive abilities. By now functional managers have taken over some of the entrepreneur's duties. The company at this stage may be incorporated, but it is still primarily owned by the founder or founder's family. Consequently the board of directors is either a rubber stamp for the entrepreneur or a forum for family squabbles. Growth strategies are not pursued because either the market niche will not allow growth or the owner is content with the company at a size he or she can still manage comfortably. Strategic decisions make limited use of objective information and tend to be intuitive—based on personal desires and the founder's background.[45]

C(2) Growth   The entrepreneur risks all available cash and the established borrowing power of the company in financing further growth. Strategic as well as operational planning is extensive and deeply involves the owner. Managers with an eye to the company's future rather than for its current situation are hired. This is an entrepreneurial high-growth firm aiming to be included in the *Inc.* 500. The emphasis now is on teamwork rather than on the entrepreneur's personal actions and energy. The personal values and philosophy of the founder are slowly transferred into a developing corporate culture.

Stage D: Take-Off

The key problems in this stage are how to grow rapidly and how to finance that growth. By now the firm is incorporated and has sold or is planning to sell stock in its company via an initial public offering (IPO) or via a direct public offering (DPO).[46] The entrepreneur must learn to delegate to specialized professional managers or to a team of managers who now form the top management of the company.[47] A functional structure of the organization should now be solidly in place. Operational and strategic planning greatly involve the hired managers, but the company is still dominated by the entrepreneur's presence and stock control. Vertical and horizontal growth strategies are being seriously considered as the firm's management debates when and how to grow. The company is now included in the *Inc. 500* select group of firms.

At this point, the entrepreneur either is able to manage the transition from a small to a large company or recognizes personal limitations, sells his or her stock for a profit, and leaves the firm. The composition of the board of directors changes from dominance by friends and relatives of the owner to a large percentage of outsiders with managerial experience who can help the owner during the transition to a professionally managed company. The biggest danger facing the firm in this stage is the owner's desire to remain in total control (not willing to delegate) as if it were still a small entrepreneurial venture, even though he or she lacks the managerial skills necessary to run an established corporation.

Stage E: Resource Maturity

It is at this point that the small company has adopted most of the characteristics of an established, large company. It may still be a small-to-medium-sized company, but it is recognized as an important force in the industry and a possible candidate for the *Fortune 500* someday. The greatest concerns of a company at this stage are controlling the financial gains brought on by rapid growth and retaining its flexibility and entrepreneurial spirit. In terms of the stages of organizational growth and development discussed in **Chapter 8**, the company has become a full-fledged Stage II functional corporation.

TRANSFER OF POWER AND WEALTH IN FAMILY BUSINESSES

Small businesses are often **family businesses**. It is estimated that over a third of the U.S. *Fortune 500* companies are either family owned or dominated. For the world, the percentage is over half.[48] Even though the founders of the companies are the primary forces in starting the entrepreneurial ventures, their needs for business support and financial assistance will cause them to turn to family members, who can be trusted, over unknown outsiders of questionable integrity, who may demand more salary than the enterprise can afford. Sooner or later, the founder's spouse and children are drafted into business operations either because the family standard of living is directly tied to the business or the entrepreneur desperately needs help just to staff the operation. The children are guaranteed summer jobs, and the business changes from dad's or mom's company to "our" company. The family members are extremely valuable assets to the entrepreneur because they are often also willing to put in long hours at low pay to help the business succeed. Even though the spouse and children might have no official stock in the company, they know that they will somehow share in its future and perhaps even inherit the business. The problem is that only 30% of family firms in the United States make it to the second generation, and just 13% survive to the third generation.[49] A common saying among European family businesses is: "The first generation creates, the second inherits, and the third destroys."[50]

Table 12–4 Transfer of Power in a Family Business

Phase 1   **Owner-Managed Business:** Phase 1 begins at start-up and continues until the entrance of another family member into the business on a full-time basis. Family considerations influence but are not yet a directing part of the firm. At this point, the founder (entrepreneur) and the business are one.

Phase 2   **Training and Development of New Generation:** The children begin to learn the business at the dining room table during early childhood and then through part-time and vacation employment. The family and the business become one. Just as the entrepreneur identified with the business earlier, the family now begins to identify itself with the business.

Phase 3   **Partnership Between Generations:** At this point, a son or daughter of the founder has acquired sufficient business and managerial competence so that he or she can be involved in key decisions for at least a part of the company. The entrepreneur's offspring, however, has to first gain respect from the firm's employees and other managers and show that he or she can do the job right. Another issue is the lack of willingness of the founder to share authority with the son or daughter. Consequently a common tactic taken by sons and daughters in family businesses is to take a job in a large, established corporation where they can gain valuable experience and respect for their skills.

Phase 4   **Transfer of Power:** Instead of being forced to sell the company when he or she can no longer manage the business, the founder has the option in a family business of turning it over to the next generation as part of their inheritance. Often the founder moves to the position of Chairman of the Board and promotes one of the children to the position of CEO. Unfortunately some founders cannot resist meddling in operating affairs and unintentionally undermine the leadership position of the son or daughter. To avoid this problem, the founder should sell his or her stock (probably through a leveraged buy-out to the children) and physically leave the company and allow the next generation the freedom it needs to adapt to changing conditions.

Source: N. C. Churchill and K. J. Hatten, "Non-Market-Based Transfer of Wealth and Power: A Research Framework for Family Businesses," *American Journal of Small Business* (Winter 1987), pp. 51–64. Reprinted with the permission of Baylor University. All rights reserved.

Churchill and Hatten propose that family businesses go through four sequential phases from the time in which the venture is strictly managed by the founder to the time in which the next generation takes charge.[51] These phases are detailed in **Table 12–4**. Each of these phases must be well managed if the company is to survive past the third generation. Some of the reasons why family businesses may fail to successfully transfer ownership to the next generation are (1) inherited wealth destroys entrepreneurial drive, (2) the entrepreneur doesn't allow for a changing firm, (3) emphasis on business means the family is neglected, (4) the business's financial growth can't keep up with rising family lifestyles, (5) family members are not prepared to run a business, and (6) the business becomes an arena for family conflicts.[52] In addition, succession planning may be ignored because of the founder's or family's refusal to think about the founder's death, the founder's unwillingness to let go of the firm, the fear of sibling rivalry, or intergenerational envy.

12.6 Issues in Evaluation and Control

As a means by which the corporation's implementation of strategy can be evaluated, the control systems of large corporations have evolved over a long period of time in response to pressures from the environment (particularly the government). Conversely the entrepreneur creates what is needed as the business grows. Because of a personal involvement in decision making, the entrepreneur managing a small business has little need for a formal, detailed reporting system. Thus the founder who has little understanding of accounting and a shortage of cash might employ a bookkeeper instead of an accountant. A formal personnel function might never appear because the entrepreneur lumps it in with simple bookkeeping and uses a secretary to handle personnel files. As an entrepreneurial venture becomes more established, it will develop more complex evaluation and control systems, but they are often not the kind used in large corporations and are probably used for different purposes.

Financial statements, in particular, tell only half the story in small, privately owned companies. The formality of the financial reporting system in such a company is usually a result of pressures from government tax agencies, not from management's desire for an objective evaluation and control system. For example, the absence of taxes in Bermuda has been given as the reason why business owners keep little documentation—thus finding it nearly impossible to keep track of inventory, monitor sales, or calculate how much they are owed.[53]

Because balance sheets and income statements do not always give an accurate picture, standard ratios such as return on assets and debt-equity are unreliable. Research reveals systematic differences among liquidity and solvency measures for small compared to large companies. The mean averages of both the current ratio and the debt ratio are systematically larger for the small companies.[54] Cash flow is widely regarded as more important for an entrepreneurial business than is the traditional balance sheet or income statement. Even though a small business may be profitable in the accounting sense, a negative cash flow could bankrupt the company. Levin and Travis provide five reasons why owners, operators, and outside observers should be wary of using standard financial methods to indicate the health of a small, privately owned company.[55]

- **The line between debt and equity is blurred.** In some instances, what appears as a loan is really an easy-to-retrieve equity investment. The entrepreneur in this instance doesn't want to lose his or her investment if the company fails. Another condition is that retained earnings seldom reflect the amount of internal financing needed for the company's growth. This account may merely be a place in which cash is left so that the owner can avoid double taxation. To avoid other taxes, owner/managers may own fixed assets that they lease to the corporation. The equity that was used to buy those assets is really the company's equity, but it doesn't appear on the books.

- **Lifestyle is a part of financial statements.** The lifestyle of the owner and the owner's family is often reflected in the balance sheet. The assets of some firms include beach cottages, mountain chalets, and automobiles. In others, plants and warehouses that are used for company operations are not shown because they are held separately by the family. Income statements may not reflect how well the company is operating. Profitability is not so important in decision making in small, private companies as it is in large, publicly held corporations. For example, spending for recreation or transportation and paying rents or salaries above market rates to relatives put artificially high costs on the books of small firms. The business might appear to be poorly managed to an outsider, but the owner is acting rationally. The owner/manager wants dependable income or its equivalent with the least painful tax consequences. Because the standard profitability measures such as ROI are not useful in the evaluation of such a firm, Levin and Travis recommend return on current assets as a better measure of corporate productivity.

- **Standard financial formulas don't always apply.** Following practices that are in contrast to standard financial recommendations, small companies often use short-term debt to finance fixed assets. The absence of well-organized capital markets for small businesses, along with the typical banker's resistance to making loans without personal guarantees, leaves the private owner little choice. Even though a large amount of long-term debt is considered to be a good use of financial leverage by a large publicly held firm, it can drive a smaller firm into bankruptcy by raising its break-even point.

- **Personal preference determines financial policies.** Because the owner is often the manager of the small firm, dividend policy is largely irrelevant. Dividend decisions are based not on stock price (which is usually unknown because the stock is not traded), but on the owner's lifestyle and the tradeoff between taking wealth from the corporation and double taxation.

- **Banks combine personal and business wealth.** Because of the large percentage of small businesses that go bankrupt every year, bank loan officers are reluctant to lend money to a small business unless the owner also provides some personal guarantees for the loan. In some instances, part of the loan may be composed of a second mortgage on the owner's house. If the owner does not want to succumb to this pressure by lenders to include the owner's personal assets as part of the collateral, the owner/manager must be willing to pay high interest rates for a loan that does not put the family's assets at risk.

12.7 Impact of the Internet on Entrepreneurial Ventures and Small Business

The years from 1998 to 2000 were glory years for Internet-based entrepreneurial ventures. Most subsequently failed during 2000 and 2001 when venture capitalists and others began to doubt that many of these ventures would ever achieve profitability. Recent graduates had been founding Internet start-ups by the thousands. Some college students were even wooed by these Internet entrepreneurial ventures to leave school (at least temporarily) and join the dot-com boom. In his own words, this is one college student's story of his experience being a part of an Internet-based entrepreneurial venture:

> There I was, walking into some unknown building, about to meet some unknown people, and working for a company I barely knew. I wondered how I had gotten myself into this mess in the first place. I say "mess" jokingly because I did enjoy the experience and wouldn't trade it for the world. Life just never goes quite according to plan.
>
> I had been working for this small operation since last October (1999). It started off as just a little side job to make ends meet. In February (2000), I received a phone call from the founder of the company. He told me that the company was currently working with a venture capital firm to secure a few million dollars in funding. The founder wanted me to come to Chicago to work full time in March. Even though I saw huge potential for the company's future, I was still extremely hesitant to drop out of school and go chase after this opportunity. He then laid out his plan for the company: Get the funding, build up the company over the following months, and then sell it off for a large amount by the end of the year. It sounded fairly reasonable to me at the time. I started to sway, but I still wasn't convinced. We then looked at the track record of many other Internet start-ups over the past few years. All of our competitors had been bought out for substantial amounts with a year of VC funding. Almost all of them were acquired just after Christmas (1999). The potential numbers plus the amazing opportunity to work for a start-up as an undergraduate far outweighed the risks.
>
> At this time in my life, I had nothing to lose. Worst-case scenario: the company flops. In this worst case, I would still have a few months salary in the bank and I'd be back in school the next semester with a shiny new addition to my resume. Best-case scenario: I would own 1% of a company that was worth a few hundred million dollars. After much thought, advice from others, and a few loose ends to tie up, I decided to go for it.
>
> Things had been falling into place perfectly except the company was a little behind schedule. In the first week of March, the VC offered to fund us. It was the beginning of what they call "due diligence." A deal falling through at this point is so rare that due diligence is often accompanied with a term sheet (letter of intent) and a bridge note (3–5% of the capital). The second week of

March (2000) was my deadline to withdraw from school, so I did. The third week of March, the improbable happened; our deal with the VC fell apart.

The month that followed turned this once-in-a-lifetime opportunity into a giant mess. We ended up firing our financial advisor, who was ultimately to blame for the VC funding falling through. Shortly after that, the CTO/Cofounder decided to leave the company. To make things worse, the stock market fell. The technology sector, most notably, Internet companies, was to blame for the crash. We were down to three people on this project, the founder, the acting CEO, and me. That brings me to where I began this story—walking into a meeting to meet these two for the first time.

We were in Chicago trying to figure out what to do. Actually, I didn't have the slightest clue what to do, so I just sat, listened, and nodded my head. It was decided that we would bring in a "turnaround" guy. I nicknamed him "The Cleaner," pun and allusion intended. Once he stepped in, he devised a plan and re-established a connection with the Cofounder and some other people that were involved. He also brought in a new CEO and a new Chairman of the Board. His plan was to change the direction of the company in a way that was more appealing to investors. We could then obtain VC and angel funding. There were still thoughts of selling the company off sometime in the future, but it was no longer a goal. The biggest change was to our business model. We took our business plan, placed it in the paper shredder, and hit "mutilate."

Our original business model was a typical business to consumer model. We provided a service—price comparison-based Internet shopping. We had a few edges that let us stay competitive, such as superior technology, additional services, and a media partner program. The media partner program is worth explaining. We partner with content-driven Web sites and embed our technology into their sites. The Web sites can then participate in our revenue stream. Our original goal was to build a brand name doing this. For example, we could partner with MTV.com. Every time their site would bring up a music CD, there would be a button that would allow the customer to buy it online for the lowest price. The turnaround guy saw this as our primary asset and our best idea. So overnight, we changed from an Internet e-commerce company to an infrastructure technology company. Our financial model also dramatically changed.

Instead of spending millions of dollars on direct advertising to build a brand name (the number one reason why dot-coms are failing now), we would utilize our partner's existing traffic. A big Web site like MTV.com gets millions of hits a day. Of those, a certain percentage will click on our button to compare prices. A certain percentage of those will buy the item. We get a commission from every sale the retailer makes. As an incentive, we give a percentage of what we make back to the partner site. We end up with a small piece of the pie, but the pie is huge and growing every day. We packaged these ideas with a lot of other ones into a 50-page business plan. With our new business plan and a very impressive management team, we were now ready to go back to a VC.

It was at this time I decided to go back to school. Despite how bright things were looking now, we still had no money. The paychecks were smaller and the fall semester was about to start. Everyone on the team agreed that for the time being, it was a smart move for me. There was no telling if and when the funding would come through. Today, as far as things stand, we are scheduled to close with a VC from Florida sometime in November (2000). Our new Chairman has been aggressively pursuing angel funding and should have some capital within the next week or two. If the VC funding works out, I will have a plethora of options of how I want to be involved in the company. Likely, I will stay in school and become an independent consultant to the company part-time. That is generally what my role is now.

For a while the company was only a handful of people. Being one of those people, I had to, rather was able to work in many different areas outside my original position. I helped lay the original groundwork for the company, which was very exciting. My official title was Director of Content Development. My primary role was to lead the content team, which consisted of one other individual and me. My team was responsible for maintaining the external Web pages, running promotions, and keeping positive relations with our customers and retailers. One thing I really

> *learned was that when you are working in a small company, everyone does everything. If there is something that needs to get done, everyone helps out. I've had the President of the company help me update Web pages. I've helped out the CEO with a PowerPoint presentation for potential investors. I've also helped the CFO with the financial planning; the CTO with java scripts, and explained the technology to potential partners. All of us worked on and wrote the business plan.*
>
> *Looking back at the roller coaster ride this company has taken me on, I'm glad to have been and still be a part of it. This experience has raised my understanding to a whole new level of how the world works. I can't, nor would I want to, imagine how my life would be if I hadn't decided to take a risk and jump on this opportunity.*[56]

Projections for the 21st Century

- From 1994 to 2010, the number of golf courses in the United States will increase from 14,648 to 16,800.
- From 1994 to 2010, gambling revenues will grow in the United States from $39.5 billion to $125.6 billion.[57]

Discussion Questions

1. In terms of strategic management, how does a new venture's situation differ from that of an ongoing small company?

2. How should a small entrepreneurial company engage in environmental scanning? To what aspects of the environment should management pay most attention?

3. What are the characteristics of an attractive industry from an entrepreneur's point of view? What role does innovation play?

4. What considerations should small-business entrepreneurs keep in mind when they are deciding if a company should follow a growth or a stability strategy?

5. How does being family owned (as compared to being publicly owned) affect a firm's strategic management?

Strategic Practice Exercise

Amazon.com began a new era in July 1995 when it offered a new proposition to the consumer: easy access to convenient ordering with seemingly endless selection. No longer did people need to drive to a local book store to search for and buy a book or CD. Amazon simplified the selection process through its search engines and huge databases. This Internet advantage was undermined, however, by an advantage only a bricks and mortar retailer like Barnes & Noble could offer: the ability for the customer to take home the book as soon as it is paid for.

In the United States, 55% of Internet deliveries are currently made by UPS, 32% by the Postal Service, and 10% by FedEx. The remaining 3% is composed of a new type of Internet service company—the Internet delivery firm. Entrepreneurial ventures like Webvan, Kozmo.com, Urbanfetch, and Pink Dot offer same-day delivery in cer-

tain locations. By combining the convenience of online ordering with nearly instant gratification, they offer a superior value proposition to those firms shipping by conventional means. Most of the Internet retailers offering same-day delivery typically focus on a mix of two broad product categories, impulse items such as videos, books, snacks, and routine necessities like grocery and household items. All offer delivery 24 hours a day, 7 days a week. Although most offer free delivery, some price their offerings to discourage small orders. The trade off with this type of business is speed of delivery versus variety of offerings. To achieve fast response, the local deliverer must hold product locally, rather than in large national distribution centers, like mass merchandisers and large catalogue companies. The speed advantage from being local means a decrease in variety. For example, Kozmo offered about

15,000 items in total versus more than 10 million total items at Amazon.[58]

1. Are there any Internet same-day local delivery firms in your city or town? How successful are they?

2. Evaluate the growth potential of the Internet same-day delivery company. It this the type of business you would like to start? If you were a venture capitalist, would you invest in this type of firm?

3. Who is the competition of the Internet same-day delivery firm? Large Internet firms such as Amazon? Local bricks and mortar retailers? National delivery operations such as UPS and the Postal Service?

4. How might new developments in technology effect this type of business?

Key Terms

advisory board (p. 308)
business model (p. 304)
business plan (p. 306)
entrepreneur (p. 303)
entrepreneurial characteristics (p. 312)

entrepreneurial venture (p. 303)
factors affecting new venture success (p. 311)
family businesses (p. 315)
lifestyle company (p. 314)
small-business firm (p. 303)

sources of innovation (p. 310)
strategic decision-making process for entrepreneurial ventures (p. 305)
substages of small business development (p. 314)

Notes

1. J. Norman, "Great Idea? That's the Easy Part," *Des Moines Register* (November 12, 1995), p. 3G.
2. J. Kahn, "Suddenly, Startups Are Chic," *Fortune* (February 15, 1999), p. 110.
3. *The State of Small Business: A Report to the President* (Washington, DC: U.S. Government Printing Office, 1987), p. 117.
4. B. Keats and J. Bracker, "Toward a Theory of Small Firm Performance: A Conceptual Model," *American Journal of Small Business* (Spring 1988), pp. 41–58; D. Dougherty, "A Practice-Centered Model of Organizational Renewal Through Product Innovation," *Strategic Management Journal* (Summer 1992), pp. 77–92.
5. J. Castro, J. McDowell, and W. McWhirter, "Big vs. Small," *Time* (September 5, 1988), p. 49.
6. B. Bowers, "This Store Is a Hit But Somehow Cash Flow Is Missing," *Wall Street Journal* (April 13, 1993), p. B2.
7. M. J. Foster, "Scenario Planning for Small Businesses," *Long Range Planning* (February 1993), p. 123; M. S. S. El-Namacki, "Small Business—The Myth and the Reality," *Long Range Planning* (August 1990), p. 79.
8. According to a study by Dun & Bradstreet of 800,000 small U.S. businesses started in 1985, 70% were still in business in March 1994. Contrary to other studies, this study only counted firms as failures if they owed money at the time of their demise. Also see J. Aley, "Debunking the Failure Fallacy," *Fortune* (September 6, 1993), p. 21.
9. R. N. Lussier, "Startup Business Advice from Business Owners to Would-Be Entrepreneurs," *SAM Advanced Management Journal* (Winter 1995), pp. 10–13.
10. J. W. Carland, F. Hoy, W. R. Boulton, and J. A. C. Carland, "Differentiating Entrepreneurs from Small Business Owners: A Conceptualization," *Academy of Management Review* (April 1984), p. 358; J. W. Carland, J. C. Carland, F. Hoy, and W. R. Boulton, "Distinctions Between Entrepreneurial and Small Business Ventures," *International Journal of Management* (March 1988), pp. 98–103.
11. S. P. Galante, "Counting on a Narrow Market Can Cloud Company's Future," *Wall Street Journal* (January 20, 1986), p. 17. Sexton's statement that entrepreneurial firms engage in more sophisticated strategic planning than do small businesses is supported by C. H. Matthews and S. G. Scott, "Uncertainty and Planning in Small Entrepreneurial Firms: An Empirical Assessment," *Journal of Small Business Management* (October 1995), pp. 34–52. See also W. H. Stewart, Jr., W. E. Watson, J. C. Carland, and J. W. Carland, "A Proclivity for Entrepreneurship: A Comparison of Entrepreneurs, Small Business Owners, and Corporate Managers," *Journal of Business Venturing* (March 1999), pp. 189–214.
12. D. Fields, "Mrs. Fields' Weekends," *USA Weekend* (February 3–5, 1989), p. 16; M. Alpert, "In the Chips," *Fortune* (July 17, 1989), pp. 115–116.
13. J. S. Bracker, B. W. Keats, and J. N. Pearson, "Planning and Financial Performance Among Small Firms in a Growth Industry," *Strategic Management Journal* (November–December 1988), pp. 591–603; J. Kargar and J. A. Parnell, "Strategic Planning Emphasis and Planning Satisfaction in Small Firms: An Empirical Investigation," *Journal of Business Strategies* (Spring 1996), pp. 120; C. R. Schwenk and C. B. Shrader, "Effects of Formal Strategic Planning on Financial Performance in Small Firms: A Meta-Analysis," *Entrepreneurship Theory & Performance* (Spring 1993), pp. 53–64; L. W. Rue and N. A. Ibrahim, "The Relationship Between Planning Sophistication and Performance in Small Businesses," *Journal of Small Business Management* (October 1998), pp. 24–32.
14. W. H. Baker, H. Lon, and B. Davis, "Business Planning in Successful Small Firms," *Long Range Planning* (December 1993), pp. 82–88.
15. A. Thomas, "Less Is More: How Less Formal Planning Can Be Best," in *The Strategic Planning Management Reader*, edited by L. Fahey (Upper Saddle River, NJ: Prentice Hall, 1989), pp. 331–336; C. B. Shrader, C. L. Mulford, and V. L. Blackburn, "Strategic and Operational Planning, Uncertainty, and Performance in Small Firms," *Journal of Small Business Management* (October 1989), pp. 45–60.

16. R. B. Robinson, Jr., and J. A. Pearce II, "The Impact of Formalized Strategic Planning on Financial Performance in Small Organizations," *Strategic Management Journal* (July–September 1983), pp. 197–207; R. Ackelsberg and P. Arlow, "Small Businesses Do Plan and It Pays Off," *Long Range Planning* (October 1985), pp. 61–67.

17. M. Berry, "Strategic Planning in Small High-Tech Companies," *Long Range Planning* (June 1998), pp. 455–466.

18. T. Mazzarol, "Do Formal Business Plans Really Matter? A Survey of Small Business Owners in Australia," Paper presented to the *45th International Conference on Small Business (ICSB) World Conference 2000*, Brisbane, Australia (June 7–10, 2000).

19. V. Fowler, "Business Study Focuses on Failures," *Des Moines Register* (August 9, 1992), p. G1. For information on preparing a business plan, see R. Hisrich and M. Peters, *Entrepreneurship*, 4th edition (New York: Irwin/McGraw-Hill, 1998).

20. L. W. Busenitz, D.D. Moesel, J. O. Fiet, and J. B. Barney, "The Framing of Perceptions of Fairness in the Relationship Between Venture Capitalists and New Venture Teams," *Entrepreneurship Theory & Practice* (Spring 1997), pp. 5–21.

21. V. H. Fried, G. D. Bruton, and R. D. Hisrich, "Strategy and the Board of Directors in Venture Capital-Backed Firms," *Journal of Business Venturing* (November 1999), pp. 493–503.

22. D. L. Sexton and F. I. Steele, *Leading Practices of Fast Growth Entrepreneurs* (Kansas City, Mo.: National Center for Entrepreneurship Research, 1997).

23. D. J. Garsombke and T. W. Garsombke, "An Empirical Investigation of the Utilization of External and Internal Boards of Directors and Management Advisory Assistance on the Performance of Small Businesses," *Journal of Business Strategies* (Fall 1996), pp. 167–184.

24. J. C. Shuman and J. A. Seeger, "The Theory and Practice of Strategic Management in Smaller Rapid Growth Firms," *American Journal of Small Business* (Summer 1986), p. 14.

25. R. C. Pineda, L. D. Lerner, M. C. Miller, and S. J. Phillips, "An Investigation of Factors Affecting the Information-Search Activities of Small Business Managers," *Journal of Small Business Management* (January 1998), pp. 60–71.

26. S. Birley and P. Westhead, "Growth and Performance Contrasts Between 'Types' of Small Firms," *Strategic Management Journal* (November–December 1990), pp. 535–557; J. L. Ward and C. E. Aronloff, "How Family Affects Strategy," *Small Business Forum* (Fall 1994), pp. 85–90.

27. P. F. Drucker, *Innovation and Entrepreneurship* (New York: HarperCollins, 1985), pp. 30–129.

28. F. Donnely, "Let zBox Accept Deliveries," *Des Moines Register* (October 31, 2000), p. TW1.

29. D. Stipp, "Inventor on the Verge of a Nervous Breakthrough," *Fortune* (March 29, 1999), pp. 104–117.

30. D. Whitford, "Taking BET Back From the Street," *Fortune* (November 9, 1998), pp. 167–170.

31. A. Bianchi, "Medical-Food Start-Up Offers Tasty Treatments," *Inc.* (January 1997), p. 15.

32. C. W. Hofer and W. R. Sandberg, "Improving New Venture Performance: Some Guidelines for Success," *American Journal of Small Business* (Summer 1987), pp. 12–23. See also J. J. Chrisman and A. Bauerschmidt, "New Venture Performance: Some Critical Extensions to the Model," Paper presented to *State-of-the-Art Symposium on Entrepreneurship*, Iowa State University (April 12–14, 1992).

33. K. C. Robinson, "An Examination of the Influence of Industry Structure on Eight Alternative Measures of New Venture Performance for High Potential Independent New Ventures," *Journal of Business Venturing* (March 1999), pp. 165–187.

34. Interview with C. Bagley by J. Useem, "Forget Patents, Says Stanford Prof," *Inc.* (October 1996), p. 23.

35. K. C. Robinson.

36. J. Wade, "A Community-Level Analysis of Sources and Rates of Technological Variation in the Microprocessor Market," *Academy of Management Journal* (October 1996), pp. 1218–1244.

37. Supported by R. C. Shrader and M. Simon, "Corporate Versus Independent New Ventures: Resources, Strategy, and Performance Differences," *Journal of Business Venturing* (January 1997), pp. 47–66, and R. Tonge, P. C. Larsen, and M. Sto, "Strategic Leadership in Super-Growth Companies—A Reappraisal," *Long Range Planning* (December 1998), pp. 838–847.

38. A. C. Cooper, G. E. Willard, and C. Y. Woo, "A Reexamination of the Niche Concept," in *The Strategy Process: Concepts, Contexts, and Cases*, 2nd edition, edited by H. Mintzberg and J. B. Quinn (Upper Saddle River, N.J.: Prentice Hall, 1991), pp. 619–628; P. P. McDougal, J. G. Covin, R. B. Robinson, Jr., and L. Herron, "The Effects of Industry Growth and Strategic Breadth on New Venture Performance and Strategy Content," *Strategic Management Journal* (September 1994), pp. 537–554; C. E. Bamford, T. J. Dean, and P. P. McDougall, "Initial Strategies and New Venture Growth: An Examination of the Effectiveness of Broad vs. Narrow Breadth Strategies," in *Frontiers of Entrepreneurial Research*, edited by P. D. Reynolds, et al. (Babson Park, MA: Babson College, 1997), pp. 375–389; G. H. Lim, K. S. Lee, and S. J. Tan, "SMEs' Market Entry Strategy: Substitution Instead of Niching," paper presented to the *International Council for Small Business Conference*, 1999.

39. H. P. Welsch, "Entrepreneurs' Personal Characteristics: Causal Models," Paper presented to *State-of-the-Art Symposium on Entrepreneurship*, Iowa State University (April 12–14, 1992); A. Rahim, "Stress, Strain, and Their Moderators: An Empirical Comparison of Entrepreneurs and Managers," *Journal of Small Business Management* (January 1996), pp. 46–58.

40. M. Kets de Vries, "The Dark Side of Entrepreneurship," *Harvard Business Review* (November–December 1985), pp. 160–167.

41. A. C. Cooper, F. J. Gimeno-Gascon, and C. Y. Woo, "Initial Human and Financial Capital as Predictors of New Venture Performance," *Journal of Business Venturing* (Vol. 9, 1994), pp. 371–395; H. R. Feeser and G. E. Willard, "Founding Strategies and Performance in High-Tech Firms," in *Handbook of Business Strategy, 1991/92 Yearbook*, edited by H. E. Glass and M. A. Hovde (Boston: Warren, Gorham & Lamont, 1991), pp. 2.1–2.18.

42. R. Ricklefs and U. Gupta, "Traumas of a New Entrepreneur," *Wall Street Journal* (May 10, 1989), p. B1.

43. N. C. Churchill and V. L. Lewis, "The Five Stages of Small Business Growth," *Harvard Business Review* (May–June 1983), pp. 30–50. The life cycle concept is supported by research by M. Beverland, "Organizational Life Cycles in Small Enterprises," paper presented to the *45th International Conference on Small Business (ICSB) World Conference*, Brisbane, Australia (June 7–10, 2000).

44. J. W. Petty and W. D. Bygrave, "What Does Finance Have to Say to the Entrepreneur?" *Journal of Small Business Finance* (Spring 1993), pp. 125–137.

45. K. D. Brouthers, F. Andriessen, and J. Nicolaes, "Driving Blind: Strategic Decision-Making in Small Companies," *Long Range Planning* (February 1998), pp. 130–138.

46. See C. Farrell, K. Rebello, R. D. Hof, and M. Maremont, "The Boom in IPOs," *Business Week* (December 18, 1995), pp. 64–72; S. Gruner, "When Mom & Pop Go Public," *Inc.* (December 1996), pp. 66–73.

47. A. Caruana, M. H. Morris, and A. J. Vella, "The Effect of Centralization and Formalization on Entrepreneurship in Export Firms," *Journal of Small Business Management* (January 1998), pp. 16–29.

48. J. Magretta, "Governing the Family-Owned Enterprise: An Interview with Finland's Krister Ahlstrom," *Harvard Business Review* (January–February 1998), pp. 113–123.

49. J. Ward, *Keeping the Family Business Healthy* (San Francisco: Jossey-Bass, 1987), as reported by U. Gupta and M. Robichaux, "Reins Tangle Easily at Family Firms," *Wall Street Journal* (August 9, 1989), p. B1.

50. J. Magretta, p. 119.

51. N. C. Churchill and K. J. Hatten, "Non-Market-Based Transfers of Wealth and Power: A Research Framework for Family Businesses," *American Journal of Small Business* (Winter 1987), pp. 51–64.

52. J. L. Ward and C. E. Aronoff, "Shirt Sleeves to Shirt Sleeves," *Nation's Business* (September 1992), pp. 62–63.

53. J. Applegate, "Business People in Bermuda Get Sloppy Without Taxes," *Des Moines Register* (July 6, 1992), p. 8B.

54. P. L. Huff, R. M. Harper, Jr., and A. E. Eikner, "Are There Differences in Liquidity and Solvency Measures Based on Company Size?" *American Business Review* (June 1999), pp. 96–106.

55. R. I. Levin and V. R. Travis, "Small Company Finance: What the Books Don't Say," *Harvard Business Review* (November–December 1987), pp. 30–32.

56. T. Atkins, "My Entrepreneurial Experience," paper submitted to Management 310, *Entrepreneurship & Innovation*, taught by J. David Hunger at Iowa State University (October 2000). Reprinted by permission of Todd Atkins.

57. J. Warner, "21st Century Capitalism: Snapshot of the Next Century," *Business Week* (November 18, 1994), p. 194.

58. T. Laseter, P. Houston, A. Chung, S. Byrne, M. Turner, and A. Devendran, "The Last Mile to Nowhere," *Strategy + Business*, Issue 20 (3rd Quarter, 2000), pp. 41–48.

chapter 13

Strategic Issues in Not-For-Profit Organizations

The New York City chapter of the American Heart Association (AHA) was in a difficult situation. Although it was one of 56 affiliates of the AHA, it had to generate revenue to put into its own projects. In recent years, the number of charitable organizations asking for corporate and foundation funds had proliferated at the same time that government dollars for human services and the arts were being drastically cut. Increasing costs had meant that the chapter would have to either increase its funding through more donations or drop some of its programs. The chapter's Board of Directors and management was unwilling to cut the chapter's programs on reducing death and disability from heart attacks and strokes. Unfortunately they would then have to raise an additional $1 million on top of the current budget—an impossible goal.[1] What should the organization do?

The American Heart Association was not alone in this situation. By the mid-1990s, most not-for-profit organizations were turning to strategic management and other concepts from business to ensure their survival. This was a significant change because most not-for-profit managers had traditionally felt that business concepts were not relevant to their situation. According to Peter Drucker:

> Twenty years ago, management was a dirty word for those involved in nonprofit organizations. It meant business, and nonprofits prided themselves on being free of the taint of commercialism and above such sordid considerations as the bottom line. Now most of them have learned that nonprofits need management even more than business does, precisely because they lack the discipline of the bottom line.[2]

A knowledge of not-for-profit organizations is important if only for the sole reason that they account for an average of 1 in every 20 jobs in nations throughout the world. A study by the Johns Hopkins University Institute for Policy Studies found that in 9 countries between 1990 and 1995, nonprofit jobs grew by 23% compared to 6.2% for the whole economy.[3] Not-for-profits employ over 25% of the U.S. workforce and own approximately 15% of the nation's private wealth.[4] In the United States alone, in addition to various federal, state, and local government agencies, there are about 10,000 not-for-profit hospitals and nursing homes (85% of all hospitals), 4,600 colleges and universities, over 100,000 private and public elementary and secondary schools, and almost 350,000 churches and synagogues, plus many thousands of charities and service organizations.[5]

Typically **not-for-profit organizations** include **private nonprofit corporations** (such as hospitals, institutes, private colleges, and organized charities) as well as **public governmental units or agencies** (such as welfare departments, prisons, and state universities). Traditionally studies in strategic management have dealt with profit-making firms to the exclusion of nonprofit or governmental organizations. This, however, is changing. Not-for-profit organizations are adopting strategic management in increasing numbers.

Scholars and practitioners are concluding that many strategic management concepts and techniques can be successfully adapted for not-for-profit organizations.[6] Although the evidence is not yet conclusive, there appears to be an association between strategic planning efforts and performance measures such as growth.[7] The purpose of this chapter is, therefore, to highlight briefly the major differences between the profit-making and the not-for-profit organization, so that the effects of their differences on the strategic management process can be understood.

13.1 Why Not-For-Profit?

The not-for-profit sector of an economy is important for several reasons. First, society desires certain goods and services that profit-making firms cannot or will not provide. These are referred to as **public or collective goods** because people who might not have paid for the goods receive benefits from them. Paved roads, police protection, museums, and schools are examples of public goods. A person cannot use a private good unless she or he pays for it. Generally once a public good is provided, however, anyone can use or enjoy it.

Certain aspects of life do not appear to be served appropriately by profit-making business firms yet are often crucial to the well-being of society. These aspects include areas in which society as a whole benefits from a particular service, but in which a particular individual benefits only indirectly. It is in these areas that not-for-profit organizations have traditionally been most effective. Libraries and museums are examples. Although most people do not visit libraries or museums very often, they are usually willing to pay taxes and/or donate funds to support their existence. They do so because these people believe that these organizations act to uplift the culture and quality of life of the region. To fulfill their mission, entrance fees (if any) must be set low enough to allow everyone admission. These fees, however, are not profitable—they rarely even cover the costs of the service. The same is true of animal shelters managed by the Humane Society. Although few people want abandoned pets running wild through city streets, fees charged from the sale of these animals cannot alone pay the costs of finding and caring for them. Additional revenue is needed—either in the form of donations or public taxation. Such public or collective services cannot generate a profit, yet they are necessary for any successful civilization. Which aspects of society are most suited for being served by not-for-profit organizations rather than by profit-making business organizations? This is the issue being faced by govern-

Global Issue

Which Is Best for Society: Business or Not-For-Profit?

$\mathbf{M}$any nations throughout the world are attempting to privatize state-owned enterprises to balance their budgets. **Privatization** is (1) the selling of state-owned enterprises to private individuals or corporations or (2) the hiring of a private business to provide services previously offered by a state agency. The British government, for example, sold British Airways, its state-owned airline to private investors. In the United States, many city governments now allow private companies to collect and dispose of trash—something that had previously been done by the city.

Problems can result, however, if privatization goes too far. For example, in converting from a communist-oriented, centrally managed economy to a more democratic, free-market economy, Eastern European countries are finding that profit-making business firms are unable to satisfy all of society's needs. What used to be provided by the state free of charge (tax-supported) in Russia and other countries may now be provided only for the rich or not at all. The same problem is evident in

the United States in the controversies over the provision of health care, retirement benefits, and private versus public education.

Some of the aspects of life that cannot easily be privatized and are often better managed by not-for-profit organizations are as follows:

- Religion
- Education
- Charities
- Clubs, interest groups, unions
- Health care
- Government

The privatization of state-owned business enterprises is likely to continue globally because most of these enterprises must expand internationally in order to survive in the increasing global environment. They cannot compete successfully if they are forced to follow inefficient, socially oriented policies and regulations (emphasizing employment over efficiency) rather than economically oriented, international practices (emphasizing efficiency over employment). The global trend toward privatization will probably continue until each country reaches the point where the efficiency of business is counterbalanced by the effectiveness of the not-for-profit sector of the economy. As political motives overcome economic ones, government will likely intervene in that decision.

ments when they privatize what was previously provided by the state. See the 🌐 **Global Issue** feature to learn more about this development.

A second reason why the not-for-profit sector is important is that a private nonprofit organization tends to receive benefits from society that a private profit-making firm cannot obtain. Preferred tax status to nonstock corporations is given in section 501(c)(3) of the U.S. Internal Revenue code in the form of exemptions from corporate income taxes. Private nonprofit firms also enjoy exemptions from various other state, local, and federal taxes. Under certain conditions, these firms also benefit from the tax deductibility of donors' contributions and membership dues. In addition, they qualify for special third-class mailing privileges.[8] These benefits are allowed because private nonprofit organizations are typically service organizations, which are expected to use any excess of revenue over costs and expenses (a surplus rather than a profit) either to improve service or to reduce the price of their service. This service orientation is reflected in the fact that not-for-profit organizations do not use the term "customer" to refer to the recipient of the service. The recipient is typically referred to as a patient, student, client, case, or simply "the public."

13.2 Importance of Revenue Source

The feature that best differentiates not-for-profit (NFP) organizations from each other as well as from profit-making corporations is their **source of revenue**.[9] The **profit-making firm** depends on revenues obtained from the sale of its goods and services to customers, who typically pay for the costs and expenses of providing the product or service plus a profit. The not-for-profit organization, in contrast, depends heavily on dues, assessments, or donations from its membership, or on funding from a sponsoring agency such as the United Way or the federal government to pay for much of its costs and expenses.

SOURCES OF NOT-FOR-PROFIT REVENUE

Revenue is generated from a variety of sources—not just from clients receiving the product or service from the NFP. It can come from people who do not even receive the services they are subsidizing. One study of Minnesota nonprofits found that donations accounted for almost 40%, government grants for around 25%, and program service fees for about 35% of total revenues.[10] In other types of not-for-profit organizations—such as unions and voluntary medical plans—revenue comes mostly from the members, the people who receive the service. Nevertheless, the members typically pay dues in advance and must accept later whatever service is provided whether they choose it or not, whether it is what they expected or not. The service is often received long after the dues are paid.

In profit-making corporations, there is typically a simple and direct connection between the customer or client and the organization. The organization tends to be totally dependent on sales of its products or services to the customer for revenue and is therefore extremely interested in pleasing the customer. As shown in **Figure 13–1**, the profit-making organization (*organization A*) tries to influence the customer (through advertising and promotion) to continue to buy and use its services. Either by buying or not buying the item offered, the customer, in turn, directly influences the organization's decision-making process. The business is thus market oriented.

In the case of the typical not-for-profit organization, however, there is likely to be a very different sort of relationship between the organization providing and the person receiving the service. Because the recipient of the service typically does not pay the entire cost of the service, outside sponsors are required. In most instances, the sponsors receive none of the service but provide partial to total funding for the needed revenues. As indicated earlier, these sponsors can be the government (using taxpayers' money) or charitable organizations, such as the United Way (using voluntary donations). As shown in **Figure 13–1**, the not-for-profit organization can be partially dependent on sponsors for funding (*organizations B and C*) or totally dependent on the sponsors (*organization D*). The less money it receives from clients receiving the service or product, the less market oriented is the not-for-profit organization.

PATTERNS OF INFLUENCE ON STRATEGIC DECISION MAKING

The **pattern of influence** on the organization's strategic decision making derives from its sources of revenue.[11] As shown in **Figure 13–1**, a private university (*organization B*) is heavily dependent on student tuition and other client-generated funds for about 70% of its revenue. Therefore, the students' desires are likely to have a stronger influence (as shown by an unbroken line) on the university's decision making than are the desires of the various sponsors such as alumni and private foundations. The sponsors' relatively marginal influence on the organization is reflected by a broken line. In contrast, a public university (*organization C*) is more heavily dependent on outside sponsors such as a state legislature for revenue funding. Student tuition and other client-generated funds form a small percentage (typically less than 40%) of total revenue. Therefore, the university's decision making is heavily influenced by the sponsors (unbroken line) and only marginally influenced directly by the students (broken line).

In the case of *organization D*, however, the client has no direct influence on the organization because the client pays nothing for the services received. In this situation, the organiza-

Figure 13–1

The Effects of Sources of Revenue on Patterns of Client-Organization Influence

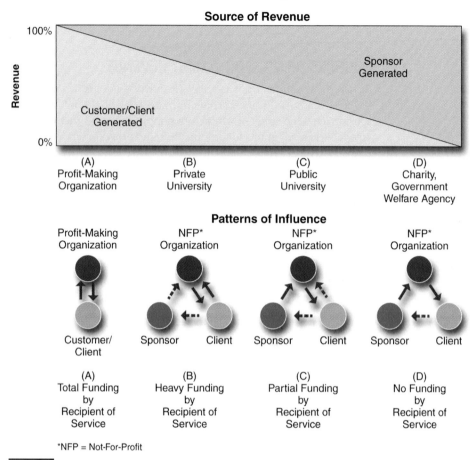

Source: Thomas L. Wheelen and J. David Hunger, "The Effect of Revenue Upon Patterns of Client-Organization Influence." Copyright ©1982 by Wheelen and Hunger Associates. Revised 1991. Reprinted by permission.

tion tends to measure its effectiveness in terms of sponsor satisfaction. It has no real measure of its efficiency other than its ability to carry out its mission and achieve its objectives within the dollar contributions it has received from its sponsors. In contrast to other organizations in which the client contributes a significant proportion of the needed revenue, *organization D* actually might be able to increase its revenue by heavily lobbying its sponsors while reducing the level of its service to its clients!

Regardless of the percentage of total funding that the client generates, the client may attempt to indirectly influence the not-for-profit organization through the sponsors. This is depicted by the broken lines connecting the client and the sponsor in *organizations B, C, and D* in **Figure 13–1**. Welfare clients or prison inmates, for example, may be able to indirectly improve the services they receive if they pressure government officials by writing to legislators or even by rioting. Students at public universities can lobby state officials for student representation on governing boards.

The key to understanding the management of a not-for-profit organization is thus learning who pays for the delivered services. If the recipients of the service pay only a small proportion of the total cost of the service, strategic managers are likely to be more concerned with satisfying the needs and desires of the funding sponsors or agency than those of the people receiving the service. The acquisition of resources can become an end in itself.

USEFULNESS OF STRATEGIC MANAGEMENT CONCEPTS AND TECHNIQUES

Some strategic management concepts can be equally applied to business and not-for-profit organizations, whereas others cannot. The marketplace orientation underlying portfolio analysis, for example, does not translate into situations in which client satisfaction and revenue are only indirectly linked. Industry analysis and competitive strategy are primarily relevant to not-for-profits that obtain most of their revenue from user fees rather than from donors or taxpayers. For example, as hospitals find themselves relying increasingly on patient fees for their revenue, they use competitive strategy to gain advantage versus other hospitals. Smaller NFP hospitals stress the "high touch" of their staff over the "high tech" of competitors having better diagnostic machinery. The concept of competitive advantage is less useful to the typical not-for-profit than the related concept of institutional advantage, which sets aside the profit-making objective of competitive advantage. A not-for-profit can be said to have **institutional advantage** when it performs its tasks more effectively than other comparable organizations.[12]

SWOT analysis, mission statements, stakeholder analysis, and corporate governance are, however, just as relevant to a not-for-profit as they are to a profit-making organization.[13] Portfolio analysis can be very helpful, but is used very differently from business firms. (See strategic piggybacking later in the chapter.) As with any corporation, nonprofits usually have boards of directors whose job is to ensure that the paid executive director and staff work to fulfill the organization's mission and objectives. Unlike the boards of most business firms, not-for-profit boards are often required, however, to take primary responsibility for strategic planning and fund-raising. Many not-for-profits are finding a well-crafted mission statement not only helps in finding donors, but also in attracting volunteers. Take the example of the mission statement of a local animal shelter:

> To shelter and care for stray, lost, or abandoned animals and to responsibly place animals in new homes and enforce animal laws. We are also here to better educate people in ways to be solutions to animal problems, not causes.[14]

Strategic management is difficult to apply when the organization's output is difficult to measure objectively, as is the case with most not-for-profit organizations. Thus it is very likely that many not-for-profit organizations have not used strategic management because its concepts, techniques, and prescriptions do not lend themselves to situations where sponsors, rather than the marketplace, determine revenue. The situation, however, is changing. The trend toward privatizing public organizations, such as converting subsidized community hospitals to independent (nonsubsidized) status, usually means that the clients/patients pay a larger percentage of the costs. As these not-for-profits become more market oriented (and thus client oriented), strategic management becomes more applicable and more increasingly used.[15] Nevertheless, various constraints on not-for-profits mean that strategic management concepts and techniques must be modified to be effective.

13.3 Impact of Constraints on Strategic Management

Several characteristics peculiar to the not-for-profit organization constrain its behavior and affect its strategic management. Newman and Wallender list the following five **constraints on strategic management:**

1. **Service is often intangible and hard to measure.** This difficulty is typically compounded by the existence of multiple service objectives developed to satisfy multiple sponsors.

2. **Client influence may be weak.** Often the organization has a local monopoly, and clients' payments may be a very small source of funds.

3. **Strong employee commitments to professions or to a cause may undermine allegiance** to the organization employing them.

4. **Resource contributors may intrude on the organization's internal management.** Such contributors include fund contributors and government.

5. **Restraints on the use of rewards and punishments** may result from constraints one, three, and four.[16]

It is true that several of these characteristics can be found in profit-making as well as in not-for-profit organizations. Nevertheless, as Newman and Wallender state, the ". . . frequency of strong impact is much higher in not-for-profit enterprises."[17]

IMPACT ON STRATEGY FORMULATION

The long-range planning and decision making affected by the listed constraints serve to add at least four **complications to strategy formulation.**

■ **Goal conflicts interfere with rational planning.** Because the not-for-profit organization typically lacks a single clear-cut performance criterion (such as profits), divergent goals and objectives are likely, especially with multiple sponsors. Differences in the concerns of various important sponsors can prevent management from stating the organization's mission in anything but very broad terms, if they fear that a sponsor who disagrees with a particular, narrow definition of mission might cancel its funding. For example, a study of 227 public Canadian hospitals found that over half had very general, ambiguous, and unquantified objectives.[18] According to Heffron, an authority in public administration: "The greater openness within which they are compelled to operate—the fishbowl atmosphere—impedes thorough discussion of issues and discourages long-range plans that might alienate stakeholders."[19] In such organizations, it is the reduced influence of the clients that permits this diversity of values and goals to occur without a clear market check. For example, when a city council considers changing zoning to implement a strategic plan for the city, all sorts of people (including the press) will demand to be heard. A decision might be made based on pressure from a few stakeholders (who make significant contributions or who threaten to stir up trouble) to the detriment of the community as a whole.

■ **An integrated planning focus tends to shift from results to resources.** Because not-for-profit organizations tend to provide services that are hard to measure, they rarely have a net bottom line. Planning, therefore, becomes more concerned with resource inputs, which can easily be measured, than with service, which cannot. Goal displacement (explained earlier in **Chapter 10**) becomes even more likely than it is in business organizations.[20]

■ **Ambiguous operating objectives create opportunities for internal politics and goal displacement.** The combination of vague objectives and a heavy concern with resources allows managers considerable leeway in their activities. Such leeway makes possible political maneuvering for personal ends. In addition, because the effectiveness of the not-for-profit organization hinges on the satisfaction of the sponsoring group, management tends to ignore the needs of the client while focusing on the desires of a powerful sponsor. University administrators commonly say that people will donate money for a new building (which will carry the donor's name), but not for other more pressing needs, such as the maintenance of existing buildings. In this situation, powerful department heads might wine and dine the donor, hoping to get the money for their pet projects. This problem is compounded by the common practice of selecting people to boards of trustees/directors not on the basis of their managerial experience, but on the basis of their ability to contribute money, raise funds, and work with politicians. (A major role of the not-for-profit board is to ensure adequate resources—usually translated to mean fund-raising.)[21] Directors usually receive no compensation for serving on the board. Their lack of interest in overseeing management is reflected in an overall not-for-profit board-meeting attendance rate of only 50%, compared with 90% for boards of directors of business corporations. This is one reason why boards of not-for-profits tend to be larger than are boards of business corporations. Eckerd College, for example, has a 52-member, extremely passive board of directors.[22] Board members of not-for-profit organizations tend to ignore the task of determining strategies and policies—often leaving this to the paid (or sometimes unpaid) executive director. The larger the board, the less likely it is to exercise control over top management.[23]

- **Professionalization simplifies detailed planning but adds rigidity.** In not-for-profit organizations in which professionals play important roles (as in hospitals or colleges), professional values and traditions can prevent the organization from changing its conventional behavior patterns to fit new service missions tuned to changing social needs. This rigidity, of course, can occur in any organization that hires professionals. The strong service orientation of most not-for-profit organizations, however, tends to encourage the development of static professional norms and attitudes. As not-for-profits attempt to become more businesslike, this may be changing. One study of Minnesota nonprofits revealed that 29% of the program directors and 15% of the staff had degrees or experience in business administration.[24]

IMPACT ON STRATEGY IMPLEMENTATION

The five constraining characteristics also affect how a not-for-profit organization is organized in both its structure and job design. Three **complications to strategy implementation** in particular can be highlighted:

1. **Decentralization is complicated.** The difficulty of setting objectives for an intangible, hard-to-measure service mission complicates the delegation of decision-making authority. Because of the heavy dependence on sponsors for revenue support, the top management of a not-for-profit organization must be always alert to the sponsors' view of an organizational activity. This necessary caution leads to **defensive centralization**, in which top management retains all decision-making authority so that low-level managers cannot take any actions to which the sponsors may object.

2. **Linking pins for external-internal integration become important.** Because of the heavy dependence on outside sponsors, a special need arises for people in buffer roles to relate to both inside and outside groups. This role is especially necessary when the sponsors are diverse (revenue comes from donations, membership fees, and federal funds) and the service is intangible (for instance, a "good" education) with a broad mission and multiple shifting objectives. The job of a "Dean for External Affairs," for example, consists primarily of working with the school's alumnae and raising funds.

3. **Job enlargement and executive development can be restrained by professionalism.** In organizations that employ a large number of professionals, managers must design jobs that appeal to prevailing professional norms. Professionals have rather clear ideas about which activities are, and which are not, within their province. Enriching a nurse's job by expanding his or her decision-making authority for drug dosage, for example, can cause conflict with medical doctors who believe that such authority is theirs alone. Because a professional often views managerial jobs as nonprofessional and merely supportive, promotion into a management position is not always viewed positively.

IMPACT ON EVALUATION AND CONTROL

Special **complications to evaluation and control** arising from the constraining characteristics affect how behavior is motivated and performance is controlled. Two problems, in particular, are often noticed:

1. **Rewards and penalties have little or no relation to performance.** When desired results are vague and the judgment of success is subjective, predictable and impersonal feedback cannot be established. Performance is judged either intuitively ("You don't seem to be taking your job seriously") or on the basis of whatever small aspects of a job can be measured ("You were late to work twice last month").

2. **Inputs rather than outputs are heavily controlled.** Because its inputs can be measured much more easily than outputs, the not-for-profit organization tends to focus more on the resources going into performance than on the performance itself.[25] The emphasis is thus on setting maximum limits for costs and expenses. Because there is little to no reward for staying under these limits, people usually respond negatively to such controls.

Because of these and other complications, not-for-profits can waste money in many ways, especially on administrative costs and expenses. Because of this, it is becoming increasingly common to calculate ratios comparing total support and revenue with the amounts spent on specific service activities. For example, analysts become concerned when the total spent on the mission of the organization (e.g., community service or whatever) is less than 50% of total income received from sponsors and activities. Other rules of thumb are that a not-for-profit should not spend more than 35% on administrative expenses and that the costs of fundraising should not account for more than 15% of total income.[26]

13.4 Popular Not-for-Profit Strategies

Because of various pressures on not-for-profit organizations to provide more services than the sponsors and clients can pay for, these organizations are developing strategies to help them meet their desired service objectives. In addition to a heavy use of volunteers to keep costs low, NFPs are choosing the strategies of strategic piggybacking, mergers, and strategic alliances.

STRATEGIC PIGGYBACKING

Coined by Nielsen, the term **strategic piggybacking** refers to the development of a new activity for the not-for-profit organization that would generate the funds needed to make up the difference between revenues and expenses.[27] The new activity is related typically in some manner to the not-for-profit's mission, but its purpose is to help subsidize the primary service programs. It appears to be a form of concentric diversification, but it is engaged in only for its money-generating value. In an inverted use of portfolio analysis, the organization invests in new, safe cash cows to fund its current cash-hungry stars, question marks, and dogs.

Although this strategy is not new, it has recently become very popular. As early as 1874, for example, the Metropolitan Museum of Art retained a professional to photograph its collections and to sell copies of the prints. Profits were used to defray the museum's operating costs. More recently, various income-generating ventures have appeared under various auspices, from the Girl Scouts to UNICEF, and in numerous forms, from cookies and small gift shops to vast real estate developments. A study by the U.S. General Accounting Office revealed that the amount of funds resulting from income-producing activities has significantly increased since the 1970s. Hospitals are offering wellness programs, ranging from meditation classes to aerobics. Some 70% of colleges and universities now offer "auxiliary" services, such as bookstores, conference rooms, and computer centers as sources of income.[28] The American Cancer Society earns millions annually from allowing its name to appear on products sold by private drug companies, such as Smith-Kline Beecham's Nicoderm chewing gum. The Metropolitan Museum of Art now has 16 stores outside the main museum and a fast-growing Web site—all of which generate money. The Baptist Hospital of Nashville, Tennessee, built and operates a $15 million, 18-acre office and training-field complex, which it rents to Nashville's professional football team.

The Small Business Administration, however, views this money-making activity as "unfair competition." The U.S. Internal Revenue Service (IRS) advises that a not-for-profit that engages in a business "not substantially related" to the organization's exempt purposes may jeopardize its tax-exempt status, particularly if the income from the business exceeds approximately 20% of total organizational revenues. The IRS requires not-for-profits to pay an unrelated business income tax on commercial activities that don't relate to the organization's central mission. So far, not-for-profits are still considered tax-exempt if their businesses are staffed by volunteers or if almost all their merchandise is donated. According to Marcus Owens, Director of tax-exempt organizations for the IRS, "The ultimate question is should these institutions continue as tax-exempt entities. And it's being raised more than ever before."[29]

Although strategic piggybacks can help not-for-profit organizations self-subsidize their primary missions and better use their resources, according to Nielsen, there are several potential drawbacks.[30] *First*, the revenue-generating venture could actually lose money, especially in the short run. *Second*, the venture could subvert, interfere with, or even take over the primary mission. *Third*, the public, as well as the sponsors, could reduce their contributions because of negative responses to such "money-grubbing activities" or because of a mistaken belief that the organization is becoming self-supporting. *Fourth*, the venture could interfere with the internal operations of the not-for-profit organization. To avoid these drawbacks, a not-for-profit should first carefully evaluate its resources before choosing this strategy. See the **boxed feature** to see the resources needed for a piggyback.

The U.S. National Association of College and University Business Officers predicts that within a few years over 90% of colleges and universities in the United States will be using strategic piggybacks.[31] Expect a similar trend for other not-for-profits that heavily rely on donations and taxpayer support for their revenue.

MERGERS

Dwindling resources are leading an increasing number of not-for-profits to consider mergers as a way of reducing costs. For example, the merger of Baptist Health Systems and Research Health Services created Health Midwest in Kansas City. The New York Hospital—Cornell Medical Center and Columbia-Presbyterian Medical Center combined to form the New York and Presbyterian Hospitals Health Care System. Between 1980 and 1991, more than 400 U.S. hospitals were involved in mergers and consolidations—more than half of them happening after 1987.[32]

STRATEGIC ALLIANCES

Strategic alliances involve developing cooperative ties with other organizations. Alliances are often used by not-for-profit organizations as a way to enhance their capacity to serve clients or to acquire resources while still enabling them to keep their identity.[33] Services can be pur-

---

Resources Needed for Successful Strategic Piggybacking

Based on his experience as a consultant to not-for-profit organizations, Edward Skloot suggests that a not-for-profit should have five resources before engaging in strategic piggybacking:

1. **Something to Sell:** The organization should assess its resources to see if people might be willing to pay for goods or services closely related to the organization's primary activity. Repackaging the Boston Symphony into the less formal Boston Pops Orchestra created a way to subsidize the deficit-creating symphony and provide year-round work for the musicians.

2. **Critical Mass of Management Talent:** Enough people must be available to nurture and sustain an income venture over the long haul. This can be very difficult, given that the most competent not-for-profit professionals often don't want to be managers.

3. **Trustee Support:** If the trustees have strong feelings against earned-income ventures, they could actively or passively resist commercial involvement. When the Children's Television Workshop began licensing its Sesame Street characters to toy companies and theme parks, many people criticized it for joining business in selling more things to children.

4. **Entrepreneurial Attitude:** Management must be able to combine an interest in innovative ideas with businesslike practicality.

5. **Venture Capital:** Because it often takes money to make money, engaging in a joint venture with a business corporation can provide the necessary start-up funds as well as the marketing and management support. For example, Massachusetts General Hospital receives $50 million from Hoechst, the German chemical company, for biological research in exchange for exclusive licenses to develop commercial products from particular research discoveries.

Source: E. Skloot, "Should Not-for-Profits Go into Business?" *Harvard Business Review* (January–February 1983), pp. 20–24. Copyright © 2001 by the President and Fellows of Harvard College, all rights reserved.

---

chased and provided more efficiently through cooperation with other organizations than if they were done alone. For example, four Ohio universities agreed to create and jointly operate a new school of international business. Alone, none of the business schools could afford the $30 million to build the school. The Collaborative Ventures Program of the Teagle Foundation has given more than $4 million in grants to help colleges set up money-saving collaborations. While only a handful of consortia existed in 1995, by 1998 there were at least 21 representing 125 colleges and universities.[34]

Strategic alliances and mergers are becoming commonplace among not-for-profit organizations. The next logical step is strategic alliances between business firms and not-for-profits. Already business corporations are forming alliances with universities to fund university research in exchange for options on the results of that research. Business firms find it cheaper to pay universities to do basic research than to do it themselves. Universities are in need of research funds to attract top professors and to maintain expensive labs. Such alliances of convenience are being criticized, but they are likely to continue.

13.5 **Impact of the Internet on Not-for-Profit Organizations**

The Internet is just beginning to have an impact on not-for-profit organizations. By far, the most impact has been upon government activities—especially in terms of taxation and the provision of services.

Taxation

The first impact of the Internet upon not-for-profit organizations (especially government) was the issue of taxation. Businesses in the United States must collect and pay sales taxes to the government of each state in which they operate. Mail order retailers—both catalogue and Internet—generally collect state sales tax from consumers only if the company operates a facility in the state where the merchandise is being sent. Since Internet companies usually don't have brick-and-mortar operations, they collect little sales tax. Many state and local government officials fear that as more of the economy shifts online, they will lose tax revenue needed for schools, police officers, and other basic services. These government officials have been supported by traditional retailers fearing that they will not be able to compete with Internet rivals who receive special tax advantages. Antitax activists and some business leaders have responded that the lack of tax has accelerated the growth of electronic commerce. According to them, a complex tax structure dealing with more than 6,000 different tax jurisdictions would stifle the growth of the Internet retail industry and hurt the overall economy. The U.S. Congress agreed in 1998 to a three-year moratorium on the taxation of sales by purely Internet-based businesses.[35]

The European Union (EU) is also concerned that the Internet will reduce its tax revenues. For example, if a German buys a CD from an American Internet retailer who delivers it by post, the German escapes paying the 16% value added tax (VAT) paid at the local shop. In addition, Internet businesses can avoid taxes by moving to low-tax countries or to tax havens, just as British gambling firms have done with online gambling. The European Commission has proposed that foreign companies with annual online sales of more than 100,000 Euros in the EU should register for VAT in at least one EU country and then collect the tax on all services downloaded from the Internet. According to *The Economist*, this tax would be almost impossible to enforce.[36]

Improvement of Government Services

After e-commerce (B2C) and business to business (B2B), the next Internet revolution will be in government services (G2C). The Internet can play an important role in helping government reduce its costs and improve its services. For example, a pioneering project called ServiceArizona allows the residents of Arizona to conduct transactions on the Web, from ordering personalized license plates for their cars to replacing lost identification cards. Instead of standing in line for hours, people can renew their registrations with the motor vehicle department in just a few minutes any hour or day of the week. The Web site was built, maintained, and hosted by IBM in return for 2% of the value of each transaction (about $4 for an auto registration). Because processing an auto registration costs only $1.60 compared to $6.60 in person, the state saves money. With 15% of renewals now being processed by ServiceArizona, the motor vehicles department saves around $17 million annually.

Governments around the world are realizing that they will need to construct Internet portals, similar to that of Yahoo! that can provide one location to satisfy all of its citizens' needs. A central government portal has been launched in Singapore; another is being developed in Austria. In Britain, BT won the contract to build UK Online, a portal to offer government services. Just as businesses are pushing their suppliers into doing business with them online, so can governments—thus streamlining the activities of government agencies. For example, EDS developed a Web-based intranet for the naval airbase at Corpus Christi, Texas, so that its mechanics could have access to spare parts anywhere in the world. IBM worked with Emekli Sandigi, a Turkish government social security organization to develop an intranet to link 17,000 pharmacies so that they can check the validity of a customer's health card and other factors. The new system reduces the amount of time pharmacists are paid from two months to less than a week. The Internet can also improve the quality of the relationship between a government and its citizens. For example, a Democratic primary in Arizona in which online voting was allowed boosted voter turnout to six times its usual level.[37]

Impact on Other Not-For-Profit Organizations

The Internet is also having an impact on not-for-profits other than government. Although the media tends to talk mostly of dot-coms (.com), three major Internet domains have

Internet Issue

The Not-For-Profit Organizations That Rule the Internet

There is a myth that the Internet has grown because of a complete absence of rules or regulations. In reality, the Internet is a highly organized place. What is unique about the Internet is that its regulation has developed from the bottom-up instead of from the top-down. The Internet Engineering Task Force (IETF) develops agreed technical standards, such as communication protocols. The Internet Corporation for Assigned Names and Numbers (ICANN) oversees the system of domain names, such as com (business), edu (education), gov (government), and org (nonprofit organizations). The World Wide Web Consortium (W3C) also oversees Internet standards. Without such global standards, there would be no way to connect modems to computers for Internet access or for viewers to read Web sites, let alone download files or host chat rooms. These not-for-profit bodies are largely self-created and self-governing. They are open in membership and willing to hear all arguments on an issue. According to David Clark of MIT, a member of IETF, "We reject kings, presidents, and voting. We believe in rough consensus and running code." Anyone can become a member of the IETF simply by signing up at the task force's Web site to a working group's mailing list. Anyone can come to the three meetings held annually by the task force.

These organizations seem to work so well because they are composed of like-minded individuals who have common interests even if located in various parts of the world. Very function-oriented, IETF decisions are based on effectiveness and efficiency. Since anyone can access all proposals, the process is very hard to manipulate. In 1999, the IETF argued about how far it should go to help law enforcement conduct wiretaps and eventually decided not to "consider requirements for wire-tapping." W3C is an organization founded by Tim Berners-Lee, the inventor of the World Wide Web, to develop standards for the Web. Most of the 400-plus members are companies paying $50,000 per year for membership. It also upholds the consensus principle in decision making. It has developed more than 20 technical specifications, including one on XML (Extensible Markup Language), which may replace HTML as the language used in Web sites. ICANN wrested monopoly control of Internet domain names from Network Solutions and has accredited over 120 registers who can sell domain names. It recently added a number of new top-level domains to the usual com, edu, gov, org, and net. ICANN also helps resolve conflicts over who has the right to a domain name. The World Intellectual Property Organization, one of four dispute-resolution bodies accredited by ICANN, recently ruled that Internet addresses bearing the names of British author, Jeanette Winterson, and the American actress, Julia Roberts, should be returned to their rightful owners. Both addresses had been registered by Internet "squatters" who had argued that the names of living people are not trademarks.

Source: "Regulating the Internet: The Consensus Machine," *The Economist* (June 10, 2000), pp. 73–79. Copyright © 2000. The Economist Newspaper Group, Inc. Reprinted with permission. Further reproduction prohibited ⟨www.economist.com⟩.

been edu, gov, and org. Along with net, these have been the primary Internet domains until the number of domains were increased in 2000 by ICANN. (See the ▨ **Internet Issue** feature for who regulates the Internet.) Most every nonprofit organization now has its own Web site to provide services to its members and to interested outsiders.

According to Peter Drucker, the greatest impact of the Internet may be upon higher education and health care (85% of U.S. hospitals are nonprofit).[38] Internet access can enable medical practitioners to access the knowledge of specialists in distant locations. Patients can learn more about their illness by talking in Internet *chat rooms* with other people having the same illness. Around 75% of U.S. colleges and universities have Web sites enabling students to access course information (including the syllabus) and download assignments. Such Web sites are replacing library reserve rooms. Although 1.4 million people were enrolled in distance education courses during the 1997–1998 academic year, that number has risen considerably during the following years.[39] Some universities, like the University of Phoenix, are offering complete courses and degree programs over the Internet.

Projections for the 21st Century

- From 1994 to 2010, the number of AIDS cases worldwide will grow from 20 million to 38 million.
- From 1994 to 2010, the cost of a Wharton MBA will increase from $84,200 to $257,200.[40]

Discussion Questions

1. Are not-for-profit organizations less efficient than profit-making organizations? Why or why not?

2. How does the lack of a clear-cut performance measure, such as profits, affect the strategic management of a not-for-profit organization?

3. What are the pros and cons of strategic piggybacking? In what way is it "unfair competition" for NFPs to engage in revenue generating activity?

4. What are the pros and cons of mergers and strategic alliances? Should not-for-profits engage in alliances with business firms?

5. Recently, many not-for-profit organizations in the United States have been converting to profit making. Why would a not-for-profit organization want to change its status to profit making? What are the pros and cons of doing so?

Strategic Practice Exercise

1. Read the **Global Issue** feature in this chapter on page 326. It lists six aspects of society that it proposes are better managed by not-for-profit organizations than by profit-making organizations. Do you agree with this list? Should some aspects be deleted from the list? Should other aspects be added?

2. Examine a local college or university—perhaps the one you may be currently attending. What strategic issues is it facing? Develop a SFAS Table (**Figure** 5–1) of strategic factors. Is it attempting to use any strategic management concepts? If so, which ones? What sorts of strategies should it be considering for continued survival and future growth? Is it currently using strategic piggybacks to obtain additional funding? What sorts of additional piggybacks should it consider? Are strategic alliances with another college or university or business firm a possibility?

Key Terms

complications to evaluation and control (p. 332)

complications to strategy formulation (p. 330)

complications to strategy implementation (p. 331)

constraints on strategic management (p. 329)

defensive centralization (p. 331)

institutional advantage (p. 329)

not-for-profit organization (p. 325)

patterns of influence (p. 327)

private nonprofit corporations (p. 325)

privatization (p. 326)

profit-making firm (p. 326)

public governmental units or agencies (p. 325)

public or collective goods (p. 325)

source of revenue (p. 326)

strategic alliances (p. 333)

strategic piggybacking (p. 332)

Notes

1. B. Wiesendanger, "Profitable Pointers from Non-Profits," *Journal of Business Strategy* (July/August 1994), pp. 33–39.
2. P. F. Drucker, "What Business Can Learn from Nonprofits," *Harvard Business Review* (July–August 1989), p. 89.
3. "The Non-Profit Sector: Love or Money," *The Economist* (November 14, 1998), pp. 68–73.
4. G. Rudney, "The Scope and Dimensions of Nonprofit Activity," in *The Nonprofit Sector: A Research Handbook*, edited by W. W. Powell (New Haven: Yale University Press, 1987), p. 56; C. P. McLaughlin, *The Management of Nonprofit Organizations* (New York: John Wiley & Sons, 1986), p. 4.
5. M. O'Neill, *The Third America* (San Francisco: Jossey–Bass, 1989).
6. K. Ascher and B. Nare, "Strategic Planning in the Public Sector," *International Review of Strategic Management*, Vol. 1, edited by D. E. Hussey (New York: John Wiley & Sons, 1990), pp. 297–315; I. Unterman and R. H. Davis, *Strategic Management of Not-for-Profit Organizations* (New York: Praeger Press, 1984), p. 2.
7. P. V. Jenster and G. A. Overstreet, "Planning for a Non-Profit Service: A Study of U.S. Credit Unions," *Long Range Planning* (April 1990), pp. 103–111; G. J. Medley, "Strategic Planning for the World Wildlife Fund," *Long Range Planning* (February 1988), pp. 46–54.
8. J. G. Simon, "The Tax Treatment of Nonprofit Organizations: A Review of Federal and State Policies," in *The Nonprofit Sector: A Research Handbook*, edited by W. W. Powell (New Haven: Yale University Press, 1987), pp. 67–98.
9. B. P. Keating and M. O. Keating, *Not-for-Profit* (Glen Ridge, NJ: Thomas Horton & Daughters, 1980), p. 21.
10. K. A. Froelich, "Business Management in Nonprofit Organizations," paper presented to the *Midwest Management Society* (Chicago, 1995).
11. J. D. Hunger and T. L. Wheelen, "Is Strategic Management Appropriate for Not-for-Profit Organizations?" in *Handbook of Business Strategy, 1989/90 Yearbook*, edited by H. E. Glass (Boston: Warren, Gorham and Lamont, 1989), pp. 3.1–3.8. The contention that the pattern of environmental influence on the organization's strategic decision making derives from the organization's source(s) of income agrees with the authorities in the field. See R. E. Emerson, "Power-Dependence Relations," *American Sociological Review* (February 1962), pp. 31–41; J. D. Thompson, Organizations in Action (New York: McGraw-Hill, 1967), pp. 30–31; and J. Pfeffer and G. R. Salancik, *The External Control of Organizations: A Resource Dependence Perspective* (New York: HarperCollins, 1978), p. 44.
12. M. Goold, "Institutional Advantage: A Way into Strategic Management in Not-for-Profit Organizations," *Long Range Planning* (April 1997), pp. 291–293.
13. Ascher and Nare, "Strategic Planning in the Public Sector," pp. 297–315; R. McGill, "Planning for Strategic Performance in Local Government," *Long Range Planning* (October 1988), pp. 77–84.
14. Lorna Lavender, Supervisor of Ames (Iowa) Animal Shelter, quoted by K. Petty, "Animal Shelter Cares for Homeless," *ISU Daily* (July 25, 1996), p. 3.
15. E. Ferlie, "The Creation and Evolution of Quasi Markets in the Public Sector: A Problem for Strategic Management," *Strategic Management Journal* (Winter 1992), pp. 79–97. Research has found that for-profit hospitals have more mission statement components dealing with principal services, target customers, and geographic domain than do not-for-profit hospitals. See R. Subramanian, K. Kumar, and C. C. Yauger, "Mission Statements of Hospitals: An Empirical Analysis of Their Contents and Their Relationship to Organizational Factors," *Journal of Business Strategies* (Spring 1993), pp. 63–78.
16. W. H. Newman and H. W. Wallender III, "Managing Not-for-Profit Enterprises," *Academy of Management Review* (January 1978), p. 26.
17. Ibid., p. 27. The following discussion of the effects of these constraining characteristics is taken from pp. 27–31.
18. J. Denis, A. Langley, and D. Lozeau, "Formal Strategy in Public Hospitals," *Long Range Planning* (February 1991), pp. 71–82.
19. F. Heffron, *Organization Theory and Public Administration* (Upper Saddle River, NJ: Prentice Hall, 1989), p. 132.
20. Heffron, pp. 103–115.
21. R. T. Ingram, *Ten Basic Responsibilities of Nonprofit Boards*, 2nd edition (Washington, DC: National Center for Nonprofit Boards, 1997), pp. 9–10.
22. A. C. Smith, "Endowment Use Overlooked," *St. Petersburg Times* (June 23, 2000), p. 3B. Eckerd's board was strongly criticized because it had tolerated improper financial practices on the part of the President and had allowed the college's endowment to dissipate.
23. I. Unterman and R. H. Davis, *Strategic Management of Not-for-Profit Organizations* (New York: Praeger Press, 1984), p. 174; J. A. Alexander, M. L. Fennell, and M. T. Halpern, "Leadership Instability in Hospitals: The Influence of Board–CEO Relations and Organizational Growth and Decline," *Administrative Science Quarterly* (March 1993), pp. 74–99.
24. Froelich, "Business Management in Nonprofit Organizations," p. 9.
25. R. M. Kanter and D. V. Summers, "Doing Well While Doing Good: Dilemmas of Performance Measurement in Nonprofit Organizations and the Need for a Multiple-Constituency Approach," in *The Nonprofit Sector: A Research Handbook*, edited by W. W. Powell (New Haven: Yale University Press, 1987), p. 163.

26. J. P. Dalsimer, *Understanding Nonprofit Financial Statement: A Primer for Board Members*, 2nd edition (Washington, DC: National Center for Nonprofit Boards, 1997), p. 17.

27. R. P. Nielsen, "SMR Forum: Strategic Piggybacking—A Self-Subsidizing Strategy for Nonprofit Institutions," *Sloan Management Review* (Summer 1982), pp. 65–69; R. P. Nielsen, "Piggybacking for Business and Nonprofits: A Strategy for Hard Times," *Long Range Planning* (April 1984), pp. 96–102.

28. D. C. Bacon, "Nonprofit Groups: An Unfair Edge?" *Nation's Business* (April 1989), pp. 33–34; "Universities Push Auxiliary Services to Generate More Revenue," *Wall Street Journal* (April 27, 1995), p. A1.

29. M. Langley, "Nonprofit Hospitals Sometimes Are That in Little but Name," *Wall Street Journal* (July 14, 1997), p. A1, A6; D. Brady, "When Nonprofits Go After Profits," *Business Week* (June 26, 2000), pp. 173–178.; E. Skloot, "Should Not-for-Profits Go into Business?" *Harvard Business Review* (January–February 1983), p. 21; E. Felsenthal, "As Nonprofits Add Sidelines, IRS Takes Aim," *Wall Street Journal* (May 3, 1996), p. B1.

30. R. P. Nielsen, "Piggybacking Strategies for Nonprofits: A Shared Costs Approach," *Strategic Management Journal* (May–June 1986), pp. 209–211.

31. "Universities Push Auxiliary Services to Generate More Revenue," (Business Bulletin) *Wall Street Journal* (April 27, 1995), p. A1.

32. S. Collins, "A Bitter Financial Pill," *U.S. News & World Report* (November 29, 1993), pp. 83–86.

33. K. G. Provan, "Interorganizational Cooperation and Decision Making Autonomy in a Consortium Multihospital System," *Academy of Management Review* (July 1984), pp. 494–504; R. D. Luke, J. W. Begun, and D. D. Pointer, "Quasi-Firms: Strategic Interorganizational Forms in the Health Care Industry," *Academy of Management Review* (January 1989), pp. 9–19.

34. "More Colleges Are Opting for Mergers," *The (Ames, IA) Daily Tribune* (August 12, 1998), p. B3.

35. H. Fineman, "The Tax War Goes Online," *Newsweek* (December 20, 1999), p. 31; R. Chandrasekaran, "Tax Debate Heats Up Over On-line Sales," *International Herald Tribune* (December 14, 1999), p. B2; G. R. Simpson, "Internet Panel Pushes Reform of Sales Taxes," *Wall Street Journal* (December 16, 1999), p. A3.

36. "The End of Taxes?" *The Economist: A Survey of the New Economy* (Special insert: September 23, 2000), p. 30.

37. "The Next Revolution" and "Quick Fixes," *The Economist: A Survey of Government and the Internet* (Special insert: June 24, 2000), pp. 3–9, 13.

38. M. Williams, "Prophet Sharing," *Red Herring* (January 30, 2001), pp. 100–107.

39. A. Levinson, "Students Attend College Online," *The (Ames, IA) Tribune* (January 29, 2001), p. A2.

40. J. Warner, "21st Century Capitalism: Snapshot of the Next Century," *Business Week* (November 18, 1994), p. 194.

chapter 14

Suggestions for Case Analysis

A few years ago, AlliedSignal's free cash flow measure turned negative. Although the company reported a 16% gain in net income for the second quarter, the free cash flow was a negative $90 million. Top management dismissed the cash flow situation as only temporary, arguing that capital spending and increasing inventory during the first part of the year was needed to fuel the company's sales growth expected later in the year. A company spokesman predicted that the free cash flow for the year should hit $300 million and concluded, "There's no problem with cash flow here."

"Not so!" responded Jeffrey Fotta, President of Boston's Ernst Institutional Research. Fotta contended that Allied's growing sales and earnings masked a serious problem in the company. Over the past year, Allied's push to boost sales had caused it difficulty in meeting its cash needs from operations. "They're growing too fast and not getting the returns from capital investments they used to get. Allied peaked in mid 1995, and returns have been deteriorating since." Fotta predicted that without major changes, AlliedSignal would have increasing difficulty continuing its double-digit sales growth.[1]

This is an example of how one analyst used a performance measure to assess the overall health of a company. You can do the same type of in-depth analysis on a comprehensive strategic management case. This chapter provides you with various analytical techniques and suggestions for conducting this kind of case analysis.

14.1 The Case Method

The analysis and discussion of case problems has been the most popular method of teaching strategy and policy for many years. The case method provides the opportunity to move from a narrow, specialized view that emphasizes functional techniques to a broader, less precise analysis of the overall corporation. Cases present actual business situations and enable you to examine both successful and unsuccessful corporations. In case analysis, you might be asked to critically analyze a situation in which a manager had to make a decision of long-term corporate importance. This approach gives you a feel for what it is like to be faced with making and implementing strategic decisions.

14.2 Researching the Case Situation

Don't restrict yourself only to the information written in the case. You should undertake outside research into the environmental setting. Check the decision date of each case (typically the latest date mentioned in the case) to find out when the situation occurred and then screen the business periodicals for that time period. Use computerized company and industry information services such as COMPUSTAT, Compact Disclosure, and CD/International, available on CD-ROM or online at the library. On the Internet, Hoover's On Line Corporate Directory ⟨www.hoovers.com⟩ and the Security Exchange Commission's Edgar database ⟨www.sec.gov⟩ provide access to corporate annual reports and 10-K forms. This background will give you an appreciation for the situation as it was experienced by the participants in the case.

A company's annual report and 10-K form from the year of the case can be very helpful. According to the Yankelovich Partners survey firm, 8 out of 10 portfolio managers and 75% of security analysts use annual reports when making decisions.[2] They contain not only the usual *income statements* and *balance sheets*, but also *cash flow statements* and notes to the financial statements indicating why certain actions were taken. 10-K forms include detailed information not usually available in an annual report. An understanding of the economy during that period will help you avoid making a serious error in your analysis, for example, suggesting a sale of stock when the stock market is at an all-time low or taking on more debt when the prime interest rate is over 15%. Information on the industry will provide insights on its competitive activities. Some resources available for research into the economy and a corporation's industry are suggested in **Appendix 14.A**.

14.3 Financial Analysis: A Place to Begin

Once you have read a case, a good place to begin your analysis is with the financial statements. **Ratio analysis** is the calculation of ratios from data in these statements. It is done to identify possible financial strengths or weaknesses. Thus it is a valuable part of SWOT analysis. A review of key financial ratios can help you assess the company's overall situation and pinpoint some problem areas. Ratios are useful regardless of firm size and enable you to compare a company's ratios with industry averages. **Table 14–1** lists some of the most important financial ratios, which are (1) **liquidity ratios**, (2) **profitability ratios**, (3) **activity ratios**, and (4) **leverage ratios**.

ANALYZING FINANCIAL STATEMENTS

In your analysis, do not simply make an exhibit including all the ratios, but select and discuss only those ratios that have an impact on the company's problems. For instance, accounts receivable and inventory may provide a source of funds. If receivables and inventories are double the industry average, reducing them may provide needed cash. In this situation, the case report should include not only sources of funds, but also the number of dollars freed for use. Compare these ratios with industry averages to discover if the company is out of line with others in the industry. A typical financial analysis of a firm would include a study of the operating statements for five or so years, including a trend analysis of sales, profits, earnings per share, debt-to-equity ratio, return on investment, and so on, plus a ratio study comparing the firm under study with industry standards.

- **Scrutinize historical income statements and balance sheets.** These two basic statements provide most of the data needed for analysis. Statements of cash flow may also be useful.
- **Compare historical statements over time** if a series of statements is available.
- **Calculate changes that occur in individual categories from year to year**, as well as the cumulative total change.
- **Determine the change as a percentage** as well as an absolute amount.
- **Adjust for inflation** if that was a significant factor.

Examination of this information may reveal developing trends. Compare trends in one category with trends in related categories. For example, an increase in sales of 15% over three years may appear to be satisfactory until you note an increase of 20% in the cost of goods sold during the same period. The outcome of this comparison might suggest that further investigation into the manufacturing process is necessary. If a company is reporting strong net income growth but negative cash flow, this would suggest that the company is relying on something other than operations for earnings growth. Is it selling off assets or cutting R&D? If accounts receivable are growing faster than are sales revenues, the company is not getting paid for the products or services it is counting as sold. Is the company dumping product on its distributors at the end of the year to boost its reported annual sales? If so, expect the distributors to return the unordered product the next month—thus drastically cutting the next year's reported sales. The Securities and Exchange Commission brought 90 accounting fraud cases against U.S. companies during 1999, more than half involving falsifying revenue.[3]

Other "tricks of the trade" need to be examined. Until June, 2000, firms growing through acquisition were allowed to account for the cost of the purchased company through the pooling of both companies' stocks. This approach was used in 40% of the value of mergers between 1997 and 1999. The pooling method enabled the acquiring company to disregard the premium it paid for the other firm (the amount above the fair market value of the purchased company often called "good will"). Thus, when PepsiCo agreed to purchase Quaker Oats for $13.4 billion in PepsiCo stock, the $13.4 billion was not found on PepsiCo's balance sheet. As of June, 2000, merging firms must use the "purchase" accounting rules in which the true purchase price is reflected in the financial statements.[4]

Note that multinational corporations follow the accounting rules for their home country. As a result, their financial statements may be somewhat difficult to understand or to use for comparisons with competitors from other countries. For example, British firms such as British Petroleum and The Body Shop use the term "turnover" rather than sales revenue. In the case of AB Electrolux of Sweden, a footnote to the annual report indicates that the consolidated accounts have been prepared in accordance with Swedish accounting standards, which

Table 14–1 Financial Ratio Analysis

	Formula	How Expressed	Meaning
1. Liquidity Ratios			
Current ratio	$$\frac{\text{Current assets}}{\text{Current liabilities}}$$	Decimal	A short-term indicator of the company's ability to pay its short-term liabilities from short-term assets; how much of current assets are available to cover each dollar of current liabilities.
Quick (acid test) ratio	$$\frac{\text{Current assets} - \text{Inventory}}{\text{Current liabilities}}$$	Decimal	Measures the company's ability to pay off its short-term obligations from current assets, excluding inventories.
Inventory to net working capital	$$\frac{\text{Inventory}}{\text{Current assets} - \text{Current liabilities}}$$	Decimal	A measure of inventory balance; measures the extent to which the cushion of excess current assets over current liabilities may be threatened by unfavorable changes in inventory.
Cash ratio	$$\frac{\text{Cash} + \text{Cash equivalents}}{\text{Current liabilities}}$$	Decimal	Measures the extent to which the company's capital is in cash or cash equivalents; shows how much of the current obligations can be paid from cash or near-cash assets.
2. Profitability Ratios			
Net profit margin	$$\frac{\text{Net profit after taxes}}{\text{Net sales}}$$	Percentage	Shows how much after-tax profits are generated by each dollar of sales.
Gross profit margin	$$\frac{\text{Sales} - \text{Cost of goods sold}}{\text{Net sales}}$$	Percentage	Indicates the total margin available to cover other expenses beyond cost of goods sold, and still yield a profit.
Return on investment (ROI)	$$\frac{\text{Net profit after taxes}}{\text{Total assets}}$$	Percentage	Measures the rate of return on the total assets utilized in the company; a measure of management's efficiency, it shows the return on all the assets under its control regardless of source of financing.
Return on equity (ROE)	$$\frac{\text{Net profit after taxes}}{\text{Shareholders' equity}}$$	Percentage	Measures the rate of return on the book value of shareholders' total investment in the company.
Earnings per share (EPS)	$$\frac{\text{Net profit after taxes} - \text{Preferred stock dividends}}{\text{Average number of common shares}}$$	Dollars per share	Shows the after-tax earnings generated for each share of common stock.
3. Activity Ratios			
Inventory turnover	$$\frac{\text{Net sales}}{\text{Inventory}}$$	Decimal	Measures the number of times that average inventory of finished goods was turned over or sold during a period of time, usually a year.
Days of inventory	$$\frac{\text{Inventory}}{\text{Cost of goods sold} \div 365}$$	Days	Measures the number of one day's worth of inventory that a company has on hand at any given time.
Net working capital turnover	$$\frac{\text{Net sales}}{\text{Net working capital}}$$	Decimal	Measures how effectively the net working capital is used to generate sales.
Asset turnover	$$\frac{\text{Sales}}{\text{Total assets}}$$	Decimal	Measures the utilization of all the company's assets; measures how many sales are generated by each dollar of assets.

Table 14-1 (continued)

	Formula	How Expressed	Meaning
Fixed asset turnover	$\dfrac{\text{Sales}}{\text{Fixed assets}}$	Decimal	Measures the utilization of the company's fixed assets (i.e., plant and equipment); measures how many sales are generated by each dollar of fixed assets.
Average collection period	$\dfrac{\text{Accounts receivable}}{\text{Sales for year} \div 365}$	Days	Indicates the average length of time in days that a company must wait to collect a sale after making it; may be compared to the credit terms offered by the company to its customers.
Accounts receivable turnover	$\dfrac{\text{Annual credit sales}}{\text{Accounts receivable}}$	Decimal	Indicates the number of times that accounts receivable are cycled during the period (usually a year).
Accounts payable period	$\dfrac{\text{Accounts payable}}{\text{Purchases for year} \div 365}$	Days	Indicates the average length of time in days that the company takes to pay its credit purchases.
Days of cash	$\dfrac{\text{Cash}}{\text{Net sales for year} \div 365}$	Days	Indicates the number of days of cash on hand, at present sales levels.

4. Leverage Ratios

	Formula	How Expressed	Meaning
Debt to asset ratio	$\dfrac{\text{Total debt}}{\text{Total assets}}$	Percentage	Measures the extent to which borrowed funds have been used to finance the company's assets.
Debt to equity ratio	$\dfrac{\text{Total debt}}{\text{Shareholders' equity}}$	Percentage	Measures the funds provided by creditors versus the funds provided by owners.
Long-term debt to capital structure	$\dfrac{\text{Long--term debt}}{\text{Shareholders' equity}}$	Percentage	Measures the long-term component of capital structure.
Times interest earned	$\dfrac{\text{Profit before taxes} + \text{Interest charges}}{\text{Interest charges}}$	Decimal	Indicates the ability of the company to meet its annual interest costs.
Coverage of fixed charges	$\dfrac{\text{Profit before taxes} + \text{Interest charges} + \text{Lease charges}}{\text{Interest charges} + \text{Lease obligations}}$	Decimal	A measure of the company's ability to meet all of its fixed-charge obligations.
Current liabilities to equity	$\dfrac{\text{Current liabilities}}{\text{Shareholders' equity}}$	Percentage	Measures the short-term financing portion versus that provided by owners.

5. Other Ratios

	Formula	How Expressed	Meaning
Price/earnings ratio	$\dfrac{\text{Market price per share}}{\text{Earnings per share}}$	Decimal	Shows the current market's evaluation of a stock, based on its earnings; shows how much the investor is willing to pay for each dollar of earnings.
Divided payout ratio	$\dfrac{\text{Annual dividends per share}}{\text{Annual earnings per share}}$	Percentage	Indicates the percentage of profit that is paid out as dividends.
Dividend yield on common stock	$\dfrac{\text{Annual dividends per share}}{\text{Current market price per share}}$	Percentage	Indicates the dividend rate of return to common shareholders at the current market price.

Note: In using ratios for analysis, calculate ratios for the corporation and compare them to the average and quartile ratios for the particular industry. Refer to Standard and Poor's and Robert Morris Associates for average industry data. Special thanks to Dr. Moustafa H. Abdelsamad, Dean, Business School, Texas A&M University–Corpus Christi, Corpus Christi, Texas, for his definitions of these ratios.

differ in certain significant respects from United States generally accepted accounting principles (U.S. GAAP). For one year, net income of 4,830m SEK (Swedish kronor) approximated
5,655 SEK according to U.S. GAAP. Total assets for the same period were 84,183m SEK according to Swedish principle, but 86,658 according to U.S. GAAP.

For further information, see ⟨www.prenhall.com/wheelen⟩ to download "Understanding
Financial Statements" by M. M. Rouse.

COMMON-SIZE STATEMENTS

Common-size statements are income statements and balance sheets in which the dollar figures have been converted into percentages. For the income statement, net sales represent
100%: calculate the percentage of each category so that the categories sum to the net sales
percentage (100%). For the balance sheet, give the total assets a value of 100%, and calculate
other asset and liability categories as percentages of the total assets. (Individual asset and liability items, such as accounts receivable and accounts payable, can also be calculated as a percentage of net sales.)

When you convert statements to this form, it is relatively easy to note the percentage that
each category represents of the total. Look for trends in specific items, such as cost of goods
sold, when compared to the company's historical figures. To get a proper picture, however,
make comparisons with industry data, if available, to see if fluctuations are merely reflecting
industrywide trends. If a firm's trends are generally in line with those of the rest of the industry, problems are less likely than if the firm's trends are worse than industry averages.
(Raymond Morris Associates provides common-size statements for various industries.)
Common-size statements are especially helpful in developing scenarios and pro forma statements because they provide a series of historical relationships (for example, cost of goods sold
to sales, interest to sales, and inventories as a percentage of assets) from which you can estimate the future with your scenario assumptions for each year.

Z-VALUE, INDEX OF SUSTAINABLE GROWTH, AND FREE CASH FLOW

If the corporation being studied appears to be in poor financial condition, use **Altman's
Bankruptcy Formula** to calculate its **Z-value**. The Z-value formula combines five ratios by
weighting them according to their importance to a corporation's financial strength. The formula is:

$$Z = 1.2x_1 + 1.4x_2 + 3.3x_3 + 0.6x_4 + 1.0x_5$$

where:

x_1 = Working capital/Total assets (%)
x_2 = Retained earnings/Total assets (%)
x_3 = Earnings before interest & taxes/Total assets (%)
x_4 = Market value of equity/Total liabilities (%)
x_5 = Sales/Total assets (number of times)

Scores below 1.81 indicate significant credit problems, whereas a score above 3.0 indicates a
healthy firm. Scores between 1.81 and 3.0 indicate question marks.[5]

The **index of sustainable growth** is useful to learn if a company embarking on a
growth strategy will need to take on debt to fund this growth. The index indicates how

much of the growth rate of sales can be sustained by internally generated funds. The formula is:

$$g^* = \frac{[P(1-D)(1+L)]}{[T - P(1-D)(1+L)]}$$

where:

P = (Net profit before tax/Net sales) $\times$ 100
D = Target dividends/Profit after tax
L = Total liabilities/Net worth
T = (Total assets/Net sales) $\times$ 100

If the planned growth rate calls for a growth rate higher than its g^*, external capital will be needed to fund the growth unless management is able to find efficiencies, decrease dividends, increase the debt/equity ratio, or reduce assets by renting or leasing arrangements.[6]

Takeover artists and LBO (leveraged buy-out) specialists look at a corporation's financial statements for **operating cash flow**: the amount of money generated by a company before the cost of financing and taxes. This is the company's net income plus depreciation plus depletion, amortization, interest expense, and income tax expense. LBO specialists will take on as much debt as the company's operating cash flow can support. A similar measure, **EBITDA** (**E**arnings **B**efore **I**nterest, **T**axes, **D**epreciation, and **A**mortization), is sometimes used, but is *not* determined in accordance with generally accepted accounting principles and is thus subject to varying calculations. Although operating cash flow is a broad measure of a company's funds, some takeover artists look at a much narrower **free cash flow**: the amount of money a new owner can take out of the firm without harming the business. This is net income plus depreciation, depletion, and amortization less capital expenditures and dividends. The free cash flow ratio is very useful in evaluating the stability of an entrepreneurial venture.[7] The danger in using these instruments is that they appear to be the same as cash flow—which they are not. According to Martin Fridson, chief of high-yield research with Merrill Lynch, "A capital intensive company isn't earning a profit if its assets are wearing down from wear and tear."[8]

USEFUL ECONOMIC MEASURES

If you are analyzing a company over many years, you may want to adjust sales and net income for inflation to arrive at "true" financial performance in constant dollars. **Constant dollars** are dollars adjusted for inflation to make them comparable over various years. See the 🌐 **Global Issue** feature to learn why inflation can be an important issue for multinational corporations. One way to adjust for inflation in the United States is to use the Consumer Price Index (CPI), as given in **Table 14–2**. Dividing sales and net income by the CPI factor for that year will change the figures to 1982–1984 constant dollars (when the CPI was 1.0).

Another helpful analytical aid provided in **Table 14–2** is the **prime interest rate**, the rate of interest banks charge on their lowest risk loans. For better assessments of strategic decisions, it can be useful to note the level of the prime interest rate at the time of the case. A decision to borrow money to build a new plant would have been a good one in 1993 at 6%, but less practical in 2000 when the rate reached 9.5%.

In preparing a scenario for your pro forma financial statements, you may want to use the **gross domestic product (GDP)** from **Table 14–2**. GDP is used worldwide and measures the total output of goods and services within a country's borders. The amount of change from one year to the next indicates how much that country's economy is growing. Remember that scenarios have to be adjusted for a country's specific conditions.

Global Issue

Why Consider Inflation in Case Analysis?

Inflation is a recent problem in the United States. Between 1800 and 1940, there was no clear trend up or down in the overall cost of living. A moviegoer in the late 1930s watching a drama set in the early 1800s would not notice prices to be unusual. For example, the cost of a loaf of bread in the late 1930s was roughly the same as in 1800. With the minor exceptions of 1949 and 1955, prices have risen every year since 1945. The Consumer Price Index (a generally used measure of the overall cost of living in the United States) increased nine times from 1945 to 1996. (Watch the movie *It's a Wonderful Life* to see how much prices have changed since 1948.) From 1970 to 1980, the CPI more than doubled. After an average rate of 7.1% during the 1970s, inflation slowed to 5.5% in the 1980s, and 3.4% during the 1990s. Inflation seemed to be under control in the United States. Although people complained about the rising price of retail gasoline, the average price in constant dollars in 2000 was the same as in 1970—before the OPEC oil embargo. Nevertheless, economist Milton Friedman warns of an increase in inflation. "We're in a period like the 1960s, when no one paid any attention to the money supply. Then we got inflation," says Friedman.

The rate of inflation in other countries varies and has a significant impact on a multinational corporation's profits. Although most countries in the developed parts of the world kept inflation under control during the five-year period from 1994 to 1999, the developing nations did not fare as well. For example, the average annual inflation rate in Turkey during 1994–1999 was

81%. Supermarkets were forced to list prices on electronic displays rather than on printed labels. Turkey's rate of inflation was high, but was a far cry from Bolivia's astounding annual rate during 1985 of 25,000%! During 1994–1999, the countries of the European Union had an inflation rate of around 2–3%, while Eastern European countries were dealing with higher rates, such as 64% in Russia and 19% in Hungary. During 1997 alone, Romania's annual inflation rate was 170%, while Bulgaria's was 1,268%. During the 1994–1999 time period in Latin America, Mexico's annual rate was 24%, Columbia's was 18%, and Brazil's was 17%. Although most Asian countries had a low rate of inflation (Singapore, Taiwan, and Malaysia increased less than 5%), Indonesia's increased 20% and India's increased 8%.

Before inflation is declared dead by politicians anxious to reduce cost-of-living increases to Social Security payments (to reduce government expenditures and thus government debt), note what happens with a relatively constant 3.4% rate of inflation. Through the working of compound interest, the price level rose about 40% during the 1990s. This means that companies have to be constantly monitoring not only their costs, but also the prices of the products they offer. Unless a company's dollar sales are increasing over 3.5% annually, its sales are actually falling (in constant dollars)! The same is true for net income. This point is often overlooked by the chief executive officers of troubled companies who are anxious to keep their jobs by fooling both the board and the shareholders.

Sources: P. W. Boltz, "Is Inflation Dead?" *T. Rowe Price Report* (Winter 1997), pp. 10–11; P. Brimelow with M. Friedman, "Beware the Funny Money," *Forbes* (May 3, 1999), pp. 138–141; "Managing Inflation: Talking Turkey," *The Economist* (October 11, 1997), p. 95; "Emerging Market Indicators," *The Economist* (December 9, 2000), p. 116; J. T. Allen and D. McGraw, "The Gas Crisis that Isn't—Yet," *U.S. News & World Report* (April 3, 1990), p. 22.

14.4 Format for Case Analysis: The Strategic Audit

There is no one best way to analyze or present a case report. Each instructor has personal preferences for format and approach. Nevertheless, we suggest an approach for both written and oral reports in **Appendix 14.B**, which provides a systematic method for successfully attacking a case. This approach is based on the **strategic audit**, which was presented at the end of **Chapter 10** in **Appendix 10.A**. We find that this approach provides structure and is very helpful for the typical student who may be a relative novice in case analysis. Regardless of the

Table 14–2 U.S. Economic Indicators: Gross Domestic Product (GDP) in Billions of Dollars; Consumer Price Index for All Items (CPI) (1982–1984 = 1.0); Prime Interest Rate (PIR)

Year	GDP	CPI	PIR
1983	3,514.5	.996	10.79
1984	3,902.4	1.039	12.04
1985	4,180.7	1.076	9.93
1986	4,422.2	1.096	8.33
1987	4,693.3	1.136	8.21
1988	5,049.6	1.183	9.32
1989	5,483.7	1.240	10.87
1990	5,743.8	1.307	10.01
1991	5,916.7	1.362	8.46
1992	6,244.4	1.403	6.25
1993	6,553.0	1.445	6.00
1994	6,935.7	1.482	7.15
1995	7,253.8	1.524	8.83
1996	7,661.6	1.569	8.27
1997	8,318.4	1.605	8.44
1998	8,790.2	1.630	8.35
1999	9,299.2	1.666	8.00
2000	9,965.7	1.720	9.23

Sources: Gross Domestic Product from *Survey of Current Business* (February 2001), Vol. 81, No. 2, Table 1.1, p. D-3. Consumer Price Index from U.S. Department of Commerce, *1997 Statistical Abstract of the United States,* 117th edition, Chart no. 752, p. 487; U.S. Bureau of Labor Statistics, *Monthly Labor Review* (October 1998), Chart no. 28, p. 74; *Survey of Current Business* (September 2000), Vol. 80, No. 9, Table D.1, p. D-41. Prime Interest Rates from D.S. Benton, "Banking and Financial Information," Table 1–2, p. 3 in *Thorndike Encyclopedia of Banking and Financial Tables,* 3rd. ed., 1998 Yearbook (Boston: Warren, Gorham and Lamont, 1998); *Survey of Current Business* (February 2001), Vol. 81, No. 2, Table D.1, p. D-41. Web sites of the Bureau of Economic Analysis, Economics & Statistics Administration, U.S. Department of Commerce ⟨www.stat-usa.gov⟩ and ⟨www.bea.doc.gov⟩.

format chosen, be careful to include a complete analysis of key environmental variables—especially of trends in the industry and of the competition. Look at international developments as well.

If you choose to use the strategic audit as a guide to the analysis of complex strategy cases, you may want to use the strategic audit worksheet in **Figure 14–1. You can download the Strategic Audit Worksheet from this book's Web site at ⟨www.prenhall. com/wheelen⟩.** Print a copy of the worksheet to use to take notes as you analyze a case. See **Appendix 14.C** for an example of a completed student-written analysis of a 1993 Maytag Corporation case (not the later 1996 version in the case portion of this book) done in an outline form using the strategic audit format. This is one example of what a case analysis in outline form may look like.

Case discussion focuses on critical analysis and logical development of thought. A solution is satisfactory if it resolves important problems and is likely to be implemented successfully. How the corporation actually dealt with the case problems has no real bearing on the analysis because management might have analyzed its problems incorrectly or implemented a series of flawed solutions.

Figure 14–1
Strategic Audit
Worksheet

Strategic Audit Heading	Analysis		Comments
	(+) Factors	**(−) Factors**	
I. **Current Situation**			
A. Past Corporate Performance Indexes			
B. Strategic Posture: Current Mission Current Objectives Current Strategies Current Policies			
SWOT Analysis Begins:			
II. **Corporate Governance**			
A. Board of Directors			
B. Top Management			
III. **External Environment (EFAS):** **Opportunities and Threats (SWOT)**			
A. Societal Environment			
B. Task Environment (Industry Analysis)			
IV. **Internal Environment (IFAS):** **Strengths and Weaknesses (SWOT)**			
A. Corporate Structure			
B. Corporate Culture			
C. Corporate Resources			
1. Marketing			
2. Finance			
3. Research and Development			
4. Operations and Logistics			
5. Human Resources			
6. Information Systems			
V. **Analysis of Strategic Factors (SFAS)**			
A. Key Internal and External Strategic Factors (SWOT)			
B. Review of Mission and Objectives			

Figure 14–1
Strategic Audit
Worksheet
(*continued*)

SWOT Analysis Ends. Recommendation Begins:			
VI. **Alternatives and Recommendations**			
A. Strategic Alternatives—pros and cons			
B. Recommended Strategy			
VII. **Implementation**			
VIII. **Evaluation and Control**			

Note: See the complete Strategic Audit on page 265–272. It lists the pages in the book that discuss each of the eight headings.

Source: T. L. Wheelen and J. D. Hunger, "Strategic Audit Worksheet." Copyright © 1989 by Wheelen and Hunger Associates. Revised 1991, 1994, and 1997. Reprinted by permission. Additional copies available for classroom use in Part D of *Case Instructors Manual* and on the Prentice Hall Web site ⟨www.prenhall.com/wheelen⟩.

14.5 Impact of the Internet on Case Analysis

The Internet is an excellent source of information about industries as well as individual companies. It can be especially useful if your instructor gives you the assignment to either update a case or to research an industry. To begin, you only need access to the Internet and a browser like Netscape Navigator or Microsoft's Internet Explorer. When "surfing" the net, you will be amazed by the amount of information (much of it worthless) you can find. A word of caution: Beware of getting caught by an online confidence game. (See the Internet Issue feature for the top 10 Internet scams.)

Finding a Company's Web Site

If you are looking for information about a particular company, you can first try using a simplified version of the firm's name to directly get to the firm's home (primary) Web page. For example, first type in the protocol—the standard first part of the **url** (uniform resource locator)—http://www. Don't capitalize any letters in the url. Then type in a likely name for the firm, such as maytag, ibm, toyota, hp (Hewlett-Packard), ti (Texas Instruments), or prenhall (Prentice Hall). This is referred to as the company's server name. Follow this name with the suffix .com. This is called a **domain**. In the United States, most business urls still end with the domain name .com. The same is true for other urls, such as edu for schools and colleges, gov for government agencies, org for not-for-profit organizations, and mil for the military. Outside of the United States each country has its own suffix, such as .uk for Great Britain, .au for Australia, .ca for Canada, .de for Germany, and .pe for Peru. This string of words and letters usually completes the url. For example, try typing ⟨http://www.maytag.com⟩ in the location line of your Internet browser and tap the Enter key. This takes you directly to Maytag's home Web page. In some instances, the url may also contain a more specific Web page beyond the company's home page. In this case, the .com is followed by /xxxx.html (xxxx can be anything). This indicates that this is another Web page that uses the html (hypertext markup language) of the World Wide Web.

Internet Issue

Top 10 Internet Scams

- **Home Business** (3%): Pay a fee but earn nothing.
- **Travel Bargains** (2%): Inexpensive trip is either not what was promised or is nonexistent.
- **Sell Special Products** (2%): Sells product at low price, but there are no buyers.
- **Invest Now** (1%): Promises stock appreciation, but little actually happens after stock purchase.
- **Health Products** (1%): Miracle medicines sold as Internet "snake oil" to solve all problems.

The U.S. Federal Trade Commission reports the following list of most popular Internet-related complaints regarding confidence games being played on unsuspecting visitors to the information highway.

- **Auctions** (45%): Buyer pays but gets wrong item or none at all.
- **Internet Access** (21%): Supposedly "free" Internet access has hidden charges and high cancellation fees.
- **Credit Card Fraud** (9%): Adult-only sites ask for credit card data to verify age—resulting in unauthorized charges.
- **Personal Web Site** (5%): Offers free Web site for 30 days but charges via the phone bill.
- **Modem Scam** (5%): Download a "free" dialer to access adult sites but high charges soon follow.

The modem scam is especially ingenious. A pornographic Web site offers to download a special "viewer" or "dialer" program to see nude photos. When the file is downloaded, the Internet connection is disconnected and the program makes the computer dial a phone number to a small island in the southwest Pacific called Vanuatu (formerly New Hebrides) at a rate of $2 to $7 per minute. Few people report this scam because they don't want others to know they were visiting pornographic Web sites!

Sources: "Top Ten Scams on the Information Highway," *U.S. News & World Report* (November 13, 2000), p. 16; S. S. Woo, "Scam Prompts Surf Warning," *Des Moines Register* (February 17, 2001), pp. D1, D6.

Using a Search Engine

If typing in an obvious company name doesn't work, use a search engine. This is especially the case if you are investigating a non-U.S. corporation like AB Electrolux of Sweden. **Search engines** are services that act like a library's card file to help you find information on a topic. Type in http://www. followed by the search engine's url. Some of the common search engines are Yahoo! ⟨yahoo.com⟩, Alta Vista ⟨altavista.com⟩, Lycos ⟨lycos.com⟩, Google ⟨google. com⟩, Northern Light ⟨northernlight.com⟩, and Excite ⟨excite.com⟩. This url will take you to the search engine's Web page where you can type in the name of a company. The search engine finds any references to that firm. One of these references should include the company's url. Use it to get to the company's home Web page.

Finding More Information

Getting to the company's home Web page does not necessarily mean that you now have access to the firm's financials. If the Web site does include a link to a Web page containing the company's financials, that page will probably have only financials for the most recent year or two. In that case, try related business directories such as Hoover's On-Line ⟨hoovers.com⟩ or the U.S. Securities and Exchange Commission Edgar database ⟨sec.gov⟩. If the company's stock is publicly traded and listed on one of the major stock exchanges, these business directories should get you to the database containing the latest annual reports and 10-K reports, as well as quarterly reports. Other sites offering valuable information relating to business firms are:

- Annual Report Gallery ⟨www.reportgallery.com⟩
- Web 100 ⟨www.w100.com⟩
- CEO Express ⟨www.ceoexpress.com⟩
- Wall Street Research Net ⟨www.wsrn.com⟩
- Companies Online ⟨www.companiesonline.com⟩
- Corporate Financials Online ⟨www.cfonews.com⟩
- Corporate Information ⟨www.corporateinformation.com⟩
- Kompass International ⟨www.kompass.com⟩
- CorpTech Database of Technology Companies ⟨www.corptech.com⟩
- ZDNet Company Finder ⟨www.companyfinder.com⟩

Additional Web sites are listed in **Appendix 14.A** and at the Web site ⟨www.prenhall.com/wheelen⟩. Note that Web sites constantly change. Just because a particular url works one time does not mean that it will work a year or two later. If the company is doing a good job of managing its Web sites, it will leave a message on its abandoned Web page sending you to a new page. If nothing works, simply go to one of the search engines and begin again. Good luck!

Projections for the 21st Century

- From 1994 to 2010, expect consumer inflation to decline from 4.3% to 2.5%.
- From 1994 to 2010, expect the international value of the U.S. dollar to increase from 1.0 to 9.33.[9]

Discussion Questions

1. Why should you begin a case analysis with a financial analysis? When are other approaches appropriate?
2. What are common-size financial statements? What is their value to case analysis? How are they calculated?
3. When should you gather information outside the case by going to the library or using the Internet? What should you be looking for?
4. When is inflation an important issue in conducting case analysis? Why bother?
5. How can you learn the date a case took place?

Strategic Practice Exercise

Convert the following two years of income statements from the Maytag Corporation into common-size statements. The dollar figures are in thousands. What does converting to a common size reveal?

	1992	%	1991	%
Net sales	$3,041,223		$2,970,626	
Cost of sales	2,339,406		2,254,221	
Gross profits	701,817		716,405	
Selling, general, and admin.				
expenses	528,250		524,898	
Reorganization expenses	95,000		—	
Operating income	78,567		191,507	
Interest expense	(75,004)		(75,159)	
Other—net	3,983		7,069	
Income before taxes				
and accounting changes	7,546		123,417	
Income taxes	(15,900)		(44,400)	
Income before accounting				
changes	(8,354)		79,017	
Effects of accounting changes for				
post-retirement benefits	(307,000)		—	
Net income (loss)	$(315,354)		$79,017	

Key Terms

activity ratios (pp. 342, 344–345)
Altman's Bankruptcy Formula
  (p. 346)
common-size statements (p. 346)
constant dollars (p. 347)
domain (p. 351)
EBITDA (p. 347)
free cash flow (p. 347)

gross domestic product (GDP)
  (p. 347)
index of sustainable growth (p. 346)
leverage ratios (pp. 342, 345)
liquidity ratios (pp. 342, 344)
operating cash flow (p. 347)
prime interest rate (p. 347)

profitability ratios (pp. 342, 344)
ratio analysis (p. 342)
search engines (p. 352)
strategic audit worksheet
  (pp. 349–351)
url (p. 351)
Z-value (p. 346)

Resources for Case Research

Company Information

1. Annual reports
2. *Moody's Manuals on Investment* (a listing of companies within certain industries that contains a brief history and a five-year financial statement of each company)
3. Securities and Exchange Commission Annual Report Form 10-K (annually) and 10-Q (quarterly)
4. Standard and Poor's *Register of Corporations, Directors, and Executives*
5. Value Line's *Investment Survey*
6. *COMPUSTAT, Compact Disclosure, CD/International,* and *Hoover's Online Corporate Directory* (computerized operating and financial information on thousands of publicly held corporations)
7. Shareholders meeting notices

Economic Information

1. Regional statistics and local forecasts from large banks
2. *Business Cycle Development* (Department of Commerce)
3. Chase Econometric Associates' publications
4. U.S. Census Bureau publications on population, transportation, and housing
5. *Current Business Reports* (U.S. Department of Commerce)
6. *Economic Indicators* (U.S. Joint Economic Committee)
7. *Economic Report of the President to Congress*
8. *Long-Term Economic Growth* (U.S. Department of Commerce)
9. *Monthly Labor Review* (U.S. Department of Labor)
10. *Monthly Bulletin of Statistics* (United Nations)
11. *Statistical Abstract of the United States* (U.S. Department of Commerce)
12. *Statistical Yearbook* (United Nations)
13. *Survey of Current Business* (U.S. Department of Commerce)
14. *U.S. Industrial Outlook* (U.S. Department of Defense)
15. *World Trade Annual* (United Nations)
16. *Overseas Business Reports* (by country, published by U.S. Department of Commerce)
17. *The World Factbook* (U.S. CIA)

Industry Information

1. Analyses of companies and industries by investment brokerage firms
2. *Business Week* (provides weekly economic and business information, and quarterly profit and sales rankings of corporations)
3. *Fortune* (each April publishes listings of financial information on corporations within certain industries)

4. *Industry Survey* (published quarterly by Standard and Poor's Corporation)

5. *Industry Week* (late March/early April issue provides information on 14 industry groups)

6. *Forbes* (mid-January issue provides performance data on firms in various industries)

7. *Inc.* (May and December issues give information on fast-growing entrepreneurial companies)

8. *The Information Catalogue* (a listing by MarketResearch.com of over 11,000 studies conducted by leading research firms)

Directory and Index Information on Companies and Industries

1. *Business Periodical Index* (on computer in many libraries)

2. *Directory of National Trade Associations*

3. *Encyclopedia of Associations*

4. Funk and Scott's *Index of Corporations and Industries*

5. Thomas's *Register of American Manufacturers*

6. *Wall Street Journal Index*

Ratio Analysis Information

1. *Almanac of Business and Industrial Financial Ratios* (Prentice Hall)

2. *Annual Statement Studies* (Robert Morris Associates)

3. *Dun's Review* (Dun and Bradstreet; published annually in September–December issues)

4. *Industry Norms and Key Business Ratios* (Dun and Bradstreet)

Online Information

1. *Hoovers Online*—Financial statements and profiles of public companies ⟨www.hoovers.com⟩

2. *U.S. Securities & Exchange Commission*—Official filings of public companies in Edgar database ⟨www.sec.gov⟩

3. *Fortune 500*—Statistics for largest U.S. corporations ⟨www.pathfinder.com⟩

4. *Dun & Bradstreet's Online*—Short reports on 10 million public and private U.S. companies ⟨www.dbisna.com/dnb/dnbhome.htm⟩

5. *Ecola's 24-Hour Newsstand*—Links to Web sites of 2,000 newspapers, journals, and magazines ⟨www.ecola.com/news⟩

6. *Competitive Intelligence Guide*—Information on company resources ⟨www.fuld.com⟩

7. *The Economist*—Provides international information and surveys ⟨www.economist.com⟩

8. *Web 100*—Information on 100 largest U.S. and international companies ⟨www.w100.com⟩

9. *Bloomberg*—Information on interest rates, stock prices, currency conversion rates, and other general financial information ⟨www.bloomberg.com⟩

10. *The World Factbook*—Profiles of many countries ⟨www.odci.gov/cia/publications/factbook/index.html⟩

appendix 14.B

Suggested Case Analysis Methodology Using the Strategic Audit

1. READ CASE

First Reading of the Case

- Develop a general overview of the company and its external environment.
- Begin a list of the possible strategic factors facing the company at this time.
- List the research information you may need on the economy, industry, and competitors.

2. READ THE CASE WITH THE STRATEGIC AUDIT

Second Reading of the Case

- Read the case a second time using the strategic audit as a framework for in-depth analysis. (See **Appendix 10.A** on pages 265–272.) You may want to make a copy of the strategic audit worksheet (**Figure 14–1**) to use to keep track of your comments as you read the case.
- The questions in the strategic audit parallel the strategic decision making process shown in **Figure 1–5** (pages 20–21).
- The audit provides you with a conceptual framework to examine the company's mission, objectives, strategies, and policies as well as problems, symptoms, facts, opinions, and issues.
- Perform a financial analysis of the company using ratio analysis (see **Table 14–1**) and do the calculations necessary to convert key parts of the financial statements to a common-size basis.

3. DO OUTSIDE RESEARCH

Library and Online Computer Services

- Each case has a decision date indicating when the case actually took place. Your research should be based on the time period for the case.
- See **Appendix 14.A** for resources for case research. Your research should include information about the environment at the time of the case. Find average industry ratios. You may also want to obtain further information regarding competitors and the company itself (10-K forms and annual reports). This information should help you conduct an industry analysis. Check with your instructor to see what kind of outside research is appropriate for your assignment.
- Don't try to learn what actually happened to the company discussed in the case. What management actually decided may not be the best solution. It will certainly bias your analysis and will probably cause your recommendation to lack proper justification.

4. BEGIN SWOT ANALYSIS

External Environmental Analysis: EFAS

- Analyze the four societal forces to see what trends are likely to affect the industry(s) in which the company is operating.
- Conduct an industry analysis using Porter's competitive forces from **Chapter 3**. Develop an Industry Matrix (**Table 3–3** on page 69).
- Generate 8 to 10 external factors. These should be the *most important* opportunities and threats facing the company at the time of the case.
- Develop an EFAS Table, as shown in **Table 3–4**, for your list of external strategic factors.
- **Suggestion:** Rank the 8 to 10 factors from most to least important. Start by grouping the 3 top factors and then the 3 bottom factors.

Internal Organizational Analysis: IFAS

- Generate 8 to 10 internal factors. These should be the *most important* strengths and weaknesses of the company at the time of the case.
- Develop an IFAS Table, as shown in **Table 4–2** (page 102), for your list of internal strategic factors.
- **Suggestion:** Rank the 8 to 10 factors from most to least important. Start by grouping the 3 top factors and then the 3 bottom factors.

5. WRITE YOUR STRATEGIC AUDIT: PARTS I TO IV

First Draft of Your Strategic Audit

- Review the student-written audit of an old Maytag case in **Appendix 14.C** for an example.
- Write Parts I to IV of the strategic audit. Remember to include the factors from your IFAS and IFAS Tables in your audit.

6. WRITE YOUR STRATEGIC AUDIT: PART V

Strategic Factor Analysis Summary: SFAS

- Condense the list of factors from the 16 to 20 identified in your EFAS and EFAS Tables to only the 8 to 10 most important factors.
- Select the most important EFAS and IFAS factors. Reconsider the weights of each. The weights still need to add to 1.0.
- Develop an SFAS Table, as shown in **Figure 5–1** (page 111), for your final list of strategic factors. Although the weights (indicating the importance of each factor) will probably change from the EFAS and IFAS Tables, the numerical rating (1 to 5) of each factor should remain the same. These ratings are your assessment of management's performance on each factor.
- This is a good time to reexamine what you wrote earlier in Parts I to IV. You may want to add to or delete some of what you wrote. Ensure that each one of the strategic factors you have included in your SFAS Table is discussed in the appropriate place in Parts I to IV. Part V of the audit is *not* the place to mention a strategic factor for the first time.
- Write Part V of your strategic audit. This completes your SWOT analysis.
- This is the place to suggest a revised mission statement and a better set of objectives for the company. The SWOT analysis coupled with revised mission and objectives for the company set the stage for the generation of strategic alternatives.

7. WRITE YOUR STRATEGIC AUDIT: PART VI

Strategic Alternatives and Recommendation

A. Alternatives

■ Develop around three mutually exclusive strategic alternatives. If appropriate to the case you are analyzing, you might propose one alternative for growth, one for stability, and one for retrenchment. Within each corporate strategy, you should probably propose an appropriate business/competitive strategy. You may also want to include some functional strategies where appropriate.

■ Construct a scenario for each alternative. Use the data from your outside research to project general societal trends (GDP, inflation, etc.) and industry trends. Use these as the basis of your assumptions to write pro forma financial statements (particularly income statements) for each strategic alternative for the next five years.

■ List pros and cons for each alternative based on your scenarios.

B. Recommendation

■ Specify which one of your alternative strategies you recommend. Justify your choice in terms of dealing with the strategic factors you listed in Part V of the audit.

■ Develop policies to help implement your strategies.

8. WRITE YOUR STRATEGIC AUDIT: PART VII

Implementation

■ Develop programs to implement your recommended strategy.

■ Specify who is to be responsible for implementing each program and how long each program will take to complete.

■ Refer to the pro forma financial statement you developed earlier for your recommended strategy. Do the numbers still make sense? If not, this may be a good time to rethink the budget numbers to reflect your recommended programs.

9. WRITE YOUR STRATEGIC AUDIT: PART VIII

Evaluation and Control

■ Specify the type of evaluation and controls that you need to ensure that your recommendation is carried out successfully. Specify who is responsible for monitoring these controls.

■ Indicate if sufficient information is available to monitor how the strategy is being implemented. If not, suggest a change to the information system.

10. PROOF AND FINE-TUNE YOUR AUDIT

Final Draft of Your Strategic Audit

■ Check to ensure that your audit is within the page limits of your professor. You may need to cut some parts and expand others.

■ Make sure that your recommendation clearly deals with the strategic factors.

■ Attach your EFAS, IFAS, and SFAS Tables plus your ratio analysis and pro forma statements. Label them as numbered exhibits and refer to each of them within the body of the audit.

■ Proof your work for errors. If on a computer, use a spell checker.

Special Note: Depending on your assignment, it is relatively easy to use the strategic audit you have just developed to write a written case analysis in essay form or to make an oral presentation. The strategic audit is just a detailed case analysis in an outline form and can be used as the basic framework for any sort of case analysis and presentation.

Example of Student-Written Strategic Audit

(For the 1993 Maytag Corporation Case—Not in This Book)

I. CURRENT SITUATION

A. Current Performance

Poor financials, high debt load, first losses since 1920s, price/earnings ratio negative.

B. Strategic Posture

1. **Mission**
   - Developed in 1989 for the Maytag Company: "To provide our customers with products of unsurpassed performance that last longer, need fewer repairs, and are produced at the lowest possible cost."
   - Updated in 1991: "Our collective mission is world class quality." Expands Maytag's belief in product quality to all aspects of operations.

2. **Objectives**
   - "To be profitability leader in industry for every product line Maytag manufactures." Selected profitability rather than market share.
   - "To be number one in total customer satisfaction."
   - "To grow the North American appliance business and become the third largest appliance manufacturer (in unit sales) in North America."
   - To increase profitable market share growth in North American appliance and floor care business, 6.5% return on sales, 10% return on assets, 20% return on equity, beat competition in satisfying customers, dealer, builder and endorser, move into third place in total units shipped per year.

3. **Strategies**
   - Global growth through acquisition and alliance with Bosch Siemens.
   - Differentiate brand names for competitive advantage.
   - Create synergy between companies, product improvement, investment in plant and equipment.

4. **Policies**
   - Cost reduction is secondary to high quality.
   - Promotion from within.
   - Slow, but sure R&D: Maytag slow to respond to changes in market.

II. STRATEGIC MANAGERS

A. Board of Directors

1. Fourteen members—eleven are outsiders.
2. Well-respected Americans, most on board since 1986 or earlier.
3. No international or marketing backgrounds.
4. Time for a change?

B. Top Management

1. Top management promoted from within Maytag Company.
2. Very experienced in the industry.
3. Responsible for current situation.
4. May be too parochial for global industry—may need new blood.

III. EXTERNAL ENVIRONMENT (EFAS see Exhibit 1)

A. Societal Environment

1. **Economic**
   a. Unstable economy but recession ending, consumer confidence growing—could increase spending for big ticket items like houses, cars, and appliances.
   b. Individual economies becoming interconnected into a world economy.
2. **Technological**
   a. Fuzzy logic technology being applied to sense and measure activities.
   b. Computers and information technology increasingly important.
3. **Political-Legal**
   a. NAFTA, European Union, other regional trade pacts opening doors to markets in Europe, Asia, Latin America that offer enormous potential.
   b. Breakdown of communism means less chance of world war.
   c. Environmentalism being reflected in laws on pollution and energy usage.
4. **Sociocultural**
   a. Developing nations desire goods seen on TV.
   b. Middle-aged baby boomers want attractive, high quality products, like BMWs and Maytag.
   c. Dual career couples increases need for labor-saving appliances, second cars, and day care.
   d. Divorce and career mobility means need for more houses and goods to fill them.

B. Task Environment

1. North American market is mature and extremely competitive—vigilant consumers demand high quality with low price in safe, environmentally sound products.
2. Industry going global as North American and European firms expand internationally.
3. *Rivalry High*: Whirlpool, AB Electrolux, GE have enormous resources and developing global presence.
4. *Buyers' Power Low*: Technology and materials used in manufacture can be sourced worldwide.
5. European design popular and consumer desire for technologically advanced appliances.
6. *Power of Other Stakeholders Medium*: Quality, safety, environmental regulations increasing.

7. *Distributors' Power High*: Super retailers more important, mom and pop dealers less.

8. *Substitutes unlikely.*

9. *Entry Barriers High*: New entrants unlikely; only large appliance firms can enter other markets.

IV. INTERNAL ENVIRONMENT (IFAS see Exhibit 2)

A. Corporate Structure

1. Divisional structure: appliance manufacturing and vending machines. Floor care managed separately.

2. Centralized major decisions by Newton corporate staff with a timeline of about three years.

B. Corporate Culture

1. Quality key ingredient—commitment to quality shared by executives and workers.

2. Much of corporate culture is based on founder F. L. Maytag's personal philosophy, including concern for quality, employees, local community, innovation, and performance.

3. Acquired companies, except for European, seem to accept dominance of Maytag culture.

C. Corporate Resources

1. **Marketing**

   a. Maytag brand lonely repairman advertising successful.

   b. Efforts focus on distribution—combining three sales forces into two, concentrating on major retailers. (Cost $95 million for this reconstructing.)

   c. Hoover's well-publicized marketing fiasco involving airline tickets.

2. **Finance** (see **Exhibits 4 and 5**)

   a. Revenues are up slightly, operating income is down significantly.

   b. Some key ratios are troubling, such as a 57% debt/asset ratio, 132% long-term debt/equity ratio. No room for more debt to grow company.

   c. Net income is 400% less than 1988, based on common-size income statements.

3. **R&D**

   a. Process-oriented with focus on manufacturing process and durability.

   b. Maytag is becoming a technology follower, taking too long to get product innovations to market (competitors put out more in last six months than prior two years combined), lagging in fuzzy logic and other technological areas.

4. **Operations**

   a. Maytag's core competence—continual improvement process kept it dominant in the U.S. market for many years.

   b. Plants are aging and may be losing competitiveness as rivals upgrade facilities.

5. **Human Resources**

   a. Traditionally very good relations with unions and employees.

   b. Labor relations increasingly strained, with two salary raise delays, and layoffs of 4,500 employees at Magic Chef.

   c. Unions express concern at new, more distant tone from Maytag Corporation.

6. **Information Systems**

   a. Not mentioned in case; Hoover fiasco in Europe suggests information systems need significant upgrading.

   b. Critical area where Maytag may be unwilling or unable to commit resources needed to stay competitive.

V. ANALYSIS OF STRATEGIC FACTORS

A. Situational Analysis (SWOT) (SFAS see **Exhibit 3**)

1. **Strengths**
   a. Quality Maytag culture.
   b. Maytag well-known and respected brand.
   c. Hoover's international orientation.
   d. Core competencies in process R&D and manufacturing.

2. **Weaknesses**
   a. Lacks financial resources of competitors.
   b. Poor global positioning; Hoover weak on continent.
   c. Product R&D and customer service innovation areas of serious weakness.
   d. Dependent on small dealers.

3. **Opportunities**
   a. Economic integration of European Community.
   b. Demographics favor quality.
   c. Trend to superstores.

4. **Threats**
   a. Trend to superstores.
   b. Aggressive rivals—Whirlpool and Electrolux.
   c. Japanese appliance companies—new entrants?

B. Review of Current Mission and Objectives

1. Current mission appears appropriate.
2. Some of the objectives are really goals and need to be quantified and given time horizons.

VI. STRATEGIC ALTERNATIVES AND RECOMMENDED STRATEGY

A. Strategic Alternatives

1. *Growth Through Concentric Diversification:* Acquire a company in a related industry like commercial appliances.
   a. *Pros:* Product/market synergy created by acquisition of related company.
   b. *Cons:* Maytag does not have the financial resources to play this game.

2. *Pause Strategy:* Consolidate various acquisitions to find economies and to encourage innovation among the business units.
   a. *Pros:* Maytag needs to get its financial house in order and get administrative control over its recent acquisitions.
   b. *Cons:* Unless it can grow through a stronger alliance with Bosch Siemens or some other backer, Maytag is a prime candidate for takeover because of its poor financial performance in recent years, and it is suffering from the initial reduction in efficiency inherent in acquisition strategy.

3. *Retrenchment:* Sell Hoover's foreign major home appliance businesses (Australia and the United Kingdom) to emphasize increasing market share in North America.
   a. *Pros:* Divesting Hoover improves bottom line and enables Maytag Corp. to focus on North America while Whirlpool, Electrolux, and GE are battling elsewhere.
   b. *Cons:* Maytag may be giving up its only opportunity to become a player in the coming global appliance industry.

B. Recommended Strategy

1. Recommend pause strategy, at least for a year, so Maytag can get a grip on its European operation and consolidate its companies in a more synergistic way.

2. Maytag quality must be maintained and continued shortage of operating capital will take its toll, so investment must be made in R&D.

3. Maytag may be able to make the Hoover U.K. investment work better since the recession is ending and the EU countries are closer to integrating than ever before.

4. Because it is only an average competitor, Maytag needs the Hoover link to Europe to provide a jumping off place for negotiations with Bosch-Siemens that could strengthen their alliance.

VII. IMPLEMENTATION

A. The only way to increase profitability in North America is to further involve Maytag with the superstore retailers, sure to anger the independent dealers, but necessary for Maytag to compete.

B. Board members with more global business experience should be recruited with an eye toward the future, especially with expertise in Asia and Latin America.

C. Product R&D needs to be improved, as does marketing, to get new products on line quickly.

VIII. EVALUATION AND CONTROL

A. MIS needs to be developed for speedier evaluation and control. While the question of control vs. autonomy is "under review," another Hoover fiasco may be brewing.

B. The acquired companies do not all share the Midwestern work ethic or the Maytag Corporation culture and Maytag's managers must inculcate these values into the employees of all acquired companies.

C. Systems should be developed to decide if the size and location of Maytag manufacturing plants is still correct and to plan for the future; industry analysis indicates that smaller automated plants may be more efficient now than in the past.

© Thomas L. Wheelen and J. David Hunger. Reprinted by permission of the authors.

Note: The following exhibits were originally attached in their entirety to this strategic audit, but for reasons of space only their titles are listed here:

Exhibit 1: EFAS Table

Exhibit 2: IFAS Table

Exhibit 3: SFAS Table

Exhibit 4: Ratio Analysis for five Years

Exhibit 5: Common-Size Income Statements

Notes

1. J. A. Sasseen, "Are Profits Shakier Than They Look?" *Business Week* (August 5, 1996), pp. 54–55.

2. M. Vanac, "What's a Novice Investor to Do?" *Des Moines Register* (November 30, 1997), p. 3G.

3. E. Iwata, "More Firms Falsify Revenue to Boost Stocks," *USA Today* (March 29, 2000), p. B1.

4. A. R. Sorking, "New Path on Mergers Could Contain Loopholes," *The (Ames, IA) Daily Tribune* (January 9, 2001), p. B7; "Firms Resist Effort to Unveil True Costs of Doing Business," *USA Today* (July 3, 2000), p. 10A.

5. M. S. Fridson, *Financial Statement Analysis* (New York: John Wiley & Sons, 1991), pp. 192–194.

6. D. H. Bangs, *Managing by the Numbers* (Dover, NH: Upstart Publications, 1992), pp. 106–107.

7. J. M. Laderman, "Earnings, Schmernings Look at the Cash," *Business Week* (July 24, 1989), pp. 56–57.

8. H. Greenberg, "EBITDA: Never Trust Anything That You Can't Pronounce," *Fortune* (June 22, 1998), pp. 192–194.

9. J. Warner, "21st Century Capitalism: Snapshot of the Next Century," *Business Week* (November 18, 1994), p. 194.

Glossary

80/20 rule A rule stating that one should monitor those 20% of the factors that determine 80% of the results. p. 259

absorptive capacity A firm's ability to value, assimilate, and utilize new external knowledge. p. 288

action plan A plan that states what actions are going to be taken, by whom, during what time frame, and with what expected results. p. 229

activity-based costing (ABC) An accounting method for allocating indirect and fixed costs to individual products or product lines based on the value-added activities going into that product. p. 245

adaptive mode A decision-making mode characterized by reactive solutions to existing problems rather than a proactive search for new opportunities. p. 19

advisory board A group of external business people who voluntarily meet periodically with the owners/managers of the firm to discuss strategic and other issues. p. 308

agency theory A theory which states that problems arise in corporations because the agents (top management) are not willing to bear responsibility for their decisions unless they own a substantial amount of stock in the corporation. p. 29

assessment center An approach to evaluate the suitability of a person for a position. p. 222

autonomous work teams A group of people who work together without a supervisor to plan, coordinate, and evaluate their own work. p. 97

balanced scorecard A measure that combines financial measures with operational measures of customer satisfaction, internal processes, and the corporation's innovation and improvement activities. p. 250

basic research and development (R&D) Research and development with focus on theoretical problem areas. p. 93

behavior control A control that specifies how something is to be done through policies, rules, standard operating procedures, and orders from a superior. p. 243

behavior substitution A phenomenon that occurs when people substitute activities that do not lead to goal accomplishment for activities that do lead to goal accomplishment because the wrong activities are being rewarded. p. 258

benchmarking The process of measuring products, services, and practices against those of competitors or companies recognized as industry leaders. p. 254

brainstorming The process of proposing ideas in a group without first mentally screening them. p. 72

budget A statement of a corporation's programs in terms of money required. p. 15

business model The mix of activities a company performs to deliver goods and services to customers. p. 304

business plan A written strategic plan for a new entrepreneurial venture. p. 306

Business Policy A previous name for strategic management; has a general management orientation and tends to look inward with concern for integrating the corporation's many functional activities. p. 2

Business Strategy A competitive and cooperative strategy at the business unit or product level that emphasizes improvement of the competitive position of a corporation's products or services in the specific industry or market segment served by that business unit. p. 13

cannibalize To replace popular products before they reach the end of their life cycle and become cash cows. p. 68

capability Something that a corporation can do exceedingly well, a key strength, a constituent skill. p. 165

capital budgeting The process of analyzing and ranking possible investments in terms of the additional outlays and additional receipts that will result from each investment. p. 92

cash cow A product that brings in far more money than is needed to maintain its market share. p. 152

categorical imperatives Kant's two principles to guide actions: A person's action is ethical only if that person is willing for that same action to be taken by everyone who is in a similar situation and a person should never treat another human being simply as a means but always as an end. p. 44

cellular organization A structure composed of cells (self-managing teams, autonomous business units, etc.) that can operate alone but can interact with other cells to produce a more potent and competent business mechanism. p. 207

center of gravity The part of the industry value chain that is most important to the company and the point where the company's greatest expertise and capabilities lay. p. 85

code of ethics A code that specifies how an organization expects its employees to behave while on the job. p. 43

codetermination The inclusion of a corporation's workers on its board of directors. p. 32

collusion The active cooperation of firms within an industry to reduce output and raise prices in order to get around the normal economic law of supply and demand. This practice is usually illegal. p. 126

common-size statements Income statements and balance sheets in which the dollar figures have been converted into percentages. p. 346

competitive intelligence A formal program of gathering information about a company's competitors. p. 70

competitive scope The breadth of a company's or a business unit's target market. p. 118

competitive strategy A strategy that states how a company or a business unit will compete in an industry. p. 117

complementor A company or an industry whose product works well with another industry's or firm's product and without which a product would lose much of its value. p. 64

concurrent engineering A process in which specialists from various functional areas work side-by-side rather than sequentially in an effort to design new products. p. 97

conglomerate structure A variant of the divisional structure, sometimes called a holding company. A conglomerate structure is typically an assemblage of legally independent firms (subsidiaries) operating under one corporate umbrella but controlled through the subsidiaries' boards of directors. p. 88

consolidated industry An industry in which a few large companies dominate. p. 122

constant dollars Dollars adjusted for inflation. p. 347

constraints on strategic management Characteristics peculiar to a not-for-profit organization that constrain its behavior and affect its strategic management. p. 329

continuous improvement A system developed by Japanese firms in which teams strive constantly to improve manufacturing processes. p. 172

cooperative strategies Strategies that involve working with other firms to gain competitive advantage within an industry. p. 126

core competency A corporate capability, something that a corporation can do exceedingly well. p. 82

corporate culture A collection of beliefs, expectations, and values learned and shared by a corporation's members and transmitted from one generation of employees to another. p. 89

corporate entrepreneurship Also called intrapreneurship; the creation of a new business within an existing organization. p. 291

corporate governance The relationship among the board of directors, top management, and shareholders in determining the direction and performance of a corporation. p. 26

corporate scenarios Pro forma balance sheets and income statements that forecast the effect that each alternative strategy will likely have on return on investment. p. 178

corporate stakeholders Groups that affect or are affected by the achievement of a firm's objectives. p. 40

corporate strategy A strategy that states a company's overall direction in terms of its general attitude toward growth and the management of its various business and product lines. p. 13

corporation A mechanism established to allow different parties to contribute capital, expertise, and labor for their mutual benefit. p. 26

cost focus A low-cost competitive strategy that concentrates on a particular buyer group or geographic market and attempts to serve only that niche. p. 119

cost leadership A low-cost competitive strategy that aims at the broad mass market. p. 118

cost proximity A process that involves keeping the higher price a company charges for higher quality close enough to that of the competition so that customers will see the extra quality as being worth the extra cost. p. 120

crisis of autonomy A time when people managing diversified product lines need more decision-making freedom than top management is willing to delegate to them. p. 200

crisis of control A time when business units act to optimize their own sales and profits without regard to the overall corporation. p. 200 *See also* suboptimization.

crisis of leadership A time when an entrepreneur is personally unable to manage a growing company. p. 200

cross-functional work team A work team composed of people from multiple functions. p. 97

defensive centralization A process in which top management of a not-for-profit retains all decision-making authority so that lower-level managers cannot take any actions to which the sponsors may object. p. 331

defensive tactic A tactic in which a company defends its current market. p. 125

Delphi technique A forecasting technique in which experts independently assess the probabilities of specified events. These assessments are combined and sent back to each expert for fine-tuning until agreement is reached. p. 72

devil's advocate An individual or a group assigned to identify the potential pitfalls and problems of a proposal. p. 183

dialectical inquiry A decision-making technique which requires that two proposals using different assumptions be generated for each alternative under consideration. p. 184

differentiation focus A differentiation competitive strategy that concentrates on a particular buyer group, product line segment, or geographic market. p. 119

differentiation strategy A strategy that involves providing unique and superior value to the buyer in terms of product quality, special features, or after-sale service. p. 118

distinctive competencies Capabilities of a firm that are superior to those of competitors. p. 82

divisional structure An organizational structure in which employees tend to be functional specialists organized according to product/market distinctions. p. 87

domain The suffix to a URL, such as .com, .gov, or .edu. p. 351

downsizing Planned elimination of positions or jobs. p. 222

due care The obligation of board members to closely monitor and evaluate top management. p. 27

durability The rate at which a firm's underlying resources and capabilities depreciate or become obsolete. p. 82

earnings per share (EPS) A calculation dividing net earnings by the number of shares of common stock issued. p. 246

EBITDA An acronym standing for earnings before interest, taxes, depreciation, and amortization. p. 347

economic value added (EVA) A shareholder value method of measuring corporate and divisional performance. EVA measures after-tax operating income minus the total annual cost of capital. p. 249

economies of scale A process in which unit costs are reduced by making large numbers of the same product. p. 97

economies of scope A process in which unit costs are reduced when the value chains of two separate products or services share activities, such as the same marketing channels or manufacturing facilities. p. 87

EFAS table External Factors Analysis Summary table, a table that organizes external factors into opportunities and threats and how well management is responding to these specific factors. p. 73

enterprise resource planning (ERP) software Software that unites all of a company's major business activities, from order processing to production, within a single family of software modules. p. 256

entrepreneur A person who initiates and manages a business undertaking and who assumes risk for the sake of a profit. p. 303

entrepreneurial mode A strategy made by one powerful individual in which the focus is on opportunities and problems are secondary. p. 18

entrepreneurial venture A new business whose primary goals are profitability and growth and that can be characterized by innovative strategic practices. p. 303

entry barrier An obstruction that makes it difficult for a company to enter an industry. p. 61

environmental scanning The monitoring, evaluation, and dissemination of information from the external and internal environments to key people within the corporation. p. 52

environmental uncertainty The degree of complexity plus the degree of change existing in an organization's external environment. p. 52

ethics The consensually accepted standards of behavior for an occupation, a trade, or a profession. p. 43

evaluation and control A process in which corporate activities and performance results are monitored so that actual performance can be compared with desired performance. p. 16

executive leadership The directing of activities toward the accomplishment of corporate objectives. p. 36

executive succession The process of grooming and replacing a key top manager. p. 221

executive type An individual with a particular mix of skills and experiences. p. 220

exit barrier An obstruction that keeps a company from leaving an industry. p. 62

experience curve A conceptual framework which states that unit production costs decline by some fixed percentage each time the total accumulated volume of production in units doubles. p. 96

expert opinion A nonquantitative forecasting technique in which experts in a particular area attempt to forecast likely developments. p. 72

explicit knowledge Knowledge that can be easily articulated and communicated. p. 83

external environment Forces outside an organization that are not typically within the short-run control of top management. p. 9

external strategic factors Environmental trends with both high probability of occurrence and high probability of impact on the corporation. p. 60

extranet An information network within an organization that is available to key suppliers and customers. p. 100

extrapolation A forecasting technique that extends present trends into the future. p. 72

financial leverage The ratio of total debt to total assets. p. 92

financial strategy A functional strategy to make the best use of corporate monetary assets. p. 169

first mover The first company to manufacture and sell a new product or service. p. 124

flexible manufacturing A type of manufacturing that permits the low-volume output of custom-tailored products at relatively low unit costs through economies of scope. p. 97

fragmented industry An industry in which no firm has large market share and each firm serves only a small piece of the total market. p. 64

free cash flow The amount of money a new owner can take out of a firm without harming the business. p. 347

functional strategy An approach taken by a functional area to achieve corporate and business unit objectives and strategies by maximizing resource productivity. This approach is concerned with developing and nurturing a distinctive competence to provide a company or business unit with a competitive advantage. p. 13

functional structure An organizational structure in which employees tend to be specialists in the business functions important to that industry, such as manufacturing, sales, or finance. p. 87

geographic-area structure A structure that allows a multinational corporation to tailor products to regional differences and to achieve regional coordination. p. 211

global industry An industry in which a company manufactures and sells the same products, with only minor adjustments for individual countries around the world. p. 65

goal An open-ended statement of what one wants to accomplish, with no quantification of what is to be achieved and no time criteria for completion. p. 12

goal displacement Confusion of means with ends, which occurs when activities originally intended to help managers attain corporate objectives become ends in themselves or are adapted to meet ends other than those for which they were intended. p. 258

gross domestic product (GDP) A measure of the total output of goods and services within a country's borders. p. 347

hierarchy of strategies A nesting of strategies by level from corporate to business to functional, so that they complement and support one another. p. 13

horizontal growth A corporate growth concentration strategy that involves expanding the firm's products into other geographic locations and/or increasing the range of products and services offered to current markets. p. 142

horizontal integration The degree to which a firm operates in multiple geographic locations at the same point in an industry's value chain. p. 142

horizontal strategy A corporate parenting strategy that cuts across business unit boundaries to build synergy across business units and to improve the competitive position of one or more business units. p. 159

human resource management (HRM) strategy A functional strategy that makes the best use of corporate human assets. p. 175

hypercompetition An industry situation in which the frequency, boldness, and aggressiveness of dynamic movement by the players accelerates to create a condition of constant disequilibrium and change. p. 68

IFAS table Internal Factor Analysis Summary table, a table that organizes internal factors into strengths and weaknesses and how well management is responding to these specific factors. p. 101

imitability The rate at which a firm's underlying resources and capabilities can be duplicated by others. p. 82

index of R&D effectiveness An index that is calculated by dividing the percentage of total revenue spent on research and development into new product profitability. p. 294

index of sustainable growth A calculation that shows how much of the growth rate of sales can be sustained by internally generated funds. p. 346

individual rights approach An approach which proposes that human beings have certain fundamental rights that should be respected in all decisions. p. 44

industry A group of firms that produce a similar product or service. p. 60

industry analysis An in-depth examination of key factors within a corporation's task environment. p. 53

industry matrix A chart that summarizes the key success factors within a particular industry. p. 69

industry scenario A forecasted description of an industry's likely future. p. 72

information systems strategy A functional strategy that uses information systems technology to provide competitive advantage. p. 176

input control A control that specifies resources, such as knowledge, skills, abilities, values, and motives of employees. p. 243

inside director An officer or executive employed by a corporation who serves on that company's board of directors; also called management director. p. 29

institution theory A theory which proposes that organizations adapt to changing conditions by imitating other successful organizations. p. 7

integration A process that involves a relatively balanced give-and-take of cultural and managerial practices between merger partners, with no strong imposition of cultural change on either company. p. 227

interlocking directorate A conditions that occurs when two firms share a director or when an executive of one firm sits on the board of a second firm. p. 33

internal environment Variables within an organization that are not usually within the short-run control of top management. p. 9

internal strategic factors Strengths (core competencies) and weaknesses that are likely to determine whether a firm will be able to take advantage of opportunities while avoiding threats. p. 81

intranet An information network within an organization that also has access to the Internet. p. 100

investment center A unit in which performance is measured in terms of the difference between the unit's resources and its services or products. p. 253

issues priority matrix A chart that ranks the probability of occurrence versus the probable impact on the corporation of developments in the external environment. p. 59

job characteristics model An approach to job design that is based on the belief that tasks can be described in terms of certain objective characteristics and that those characteristics affect employee motivation. p. 209

job design The design of individual tasks in an attempt to make them more relevant to the company and to the employee. p. 208

job enlargement Combining tasks to give a worker more of the same type of duties to perform. p. 208

job enrichment Altering jobs by giving the worker more autonomy and control over activities.p. 208

job rotation Moving workers through several jobs to increase variety. p. 208

joint venture An independent business entity created by two or more companies in a strategic alliance. p. 128

justice approach An approach which proposes that decision makers be equitable, fair, and impartial in the distribution of costs and benefits to individuals and groups. p. 44

just-in-time (JIT) A purchasing concept in which parts arrive at the plant just when they are needed rather than being kept in inventories. p. 174

key performance measures Essential measures for achieving a desired strategic option. p. 251

key success factors Variables that significantly affect the overall competitive position of a company within a particular industry. p. 69

late movers The later companies to manufacture and sell a new product or service. p. 124

law A formal code that permits or forbids certain behaviors. p. 43

lead director An outside director who coordinates the annual evaluation of the CEO. p. 34

lead user A customer who is ahead of market trends and has needs that go beyond those of the average user. p. 281

lead To provide direction to employees to use their abilities and skills most effectively and efficiently to achieve organizational objectives. p. 225

learning organization An organization that is skilled at creating, acquiring, and

transferring knowledge and at modifying its behavior to reflect new knowledge and insights. p. 8

level of moral development One of Kohlberg's proposed three levels of moral development through which a person progresses: the preconventional level, the conventional level, and the principled level. p. 42

leveraged buy out An acquisition in which a company is acquired in a transaction financed largely by debt—usually obtained from a third party, such as an insurance company or an investment banker. p. 170

licensing arrangement An agreement in which the licensing firm grants rights to another firm in another country or market to produce and/or sell a product. p. 129

lifestyle company A small business in which the firm is purely an extension of the owner's lifestyle. p. 314

liquidation The termination of a firm in which all its assets are sold. p. 150

logical incrementalism A decision-making mode that can be viewed as a synthesis of planning, adaptive, and entrepreneurial modes. p. 19

logistics strategy A functional strategy that deals with the flow of products into and out of the manufacturing process. p. 174

long-term evaluation method A method in which managers are compensated for achieving objectives set over a multiyear period. p. 260

long-term orientation The extent to which society is oriented toward the long term versus the short term. p. 233

lower cost strategy A strategy in which a company or business unit designs, produces, and markets a comparable product more efficiently than its competitors. p. 118

management audit A technique used to evaluate corporate activities. p. 252

management by objectives (MBO) An organizationwide approach to ensuring purposeful action toward desired objectives. p. 231

management contracts Agreements through which a corporation uses some of its personnel to assist a firm in another country for a specified fee and period of time. p. 146

market development A marketing functional strategy in which a company or business unit captures a larger share of an existing market for current products through market penetration or develops new markets for current products. p. 168

market location tactics Tactics that determine where a company or business unit will compete. p. 125

market position Refers to the selection of specific areas for marketing concentration and can be expressed in terms of market, product, and geographical locations. p. 90

market research A means of obtaining new product ideas by surveying current or potential users regarding what they would like in a new product. p. 282

market segmentation The division of a market into segments to identify available niches. p. 90

market value added (MVA) The difference between the market value of a corporation and the capital contributed by shareholders and lenders. p. 250

marketing mix The particular combination of key variables (product, place, promotion, and price) that can be used to affect demand and to gain competitive advantage. p. 90

marketing strategy A functional strategy that deals with pricing, selling, and distributing a product. p. 168

mass customization The low-cost production of individually customized goods and services. p. 97

mass production A system in which employees work on narrowly defined, repetitive tasks under close supervision in a bureaucratic and hierarchical structure to produce a large amount of low-cost, standard goods and services. p. 172

matrix of change A chart that compares target practices (new programs) with existing practices (current activities). p. 194

matrix structure A structure in which functional and product forms are combined simultaneously at the same level of the organization. p. 204

mission The purpose or reason for an organization's existence. p. 10

mission statement A statement that defines the fundamental, unique purpose that sets a company apart from other firms of its type and identifies the scope of the company's operations in terms of products offered and markets served. pp. 10–11

modular manufacturing A system in which pre-assembled subassemblies are delivered as they are needed to a company's assembly-line workers, who quickly piece the modules together into finished products. p. 173

moral relativism A theory which proposes that morality is relative to some personal, social, or cultural standard, that there is no method for deciding whether one decision is better than another. p. 42

morality Precepts of personal behavior that are based on religious or philosophical grounds. p. 43

multidomestic industry An industry in which companies tailor their products to the specific needs of consumers in a particular country. p. 64

multinational corporation (MNC) A company that has significant assets and activities in multiple countries. p. 56

multiple sourcing A purchasing strategy in which a company orders a particular part from several vendors. p. 173

mutual service consortium A partnership of similar companies in similar industries that pool their resources to gain a benefit that is too expensive to develop alone. p. 128

net present value A calculation of the value of a project that is made by predicting the project's payouts, adjusting them for risk, and subtracting the amount invested. p. 181

network structure An organization (virtual organization) that outsources most of its business functions. p. 206

new entrants Businesses entering an industry that typically bring new capacity to an industry, a desire to gain market share, and substantial resources. p. 61

no-change strategy A decision to do nothing new, to continue current operations and policies for the foreseeable future. p. 147

not-for-profit organizations Private nonprofit corporations and public governmental units or agencies. p. 325

objectives The end results of planned activity, which are quantified and have time horizons. p. 12

offensive tactic A tactic that calls for competing in an established competitor's current market location. p. 125

operating budget A budget for a business unit that is approved by top management during strategy formulation and implementation. p. 252

operating cash flow The amount of money generated by a company before the costs of financing and taxes are figured. p. 347

operating leverage The impact of a specific change in sales volume on net operating income. p. 96

operations strategy A functional strategy that determines how and where a product or service is to be manufactured, the level of vertical integration in the production process, and the deployment of physical resources. p. 171

organization slack Unused resources within an organization. p. 139

organizational analysis Internal scanning concerned with identifying an organization's strengths and weaknesses. p. 81

organizational life cycle How organizations grow, develop, and eventually decline. p. 201

organizational structure The formal setup of a business corporation's value chain components in terms of work flow, communication channels, and hierarchy. p. 87

output control A control that specifies what is to be accomplished by focusing on the end result of the behaviors through the use of objectives and performance targets. p. 243

outside directors Members of a board of directors who are not employees of the board's corporation; also called nonmanagement directors. p. 29

outsourcing A process in which resources are purchased from others through long-term contracts instead of being made within the company. p. 142

parallel sourcing A process in which two suppliers are the sole suppliers of two different parts, but they are also backup suppliers for each other's parts. p. 174

parenting-fit matrix A summary of various judgments regarding corporate/business unit fit for a corporation as a whole. p. 157

patterns of influence A concept stating that influence in strategic management derives from a not-for-profit organization's sources of revenue. p. 327

pause/proceed with caution strategy A corporate strategy in which nothing new is attempted; an opportunity to rest before continuing a growth or retrenchment strategy. p. 147

penetration pricing A marketing strategy to hasten market development that offers a pioneer the opportunity to use the experience curve to gain market share. p. 169

performance The end result of activities, actual outcomes of a strategic management process. p. 16

performance appraisal system A system to systematically evaluate employee performance and promotion potential. p. 221

periodic statistical reports Reports summarizing data on key factors such as the number of new customer contracts, volume of received orders, and productivity figures. p. 252

pioneer p. 124 *See* first mover.

piracy The making and selling counterfeit copies of well-known name-brand products. p. 255

planning mode A decision-making mode that involves the systematic gathering of appropriate information for situation analysis, the generation of feasible alternative strategies, and the rational selection of the most appropriate strategy. p. 19

policy A broad guideline for decision making that links the formulation of strategy with its implementation. p. 14

political strategy A strategy to influence a corporation's stakeholders. p. 181

population ecology A theory which proposes that once an organization is successfully established in a particular environmental niche, it is unable to adapt to changing conditions. p. 7

portfolio analysis An approach to corporate strategy in which top management views its product lines and business units as a series of investments from which it expects a profitable return. p. 151

pressure-cooker crisis A situation that exists when employees in collaborative organizations eventually grow emotionally and physically exhausted from the intensity of teamwork and the heavy pressure for innovative solutions. p. 201

prime interest rate The rate of interest banks charge on their lowest-risk loans. p. 347

privatization The selling of state-owned enterprises to private individuals or corporations or the hiring of a private business to provide services previously offered by a state agency. p. 326

pro forma financial statements Financial statements projected into the future. p. 178

procedures A list of sequential steps or techniques that describe in detail how a particular task or job is to be done. Procedures detail the various activities that must be carried out in order to complete a corporation's programs. p. 15

process innovations Improvements to the making and selling of current products. p. 287

product champion A person who generates a new idea and supports it through many organizational obstacles. p. 291

product development A marketing strategy in which a company or unit develops new products for existing markets or develops new products for new markets. p. 169

product life cycle A graph showing time plotted against dollar sales of a product as it moves from introduction through growth and maturity to decline. p. 90

product R&D Research and development concerned with product or product-packaging improvements. p. 93

product/market evolution matrix A table in which products are plotted in terms of their competitive positions and their stages of product/market evolution. p. 289

product-group structure A structure of a multinational corporation that enables the company to introduce and manage a similar line of products around the world. p. 211

production sharing The process of combining the higher labor skills and technology available in developed countries with the lower-cost labor available in developing countries. p. 145

profit center A unit's performance, measured in terms of the difference between revenues and expenditures. p. 253

profit strategy A strategy that artificially supports profits by reducing investment and short-term discretionary expenditures. p. 147

program A statement of the activities or steps needed to accomplish a single-use plan in strategy implementation. p. 15

propitious niche A portion of a market that is so well suited to a firm's internal and external environment that other corporations are not likely to challenge or dislodge it. p. 112

public or collective goods Certain goods that are available to all in a society that profit-making firms cannot or will not provide. p. 325

pull strategy A marketing strategy in which advertising pulls the products through the distribution channels. p. 169

purchasing power parity (PPP) A measure of the cost, in dollars, of the U.S.-produced equivalent volume of goods that another nation's economy produces. p. 58

purchasing strategy A functional strategy that deals with obtaining the raw materials, parts, and supplies needed to perform the operations function. p. 173

push strategy A marketing strategy in which a large amount of money is spent on trade promotion in order to gain or hold shelf space in retail outlets. p. 169

quality of work life A concept that emphasizes improving the human dimension of work to improve employee satisfaction and existing union relations. p. 98

quasi-integration A type of vertical growth/integration in which a company does not make any of its key supplies but purchases most of its requirements from outside suppliers that are under its partial control. p. 141

question marks New products that have the potential for success and need a lot of cash for development. Also called problem children or wildcats. p. 151

R&D intensity A company's spending on research and development as a percentage of sales revenue. p. 92

R&D mix The balance of basic, product, and process research and development. p. 93

R&D strategy A functional strategy that deals with product and process innovation. p. 170

ratio analysis The calculation of ratios from data in financial statements to identify possible strengths or weaknesses. p. 342

real options An approach to new project investment when the future is highly uncertain. p. 181

red tape crisis A crisis that occurs when a corporation has grown too large and complex to be managed through formal programs. p. 201

reengineering The radical redesign of business processes to achieve major gains in cost, service, or time. p. 207

repatriation of profits The transfer of profits from a foreign subsidiary to a corporation's headquarters. p. 53

replicability The ability of competitors to duplicate resources and imitate another firm's success. p. 83

resource An asset, a competency, a process, a skill, or knowledge that is controlled by a corporation. p. 81

responsibility center A unit that is isolated so that it can be evaluated separately from the rest of the corporation. p. 252

retrenchment strategies Corporate strategies to reduce a company's level of activities and to return it to profitability. p. 138

return on equity (ROE) A measure of performance that is calculated by dividing net income by total equity. p. 247

return on investment (ROI) A measure of performance that is calculated by dividing net income before taxes by total assets. p. 246

revenue center A responsibility center in which production, usually in terms of unit or dollar sales, is measured without consideration of resource costs (e.g., salaries). p. 252

reverse engineering Taking apart a competitor's product in order to find out how it works. p. 82

risk A measure of the probability that one strategy will be effective, the amount of assets the corporation must allocate to that strategy, and the length of time the assets will be unavailable. p. 180

scenario writing A forecasting technique in which focused descriptions of different likely futures are presented in a narrative fashion. p. 72

SFAS matrix Strategic Factors Analysis Summary matrix, a chart that summarizes an organization's strategic factors by combining the external factors from an EFAS table with the internal factors from an IFAS table. p. 110

shareholder value The present value of the anticipated future stream of cash flows from a business plus the value of the company if it were liquidated. p. 248

simple structure A structure for new entrepreneurial firms in which the employees tend to be generalists and jacks-of-all-trades. p. 87

skim pricing A marketing strategy in which a company charges a high price while a product is novel and competitors are few. p. 169

social responsibility The ethical and discretionary responsibilities a corporation owes its stakeholders. p. 39

societal environment Economic, technological, political–legal, and sociocultural environmental forces that do not directly touch on the short-run activities of an organization but influence its long-run decisions. p. 52

sole sourcing Relying on only one supplier for a particular part. p. 174

sources of innovation Drucker's proposed seven sources of new ideas that should be monitored by those interested in starting entrepreneurial ventures. p. 310

sponsor A department manager who recognizes the value of a new idea, helps obtain funding to develop the innovation, and facilitates the implementation of the innovation. p. 291

stability strategies Corporate strategies to make no change to the company's current direction or activities. p. 138

staffing Human resource management priorities and use of personnel. p. 218

stages of corporate development A pattern of structural development that corporations follow as they grow and expand. p. 198

stages of international development The stages through which international corporations evolve in their relationships with widely dispersed geographic markets and the manner in which they structure their operations and programs. p. 210

stages of new product development The stages of getting a new innovation into the marketplace. p. 290

staggered board A board on which directors serve terms of more than one year so that only a portion of the board of directors stands for election each year. p. 34

stakeholders See corporate stakeholders.

stakeholder measures Various criteria used by each stakeholder category to determine how well a corporation is performing. p. 247

stakeholder priority matrix A chart that categorizes stakeholders in terms of their interest in a corporation's activities and their relative power to influence the corporation's activities. p. 181

standard cost center A responsibility center that is primarily used to evaluate the performance of manufacturing facilities. p. 252

standard operating procedures (SOPs) Plans that detail the various activities that must be carried out to complete a corporation's programs. p. 196

stars Market leaders that are able to generate enough cash to maintain their high shares of the market. p. 151

statistical modeling A quantitative technique that attempts to discover causal or explanatory factors that link two or more time series together. p. 72

steering controls Measures of variables that influence future profitability. p. 243

stewardship theory A theory which suggests that executives tend to be more motivated to act in the best interests of the corporation than for their own self-interests. p. 30

strategic alliance A partnership of two or more corporations or business units to achieve strategically significant objectives that are mutually beneficial. p. 127

strategic audit A checklist of questions by area or issue that enables a systematic analysis of various corporate functions and activities. pp. 252, 262

strategic business unit (SBU) A division or group of divisions composed of independent product-market segments that are given primary authority for the management of their own functions. p. 87

strategic choice The evaluation of strategies and selection of the best alternative. p. 183

strategic choice perspective A theory which proposes that organizations adapt to a changing environment and have the opportunity and power to reshape their environment. p. 8

strategic decisions Decisions that deal with the long-run future of an entire organization and are rare, consequential, and directive. p. 18

strategic factors External and internal factors that determine the future of a corporation. p. 9

strategic group A set of business units or firms that pursue similar strategies and have similar resources. p. 66

strategic inflection point A point in time when a major change takes place in an industry due to the introduction of new technologies, a change in regulatory environment, a change in customer's values, or a change in what customers prefer. p. 17

strategic management A set of managerial decisions and actions that determine the long-run performance of a corporation. p. 2

strategic myopia The willingness to reject unfamiliar as well as negative information. p. 59

strategic piggybacking The development of a new activity for a not-for-profit organization that would generate the funds needed to make up the difference between revenues and expenses. p. 332

strategic planning staff A group of people charged with supporting both top management and business units in the strategic planning process. p. 37

strategic rollup A means of consolidating a fragmented industry in which an entrepreneur acquires hundreds of owner-operated small businesses, resulting in a large firm with economies of scale. p. 122

strategic type A category of firms based on a common strategic orientation and a combination of structure, culture, and processes that are consistent with that strategy. p. 66

strategic vision A description of what a company is capable of becoming. p. 36

strategic window A unique market opportunity that is available only for a particular time. p. 112

strategic-funds method An evaluation method that encourages executives to look at development expenses as being different from expenses required for current operations. p. 260

strategy A comprehensive plan that states how a corporation will achieve its mission and objectives. p. 13

strategy formulation Development of long-range plans for the effective management of environmental opportunities and threats in light of corporate strengths and weaknesses. p. 10

strategy implementation A process by which strategies and policies are put into action through the development of programs, budgets, and procedures. p. 15

strategy shadow committee An approach for generating a series of strategic alternatives via a committee that is composed of employees at least two echelons below the executive-level strategy committee. p. 184

structure *See* organizational structure.

stuck in the middle A term that refers to a situation in which a company or business unit has not achieved a generic competitive strategy and has no competitive advantage and is therefore doomed to below-average performance. p. 120

suboptimization A phenomenon in which a unit optimizes its goal accomplishment to the detriment of the organization as a whole. p. 259

substitute products Products that appear to be different but can satisfy the same need as other products. p. 62

supply chain management The formation of networks for sourcing raw materials, manufacturing products or creating services, storing and distributing goods, and delivering goods or services to customers and consumers. p. 102

support activities Activities which ensure that the primary value-chain activities operate effectively and efficiently. p. 86

SWOT analysis Analysis that involves the strengths, weaknesses, opportunities, and threats that may be strategic factors for a specific company. p. 9

synergy A concept which states that the whole is greater than the sum of its parts, that two units will achieve more together than they could separately. p. 143

tacit knowledge Knowledge that is not easily communicated because it is deeply rooted in employee experience or in a corporation's culture. p. 83

taper integration A type of vertical integration in which a firm internally produces less than half of its own requirements and buys the rest from outside suppliers. p. 141

task environment The part of the business environment that includes the elements or groups that directly affect the corporation and, in turn, are affected by it. p. 53

technological competence A corporation's proficiency in managing research personnel and integrating their innovations into its day-to-day operations. p. 92

technological discontinuity The displacement of one technology by another. p. 94

technology transfer The process of taking a new technology from the laboratory to the marketplace. p. 93

time to market The time from inception to profitability of a new product. p. 284

timing tactic A tactic that determines when a business will enter a market with a new product. p. 124

total quality management (TQM) An operational philosophy that is committed to customer satisfaction and continuous improvement. p. 232

TOWS matrix A chart that illustrates how the external opportunities and threats facing a corporation can be matched with that company's internal strengths and weaknesses to result in four sets of strategic alternatives. p. 114

tracking stock A type of common stock that is tied to one portion of a corporation's business. p. 170

transaction cost economics A theory which proposes that vertical integration is more efficient than contracting for goods and services in the marketplace when the transaction costs of buying goods on the open market become too great. p. 140

transfer pricing A practice in which one unit can charge a transfer price for each product it sells to a different unit within a company. p. 253

transfer pricing, international A practice that involves selling goods from one unit to another unit (in a different country) within the same multinational corporation in order to minimize taxes. p. 255

transferability The ability of competitors to gather the resources and capabilities necessary to support a competitive challenge. p. 83

transparency The speed with which other firms can understand the relationship of resources and capabilities supporting a successful firm's strategy. p. 82

Triad The three developed markets of Japan, North America, and Western Europe, which form a single market with common needs. p. 56

triggering event Something that acts as a stimulus for a change in strategy. p. 17

turnaround specialist A manager who is brought into a weak company to salvage that company in a relatively attractive industry. p. 220

turnaround strategy A plan that emphasizes the improvement of operational efficiency when a corporation's problems are pervasive but not yet critical. p. 148

turnkey operations Contracts for the construction of operating facilities in exchange for a fee. p. 145

utilitarian approach A theory which proposes that actions and plans should be judged by their consequences. p. 43

value chain A linked set of value-creating activities that begins with basic raw materials coming from suppliers and ends with distributors getting the final goods into the hands of the ultimate consumer. p. 84

value trap businesses Units that fit well with parenting opportunities but are misfits with the parent's understanding of the units' strategic factors. p. 158

value-chain partnership A strategic alliance in which one company or unit forms a long-term arrangement with a key supplier or distributor for mutual advantage. p. 129

vertical growth A corporate growth strategy in which a firm takes over a function previously provided by a supplier or distributor. p. 139

vertical integration The degree to which a firm operates in multiple locations on an industry's value chain, from extracting raw materials to retailing. p. 140

virtual organization An organizational structure that is composed of a series of project groups or collaborations linked by changing nonhierarchical, cobweb-like networks. p. 206

virtual teams Groups of geographically and/or organizationally dispersed co-workers that are assembled using a combination of telecommunications and information technologies to accomplish an organizational task. p. 103

VRIO framework Barney's proposed analysis to evaluate a firm's key resources in terms of value, rareness, imitability, and organization. p. 81

weighted-factor method A method that is appropriate for measuring and rewarding the performance of top SBU managers and group-level executives when performance factors and their importance vary from one SBU to another. p. 260

whistleblower An employee who reports questionable behavior by other employees of the same company to a higher authority or to the media. p. 43

z-value A formula that combines five ratios by weighting them according to their importance to a corporation's financial strength to predict the likelihood of bankruptcy. p. 346

Name Index

AA & Co. (Arthur Anderson), 40
ABB Asea Brown Boveri AG, 89, 90. *See also* Asea Brown Boveri (ABB)
ABC, 177
Abdelsamad, Moustafa H., 345n
AB Electrolux. *See* Electrolux AB
Abraham, S. C., 23n, 189n
A. C. Nielsen Co. *See* Nielsen, A. C., Co.
Accrue, 185
Ace Hardware, 175
Ackelsberg, R., 322n
Adidas, 60
Admiral, 228, 229
Aeppel, T., 273n
Aerospatiale of France, 127
Affrim, H., 273n
Agle, B. R., 43n
Ahrader, R. C., 322n
Ainuddin, R., 273n
Airbus, 61, 77, 181
Aircraft Engine Group (GE), 219
Akerson, D., 183
Alamo Rent-A-Car, 119
Alcatel-Alsthom NV, 90
Alchemy, 150
Aldred, D. and M., 51–52
Aldrich, H., 24n
Alexander, J. A., 338n
Alexander, K., 299n
Alexander, L. D., 215n
Alexander, M., 156, 157, 158, 162n, 163n
Aley, J., 321n
Allen, J. T., 348n
Alley, J., 134n
AlliedSignal, 139, 221, 341
Almanac of Business and Industrial Financial Ratios, 358
Almeida, P., 299n
Alpert, M., 321
Alta Vista, 75, 352
Altman, 346
Amabile, T. M., 239n
Amason, A. C., 189n
Amazon.com, 22, 128, 131, 185, 248, 320
Amburgey, T. L., 215n
Amerco, 264
American Airlines, 5, 77, 80, 81, 143
American Cancer Society, 333
American Can Company, 65
American Cyanamid, 211
American Express, 228, 301

American Heart Association, 324
American Hospital Supply (AHS), 100
American Management Association, 167, 262
American Productivity & Quality Center, 74, 254
American Society of Industrial Security, 71
American Standard, 285
America Online (AOL), 18, 150
Amidon, D. M., 143, 272n, 273n
Amoco, 85
Amoco Chemical, 174
Amodio, Mark, 192
Amram, M., 188n
AMR Corporation, 143
AMR Research, 6
Amy's Bread, 132
Anchor Steam, 310
Andersen, T. J., 23n
Anderson, C. A., 162n, 182n, 189n
Andrews, K. Z., 135n, 272n, 300n
Andriesen, F., 322n
Angara, 186
Angwin, D., 188n
Anheuser-Busch, 125, 127, 129, 144, 184, 253
Annual Report Gallery, 353
Annual Statement Studies, 353
Annuncio, 185
Ansoff, H. I., 78n
Anterasian, C., 163n
Apple Computer, 13, 36, 62, 93, 119, 149, 166, 201, 253, 257, 283
Applegate, J., 323n
Apria Healthcare, 29
Archer Daniels Midland (ADM), 127
Argus Systems Group, 294, 295
Aristotle, 184
Arlow, P., 41n, 322n
Armenakis, A. A., 239n
Arm & Hammer, 112, 159, 164–165, 188
Armstrong, L., 273n
Arndt, M., 39n
Aronloff, C. E., 322n, 323n
Arthur D. Little, Inc., 65, 283
Art Technology Group, 186
Ascarelli, S., 273n
Ascher, K., 338n
Asda Group, 144
Asea Brown Boveri (ABB), 211
Ashcroft, Michael, 26
Ashkenas, R. N., 239n

Ashman, D. P., 189n
Associated Consultants International, 65
Association of South East Asian Nations (ASEAN), 6
AT&T, 125, 136–137, 166, 170, 222, 228–229, 248, 279
AT&T Cable Services, 137
AT&T Wireless, 170
Atkins, T., 323n
Atwater, H. B., 155
Aupperle, K. E., 39n, 105n
Automotive Resources, 255
Avakian, P. N., 78n
Avis, 217
Avon Products, 21, 71, 165, 176
Axion, 169

Baan, 256
Babineck, M., 104n
Bachman, J., 105n
Bachmann Industries, 203
Bacon, D. C., 339n
Baden-Fuller, C. W. F., 78n, 215n
BAE Systems, 131
Bagley, C., 311, 322n
Bain & Company, 4, 221, 254
Baird, I. S., 24n
Baker, S., 299n
Baker, W. H., 321n
Baldwin, T. T., 24n, 239n
Baldwin Locomotive, 52
Baldwin-United, 203
Balfour, F., 255n
Balkin, D. B., 273n
Bamford, C. E., 322n
Banbury, C., 214
Bangs, D. H., 366n
Banker, R. D., 188n
Bankers Trust, 221, 223
Baptist Health Systems (Kansas City), 333
Baptist Hospital (Nashville), 333
Barkema, H., 162n
Barker, R., 248n
Barnes, F. C., 272n
Barnes and Noble, 22
Barnett, W. P., 215n
Barnevik, P., 90
Barney, J. B., 81, 104n, 105n, 135n, 188n, 322n
Barrett, A., 239n
Barrett, M., 5

Bartholomew, D., 105n
Bartlett, C. A., 216n
Baucus, D. A., 38n
Baucus, M. S., 38n
Bauerschmidt, A., 322n
Baum, J. A. C., 24n, 32n
Bay Networks, 289
Beamish, P. W., 135n, 162n
Bean, L. L., 254
Beaver, G., 34n
Bechtel Corporation, 235
Bechtel Group, Inc., 21
Bechtel Systems & Infrastructure (BSII), 235
Beckstead, S. M., 300n
Bedeian, A. G., 239n
Begun, J. W., 339n
Behling, O. C., 240n
BellCore, 294
Bell Labs, 293
Bell South, 136
Belluzzo, Richard, 293
Benetton, 206
Ben & Jerry's Homemade Inc., 39
Beresford, L., 163n, 312n
Bergh, D. D., 162n
Berkeley, S., 45n
Berkshire Hathaway, 264
Berle, A. A., Jr., 30n
Berman, Joshua, 26
Berners-Lee, T., 336
Berry, M., 322n
Best Buy, 69
Bestfoods Asia Ltd., 255
Bettis, R. A., 78n, 163n
Beverland, M., 322n
Bewrnstein, A., 105n
Beyer, J. M., 78n
B. F. Goodrich, 293
Bianchi, A., 322n
Bianco, A., 239n
Bierly, P. E., III, 104n
Bigness, J., 188n
Bijur, P., 212
Birkinshaw, J., 299n
Birley, S., 322n
Biz, 169
Black, J. S., 224, 239n, 240n
Blackburn, V. L., 321n
Black Entertainment Television, Inc. (BET), 310
Blackhat, 295
Blanning, R., 24n
Blaze Software, 186
Bleakley, F. R., 188n
Bleeke, J., 135n
Blodgett, L. L., 135n
Bloomberg, 356
Blumberg, P., 236
BMW (Bayerische Motoren Werke AG), 22, 148, 150, 282

Boardman, B., 235
Body Shop, The, 36, 342
Boeing, 7, 13, 61, 77, 97, 127, 131, 206
Boeker, W., 163n, 239n
Boltz, P. W., 348n
Bond, M. H., 240n
Boo.com, 203
Booz-Allen & Hamilton, 5
Boroughs, D. L., 105n
Bose Corporation, 174
Boston Consulting Group, 3, 151
Boston Pops Orchestra, 334
Boston Symphony, 334
Boulton, W. R., 321n
Bower, J. L., 36n, 299n
Bowers, B., 321n
Bowles, J., 24n
Boyd, B. K., 78n
BP Amoco, 45, 140
Bracker, J. S., 321n
Bradford, M., 272n
Brady, A., 299n
Brady, D., 189n, 339
Brady Bunch, The, 56
Brancato, C. K., 272n, 273n
Brellis, M., 104n
Bremner, B., 135n
Bresser, R. F., 23n
Brewer, P. C., 272n
Bridgestone, 131, 145
Brimelow, P., 188n, 348n
Bristol Myers Squibb, 221
British Aerospace, 127
British Airways, 5, 326
British Petroleum, 85, 342
Broadbase Software, 185
BroadVision, 186
Brodsky, N., 121, 134n
Brouthers, K. D., 322n
Brown, D., 190, 274
Brown, T., 134n
Brull, S. V., 240n
Brunswick, 55
Brusger, J., 50, 106, 190, 274
Bruton, G. D., 239n, 322n
Bryan, N. B., Jr., 46n
Brynjolfsson, E., 194, 195n, 215n
Buchholtz, A. K., 189n
Buchko, A. A., 239n
Budweiser, 129, 255
BuildPoint, 6
Burgelman, R. A., 292n, 300n
Burger King, 66
Burns, C. S., 132
Burrows, P., 17n, 46n, 134n
Burton, T. M., 135n, 234n
Busch Gardens, 55
Busenitz, L. W., 188n, 322n
Busija, E. C., 163n
Business Cycle Development, 355
Business Environment Risk Index, 65

Business International's Country Assessment Service, 65
Business Periodical Index, 356
Business Roundtable, 3, 42
Business Week, 355
Butler, R. J., 24n
Bygrave, W. D., 322n
Byrne, J. A., 188n, 215n, 239n, 299n
Byrne, S., 323n
Byrnes, N., 26n, 248n

Cadbury, A., 34n
Cadillac, 15
California Public Employees' Retirement System (CalPERS), 34
Callahan, C. V., 24n
Calvin Klein, 185
Campbell, A., 24n, 156, 157, 158, 162n, 163n, 215n
Campbell, M., 186, 197
Campbell-Hunt, C., 134n
Campbell Software, 186
Cannella, A. A., Jr., 30n, 239n
Cannondale, 132
Canon, 142
Cantrell, R. S., 31n
Cardinal, L. B., 23n, 162n
Caremark Rx, 264
Carey, D. C., 239n
Carey, J., 300n
Carland, J. C., 321n
Carland, J. W., 321n
Carnival Cruise Lines, 55
Carper, W. B., 162n
Carr, L. L., 29n
Carroll, A. B., 37–39
Carroll's Foods, 140, 141
Carter, N. M., 134n
Carter, R., 230–231
Caruana, A., 322n
Cascio, W. F., 163n
Case, 54
Case, Steve, 18
Casey's General Stores, 108–109, 119, 184
Castro, J., 321n
Caterpillar, Inc., 208
Cavanagh, G. F., 43n
Caves, R. E., 134n
CD/International, 342, 355
Celestial Seasonings, 23
Celestica, 166–167
Census, U.S., 56, 355
CEO Express, 353
Chae, M. S., 36n
Chambers, J., 36
Champion, D., 188n
Champion, M., 163n
Chan, P. S., 299n
Chandler, A. D., 197–198, 201, 215n, 220
Chandra, G., 272n
Chandraeskaran, R., 339

Charan, R., 35n, 251, 273n
Charmin, 159
Chase Econometric Associates, 355
Chase Manhattan Corporation, 35
Chattopadhyay, P., 78n, 189n
Chaudhuri, S., 300n
Chawla, S. K., 273n
Chefs Unlimited, 51–52
Chelsea Market, 132
Chen, M. J., 35n
Chesapeake & Ohio Railroad, 228
Chevron, 181
Chi, P. C. K., 134n
Children's Place, 192
Children's Television Workshop, 334
Chinta, R., 299n
Cho, D. S., 134n
Cho, T. S., 35n
Choi, T. Y., 240n
Choudhury, N., 163n
Chrisman, J. J., 134n, 322n
Christensen, C. M., 95, 105n, 296, 299n
Chrysler Corporation, 5, 32, 97, 131, 171, 173, 205, 282, 291
CHS Electronics, 264
Chung, A., 323n
Chung, H. M., 24n
Chung, S. Y., 134n
Church & Dwight Company, 112, 164–165, 169
Churchill, N. C., 313, 316, 322n
Chussil, M. J., 299n
CIGNA, 251
CISC (Complex Instruction Set Computing), 288
Cisco Systems, 36, 129, 130, 140, 160, 264
Citicorp, 221
CKE Restaurants, 264
Clark, D., 188n, 273n, 336
Clark, Martire & Bartolomeo, 264
Clark, S. M., 78n
Clegg, S. R., 24n, 215n
Clorox Company, 126
Cluetrain Manifesto, 212
CNN, 36
Coase, 141
Coca-Cola Company, 99, 128, 150, 194, 248, 250, 257
Cohen, W. M., 300n
Coker, M., 44n
Coleman, H. J., Jr., 215n
Coles, J. W., 34n
Colgate-Palmolive, 165, 168–169, 290
Collins, S., 339n
Collis, D. J., 163n
Colt's Manufacturing, 203
Columbia-Presbyterian Medical Center, 333
Colvin, G., 40n, 105n
Communications Workers of America, 98
Compact Disclosure, 342, 355
Compaq Computer, 62, 131, 147, 149

Competitive Intelligence Guide, 356
Comptronix, 166
COMPUSTAT, 342, 355
ConAgra, 183
Conference Board's Global Corporate Governance Research Center, 31
Congress, U.S., 282
Conlin, M., 46n
Construcciones Aeronáuticas, 127
Contardo, I., 188n
Conti, R., 239n
Continental Airlines, 80, 177
Converse, 60
Cooper, A. C., 135n, 322n
Cooper, C. L., 40, 239n
Cooper and Lybrand, 127
Corcoran, E., 23n
Coremetrics, 185
Corkindale, D. R., 299n
Corning, Inc., 208–209, 219
Corporate Financials Online, 353
Corporate Information, 353
Corporate Watch, 45
CorpTech Database of Technology Companies, 353
Corriher, S. E., 42n
Cortese, A., 105n
Cosby Show, The, 56
Cosco, 39
Cosco, J., 24n
Cosier, R. A., 189n
COSMOS, 252
Council of Europe, 45
Cover Girl, 139
Covin, J. G., 300n, 322n
Covisint, 131
Cowen, J. L., 202
Coy, P., 39n, 188n
Cray, D., 24n
Cringely, R. X., 36n
Crockett, R. O., 134n, 160n, 300n
Cronin, M. J., 240n
Crosier, D., 174, 175
CSX Corporation, 143, 228
Cullen, D., 310
Cummings, S., 24n
Cummins Engine Co., 287
Curran, J. J., 163n
Cyrix Corporation, 125

Dacin, M. T., 189n, 215n
Daft, D., 99
Daily, C. M., 34n, 48n
Daimler-Benz, 5
Dale, K., 174
Dalsimer, J. P., 339n
Dalton, D. R., 34n
Dana Corporation, 131
Daniels, J. D., 273n
Danielson, C., 239n
Danjou, T., 285

Dart Industries, 39
Das, T. K., 135n
Datta, D. K., 239n
D'Aveni, R. A., 8, 24n, 68, 78n, 122–123, 134n
David, G., 205, 215n
David, J. H., 36n
Davidson, W. N., III, 34n
Davies, J., 24n
Davis, B., 321n
Davis, J. H., 30n
Davis, R. H., 338n
Davis, S. M., 205, 215n
Dayton-Hudson, 21, 39
Dean, H., 171
Dean, J. W., Jr., 24n
Dean, T. J., 322n
Dean Foods Company, 171
DeCastro, J. O., 134n
Dechant, K., 188n
DeDee, J. K., 163n
Deere, John, 169
Deere & Company, 12, 54, 235
Defense, U.S. Department of, 7
Delios, A., 162n
Dell, M., 147
Dell Computer Corporation, 22, 55, 62, 120, 131, 142, 147, 149, 211, 264
Deloitte & Touche Consulting Group, 58
Delta Airlines, 15, 16, 80
DeMarie, S. M., 24n, 105n, 188n
Demb, A., 27n
Deming, W. E., 174
Denis, J., 338n
DeStephano, J. J., 135n
Deutsche Aerospace, 127
Devanna, M. A., 239n
Devendran, A., 323n
Diamond Multimedia Systems, 202
digiMine, 185
Dinne, S. P., 163n
Director of National Trade Associations, 356
Disney, Walt, Company, 177
Disney, Walt, Productions, 119, 201
DiStephano, J. J., 135
DiVerde, D., 239n
Dixon, L., 174
Dobbin, F., 78n
Doll Collection, The, 160, 312
Domino's, 122
Donaldson, G., 273n
Donaldson, L., 30n, 215n
Donnely, F., 322n
Dougherty, D., 300n, 321n
Douma, S., 162n
Dow, D., 273n
Dowd, F., 78n
Dowd, T. J., 78
Drazin, R., 239n
Dreese, M., 50, 106, 190, 274
Drew, A. W., 273
Drew, S., 216n

Drew, S. A. W., 273n
Drucker, P. F., 145, 309, 322n, 324, 337, 338n
Drugstore.com, 248
Duchan, D., 189n
Due, T., 188n
Dugal, S. S., 299n
Dun & Bradstreet, 321
Dun & Bradstreet Online, 356
Dunlap, A. J., 220
Dun's Review, 356
DuPont, 166, 176, 197, 198, 201, 245
Durant, W., 201

EASDAQ, 302
Eastern Airlines, 203
Eastman Kodak, 223
Eaton Corporation, 260
eBay, 17, 203, 295, 313
Eckberg, J., 234
Eckerd College, 331, 338n
Eckerd Drugs, 170
Ecola's 24-Hour Newsstand, 356
Economic Espionage Act, 71
Economic Indicators, 355
Economic Report of the President, 356
Economist, The, 325, 356
Economist Intelligence Unit, 5
Edgar database, 342
EDS, 336
Edwards, C., 215n
Edwards, J. D., 256
Ehitex.com, 131
Ehrbar, A., 272n
Eikner, A. E., 323n
Eisenmann, T. R., 36n
Elango, E., 162n
Electrolux AB, 31, 123, 145, 225, 342, 352
Eli Lilly, 248
Eller, R., 295
Ellison, L., 200
Ellstrand, A. E., 34n
El-Namacki, M. S. S., 321n
Elsass, P. M., 189n
Elstrom, P. 240n
E-marketing, 185
Emekli Sandigi. *See* Sandigi, Emekli
Emerson, R. E., 338n
Emerson Electric, 159–160
Encyclopedia Britannica, Inc., 19
Encyclopedia of Associations, 356
Engardio, P., 255n
England, G. W., 41n
Enhanced Tracker software, 252
Enron, 26, 27, 40
Enterprise Rent-A-Car, 217–218
E-piphany, 185
Equal Employment Opportunity
    Commission (EEOC), 225
Erhardt, W., 218
Erickson, T. J., 299n
Ericsson, 142

Ernst, D., 135n
Ernst & Young, 278
Ernst Institutional Research, 341
e-Steel, 6
Estee Lauder, 55
eToys, 191, 192
ETrade, 2
ETrade Zone, 2
European Commission, 325
European Union (EU), 6, 56, 176, 325, 348
Excite, 352
Export Hotline, 65

Fadal Engineering, 119
Fahey, L., 135n, 321n
Falshaw, J. R., 134n
Fang, Y., 209n
Fannin, W. R., 273n
Farrell, C., 322n
Fashionmall.com, 203
Federal Security Bureau (FSB), 44
Federal Trade Commission (FTC), 131,
    352
Federated Department Stores, 191–192,
    197
FedEx Corporation, 15, 62, 100, 157, 165,
    176, 210, 211, 252, 263, 310
Feeser, H. R., 322n
Felsenthal, E., 339n
Fennell, M. L., 338n
Fenton, J., 273n
Ferland, C. A., 299n
Ferlie, E., 338n
Fernandez, P., 185
Fiat, 146
Fiegenbaum, A., 78n
Field, J. M., 188n
Fields, D., 303, 321n
Fiet, J. O., 322n
FIND/SVP. *See* MarketResearch.com
Fineman, H., 339n
Fingerhut Company, 191–192, 193, 197
Finkelstein, S., 31n, 35n
Finsbury Data Services, 71
Fiorina, C., 19
Firestone, 39, 145
Fishburne, R., 105n
Fisher, A. B., 273n
Fisher, G., 139
Flanagan, D. J., 162
Fleisher, C., 39n
Fletcher, J., 78n
Flora, B., 79n
Flynn, E. J., 299n
Fogg, C. D., 36n
Fombrun, C. J., 239n
Forbes, 278, 356
Ford, H., 84, 139, 201
Ford Motor Company, 84, 98, 114, 131, 150,
    173, 201, 236, 282, 287
Ford of Britain, 210

Formichelli, Joseph, 149
Forrester Research, Inc., 255
Fort, John, 26
Fortune, 191, 264, 356
Fortune 500, 251, 315, 356
Foss, Stephen, 26
Foster, M. J., 321n
Foster, R., 94, 95
Fotta, J., 341
Fouts, P. A., 39n
Fowler, K. L., 273n
Fowler, V., 322n
Fox, V., 6
France, M., 44n
Francis, S. C., 239n
Frank, R., 234n
Frank J. Zamboni & Company. *See* Zamboni,
    Frank J., & Company
Franko, L. G., 299n
Fraser, D., 58n
Frazier, M., 2
Freedman, D. H., 299n
Freeman, R. E., 39n, 249n
Freundlich, N., 300n
Fridson, M. S., 347, 366n
Fried, V. H., 162n, 322n
Friedman, M., 37, 38–39, 348
Friesen, P. H., 215n
Frigidaire, 145
Frito-Lay, 194
Froelich, K. A., 338n
Frost and Sullivan, 65
Fruit of the Loom, 264
Fujitsu Ltd., 177
Fulk, J., 78n
Fulmer, R. M., 222n
FunZone, 301, 303

Gable, M., 41n
Gadella, J. W., 215n
Gadiesh, O., 104n
Galante, S. P., 321n
Galbraith, C. S., 189n, 273n
Galbraith, J. R., 84n, 104n, 300n
Garage.com, 192
Garcia, F., 215n
GarnerGroup, 7
Garsombke, D. J., 322n
Garsombke, T. W., 322n
Garten, J. E., 211n
Garud, R., 299n
Garvin, D. A., 24n, 121
Gashurov, I., 215n
Gates, W., 36, 68
Gateway Computers, 55, 62, 120, 149
Gebelein, C., 24n
GE Financial Assurance (GEFA), 2
Geiner, P., 144
Geletkaycz, M. A., 189n
Gembicki, M. P., 79n
General Accounting Office, 333

General Electric, 1–2, 4, 14, 21, 29, 35, 90, 97, 123, 127, 142, 153, 156, 167, 177, 184, 201, 219, 221, 222, 248, 250, 253–254, 261, 264
General Electric Financial Network, 2
General Foods, 88
General Mills, 61, 70, 155, 279
General Motors, 14, 87, 114, 128, 131, 140, 148, 168, 173, 183, 197, 198, 201, 203, 225, 227, 250
Genetech, 261
George, E., 78n
George Washington University, 54
Georgia-Pacific, 174, 248
Gerber, 279
Geringer, J. M., 135n
Gerlach, M. L., 32n
Gerstner, L., 149
Getz, G., 299n
Ghemawat, P., 134n
Ghoshal, S., 216n
Giampapa, D., 301, 305
Gibbs, P. A., 222n
Gibson, R., 162n
Gilbert, D. R., 39n
Gilbert, J. L., 104n
Gillette, 82, 83–84, 255, 279
Gimeno, J., 163n
Gimeno-Gascon, F. J., 322n
Ginsberg, A., 291, 300n
Gioia, D. A., 78n
Girl Scouts, 332
GIS. *See* Global Information Solutions (GIS)
Gladwin, T. N., 78n
Glain, S., 285n
Glaister, K. W., 134n
Glass, H. E., 162n, 163n, 188n, 322n, 338n
Glick, W. H., 78n, 189n
Global Aerospace & Defense Trading Exchange, 131
Global Competitiveness Report, 302
Global Crossing, 27
Global Enterprise Data Warehouse, 175
Global Information Solutions (GIS), 229
Global Supply Chain Management Forum, 131
Gluck, F. W., 23n
Gogoi, P., 162n
Goizueta, R., 250
Gold, I., 24n
Goldenberg, D. I., 272n, 273n
Golder, P. N., 134n
Goldsmith, M., 222n
Gomes-Casseres, B., 130n
Gomez-Mejia, L. R., 273n
Gooding, R. Z., 189n
Goodstein, J., 163n, 239
Goodyear Tire & Rubber, 131, 257
Goold, M., 156, 157, 158, 162n, 163n, 197, 215n, 338n, 352
Gopinath, C., 239n

Gordon, G. G., 240n
Govindarajan, V., 272n
Graham, J. L., 163n
Grant, L., 24n, 162n
Grant, R. M., 23n, 82, 104n
Graves, S. B., 39n, 299n
Greco, J., 78n, 188n, 239n
Green, H., 135n
Green, J., 215n
Greenberg, H., 366n
Green Book, 235
Greene, J., 46n
Greening, D. W., 39n
Greenlight.com, 248
Greenpeace's Shareholders Against New Exploration (SANE), 45
Gregersen, H. B., 224, 239n, 240n
Greiner, L. E., 201–202, 215n
Greve, H. R., 78n
Grey-Wheelright, 238
Griffin, R. W., 209n
Grimm, C. M., 23n, 134n, 239n
Grint, K., 216n
Grossman, D., 149
Grossman, L. M., 78n, 79n
Grossman, W., 273n
Grove, A. S., 17, 36, 64, 78n, 180
Grover, R., 188n, 299n
Gruber, R., 272n
Gruner, S., 322n
Grupo Transportacion Ferroviaria Mexicana (TFM), 145
Gulati, R., 299n
Gupta, A. K., 215n
Gupta, U., 240n, 322n
Guth, W. D., 41n, 78n, 291, 300n
Guthrie, J. P., 239n
Guyon, J., 90n, 162n

Hackman, J. R., 209n
Hadley, L., 229
Halal, W. E., 78n
Hall, E. H., Jr., 299n
Hallmark, 279
Halpern, M. T., 338n
Hambrick, D. C., 30n, 31n, 35n, 189n
Hamel, G., 149n, 188n, 189n, 299n
Hamermesh, R. G., 163n
Hamilton, D. P., 134n
Hamilton, R. D., III, 272n
Hammer, M., 207–208, 215n
Hanaoka, M., 239n
Handy, C., 24n
Hanks, T., 187
Harback, H. F., 239n
Hardee's, 66
Hardy, C., 215n, 300n
Harley-Davidson, 208, 223
Harman, C. L., 39n
Harper, R. M., Jr., 323n
Harrell, G. D., 155n, 163n

Harrigan, K. R., 140, 162n
Harris, D., 34n
Harris, L. C., 105n
Harrison, D. A., 189n
Harrison, J. S., 284, 299n
Hartman, R. I., 239n
Harvey, L., 186
Hasbro, 203, 206
Hatfield, J. D., 39n
Hatten, K. J., 78n, 316, 322n
Hatten, M. L., 78n
Havens, C., 24n, 163n
Hayes, D., 201, 202, 203
Hayes Corporation, 202
Hayes Microcomputer Products, 201, 202, 203
Hayes Smartmodem, 202
Hayes Standard AT Command Set, 202
Hayward, M. L., 30n
Health Midwest (Kansas City), 333
Heartherington, D., 202
Hebert, F. J., 240n
Hedley, B., 152n, 163n
Heeley, M. B., 300n
Heene, A., 188n
Heffron, F., 338n
Hegel, 184
Heiens, R. A., 134n
Heineken Beer, 102
Helfat, C. E., 34n
Henderson, P., 310
Hendrickson, A. R., 105n
Henkoff, R., 135n, 239n
Herbert, F. J., 240
Herbert, T. T., 240n
Herron, L., 322n
Hershey Foods, 257
Hertz, 217
Hesterly, W. S., 34n
Hewitt Associates, 227
Hewlett-Packard (HP), 8, 14, 19, 120, 127, 131, 142, 149, 174, 175, 221, 245, 288, 293, 294, 351
Hickson, D. J., 24n
Higgins, J. M., 247n
Hill, C. W. L., 105n, 273n, 299n
Hill, G. C., 299n
Hill, J. S., 36n
Hill, T., 134n
Hisrich, R., 322n
Hitt, M. A., 23n, 24n, 163n, 188n, 189n, 239n, 284, 299n, 300n
Hock, C. A., 272n
Hodgetts, R. M., 134n, 240n, 273n
Hoechst, 334
Hoerr, J., 216n, 239n
Hof, R. D., 299n, 300n, 322n
Hofer, C. W., 79n, 289n, 311–313, 322n
Hofstede, G., 232–233, 240n
Holstein, W. J., 135n
Home Depot, 169, 257
Honda, 121, 145, 166

Honeywell, 129, 174
Hoover, 5, 185
Hoover, R., 219
Hoover Europe, 115
Hoovers Online Corporate Directory, 75, 185, 342, 353, 355, 356
Horlstein, W. J., 300n
Hormozi, A. M., 272
Hornsby, J. S., 299n
Hoskisson, R. E., 23n, 273n, 284, 299n, 300n
HotOffice, 236
House, D., 289
Houston, P., 323n
Hovde, M. A., 162n, 163n, 188n, 322n
Howard, W., 188n
Hoy, F., 321n
Hrebiniak, L. G., 215n
Huber, G. P., 189n
Huellmantel, A. B., 23n
Huff, P. L., 323n
Humana, 264
Humane Society, 325
Hunger, J. D., 20n, 28n, 69n, 74n, 102n, 111n, 168n, 172n, 179n, 265n, 273n, 323n, 328, 338n, 351n
Hunter, D., 131
Hussey, D. E., 78n, 162n, 215n
Hwang, P., 273n

IBM, 17, 62, 128, 141, 147, 149, 174, 177, 200, 222, 235, 280, 336
Ibrahim, N. A., 24n, 321n
Ibuka, M., 280
ICANN. See Internet Corporation for Assigned Names and Numbers
Ilinich, A. Y., 162n
iMac, 13
Imation, 204
Inc., 356
Inc. 500, 315
Index of Corporations and Industries, 356
Industry Norms and Key Business Ratios, 356
Industry Survey, 356
Industry Week, 356
In Focus Systems, 141
Information Catalogue, The, 355–356
Infoseek, 75
Ingersol-Rand, 174
Ingram, T., 338n
Inkpen, A. C., 130n, 163n
Inland Steel Company, 8
Inner City Entertainment (ICE), 119
Institute for Scientific Information, 294
Institute of the Future, 262
Integra, 292–293
Intel Corporation, 8, 14, 15, 17, 36, 60, 82, 127, 160, 180, 250, 279, 288
Intel's Pentium, 82, 127, 180
Intercontinental Hotels, 177
Internal Revenue Service (IRS), 26, 326, 333

International Benchmarking Clearinghouse, 254
International Harvester, 203
International Specialty Products, 291
International Staffing, 224
International Strategies, 65
Internet Corporation for Assigned Names and Numbers (ICANN), 336
Internet Engineering Task Force (IETF), 45, 336
Internet Explorer, 280, 351
Intira Corp., 160
Investment Survey, 355
Iomega, 286
ISO 9000, 245
It's a Wonderful Life, 348
Ittner, C. D., 272n
i2 Technologies, 6
Iverson, K. F., 241–242, 272n
Ivey, M., 299n
Iwata, E., 366n
Izumi, H., 204n

Jackson, J., 187
Jackson, M., 150
Jassawalla, A. R., 105n
JC Penney. See Penney, JC
Jennings, D. F., 215n
Jenster, P. V., 338
J. G. Edwards, 256
Jobs, S., 36, 93, 201, 283
Johannet, J., 50, 106
Johns, G., 209n
Johns Hopkins University Institute for Policy Studies, 325
Johns-Mansville, 203
Johnson, J. L., 34n
Johnson, J. M., 255
Johnson, P., 188n
Johnson, R. A., 300n
Johnson, W. A., 273n
Johnson & Johnson, 159
Jonash, R., 299n
Jones, D., 273n
Jones, P., 24n, 279n
Jones, W. A., Jr., 46n
Jordan, J., 189n
Jordan Industries Inc., 159
Joyce, T., 273n
Joyce, W. F., 215n
Judge, W. Q., Jr., 28n
Just Toys, 206
Justice, U.S. Department of, 127

Kahaner, L., 24n, 79n, 279n
Kahn, J., 302n, 321n
Kansas City Southern Railroad, 145
Kant, I., 43
Kanter, R. M., 24n, 128n, 135n, 338n
Kaplan, R. S., 250, 273n
Kargar, J., 321n

Kaske, K., 284
Katey, B., 189n
Kaufman, S. P., 23n
Kazanjian, R. K., 239n
Keating, B. P., 338n
Keating, M. O., 338n
Keats, B. W., 24n, 188n, 239n, 321n
Keebler, 283
Keels, J. K., 239n
Keenan, F., 188n
Keirsey, D., 240n
Keirsey Temperament Sorter, 238
Kelleher, H., 36
Keller, J. J., 240n
Kelley, B., 188n
Kellogg Company, 169
Kelly, K., 239n, 299n
Kennedy, R. J., 273n
Keogh, J., 42n
KeraVision, Inc., 251–252
Kerstetter, J., 46n
Kerwin, K., 299n
Kets de Vries, M., 322n
Khan, Z. U., 273n
Kids Kab, 310
Kiefer, R. O., 155n, 163n
Killing, J. P., 135n
Kilmann, R. H., 240n
Kim, D-J., 134n
Kim, H., 239n
Kim, L., 144
Kim, W. C., 273n
Kimberly-Clark, 159
King, D., 24n
King, P. S., 141n
Kinloch, J., 98
Kirchner, J., 160n
Kirin, 127
Kirkman, B. L., 188n
Kirsch, R. J., 273n
Klein, C., 76n
Klein, H. E., 79n
Kleiner, A., 216
Kleiner Perkins, 32
KLM, 142, 143
Kmart, 33
Knapp, E., 24n, 163n
Kochhar, R., 188n
Kocurek, P. F., 134n
Kohlberg, L., 42, 43
Kohut, G. F., 42n
Kompass International, 353
Kono, T., 240n
Korn/Ferry International, 28, 31
Kotler, P., 91n
Kotulic, A. G., 24n
Koza, M. P., 215n
Kozlowski, Dennis, 25–26, 27
Kozmo.com, 320
KPMG, 193
Kraatz, M. S., 23n

Krause, A., 249
Krause, I., 295n, 300n
Kremer, L., 172
Kroll, M., 134n
Krugman, P., 189n
Krum, D., 4
Kuczmarski & Associates, 279
Kulatilaka, N., 188n
Kumar, K., 41n, 338n
Kunstler, B., 298n
Kuratko, D. F., 24n, 299n
Kvinnsland, S., 234

Labatt, 127
Labich, K., 188n
Laderman, J. M., 366n
L. A. Gear, 150
Lakey, C., 185
Lamberti, D., 108–109
Lamont, B. T., 162n
Land, E., 201
Land Rover, 150
Lands' End, 173
Lane, H. W., 135n
Lane, P. J., 30n, 300n
Lane, R., 12
Langley, A., 338n
Langley, M., 339n
Langowitz, N. S., 299n
Lansing, W., 193, 196
Larcker, D. F., 272n
Larsen, P. C., 322n
Laseter, T., 323n
Lasserre, P., 78n
Lau, R. S. M., 24n
Lavelle, L., 29n, 239n
Lavender, L., 338n
Lawler, E. E., 105n
Lawrence, P. R., 205, 215n
Lay, Kenneth, 40
Lederman, L. L., 59n
Ledford, G. E., Jr., 105, 105n
Lee, H., 131, 134n
Lee, J., 24n, 105n, 255n
Lee, K. S., 322n
Lee, L., 23n
Lehn, K., 272n, 273n
Lei, D. T., 24n, 162n, 163n, 188n, 273n
Lengnick-Hall, C. A., 300n
Leontiades, M., 105n
Lerner, L. D., 322n
Lerwin, A. Y., 215
Lestoil, 283
Leuchter, M., 189n, 239n
Lever Brothers, 165
Levin, J. B., 300n, 317
Levin, R. I., 323n
Levine, M., 292–293
Levine, R., 212, 213, 216n
Levinson, A., 339n
Levinthal, D. A., 300n

Levi Strauss, 39, 173
Levy, D., 310
Lewin, A. Y., 24n, 215n
Lewis, F. L., 314, 322
Lewis, J., 230, 231
Lewis, M., 215n
Lewis, V. L., 314, 322n
Li, K-Q., 130n
Li, M., 105n
Lickona, T., 42n
Liemandt, J., 277
Light, L., 27n
Lim, G. H., 322n
Linneman, R. E., 79n
Lionel, 202–203
Lipton, M., 34n, 36n, 150
Little, D., 163n, 175n
Liu, J., 295n, 300n
Livington, R., 177
L. L. Bean. See Bean, L. L.
Loarie, T., 252
Locke, C., 212, 216n
Lockheed Martin, 7, 131
Loewen Group, 122
Lon, H., 321n
Lorange, P., 135n, 239n
Lorenzoni, G., 215n
Lorsch, J. W., 34n
Lotus, 236, 280
Lotus Notes, 235
Lotus Translation Services, 176
Love, L. G., 104n
Low, J., 272n
Lozeau, D., 338n
Lubatkin, M. H., 30n, 239n, 240n, 300n
Lublin, J. S., 35n, 240n
Lucent Technology, 238, 293
Ludwig, P., 129
Luehrman, T. A., 188n-189n
Luke, R. D., 339n
Lussier, R. N., 321n
Lycos, 75, 352
Lyles, M. A., 24n
Lynch, R. P., 135n
Lynn, G. S., 299n

Machrone, C., 273n
Mach 3, 82
Macintosh, 235
Macy, B., 204n
Macy's Department Stores, 203
Maddox, R., 203
Magic Chef, 13
Magnusson, P., 255n
Magretta, J., 322n
Mahon, J. F., 135n
Mahoney, J. T., 162n
Makadok, R., 134n
Makhija, A. K., 272n, 273n
Malekzadeh, A. R., 228n, 240n
Mallory, G. R., 24n

Malone, M. S., 105n, 299n
Manco, Inc., 254
Mandel, M. J., 40n, 188n
Mann, L., 273n
Mansfield, E., 299n
March, J. G., 215n
Maremont, M., 322n
MarketResearch.com, 71, 355
Marlboro, 255
Marriott, 174
Marsico Capital Management, 248
Martin, C., 236
Mary Kay Corporation, 71
Masakowski, E., 141n
Mascarenhas, B., 134n
Massachusetts General Hospital, 334
Masterson, S. S., 240n
Mathews, J. A., 215n
Matsushita, 286, 288
Mattel, 173, 206
Matthews, C. H., 321n
Matusik, S. F., 105n
MaxiShips, 176
Mayer, R., 36n
Maytag Company, 14, 39, 40, 122, 129, 166, 171, 229
Maytag Corporation, 4, 5, 11, 13, 40, 41, 74, 101–102, 114–117, 119, 122–123, 128, 145, 228, 287, 292, 349, 351, 361–365
Mazzarol, T., 322n
MCA, 136
McAlary, S., 273n
McCann, J. E, III, 162n
McDermott, D., 202n
McDonald's, 66, 175, 176, 196, 221
McDougall, P. P., 322n
McDowell, J., 321n
McGee, J. E., 104n
McGill, M., 162n
McGill, R., 338n
McGrath, R. G., 189n
McGraw, D., 348n
MCI, 125, 136
McKenna, M. G., 134n
McKinsey & Company, 94, 153, 221
McLaughlin, C. P., 338n
McNealy, S., 17
McQuaid, K. L., 163n
McWhirter, W., 321n
McWilliams, A., 39n
Mead Corporation, 29
Means, G. C., 30n
Medford, C., 189n
Media One, 137
Medical Foods, 310–311
Medley, G. J., 338n
Melrose, K., 143
Mendenhall, M., 240n
Menon, K., 239n
Mercedes-Benz, 119, 239, 255
Merck & Co., 279

Mercosur (Mercosul), 6, 56
Meredith, G. G., 189n
Merrill, G. B., 189n
Merrill Lynch, 257, 347
Merrit, J., 239n
Mesa Airlines, 142
Metacrawler, 75
Metcalfe, B., 105
Metro AG, 144
Metropolitan Museum of Art, 333
Metz, C., 240n
Meyer, H., 39n, 135n
MG Car Company, 150
Michaels, C. E., 307
Michelin, 131
Micron, 140
Microsoft Corporation, 36, 62, 68, 93, 113,
    124–125, 221, 250, 256–257, 263, 280,
    282, 283, 294, 295, 351
Microsoft Office, 280
Microstrategy, 185
Midwest Express, 77
Miles, G., 215n
Miles, R. E., 66, 78n, 207, 215n
Miller, C. C., 23n, 162n, 189n
Miller, D., 105n, 215n
Miller, M. C., 322n
Miller, S., 163n
Miller, S. H., 79n, 163
Minow, N., 26n
Mintzberg, H., 16, 18–19, 24n, 84n, 104n,
    304, 322n
Mirvis, P. H., 163n
Mishra, A. K., 239n
Mishra, K. E., 239n
Mitchell, R. K., 43n
Mitchell, W., 24n
Mitsubishi Corporation, 225
Mitsubishi Trading Company, 65
Modelo, 127
Modem Express, 202
Moesel, D. D., 300n, 322n
Mohrman, S. A., 105n
Money, R. B., 163n
Monks, R. A. G., 26n, 31n
Monsanto, 18
Montagno, R. V., 299n
Montgomery Ward, Inc., 203, 220
Monthly Bulletin of Statistics, 355
Monthly Labor Review, 355
Moody's Industrials, 75
Moody's Manuals on Investment, 355
Moore, G., 94
Moore, P. L., 23n
Moore's Law, 94
Morgan Motor Car Company, 119
Morita, A., 279, 280
Morone, J. G., 299n
Morris, J. R., 163n
Morris, M. H., 322n
Morrison Knudsen, 166

Moss, J., 295
Mossville Engine Center, 208
Motorola, Inc., 8, 97, 139, 141, 142, 166–167,
    219, 280, 292
Mr. Donut, 165
Mroczkowski, T., 239n
Mrs. Fields Cookies, 303
Muir, N. K., 189n
Mulford, C. L., 321n
Mullaney, T. J., 187, 189n
Muller, J., 105n
Mulvey, P. W., 189n
Muralidharan, R., 245, 272n
Murmann, J. P., 163n
Murphy, D., 239n
Murray, E. A., Jr., 135n
Myers-Briggs, 238

Naffziger, D. W., 299n
Nahavardi, A., 228n, 240n
Naisbitt, J., 78n, 162n
Napster, 255
Nare, B., 338n
Nargundkar, R., 299n
NASDAQ, 302
Nathan, M., 189n
National, 217
National Energy Associates, 303
National Organization for Women, 225
National Security Agency (NSA), 263
National Semicondutor Corporation, 211
NatWest Markets, 235–236
Navistar, 257
Navy, U.S., 268
Nayak, P. R., 299n, 300n
Naylor, J., 215n
Nayyar, P. R., 299n
NCR Corporation, 97, 228–229
Neale, M. R., 299n
NECX, 6
Nemec, C., 34n
Nestea, 150
Nestlé, 211
NetGenesis, 185
Net Perceptions, 185
Netscape, 124–125, 280, 282, 351
Neubauer, F. F., 27n
Newbury Comics, Inc., 50, 106, 190, 274–275
New Hampshire, State of, 26
Newman, W. H., 134n, 329–330, 338n
Newport News Shipbuilding, 12
New York and Presbyterian Hospitals Health
    Care System, 333
New York Hospital-Cornell Medical Center,
    333
New York Stock Exchange (NYSE), 29
Nextel, 183
Nicoderm, 333
Nicolaes, J., 322n
Nielsen, A. C., Co., 71
Nielsen, R. P., 322, 332, 339n

Nightmare at 43 Hillcrest, 187
Nike, Inc., 60, 119, 150, 171, 206, 221
Nissan, 121, 145
NiteBite, 311
Nixon, R. D., 239n
Nobel, R., 299n
Nohria, N., 299n
Nord, W. R., 24n, 215n
Nordstrom, 14, 89
Norman, J., 321n
Nortel Networks, 289, 296
North American Free Trade Agreement
    (NAFTA), 6
North American Free Trade Zone, 56
Northern Light, 352
Northern Telecom, 166, 288–289
Northwest Airlines, 32, 77, 80, 142,
    143
Norton, D. P., 250, 273n
Novak, R. S., 188n
Noxell Corporation, 139
Noxema, 139
Nucor Corporation, 241–242, 243
Nueno, P., 299n
Nummi Corporation, 128
Nutrasweet, 62
Nutt, P. C., 134n

O'Boyle, T. F., 299n
Ocasio, W., 239n
Oddou, G., 240n
Oden, H. W., 291n
O'Donnell, M., 235
Ogbonna, E., 105n
Ogden, D., 239n
Ohmae, K., 56, 78n
Ohsone, K., 282
Oil of Olay, 139
Oldham, G. R., 209n
Olive Garden, 66
Oliver, C., 32n
Ollinger, M., 215n
Olson, E. M., 300n
O'Neill, H. M., 163n, 189n, 338n
Oosterveld, J., 299n
OPEC, 348
Oracle Corporation, 100, 200, 256
O'Reilly, B., 105n, 239n
Orion Pictures, 203
Orris, J. B., 24n
Oster, S. M., 188n
Ouchi, W. G., 272n
Overseas Business Reports, 355
Overstreet, G. A., 338n
Owens, M., 333
Owens-Corning, 257

Paikeday, T., 310
Palich, L. E., 162n
Palmer, T. B., 188n
Palto Alto Research Center (PARC), 93, 283

Pan, Y., 134n
Pan Am Building, 177
Pan American Airlines, 77, 177, 203
Paper, D., 216n
Parducci, Anne, 173
Pare, T. P., 272n
Parish, W., 303
Park, D., 189n
Parnell, J. A., 239n, 321n
Party HOLDems, 301
Pascarella, P., 94n, 105n
Pasternack, B. A., 24n
Patricia Seybold Group, 186
Patrick, J., 149
Patterson, M. L., 286n
Paulson, A. S., 299n
PC DOS, 283
Pearce, J. A., II, 28n, 163n, 322n
Pearson, J. N., 321n
Pekar, P., Jr., 23n
Pellengahr, H., 144
Penney, JC, 170
Pennings, J. M., 162n
Pentium. *See* Intel's Pentium
PeopleSoft, 256
PepsiCo, 150, 194, 196, 221, 254, 343
Percy Barnevik, 90
Perkins, J., 162n
Personify, 185
Peters, M., 322n
Peters, T. J., 260, 273n
Petty, J. W., 322n
Petty, K., 338n
Pfeffer, J., 338n
Pfizer, 29, 221
Pharmacia AB, 234
Pharmacia & Upjohn, Inc., 92, 234
Phatak, A. V., 273n
Philips, 166
Phillips, D., 78n
Phillips, S. J., 322n
Phoenix, University of, 337
Pickton, D., 272n
Pine, B. J., 105n
Pineda, R. C., 322n
Pink Dot, 320
PitBull, 294–295
Pittiglio Rabin Todd McGrath, 294
Pitts, R. A., 24n, 239n
Pizza Hut, 122
Plato, 184
Pointer, D. D., 339n
Poirer, C. C., 105n
Polanyi, M., 104n
Polaroid Corporation, 177, 201, 248
Polek, D., 188n
Political System Stability Index, 65
Pollock, T. G., 273n
Poon, J. M. L., 273n
Pope, J., 295n
Popular Club, 192

Porac, J. F., 273n
Port, O., 300n
Porter, M. E., 60–62, 61n, 62–63, 78n, 79n,
    85–87, 105n, 118, 120n, 121, 123, 124,
    126, 134n, 135n, 154, 162n, 163n, 171, 311
Porterba, J. M., 105n
POSCO. *See* Pohang Iron & Steel Company,
    Ltd. (POSCO)
Post 300, 251
Pouder, R. W., 31n, 189n
Powell, T. C., 240n
Powell, W. W., 338n
Power, C., 299n
PowerShip, 176
Prahalad, C. K., 78n, 299n
Prahalad, S. K., 78, 188n, 299
Precision Thermoforming & Packaging,
    150
Preece, S., 39n
Prentice Hall, 351
Priem, R. L., 24n, 189n
PRISM software, 257
Probert, J., 78n
Procter & Gamble (P&G), 13, 39, 57, 61, 71,
    83, 85, 102–103, 120, 126, 132, 139, 159,
    165, 168–169, 198, 205, 221, 227, 255,
    278, 282, 283, 296
Provan, K. G., 339n
Puffer, S. M., 24n
Pugliese, D., 78n

Quaker Oats, 150, 248, 343
Quinn, J. B., 18, 19, 24n, 84n, 104n, 167,
    188n, 322n
Qwest, 27

Radebaugh, L. H., 273n
Radiata, Inc., 140
Rahim, A., 322
Rajagopalan, N., 239n
Rajan, M. V., 272n
Ramaswamy, K., 162n, 239n
Rao, S. S., 272n
Rappaport, A., 188n, 273n
Rasheed, A. M. A., 24n
Raymond Morris Associates, 346
Raynor, M., 58n
Raytheon, 131
Rebello, K., 322n
Rechner, P. L., 39n, 189n
Redmond, W., 188n
Reebok International, 5, 42, 60, 150, 206
Register of American Manufacturers, 356
Register of Corporations, Directors and
    Executives, 366
Reichert, A., 163n
Reilly, B., 239n
Reimann, B. C., 163n
Renshaw, A. A., 194, 195n, 215n
Rensi, E., 176
Research Health Services, 333

Responsys.com, 185
Revlon, 264
Reynolds, P. D., 134n, 322n
Rhee, D. K., 134n
Richard, O. C., 188n
Richards, B., 273n
Richardson, J., 188n
Richardson-Vicks, 139
Ricklefs, R., 322n
Rigdon, J. I., 215n
Ring, P. S., 141
RISC (Reduced Instruction Set Computing),
    288
Rite Aid, 264
River Rouge Plant (Ford Motor Co.), 139
RJR Nabisco, 250
Roach, R., & Associates, 104
Roadway, 175
Robbins, D. K., 163n
Robbins, S. M., 273n
Robert, M., 299n
Roberts, D., 255n
Roberts-Witt, S. L., 188n, 189n
Robichaux, 322
Robinson, G., 188n
Robinson, K. C., 322n
Robinson, R. B., Jr., 322n
Rockwell International Corporation, 13
Roddick, A., 36
Rodrigues, A. F., 273n
Rogers, E. M., 290, 300n
Rolm and Haas, 29
Roman Catholic Church, 183
Romanelli, E., 24n
Roon, J. M. L., 273
Rosen, B., 188n
Ross, D., 218
Ross, J., 189n
Rosser, B., 105n
Roth, J., 289
Roth, K., 39n, 240n
Rothman, H., 273n
Rothschild, W. E., 239n
Rouse, M. M., 346
Rousseau, D. M., 105n
Roussel, P. A., 299n
Rowe, D., 300n
Rowe, W. G., 272n
Roy, M. H., 299n
Royal Dutch Shell, 72, 140, 296
RSD, 128
Rubbermaid, 39, 72, 254, 278
Rubbernetwork.com, 131
Rudney, G., 338n
Rue, L. W., 24n, 321n
Rumelt, R. P., 78n, 162n
Russo, M. V., 39n
Ryberg, W., 24n

Saad, K. N., 299n
SABRE Travel Information Network, 143

Saffo, P., 262–263
Safieddine, A., 188n
Sager, I., 149n
Salancik, G. R., 338n
Sametime, 236
Samson, D., 273n
Sanchez, C. M., 239n
Sanchez, J. I., 239n
Sanchez, R., 105n
Sandberg, W. R., 189n, 311–313, 322n
Sandigi, E., 336
Sandone, R., 295
SAP AG, 100, 211, 256
Sapet, C., 302
Sapienza, H. J., 189n
Saporito, B., 78n
Sara Lee Corporation, 169
Sarason, Y., 214
Sarma, A., 163
Sashittal, H. C., 105n
Sasseen, J. A., 366n
Saturn Division (General Motors), 227
Savage, R., 260
Saxton, M. J., 240n
Sayles, L. R., 300n
Schein, E. H., 105n
Schellhardt, T. D., 273n
Schendel, D. E., 78n, 79n, 162n, 289n
Scherreik, S., 188n
Schiller, Z., 135n
Schilling, M. A., 299n
Schine, E., 273n
Schlender, B. R., 299n
Schlitz Brewing Company, 31
Schmidt, D. R., 273n
Schmidt, J. A., 244n
Schneider, B., 105n
Schoenecker, T. S., 135n
Schomburg, A., 134n
Schonberger, R. J., 240n
Schonfeld, E., 188n, 248n
Schoorman, F. D., 30n, 36n
Schroeder, M., 300n
Schroeder, R. G., 188n
Schuling, M. A., 299
Schumpeter, J., 302
Schwartz, K. B., 239n
Schwartz, M., 299n
Schweiger, D. M., 189n, 239n, 240n
Schwenk, C. R., 189n, 321n
Scott, S. G., 321n
Scott Paper, 159, 220
SDNet Company Finder, 353
Seaboard Railroad, 228
Seaman, S. L., 215n
Searls, D., 212, 216n
Sears, Roebuck & Co., 69, 144, 197, 222, 259, 269
Securities and Exchange Commission (SEC), 26, 76, 356
   Edgar database, 353

Seeger, J. A., 322n
Segil, L., 130, 135n
Senge, P. M., 24n
Sensor, 82
Serpa, R., 240n
ServiceArizona, 325
Service Corporation International, 122
Sesame Street, 334
Sexton, D. L., 303, 321n, 322n
Shaker, S. M., 79n
Shanghai Automotive, 225
Shank, J. K., 272n
Shapiro, D. L., 188n
Sharfman, M. P., 24n
Sharif, M. F., 273n
Sharma, A., 163n
Sharpe, R., 239n
Shaver, J. M., 24n
Shaw, M. J., 24n
Shearson, 228
Sherman, S., 162n
Shleifer, A., 78n
Shook, C. L., 239n
Shrader, C. B., 321n
Shrader, R. C., 322n
Shuman, J. C., 322n
Shuttle by United, 81
Siegel, D., 39n
Siemens AG, 90, 128, 142, 284
Siesfeld, T., 272n
Signal Companies, 139
Silva, M., 299n
Simerly, R. L., 105n
Simmonds, P. G., 162n
Simon, H. A., 24n
Simon, J. G., 338n
Simon, M., 322n
Simpson, G. R., 339n
Simpson, R. L., 134n
Simpson Industries, 148
Singer, D., 149
Singer-Loomis, 238
Sinha, D. K., 163n, 188n
Sinha, K. K., 188n
Sirower, M. L., 162n, 188n
Sjögren, B., 299n
Skloot, E., 334, 339n
Skyrme, D. J., 272n, 273n
Slater, R. W., 273n
Sloan, A. P., 183, 198, 215n
Slocum, J. W., Jr., 24n, 162n, 273n
Small Business Administration, 333
Smart, T., 135n, 188n
Smircich, L., 105n
Smith, A. C., 338n
Smith, F., 211
Smith, G., 23n, 46n, 162n, 273n
Smith, J. A., 24n, 78n
Smith, K. G., 23n, 134n, 239n
Smith, M., 239n
Smith, M. F., 273n

Smithfield Foods, 141
Smith-Kline Beecham, 333
Snapple, 150
Snow, C. C., 66, 78n, 207, 215n, 273n
Snow Brand, 39, 66
Snyder, N., 299n
Society of Competitive Intelligence Professionals, 71, 74
Sommerlatte, T., 299n
Sonnack, M., 299n
Sonnenfeld, J. A., 43n
Sony Corporation, 279, 280, 282, 288
Soper, B., 273n
Sorensen, J. B., 299n
Sorking, A. R., 366n
South African Breweries (SAB), 113
South Dekalb Mall, 56
Southern California Edison, 303
Southwest Airlines, 36, 77, 80–81, 82, 84, 119, 264
Spector, P. E., 239n
Sperlich, H., 282
Spreitzer, G. M., 239n
Springer, M., 188n
Sprint (SprintPCS), 125, 136, 170, 248
SSA, 256
Stafford, E. R., 39n
Stalk, G., Jr., 299n
Standard Oil, 197, 222
Standard & Poor's, 75
Stanley Works, 257
Staples, 170, 174, 175
Starkey, M., 272n
Starks, A. and D., 119
Statistical Abstract of the United States, 355
Statistical Yearbook, 355
Staw, B. M., 189n
Stearns, T. M., 134n
Steele, F. I., 322n
Steensen, J., 160
Steensma, H. K., 189n
Stepanek, M., 300n
Stephan, J., 163n
Stern, G., 240n
Stern Stewart & Company, 248
Stevens, S., 135n, 188n
Stewart, E., 80
Stewart, G. B., III, 272n
Stewart, T. A., 240n, 273n, 300n
Stewart, W. H., Jr., 321n
Stewart Enterprises, 122
Stipp, D., 322n
Stivers, B. P., 273n
Sto, M., 322n
Stobaugh, R. B., 273n
Stofford, J. M., 78n
Stoner, C. R., 239n
Stonich, P. J., 261n, 273n
Strader, T., 24n
Stuart, T. E., 299n

Subramanian, R., 239n, 338n
Sullivan, A., 216n
Sullivan, J., 98
Summers, D. V., 338n
Summers, L. H., 105n
Sunbeam Corporation, 220
Sun Microsystems, 17
Suris, O., 134n
Survey of Current Business, 355
Svetcov, D., 189n
Swartz, Mark, 26
Switchboard, 75
Symonds, W. C., 26n, 27n

Tabrizi, B., 300n
Taggart, J. H., 216n
Taisei Corporation, 21
Tan, H. H., 36n
Tan, S. J., 322n
Tancredi, J., 291
Tannenbaum, J. A., 134n
Tavakolian, H., 215n
Taylor, A., 218
Taylor, M. S., 240n
TCI, 137
Teagle Foundation, 334
Teece, D. J., 78n, 162n, 163n
Teledyne, 248
Tellis, G. J., 134n
Teng, B-S., 135n
Tenneco, 248
Tennessee Valley Authority, 181
Teradyne, 292–293
Tertkauf, 144
Tetenbaum, T. J., 240n
Texaco, Inc., 85, 211–212
Texas Instruments, 29, 290, 351
Textron, 261
Thain, D. H., 199n
Thilgen, T., 162n
Thomas, A., 321n
Thomas, A. S., 239n
Thomas, H., 78n
Thomas, J. B., 78n
Thomas, L. G., III, 189n
Thomke, S., 299n
Thompson, J. D., 338
Threat, H., 273n
3M (Minnesota Mining & Manufacturing
    Company), 14, 29, 132, 175, 211, 245,
    254, 278, 279, 281, 290, 294
Tichy, N. M., 35n, 239n
Tide, 255, 290
Timex, 119
Titman, S., 188n
TLCi, 236
Toccacelli, J., 39n
Tomsho, R., 134n
Tonge, R., 322n
Toro Company, 143
Toshiba, 128, 142

Total System Services, 166
Toto Ltd., 285
Towner, S. J., 299n
Townsend, A. M., 105n
Toyota Motor Corporation, 114, 121, 128,
    145
Toys "R" Us, 128, 131, 144, 256
TradeMatrix, 6
Trading Process Network, 177
Transmet Corporation, 310
Transportacion Maritima Mexicana, 145
Trans World Airlines (TWA), 80, 264
Travis, V. R., 323n
Treece, J. B., 163n
Trevino, L. K., 42n
Trilogy Software, Inc., 277
Trotman, A., 114
Trump Resorts, 264
TRW Systems, 206
Tsang, E. W. K., 302n
Tully, S., 272n, 273n
Tung, R. L., 240n
Tupperware, 71–72
Turban, E., 24n
Turner, D. B., 39n
Turner, Lyn, 26
Turner, M., 323n
Turner, T., 36
Tushman, M. L., 24n
Tyco International Ltd., 25–26, 27, 29, 31, 40
Tyler, B. B., 189n

UBS Warburg, 248
UK Online, 325
Ullmann, A. A., 172n
UNICEF, 332
Unilever, 168–169, 224
Union Carbide, 174
United Airlines (UAL), 32, 77, 80–81, 142
United Auto Workers, 32, 98
United Express, 142
United Parcel Service (UPS), 98, 263, 310,
    320
U.S. Census, 56, 355
U.S. Congress, 282
U.S. Constitution, 4
U.S. Defense Department, 7
U.S. Department of Justice, 127
U.S. Equal Employment Opportunity
    Commission, 225
U.S. Federal Trade Commission, 131, 352
U.S. General Accounting Office, 333
U.S. Industrial Outlook, 355
U.S. Internal Revenue Service (IRS), 326,
    333
U.S. National Association of College and
    University Business Officers, 333
U.S. Navy, 268
U.S. Robotics, 202
U.S. Securities and Exchange Commission,
    76, 356

U.S. Securities and Exchange Commission
    Edgar database, 353
United Way, 327
University of Phoenix, 337
UNIX, 149
Unterman, I., 338n
Upjohn Pharmaceuticals, 234
Urbanfetch, 320
Urschel Laboratories, 170
Useem, J., 322n
US West, 136
Uzumeri, M. V., 272n

Vaghefi, M. R., 23n
Value Line, 75
Vanac, M., 366n
Van Alstyne, M., 194, 195n, 215n
Van Der Linde, B. 246
Van De Ven, A. H., 141n
Varchaver, N., 26n
Varian, T., 272n
Vedder, R. G., 79n
Veiga, J. F., 189n
Vella, A. J., 322n
Verdin, P. J., 188n
Veridicom, 293
Versteeg, A., 105n
VerticalNet, 6
Veterinary Centers of America, 122
Vidal Sassoon, 139
Viskny, R. W., 78n
Visual Insights, 293
Voloberda, H. W., 24n
Von Bergen, C. W., 273n
Von der Embse, T. J., 42n
Von Hippel, E., 79n, 281, 299n
Vorhies, D. W., 163n
Voss, B., 162n, 215n

Waddock, S. A., 39n
Wade, J., 273n, 299n, 322n
Wagley, R. A., 42n
Wagner, J. A., III, 189n
Wagner, S., 299n
Wagner, T., 203
Walal, W. E., 78
Wallace, B., 273n
Walleck, A. S., 23n
Wallender, H. W., III, 329–330, 338n
Wall Street Journal Index, 356
Wall Street Research Net, 353
Wal-Mart, 83, 102–103, 108, 119, 132, 143,
    144, 147, 186, 191, 211, 254, 256
Walmart.com, 187
Walsh, Frank, Jr., 26
Walt Disney entries. *See* Disney entries
Wan, W. P., 23n
Ward, D., 273n
Ward, J. L., 322n, 323n
Ward, V., 235–236
Waring, G., 189n

Warner, J., 24n, 46n, 79n, 105n, 135n, 163n, 189n, 216n, 240n, 273n, 300n, 323n, 339n, 366n
Warner, M., 32n
Warner-Lambert, 21, 131
Wasson, C. R., 91n
Waterman, R. H., 273n
Watkins, Sherron, 40
Watson, W. E., 321n
Webb, J., 292
Webber, A. M., 299n
WebCrawler, 75
Weber, H. R., 26n
Weber, P. S., 132
Weber, Y., 239n, 240n
Web 100, 353, 356
Webvan, 320
Weihrich, H., 115
Weinberg, N., 135n
Weinberger, D., 212, 216n
Welch, D., 24n
Welch, J., 1–2, 35n, 156, 184
Welsch, H. P., 322n
Westbrook, R., 134n
Westhead, P., 322n
Westinghouse, 127
Weyerhauser, 85
Wharton School of Business, 278
Wheatley, J., 188n
Wheelen, T. L., 20n, 28n, 69n, 74n, 102n, 111n, 168n, 172n, 179n, 265n, 273n, 307, 308n, 328, 338n, 351n
Wheeling-Pittsburgh Steel, 32, 203
Whinston, A., 24n
Whirlpool, 29, 123, 166, 172, 248, 257, 287

White, J. B., 273n
White, M. C., 239n
White Consolidated Industries, 145
Whitford, D., 322n
Whitman, M., 17, 203, 313
Who Wants To Be a Millionaire, 177
Whyte, G., 189n
Wiesendanger, B., 338n
Wiggenhorn, W., 239n
Willard, G. E., 300n, 322n
Williams, J. R., 83n, 188n
Williams, M. L., 134n, 339n
Williamson, O. E., 141
Williamson, P. J., 188n
Wilson, D. C., 24n
Wilson, I., 23n
Winter, S. G., 141n
Winterson, J., 336
Wiseman, R. M., 188n
Wisendanger, B., 338
Wolf, C., 248
Woo, C. Y., 163n, 248, 300n, 322n
Woo, S. S., 352
Wooldridge, J. R., 273n
WordPerfect, 280
WorldCom, 27, 40, 160
World Economic Forum's, 302
World Fact Book, The, 355–356
World Intellectual Property Organization, 336
World Trade Annual, 355
World Wide Web Consortium (W3C), 336
Worrell, D. L., 34n
Wortman, M. S., 273n
Wright, P. M., 134n, 272n

Wyatt, J., 78n
Wynett, C., 296

Xerox Corporation, 93, 141, 166, 223, 254, 283, 293
Xie, J. L., 209n

Yahoo!, 45, 75, 295, 325, 352
Yamada, K., 299n
Yamaha, 255
Yang, D. J., 105n
Yankelovich Partners, 342
Yauger, C. C., 338n
Yellow Pages, 235
Yeung, B., 24n
Yeung, S., 24n
Yiu, D., 23n
Yoder, S. K., 300n
Young, C. E., 163n
Young, S., 225
Yuengling, 310

Zabriskie, Dr., 234
Zachary, G. P., 273n
Zahra, S. A., 28n, 300n
Zajac, E. J., 23n
Zamboni, F., 112
Zamboni, Frank J., & Company, 112
Zander, Edward, 17
Zangwill, W. I., 299n
zBox Company, 310
Zeithaml, C. P., 28n, 162n, 163n
Zellner, W., 39n, 40, 189n, 273n
Ziegler, B., 149n
Zoom Telephonics, 202

Subject Index

ABC. *See* Activity-based costing (ABC)
Absorptive capacity, 288
Accounting
    for multinational corporations, 343–346
    traditional cost accounting vs. ABC,
      245–246
Accounts payable period, 345
Accounts receivable turnover, 345
Acquisitions, 139
    international markets entry and, 145
    managing corporate cultures after,
      227–229
    technological competence and, 288–289
Action plan, for strategy implementation,
    229–231
Activity-based costing (ABC), 245–256
Activity ratios, 342, 344–345
Adaptive mode, of strategic decision making,
    18–19
Advanced Manufacturing Technology
    (AMT), 171–172
Advertising, push/pull marketing strategies
    for, 169
Advisory board, for small
    businesses/entrepreneurial ventures,
    308–309
Affiliated directors, 31
Affirmative action, 43
Agency theory, 29, 30
Alien territory businesses, 158
Alliances. *See* Strategic alliances
Allport-Vernon-Lindzey Study of Values test,
    41
Altman's Bankruptcy Formula, 346
Ambiguity, 312
Analysis
    industry, 60–70
    organizational, 80–103
    of societal environment, 57–59
    SWOT, 109–113
    VRIO framework of, 81
Analytical portfolio manager (executive
    type), 220
Analytics software, 185
Analyzers, 67
Arms Race strategy, 177
ASEAN. *See* Association of South East Asian
    Nations (ASEAN)
ASEAN Free-Trade Area (AFTA), 6
Assessment centers, 222
Asset turnover, 344

Assimilation, of corporate cultures after
    acquisitions, 228, 229
Association of South East Asian Nations
    (ASEAN), 6
Assumptions, 71
Attitude Toward Risk, 180
Audits
    management, 252
    strategic (*See* Strategic audit)
Autonomous (self-managing) work teams,
    97
Average collection period, 345

Baby boom, 55
Backward integration, 140
Balanced scorecard, 250–251
Ballast businesses, in parenting-fit matrix,
    158
Banking Act (1933), 32
Bankruptcy, 150, 203
    Altman's Formula for, 346–347
Bargaining power of buyers, 63
Bargaining power of suppliers, 63
Barriers. *See* Entry barriers; Exit barriers
Basic R&D, 93
BCG (Boston Consulting Group) Growth-
    Share Matrix, 151–153
    advantages and limitations of,
      152–153
    cash cows, 152
    dogs, 152
    question marks, 151
    stars, 151
    vs. GE Business Screen, 154
Behavior controls, 243
    ISO 9000 Standards Series, 245
Behavior substitution, 258–259
Benchmarking, 254
Benefits of strategic management, 4
Best practices, for improving R&D, 294,
    295
Bill of Rights, 43
Blocks to changing stages, 201
Board of directors
    compensation committee, 258
    in corporate governance, 26–29, 31–35
    employees on, 32
    of entrepreneurial firms, 308
    members of, 29, 31–32
    nomination and election of members,
      32–33

    organization of, 33–34
    responsibilities of, 27
    in strategic management, 27–28
Board of directors continuum, 28–29
Boomlet, Generation Y, 55
BOT (Build, Operate, Transfer) concept,
    international markets entry and,
    146
Brainstorming, 72
Brand extension, 169
Brand management, 205
Broad target strategy, 120
B2B. *See* Business to business (B2B)
B2B consortiums, 131
Budget, 196, 395
    defined, 15
    operating, 252
Budgeting, capital, 92
Business
    cultural differences in role of, 53
    pace of, 7
    responsibilities of, 37–38
    traditional view of, 37
Business directories, on Internet, 353
Business model, 304
Business plan, for entrepreneurial ventures,
    306–307, 308
Business policy, defined, 2
Business screen, GE, 153
Business strategy, 13, 115–130
    competitive, 115–117, 117–126
    cooperative, 117, 126–130
    Internet and, 131–132
    new venture success and, 311–312
    Porter's competitive strategies, 117–126
    strategies to avoid, 177
Business to business (B2B), 6
    defined, 131
    developmental stages of, 131–132
Business to consumer (B2C), 131
Buyers, as competitive force, 63
Bypass attack, 125

CAD/CAM. *See* Computer-Assisted Design
    and Computer-Assisted Manufacturing
    (CAD/CAM)
Cannibalization, of products, 68
Capabilities, 82
    core, 165
Capacity, intense firm rivalry and, 62
Capital budgeting, 92

Capital requirements, as barrier to entry, 61
Capital structure, 91
Captive company strategy, 148
Case analysis, 341–353
    case method, 342
    common-size statements, 346
    economic measures, 347, 349
    financial statements analysis, 342–347
    free cash flow in, 347
    index of sustainable growth in, 346–347
    inflation and, 348
    Internet and, 351–353
    research for, 342
    research resources for, 355–356
    strategic audit format for, 348–351,
        357–359
    Strategic Audit worksheet, 350–351
    trends comparison, 343
    Z-value calculation, 346
Case Method, 342
Case Research, 342
    resources, 355
Cash cows, in BCG Growth-Share Matrix, 152
Cash ratio, 344
Categorical imperatives, 43
Cautious profit planner (executive type), 220
Cellular organization, 207
Center of gravity, 85
Centers, responsibility, 252
Centralization, 210
    defensive, 331
    vs. decentralization in MNCs, 211–212
Centralized logistics group, 175
CEO. See also Executive(s); Top management
    in articulating strategic vision, 36
    as chairman of the board, 29
    compensation contingencies for, 261
    corporate development stages and, 200, 201
    evaluation of, 251–252
    information manipulation by, 258
    nomination and election of board
        members by, 32–33
    as outside director, 31
    strategy implementation and, 220–221
Characteristics
    of entrepreneur, 312
    product/service, intense firm rivalry and,
        62
Charities, 325
Chief executive officer. See CEO (chief
    executive officer)
Chief operating officer (COO). See COO
    (chief operating officer)
Churches, 325
Clayton Act, 32
Client-organization influence, sources of
    revenue and, 327–329
Cluetrain Manifesto, 212
Codes of ethics, 42
Codetermination, 32
Collective goods, 325
Colleges, 325

Collusion, 126–127
Common-size financial statements, 178–179,
    346
Communication, cultural change
    management and, 227
Companies. See also Corporate entries;
    Industries
    directory and index information, 356
    Internet resources for, 352–353, 355
    locating Web sites of, 351
Compensation committees, 251
Compensatory justice, 43
Competency(ies), 82
    core, 165
    distinctive, 165
Competition, 7. See also Competitive forces,
    in Porter's industry analysis;
    Hypercompetition
Competitive advantage
    competitive scope and, 118
    Porter's generic competitive strategies
        and, 118
    R&D and, 285
    R&D strategy and, 171
    resources and, 82
    strategic alliances and, 128
    sustainability of, 82–83
Competitive forces, in Porter's industry
    analysis, 60–64
    bargaining power of buyers, 63
    bargaining power of suppliers, 63
    new entrants, 61–62
    relative power of unions, governments,
        etc., 63–64
    rivalry among existing firms, 62
    threat of substitute products/services,
        62–63
Competitive intelligence, 70–71
Competitive scope, 118
Competitive strategy, 115–117, 117–126
    broad target, 120
    cost focus, 119, 120
    cost leadership, 118–119, 120
    differentiation, 119, 120
    differentiation focus, 119, 120
    differentiation strategy, 118
    hypercompetition and, 122–123
    knowledge and, 7
    lower cost strategy, 118
    market location tactics for, 125–126
    narrow target, 120
    Porter's, 117–126
    requirements for, 123, 124
    risks in, 119–120
    timing tactics for, 124–125
Competitive strengths, in international
    portfolio analysis, 154, 155
Competitive tactics, 123–124
Competitor information, available on
    Internet, 76
Competitors, intense firm rivalry and, 62
Complement, 64

Complications
    to evaluation and control, 332
    to strategy formulation, 330–331
    to strategy implementation, 331
Computer-Assisted Design and Computer-
    Assisted Manufacturing (CAD/CAM),
    97
Computer disk drive manufacturers,
    technological discontinuity and, 95
Computer hackers, 263, 295
Computer-integrated design and
    manufacturing (CAD/CAM), 171
Concentration, 139–142
    horizontal growth and, 142
    vertical growth and, 139–142
Concentric diversification, 142–143
Concurrent engineering, 97
Conglomerate diversification, 143
Conglomerate structure, 88
Connected line batch flow, 172
Consensus, 183
Consolidated industry, 64, 122
Consolidation, 148
Constant dollars, 347
Constitution, U.S., 4, 43
Constraints on strategic management,
    329–330
    complications to strategy formulation
        and, 330–331
    strategy implementation and, 331
Consumer Price Index (CPI), 347, 348
Consumers, 7
Continual process improvements, 287
Continuous improvement system, 172–173
Continuous systems, 96
Continuum of sustainability, 83–84
Contracting, for corporate entrepreneurship,
    293
Contraction, 148
Contracts, long-term, 142
Control(s), 16. See also Evaluation and
    control process
    types of, 243–245
Conventional level, of moral development, 42
COO (Chief Operating Officer)
    as outside director, 31
Cooperative contractual relationships, 142
Cooperative strategies, 117, 126–130
    collusion, 126–127
    strategic alliances, 127–130
Core capability, 165. See also Core
    competencies
Core competencies, 82. See also Distinctive
    competencies
    as distinctive competencies, 165–166
    imitability and, 82–83
    replicability and, 83
    transferability, 83
    transparency and, 82
Corporate 10-K forms, for case research, 342
Corporate annual reports, for case research,
    342

Corporate capabilities, 82. *See also* Distinctive competencies
Corporate culture(s), 88–89
  as competitive advantage, 90
  integration, 89
  intensity and, 89
  leading after international mergers, 233–234
  management of (*See* Managing corporate culture)
  managing after acquisitions, 227–229
Corporate culture pressures, strategic choice and, 181–182
Corporate development, stages of. *See* Stages of corporate development
Corporate diversification strategy. *See* Diversification
Corporate entrepreneurship, 291–294
Corporate governance, 26
  agency vs. stewardship theory in, 30
  board of directors in, 26–29, 31–35
  impact of Internet on, 44–45
  of small businesses/entrepreneurial ventures, 308–309
  top management in, 35–37
  trends in, 34–35
Corporate headquarters, role in corporate parenting, 156
Corporate New Ventures (CNV) unit, at P&G, 296
Corporate parenting, 137, 156–159
  horizontal strategy and, 159
  multipoint competition and, 159
  parenting-fit matrix in, 157–158
  strategy development, 156–157
Corporate performance
  balanced scorecard approach, 250–251
  information systems/technology and, 100
  shareholder value, 248–250
  stakeholder measures of, 247
  strategic audit evaluation of, 262
  top management evaluation, 251–252
  traditional financial measures for, 246–247
Corporate scenarios. *See* Scenarios, corporate
Corporate stakeholders, 39–40. *See also* Stakeholder(s)
Corporate strategy, 13
  at AT&T, 136–137
  defined, 137–138
  directional strategy and, 137, 138–150
  Internet and, 159–160
  parenting strategy and, 156–159
  portfolio analysis and, 137, 151–155
  strategies to avoid, 177
Corporate value chain analysis, 85–87
Corporation(s), 26. *See also* Companies; Industries; Multinational corporation (MNC)
  links among, 7

Cost focus, 119
Cost leadership, 118–119
Cost proximity, 120
Costs
  as barriers to entry, 61, 62
  disadvantages independent of size, 62
  fixed, 62
  switching, 61
Country's attractiveness, in international portfolio analysis, 154, 155
Creativity, 297
Crisis of autonomy, 200
Crisis of control, 200
Crisis of leadership, 200
Criticisms of SWOT analysis, 109
Cross-functional work teams, 97–98
Cross-impact analysis (CIA), 72
Cultural change, communication and, 227
Cultural differences
  staffing and, 224
  strategy implementation and, 234
Cultural integration, 89
Cultural intensity, 89
Culture(s)
  corporate (*See* Corporate culture[s])
  entrepreneurial, 290
  national, 232–233
Culture trends. *See* International societal environment
Current ratio, 344
Customization, mass, 97, 173
Cybersquatting, 44

Days of cash, 345
Days of inventory, 345
Debt to asset ratio, 345
Debt to equity ratio, 345
Decentralization, vs. centralization in MNCs, 211–212
Decision making
  ethical, 40–43
  social responsibilities of strategic, 37–40
  strategic, 18–21
Deculturation, after acquisitions, 228–229
Dedicated transfer lines, 172
Defenders, 66
Defensive centralization, 331
Defensive tactics, 126
Delphi technique, 72
Demographics, 310
Demographic trends, 54
Developed nations, Triad and, 56–57
Developing nations, identifying potential markets in, 57, 58
Developing policies. *See* Policy development
Devil's advocate technique, 183
Dialectical inquiry, 184
Differentiation, 119
Differentiation focus, 119
Differentiation strategy, 118–119
Digital signature, 263
Dimensions of national culture, 232–233

Direct integration, for corporate entrepreneurship, 292
Directional strategy, 137
  growth strategies, 138–146
  retrenchment strategy and, 148–150
  stability strategy and, 138, 146–147
Directory and index information on companies and industries, 356
Direct public offering (DPO), 315
Discretionary expenses, 253
Discretionary responsibilities, 38
Disintermediation, 7
Disruptive technology, 95
Distinctive competencies, 165–166
  defined, 82
  durability, 82
  imitability, 82–83
  resources and capabilities as, 83–84
  SWOT analysis and, 109
Distribution, marketing strategies for, 169
Distribution channels, 7
  access to, as barrier to entry, 62
Diverse cultures, 227
Diversification, 139
  concentric, 142–143
  conglomerate, 143
  financial strategy and, 170
Diversity, human, 98–99, 176
Divestment, 150. *See also* Sell out
Dividend payout ratio, 345
Dividends, financial strategy and, 170
Dividend yield on common stock, 345
Divisional and functional performance measures, 252–254
  benchmarking, 254
  responsibility centers, 252–254
Divisional structure, 87, 88, 200–201
Do Everything strategy, 177
Dogs, in BCG Growth-Share Matrix, 152
Domain, 336–337, 351
Domestic company, stages of international development for, 210
Dot-Com Deathwatch, 203
Dot.coms. *See* Internet
Downsizing, 222–223
  guidelines, 223
Due care, 27
Durability, 82
Dynamic industry expert (executive type), 220
Dynamic intranets, 235, 236
Dynamic pricing, e-CRM software and, 186

Earnings per share (EPS), 246–247, 344
EBITDA (Earnings Before Interest, Taxes, Depreciation, and Amortization), 347
E-commerce. *See* Electronic commerce
Economic Creativity Index (World Economic Forum), 302
Economic Espionage Act (1996), 71
Economic forces, 52
Economic information, resources, 355

Economic responsibilities of business organization, 37
Economics, transaction cost, 140
Economic societal environment, 52, 53
  international, 57
  trends in, 54
Economic value added (EVA), 248–250
Economies of scale, 97
  as barrier to entry, 61
Economies of scope, 87, 97
E-CRM software. *See* Electronic customer relationship management (e-CRM) software
Edge-of-heartland businesses, 158
  in parenting-fit matrix, 158
Education, Internet and, 337
EFAS (External Factors Analysis Summary) Table, 73–74, 110
80/20 rule, 259
Electronic commerce, 5–6
Electronic customer relationship management (e-CRM) software, 185–186
Electronic networking, 7, 54
E-marketing software, 185
Embrace and extend strategy, 283
Employees. *See also* Human resource management (HRM) entries
  on boards of directors, 32
  monitoring of Internet usage, 262–263
Employee stock ownership plans (ESOPs), 32
Encirclement, 125
Energy sources, alternative, 54
Engineered expenses, 253
Engineering, concurrent, 97
Engineering (process) R&D, 93
Enterprise resource planning (ERP), 256–257
Entrepreneur(s)
  in simple structure stage, 199–200
  as strategist, 303–304
Entrepreneurial characteristics, for new venture success, 312–313
Entrepreneurial culture, development of, 290–291
Entrepreneurial mode, of strategic decision making, 18
Entrepreneurial ventures. *See also* Small-business firms
  business model and, 304
  business plan for, 306–307, 308
  corporate governance and, 308–309
  defined, 303
  environmental scanning and strategy formulation for, 309–313
  evaluation and control process for, 316–318
  factors affecting success of, 311–313
  focus strategies for, 121
  FunZone as, 301, 303
  guidelines for success, 313
  importance of, 301–303
  informal questions for strategic management process, 305

Internet and, 318–320
  sources of innovation for, 309–311
  strategic audit for, 307
  strategic decision-making process for, 305–307
Entrepreneurship, 301
  corporate, 291–294
  global, 302
  strategy formulation, 309
Entry barriers, 61–62
  as defensive tactics, 126
  SAS and, 113
Environment
  external, 9–10
  internal, 10
  variables in, 11
Environmental awareness, 55
Environmental scanning, 9–10, 52–60. *See also* EFAS (External Factors Analysis Summary) Table; Industry analysis
  Chefs Unlimited and, 51–52
  competitive intelligence and, 70–71
  defined, 52
  external environmental variables, 52–59
  external strategic factors, 59–60
  forecasting and, 71–72
  Internet and, 74–76
  of Newbury Comics, Inc., 106–107
  for small businesses/entrepreneurial ventures, 309–313
  of societal environment, 52, 53–57
  of task environment, 57–59
  technology and innovation management and, 280–284
Environmental uncertainty, 52
Ethical behavior
  encouraging, 42
  guidelines for, 42–43
Ethical decision making, 40–43
Ethical responsibilities, 38
EU. *See* European Union (EU)
European Commission, Internet, tax revenues, and, 335
European Union (EU), 5, 6
  Internet, tax revenues, and, 335
  ISO 9000 certification and, 245
  MNCs and, 56
Euros, 335
Evaluation and control information, 243
Evaluation and control process, 16
  complications to, 332
  control guidelines, 259–260
  for entrepreneurial ventures/small businesses, 316–318
  five-step feedback model for, 242
  Internet and, 262–263
  at Nucor Corporation, 241–244
  performance measurement and, 243–259
  strategic incentive management and, 260–262
  in strategic management, 243, 244
  technology and innovation management and, 294–295

Executive(s). *See also* CEO; Top management
  strategic choice and, 182–183
Executive committee, 34
Executive development, 331
Executive leadership, 35
Executive succession, 221
Executive type, strategy implementation and, 220–221
Existing markets, product development for, 169
Exit barriers, 62
Expense centers, 253
Experience curve, 96
  BCG Growth-Share Matrix and, 152
Expert opinion, 72
Explicit collusion, 126–127
Explicit knowledge, 83
Exporting, international markets entry and, 143
External environment, 9–10
  analysis of, 57–59
  environmental scanning of, 52–59
  issues priority matrix and, 59, 60
  strategic factors identified in, 59–60
  variables identified in, 52–59
External Factors Analysis Summary. *See* EFAS (External Factors Analysis Summary) Table
External-internal integration, 331
Externally oriented planning. *See* Strategic planning
External scanning
  stakeholders and, 281
  technological developments and, 280–281
External strategic factors, 59–60
  defined, 60
Extranet, 100
  intranets connected via, 257
Extrapolation, 72

Factors affecting new venture success, 311–313
  business strategy, 311–312
  entrepreneurial characteristics, 312–313
  guidelines for, 313
  industry structure, 311
Family businesses, transfer of power and wealth in, 315–316
Family directors, 31
Farming, precision, 54
Fast-cycle resources, 83, 84
Feedback/learning process, 16
Finance, 169
  measures, 246–247
Financial issues, 91–92
  capital budgeting, 92
Financial leverage, 92
Financial manager, 91
Financial methods, standard, use in small business evaluation, 317–318
Financial planning, 3
Financial ratio analysis, 344–345
Financial risk, strategic alliances and, 127

Financial statements
  analyzing, 342–347
  locating on Internet, 352–353
Financial strategy, 169–170
  dividends management and, 170
  leveraged buy out, 170
  tracking stock, 170
First mover, 124
Fixed asset turnover, 345
Fixed costs, 62
Flanking maneuver, 125
Flexible manufacturing, 97, 172
Focus strategies, 119, 120, 121
Follower R&D functional strategy, 171
Follow the Leader strategy, 177
Follow-the-sun management, 176
Forecast-based planning, 3
Forecasting, 71–72
  faulty assumptions and, 71–72
  techniques for, 72–73
Foreign assignments. *See* International
    assignments
Formality of strategic planning, 304
Forward integration, 140
Founder of company, as block to corporate
    development, 201, 202
Fragmented industry, 64, 121–122
  strategic rollup and, 122
Franchising, international markets entry
    and, 144
Fraud, 44
Free cash flow, 347
Free trade associations, 6
Frontal assault, 125
FTA. *See* Free trade associations
Fuel cells, 54
Full integration, 140
Functional performance measures. *See*
    Divisional and functional performance
    measures
Functional strategy, 13
  at Church & Dwight Company, 164–165
  core competencies and, 165–166
  defined, 165
  financial strategy, 169–170
  human resource management strategy,
      175–176
  information systems strategy, 176–177
  Internet and, 184–188
  logistics strategy, 174–175
  marketing strategy, 168–169
  operations strategy, 171–173
  policy development, 184
  purchasing strategy, 173–174, 175
  R&D strategy, 170–171
  selection of (*See* Strategic choice)
  sourcing decision, 166–168
  strategies to avoid, 177
Functional structure, 87, 88, 200
Fuzzy logic technology, 287

GE Business Screen, 153–154
  shortcomings of, 154

Generation Y boomlet, 55
Generic competitive strategies, 118. *See also*
    Competitive strategy
Genetically altered organisms, 54
Geographic-area structure, 211–212
Global communication/transportation
    systems, human resources and, 99
Global Competitiveness Report (World
    Economic Forum), 302
Global industries, 65
Global Internet economy, 99
Globalization, defined, 5
Global markets, Web sites for local business
    presence in, 312
Global MNC, control and reward systems in, 256
Goal, 12
Goal conflicts, 330
Goal displacement, 258–259
Government(s)
  as barrier to entry, 62
  Internet and, 335–336
Government services (G2C), Internet and,
    335–336
Green-field development, international
    markets entry and, 145, 178
Gross domestic product (GDP), 347
  PPP and, 58
  for U.S. (1983–2000), 349
Gross profit margin, 344
Growth
  horizontal, 142
  vertical, 139–142
Growth-share matrix, BCG, 151
Growth strategies, 138–146
  concentration, 139–142
  controversies in, 146
  diversification, 142–143
  international entry options, 143–146
Guerrilla warfare, 125
Guidelines
  for downsizing, 223
  for new venture success, 313
  for proper control, 259–260

Hackers, computer, 263, 295
Health care, Internet and, 337
Heartland businesses, 158
  in parenting-fit matrix, 158
Hierarchy of strategy, 13
High force, 60
Hiring, strategy implementation and, 219
Hit Another Home Run strategy, 177
Horizontal growth, 142
Horizontal integration, 142
Horizontal strategy, 158
Hospitals, 325
Households, changing composition of, 56
HRM. *See* Human resource management
    (HRM) entries
Human diversity, 98–99, 176
Human resource management (HRM), 97–99
  global communication/transportation
      systems and, 99

human diversity and, 98–99, 176
  quality of work life, 98
  teams usage, 97–98
  temporary workers, 98
  union relations, 98
Human resource management (HRM)
    strategy, 175–176
Human resource manager, 97
Hypercompetition, 67–68
  competitive strategy and, 122–123
  defined, 68
  Microsoft in, 68
  multipoint competition, horizontal
      strategy, and, 158
Hyperlinked organization, 212

Identifying abilities and potential, 221
IFAS (Internal Factor Analysis Summary)
    Table, 101–102, 110
  total weighted score in, 101
Imitability, 82–83
Implementation. *See* Strategy
    implementation
Incentive programs, 260. *See also* Strategic
    incentive management
Independent business units, for corporate
    entrepreneurship, 293
Independent contractors, 176
Index of R&D effectiveness, 294
Index of sustainable growth, 346–347
Individualism-collectivism (I-C), 233
Individual rights approach, to ethical
    behavior, 43
Industrial espionage, 71
Industries. *See also* Corporate entries; Industry
    analysis; International industries
  competitive forces in, 60–61
  consolidated, 64, 122
  defined, 60
  directory and index information, 356
  evolution of, 64
  fragmented, 64, 121–122
  global, 65
  information resources for, 355–356
  multidomestic, 64–65
  new entrants in, 61–62
  strategic rollup and, 122
Industry analysis, 53, 60–70. *See also* EFAS
    (External Factors Analysis Summary)
    Table; Environmental scanning
  continuum of international industries,
      64–65
  forces driving competition, 61
  hypercompetition, 67–68
  industry evolution and, 64
  international risk assessment, 65–66
  Internet and, 74–76
  key success factors and industry matrix
      creation, 69–70
  Porter's approach, 60–64
  strategic groups, 66
  strategic types, 66–67
Industry matrix, key success factors and, 69–70

Industry scenario, 72–73, 178
Industry structure, 121
  new venture success and, 311
Industry value chain analysis, 84–85
Inflation, case analysis and, 347, 348
Information
  company, 355
  directory/index information on
    companies/industries, 356
  economic, 355
  evaluation and control, 243
  industry, 355–356
  online, 356
  ratio analysis, 356
Information systems (IS), strategic, 256–257
Information systems strategy, 176–177
Information systems/technology, 99–100
  corporate performance and, 100
  global Internet economy and, 99
Information technology
  international business and, 211
  Moore's Law and, 94
Initial public offering (IPO), 315
Innovation(s). *See also* Technology and
  innovation management
  corporate entrepreneurship and, 291–294
  "knowledge market" approach to, 296
  lead users and, 281–282
  product and process, 285–286, 287
  sources for entrepreneurial ventures,
    309–311
  stakeholders and, 281
Innovation life cycle, product and process
  R&D in, 286
Input controls, 243, 245
Inside directors, 29, 31
Institutional advantage, 329
Institution theory, 7–8
Integrated planning focus, 330
Integration
  after acquisitions, 227–228
  cultural, 89
  forms of, 140–142
Intelligence agencies, Echelon system of, 263
Intensity, cultural, 89
Interest rate, prime, 347
Interlocking directorate, 32
Intermittent systems, 95–96
Internal development, technological
  competence and, 288–289
Internal environment, 10
Internal Factor Analysis Summary. *See* IFAS
  (Internal Factor Analysis Summary)
  Table
Internal scanning. *See also* Organizational
  analysis
  innovation and, 283
Internal strategic factors, 81
International assignments, 225
  organizational learning and, 224
International Benchmarking Clearinghouse,
  254

International business. *See also*
  Multinational corporation (MNC)
  FedEx, information technology, and, 211
International development, stages of, 210
International entry options
  acquisitions, 145
  BOT concept, 146
  exporting and, 143
  franchising, 144
  green-field development, 145
  joint venture, 145
  licensing, 144
  management contracts, 146
  production sharing, 145
  turnkey operations, 145–146
International expansion, staffing for, 224–225
International industries, continuum of, 65
International leading, 232–234
International markets. *See also* International
  entry options
  Internet and entry into, 160
  Wal-Mart entry into, 144
International performance evaluation, 254–256
International portfolio analysis
  country attractiveness and, 154
  matrix for plotting products by country,
    155
  product's competitive strength and, 154
International risk assessment, 65–66
International societal environment, 56–57
International staffing, 224–225
International Standards Association, 245
International strategies, 65
International trade, piracy in, 255
International transfer pricing, 255
Internet, 5–6, 6–7. *See also* Business to
  business (B2B); Web sites; World Wide
  Web (WWW)
  B2B transactions on, 6
  business directories on, 353
  business strategy and, 131–132
  case analysis and, 351–353
  competitor information on, 76
  computer security, hackers, and, 263, 295
  corporate strategy and, 159–160
  delivery firm, 320
  Dot-Com Deathwatch, 203
  e-CRM software and, 185–186
  education, health care, and, 337
  environmental scanning, industry
    analysis, and, 74–76
  evaluation and control process and, 262–263
  functional strategy and, 185–186
  global economy and, 99
  global online population, 160
  government regulation of, 45
  impact of, on corporate governance and
    social responsibility, 44–45
  locating company's Web site, 351
  logistics strategy and, 175
  marketing and, 100
  not-for-profits and, 335–337

online resources for case research, 356
organizational design/structure and,
  212–213
outside case research using, 342
privacy issues, 262–263
purchasing strategy and, 174, 175
regulation of, 336
scams on, 352
search engines, 352
staffing, leading, and, 235–237
strategic management and, 22
supply chain management and, 102–103
technology and innovation management
  and, 296
triggering event at Sun Microsystems, 17
virtual teams and, 103, 236
Internet domains, 336–337, 351
Internet Engineering Task Force (IETF), 336
Internet value-chain partnership, 130
Intranets, 100
  advantages/disadvantages, 237
  connected via extranets, 257
  defined, 235
  dynamic, 235, 236
  static, 235–236
Intrapreneurship, 291
Inventories, Internet and replenishment of,
  174, 175
Inventory turnover, 344
Investment centers, 253
ISO 9000 Standards Series, 245
Issues priority matrix, 59–60

Japan, as market, 56–57
Job characteristics model, 209
Job design
  at Corning, Inc., 208–209
  defined, 208
Job enlargement, 208, 331
Job enrichment, 208
Job rotation, 208, 222
Job shop, 95–96, 172
Joint venture, 128–129
  international markets entry and, 145
Justice approach, to ethical behavior, 43
Just-In-Time (JIT) concept, 174

Key managers. *See* CEO; Executive(s); Top
  management
Key performance measures, 251
Key success factors, industry matrix and,
  69–70
Knowledge
  as asset, 7
  explicit, 83
  tacit, 83
"Knowledge market" approach, to
  innovation, 296

Late movers, 124–125
Law, defined, 42
Leader R&D functional strategy, 171

Leading, 218, 225–234
    action planning and, 229–231
    defined, 225
    international, 232–234
    Internet and, 235–237
    Management By Objectives and, 231
    managing corporate culture, 225–229
    Total Quality Management and, 232
Lead director, 34
Leadership, executive, 35–37
Lead user
    innovation and, 281–282
    teams, 281
Learning curve. *See* Experience curve
Learning organization, 8–9
Learning process, feedback and, 16
Legal responsibilities, 38
Leveraged buy out (LBO), 170, 347
Leverage ratios, 342, 345
Library, 357
Licensing, 129
    international markets entry and, 144
Licensing arrangement, 129
Life, changing pace and location of,
    55–56
Life cycle
    organizational, 201
    product, 90
Lifestyle, 317
    company, 314
Linkages, 86
Linking pins, 331
Liquidation, 150
Liquidity ratios, 342, 344
Locus of control, 312
Logical incrementalism, as decision-making
    mode, 19
Logistics strategy, 174–175
Long-range planning. *See* Strategy
    formulation
Long-run evaluations, 258
Long-term contracts, 142
Long-term evaluation method, 260
Long-term orientation (LT), 233
Losing Hand strategy, 177
Lower cost strategies
    cost focus, 119
    cost leadership, 118–119
    defined, 118
Low force, 60

Management. *See also* Leading; Strategic
    management
    role in technology and innovation,
    278–280
    supply chain, 102–103
    of technology and innovation, 277–296
Management audits, 252
Management Buy Outs (MBOs), 170
Management By Objectives (MBO), 231, 233
Management contracts, international
    markets entry and, 146

Management, role of top, in corporate
    governance, 35–37
Managers. *See also* Management
    needs and desires, 182
Managing, technology, 290, 294
Managing corporate culture, 225–229
    communication and, 227
    strategy-culture compatibility assessment,
    226–227
Manufacturing
    continuous systems, 96
    flexible, 97
    intermittent systems, 95–96
    modular, 173
Manufacturing capabilities, strategic
    alliances and, 127
Manufacturing manager, 95
Manufacturing strategy. *See also* Operations
    strategy
    product's life cycle, 172
Market(s)
    diversity in, 56
    identifying in developing nations, 57, 58
    product development for, 169
    Triad as, 56–57
Market access, strategic alliances and, 127
Market development, 168–169
Marketing, 89–91
    product life cycle and, 90, 91
    strategic marketing issues, 89
Marketing channels, 7
Marketing manager, 89
Marketing mix, 90
    variables, 91
Marketing strategy, 168–169
    market development, 168–169
    product development, 169
    push/pull strategies, 169
Market location tactics
    defensive, 126
    offensive, 125
Market position, 90
Market research
    new product experimentation and, 283
    product innovation and, 282–283
Market segmentation, 90
Market value added (MVA), 248–249, 250
Masculinity-femininity (M-F), 233
Mass customization, 97, 173
Mass market, decline of, 55
Mass production, 172
Matrix of change, 194–196
Matrix stage, in corporate development, 201
Matrix structures, 204–206
    phases in, 205–206
MBO. *See* Management By Objectives
    (MBO)
Measurement, international, 254
Measures
    financial, 246–247, 248
    of performance, 243–256
    stakeholder, 247

Medium force, 60
Mercosur (Mercosul), 6
    MNCs and, 56
Mergers, 139
    for not-for-profits, 333
Micro new ventures department, for
    corporate entrepreneurship, 293
Minority groups
    in markets and workforce, 56
    in U.S. workforce, 98–99
MIS, 176. *See also* Information systems strategy
Mission, 10
Mission statements, 10–12, 114
    innovation emphasis in, 279, 280
    for not-for-profit organizations, 329
MNC. *See* Multinational corporation
    (MNC)
Modes of strategic decision making, 18–19
Modular manufacturing, 173
Moore's Law, 94
Moral development levels, 41–42
Morality, defined, 42
Moral relativism, 41
Multidomestic industries, 64–65
    movement to global, 209
Multidomestic MNC, control and reward
    systems in, 256
Multinational corporation (MNC), 56. *See
    also* Stages of international
    development
    accounting rules of, 343–346
    centralization versus decentralization in,
    210–212
    control and reward systems in, 256
    geographic-area structure and, 211–212
    as global, 209
Multinational corporation (MNC) *(cont.)*
    inflation and, 348
    information systems strategies of, 176
    international transfer pricing, taxes, and,
    255
    organizational learning, international
    assignments, and, 224
    product-group structure and, 211–212
    repatriation of profits by, 255
    self-managing work teams in, 175–176
    staffing from host country and, 224–225
    strategic alliances and, 209
    third country nationals and, 225
    Triad and, 57
Multiple sourcing, 173–174
Multipoint competition, 158
Mutual service consortium, 128

NAFTA. *See* North American Free Trade
    Agreement (NAFTA)
Narrow target strategy, 120
National cultures
    clash with corporate cultures in
    international mergers, 233–234
    dimensions of, 232–233
Need for achievement, 312

Net present value (npv), 181
Net profit margin, 344
Net working capital turnover, 344
Network stage, in corporate development, 201
Network structure, 206
New business model, 304
New entrants, threat of, 61–62
New markets, product development for, 169
New product business department, for corporate entrepreneurship, 292
New product development, stages of, 290, 291
New product experimentation, 283
New venture(s). *See* Entrepreneurial ventures; Small-business firms
New venture division, for corporate entrepreneurship, 293
New venture success
   factors affecting, 311–313
   guidelines for, 313
Niche, 55
   changes in, 113
   growth in, 112–113
   propitious, 112
No change strategy, 147
Nonfinancial performance measures, 250–251
Non-profit corporations, 325
North America, as market, 56–57
North American Free Trade Agreement (NAFTA), 6
North American Free Trade Zone, MNCs and, 56
Not-for-profit organizations, 324–337
   American Heart Association as, 324
   evaluation and control complications, 332
   institutional advantage and, 329
   Internet and, 335–337
   mergers and, 333
   need for, 325–326
   private nonprofit corporation, 325
   public governmental units/agencies, 325
   public or collective goods and, 325
   revenue sources for, 326–327
   strategic alliances and, 333–334
   strategic decision making and, 327–329
   strategic management constraints, 329–332
   strategic piggybacking, 332–333, 334
   strategy formulation complications, 330–331
   strategy implementation complications, 331
   taxation and, 335
   vs. business, 326
Nursing homes, 325
Nurturing and contracting, for corporate entrepreneurship, 293

Objectives, 12, 305, 330
   management by, 231
   review of, 114

Offensive tactics, 125
Online computer services, 357
Online information, 356
Operating budgets, 252
Operating cash flow, 347
Operating leverage, 96
Operating objectives, ambiguous, 330–331
Operations issues
   continuous systems, 96
   experience curve, 96
   flexible manufacturing for mass customization, 97
   intermittent systems, 95–96
Operations manager, 95
Operations strategy, 171–173
   Advanced Manufacturing Technology (AMT) and, 171–172
   international differences, 172
Opportunity, SWOT analysis and, 109
Options, real, 181
Orchestrator, 291
Organizational analysis, 106
   in airline industry, 80–81
   IFAS, 101–102
   Internet and, 102–103
   resource-based approach to, 81–84
   scanning functional resources, 87–100
   strategic audit and, 100–101
   value chain analysis and, 84–87
Organizational design. *See also* Organizational structure(s)
   for corporate entrepreneurship, 292–294
Organizational learning, international assignments and, 224
Organizational learning theory, 8
Organizational life cycle, 201–203
Organizational scanning, of Newbury Comics, Inc., 106–107
Organizational structure(s). *See also* Organizational life cycle
   cellular organization, 207
   conglomerate structure, 88
   divisional structure, 87, 88, 200–201
   functional structure, 87, 88, 200
   hyperlinked organization, 212–213
   industry, 121
   matrix structure, 204–206
   network structure/virtual organization, 206
   simple structure, 87, 88, 199–200
   stages of corporate development in, 198–201
   strategic business units, 87–88, 200–201, 257
   structure follows strategy concept and, 197–198
Organization slack, 139
Output controls, 243, 245
Outside directors, 29, 31
Outsourcing, 142
   defined, 166
   of logistics, 175
   matrix, 168
   outsourced activities, 167

technology (*See* Technology sourcing)
   unsuccessful, 168

Pacific Rim area, societal environments in, 53
Parallel sourcing, 174
Parenting-fit matrix, 157–158
Parenting strategy. *See* Corporate parenting
Participative problem solving, 98
Partnership, value-chain, 129
Part-time employees, 176
Pattern of influence, on strategic decision making, 327–329
Pause/proceed with caution strategy, 147
Penetration pricing, 169
Performance, 16, 243
Performance appraisal system, 221–222
Performance gap, 17
Performance measures, 243–259, 305
   activity-based costing, 245–246
   at Amazon.com, 248
   control guidelines, 259–260
   control types, 243–245
   of corporate performance, 246–252
   of divisional and functional performance, 252–254
   goal displacement and, 258–259
   international, 254–256
   problems in, 257–259
   short-term orientation of, 258
   steering controls and, 243
Periodic statistical reports, 252
Personalization software, 185–186
Phantom/rubber stamp board of directors, 29
Phantom stock, 296
Phases of strategic management, 3
Pioneer, 124
Piracy, in international trade, 255
Place, as marketing mix variable, 90, 91
Planning mode, of strategic decision making, 19
Policy, 14, 305
Policy development
   strategy formulation and, 184
   technology, innovation, and, 278–279
Political-legal societal environment, 52, 53
   international, 57
   trends in, 54
Political risk, strategic alliances and, 128
Political strategy, 181
Population ecology, 7
Portable information devices, 54
Porter's approach to industry analysis, 60–64
Porter's competitive business strategies, 117–126
   generic, 118
   industry structure and, 121–122
   issues in, 120–121
   organizational requirements for, 123, 124
   risks in, 119–120
   skill and resource requirements for, 123, 124

Portfolio analysis, 151–155, 329
  advantages and limitations of, 155
  BCG Growth-Share Matrix, 151–153
  defined, 151
  GE Business Screen and, 153–154
  international, 154
  managing innovation, 289
  matrix for plotting products by country, 155
  product portfolio, 289
Portfolio strategy, 137
Power, transfer in family businesses, 315–316
Power distance (PD), 233
PPP. See Purchasing power parity (PPP)
Precision farming, 54
Preconventional level, 42
Presidents, 31
Pressure-cooker crisis, 201
Price, as marketing mix variable, 90, 91
Price/earnings ratio, 345
Pricing
  e-CRM software and dynamic, 186
  international transfer, 255
  penetration, 169
  skim, 169
  transfer, 253
Primary activities, 85
Prime interest rate, 347, 349
Principled level, 42
Privacy issues
  confidential corporate information on Internet, 263
  monitoring employees on Internet, 262–263
Private nonprofit corporations, 325
Privatization, 326
Procedures, 305
  defined, 15
  development of, 196
Process innovations, 285–286, 287
Process R&D, 285
Product(s)
  cannibalizing of, 68
  as marketing mix variable, 90, 91
Product champion, 291
Product development, 169, 291
Product differentiation, as barrier to entry, 61
Product-group structure, 211–212
Product innovations, 285–286, 287
Production, mass, 172
Production costs, experience curve and, 96
Production sharing, international markets entry and, 145
Product life cycle, 90, 91
  BCG Growth-Share Matrix and, 151–152
Product management, 205
Product/market evolution portfolio matrix, 289–290
Product R&D, 93, 285
Product's competitive strengths, in international portfolio analysis, 154, 155
Professionalism, 331

Professionalization, 331
Professional liquidator (executive type), 220
Profitability ratios, 342, 344
Profit centers, 253
Profit-making firm, 326–327
Profits, repatriation of, 53
Profit strategy, 147
Pro forma financial statements, 178, 179–180
  common-size statements and, 346
  GDP and, 347
Program, 305
  defined, 15
  development of, 194–196
Promotion
  as marketing mix variable, 90, 91
  push/pull marketing strategies for, 169
Propitious niche, 112
  SAS and, 113
Prospectors, 67
Public governmental units or agencies, 325
Public interest, 44
Public or collective goods, 325
Pull strategy, 169
Purchase accounting rules, 343
Purchasing, 173
Purchasing power parity (PPP), 58
Purchasing strategy, 173–174
  Internet and, 174, 175
  multiple sourcing, 173–174
  parallel sourcing, 174
  sole sourcing, 174
Push strategy, 169

Quality
  differentiation strategy and, 118, 120
  eight dimensions of, 121
Quality of work life, 98
Quasi-integration, 141–142
Question marks, in BCG Growth-Share Matrix, 151
Quick (acid test) ratio, 344

R&D effectiveness, index of, 294
R&D intensity, 92, 283
R&D manager, 92, 94
R&D mix, 93
Rate of industry growth, intense firm rivalry and, 62
Ratio analysis
  example, 344–345
  resources for, 356
  types of ratios, 342
Rational approach, to strategic decision making, 20–21
Rational planning, 330
Reactors, 67
Real options approach, 181
Red tape crisis, 201
Reengineering, strategy implementation and, 207–208
Regional trade associations, 5, 6
Related diversification. See Concentric diversification

Repatriation of profits, 53, 255
Replicability, 83
Research, for case analysis, 342
Research and development (R&D). See also R&D entries; Technology and innovation management
  best practices for, 294, 295
  competitive advantage in China and, 285
  intensity, 92
  Internet usage for, 296
  mix, 93
  product versus process, 285–286
  resource allocation and, 283–284
  technological competence and, 92
  technological discontinuity and, 94–95
  technology sourcing and, 286–288
  technology transfer and, 93
  time to market and, 284
Research and development (R&D) strategy, 170–171
  competitive advantage and, 171
Resource(s)
  for case research, 355–356
  competitive advantage and, 82
  defined, 81
  fast-cycle, 83
  functional, 87–100
  slow-cycle, 83
  standard-cycle, 83
  sustainability of, 82–84
  VRIO framework for evaluation of, 81
Resource allocation
  for research and development, 283–284
  time to market and, 284
Resource-based approach, 81
Responsibility centers, 252–254
Retaliation tactic, 126
Retired directors, 31
Retrenchment strategies, 148–150
  bankruptcy/liquidation, 150
  captive company, 148
  downsizing and, 222–223
  sell-out/divestment, 148–150
  turnaround, 148, 149
Retributive justice, 43
Return on equity (ROE), 247
Return on investment (ROI), 198, 243, 246
  advantages/disadvantages of using as corporate performance measure, 247, 258
  investment centers and, 253
Revenue centers, 252–253
Revenue sources for not-for-profit organizations, 326–327
  pattern of influence and, 327–329
Reverse engineering, 82
Reward systems, 98. See also Strategic incentive management
Rightsizing. See Downsizing
Risk
  political, 128
  real options approach and, 181
  strategic choice and, 180

Risk assessment, 65–66
Rivalry among existing firms, as barrier to entry, 62
Robots, 54
Rollup, strategic, 122
R/3 software system, 256–257

Scams, on Internet, 352
Scanning
    environmental, 51–76
    functional resources, 87–100
    internal, 80–103
    societal environment, 53–56
    task environment, 57–59
Scenarios, corporate, 178–180
    common-size statements and, 346
    GDP and, 347
Scenario writing, 72
Schools, 325
Scope, competitive, 118
Search engines, 75, 352
Security, on Internet, 263, 295
Segmentation, market, 90
Self-managing work teams, 97, 175–176
Self-subsidization for not-for-profits, strategic piggybacks and, 333
Sell out, 148. *See also* Divestment
Seniors market, growth in, 55
Separation, of corporate cultures after acquisitions, 228
Service manager, 95
SFAS (Strategic Factors Analysis Summary) Matrix, 110–112
Shadow Committee, 184
Shareholder value
    defined, 248–249
    economic value added (EVA), 248–250
    market value added (MVA), 248–249, 250
Short-term orientation, accounting-based measures and, 258
Simple structure, 87, 88, 199–200
Simplification, in manufacturing, 287
Situational analysis, SWOT analysis and, 108, 109–113
Skim pricing, 169
Slow-cycle resources, 83, 84
Small-business firms. *See also* Entrepreneurial ventures
    corporate governance of, 308–309
    defined, 303
    developmental substages, 313–315
    environmental scanning and strategy formulation for, 309–313
    evaluation and control process for, 316–318
    as family businesses, 315–316
    importance of, 301–303
    informal questions for strategic management process, 305
    Internet and, 318–320
    lack of strategic planning in, 304
    strategic planning and management for, 304–308

    strategy formulation issues for, 313–316
    Web sites providing global presence for, 312
SO, ST, WO, WT Strategies, 115
Social responsibility, 37
    Internet impact on, 44–45
    of strategic decision makers, 37–40
Societal environment
    analysis of, 58
    international, 56–57
    scanning, 53–56
    variables in, 52, 53
Sociocultural societal environment, 53
    forces, 52
    international, 57
    trends in, 55–56
Software
    analytics, 185
    e-CRM, 185–186
    e-marketing, 185
    information systems strategies and, 176
    personalization, 185–186
Software industry
    beta testing in, 294
    evaluation and testing at Argus Systems Group, 295
    product evaluation and marketing in, 294
Sole sourcing, 174
Sources of innovation, for entrepreneurial ventures, 309–311
Sources of revenue for not-for-profits, 326–327
    patterns of client-organization influence and, 328
    patterns of influence and, 327–329
Sourcing, 166, 174
    technology, 286–288
Sourcing decision, 166–168
Special business units, for corporate entrepreneurship, 292–293
Spin-off, complete, for corporate entrepreneurship, 293–294
Sponsor, 291
Stability strategies, 146–147
    no change strategy, 147
    pause/proceed with caution, 147
    profit, 147
Staffing
    abilities and potential identification, 221–222
    downsizing and, 222–223
    at Enterprise Rent-A-Car, 217–218
    executive succession process and, 221
    executive type and, 220
    growth strategies and, 218–219
    at Hewlett-Packard, 222
    hiring and training requirements, 219
    international, 224–225
    Internet and, 235–237
    manager/strategy match, 220–221
    selection and management development, 221–222
Staffing follows strategy concept, 219–221

Stages of corporate development, 198–201
    blocks to development, 201, 202
    divisional structure, 200–201
    functional structure, 200
    matrix/network stage, 201
    simple structure, 199–200
Stages of international development, 210
Stages of new product development. *See* New product development
Staggered board, 33
Stakeholder(s), 39–40
    as competitive forces, 63–64
    strategic choice and pressures from, 181
    in task environment, 60
Stakeholder measures, of corporate performance, 247, 249
Stakeholder Priority Matrix, 181, 182
Standard cost centers, 252
Standard Operating Procedures (SOP), 15, 196
Stars, in BCG Growth-Share Matrix, 151
Statement of mission. *See* Mission statements
Static intranets, 235–236
Statistical modeling, 72
Statistical Process Control (SPC), 243
Steering controls, 243
Stewardship theory, 29, 30
Strategic alliances
    defined, 127
    growth and, 139
    Internet value-chain partnership, 130
    joint venture, 128–129
    licensing arrangement, 129
    between MNC and local partner, 209
    mutual service consortium, 128
    for not-for-profits, 333–334
    for R&D, 287–288
    reasons for forming, 127–128
    success factors, 130
    value-chain partnership, 129
Strategic audit, 100–101, 262
    Analysis of Strategic Factors (SWOT), 271
    as case analysis format, 348–351, 357–359
    Corporate Governance, 265–266
    Current Situation, 265
    for entrepreneurial ventures, 307
    Evaluation and Control, 272
    External Environment: Opportunities and Threats (SWOT), 266
    Implementation, 271–272
    Internal Environment: Strengths and Weaknesses (SWOT), 267–270
    sample, 265–272
    Strategic Alternatives and Recommended Strategy, 271
    student-written (1993 Maytag Corporation case), 361–365
Strategic audit worksheet, 349–351
Strategic business units (SBUs), 87–88
    in divisional structure, 200–201
    IS support and, 257
Strategic choice, 177–184
    corporate culture and, 181–182
    corporate scenarios for, 178–180

devil's advocate technique and, 183
dialectical inquiry and, 184
process of, 183–184
risk and, 180–181
stakeholders and, 181
strategy shadow committee and, 184
top management and, 182–183
Strategic choice perspective, 8
Strategic decision making, 18–21
Mintzberg's modes of, 18–19
patterns of influence on, 327–328
Strategic decision-making process, 19–21
for entrepreneurial ventures, 305–307
situation analysis in, 109
Strategic factor analysis summary. *See* SFAS
(Strategic Factors Analysis Summary)
Matrix
Strategic factors, 9
compared to key success factors, 69
external, 59–60
internal, 81
Strategic-funds method, 260–261
Strategic groups, 66
mapping, 66, 67
Strategic incentive management, 260–261
Strategic inflection point, 17
Strategic information systems (IS)
at divisional (SBU) level, 257
enterprise resource planning and,
256–257
Strategic management, 3–4
basic model of, 9–16
benefits of, 4
board of directors' role in, 27–28
constraints on, 329–330
defined, 2
evaluation and control in, 243, 244
financial issues, 91–92
human resource management issues,
97–99
information systems/technology, 99–100
marketing, 89–91
operation issues, 95–97
R&D issues, 92–95
for small businesses, 304–308
Strategic management model, for small
businesses and entrepreneurial
ventures, 305
Strategic myopia, 59
Strategic piggybacking, 332–333
resources for, 334
Strategic planning, 3. *See also* Strategy
formulation
for small businesses, 304–308
Strategic planning process, managing, 36–37
Strategic planning staff, 37
Strategic R&D alliance, 287
Strategic rollup, 122
Strategic types
analyzers, 67
defenders, 66
prospectors, 67
reactors, 67

Strategic vision, 35
Strategic window, 112
Strategy(ies), 13. *See also* specific types
alternative, 114
to avoid, 177
business, 13, 115–132
competitive strategy, 115–117, 117–126
cooperative, 117, 126–130
corporate, 13, 137–160
directional, 137–150
financial, 169–170
functional, 13, 164–188
growth, 138
hierarchy of, 13
HRM, 175–176
information systems, 176–177
initiation of, 16–17
logistics, 174–175
marketing, 168–169
of Newbury Comics, Inc., 50
operations, 171–173
purchasing, 173–175
R&D, 170–171
retrenchment, 148
SO, ST, WO, WT, 115
stability, 146
Strategy-culture compatibility, 226–227
Strategy formulation, 10–14, 108–132
business strategies and, 115–130
for Casey's General Stores, 108–109
complications to, 330–331
corporate strategy, 136–160
functional strategy, 164–177
Internet and business strategy, 131–132
mission and objectives review, 114
for Newbury Comics, Inc., 190
propitious niche identification, 112–113
SFAS Matrix and, 110–112
situation analysis and SWOT analysis,
109–112
for small businesses, 313–316
for small businesses/entrepreneurial
ventures, 309–313
strategic choice and, 177–184
in technology and innovation
management, 285–290
TOWS Matrix and, 114–115
Strategy implementation, 15
budget process, 196
complications to, 331
defined, 192–193
at Fingerhut Company, 191–192
international, 209–212, 224–225,
232–234
Internet and, 212–213, 235–237
job design for, 208–209
leading and, 225–234
organizational structure and, 197–209
people involved in, 193–194
problems in, 193
procedures development, 196–197
program development, 194–196
reengineering and, 207–208

staffing and, 217–225
synergy in, 196–197
Strategy shadow committee, 184
Structure. *See* Organizational structure(s)
Structure follows strategy concept,
197–198
Stuck in the middle, of competitive
marketplace, 120
Suboptimization, 259
Substages of small business development,
313–315
Substitute products/services, as competitive
forces, 62–63
Succession, executive, 221
Suppliers, as competitive force, 63
Supply chain management, 102–103
Support activities, 86
Sustainability, of competitive advantage,
82–84
continuum of sustainability, 83–84
Switching costs, as barrier to entry, 61
SWOT analysis, 9, 108–109, 109–113, 209,
329. *See also* EFAS (External Factors
Analysis Summary) Table; IFAS
(Internal Factor Analysis Summary)
Table; SFAS (Strategic Factors Analysis
Summary) Matrix
criticisms of, 109
opportunity and, 109
propitious niche and, 112–113
for small entrepreneurial businesses,
309
TOWS Matrix and, 114–115
Synagogues, 325
Synergy, 143
corporate headquarters and, 156
forms of, 197
horizontal strategy and, 158
in strategy implementation, 196–197
Synergy Game, 214

Tacit collusion, 127
Tacit knowledge, 83
Tactics
defined, 123–124
market location, 125–126
timing, 123–124
Taper integration, 141
Task environment, 53
industry analysis and, 60–70
scanning, 57–59
Taxation, 44
international transfer pricing and, 255
not-for-profits, Internet, and, 335
Teams
autonomous (self-managing) work, 97
cross-functional work, 97–98
virtual, 103
Technological competence, 92, 288–289
Technological discontinuity, 94–95, 282, 287
disruptive technology and, 95
Technological follower, 171
Technological forces, 52

Technological leader, 171
Technological societal environment, 52, 53
   international, 57
   trends in, 54
Technology, information systems, 99–100
Technology and innovation management,
   277–296. *See also* Research and
   development (R&D)
   corporate entrepreneurship
      (intrapreneurship) and, 291–294
   entrepreneurial culture development, 290
   environmental scanning and, 280–284
   evaluation and control process and,
      294–295
   executives survey on, 278
   external scanning, 280–281
   internal scanning and, 283
   Internet and, 296
   lead users and, 281–282
   management's role in, 278–280
   market research and, 282–283
   mission statement and, 279, 280
   new product development and, 290, 291
   product and process innovation, 285–286,
      287
   product/market evolution portfolio
      matrix, 289–290
   resource allocation issues, 283–284
   strategy formulation and, 284–290
   strategy implementation and, 290–294
   at Trilogy Software, Inc., 277
Technology capabilities, strategic alliances
   and, 127
Technology sourcing, 286–288
Technology transfer, 93
   at Xerox, 93
Temporary workers, 98, 176
Theories of Organizational Adaptation, 7
Threat
   of new entrants, 61
   of substitute products/services, 62
Time interest earned, 345
Time to market, 284
Timing tactics, 124–125
Top-down strategic planning, 36
Top management. *See also* CEO
   as blocks to corporate development, 201,
      202

evaluation of, 251–252
   role in technology and innovation, 278–280
   strategic choice and, 182–183
   strategy implementation and, 220–221
Total Quality Management (TQM), 232
Total weighted score, 101
TOWS Matrix, 114–115
   for Maytag Corporation, 116–117
TQM. *See* Total Quality Management
   (TQM)
Tracking stock, 170
Trade, regional associations, 5
Trade barriers, regional trade associations
   and, 6
Traditional cost accounting, vs. ABC,
   245–246
Training, strategy implementation and,
   219
Transaction cost economics, 140
   vertical growth strategy and, 141
Transferability, 83
Transfer of power, 216
Transfer pricing, 253
   international, 255
Transparency, 82
Trend-impact analysis (TIA), 72
Trends
   in international societal environments, 56
   societal, 53–56
Triad, 56–57
Triggering event, 17
Trigger point, 58
Turnaround specialist, 220
Turnaround strategy, 148
   at IBM, 149
Turnkey operations, international markets
   entry and, 145–146

Uncertainty avoidance, 233
Unethical behavior, reasons for, 41–42
Unions, human resource managers and, 98
Universities, 325
Unrelated diversification. *See* Conglomerate
   diversification
Url (uniform resource locator), 351
User. *See* Lead user
Utilitarian approach, to ethical behavior, 43
Utility, 43

Value chain, 84
Value chain analysis
   corporate, 85–87
   industry, 84–85
Value-chain partnership, 129
   Internet, 130
Value trap businesses, 158
   in parenting-fit matrix, 158
Venture capitalists, 309
Vertical growth, 139–142
   transaction cost economics and, 141
   vs. cooperative contractual relationships,
      142
Vertical integration
   continuum, 140
   defined, 140
Vice presidents, 31
Virtual organization, 206
Virtual personal assistants, 54
Virtual teams, 103
   Internet and, 236
VRIO (Value, Rareness, Imitability, and
   Organization) framework of analysis,
   81, 101

Wealth, transfer in family businesses,
   315–316
Web. *See* World Wide Web (WWW)
Web sites, 2, 353. *See also* Internet
   evaluation and reliability of industry
      information on, 75
   for local businesses' global presence, 312
   locating companies', 351
Weighted-factor method, 260, 261
Western Europe, as market, 56–57
Whistleblowers, 40
Women, in U.S. workforce, 98–99
Woofies, 55
Work environment, 98
Workforce, diversity and, 56, 98–99, 176
Work restructuring, 98
World industries. *See* International
   industries
World Wide Web (WWW), 2. *See also*
   Internet; Web sites
   global online population, 160

Z-value, 346